GODFREY OF BULLOIGNE

This is that Godfrey by whose valiant hand
God freed from Saracens, the Holie Land.

Portrait facing title-page of 1624 edition

GODFREY OF BULLOIGNE

A critical edition of
Edward Fairfax's translation of
Tasso's *Gerusalemme Liberata*,
together with Fairfax's
Original Poems

EDITED BY

KATHLEEN M. LEA

AND

T. M. GANG

OXFORD
AT THE CLARENDON PRESS
1981

Oxford University Press, Walton Street, Oxford OX2 6DP

London Glasgow New York Toronto
Delhi Bombay Calcutta Madras Karachi
Kuala Lumpur Singapore Hong Kong Tokyo
Nairobi Dar es Salaam Cape Town Salisbury
Melbourne Auckland
and associate companies in
Beirut Berlin Ibadan Mexico City

Published in the United States
by Oxford University Press, New York

British Library Cataloguing in Publication Data

Tasso, Torquato
  Godfrey of Bulloigne. – (Oxford English
  texts)
  I. Title II. Godfrey of Bulloigne
  III. Fairfax, Edward
  IV. Lea, Kathleen Marguerite
  V. Gang, T. M. VI. Series
  851'.4   PQ4642.E21   79-40838

ISBN 0-19-812480-5

Printed in Great Britain
at the University Press, Oxford
by Eric Buckley
Printer to the University

To
Ethel Seaton and Rosemond Tuve
who loved learning and
spared no pains

ACKNOWLEDGEMENTS

THE editors would like to express their gratitude to the following: Mr. C. G. Bell; Miss Jonquil Bevan; Mrs. Jean Bromley; Mr. John Buxton; the Rt. Hon. Lord Cornwallis; Mr. C. T. d'Alessandro; Professor Eric Dobson; the Dowager Lady Fairfax; Major Sir Joslan Ingilby; the late J. C. Maxwell; the late A. N. L. Munby; Miss Felicity Ranger; Messrs. Sotheby; Thoresby Society, Hon. Joint Editor; Professor Edward Weismiller; Mr. Derek Wood.

Their gratitude is also due to the librarians of the Bodleian Library; the British Library; Cambridge University Library; Christ Church, Oxford; Dulwich College; Houghton Library, Harvard University, Henry E. Huntington Library, California; the Lambeth Palace Library; Newcastle University Library; the Public Record Office; the Taylorian Institute, Oxford; the Victoria and Albert Museum Library; and Worcester College, Oxford.

CONTENTS

LIST OF PLATES

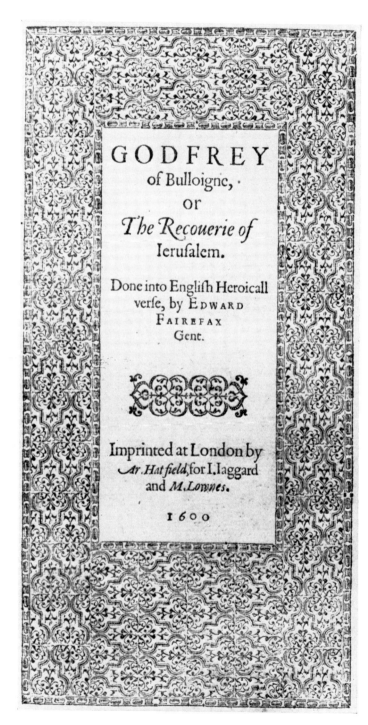

GODFREY
of Bulloigne,
or
The Recouerie of
Ierusalem.

Done into Englifh Heroicall
verfe, by EDWARD
FAIREFAX
Gent.

Imprinted at London by
Ar. Hatfield, for I. Iaggard
and *M. Lownes.*

1600

Title-page of 1600 edition

GENERAL
INTRODUCTION

I. THE LIFE OF EDWARD FAIRFAX

In 1631, we are told, the antiquary Roger Dodsworth noted in his manuscript book *Sancti et Scriptores Eboracenses:*

Edward Fairfax of fuyston Esqr in the Forest of Knaresborow . . . brother of Sir. Thos. Lord ff. of Denton. He translated Godfrey of Bullen out of Italian into English verse. Writ the History of Edward the Black Prince, and other witty Eclogues not printed. He is accounted a singular Schollar in all kinds of learning, and yet liveth 1631.

The note is quoted by Brian Fairfax the younger in a biographical sketch that has formed the basis of all subsequent accounts of the poet.[1] Brian speaks of the military prowess of Edward's brothers, and continues:

While his brothers were thus honorably employd abroad, he stayd at home, at his Book, and thereby made himselfe fit for any employment in Church or State, but an invinceable Modesty and Love of a retired Life made him prefer the shady groves, and natural cascades of Denton and the forest of Knaresborow, before all the diversions of Court or Camp.

He did not pass his time *ignobili otio*, as appears by the many valuable manuscripts he has left in the library of my Lord FF at Denton, both in verse and Prose . . .

He was very serviceable to his Brother my Lord Fairfax in the education of his Children, and the Government of his Family, and in all his affairs the success appeard in haveing all his Children bred Schollars, and well principled in Religion and vertue. His house famed for hospitallity and his estate flourishing.

What his Principles were, appears by this Character he gives of himselfe in his booke called Demonology:

'For my selfe I am in Religion neither a Fantastic Puritan nor a super-'stitious Papist, but so settled in Conscience that I have the sure ground 'of Gods word to warrant all I Believe, and the commendable ordinances of 'our English Church to approve all that I practice. In which course I live 'a Faithfull Christian and an obedient Subject, and so teach my Family . . .'

Mr E. F. had several Children, sons and daughters, the eldest son William

---

[1] Letter to Francis Atterbury, 12 Mar. 1704/5, British Library MS. Add. 5144, fos. 92–8 (printed in *The Epistolary Correspondence of Francis Atterbury* (1783–90), iii. 255–69). We have not been able to find Dodsworth's MS. volume.

was a Schollar, of the same temper as his father, but more Cynicall. He translated Diogenes Laertius the life of the old Philosophers out of Greek into English.

Edwd dyed about the yeare 1632, at his owne house called New Hall, in the parish of Fuystone between Denton and Knaresbury, and lies under a marble stone, but deserved a Monument nere Godfrey of Bullen in the Temple of Jerusalem.

Though later research has not added as much to our knowledge of the man and his life as one might have hoped, the facts we possess imply an image that is at once less ideal and more interesting than that which is presented in Brian's pious delineation.

Edward Fairfax belonged to the younger branch of the ancient Yorkshire family of Fairfax—the branch which was settled at Steeton and Bolton Percy in the fifteenth century, and which numbered among its scions the great Lord Fairfax of the Civil War. Edward's grandfather, Sir William Fairfax of Steeton, eloped in 1518 with an heiress called Isabella Thwaites, who was a ward of the abbess of Nun Appleton. (The story is alluded to in Marvell's poem *Upon Appleton House*.) Among other properties which Sir William acquired by this romantic exploit was Denton, an estate in Wharfedale, and this was inherited by his eldest son, Thomas. It was this Sir Thomas Fairfax of Denton who was the father of Edward Fairfax. Among Sir Thomas's other children were Sir Thomas the younger, later to be created Baron Fairfax of Cameron, and Charles Fairfax, a gallant soldier.[1]

Edward and Charles were both illegitimate.[2] This perhaps accounts for the paucity of evidence for the date of Edward's birth. A modern source, which seems in other ways well informed,

[1] [C. R. Markham], 'Genealogies of the Fairfaxes', *Herald and Genealogist*, vi (1870), 385–407; corrected by 'W. H. W.', ibid. vii (1873), 145–63. See also *The Scots Peerage*, ed. Sir James Balfour Paul, iii (1906), 595–6; Thomas Parkinson, D.D., *Lays and Leaves of the Forest*, 1882; Joseph Hunter, *Chorus Vatum Anglicanorum*, British Library MS. Add. 24487–92 (i. 193). The ultimate source of much of this information is the MS. book 'Analecta Fairfaxiana' compiled by Charles Fairfax of Menston *c.* 1660. Two copies of this are at present in the possession of the family.

[2] 'Analecta Fairfaxiana', which describes Edward as 'Esquire for the Body' to Queen Elizabeth, joins both his and Charles's name to the family tree with a wavy line. Edward's illegitimacy was disputed by some nineteenth-century biographers, but established beyond doubt by G. C. Bell, 'Edward Fairfax a Natural Son', *M.L.N.*, lxii (1947), 24–9.

gives it as 1568.[1] We know nothing of his education, though it seems possible that he may be identical with the Edward Fairfax who matriculated as a member of Clare Hall, Cambridge, in Lent 1580/1. The fact that a Charles Fairfax matriculated at the same college in 1584 lends some colour to this identification.[2] In 1597 we find Edward and his father acquiring property at Fewston and Little Timble in Wharfedale, and there is a record of Edward Fairfax receiving a licence to marry Catherine Calverley, a widow, of Otley.[3] Presumably his eldest son William was born of this marriage.[4]

It would appear that in the years 1595–9 Edward was his father's favourite son, managing the estate and conducting the greater part of the old man's private affairs. This must likewise have been the period in which he was working on his translation of Tasso. However, these no doubt happy times came to an end in January 1599/1600. On the fourth day of that month old Sir Thomas, now nearly 80 years of age and in his last sickness, made his will. In this he left 'divers legacies of good valew' to Sir Thomas the younger, his eldest legitimate son, and smaller legacies to various other people, but left the remainder to Edward, whom he appointed sole executor. He committed to Edward's care all his money, plate, goods, and chattels, as well as the keys to his trunks and chests.[5]

Young Sir Thomas, who had for several years been banished from his father's presence, now took determined action. With a force of armed men he occupied Denton Hall and its lodge, where his father was lying, assaulted Edward (pulling his beard) and

---

[1] 'Paver's Marriage Licences', *Yorkshire Archaeological Journal*, Leeds, x (1887–9), 183: a footnote by the Revd. C. B. Northcliffe refers to Edward Fairfax 'The poet, born 1568, died 1632'.

[2] J. A. Venn, *Alumni Cantabrigienses* (1922), I. ii. 116–18.

[3] 'Yorkshire Fines IV', *Yorkshire Archaeological Society, Record Series*, viii (1889), 83; 'Paver's Marriage Licences', p. 37. We have not found a record of the marriage itself.

[4] We have not been able to find any record of William's birth or baptism.

[5] The details of this complex story can be pieced together from documents in the Public Record Office (Star Chamber 5/F31/33) and a manuscript in Lambeth Palace (MS. vol. 708, fo. 212). For a fuller account see T. M. Gang, 'The Fairfax Quarrel', *Notes and Queries*, ccxiv (1969), 28–33. It was G. C. Bell who first drew attention to the Fairfax quarrel in *Notes and Queries*, cxcix (1954), 143–5.

drove him out. Edward alleges that the old man was kept incom-
municado, not even being allowed his own servants, and that he
was bullied and ill-treated, to make him draw up a new will.
Whatever means young Sir Thomas may have used, a new will
was indeed signed on 13 January: old Sir Thomas died on
28 January,[1] but Edward, who by his expulsion from Denton had
lost valuable property and some of his writings, had meanwhile
ridden to London to seek redress on his own and his father's behalf.
He petitioned the Lords of the Privy Council to instruct the Lord
President of the Council of the North to remove the intruders; and
they in turn instructed the Lord President to investigate the case.
Young Sir Thomas (who was in fact a member of the Learned
Council of the Lord President of the North) used various legalistic
delaying tactics, and when he finally did attend the Lord President's
court he carried the day.

The Lord President reported to the Privy Council on 6 February:

With reference to the complaint made by Edward Fairfax, base son to Old
Sir Thomas Fairfax, against Sir Thomas Fairfax, elder brother of the house,
in accordance with your directions I have called the parties before me, with
their witnesses, and find the complaint unsuitable to the nature of the
gentleman accused and to the truth. He is a very dutiful and natural son,
and as to this particular charge, you shall understand that it was made in
his father's name yet without his privity, who was so moved at the insolence
of his base son, as calling forth his will, he would have quite put him out of
it had not Sir Thomas his son entreated him.[2]

Edward turned to Star Chamber for redress, and was given leave
to present a new plea. He eloquently set forth his wrongs, but to
no avail. On 10 April 1600, young Sir Thomas was able to write
to Sir Robert Cecil, thanking him for his 'favourable speech when
one Edw. Fairfax, to whom my father sometimes gave the name of
his base son, did exhibit a slanderous petition against me to the
Privy Council'.[3]

[1] Parkinson, *Lays and Leaves*, pp. 106–7. See also W. Grainge's introduction to his
edition of Edward Fairfax, *Daemonologia* (Harrogate, 1881), pp. 24–5; *Scots Peerage*,
vol. cit., p. 596. There is a transcript of the will in 'Analecta Fairfaxiana' (MS.
Phillipps 10308).

[2] *Ninth Report of the Historical Manuscripts Commission (Salisbury 10)*, p. 32. The
wording and date of the will do not seem consistent with this account.

[3] Ibid., p. 242.

By his own estimate, the new will left Edward £1,500 less well off than the old will would have done. All he received was Newhall (the property at Fewston) and the sum of £150. The new will states that old Sir Thomas left him Newhall 'at the request of my said son Sir Thomas Farfax'.[1] It must have been about the time of these troubles that Edward was seeing his *Godfrey of Bulloigne* through the press; and it was likewise about now that he made his second marriage. We do not know when his first wife died; but we do know that his second wife was Dorothy Laycock, the sister of Walter Laycock, the Chief Aulnager of the northern counties—the man whose duty it was to supervise the quality of cloth manufactured in the north.[2] From this time until 1621 the Leeds and Fewston parish registers record the baptisms and deaths of Edward Fairfax's children; thus the Leeds register chronicles the baptism of Thomas, 'child of Mr Edward ffairfax, Hunslett' on 6 September 1601; then the Fewston register tells of the baptisms of Charles (1602), Ellen (1605) and Elizabeth (1606); the last of these must have died in childhood, for the Leeds register continues the story with the baptism of another Elizabeth (1614/15), shortly followed by Mary (1616), Frances (1617) and Henry (1619). The later Leeds entries describe Edward Fairfax as a resident of Kirkgate (a street leading to St. Peter's church), and Ralph Thoresby tells us that he lived at a house called Stocks. In 1621 Edward's last-born child, Anne, was baptized and buried at Fewston.[3]

We do not know when Edward moved from Hunslet to Leeds, or how he divided his time between Leeds and Fewston; but the *Daemonologia* shows him firmly settled at the latter place. There seems no reason to doubt Brian Fairfax's assertion that he assisted Sir Thomas Fairfax in the education of his children, for in spite of

[1] Quoted by Grainge, in *Daemonologia*, loc. cit.

[2] 'Paver's Marriage Licences', p. 183, records that Edward obtained a licence in 1600; we do not know the date of the wedding. On Walter Laycock, see William Dugdale, 'Visitation of Yorkshire', *Surtees Society*, xxxvi (1859), 156.

[3] Leeds Parish Register, *Thoresby Society Publications*, Leeds, i (1889), 211; iii (1895), 17, 24, 32, 40; *The Registers of Fewston Church*, transcribed by the Revd. Thomas Parkinson, Skipton, i (1899), 10, 13, 15, 32. Parkinson states, in *Lays and Leaves*, that the baptism of a son, Edward, is recorded in the Fewston register under 1611. The poet's connection with Hunslet, a village near Leeds, is mentioned by Thoresby, *Ducatus Leodensis* (1715), p. 178; Edward's residence at Stocks is mentioned on p. 38.

the quarrel of 1600 the *Daemonologia* shows that the brothers were at least on civil terms, and Sir Thomas's son Ferdinando was a familiar visitor in Edward's house.[1] Evidently the poet did not spend all his time in scholarly pursuits, however, for it seems that he assisted his brother-in-law in his task of inspecting cloth.[2] He took an interest in local antiquities and in the affairs of Leeds parish church, and he was involved in a lawsuit in 1618;[3] but we know nothing else of how he spent his time until we come to 1621, when strange things began to happen in his household. The troubles seem to have started with the death of his little daughter Anne. Edward seems to have suspected that there was something unnatural about this. Shortly afterwards, in October 1621, his eldest daughter Ellen (or Helen) began to behave strangely. She reported seeing people whom others were unable to see, and she conversed with these visionary presences while her astonished family looked on. She also vomited pins. Edward, who narrated these events in the book known as *Daemonologia* while the strange goings-on were still in progress, is at pains to assure us that his first thought was that his daughter was merely suffering from hysteria. One day however there occurred an incident which opened his eyes. A woman with a bad reputation for witchcraft gave his wife a penny with a hole in it and said she would come back for it. It was clear that the penny was supposed to be bewitched; and Edward, who was worried by this, locked it up in his desk. When the desk was opened the penny was gone. The following day Ellen unlocked the desk, and there was the penny back again. He threw it in the fire and burnt it; and the next day it was lying in the grate. Finally he broke it into small pieces and burnt it with brimstone, and it did not reappear. From that time on Edward was convinced that he and his daughter were being persecuted by witches.

[1] *Daemonologia*, ed. Grainge, pp. 38, 48.

[2] 'West Riding Sessions Records II', *Yorkshire Archaeological Society Record Series*, liv (1915), 240.

[3] 'There hath beene a castle at Leedes, as Mr Edward Fairfax conjectureth', Thomas Dunham Whitaker, Loidis and Elmete (Leeds, 1816), p. 4: from the Roger Dodsworth MS., vol. xliv, fo. 168, now lost. Whitaker (p. 24) lists Fairfax among the signatories of a Bill of Complaint concerning the purchase of the advowson of the church. Hunter (*Chorus Vatum*, i. 193) mentions the lawsuit.

Little Elizabeth now followed her sister's example and began to converse with unseen presences. The apparitions they saw were taken to be the witches' familiars in various disguises—ranging from cats to birds to an old woman and handsomely dressed young gentlemen. The girls now formally accused a number of local women of bewitching them, and Edward felt it his duty to prosecute. In April 1622 the supposed witches were brought to trial at York assizes. In spite of the fact that Edward gave evidence of the harm they were doing, they were bailed upon sureties.

The case came up for trial at the August assizes. The grand jury found that there was a case to answer, and the jury of life and death were empanelled. As the hearing began, little Elizabeth Fairfax and a girl called Maud Jeffray, another alleged victim of the witches, fell into a trance, while Ellen spat blood. The girls were at once taken out by some justices of the bench, who returned some time later and declared that it was 'practice confessed': Maud Jeffray had admitted that the whole thing had been a hoax, devised by her father and agreed to by the Fairfax girls who hoped thereby to be 'more cherished'. The judge stopped the case, and aspersions were cast on Edward, not of dishonesty but of simplicity. Maud's father was jailed. Edward remained convinced however of the good faith of his daughters. He was sure the confession had been obtained by force and that evidence had been suppressed. He strongly suspected the justices themselves of being influenced by the witches or their powerful protectors, and regarded those of his neighbours who were sceptical about witchcraft as being, in fact, in league with the witches. He was confirmed in his belief in the genuineness of the witching by the fact that his daughters continued to report encounters with the witches and their familiars, and by other happenings difficult to explain by natural causes. Then, one day, Ellen became ill and appeared to be deaf; and when after a long period she recovered, she disclaimed all recollection of having been bewitched. Little Elizabeth kept up the pretence a little longer, but in April 1623 she reported that one of the familiars had told her that they had finished with her sister and would shortly have finished with her. At this point the *Daemonologia* comes to an abrupt end.

No record appears to survive of Edward's last years. Thoresby gives the date of his death as 1635.

Little though we know of the greater part of Edward Fairfax's life, we do at least have his own accounts of the dramatic events of 1600 and 1621–3, and these allow us to form some notion of his character. From the Star Chamber document, which is couched in formal, legal terminology, Edward seems to emerge as well-meaning, somewhat simple, and given to believing hearsay. He reports as fact a conspiracy of which he can have had no direct knowledge, and describes his brother's treatment of old Sir Thomas, though by his own account there was no means by which he could have known what passed in Denton Lodge after his brother had taken it over. But while that document allows us mere glimpses of his mixture of credulity and suspiciousness, those characteristics are strikingly displayed in the *Daemonologia*, a piece of writing so eloquently direct that we seem to hear Edward's voice speaking to us. It does not occur to him that Ellen might have removed the witches' penny from the desk and put it back again. He simply refuses to entertain the possibility that the girls might be putting on a carefully prepared act when they converse with visitors whom no one else present can hear or see. From their replies he reconstructs what the spirits must have said, and when he finds this tallies with the girls' own report of what they have heard, he takes this as proof that they have indeed spoken with spirits, and dismisses the possibility that they might have been playing a trick because he does not believe them capable of it.

Edward saw himself as a sober, rational, balanced sort of man: not a fanatic, not superstitious, but careful to refer his observations to the most respectable theories of witchcraft and demonic possession. He views the acquittal of the witches without anger: indeed, he derives some consolation from the fact that it entailed the saving of their lives. And he insists again and again on the care with which he and those around him recorded and considered the evidence. His prosecution of the witches was supported by his brother Sir Thomas; so that it was easy for Edward to see himself as pursuing a perfectly reasonable course. The *Daemonologia*, however, shows that Edward was completely carried away by the incidents he set out to describe. What his daughters told him at once became so real to him that he could not help believing in it. He narrates the words of the spirits, and describes their appearances, as if he had heard and seen them for himself. So he introduces in a factual tone the various protagonists, including for example 'a deformed thing with many feet, black of colour, the bigness of a cat, the name of it unknown', and another 'the shape of a bird, yellow of colour, about the bigness of a crow—the name of it is Tewhit'. Starting from the premiss that such creatures really did afflict his daughters he leaves himself no room for critical appraisal of the evidence. In short, Fairfax emerges from the *Daemonologia* as a man whose judgement was subdued by his imagination.

The *Daemonologia* conveys a clear picture of Edward's domestic life and circumstances at Newhall, his family's house at Fewston. It was a modest sort of existence; there seems to have been a certain amount of farming, and he owned the local flour-mill, collecting fees from those who used it. There were few servants, and the children did much of the work. Ellen for example was sent to collect money for the corn ground at the mill, and did the cooking. The family spent much of their time in the kitchen, and neighbours came into the kitchen and the parlour. Something of the flavour of life at Newhall is suggested by details such as this: 'Upon Monday, 10 November, as she [i.e. Ellen] stood by the window in the kitchen, mending an old cuff sewed with black work, she was suddenly in a trance . . .'[1]

Our sense of the physical narrowness of the family's life is confirmed by nineteenth-century accounts of Newhall, which was not pulled down until 1876. Grainge, who saw it before it was demolished and its site submerged in the waters of the Swinsty reservoir, describes it as presenting 'only a humble appearance'; it was then two storeys in height, two rooms in length, and two in breadth (though it was believed to have been considerably larger at one time).[2]

That is virtually the sum of our knowledge of Edward Fairfax the man and his life. His widow died in 1648.[3] Grainge traced the

---

[1] *Daemonologia*, ed. Grainge, p. 52.   [2] Ibid., p. 25.   [3] Ibid., p. 27.

descendants of his daughters down to the eighteenth century,[1] but
has little to tell us of the eldest son, William, or of the other sons.
William was, however, a figure of some interest in his own right.
He was tutor to Thomas Stanley, the poet and author of a cele-
brated *History of Philosophy*, to which William is said to have
contributed extensively. One of William's own poems, *The Union*,[2]
appears among Stanley's *Poems and Translations*; and a beautiful
tribute to his qualities as a tutor is presented in the pupil's *Register
of Friends*:

> Man is a walking shadow, such, in show,
> Thou did'st appear, though far from being so;
> For Nature, underneath that dark disguize,
> Veil'd her more subtle light from common Eies,
> Which, when thou spok'st, broke from the sable shrowd
> (Yet without noise) like lightning through a Cloud.

[1] *Daemonologia*, 156–69.
[2]

THE UNION

By Mr. William Fairfax

Μία ψυχὴ δύο σώματα

> As in the Chrystal Center of the sight
> Two subtle beams make but one Cone of light,
> Or when one flame twin'd with another is,
> They both ascend in one bright Pyramis;
> Our spirits thus into each other flow,
> One in our being, one in what we know,
> In what we will, desire, dislike, approve,
> In what we love, and one is that pure love.
> As in a burning glasse th'aerial Flame,
> With the producing Ray, is still the same:
> We to Loves purest quintessence refin'd,
> Do both become one undivided minde.
> This sacred fire into it self converts
> Our yielding spirits, and our melting hearts,
> Till both our souls into one spirit run,
> So several lines are in their center one.
> And when thy fair *Idea* is imprest
> In the soft tablet of my easier breast,
> The sweet reflexion brings such sympathie,
> That I my better self behold in thee;
> And all perfections that in thee combine,
> By this resultance are intirely mine;
> Thy Rayes disperse my shades who only live
> Bright in the Lustre thou art pleas'd to give.

Little in men, in Science deeply read,
None lesse than thee the living knew, none more, the Dead.
   Thou to inform my Childhood didst descend,
And the same care unto my Youth extend;
Language and Sciences thou didst bestow,
First taught me how to speak, and then to know.
Years, that insensibly-successive glide,
Rais'd me at last to Manhood, Thou my Guide.
Then what before Instruction us'd to be
Grew by degrees into Society.
With scrutiny the Greeks we often vext,
And disentangled oft the Romane Text;
The old Philosophers we did excite
To quarrell, whilst we smil'd to see the fight:
Some serious hours Historians did divide,
Our mirthfull by the Poets were supply'd.
   All these are dead with thee, whose active mind,
Alass! was within Walls so thin confin'd,
That the impatient fire devour'd the Clay,
And melted through resisting clouds its way
To that bright Sphere, from which it star-like shot;
Though born on Earth, souls are in Heav'n begot.[1]

William annotated his father's eclogues, and it was presumably his manuscript copy of them that Mrs. Cooper saw. There, however, the trail runs cold. As our records of Edward's life fade out before his death, so our knowledge of his descendants remains fragmentary and tantalizing.

It remains to say something of his works. We do not know of any writings of his earlier than *Godfrey of Bulloigne*—though it must be surmised that a man who embarked on so major an exercise of the poet's craft cannot have been a complete novice. His *Eclogues*, which were twelve in number, as Brian Fairfax and Mrs. Cooper tell us,[2] were all written in the reign of King James; two have survived intact, and a substantial portion of what is thought to be a third is extant, while a stray couplet of yet another appears

[1] The association with Stanley is mentioned by Anthony Wood, *Fasti Oxonienses*, ed. P. Bliss, i (1820), col. 516, and by Mrs. Cooper, *The Muses Library* (1737), pp. 342–4. The poems first appeared in Thomas Stanley, *Poems and Translations* (1647), sigs Λ^r and Λ 8^r. See also the edition by G. M. Crump, pp. xxi, xxiii–iv, 66, and 355–6.
[2] Brian Fairfax's *Letter to Atterbury*; Mrs. Cooper, loc. cit.

in R. Gough's edition of Camden's *Britannia*, 1789.[1] The rest do not seem to have survived. At least two other works of his are lost—the *History of Edward the Black Prince*, and his letters to one John Dorrell, 'a Romish priest then prisoner in York Castle', on such subjects as 'the Pope's Supremacy, Infallibility, Idolatry etc which deserve to be publisht'.[2] Fortunately for us, however, two other works remain: the *Daemonologia*, of which we have already spoken, and the accomplished poem on the death of King James I, which was printed by G. W. Johnson in his edition of the Fairfax correspondence.[3] Finally, there is recorded an epitaph by Edward Fairfax on the wife of Sir Thomas Fairfax the younger.[4]

In his minor verse Fairfax shows himself a skilful and imaginative poet, and one can only regret that neither he nor his family felt impelled to ensure its survival by having it printed. His prose has been less neglected, for the *Daemonologia* achieved a surprisingly wide manuscript circulation, was twice printed in the nineteenth century, and is well known to connoisseurs of the supernatural. Its literary merits however have not yet received their due.

This is not the place to enter into conjectures about the missing works of Edward Fairfax, but if, by some good fortune, they should one day come to light, they are likely to prove of more than merely antiquarian value; for as the surviving writings show, Edward Fairfax was a poet, and prose-writer, of genuine originality.

---

[1] III. 50.

[2] Brian Fairfax, loc. cit.

[3] *The Fairfax Correspondence*, ed. G. W. Johnson, i (1848), 2–3. The manuscript was purchased by Monckton Milnes, Lord Houghton, and may have perished in the fire which destroyed his library.

[4] In British Library Add. MS. 39, 992, fo. 384[r].

II. GODFREY OF BULLOIGNE
THE TRANSLATION

ACCORDING to John Payne Collier, Coleridge, Wordsworth, Hazlitt, and the Lambs once talked together about Tasso's *Jerusalem Delivered*, and Spenser's obligations to the Italian were discussed:

'Lamb mentioned the translation of Tasso by Fairfax, of which Wordsworth said he had no copy, and was not well acquainted with it. Lamb gave it as his opinion that it was the very best, yet the very worst translation in English; and, being asked for an explanation of his apparent paradox, he stammered a little, and then went on, pretty flowingly, to say that it was the best for the air of originality and ease, which marked many of the stanzas, and the worst, as far as he was able to judge (and he had been told the same by competent Italians) for literalness, and want of adherence to the text. Nothing could be more wanton than Fairfax's deviations, excepting some of those in Sir John Harington's version of Ariosto, into which whole octaves had often been thrust without need or notice.

'Aye (interposed Hazlitt,) that is an evil arising out of original genius undertaking to do unoriginal work; and yet a mere versifier, a man who can string easy rhymes, and employ smooth epithets, is sure to sacrifice the spirit and power of the poet: it is then a transfusion of wine into water, and not of one wine into another, or of water into wine . . .

'Miss Lamb adverted to the amazing pains and polishing Fairfax had bestowed upon his work; and a copy of it was after produced in which the first stanza, as first printed, and as afterwards altered, were both preserved, one having been pasted over the other. Not only so (said another of the company) but even this emendation did not satisfy Fairfax, for he changed his mind a third time, and had the whole of the first leaf cancelled, in order to introduce a third reading of the first stanza.★

★ Soon afterwards I had the pleasure of giving Wordsworth a copy of Fairfax's *Godfrey of Bulloigne*, as he entitles his translation, of the date of 1600, in which the whole of the first leaf had been reprinted, with several variations, in order that the translator's third attempt at an opening stanza might be inserted. Wordsworth thanked me in a letter containing some criticisms, which I still have by me. What became of the book on the death of the poet I do not know, but I never saw another copy with this peculiarity.[1]

[1] Collier, John Payne, in his edition of *Seven Lectures on Shakespeare and Milton* by the late S. T. Coleridge (1856), pp. xxxii–v. Collier cannot give date or place, but thinks the meeting probably occurred in Lamb's rooms in the Temple.

'Meanwhile Coleridge had been turning over the pages of the copy
produced, and observed that in one place Fairfax had been quite as much
indebted to Spenser as to Tasso, and read the subsequent stanzas from
Book XVI, with that sort of musical intonation which he always vindicated
and practised:

> 'The gentle-budding rose (quoth she) behold,
> The first scant peeping forth with virgin beams,
> Half ope, half shut, her beauties doth upfold
> In their dear leaves, and less seen fairer seems;
> And after spreads them forth more broad and bold,
> Then languisheth, and dies in last extremes:
>   Nor seems the same that decked bed and bower
> Of many a lady late, and paramour.
>
> 'So in the passing of a day doth pass
> The bud and blossom of the life of man,
> Nor e'er doth flourish more, but, like the grass
> Cut down, becometh wither'd pale and wan.
> O! gather then the rose while time thou has:
> Short is the day, done when it scant began,
>   Gather the rose of love while yet thou may'st,
> Loving be lov'd, embracing be embrac'd.

'Nobody was prepared to say from memory, how far the above was or was
not a literal rendering of Tasso's original; but nobody doubted that it was
very like Spenser, in the Canto which Wordsworth not long before so
warmly praised. Coleridge repeated, with a very little prompting, the
following stanza from Book II, c. 12, of the *Faery Queen*, for the purpose of
proving how closely Fairfax had followed Spenser.

> 'So passeth, in the passing of a day,
> Of mortall life the leaf, the bud, the flower,
> Ne more doth flourish after first decay,
> That erst was sought to decke both bed and bower,
> Of many a lady, and many a paramour.
> Gather therefore the rose whilst yet is prime,
> For soone comes age, that will her pride deflower:
> Gather the rose of love, whilst yet is time
> Whilst loving thou may'st loved be with equal crime.

'It was held, on all hands, sufficiently established, that Fairfax, in trans-
lating Tasso, must have had Spenser in his memory, if not in his eye; and
it was contended by Hazlitt, that it would have been impossible for Fairfax
to have done better: moreover, he insisted that in translating this part of
the *Gerusalemme Liberata*, he could not have acquitted himself at all

adequately, without approaching so near Spenser as absolutely to tread upon his heels. But, (added Lamb stuttering) he has not only trodden upon his heels, but upon his toes too: I hope he had neither kibes nor corns.'

If Collier's report may be suspected of a little tidying and tightening there is some confirmatory evidence in two of Lamb's letters.

Fairfax I have been in quest of a long time. Johnson in his life of Waller gives a most delicious specimen of him, and adds, in the true manner of that delicate critic, as well as amiable man, 'it may be presumed that this old version will not be much read after the elegant translation of my friend, Mr. Hoole'. I endeavour'd—I wish'd to gain some idea of Tasso from this Mr. Hoole, the great boast and ornament of the India House, but soon desisted. I found him more vapid than smallest small beer sun-vinegared.
(5 Feb. 1797)

And to H. F. Cary,

Fairfax's Tasso is no translation at all. It's better in some places; but it merely observes the number of stanzas; as for images, similes, etc., he finds 'em himself, and never 'troubles Peter for the matter'.
(9 Sept. 1833)

But long before on 15 April 1797 he had reported 'By the way, I have lit upon Fairfax's *Godfrey of Bullen* for half-a-crown. Rejoice with me.'

These extracts are given in full because they touch upon many of the matters which this Introduction must take up, such as the character and quality of the version; the evidence for a double revision of the opening of the poem; the relation between Tasso, Spenser, and Fairfax; the eighteenth-century preference for Hoole's rendering; the hint about Wordsworth's copy.

But to go back to the start: on 22 November 1599 Mathewe Lownes and John Jagger 'Entered for their copie under the handes of my Lord Bysshop of London and Master Man Warden / All TASSO translated out of the Italian into Englishe . Alias the Recoverie of Jerusalem by GODFREY OF BULLEN.'[1] The book was published in 1600 under the title *Godfrey of Bulloigne, or the Recoverie of Ierusalem . Done into English Heroicall verse, by Edward Fairefax Gent.* Imprinted at London by Ar. Hatfield for I. Iaggard and M. Lownes.

[1] *A Transcript of the Registers of the Company of Stationers of London. 1554–1640,* ed. Edward Arber, iii (1875), 54.

An authorized text of Tasso's whole poem appeared first in 1581, replacing a pirated version of the previous year. The textual history is unusually complicated: it will be considered later which edition, or editions, it is likely that the translator used.

Fairfax was not the first in the field. Apart from the Latin renderings of some portions by Scipio Gentili printed in England in 1584, Christopher Hunt of Exeter had offered readers in 1594 the first part of 'An Heroicall Poem' by Torquato Tasso, 'translated into English by R.C. Esquire'. The initials stood for Richard Carew of Antonie. The title, *Godfrey of Bulloigne, or the recoverie of Hierusalem*, was identical with the double title later used by Fairfax. Hunt averred at the end of February that 'it hath pleased the excellent doer of them [the verses] (for certaine causes to him-selfe best knowne) to command a staie of the rest till the sommer.' Meanwhile Hunt had 'caused the Italian to be printed together with the English, for the delight and benefit of those Gentlemen, that love that most lively language. And thereby, the learned Reader shall see how strict a course the translator hath tyed him-selfe in the whole work, usurping as little liberty as any what-soever, that ever wrote with any commendations.'

Hunt's claim for Carew's accuracy is very just, indeed better deserved than his enterprise allowed to appear, for it has been demonstrated that the text of Tasso which the printer provided facing Carew's verses was that of Osanna, 1584, and not the edition from which Carew worked.[1] Carew's close rendering, translation in the strictest sense, is more useful as a crib than immediately readable as a poem, but his procedure is always inter-esting and to be respected and he is occasionally felicitous.

Meanwhile in 1590 the most distinguished evidence of Tasso's popularity would have been apparent to the discerning in the *Faerie Queene*, Book II. The Romantic critics guessed shrewdly enough: Fairfax when he came to some of Tasso's most alluring stanzas describing the Garden of Armida must have reckoned that he could not do better than note the way in which this passage had been boldly Englished by Spenser for his Bower of Bliss. In

---

[1] Neil Dodge, R.E., 'The text of *Gerusalemme Liberata* in Carew and Fairfax', *P.M.L.A.* xliv (1929), 681–95; Bullock, W. L., *P.M.L.A.* xlv (1930), 330–5.

the translating of a few odd stanzas Fairfax was also preceded by Harington and Southwell. Fairfax was therefore the first Englishman to publish, not 'all Tasso', but at any rate Tasso's epic whole. He was by no means the last. In 1737 Mrs. Elizabeth Cooper, in the *Muses Library*, remarks that except for Dryden's praise Fairfax was neglected in her day, and she comes out strongly in his support: 'Nor could any Author, in my opinion, be justify'd for attempting Tasso anew, as long as his translation can be read.' Johnson thought otherwise, and his Life of Waller contains the reference which stirred Lamb to irony. In a letter to Thomas Cadell (2 May 1779), Johnson writes: 'As Waller professed to have imitated Fairfax, do you think a few pages of Fairfax would enrich *our edition*? Few readers can have seen it and it may please them. But it is not necessary.' Johnson selected a substantial extract of eighteen stanzas from Book VII describing Erminia's flight. It may be wondered whether his distaste for pastoral determined the choice of this passage, somewhat to disparage Fairfax who is at his weakest at the beginning and end of the extract. On the other hand, at the age of 75 Johnson apparently projected an edition of Fairfax's Translation of Tasso with notes, glossary, etc.[1] To judge by the frequency of editions, Fairfax was holding his own in a modest way. By the time Johnson wrote there had been five editions (1600, 1624, 1687, 1726, and 1749), and to complete the list seven more were to follow (1817 twice, 1844, 1858, 1890, 1962, and 1963). The number is not spectacular, but it shows that Fairfax's services were not entirely forgotten.

Meanwhile many others tried their hands at translating a poem which, as is shown in a later section, at any rate until the mid-eighteenth century was very freely read and frequently referred to. Ten versions reached print; one remains in manuscript, another in typescript, not to mention half a dozen part-translations by enterprising amateurs.

Fairfax as a translator is as self-effacing as his contemporary Harington is entertainingly obtrusive; he provides graceful verses in compliment to the Queen to preface the first edition, and was probably responsible for the other poem for Charles set before

---

[1] Boswell, J., *Life of Johnson*, ed. Hill and Powicke, iv (1934–50), 381 n.

the second edition of 1624; but there is never a word about himself. His characteristics as a translator may supplement the evidence derived from those few compositions that are original in the full sense. Every reader must have been warned by now that *Godfrey of Bulloigne* is a very free translation. But how free? How much of the most famous of Renaissance heroic poems can we trust it to convey? First it would be fair to ask what text Fairfax had to work from. The matter is vexed both by the fact that Tasso was not himself responsible for the initial publication of his poem, and also by his habit of nervous reworking. The scholarship of Angelo Solerti revealed the extent of the trouble as he assembled and scrutinized the mass of material upon which subsequent editors have worked, questioning and modifying to some extent the findings of Solerti's magnificent pioneer editing. From these investigations it is at least clear that there are two principal strains. The first was established by the text issued by Bonnà in 1581, the second derived from the text of Osanna in 1584, a text which had been attended to, and possibly somewhat adulterated, by Tasso's admiring patron Scipione Gonzaga. Osanna's was the tradition favoured for some three centuries until by the persuasion of late-nineteenth-century critics there came a renewed respect for Bonnà's line. The problems involved in establishing a text do not, however, affect the questions which are pertinent to the English translations. All that it would be in place to inquire here is what was available for an Elizabethan reader and which text, or texts, Fairfax had before him. It has been ably demonstrated by Neil Dodge and Bullock that, unlike Carew and Gentili who used Viotto, an edition in the Bonnà tradition, Fairfax used Osanna; this is clear from the number of stanzas in Cantos VII and XVI and by the preponderance of readings presenting variants in the Osanna tradition. There are, however, a few readings which suggest recourse to something other than Osanna. Dodge lists some twenty editions and tests fourteen places against the variant readings available before 1600. Judging by a close scrutiny of the fifteen editions now available in this country it would seem to us that most of the deviations could be accounted for if Fairfax had his eye on either of two Venetian editions (i.e. those of Francesco de' Franceschi Senese (1583) or Altobello Salicato (1589)), with perhaps very occasional reference to the text presented by Gratioso Perchacino (1581) or that of A. Canacci and Erasmo Viotto (Casalmaggiore and Parma 1581) or the now rare Lyons edition of Alessandro Marsilii (1581). It is impossible to press further towards certainty because of the looseness of the rendering, but the supposition that he had access to and occasionally consulted a couple of texts in addition to his standard Osanna seems reasonable, and offers a decent explanation for what might otherwise be counted to his discredit as mistakings of his author. It still leaves us to be wary of some slips, some errors, and a great number of soft renderings which blur Tasso's nice intricacies, and to remark, sometimes with amusement, occasionally with admiration, the few deliberate additions that in his character as an Englishman, or as a Protestant, or as a minor poet, he feels constrained to make. The reader who is suspicious that his Tasso is diluted and occasionally adulterated may find the Commentary which records the additions, omissions, and major changes of some use. He who reads for the fable can ignore all such probing. Meanwhile both types of reader might be interested to the extent of examining a few sample instances to show the quality, while a glance at the footnotes reveals the quantity, of these changes. A convenient way of sampling the nature and degree of the licence Fairfax allows himself (for better, for worse) is to compare some of his stanzas with Carew's close and painstaking translations; for instance, by consulting the present notes to Books I–V and especially to Book II, stanzas 14–18.

Denham, in a similar connection, once paid Fanshawe a handsome compliment on his version of Guarini's '*Il Pastor Fido*':

> That servile path thou nobly dost decline
> Of tracing word by word, and line by line.
>
> .   .   .   .   .
>
> A new and nobler way thou dost pursue
> To make Translation and Translators too.
> They but preserve the Ashes, thou the Flame,
>
> .   .   .   .   .

I conceive it a vulgar error in translating Poets to affect being *Fidus Interpres*; . . . it is not his business alone to translate Language into Language, but Poesie into Poesie; and Poesie is of so subtile a spirit, that in pouring out of one language into another, it will all evaporate; and if a new spirit be not added to the transfusion, there will remain nothing but a *Caput mortuum*, there being certain Graces and Happinesses peculiar to every Language, which gives life and energy to the words . . .[1]

In principle these remarks might well be transferred to Fairfax's way with Tasso at its best. Fairfax's style is easy as Tasso's is not. We would be right then in guessing that we pay a price for running as we read. The price, of course, is some loss of poetic distinction: *pace* Hazlitt, the wine *has* been watered a little. Fairfax seizes on any chance to secure an antithesis:

> And in this legend, all that glorious deede
> Read, whil'st you arme you; arme you, whilst you reed.
> (I. 5)

> Safe from sunnes heat, but scorcht with beauties beame
> (III. 22)

> And two large doores made for his life and breath,
> Which past, and curde hot love, with frozen death
> (XX. 120).[2]

He enjoys touching up a conceit;[3] he likes to work in a turn or *schema* of his own devising,[4] to introduce classical references of a fairly obvious kind,[5] to thread in a Biblical allusion (whether the speaker be Christian or pagan),[6] to stud his verses with moralizing sentences,[7] casting them wherever possible into proverbial form:[8] above all he is addicted to lists—lists of nouns, epithets, or verbs.

---

[1] Other instances of cultivated antithesis will be found at I. 5, 49, 56; II. 17, 34; III. 22; V. 47; VI. 64; IX. 39, 92; XIX. 17, 19; XX. 89, 120.

[2] *The Poetical Works of Sir John Denham*, ed. T. H. Banks, (2nd edn., 1969), pp. 143–4 and 159.

[3] *Conceits and metaphors.* I. 49; II. 26, 28, 31, 38, 39, 58, 62, 68[8], 70[4], 72[1–4]; III. 1, 15[8], 21[8], 43[8], 49[4], 52[8], 53[8], 69; IV. 3, 7, 16, 34, 38, 46, 51, 72, 74, 75, 76, 84, 92, 93; V. 7, 61, 63, 70; VI. 40, 60, 80, 104; VII. 79; VIII. 32; IX. 33; XII. 21, 88[6]; XIV. 64; XIX. 8, 47[3], 69, 80.

[4] *Miscellaneous figures.* I. 47; II. 53, 93[5]; IV. 94; VI. 35, 45, 84; VIII. 78, 82.

[5] *Classical allusions.* I. 61, 73, 77; II. 2, 14, 34, 40, 70, 94; III. 33, 37, 52, 75; IV. 5, 46, 76, 84, 91, 92, 93; V. 60, 66, 86; VI. 8, 22, 28, 33, 40, 79, 111; VII. 19, 57, 63; VIII. 32, 61; IX. 22, 49, 65, 71, 92; X. 17; XI. 13, 27, 28, 38; XIII. 55; XIV. 37, 43, 66, 72; XV. 15, 16; XVI. 1[8], 3, 8, 24, 68.

[6] *Biblical echoes.* I. 16, 71; II. 2, 3, 12, 54, 66, 71, 85; III. 69[8], 70; VI. 52; IX. 48; X. 33, 69; XIII. 56, 75; XIV. 36.

[7] *Moral sentences.* II. 58, 65, 77, 79; III. 10, 51; IV. 85; V. 47, 62; X. 20; XI. 40; XII. 88; XIV. 20; XIX. 111; XX. 63.

[8] *Proverbs* (or phrases with a proverbial ring). I. 62; II. 11, 15, 50; IV. 15, 45, 47, 78, 86, 89, 90; V. 73; XII. 24.

Lists fill out his line, usually the concluding line; are all too easy tricks of rhetorical amplification:

> All in that masse, that globe, and compasse see,
> Land, sea, spring, fountaine, man, beast, grasse and tree.
>
> (XIV. 9)

In moderation this device is tolerably effective; but it is used far too often, and many a sequence when scrutinized is merely verbiage and reads dangerously like an entry in a dictionary of synonyms:

> Amas'd, asham'd, disgras'd, sad, silent, trist,
>
> (XIII. 29)

> His valour boldnesse, hart and courage brave,
> To his faint body strength and vigor gave.
>
> (XIII. 32)[1]

Among these rhetorical devices there are instances of genuine poetic wit or imagination:

> In bond of vertuous love together tied,
> Together serv'd they and together died.
>
> (I. 56)

> The rose within her selfe her sweetnes closed.
>
> (II. 18^4)

> And prickt his reason on his weapons end.
>
> (II. 59^8)

> For chance assisteth oft th' ignobler part,
> We lost the field, yet lost we not our hart,
>
> (IV. 15)

> This said; the day to sable night was turned,
> That scant one could anothers armes descrie,
> But soone an hundreth lampes and torches burned,
> That cleared all the earth and all the skie;
> The castell seem'd a stage with lights adorned,
> On which men play some pompous tragedie;
> Within a tarras sat on high the Queene,
> And heard and saw, and kept her selfe unseene.
>
> (VII. 36)

> Daz'led his eies, the world on wheeles ran round.
>
> (XIX. 28^5)

---

[1] For other instances of lists, see Commentary on I. 7.

Sometimes, on the other hand, he can miss the mark and leave clumsy lines which blur or coarsen Tasso. There is little point in quoting these; when the sense is in danger it is noted in the Commentary; others are self-evident blemishes. But when the reader is caught by the movement of the poem, and it is a swift, steady current whether carrying narrative or lyrical impetus, the stylistic details, happy or inept, slip by and the total impression is one of fluency and delight in the telling. The version has this great merit that it reads well to the inner, and very tolerably aloud to the outer ear.

Fairfax has laboured to leave Englishmen a book which affords hours of agreeable entertainment. How true this may have been for inarticulate but not unintelligent readers for almost four centuries can never be fully documented. It is to be suspected, however, that although Tasso was then held in higher esteem than he is in the present century, many would still have found the fine twistings of his style beyond their command of the language and have been content to get from Fairfax's version the splendid stories which they refer to with casual ease. Here and there we find evidence of a closer response, notably on the part of Milton and Waller as a later section will make plain. Brian Fairfax told Atterbury that King James valued this book above all other poetry, and King Charles in the days of his confinement used to divert himself by reading it. It must have been and may still prove to be, both a solace and a stimulus in happier circumstances to humbler men.

III. TASSO'S REPUTATION IN ENGLAND

THE following account of Tasso's standing among English and, in particular, Elizabethan readers is often indebted to the findings of Castelli, Praz, Clark, and Brand. An article by G. C. Bell gives a basis for the investigation of the popularity of Fairfax's version.[1]

Knowledge of Tasso's life and writings came into England with remarkably little delay. In 1584 Scipio Gentili translated into Latin hexameters part of the fourth book of Tasso's *Gerusalemme Liberata* under the title of *Plutonis Concilium*, and dedicated it to Sidney.[2] In the same year John Wolfe published in London Scipio Gentili's translations into Latin of the beginning of the epic.[3] Giacomo Castelvetri, writing to Ludovico Tassoni, reports that the Queen already had some of the Italian stanzas by heart and wanted to know more.[4]

Thomas Watson put *Aminta* (1573) into Latin by 1585, and two years later Abraham Fraunce published a translation, unauthorized by Watson and with no acknowledgement as the *Lamentations of Amyntas for the death of Phillis*; he acknowledged his debt only in the edition of 1591, re-entitling it *The Countess of Pembroke's Tvychurch* and adding some matter freshly drawn from the Italian. Before 1590 Spenser had worked a sympathetic allusion to Aminta's

---

[1] Castelli, A., *'La Gerusalemme Liberata' nella Inghilterra di Spenser* (Milan, 1936); Praz, M., *The Flaming Heart* (1958); Clark, A. F. B., *Boileau and the French Classical critics in England (1660–1830)* (1925); Brand, C. P., *Torquato Tasso* (1965); Bell, G. C., 'A History of Fairfax criticism', *P.M.L.A.* lxii (1947), 644–56.

[2] Buxton, John, *Sir Philip Sidney and the English Renaissance* (1954), p. 157. See also *A Short-Title Catalogue of Books printed in England, Scotland and Ireland 1475–1640*, compiled by A. W. Pollard and G. R. Redgrave, 1926, No. 23702 for the unique Cambridge copy.

[3] Castelli, op. cit., p. 12 distinguishes between

> (1) A. Scipio Gentilis, *Torquati Tassi Solymeidos Liber Primus Latinis numeris expressus*, containing one dedication to Elizabeth and another to the Poets of Italy (British Library, 1073.g.31 1073.g.31(2)) and
> (2) *Solymeidos Libri Duo priores de Torquati Tassi Italicis expressi* containing verses in praise of Tasso and addressed to the Italian Poets (British Library, 11403.bb.32(5)).

[4] Castelli quotes from A. Solerti, *Vita di T. Tasso*, ii (1895), 204.

'wretched fate,/To whom sweet Poet's verse hath given endlesse date' into the flower passage in the Garden of Adonis.[1] As a sonneteer he found Tasso a help both at close quarters, as in *Amoretti*, 31, 72, and 73, and for more distant allusions. In Spenser's 'Letter to Raleigh' (1589) Tasso is found in company with Homer, Virgil, and Ariosto, and Spenser is apparently aware of the allegorical interpretation of Rinaldo's ethical, and Godfredo's political significance. The most famous salute from poet to poet comes in the free use made of Tasso's description of the Garden of Armida (*G.L.* XIV and XV) in the Bower of Bliss (*F.Q.* II. xii): here the relationship is closest, though not unique.[2] 'T.W. Gent' (?Thomas Watson again) worked on an English rendering of a passage from Tasso's pastoral, printed in the *Phoenix Nest*, 1593. Daniel the year before had included among his sonnets to Delia a graceful version of the first chorus, 'O bella età dell'oro'; and the image in 'Look Delia how wee steeme the half-blowne Rose', handled with felicity in Sonnet XXXI, derives from *Gerusalemme*, XVI. 14. Earlier than this, Southwell had contrived to give a religious turn to the famous rose simile and converted it into the beautiful lyric, *Optima Deo*.[3]

Daniel in his *Defence of Ryme* (?1603) hailed Tasso as 'the wonder of Italy', and his 'Jerusalem' as 'that admirable Poem . . . com-

---

[1] *Faerie Queene*, III. vi. 45.

[2] See Koeppel, E., *Anglia*, xii (1889), 103–42 for the quantity of Tasso/Spenser connections and R. M. Durling, *Comparative Literature*, vi (1954) for the quality of dependence in the Bower of Bliss.

[3]
        Behold how first the modest Rose doth prie
        Out of her somer coate in virgins hew,
        One half in sight, half-hidden from the eie;
        The lesser sene, the fairer to the view.
        But in her pride her leaves she doth display,
        And fades in fine, and semeth not the same;
        It seemes not she that was a dainty praye
        For ev'ry am'rous youth and galant Dame.
        So with the passing of a sliding day
        Of mortal life the floure and leafe doth passe;
        Ne with the new returne of flouring May
        Doth it renew the bounteous wonted glasse.
        Then croppe the morening Rose, while it is faire,
        Our day is short, the evening makes it die;
        Yield God the prime of youth, eare it empaire;
        Least he the dregges of crooked age denie.

(*The Poems of Robert Southwell. S.J.*, ed. J. H. McDonald and Nancy Pollard Brown (1967), p. 109.)

parable to the best of the ancients in any other forme than the accustomed verse';[1] and in the invocation and dedication of the *Civile Wars* and in a couple of similes Castelli heard echoes of the Italian poet.[2] Drayton, in *Robert, Duke of Normandy* (1596) gently reproved Tasso for treating his 'Great Worthy' among the Crusaders so slightly.[3] The complaint is repeated by Sir G(ilbert) T(albot), who translated the whole epic in the seventeenth century.[4] Brand finds the *Barons' Wars* often reminiscent of Tasso, and some passages in the *Muses Elizium* remind him of the Garden of Armida.[5]

It has tempted several critics who have sensed Sidney's regard for Tasso's work to conjecture that the two men met in Paris. It would appear, however, more likely that they just missed each other.[6] Tasso figures in Campion's *Licentiate Iambicks* (1602),[7]

[1] Smith, Gregory, *Elizabethan Critical Essays*, ii (1904), 369.

[2] *Civile Wars betweene the two houses of Lancaster and Yorke*, Bks. i–iv (1595), Bk. v (1599), Bks. vi and vii (1601). The similes are found in ii. 11 (cf. *G.L.* III. 32) and vi. 107 (cf. *G.L.* IX. 46).

[3] Drayton, Michael, *Works*, eds. Hebel and Hudson, i (1961), 292, stanza 157; and ii. 405.

> O thou immortall *Tasso, Aestes* glory,
> Which in thy golden booke his name hast left,
> Enrold in the great *Godfreis* living story
> Whose lines shall scape untoucht of ruins theft,
> Yet us of him thou hast not quite bereft:
> Though thy large Poems onely boast his name,
> Ours was his birth, and we will have his fame.
> Revised in 1619 as ll. 792–8:
> O wherefore then Great *Singer* of thy dayes,
> Renowned TASSO in thy Noble Story
> Wert thou so slacke in this Great *Worthy*'s prayse,
> And yet so much should'st set forth others glory?
> Methinks for this, thou canst not but be sorry,
> That thou should'st leave another to recite
> That, which so much Thou did'st neglect to write.

See also a reference to the possible influence of *G.L.* I. 44 on the description in *Robert of Normandie* (1619), ll. 722–42; op. cit. ii. 403.

[4] MS. Bodley Rawlinson Poet. 1 and 4. See Commentary, below, on I. 44 and III. 62.   [5] Brand, C.P., op. cit., p. 247.

[6] I am indebted to Jean Bromley for the following dates derived from Solerti's *Vita di Torquato Tasso*, i (1895), 135–54. Tasso arrived in Paris on 15 Nov. 1570 and left on 19/20 Mar. 1571, arriving in Ferrara on 12 Apr. Sidney came to Paris on 8 June 1572, and left after 23 Aug. He was in Venice and Padua from Oct. 1573 until 1 Aug. 1574; he visited Florence and Genoa but there is no record that he was in Ferrara or at the Este residence on 31 July when *Aminta* was first produced.

[7] Smith, Gregory, op. cit. ii. 336.

and more amusingly in his description of a Masque for the marriage
of the Earl of Somerset in 1614:

> But in our dayes, although they [Satyrs, nymphs, and their like] have not
> utterly lost their use, yet finde they so little credit, that our moderne
> writers have rather transfered their fictions to the persons of Enchanters and
> Commanders of Spirits, as that excellent Poet Torquato Tasso hath done,
> and many others.[1]

Harington refers to Tasso's own captivity in an unpleasing
epigram (II. 43),[2] but pays tribute in his *Apologie*, prefixed to the
translation of *Orlando Furioso*, to Tasso's 'pretty Prosopopeia' by
introducing his own version of the third stanza of the first book
of *Gerusalemme*.[3] Meres has a reference in 1598, but it tells us little,[4]
whereas in *Ortho-Epia Gallica* (1593) John Eliot instructs his
reader and sums up popular knowledge:

> '*Torquato Tasso*, a fine scholer truly, who is yet living, the last Italian Poet
> who is of any great fame in our age, but worthie of the first honour, besides
> that he is a divine Poet, he is also a most eloquent Oratour and Rhetoricyan,
> as his missive Epistles do shew very well. This youth fell mad for the love
> of an Italian lasse descended of a great house, when I was in Italie, . . . there
> are three Toomes of his workes printed at Ferrara, wherein there are divers
> sorts of verses of all kinds of fine inventions: a Commedie, a Tragedie, divers
> Dialogues and discourses in Prose, all worthie the reading of the wisest and
> quickest spirits of Europe.'
> 'Is that all that he hath written?'
> 'No, for he hath the pen in hand every day.'
> 'You have forgotten his *Gierusalemme liberata*.'
> 'You say, true, this child hath written in Heroicall verses one excellent
> Poeme amongst all other Italian Poesies, intituled as you say, wherein all
> the riches of the Greekes and Latines are gathered together and enchaced so
> cunningly past all other skill, with such grace, brevitie, gravitie, learning,
> livelinesse, and vivacitie that is remarqued to have bene in *Virgill* the
> Prince of Latine Poets.'[5]

The most interesting among Nashe's characteristically odd
remarks occurs in *Christ's Teares* (1593):

> Admirable Italian teare-eternizers, *Ariosto*, *Tasso* and the rest, nere had you
> such a subject to roialize your Muses with. Of a late destruction of *Ierusalem*,

---

[1] *The Works of Thomas Campion*, ed. Walter R. Davis (1967), p. 268.
[2] *The Most Elegant and Wittie Epigrams of Sir John Harington, Knight* (1633), Sig.
Qq1ᵛ.
[3] Smith, Gregory, op. cit. ii. 199.　　　　[4] Ibid. ii. 319.　　　　[5] Sig. G3ᵛ–4ʳ.

Tasso, thou wrot'st, wherein thy *Godfry of Bulloyne*, the destroyer, beareth the chiefe part of honour.[1]

Naturally Tasso was one of the authors consulted by Florio for his dictionary. Abraham Fraunce also ransacked this poet's work when compiling the *Arcadian Rhetorick* (1588), and quoted eighty-four passages. Tasso was standard reading for Lady Politique-Would-bee.[2] Thomas Churchyard pays a conventional tribute in *A Praise of Poetrie* (1595). Gabriel Harvey's *Marginalia* show his familiarity, and in *Pierce's Supererogation* (1593) he alludes to the 'surmounting rage of Tasso in his furious angoy [*sic*]'; more significantly elsewhere he asks 'And which of the Golden Rivers floweth more currently then the silver streame of the *English Ariosto*', and exclaims 'Oh that we had such an *English Tasso*'.[3]

Harvey's allusions to Tasso's personal distress may be connected with the exploitation of the sad story of the poet's life on the English stage. A play entitled *Tasso's Melancholy* stands alongside a title *2 Godfrey of Bulloigne* in the same list of plays belonging to the Admiral's Men; they are dated 13 August and 19 July 1594 respectively.[4] Dekker was paid for alterations to *Tasso's Melancholy* in November 1604. Another lost play whose title *Jerusalem* has a possible relevance was in the repertory of Strange's Men in the early 1590s. The relationship between this play and Heywood's *The Four Prentises of London with the Conquest of Ierusalem* is obscure.[5] In 1604, in *Diaphantus, or The Passions of Love . . .* by An[thony] Sc[oloker] Gentleman there is a description of a distracted lover[6] who reminds him of Hamlet. Thomas Kyd got hold of one of Tasso's minor prose tracts, *Il Padre di Famiglia* and made it over into a readable and amusing piece of domestic didacticism as *The Householder's Philosophie* (1588). R[obert] T[oft]'s effort with another

---

[1] T. Nashe, *Works*, ed. R. B. McKerrow, ii (1910), 60.

[2] Jonson, *Volpone*, III. iv. 79.

[3] *An Advertisement for Pap-Hatchet*, and *Martin Mar-Prelate* (?1592). See Gregory Smith, op. cit. ii. 283.

[4] Chambers, E. K., *Elizabethan Stage* ii (1923), 143 and 181.

[5] Ibid. ii. 122 and iii. 340.

[6] *Tasso*, he finds, by that of *Hamlet*, thinkes
Tearmes him a mad-man, than of his Inkhorne drinks.
     .   .   .   .   .
Puts off his cloathes; his shirt he onely weares,
Much like mad-*Hamlet*; thus as Passion teares.   (Sig. E4[v].)

dialogue between 'the two famous Tassi, now living, the one
Hercules the philosopher, the other Torquato, the Poet', published
in 1599 as *Of Marriage and Wiving*, is a wearisome diatribe, drawn
from a book published in Bergamo (1595), entitled *Dello Ammo-
gliarsi Piacevole Contesa Fra i due Moderni Tassi, Hercole, cioé, e
Torquato, Gentilhuomini Bergamaschi*.[1]

The opening lines of Phineas Fletcher's *Locustes* (1627) reminded
Castelli of *Gerusalemme Liberata*, IV, 2–7; there are also signs in two
places of the second canto of *Brittains Ida* (1628) (Stanzas 6 and 8)
that Fletcher took advantage of *Gerusalemme*, XVI. 9 and XVI. 62.
William Browne, too, had Tasso in mind when he fashioned the
story of Coelia and Philocel in *Britannia's Pastorals*, Bk. II, Song 5,
ll. 739–44; the fate of these lovers owes much to the story of
Sofronia and Olindo in *Gerusalemme*, II. 35 ff.[2] Drummond, com-
paring Donne's elegy, *The Anagram*, with Tasso's 'Stanze sopra
la Bellezza' remarks 'one shall hardly know who hath the best'.[3]
Drummond himself possessed most of Tasso's important works,
and took leave to use his lyrical poetry freely on occasions.[4]

Milton's respect for Tasso is clearly shown in several forms.
His visit to Manso, the patron in whose house Tasso composed
his *Sette Giornate* may also be connected with the Leonora of
Milton's Latin poem who is obviously the lady of the Tasso
legend. F. T. Prince has effectively shown the influence of Tasso's
style on Milton's versification. The Commonplace Book has an
entry to illustrate 'Mendacio' drawn from Sofronia's heroic lie
(*G.L.* II. 22). His regard for Tasso as a critic is clear from the
Reason for Church Government and *Of Education*. Readers well versed
in both literatures, and notably Milton's eighteenth-century
editors, have picked up many echoes from pastoral and lyric as
well as heroical styles.

[1] See Wilson, F. P., ed., *The Batchelors Banquet* (1929) and F. B. Williams, Jr.,
R.E.S. xiii (1937), 405–24.
[2] See also Grundy, J., 'William Browne and the Italian Pastoral', *R.E.S.* n.s. iv
(Oct. 1953), 305.
[3] Spingarn, J. E., *Critical Essays of the Seventeenth Century*, i (1908), 217, 255, and
see exposition by J. B. Leishman, *The Monarch of Wit* (1951), pp. 81–3.
[4] William Drummond of Hawthornden, ed. Kastner, L. E., *Works* (1913). For
reference to the imitations see I. 185, 188, 192, 213, 220, 230, 231, 233, 235–7, 240
and II. 398.

Throughout the seventeenth century the frequency and casualness of reference indicate that Tasso was an author commonly read. From among a number of conventional allusions remarks of more interest were made by Henry Reynolds, the translator of *Aminta* who in *Mythomystes* (1632) shows his preference for 'the grave and learned *Tasso*, in his *Sette giorni* (a divine worke) and his *Gierusalem liberata*, so farre as an excellent pile of meerely Morall Philosophy may deserve'.[1] For Sir William Alexander (*Anacrisis*, 1634), 'There is no Man doth satisfy me more than that notable *Italian, Torquato Tasso*, in whom I find no Blemish but that he doth make *Solyman*, by whose Overthrow he would grace *Rinaldo*, to die fearfully, belying the Part that he would have Personated during his Life . . .'[2] Rymer was critical of the epic's structure and sometimes curious about small details of Tasso's dependence upon Virgil.[3] Davenant, in the *Preface to Gondibert* (1650), is censorious of Tasso's treatment of the supernatural, a criticism later to be exactly reversed by Hurd. There are signs that when Cowley was at work on his *Davideis* Tasso's critical theory, and occasionally Tasso's practice were in his head. Thomas Stanley translated some of Tasso's lyrics and his connections with William Fairfax, the poet's son. Meanwhile Sir G. T., formerly supposed to be George Turbeville [*sic*], but now identifiable as the Gilbert Talbot who Englished Bonarelli's *Filli di Sciro* (left in manuscript now in the Bodleian Library), judged it worth his while to translate the entire epic, and further, to revise many of his verses, as the two handsome folios, Rawlinson Poet. MSS. 1 and 4 bear witness.

The dimming of Tasso's fame in the eighteenth century has been traced by Clark, following a hint of Hurd's, to Addison's exploitation of Boileau's damaging metaphor by which the tinsel of Tasso is contrasted with Virgilian gold. There had been an earlier sign of similar disparagement when Dryden, whose early references to Tasso were complimentary, made an adverse comment in his *Discourse concerning the Original and Progress of Satire*:

. . . he is too flatulent sometimes, and sometimes too dry; many times unequal, and almost always forced; and besides, is full of conceits, points of epigarm

---

[1] Spingarn, i. 146.
[2] Ibid. i. 185.   [3] Ibid. ii. 176.

and witticisms; all of which are not only below the dignity of heroic verse, but contrary to its nature.[1]

If, as it seems, for a couple of generations the enjoyment of Tasso was to be relegated to the private reader and find no public voice, by the second half of the century the tide was turning. Hurd's advocacy is strongly persuasive[2] and Gray amused himself by translating selected portions. Collins speaks warmly of his pleasure in reading this author. Hazlitt, it is true, in his review of Sismondi, shows some slight knowledge but little liking; and it was remarked by Collier that Coleridge 'seemed to have little admiration of Ariosto, and perhaps less of Tasso, but I think he did not know much of them'.[3] But Leigh Hunt, Scott, Byron, and Shelley all bear witness, in varying forms and degrees, of their regard for Tasso both as poet and man. Scott has Waverley complimented by Flora as a man 'so gentle, so well-informed' that '. . . he can admire the moon, and quote a stanza from Tasso' (chap. 52). Leigh Hunt made his own translation of the *Aminta*. With Shelley and Byron the concern went much deeper. Their visit to Ferrara is tellingly recorded in Shelley's letter to Peacock of 7 November 1818. He had been moved by the sight of the Tasso manuscripts:

the hand writing . . . [contrasted to Ariosto's] is large free and flowing except that there is a checked expression in the midst of its flow which brings the letters into a smaller compass than one expected from the beginning of the word. It is the symbol of an intense and earnest mind exceeding at times its own depth and admonished to return by the chillness of the waters of oblivion striking on its adventurous feet.—You know I always seek in what I see the manifestation of something beyond the present and tangible object: and as we do not agree in phisiognomy so we may not now. . . . Some of these Mss of Tasso were sonnets to his persecutor which contain a great deal of what is called flattery. . . . But to me there is much more to pity than to condemn in these entreaties and praises of Tasso. It is as a Christian prays to {and} praises his God whom he knows to [be] the most remorseless, capricious and inflexible of tyrants, but whom he knows also to be omnipotent. Tasso's situation was widely different from that of any persecuted being of the present day, for from the depths of dungeons

---

[1] *Dryden's Essays*, ed. W. P. Ker, ii (1960), 27.
[2] Hurd, R., *Letters of Chivalry and Romance* (1762), *passim*.
[3] Raysor, *Coleridge's Shakespearean Criticism*, ii (1930), 39.

public opinion might now at least be awakened to an echo that would startle the oppressor. But then there was no hope. There is something irresistibly pathetic to me in the sight of Tasso's own handwriting moulding expressions of admiration and entreaty to a deaf and stupid tyrant in an age when the most heroic virtue would have exposed its possessor to hopeless persecution, and—such is the alliance between virtue and genius—which unoffending genius could not escape.

Some months before, Shelley had told Peacock (20 April 1818), 'I have devoted this summer, and indeed the next year to the composition of a tragedy on the subject of Tasso's madness, which I find upon inspection is, if properly treated, admirably dramatic and poetical.'[1] He confided the plan to Hogg on 30 April. Of this drama, as Mrs. Shelley notes, only 'a slight fragment and a song of Tasso remain', but there is surely an oblique reference to his case in the compassionate study of dementia in *Julian and Maddalo* and a direct, challenging mention in *A Defence of Poetry*:

Let us assume that Homer was a drunkard, that Virgil was a flatterer, that Horace was a coward, that Tasso was a madman, that Lord Bacon was a peculator, that Raphael was a libertine, that Spenser was a poet laureate . . . Their errors have been weighed and found to have been dust in the balance; if their sins were as scarlet, they are now white as snow: they have been washed in the blood of the mediator and redeemer, Time.[2]

Byron, meanwhile, completed his *Lament for Tasso*, a poem which Shelley greatly admired.

For Wordsworth, Tasso was said to have been a favourite poet all his life.[3] There is a pleasing allusion to Erminia in the *Prelude*, IX. 452. But perhaps his appreciation faded so that in 1812 Crabb Robinson observed that he 'seemed to think low' of Tasso.[4] Three years later Wordsworth wrote to Southey,

Now Tasso's is a religious subject, and in my opinion, a most happy one; but I am confidently of opinion that the movement of Tasso's poem rarely corresponds with the essential character of the subject; nor do I think it possible that, written in stanzas, it should. The celestial movement cannot,

[1] *The Letters of Percy Bysshe Shelley*, ed. F. L. Jones, ii (1964), 47; 8; 15.

[2] *Complete Works of Percy Bysshe Shelley*, ed. Roger Ingpen and Walter E. Peck, vii (1930), 138.

[3] Moorman, M., *William Wordsworth. The Early Years, 1770–1803* (1957), p. 87; *The Letters of William and Dorothy Wordsworth. The Early Years 1787–1805*, ed. E. de Sélincourt, 2nd edn., rev. by C. L. Shaver (1967), p. 120, n. 4.

[4] M. L. Peacock, Jr., *The Critical Opinions of William Wordsworth* (1950), p. 363.

I think, be kept up, if the sense is to be broken in that despotic manner at the close of every eight lines. Spenser's stanza is infinitely finer than the *ottava rima*, but even Spenser's will not allow the epic movement as exhibited by Homer, Virgil and Milton. How noble is the first paragraph of the *Aeneid* in point of sound, compared with the first stanza of the *Jerusalem Delivered*! The one winds with the majesty of the Conscript Fathers entering the Senate House in solemn procession; and the other has the pace of a set of recruits shuffling on the drill-ground, and receiving from the adjutant the command to halt at every ten or twenty steps.[1]

Lamb's views have been noticed already. Keats used Fairfax's phrase 'Gather the rose' in a letter to J. H. Reynolds, 22 September 1818,[2] and has a conventional reference to Tasso in the *Ode to Apollo*, l. 36. Haydon told Keats, 'when I die I'll have my Shakespeare placed on my heart, with Homer in my right hand, and Ariosto in the other, Dante under my head, Tasso at my feet . . .'[4]

The list of translations tells its own tale; in addition to two fresh versions in the eighteenth century and the eight as published in the nineteenth we may add several private and partial versions. An article in *T.L.S.*, 14 December 1962, reviews the situation in the mid-twentieth century and asks boldly 'How good *is* Tasso?' For the reader who stays for an answer there follows a discerning critique from which it is at least apparent that some resuscitating massage is still needed.

Meanwhile what of the minor part taken by Fairfax in these fluctuations of taste for his major author?

[1] *Letters of William and Dorothy Wordsworth, 1812–20*, ed. E. de Sélincourt, rev. Moorman and Hill (1970), p. 268.

[2] *Letters*, ed. Buxton Forman (1952), p. 216.

[3] 25 Mar. 1818: ibid., p. 119.

IV. FAIRFAX'S REPUTATION

WHEN *Godfrey of Bulloigne* appeared in 1600 Robert Allott made immediate use of it in compiling his *England's Parnassus*. As against 450 extracts from Spenser, he took 50 from Fairfax. Here is certainly evidence of contemporary approval; though after this the references come sparsely. Webster seems to be recalling Fairfax twice in the *Duchess of Malfi* and possibly again in his *Monumental Column*.[1] Ben Jonson told Drummond with his usual tartness that Fairfax's translation was not well done, but the phrase 'thunderbolt of warre' (*G.L.* XVII. 31) seems to have come in useful when Jonson composed a speech for *Prince Henry's Barriers* (l. 285).[2] Dowden, editing *Cymbeline* (4th edition, 1930) records that Mr. Craig suggested Book VII of Fairfax's Tasso as a possible source for the pastoral scenes in Act III, Scene iii.

Apart from the possibility that the reflections of Tasso in the poetry of William Browne of Tavistock and Phineas Fletcher may have come by way of the English version, no other recognition of the *Gerusalemme* has been noted until the publisher of the second edition of the *Godfrey* in 1624 informs us that the poem was reprinted at the command of James I and Prince Charles, and it is to the Prince that the edition is dedicated. At about this date Waller who was an admiring pilferer began to try himself out as a poet. 'Many besides myself', Dryden tells us, 'have heard our famous Waller own that he deriv'd the harmony of his numbers from *Godfrey of Bulloign*, which was turned into English by Mr. Fairfax.'[3] To the reader who turns from Fairfax to Waller this may seem a surprising assertion, for Waller writes in couplets more often than in stanzas such as Fairfax uses. Direct borrowings are easy to detect, but this was not the debt that Waller admitted

---

[1] See Commentary for *G.L.* IV. 73; IX. 54; XX. 30.

[2] Jonson, *Works*, ed. P. Simpson (1925–51), vii. 331 and x. 516.

[3] Dryden, *Preface to the Fables*, in *Prose Works*, ed. W. P. Ker, ii (1899, reprinted 1961), 247.

to, he was referring to versification. Later we discuss the nature of Fairfax's influence in this respect.

The question of Milton's debt to Fairfax has already been remarked upon and will be amplified in the following section and substantiated in the Commentary. A glance at the list of possible correspondences will show that for all his good Italian he had also enjoyed and profited from the English version.

Edward Phillips, Milton's nephew, has a brief but complimentary entry in his *Theatrum Poetarum* (1675), The Modern Poets, p. 34:

Edmund [*sic*] Fairfax, one of the most Judicious, Elegant and haply in his time, most approved of *English* Translatours, both for his choice of so worthily Extoll'd a Heroic Poet as *Torquato Tasso*; as for the exactness of his Version, in which he is judg'd by some to have approved himself no less a Poet than in that he hath written of his own Genius.

It would seem from this that Fairfax's original poems, though unpublished, had something of a reputation at this time.

Winstanley in 1687 copies Phillips's praise in his *Lives of the Most Famous English Poets*; and in the same year Roger L'Estrange brought out the third edition of *Godfrey of Bulloigne*. His preface contains this commendation:

This translation . . . is one of the most correct Pieces, perhaps, for the Turn of the Verse; The apt and Harmonious Disposition of the Words, and the strength of Thought, that we have anywhere extant of this kind in the English Tongue.

Robert Gould's complimentary verses, printed with the preface, reveal a similar critical stance:

> So wondrous are the Actions here enroll'd!
> And in such high, Harmonious Numbers told!
>
> See here, you dull Translators, look with shame
> Upon this stately Monument of Fame.
> And, to amaze you more, reflect how long
> It is, since first 'twas taught the English Tongue,
> In what a *dark Age* it was brought to light;
> Dark? No, our *Age* is dark, and that was bright.
>
> 'Tis true, some few *exploded* Words we find,
> To which we've Obligation to be kind;
> For, if the Truth is scan'd, we must allow
> They're better than the *New* admitted now:

Our language is at best, and it will fail
As th'innovation of *French* words prevail.
Let *Waller* be our Standard, all beyond
Tho spoke at Court, is Foppery and fond.

The praise is ambivalent (as the later seventeenth-century's attitude to the age of Shakespeare so often was): how clever of one of our barbarous forefathers to write so well, and how foolish of us to think that our forefathers were barbarous!

Dryden, who elsewhere bestows a similar mixture of patronage and admiration on the Elizabethans, does full justice to Fairfax in his *Preface to the Fables*:[1]

For *Spenser* and *Fairfax* both flourished in the reign of Queen *Elizabeth*: Great Masters in our Language; and who saw much farther into the Beauties of our Numbers, than those who immediately followed them. *Milton* was the poetical son of *Spenser*, and Mr. *Waller* of *Fairfax*; for we have our Lineal Descents and Clans as well as other families.

Waller's indebtedness to Fairfax is mentioned by his early eighteenth-century editors, one of whom in 1711 asserts that in Fairfax 'there's much more Harmony than in the *Fairy Queen*'.[2] Evidently *Godfrey of Bulloigne* was still an acceptable poem in the earlier eighteenth century: L'Estrange's edition was reprinted in 1726, and in 1737 Mrs. Elizabeth Cooper included in her anthology of older English poetry, *The Muses Library*, a long extract from Book XVI. Mrs. Cooper was well informed and enthusiastic; it may be significant that she felt it necessary to argue for her poet a little. She added some biographical information, which had not hitherto appeared in print, and published the whole of the fourth Eclogue. *Eglon and Alexis*. Her critical remarks go some way beyond the conventional praise of Fairfax's numbers: 'Nor could any Author, in my Opinion, be justify'd for attempting *Tasso* anew, as long as his Translation can be read.' (p. 343). Certainly the most eloquent eighteenth-century tribute to Fairfax comes from William Collins in his *Ode on the Popular Superstitions of the Highlands of Scotland*. The poem was composed between November 1749 and the early months of 1750. That Collins was aware of the appearance of a new edition of *Godfrey* in October 1749 is evident

---

[1] *Prose Works*, ed. W. P. Ker, ii, 247.   [2] *Poems*, 1711, p. lxv.

from an entry in the *General Advertiser* for Tuesday, 27 March 1750, noted by J. S. Cunningham, announcing 'An Epistle to the Editor of Fairfax, his Translation of Tasso's *Jerusalem*. By William Collins. Printed by R. Manby and H. S. Cox, on Ludgate Hill', but of this no more is known. The complicated story behind the *Ode* is unravelled in a long note by Roger Lonsdale in his edition of the *Poems of Thomas Gray, Oliver Goldsmith and William Collins*.[1] In what is regarded as an early draft, lines 192–5 read:

> How have I trembled, when, at Tancred's side
> Like him I stalkd and all his Passions felt
> When Charm'd by Ismen thro' the Forrest wide
> Barkd in Each Plant a talking Spirit dwelt.

and lines 200–5,

> Hence sure to Charm, his Early Numbers flow
> Though strong, yet sweet—
> Though faithful sweet, tho' strong, of simple kind.
> Hence with Each Theme he bids the bosom glow
> While his warm lays an easy passage find
> Pour'd thro' Each inmost nerve,

The stanza as revised improves on the expression:

> In scenes like these, which, daring to depart
>   From sober Truth, are still to Nature true,
>   And call forth fresh delights to Fancy's view,
> Th'heroic Muse employ'd her Tasso's art!
> How have I trembled when, at Tancred's stroke,
>   Its gushing blood the gaping cypress poured;
> When each live plant with mortal accents spoke,
>   And the wild blast upheav'd the vanished sword!
> How have I sat, where piped the pensive wind,
>   To hear his harp by British Fairfax strung.
> Prevailing poet, whose undoubting mind
>   Believed the magic wonders which he sung!
> Hence at each sound imagination glows;
>   Hence his warm lay with softest sweetness flows;
> Melting it flows, pure, numerous, strong and clear,
>   And fills the impassioned heart and lulls the harmonious ear.

It appears from a letter dated 10 November 1747 that Collins had

---

[1] Longmans, 1969.

had an interest in Fairfax a couple of years earlier. He mentions to
John Gilbert Cooper 'Some MSS. of Fairfax which I can procure',
a most tantalizing hint. In *Lines to a Friend about to Visit Italy* both
poets are praised again:

> Oh, think in what sweet lays, how sweetly strong,
> Our Fairfax warbles Tasso's forceful song.

Finally, as item 41 of the section on Lost and Doubtful poems
Lonsdale records another title: *An Epistle to the Editor of Fairfax his
Translation of Tasso's Jerusalem Delivered.*

It is from about this time that a decline in Fairfax's reputation
sets in. It is significant that a number of new translations, at first
only of parts of the *Gerusalemme*, begin to appear. And although
a new edition of Fairfax's version came out in 1749, the editor now
thought it necessary to introduce considerable changes into the
text. Colloquial and proverbial expressions were replaced by neutral
or elevated ones. For example, at II. 96[8] the line is changed from
'Sung lullabie, to bring the worlde to rest' into 'Sooth'd mortal
Cares, and lull'd the World to Rest'.[1]

A new version of the complete epic, in blank verse, was produced
by Philip Doyne and published in 1761. It purported to be more
accurate than Fairfax, but it found no favour with the public.
However, in 1763 a protégé of Samuel Johnson, John Hoole,
offered a translation which was to become standard for half a
century. A reviewer who evidently found it acceptable briefly
mentions Fairfax, who 'had the powers of Genius and Fancy',
but who unhappily chose 'a species of versification which was ill-
adapted to the English language'. Hoole, who used couplets, is
evidently making the same point when he comments on Fairfax's
use of a stanza form 'that cannot be read with pleasure by the
generality of those who have a taste for English poetry'. For all
his beauties 'of expression and sentiment', Fairfax had apparently
become unreadable; Hoole believed himself to be supplying a form
of verse 'more modern, and better adapted to the ear of all readers

---

[1] It has been noted that Joseph Warton apparently approved of these 'judicious
emendations'; see his edition of Vergil, 1763, ii. 57n. Douce, on the other hand,
thought them deplorable; see MS. note in the Bodley copy (Douce T.T.65) of the
1749 edition of Fairfax.

of English poetry, except of the very few who have acquired a taste for the phrases and cadences of those times when our verse, if not our language, was in its rudiments'.[1] Johnson, who was perfectly capable of appreciating Fairfax, but sympathized with the reactions of the common reader, appended eighteen stanzas of Book VII to his *Life of Waller*, to show how great a gap there was between Waller and his supposed master in the art of versification. He adds his opinion that 'they were unlikely to be soon reprinted'. Even Hume, who praises Fairfax for his elegance and exactness ('which, for that age, are surprising') finds it necessary to complain of the stanza-form.[2] One might expect to find praise for Fairfax in the works of the Wartons; but Thomas Warton's *History of English Poetry* gives him a bare mention, while Joseph Warton, in the second edition of *Essay on the Genius and Writings of Pope* (1782) questions the justice of Fairfax's reputation as an improver of English numbers.[3] In short, there had been a complete change of attitude: for the seventeenth and early eighteenth centuries Fairfax had been a master of poetic skill; to the later eighteenth century his versifications were distasteful.

The early nineteenth century, however, brought some revival of appreciation. The conversation quoted at the beginning of this Introduction provides some evidence of this.

In a new edition of Hartley Coleridge's *Lives of Northern Worthies* prepared by his brother Derwent in 1852 and enriched by marginal observations from S. T. C., there is a substantial passage about Fairfax. After quoting the entry in Chalmers's *Biographical Dictionary*, vol. xiv Hartley continues:

So long as the Italian models continued in vogue, and the rich various, long-drawn, linked sweetness of our early versification was understood and enjoyed, Fairfax's Tasso was read and admired, as a fair exotic transplanted by a skilful hand into a congenial soil . . . Even under the detestable tyranny of French criticism, when it became fashionable to talk of the Elizabethan writers as rude stammerers in an unpolished language and unmanageable metres, the wits of the new school allowed them such modicums of praise

[1] John Hoole, 3rd edn. (1767), i. xviii.
[2] Hume, *History of England from the invasion of Julius Caesar to . . . 1688*', new edn. (London, 1864), iv. 125.
[3] ii. 422; see also a reference in his edition of Pope, iv (1797), 205.

as they were wont to accord to the poets of better times; always, however, objecting to his stanza, the *ottava rima*, as unfitted to the English tongue. In fact, their ears, accustomed to the narrow compass, quick recurring rhymes, and balanced structure of the couplet, were incapable of perceiving a prolonged and suspended harmony. The present race of critics have a much juster sense of poetic music; and though it is unlikely that Fairfax will ever again be generally read, he is no longer liable to be insulted by invidious comparisons of his stanzas with the couplets of a Mr Hoole, of the India House, who *traduced* (to borrow an expressive French phrase) Tasso and Ariosto in the English heroic verse. Fairfax was, it must be confessed, an unfaithful translator, who, if he sometimes expanded the germ of his author, to a bright consummate flower, just as often spoiled what he was trying to improve.

Of Fairfax's other poems, Hartley remarks, there were

Eclogues, composed in the first year of James I, said by his son to be so learned that no man's reading but his own was sufficient to explain the allusions in them. This filial praise does not promise much poetry. Probably the Eclogues are 'allegorical pastorals'. Now, as pastoral, *per se*, is the silliest of all compositions, so, with due deference to the Mantuan and Spenser, the allegorical is the absurdest of all pastorals. [Marginal protests from S. T. C.:] Still, they must be curious; and it is to be regretted that excepting the fourth, which appeared in Mrs Cooper's *Muses Library*, 1737, they have never been printed.[1]

A. C. Robertson records an exchange with Wordsworth on the desirability of translating the *Gerusalemme*.

'I think', said Wordsworth, 'the work you propose to attempt would be useful. I do not, however, see the use of making an entirely new translation. You ought to make Fairfax the basis of your work, and only substitute your new version when Fairfax fails, or when your own seems better than his.'

'I suppose you consider it quite essential that the translation should follow the stanza of the original?'

Wordsworth.—'I am doubtful as to that point. To be able to do so would no doubt be highly advantageous, but the unfavourable nature of the English language for finding rhymes would render this difficult, if not impossible. When I was teaching my son Latin, I translated three books of Ariosto. I did not adhere strictly to the ottava rima arrangement of the rhymes. I found I could not do so without occasionally departing widely from the original, or expressing the meaning very poorly. I never lengthened the final line; I should consider this very objectionable. Wiffen's translation of *La Gerusalemme* is a failure; Hoole's is contemptible. The meaning of the

---

[1] pp. 280–2.

Italian ought, from the structure of the English language, to be rendered in a stanza of the same length . . . If I had been younger, I would have taken some trouble about your translation; but I am now too old to make a labour of it; however, if it ever gets into print, I shall look over it, and without going into detail, will make any general observations that I think may be of use to you.'[1]

Warmer advocacy had come in the form of a scholarly and charmingly produced edition of Fairfax's translation by S. W. Singer in 1817. Collier wrote knowledgeably about this reprint in an article in the *Critical Review*, 1817, and later showed that he knew even more about the matter in his contribution to *Notes and Queries*, 1850, presented under the pseudonym of 'the Hermit of Holyport'.

Charles Knight, the other 1817 editor, deprecates eighteenth-century taste altogether, and speaks of a renewed understanding of 'the harmonious variety, enchanting simplicity, and eloquent outpourings, of our early poets'. Evidently Fairfax was now to be admired as representative of his age, by some at least, though Hunt in 1818 was still dismissing him in the usual eighteenth-century terms.

J. H. Wiffen in an essay prefixed to his own version of the fourth book of the *Jerusalem* in 1821 is condescending, but his contemporary T. Holt White is pleased to remark that 'this version of Tasso often reads with all the ease and spirit of an original. Sometimes it must be confessed, at the expense of fidelity. May it not be said of *Fairefax*, that he is a solitary example of any one gaining a high and permanent reputation as a Poet, by metrical Translation alone?'[2]

A significant comment comes from Henry Neele, who in his *Lectures on English Poetry*, 1827 (pr. 1829), speaks of the 'spirited and truly poetical production of Fairfax', and claims that it is recovering its popularity.[3]

Knight's edition was reprinted in 1844; in 1858 R. A. Wilmott put out a slightly modernized text. After these there were no further reprints for over thirty years and, apart from some remarks

---

[1] A. C. Robertson's translation of *Jerusalem Delivered* (1853), p. ix.
[2] Milton, *Areopagitica*, ed. T. Holt White (1819), p. 77, n. 6.
[3] *The Literary Remains of . . . Henry Neele* (1829), p. 57.

by C. L. Smith in the preface to his own translation in 1851, no notable allusions. Smith himself used the stanza and observes:

But there is already extant a version in the metre of the original, which no only was popular soon after it was produced, but may be said to have risen to popularity again in the present day. And certainly the *Godfrey of Bulloigne* by Fairfax is a work which is never likely to vanish from English literature. There is a charm about the ancient structure of its language which can hardly fail to allure; for the degree of its antiquity is such that it is sufficiently aged to excite feelings of veneration, and yet sufficiently modern to be intelligible to all. There is a spirit and an ease in the versification, too, which is wonderful considering the age in which it was produced; there being no more inversions of language than was almost allowable in the prose of that day, or than was hidden from notice by the antique structure and grouping of the words.

In 1889 the German scholar Koeppel published his thorough and intelligent study of English translations of Tasso, a large part of which was devoted to Fairfax,[1] and in the following year Henry Morley published a new edition of *Godfrey of Bulloigne*. However, these two events do not seem to have led to a Tasso revival. It is significant that the *Cambridge History of English Literature*, which reflects the critical attitude of the early twentieth century, mentions Fairfax in passing, but devotes some space to Harington's version of Aristo's *Orlando Furioso*. It was about to be the turn of the rough poets rather than the smooth, the bawdy rather than the chaste, the Metaphysical rather than the Elizabethan. Yet by the 1940s the undisputed reign of Donne was drawing to a close, scholars were beginning to look at Spenser again, and the critical fortunes of Fairfax, too, began to revive. C. G. Bell, between 1947 and 1954 published a series of valuable articles on Fairfax,[2] and C. S. Lewis, in his volume of the *Oxford History of English Literature*, makes two elementary but telling points: first, that although the Augustans thought of Fairfax as a precursor, he is in fact extremely un-Augustan, and second, that the poem was capable of holding his attention all the way through.[3]

---

[1] *Anglia*, xi and especially xii (1889), pp. 103–42.

[2] 'Edward Fairfax, A Natural Son', *M.L.N.* lxii (1947), 24–7; 'A History of Fairfax Criticism', *P.M.L.A.* lxii (1947), 644–56; 'Edward Fairfax—Base Son and Lost Eclogues', *N. & Q.* cxcix (Apr. 1954), 143–5; 'Fairfax's Tasso', *Journal of Comparative Literature*, vi (1954).   [3] Op. cit., p. 521.

A recently published book by C. P. Brand devotes several pages to Fairfax and judiciously assesses his merits.[1] Two distinct editions of Fairfax have recently appeared—one introduced by Roberto Weiss (1962), the other by J. C. Nelson (1963).

[1] *Torquato Tasso* (1965).

V. FAIRFAX AND THE ENGLISH POETS
THEIR MUTUAL INFLUENCE

As one might expect, Fairfax sought for diction chiefly in Spenser, but C. G. Bell detected a hint of Gower;[1] a passage of phrasing reminded him of Medieval lyric;[2] a few touches brought Chaucer to his ear;[3] and our glossary shows frequent echoes of the diction of Gavin Douglas.[4]

It is not certain whether or not Fairfax knew Carew's translation: earlier critics were persuaded that he could not have had it by him or it might have saved him from certain slips; others have pointed out a rare coincidence of phrase which may have been more than accident.[5]

All these are doubtful echoes, but there is no missing the debt to the *Faerie Queene*. Again a glance at the glossary is revealing, and for a more exhaustive display the reader may turn to Koeppel's articles in *Anglia*, vols. xi and xii. From these findings we have reproduced only those which strike us as convincing borrowings. In addition to words and some archaic usages in the form of prefixes, preterites, and circumlocutions there are some half-dozen similes, independent of any Italian original, which are very credibly raised from a good memory of Spenser's poetry. The most interesting

[1] II. 13³: 'the trompe of death' might come from Gower's *Confessio Amantis,* I. 2128. Bell notes Fairfax's father had a manuscript of this work.

[2] III. 8.   Flower of goodness, root of lasting blisse,
                         Thou well of Life,

[3] I. 38; III. 76 lists of trees, cf. *Parlement of Foules*, ll. 176 ff. and see Commentary. IV. 86³: cf. *Troylus and Criseyde*, II. 1276. IX. 46¹: 'Vesulus the colde', cf. *Clerk's Tale*, l. 58. XII. 33²: Fairfax intrudes 'when more than halfe my tappe of life was roone'; cf. *Canterbury Tales*, A.3890, 'Syn that my tappe of lif began to renne'.

[4] See Glossary under: *armipotent: eild: environ: fand: greaves: guie.*

[5] What we now believe to be stated of I. 1⁴ (first state) is very close to Carew's phrase:
Carew: 'Much in his glorious conquest sufferd hee'
Fairfax: 'Much in that glorious conquest suffered hee'.
At I. 37 Carew and Fairfax make the same mistake over Clotareo.
I. 50 Carew: 'ready t'assayle'
     Fairfax: 'Readie to charge'.
IV. i. 'Lividi occhi' is rendered as 'wannish eies' in both.

instances and the closest are found (and it causes no surprise) when the description of the Garden of Armida is put alongside that of the Bower of Bliss. Here the source is shared: Spenser's use is masterly and free, Fairfax, with another allegiance and more modest intention, seeks to do justice to the Italian by drawing some felicitous phrasing from Tasso's earlier English admirer.[1]

Turning to those poets who borrowed from Fairfax, Allott's use of the new translation has already been noted. There are signs in *Britannia's Pastorals* that William Browne may owe a little to Fairfax in the episode of Coelia and Philocel, which obviously draws on the story of Sophronia and Olindo in *Gerusalemme Liberata*, Book II, but one cannot be sure that Browne needed any intermediary.[2] The same is true of the likenesses between Tasso and Phineas Fletcher which have been detected in *Brittain's Ida*.[3]

The line in IX. 15[5]:

> The earth was fild with devils, and emptie hell

chimes with Ariel's repetition of Ferdinand's cry,

> 'Hell is empty / And all the devils are here'
> (*Tempest*, I. ii. 214).

When in XVI. 4[5,6] we read

> The waters burnt about their vessels good,
> Such flames the gold therein enchased threw,

one cannot but think of the more famous description in *Antony and Cleopatra*.

The Duchess of Malfi's splendid defiance

> 'For know whether I am doomb'd to live or die
> I can doe both like a Prince'   (III. ii. 78–9)

---

[1] See the Commentary at the following passages: I. 71 and 84; II. 39; III. 4, 43, 52, and 53[8]; IV. 5 and 7; VI. 36 and 38; VII. 18; IX. 33; X. 26; XV. 1 and 60–2; XVI. 9[8], 12, 14, and 19; XVIII. 12; XIX. 105; and XX. 103[8].

[2] See Grundy, J., 'Tasso, Fairfax and Browne', in *R.E.S.*, n.s. iii (July 1952), 268.

[3] II. 8: cf. *G.L.* XIV. 62 and XVI. 5. Drayton, Daniel, and Drummond would not need Fairfax as a channel nor, indeed, would Jonson.

has a ring of

> it resteth then
> To scorne his powre, and be it therefore seene
> *Armida* liv'd, and dide, both like a Queene
>
> (*Godfrey*, IV. 73)

F. L. Lucas, however, quotes Sidney's *Arcadia*,

> Lastly, whether your
> time call you to live or die, doo both like a prince

which may have been Webster's source.[1] It is possible, I suppose, that Fairfax helped himself by means of Sidney to turn Tasso's couplet so successfully:

> Veggio la morte, e se'l fuggirla è vano,
> incontro a lei n'andrò con questa mano.

Another expression in *The Duchess*:

> . . . and your vengeance,
> (Like two chain'd bullets), still goes arme in arme
>
> (IV. ii. 346–7)

is reminiscent of Fairfax's line:

> So from a piece two chained bullets flie
>
> (IX. 54[8])

where the comparison is Fairfax's own. Here again editors catch a different echo and cite Chapman's *Revenge of Bussy d'Ambois*, v. i. 7–9 (1613):

> who in th'act itselfe
> Includes th'infliction, which like chained shot
> Batter together still.

The allusion in XX. 133 to the hundred ways to die seems too much of a commonplace for a connection to be remarked.

R. W. Dent, editing Webster's *Monumental Column*, ll. 84–8, noted a possible connection between

> Who jestingly, would say it was his trade
> To fashion death-beds, and hath often made
> Horror looke lovely, when i'th'fields there lay
> Armes and legges, so distracted, one would say
> That the dead bodies had no bodies left

---

[1] Webster, *Works*, ed. F. L. Lucas, ii (1927), 162. Sidney, *Arcadia* (1590), ed. Feuillerat, i (1922), 25.

and Fairfax's

> Horrour it selfe in that faire fight seem'd faire,
> And pleasures flew amid sad dreed and feare.
>
> (XX. 30[1-2])[1]

Very different from these are the there plagiarisms in T. Weever's *Mirror for Martyrs* (1601), exposed by C. Crawford in his edition of *England's Parnassus* (1913). The chief examples are numbers 21, 1128, 1148, 1149, 1626, 1869, 2025, 2048: Crawford cites sixty-two.

By contrast, Waller's borrowings though often equally palpable pay Fairfax a compliment: the commentary lays them out to view, and the section on versification traces the subtler form taken by Fairfax's influence.[2]

Dryden, Englishing Boileau, in *The Art of Poetry*, ll. 115–16 introduces Fairfax as

> . . . he, who in that Darker Age,
> By his just Rules restrain'd Poetic Rage.

The direction for Song VIII from *King Arthur*, which presents two Syrens rising from the waters who 'shew themselves to the Waste, and Sing' reminds Dryden's editor of the situation in the Bower of Bliss, and particularly of Fairfax's stanzas describing a similar allurement (XV. 59 ff.).[3]

Another instance in which Dryden may owe something to Fairfax is the simile in 'Loyal London':

> Like a rich Bride does to the Ocean swim
> And on her shadow rides in floating gold.
>
> *Annus Mirabilis*, 604–5

when compared with Fairfax's:

> The waters burnt about their vessels good,
> Such flames the gold therein enchased threw,
>
> (XVI. 4[5-6])

To the metrist, Samuel Say, writing in the margin of the British Library copy of the first edition of *Godfrey*, the line

> Their father, (but no father now, alas! . . .)   (IX. 35[1])

---

[1] R. W. Dent in *John Webster's Borrowing* (1960), p. 271.

[2] See Commentary, below, under: I. 4; III. 52; VI. 38, 70, 103; VIII. 83; IX. 12, 50; XI. 52; XII. 51; XV. 12, 32, 35–6; XVI. 24; XIX. 22; XX. 98, 114, 129.

[3] *The Poems of John Dryden*, ed. James Kinsley (1958), ii. 564 and iv. 2001.

had a ring of the way Dryden turned a paradox in *Aeneid*, X. 1185:

> What time the Father, now no Father stood.

Spence tells us that Pope read Fairfax; and perhaps the end of 'Summer'

> On me love's fiercer flames forever prey,
> By night he scorches, as he burns by day

owes a little to the couplet in III. 22:

> The same that left thee by the cooling streame,
> Safe from sunnes heat, but scorcht with beauties beame.

Milton, of course, knew Tasso's *Gerusalemme Liberata*, and it is certain that he knew it in Italian, but it is more than probable that he also knew Fairfax's version, and indeed that he knew it very well. The reader of Milton who knows his Fairfax will again and again hear echoes of the *Godfrey of Bulloigne*; and yet, when he tries to prove that these are indeed recollections of that poem he will find that most of them, taken in isolation, could be explained away as translations from the Italian, or as examples of common poetic formulations. A list of 100 parallels consisting of such items as 'Shape divine—*Godfrey*, l. 15[7]: cf. Shape Divine, *Paradise Lost*, VIII. 295' would be unlikely, at first glance, to convince the sceptic that Fairfax's lines were going round in Milton's head. It is only when the parallel phrases are set in their contexts that we begin to see that they genuinely constitute echoes.

Professor Weismiller has recently divided possible Fairfax echoes in Milton into a number of categories: (*a*) conventional formulations; (*b*) expressions which, 'granting the rhythm of the sixteenth and seventeenth century English line plus the logic of what in a given situation may be said, seem all but inevitable'; (*c*) phrases 'the echoing of which seems—especially in a given context—by no means inevitable'; (*d*) those in which the echo is reinforced by the rhythm of the line (because the phrases occur in corresponding portions of the line); (*e*) correspondences in which a slight rearrangement or expansion of the material makes the echo even more compelling; (*f*) 'involuntary musical imitations'; and (*g*) uses by Milton of pronunciations which are otherwise only found in Fairfax.[1] The first two categories include such parallels as: 'flaming brand' (Godfrey, XI. 81[6]: *Paradise Lost*, XII. 644), 'in evill howre' (Godfrey, XII. 61[6]: *P.L.* IX. 1067); 'reverence done' (*Godfrey*, I. 34[5]: *P.L.* IX. 835), 'hideous fall' (*Godfrey*, I. 75[6]: *P.L.* II. 177), and very many further examples could be found, but they will not in themselves convince anyone. More interesting are those in Weismiller's third category—the 'by no means inevitable' parallels. Thus he compares,

> The sprites impure from blisse that whilome fell
> (*Godfrey*, II. 4[5])

with

> Glad was the Spirit impure as now in hope . . .
> (*Pl.* III. 630)

There is no particular reason in the context why Milton should have used that particular formula at that point; on the other hand, he might have derived the formulation from some other source, e.g. Spenser, *Hymne of Heavenly Love*, l. 98. More compelling, though still in the same category, is the parallel between:

> The doore leaves fram'd of carved silver plate,
> Upon their golden hinges turne and twine
> (*Godfrey*, XVI. 2[3–4])

and

> . . . the gate self-opend wide
> On golden hinges turning
> (*P.L.* V, 255)

Still more convincing are the examples in Weismiller's next category, where the position of the corresponding phrases in the line is parallel:

> Appeer'd the Angell, in his shape divine,
> (*Godfrey*, I. 15[7])
> One came, methought, of shape divine
> (*P.L.* VIII. 295)

or

> Well have you labour'd, well foreseene about
> (*Godfrey*, II. 3[6])

[1] Edward Weismiller, 'Materials Dark and Crude: A Partial Genealogy for Milton's Satan', *H.L.Q.* xxxi (1967), 75–92. See also A. B. Giamatti, *Revue de Littérature Comparée*, xl (1966), 613–15.

Well have ye judged, well ended long debate
(*P.L.* II. 390).

In the last example there is also a phonetic resemblance between the line-endings 'about' and 'debate'.

Perhaps the most interesting category is that in which there has been a rearrangement or expansion of material. The most convincing of these examples is one in which Fairfax has added items to a list of Tasso's, and Milton incorporates these in his version:

L'orror, la crudeltà, la tema, il lutto
(*G.L.* IX. 93[1])

Feare, crueltie, griefe, horrour, sorrow, paine
(*Godfrey*, IX. 93[1])

Anguish and doubt and fear and sorrow and pain
(*P.L* .I. 558)

The next class, 'involuntary musical imitations' is best exemplified by the evident relationship between

Fire, aire, sea, earth, man, beast, sprite, place and time
(*Godfrey*, XIV. 45[4])

and Milton's

Rocks, caves, lakes, fens, bogs, dens, and shades of death
(*P.L.* II. 621)

One might go beyond Professor Weismiller and demonstrate even more complex echoes. In the following example there are parallels of vocabulary, rhythm (or placing of words in lines), syntactic relationships, and of the interplay of all these in both passages:

Thou, who dost all thou wishest, at thy will,
And never willest ought, but what is right
(*Godfrey*, IV. 63[1–2])

and

. . . That far be from thee, Father, who art judge
Of all things made, and judgest only right
(*P.L.* III. 154–5)

On the face of it the passages seem rather different, and yet we may feel that there is some profound similarity of cadence, of the way these lines seem to run. A closer analysis confirms this.

Fairfax	*Milton*
Thou	Father (directly addressed)
who dost	who art judge of
all thou wishest	all things made
and willest	and judgest
never ought but what is	only
right	right

The skeleton of the two sentences is very similar, and this similarity is reinforced by a second set of resemblances: the sequence 'will . . . willest . . . right' corresponds to 'judge . . . judgest . . . right'. The fact that 'will' and 'judge', as well as 'right' in both cases, occur at line endings makes the resemblance even closer.

Perhaps we may add to this category the parallel noted by Koeppel:

> On Libanon at first his foote he set,
> And shooke his wings with roarie May-dewes wet.
> (*Godfrey*, I. 14).

> Like Maia's son he stood,
> And shook his plumes, that heav'nly fragrance filled
> The circuit wide. (*P.L.* V. 285–7)

where a phonetic resemblance (May-dewes, Maia's), cutting right across the more obvious parallel, makes the echo confused but insistent.

Weismiller's last category consists of the words to which both Fairfax and Milton give unusual pronunciations. These are *Aegean* (disyllabic in *Godfrey*, I. 60 and *P.L.* I. 746); *fantasme* (disyllabic, and stressed on the first syllable, in *Godfrey*, XIII. 37 and *P.L.* II. 743); and *future* (stressed on the second syllable, *Godfrey*, XVII. 88 and *P.L.* X. 840). But this evidence counts for rather less than the other kinds we have been surveying, since it is difficult, even with the help of the *Oxford English Dictionary*, to be sure how uncommon a given pronunciation was at a given time.

However, when all is said, it is clear that while Milton nowhere sets out to imitate Fairfax or to allude to him, his poetry is shot through with recollections and echoes, probably often quite inadvertent ones, of the *Godfrey of Bulloigne*.

VI. LANGUAGE, STYLE, AND
VERSIFICATION OF THE *GODFREY*

1. *Some Aspects of the Language*

ALTHOUGH Fairfax was not a great creative innovator, his language shows certain idiosyncrasies.

There is scattered but striking evidence of Fairfax's Northern background. Our Glossary notes more than a dozen words (such as *busk* and *bray*) which were certainly Northern, and there are others which were probably obsolete in Southern forms of English by 1600 but were still used in the North. There is also a number of rhymes pointing to a Northern pronunciation, and a handful of characteristically Northern spellings (e.g. *maide* for *made*) which may well have been Fairfax's rather than the printer's; but these add only an occasional Northern touch to a form of English that would not on the whole have seemed provincial.

Fairfax is sporadically archaic in his diction and in some of his grammatical forms; our glossary notes close on forty such items. Archaism had been a favourite poetic device throughout most of the sixteenth century, and was brought to a systematic extreme by Spenser, but it seems to have been rather out of fashion among Fairfax's immediate contemporaries. Some of Fairfax's archaic words (e.g. 'eft' and 'dight') had long been standard items of Elizabethan poetic diction; but others were freshly borrowed from Spenser's word-hoard, while others still were presumably taken straight from Middle English sources. Fairfax adopts a few of Spenser's pseudo-archaic forms or usages (see Glossary under *blest*, *embay*, *chevisaunce* and *yond*), and may have been responsible for coining one or two of his own (see *discoverment* and *outbraid*). Like Spenser, too, he uses a few archaic grammatical terminations; thus he retains the old -n in a few infinitives (*been*, *don*) and third person plurals (*commenden*). The noun plural *treen* is also presumably an archaism. Still, when one considers the length of the poem all this does not amount to a great harvest of archaic forms; and one may read whole pages of the *Godfrey* without coming across any. There does not seem to be any particular stylistic principle underlying the use Fairfax makes of them; and one may suspect that he sometimes found them convenient to help out with a rhyme or a foot.

Some of Fairfax's divergences from normal syntax, on the other hand, do seem to produce stylistic effects. There are two that seem to stand out: his way with past participles, and his ruthless reshuffling of the normal order of words and phrases. His peculiarity with participles is to use them in quasi-Latin constructions. For example, a past participle may be used in place of a relative clause, as 'his message, saide' (I. 18^2), which means 'the message which he said'. Elsewhere participles do the work of verbal nouns, as in

> Turkes, Persians conquer'd, Antiochia wonne
> Be glorious actes
>
> (I. 26$^{1-2}$)

While such usages were not unprecedented in sixteenth-century English, they were certainly learned rather than colloquial and impart a literary, slightly mannered flavour to the poem. But they do more: they help to produce a condensed, highly-packed effect. No doubt Tasso, who achieves compression by a variety of means, set the general example.

More directly, Tasso showed Fairfax the way in boldly disarranging the normal order of words and phrases. Some departures from normal word-order are of course found in a great deal of English poetry, and certain sixteenth-century poets, Sidney among them, produced some striking dislocations. What seems distinctive in Fairfax is his way of splitting up clauses and other still more close-knit structures and shuffling the parts with complete disregard for normal usage. He may for example split up a relative clause and transpose the parts. Readers are unlikely at first reading to realize that the line

> In height and cleerenes which the rest excell
>
> (I. 17^6)

means: 'which excel the rest in height and clearness'. Or he may split up a pair of phrases joined by 'of', putting the 'of-' phrase first. The line

> Of Sions fort to scale the noble wall
> (I. 23^2)

shows that Tasso was Fairfax's model in this, for the original line contains the phrase 'di Sion le nobil mura'. An equally drastic dislocation, for which precedents can similarly be found in Tasso, is the splitting up of phrases linked by 'and', e.g.

> His mothers heritage was this and right
> (I. 42^1)

Precedents might also be found in English verse; but one may well feel that there is more of it in Fairfax, and done with greater disregard for the reader, than in earlier English poets. He seems only too happy to combine several transpositions to produce such difficult lines as:

> I am the man; of thine intent (quoth hee)
> And purpose new, that sure conjecture hath
> (X. 10$^{1-2}$)

or, still more puzzling at first, the notorious:

> *Ismen* dead bones laid in cold graves that warmes
> And makes them speake, smell, taste, touch, see and heere
> (II. 1$^{3-4}$)

Apart from producing a knottiness that may well have been deliberate (to make the reader work hard for his reward, as it were), this mannerism allows the poet to juxtapose words to produce particular interactions of their connotations quite apart from those arising from their syntactic relationships. Thus there is an obvious point in associating 'Ismen' with 'dead bones'; and by making 'cold' precede 'warmes'; the line imitates the order of the events it narrates.

It may be worth mentioning, in this context, something that is not in fact a syntactic abnormality, the use of such participial forms as *unite* for 'united' (II. 73^3), *discomfite* for 'discomfited' (III. 36^4), and even *take* for 'taken' (XII. 73^4). All these forms, which look like infinitives or present indicatives, were perfectly normal sixteenth-century variations; but it is difficult to say whether for Fairfax's contemporaries the similarity of their forms to Latin derived participles would have had any significance.

2. Rhyme

Though most of the rhymes in the *Godfrey* would have been perfectly accurate in one or other of the forms of English spoken in London and the South-East about the year 1600, there remain a number that presuppose a provincial form of speech, as in the following instances:

(i) *aide*/*maide* (= made)/*staid* (I. 70) and similar rhymes, where the vowel descended from ME *ai* rhymes with the descendant of ME *ā*; although this was just beginning to be acceptable in educated London speech about 1600, its prevalence in the *Godfrey* suggests a Northern mode of pronunciation.

(ii) *rout* (= root)/*out*/*about* (II. 3) etc., where a descendant of ME *ǭ* rhymes with descendants of ME *ū*.

(iii) *now*/*bow* (= weapon used in archery)/*wow* (= woo) (XVI. 38), where (*a*) two descendants of ME *ū* (in *now* and *wow*) rhyme, though they would no longer have done so in Southern speech, as the initial *w* in *wow* kept the vowel from undergoing the normal Southern process of diphthongization; and (*b*) both rhyme with a descendant of ME *ǫu* which had evidently evolved via a late ME *ū*—a development more common in the North than in Southern forms of English.

(iv) *stead* (= steed)/*dead*/*spread* (XX. 51) and similar rhymes: the first of these vowels derives from ME *ẹ̄* while the other two derive from ME *ę̄*. (They remain long; the present-day pronunciation of the latter two descends from variants with a shortened vowel.)

(v) *refar*/*ar*/*war* (II. 51) etc.: although the change from *er* to *ar* was also found in Southern forms of English, it was more common in the North at this period.

(vi) *gace* (= gaze)/*cace*/*place* (II. 27); the unvoicing of the consonant in *gaze* was a Northern feature.

(vii) *smote/hote/throte* (XX. 81), where *hote* (= hot) evidently
   retains its long vowel, as in *ME*, when Southern English had
   already shortened it.

3. *Style*

A complete stylistic study of the *Godfrey* is outside the range of this
Introduction, but something needs to be said about a general
stylistic characteristic of the poem, and about some particular
rhetorical devices that contribute various stylistic effects.

One would expect an epic to maintain a lofty level of style
throughout, by the use of suitably selective vocabulary and suit-
able figures of rhetoric as well as by avoidance of too much concrete
detail, particularly of socially humble things. Tasso maintains
such a level; Fairfax does not, while the syntactic dislocations
already listed probably contribute to loftiness, other Fairfaxian
characteristics do not. For Tasso's ingenious use of generalities
Fairfax substitutes a workmanlike concern with technical detail, as
when the lines

> Si commette la mole e ricompone
> con sottili giunture in un congiunta

become

> In mortesses and sockets framed iust
> The beames, the studdes and punchions ioyn'd he fast
> $(\text{XVIII. } 44^{1-2})$

This may merely be Fairfax preferring honest fact to grand
generalities, regardless of elevation of style (a not unusual pre-
ference in sixteenth-century English poetry), but there are other
times when a sudden lowering of style serves a more particular
purpose. For example, Fairfax is fond of using homely proverbs
and idioms to undermine or deflate. Thus Armida's pretended
modesty is discredited by the colloquial tone and racy idiom of

> Sometimes she heard him, sometimes stopt her eare,
> And played fast and loose the live-long day
> $(\text{IV. } 95^{3-4})$

The tyrant Aladine's joy at finding a pretext to persecute the
Christians is ridiculed with the contemptuous proverb:

> A staffe to beat that dog he long had sought
> $(\text{II. } 11^{6})$

while poor Artemidore's self-congratulation when he is chosen to
escort Armida is mocked in the notorious line:

> Doubtlesse the Countie thought his bread well baken
>
> (v. 73⁵)

To a somewhat similar end the phrase 'carpet champion' comes at
the climax of Ubaldo's denunciation of Rinaldo's agreeable life with
Armida (XVI. 32).

Other homely expressions, however, may be used for rather
different purposes. One of the most striking instances of what looks
like deliberate indecorum is provided by the conclusion of the
penultimate stanza of Book II:

> Now spred the night her spangled canopie,
> And sommon'd euery restlesse eie to sleepe:
> On beds of tender grasse the beastes downe lie,
> And fishes slumbred in the silent deepe,
> Vnheard was serpents hisse, and dragons crie,
> Birds left to sing and Philomene to weepe,
>   Onely that noice heau'ns rolling circles kest,
>   Sung lullabie, to bring the world to rest.
>
> (II. 96)

Such a yoking together of macrocosm and nursery, which produces
its own stylistic effect (it would be wrong to call it bathos) is
foreign to Tasso, but far from uncommon in English poetry of
the period; we need not look beyond Shakespeare for examples.

Leaving the general question of 'levels of style', we turn to
particular features. We have already seen that many of Fairfax's
tropes are ready-made, being in fact common proverbs. He is equally
happy to use the ready-made tropes of literary tradition; and to
these too he gives new life. For example, he imports into the
opening lines of Book III an ancient personification which Tasso
managed to do without:

> The purple morning left her crimsen bed,
> And dond her robes of pure vermilion hew,
> Her amber locks she crown'd with roses red,
> In Edens flowrie garden gathred new.
>
> (III. 1¹⁻⁴)

But this is not a mere literary commonplace; Fairfax manages to use the image in order to suggest the range of colours that accompany the sunrise. Or he may splice together two stock literary images to create something new, as in:

> About her shoulders shone her golden locks
> Like sunnie beames, on Alablaster rocks
> (III. 21$^{7-8}$)

The point is that Fairfax, though not a great inventor of new images often manages to give some new twist to the old ones he uses, whether they are based on Tasso or imported from other sources. The additional layer of complexity may be intriguing and suggestive as in his elaboration on Tasso's description of the impact of Clorinda on Tancred's mind:

> Yet thence she fled, vncompaned, vnsought,
> And left her image in his hart ipight,
> Her sweet Idea wandred through his thought.
>   Her shape, her gesture and her place in minde
>   He kept, and blew loues fire with that winde.
> (I. 48$^{4-8}$)

It is true that this will not stand up to a rigorous analysis; but there seems to be some odd and moving appropriateness in the very inconsistency of this succession of metaphors, where Clorinda's image in Tancred's mind seems to turn, finally, into a breath. Elsewhere the inconsistency within the trope, or the return from trope to literalness may be more noticeable. For example, when Sophronia is suddenly seen as a 'siluer doue', her executioners are turned, for the instant, into 'kites', but the metaphor does not extend to their actions:

> Her vaile and mantle pluckt they off by force,
> And bound her tender armes in twisted wire:
> Dumbe was this siluer doue, while from her corse
> These hungrie kites pluckt off her rich attire.
> (II. 26$^{3-6}$)

But this slight oddity is not necessarily damaging: it merely makes us aware, for a moment, of the poet as rhetorical.

What seems to be lacking in Fairfax is the rather deeper sort of complexity that Tasso manages sometimes to convey with a simple phrase. When Argante goes up to the walls of Jerusalem in the starlight, Tasso speaks of 'l'amico silenzio de le stelle'; in Fairfax this is reduced to 'friendly star-light' (II. 95$^{5-6}$) which loses the openness and suggestiveness of Tasso's phrase. In short, while Fairfax's tropes are often more elaborate and complex than Tasso's, they sometimes seem to lack the deeper resonance, as well as the clarity, of the original.

Something needs to be said also about the other major group of stylistic devices—the figures involving the use of patterns of sound, meaning, or syntax. Fairfax is not outstandingly given to using patterns of sound; but he makes particular use of two sorts of figures based on patterns of meaning. In the first place, he is particularly fond of figures involving parallelism or antithesis—in otherwords, balance. These are found in all parts of his stanzas; but they are most strikingly seen in the concluding lines:

> So doth thy vertue, so thy powre perswaide
> (IV. 39)

> More is thy praise to make, than kill a king
> (IV. 41)

> My birth, her death; my first day, was her last
> (IV. 43)

> For on my ruine is his safetie wrought
> (IV. 60)

Sometimes such figures are extended throughout the final couplet:

> He breedes the sore, and cures vs of the paine:
> *Achilles* lance that wounds and heales againe.
> (IV. 92)

> Full seem'd her lookes of anger, and of shame;
> Yet pitie shone transparent through the same
> (IV. 94)

> Since these true champions of the Lord aboue
> Were thralles to beautie, yeelden slaues to loue
> (IV. 96)

At other times Fairfax interweaves several sets of parallels or antitheses or both, as in:

> Then in the secret creekes of fruitful Nile
> Cast in her lappe, he would sadde death awate,
> And in the pleasure of her louely smile,
> Sweeten the bitter stroake of cursed fate.
>
> (XVI. 7[1–4])

An Augustan critic might have objected to the inexact parallelism, and particularly to the false symmetry between 'fruitful Nile' and 'louely smile'. The fact is that Fairfax did not usually combine parallel meaning with parallel syntax in these figures. It was left to Waller to take up some of Fairfax's balancing figures and improve the symmetry; examples are collected below in the Commentary.

The other figures that Fairfax particularly favours are those involving strings of words of similar reference. The simplest of these are pairs and triads of synonyms or near-synonyms; the poem is studded with these, but all too often they are obviously nothing more than padding:

> *Rinaldo* was their leader, lord, and guide
>
> (XX. 10[8])

> Their leaders heard, obaid or follow'd bee
>
> (XX. 16[7])

Longer strings may produce an even more feeble effect where, as so often, there is no relationship between the individual items:

> So from his lips his words and speeches fell,
> Shrill, speedie, pleasant, sweete, and placed well.
>
> (XX. 13[7–8])

This sort of slackness is one of the obvious defects of the *Godfrey*; and yet, in context, these lists are not nearly as bad as they seem when singled out for critical comment. In the last example quoted, for instance, it looks at first sight as if the items formed some sort of orderly sequence, if one could only grasp the underlying logic of it. In fact, however, this is an illusion; for while there appears to be a particular relationship between the first and last words in the sequence (referring, as they do, to the sound of the speech and its composition respectively) the intervening items do not form a link between them. Whether the illusion of a logical sequence was intentional or accidental does not much matter; the effect is that there is much in the poem that 'works' on a rapid reading but will not stand up to close scrutiny.

Fairfax not infrequently attempts more complex figures; and the greater the complexity, the greater is his chance of getting away with major or minor illogicalities. It is not quickly obvious for example that the following *tour de force* (which combines a progressive series with some sort of parallelism) is not in fact entirely consistent:

> Sight, wonder; wonder, loue; loue bred his caire,
> O loue, O wonder; loue, new borne, new bred,
> Now growne, now arm'd this champion captiue led.
>
> (I. 47$^{6-8}$)

This looks as if it were worked out in detail so that all the bits fit into place, though in fact it will not stand up to closer analysis. Nevertheless the figure works, since it conveys the impression of rapid and astonishing developments. In fact it is the 'image' element in the figure rather than its logical structure that does most of the work. Would it be going too far to say, more generally, that Fairfax's rhetoric is characterized by apt images and a superficial appearance of logic?

4. *Versification*

One of Fairfax's claims to fame is his versification, with its alleged influence on Waller—an influence Waller himself acknowledged. Metrical analysis alone, however, will not reveal what is significant here. As Ruth Wallerstein has shown, it is the interaction of metrical and rhetorical features that give Fairfax's verse those characteristics which made it plausible to regard his octave stanzas as pointing the way towards the Augustan heroic couplet.

The most obvious 'Augustan' characteristics are, of course, found in the concluding couplets of the stanzas. These are generally self-contained; there is rarely any running-on from the first to the second line; and there is generally quite a well-marked syntactic break, around the middle of the line (i.e. after the fourth, fifth, or sixth syllable). Most important of all, this break or the line division frequently serves as the fulcrum of a balancing figure. Of course, other Elizabethan poets did exactly the same in concluding couplets of their stanzas (or even, occasionally, when they were writing pure couplet verse); but Fairfax's balancing figures are frequent and striking, and Waller evidently admired them sufficiently to imitate a good many of them.

But there is more to Waller's debt to Fairfax. Spenser (and for that matter Tasso) exploited the stanza form by drawing out the sense variously from line to line; and part of the delight of their kind of writing lies in the way in which the pattern of the line-endings cuts across the patterns produced by the syntax. It is in this sense that Milton is a poetic descendant of Spenser. Fairfax on the other hand tends to treat a pair of lines as a self-contained unit; that is to say, there is almost always a substantial syntactic break at the end of lines 2, 4, and 6; and even within the pair, there is not a great deal of running-on, and such as there is tends to be of a fairly mild kind. Again, there tends to be a syntactic break round about the middle of the line. In short, the first six lines of the Fairfax stanza tend to have the regular pace of couplet verse without having its rhyme-scheme.

Having said all this we must add that other sixteenth-century poets might have equally good claims to be regarded as ancestors of the Augustan couplet; and that, as Johnson felt, there were important ways in which Fairfax is very unlike the Augustans. It is true that a surprisingly large proportion of Fairfax's lines scan as perfect 'iambics' or depart from this pattern in minor and unobtrusive ways only (e.g. by an inverted first foot or a 'silent stress' in the body of the line)—perhaps because these are the lines in which physical conflict is portrayed. And since the *Godfrey* is much concerned with conflict, there are many such rugged lines in it. Nor is this overloading the only feature in the versification that an Augustan ear might have found harsh; but it would require a highly technical analysis to show precisely what is harsh about them—such lines, for example, as

But there drowne cities, countries, townes and towres

$$(\text{I. }43^8)$$

Even so, the lines that are easy to read outnumber the awkward ones; the stanzas that close on an impressive cadence outnumber the ones that creep to a lame and impotent conclusion (though there are enough of these, it must be admitted). When one compares the *Godfrey* with other respectable poems of the late sixteenth century—the long poems of Drayton and Daniel, for example— one finds that it is a far easier and more satisfying poem to read aloud. This is partly because for all his occasional roughness Fairfax places few serious stumbling-blocks in the reader's way; and partly because of its insistent rhythmic vitality. In the *Godfrey* there is both order and power; regularity and variety. It is doubtful whether the superior neatness and smoothness of Waller's verse would have been equally suited to so long a poem; and none of the Augustans managed to write an epic that has stood the test of time.

Title-page of 1624 edition

TEXTUAL
INTRODUCTION

I. TEXT OF THE 1600 EDITION

Two editions of the *Godfrey* appeared in Fairfax's lifetime: those of 1600 and 1624. Although the 1624 edition contains matter not in 1600 (a Dedicatory Epistle to Prince Charles, a poem to him, and a Life of Godfrey), everything else in it is merely reprinted and has no independent textual authority. A number of minor errors are, however, corrected. That 1624 lacks authority is clearly proved by a number of variants which could only have arisen through the attempts of 1624's compositor to 'correct' lines he misunderstood. Thus at I. 72^3, 1600 reads *hawberke*, which is obviously correct; 1624 emends to *halbert*. At XII. 25^2 the 1624 compositor used his initiative to disastrous effect, correcting *in roome of* to *in Rome of*. As against these changes, there are none in 1624 that in any way suggest the poet's hand.

The Stationers' Register has the following entry for 22 November 1599:

Mathewe Lownes
John Jagger
All TASSO translated out of Italian into Englishe
Alias the Recoverye of Jerusalem by GODFREY OF BULLEN[1]

This cannot refer to anything other than Fairfax's version.

Copies of this edition are not outstandingly scarce.[2] In preparing our text we have taken account of eighteen easily accessible copies, but fully collated only three (Bodleian 1 and 2, and Buxton). The following are the copies consulted, with their locations and sigla.

---

[1] E. Arber, *A Transcript of the Stationers' Registers* (1875–94), iii. 54.

[2] In addition to the copies listed on this page, there are, or, were, copies at the following locations: Birmingham Univ.; Blackburn Public Library; Cambridge Univ. Library (2 copies); Chapin Library, Williams College, Williamstown; W. A. Clark Memorial Library, Univ. of California; Univ. of Durham Library; Folger Library, Washington, D.C. (3 copies); Harvard Univ. Library; Huntington Library (2 copies); Johns Hopkins Univ. Library; King's College, Cambridge; Leeds Univ. Library; Liverpool Univ. Library; Manchester, John Rylands Library; Newberry Library; Pforzheimer Collection; Pierpont Morgan Library; St. John's College, Cambridge; Trinity College, Cambridge; Turnbull Library, Wellington; Warrington Public Library; Wellesley College, Massachusetts.

Bodl[1]	Bodleian Library, Oxford, Antiq.d.E. 1600/2.
Bodl[2]	Bodleian Library, Oxford, Malone 19.
BL	British Library, 82.g.16.
B	Copy in possession of Mr. John Buxton.
ChCh	Copy in the library of Christ Church, Oxford.
Dul[1]	Copy in the library of Dulwich College, O.a.2.
Dul[2]	Copy in the library of Dulwich College, O.a.6.
Dy	Dyce copy, in the Victoria and Albert Museum, London.
Ed	Copy in National Library of Scotland, Edinburgh.
G[1], G[2], G[3]	Copies at Gays House, Holyport, Berks.
H	Robert Hoe copy in Huntington Library, California, 69619.
M	Copy in the possession of Mr. James Maxwell.
Shef	Copy in Sheffield University Library.
Sen	Copy in Senate House, London University.
W[1]	Copy in Worcester College, Oxford, W.1.23.
W[2]	Copy in Worcester College, Oxford, LRA.5.5(A).

The title-page of 1600 is reproduced facing p. 1. The Colophon (on Ll4[v]) reads: Printed at London by Ar. Hatfield / for *John Jaggard* and / M. Lownes. / 1600.

The book is in Folio (in gatherings of 6), and the collation and contents are as follows:

A[4], B–Z[6], Aa–Kk[6], Ll[4] [the first three pages of each gathering are signed except for A1, A3, and Ll3]. 200 leaves, pp. 8, 1–392 [errors in pagination vary between copies]. Contents: [Al]: title (verso blank); A2 poem 'To her High Maiestie'; A2[v]–A4[v]: 'The allegorie of the Poem'; B1–Ll4[v]: 'Godfrey of Bulloigne' (B1–C4: Bk. i; C4–E2: Bk. ii; E2–F3[v]: Bk. iii; F4–H1[v]: Bk. iv; H1[v]–I5: Bk. v; I5–L4[v]: Bk. vi; L4[v]–N5: Bk. vii; N5–P1[v]: Bk. viii; P2–Q6: Bk. ix; Q6–S2: Bk. x; S2–T4: Bk. xi; T4–X3[v]: Bk. xii; X3[v]–Y5[v]: Bk. xiii; Y5[v]–Aa1[v]: Bk. xiv; Aa1[v]–Bb2[v]: Bk. xv; Bb2[v]–Cc4: Bk. xvi; Cc4–Ee2: Bk. xvii; Ee2–Ff6[v]: Bk. xviii; Ff6[v]–Ii2: Bk. xix; Ii2–Ll4[v]: Bk. xx; Ll4[4]: Colophon.

All books conclude with a printer's ornament, except Book xiv, and all books open with a heading in large type, except Book xv. None of the copies examined possesses a list of 'Faults Escaped'.

The text is well printed. One notable feature is the consistency with which personal proper names are italicized, while place-names are printed in roman. There are signs that as the printing proceeded the printer had to economize with paper.

Press Variants in 1600

Most of the press variants in this edition are of a fairly minor variety, and indicate an intermittently vigilant printer occasionally capable of intelligent proof-reading. They are listed below. There is, however, a major press variant on the first page of the poem, which has long been known to bibliographers, and needs to be examined in some detail.

In the first place there are two versions of the Argument. One version (which we print in our Commentary, below), has a second line which reads *Godfrey to counsell cals the Christian Peeres*. We may call this 'State a'. The version of the Argument which is found in the overwhelming majority of copies, however, differs from this in a number of points, including a second line which runs *Godfrey unites the Christian peeres and knights*. We shall refer to this as 'State b', without (at this point) implying thereby which of them is the earlier.

'State a' is in fact extremely rare (we know of only two copies which contain it: the Robert Hoe copy at the Huntington library and one of the Gays House copies); but where it occurs, it is accompanied by a version of stanza 1 which is not found in any other copies. That is the version which opens: 'I sing the sacred armies and the knight'. It will be convenient to call this 'State α'.

'State b' of the Argument, however, is found in conjunction with two distinct states of stanza 1. It was originally printed with a version which opened: 'The sacred armies and the godly knight' (State β); but a cancel slip was then printed and pasted over it in many, indeed the majority, of the extant copies. This carried a third version of stanza 1, which opened with the line: 'I sing the warre made in the Holy land' (State γ).

Bibliographical probability would lead us to suppose that the rarest version (states a+α) must be the earliest; while b+γ are obviously the latest. John Payne Collier, however, who first drew attention to the variants in a well-informed article in the *Critical*

Review, v (1817), 193–204, later asserted, without offering any evidence, that the a+α state represented Fairfax's final intention.[1] This final revision involved, as he supposed, the printing of a new cancel leaf; and he accounts for the scarcity of this version (of which he had possessed a copy, which he had later given to Wordsworth) by supposing that Fairfax was still dissatisfied with it. The inherent implausibility of this story does not seem to have struck Collier, or anyone else, and library catalogues and book-sellers consistently describe b+β as the earliest state. An examination of chain-lines and watermarks on a copy of b+β [M] has however shown that in that version, Sig. B¹ is a cancel leaf; while examination of the Robert Hoe copy in the Huntington Library has shown that in that copy (one of the a+α copies) Sig. B1 is conjugate with Sig. B6. In short, there can be no doubt that a+α is the earliest version.[2]

Our text prints the final version, b+γ, while the textual notes reproduce the earlier variants. One thing is clear: these variants represent Fairfax's striving for perfection.

Minor press variants

1. A number of minor variants are associated with the major changes on Sig. B1 discussed above.

a+α version	b versions
B1ʳ st. 2⁸ than	then
st. 3⁵ young	yong
B1ᵛ st. 4³ errours	errors
st. 5⁵ foorth	forth
st. 5⁷ deed	deede

---

[1] Replying to a note by T. N. in *Notes and Queries*, 19 Oct. (1850), p. 325, Collier put forward his theory on 26 Oct. (1850), p. 359, under the pseudonym of 'The Hermit of Holyport', and returned to the subject on 2 Nov. of the same year, p. 377.

[2] b+β is found in Bodl², ChCh, Dul¹, Dul², Durham, Ed, Gays Ho. (1 copy), Huntington (1 copy), Johns Hopkins, Liverpool, M. Newberry, Pierpont Morgan, Pforzheimer, St. John's Coll., Turnbull, Warrington, W¹, and W².

b+γ is found in Birmingham, Blackburn, Bodl¹, BL, B, Cambridge (2 copies), Chapin, Clark, Dy, Folger (3 copies), Gays Ho. (1 copy), Harvard, Huntington (1 copy), King's Coll., Leeds, Manchester, Sen, Shef, Trinity (2 copies), Wellesley

2. Other press variants.

The full collation of Bodl[1], Bodl[2], and B and the partial collation of these with the copies listed on p. 2 revealed no significant pattern of proof correction, and we do not think it necessary here to list all the copies in which a given reading is found. (N.B. the corrected version is given second.)

D3^v (II. 55^3) labour and vertues [Bodl, BL]
                labour's vertues [B, M]
D6^v (p. 36, running title) The first booke [B]
                    The second booke [H]
E5 (III. 29^2) know [Bodl[1]]
            knew [B]
F4^v (IV. 5^4) Hydrayes [M]
            Hydraes [Bodl[1]]
I4 (V. 83^2) sparled [Bodl[1]]
           sparkled [B]
L6^v (VII. 18^1) thofe [M]
            those [Bodl[1]]
L6^v (VII. 19^5) het [M]
            her [Bodl[1]]
N4^v (VII. 116^8) bnt [Bodl[1]]
            but [B]
O2 (VIII. 29^6) nouhht [Bodl[1]]
            nought [B]
P5^v (running title) eight [Bodl[1]]
            ninth [M]
T2 (page numbering) 193 [Bodl[1]]
            207 [W[1]]
Y3^v (XIII. 59^6) ganges [Bodl[1]]
            Ganges [all others]
Aa1 (XIV. 72^1) I parted [BL]
            Iparted [M]
Aa1 (XIV. 72^8) palinure [BL]
            Palinure [M]
Ff5^v (XVIII. 97^1) winkte and [Bodl[1]]
            wink'd, and [M]

Gg4^v (XIX. 37^4) breoke [Bodl^1]
           breake [ChCh]
Kkl^v (XX. 53^3) Rpread [Bodl^1]
             Spread [all others]

The errors on which all copies checked are agreed are given in the apparatus criticus.

II. SUBSEQUENT EDITIONS

THE second edition of the poem, with a spelling change in the title to *Godfrey of Boulogne*, was printed by John Bill and contained a number of items not in 1600: a portrait of Godfrey; a prose dedication 'To the most / illustrious' Prince Charles; a poem, 'The Genius of Godfrey to Prince Charles'; and a Life of Godfrey; as well as all the preliminaries of the first edition.[1] However, it would perhaps be more accurate to say that each of these items was printed for the second edition; but there is considerable variation in what any given volume of 1624 contains.

The collation of Bodley's Volume Douce T.299 is:

[Blank page] Title-page; [verso] blank; ¶2-[¶3ᵛ] to the most / illustrious . . .; [¶4ʳ] To her High Majestie; [¶4ᵛ] blank; x1–x3 The Life of Godfrey; [x3ᵛ] blank; [x4] A–A4; The Allegorie. A4ᵛ blank. B1 The first Booke. (The book is signed to Ll4ᵛ, omitting u and w, with Ll5 blank, and paginated 1–392. Bodley's Vet. A.2.d.56 has the portrait opposite the title-page and follows it with the poem, 'the Genius of Godfrey' (a1).

The 1624 text of the poem itself is a fairly good page-for-page reprint of 1600, taken from a b+β version. A number of accidentals are corrected (II. 74⁴ favout–favour; IV. 33⁵ gestnres–gestures; VI. 70⁷ seeret–secret; VI. 89⁶ sheevelesse–sleevelesse; VII. 1⁸ vaive–vaine; VII. 25² cleree–cleere; VII. 27⁶ Tacredi–Tancredi; VII. 52⁶ hean'n–heau'n; VII. 58⁵ champious–champions; X. 30⁶ seeret–secret; X. 61⁶ thar–that; XII. 59³ ease–case; XIII. 32⁵ attemps–attempts; XIV. 14⁶ strenght–strength; XVII. 51⁵ they–the; XVIII. 16³ spinkled–sprinkled (in some copies); XIX. 10⁵ orethrnowne–orethrowne; XIX. 58³ harmornies–harmonies; XIX. 61⁶ they–the; XX. 3⁴ strenght–strength; XX. 33¹ lannce–launce. In addition, errors of pagination and stanza numbering and a few incorrect running titles are also put right: thus 1600's incorrect III. 71 (for 21), III. 37 (for 63), VI. 96 (for 56), VIII. 53 (for 55);

---

[1] The 1624 preliminaries are all given below, pp. 590 ff.

XII. 95 (for 59), XV. 27 (for 25) are all correctly given in 1624; p. 82 (misnumbered 84 in 1600), is corrected; as is the incorrect running title sixth (for seventh) on p. 138.

Perhaps the most noticeable difference between 1600 and 1624 is that the later edition has abandoned the practice of giving matching spellings to rhyme-words. Where 1600 prints donne / shonne / begonne (I. 24), or foe / soe / groe (I. 36). 1624 allows these to appear as done / shun / begun and foe / so / grow. This kind of change is found over and over again. It is noted by Singer (1817) at p. xxi of his Introduction, and reference is made to G. Puttenham's *The Arte of English Poesie* (1589), Bk. 2, ch. 8.

Details of subsequent editions are as follows:

3. (1687)

(*a*) Godfrey / of / Bulloigne: or the / Recovery / of Jerusalem. / Done into English Heroical Verse, / By Edward Fairfax, Gent. / Together with the Life of the said / Godfrey /
Licensed to be reprinted, / Sept. 18. / 1686 / Ro. L'Estrange. /

London / Printed by J. M. for H. Herringman, and are to / be sold by Jos. Knight, and F. Saunders in the / Lower Walk of the New Exchange, 1687. 8 vo. A2 To the Reader; A3–A8 The Life of Godfrey; a–a7^r The Allegory of the Poem; a7^v–a8^v A Poem (by Robert Gould); B–Tt8^r Godfrey of Bulloigne (pp. 1–655).

(*b*) (Another imprint) London, Printed by J. M. for George Wells at the Sun, and / Abel Swalle at the Unicorn at the West-end / of St. Paul's Church-yard. 1687 (identical with a).

(*c*) (Another imprint) cited Chiswell, Bentley, Sawbridge, and Wells.

4. (1726)

(Title-page substantially as for 1687 except for the imprint.) Dublin: / Printed by and for A. Rhames, opposite the Pide / Horse in Capel-Street, MDCCXXVI.

A2 To the Reader; A3–A6 The Life; A7–a5^r The Allegory; a5^v–a6^v A Poem [R. Gould]; [a★]–[a4^v★] Subscribers; [a7–a8] B–Tt8 The Poem, pp. 1–659. 8vo.

5. (1749)

Tasso's / Jerusalem Delivered: / or Godfrey of Bulloign. / An Heroic Poem. / Done into English, / In the Reign of Queen Elizabeth, / By Edward Fairfax, Gent. / The Fourth edition, / With a Glossary, and Index / London: / Printed by J. Purser / for / J. Clark, at the Royal Exchange; / E. Withers, in Fleet Street: / J. Jackson, in St. James's Street; J. Millan, at Charing Cross. / MDCCXLIX.

(Dedicated to William, Earl of Harrington . . . by the Editor.)

A–A4ᵛ The Preface (an Account of the Crusade and of Tasso and of Fairfax; unsigned); a–a2ᵛ Mr. Bill's Dedication (as from 1624); bʳ–bᵛ Dedication to Queen Elizabeth (Fairfax's verses); b2–b4ᵛ The Arguments (Collected together here); B–Rrr2ᵛ Godfrey of Bulloigne (pp. 1–492). Rrr3–SssIᵛ Allegory; Sss3–Tttᵛ Glossary; Ttt2–Xxx3ʳ Index. 8vo.

This edition alters the text in numerous places, apparently to make it more acceptable to the taste of the mid-eighteenth-century readers.[1]

6. (1817) Godfrey / of / Bulloigne, / or / Jerusalem Delivered, / by /

(a) Torquato Tasso, / Translated by Edward Fairfax, Gent. Edited S. W. Singer, 2 vols. Bensley and Son; London, 1817. 12mo.

(Dedicated to Samuel Rogers. Ornamented with engravings on wood; including a sonnet by Melchiore and Tasso's reply.)

---

[1] Examples of such 'Improvements' are:

I. 59³   Fit mother for that pearle (1600)
         For that rich Pearl fit Mother (1749)
II. 20⁸   engendreth (1600)
         ingenders (1749)
II. 55³   But labour and vertues watching ease her sleepe (1600)
         But labour's vertues watching, ease her sleepe (1624)
         But virtue's Guard is Labour, Ease her Sleep; (1749)
II. 96⁸   Sung lullabie, to bring the world to rest (1600)
         Sooth'd mortal Cares, and lull'd the world to Rest (1749)
III. 73⁸ The champion *Dudons* glorious carkasse dead (1600)
         The honour'd Reliques of Great Dudon dead (1749)
IV. 3³   wastnes (1600)
         wide Wastes (1749)
IV. 4⁸   And teare the twinkling stars from trembling skie (1600)
         As they would storm the Regions of the Sky (1749)
V. 31⁵   His bloodie sword the victor wipte and drest (1600)
         The Victor sheath'd his Sword unwip'd, undrest, (1749).

(This elegant edition includes a critical introduction, Fairfax's fourth eclogue and Book IV of the version of the epic as translated by Richard Carew.)

(*b*) A limited number of copies were printed in octavo on India paper with additional illustrations. There is a copy in the British Library, C. 43.d.23.

7. (1817) Godfrey of Bulloigne. Fifth [*sic*] Edition, reprinted from the original of folio 1600, (ed. C. Knight) 2 vols. Knight and Son: Windsor, 1817. 8vo.

This edition includes a glossary and brief lives of Tasso and Fairfax, but it is found not to be as accurate as Singer's.

8. (1844) Godfrey of Bulloigne; . . . Seventh [*sic*] edition, reprinted from the original folio of 1600, ed. C. Knight, 2 vols. Knight and Son: Windsor, 1844.

This is a reprint of with some changes in the lives. 16mo. It was issued in the series of Knight's Weekly Volumes, vols. 10 and 14.

9. (1855) An American edition in 12mo cited by M. A. Scott, *Elizabethan Translations from the Italian* (1916), p. 157, which we have not seen.

10. (1858) Jerusalem Delivered, ed. R. A. Wilmott, 1858. 8vo (Routledge's British Poets). A slightly modernized text.

11. (1890) *Jerusalem Delivered* . . . translated by Edward Fairfax, edited by Henry Morley, London, George Routledge and Sons, Ltd., 1890. (Published as vol. 7 of the Carisbrooke Library.)

Introduction dealing with Tasso, Fairfax, and Godfrey in history. The text purports to be a reprint of 1600 but it is partially modernized and has many inaccuracies. 8vo.

12. (1962) *Jerusalem Delivered*. The Edward Fairfax translation newly introduced by Roberto Weiss, 1962. Centaur Classics.

13. (1963) *Jerusalem Delivered* . . . introduced by J. C. Nelson, Putnam, New York, 1963.

III. EDITORIAL PROCEDURE

THE text is set up from one of the Bodleian copies (Antiq. d. E. 1600), corrected by collation with eighteen other copies (see list, p. oo, above). The original spelling and punctuation have been retained, but long ʃ has been normalized, inverted commas have been supplied, the italicization of proper names has been completed, and a number of small slips not corrected in any of the copies consulted have been adjusted, viz.:

Sig. A3^r, l. 35 *Syrenus*, < *Sweno*,
   l. 40 unluckly < unlucky
Book I. 56^3 *Germer* < *Gernier*
 I. 71^3 clarious < clarions
 II. 18^7 the < she
 II. 63^5 that < yet (see note)
 II. 67^1 sinne < sunne (see note)
 II. 74^4 fauout < fauour (cf. 1624)
 III. 21 71 < 21 (cf. 1624)
 p. 46 48 < 46
 III. 63 37 < 63 (cf. 1624)
 IV. 29^7 *Guidos,* < *Gnidos,* (see note)
 IV. 33^5 gestnres < gestures (cf. 1624)
 p. 82 84 < 82
 V. 42^2 *Ridaldo* < *Rinaldo* (cf. 1624)
 V. 83^2 sparled < sparkled (cf. 1624)
 VI. 22^8 He < Her
 VI. 38^8 thrund'red < thund'red
 VI. 56 96 < 56 (cf. 1624)
 VI. 70^7 seeret < secret (cf. 1624)
 VI. 89^6 sheeuelesse < sleevelesse (cf. 1624)
 VII. 1^8 vaiue < vaine (cf. 1624)
 VII. 23^7 are, < eare,
 VII. 25^2 cleree < cleere (cf. 1624)

VII. 27[6] *Tacredie* < *Tancredie* (cf. 1624)

VII. 52[6] hean'n < heav'n (cf. 1624)

VII. 58[5] champious < champions (cf. 1624)

p. 138, headline, sixth < seuenth (cf. 1624)

VIII. 55 53 < 55

VIII. 73[5] spright, < spight,

X. 13[8] grearest < greatest (cf. 1624)

X. 30[6] seeret < secret (cf. 1624)

X. 61[6] thar < that (cf. 1624)

XI. 42[5] gantled < gantlet

p. 207 193 < 207 (cf. 1624)

XII. 37[6] morne < morne from

XII. 59 95 < 59 (cf. 1624)

XII. 59[3] ease < case (cf. 1624)

XIII. 24[7] oug < ought (cf. 1624)

XIII. 32[5] attemps < attempts (cf. 1624)

XIII. 49[8] brow < bow

XIV. 14[6] strenght, < strength, (cf. 1624)

XIV. 34[7] warrious < warriours (1624)

XV. 14[4] Hiperious < *Hiperions*

XV. 23[2] wandrous < wondrous

XV. 25 27 < 25 (cf. 1624)

XVI. 16[1] He . . . he < She . . . she

XVI. 53[6] ioes < ioies

XVI. 71[8] -t < at

XVII. 51[5] they < the (cf. 1624)

XVII. 65[6] Knigtly < Knightly

XVIII. 16[3] spinkled < sprinkled

XVIII. 41[4] elect, < erect,

XVIII. 61[6] lenghtned < lengthned (cf. 1624)

XIX. 10[5] orethrnowne < orethrowne (1624)

XIX. 12[4] put < but

XIX. 37[4] breoke < broke (cf. 1624)

XIX. 58[3] harmornies < harmonies (cf. 1624)

XIX. 61[6] They < The (cf. 1624)

XX. 33[1] lannce < launce (cf. 1624)

XX. 53[3] Rpread < Spread (cf. 1624)

XX. 78[5] rauning < rav'ning (cf. 1624)
XX. 84[4] strenght < strength (cf. 1624)

In addition the following irregularities of punctuation and typography have been adjusted as shown:

A 3[r], l. 6 other. < other
A 3[r], l. 45 powers, < powers
A 3[v], l. 51 *Rinaldo* < (*Rinaldo*
Book I. 2[5] wit < wit,

    I. 25[3] Whereof < Where of
    I. 25[5] no ught < nought
    I. 45[6] sight < sight;
    II. 13[8] vnbind, < vnbind.
    II. 55[3] labour and vertues < labour's vertue's (see commentary)
    II. 59[8] end, < end.
    II. 73[8] spring, < spring.
    III. 48[7] shelter, < shelter
    V. 65[1] alwaies < al waies
    VI. 92[8] sponne, < sponne.
    IX. 1[2] (Who < Who
    IX 1[3] Gainst < (Gainst
    IX. 76[6] pin, < pin),
    IX. 86[7] *Soliman*) < *Soliman*
    XIII. 59[6] ganges < Ganges
    XIV. 67[5] eieglance < eie-glance
    XV. 11[8] floate;) < floate;
    XV. 44[4] folly, < folly
    XV. 45[3] said, < said
    XVI. 33[1] vppend < vp pend (cf. 1624)
    XVII. 35[7] stands; < stands,
    XVIII. 56[5] to < To
    XVIII. 65[5] rightwell < right well
    XVIII. 96[2] appeare; < appeare.
    XVIII. 97[1] winkte < winkte,
    XIX. 30[3] vppilde < vp-pilde (cf. 1624)
    XIX. 101[8] ride, < ride.

XIX. 118^8 pilgrimage, < pilgrimage.

XX. 3^4 strenght, < strength,

XX. 87^4 vengeance, wrath, his hart; < vengeance; wrath his hart,

XX. 123^4 proue < proue,

IV. FAIRFAX'S ITALIAN TEXTS

In an article in *P.M.L.A.* xliv (1929), Neil Dodge has demonstrated that Fairfax (unlike Carew) used the Osanna text of the *Gerusalemme Liberata*, and remarked on some fourteen passages in which some other authority seems to have been consulted. These passages have been examined in fifteen editions. Four of the texts referred to by Neil Dodge we have not managed to locate; they are:

Venice, Ingegneri, 1581. (Solerti, M.2.)
Ferrara, Bonnà, 1581. (Solerti, B.2.)
Naples, Capelli, 1581. (Solerti, C.)
Naples, Salviani, 1582. (Solerti, R.)

Those examined are as follows:

1. Venice, Domenico Cavalcalupo, 1580. (Solerti, M.1.) B.L. 638.h.12.

2. Venice, Gratioso Perchacino, 1581. Bodl. Vet. F.i.e. 148.

3. Parma, Viotto, 1581. (Solerti, 1.i.) B.L. 1073.g.31(1).

4. A. Canacci and Erasmo Viotto, Casalmaggiore and Parma, 1581. (Solerti 1.2.) Bodl. Vet. F.i.e.48.

5. Lyons, Alessandro Marsilii, 1581. Rare. B.L. 11427.d.32.

6. Ferrara, Bonna, 1581. (Solerti. B.I.) B.L. 81.i.31.

7. Parma, Viotto, 1581. (Solerti. V.) B.L. C.45.e.22.

8. Venice, Perchacino, 1582. (Solerti, M.3.) B.L. 82.i.17.

9. Venice, Francesco de' Franceschi Senese, 1583. Bodl. Douce T.T. 18.i. Holkham. d.78. B.L. 1073.i.10.

10. Mantua, Francesco Osanna, 1584. (Solerti. O) B.L. 638.h.14.

11. Venice, Salicato, 1585. (Solerti. S.2.) B.L. 83.e.11.

12. Ferrara, Giulio Cesare Cagnacini e Fratelli, 1585. (Solerti. B.3.) Bodl. Holkham F.172.

13. Genova, Girolamo Bartoli, 1590. (Text as of 1584.) (Solerti. G.) B.L. 681.g.20.

14. Venice, Altobello Salicato, 1589. (Solerti. S.4.) Bodl. Vet. F.i.e.82.

15. Venice, Altobello Salicato, 1593. (Solerti. S.6.) B.L. 11426.
e.41.

Passages tested

The numbers refer to the texts as listed above, and brackets
indicate that the reading can be found as a variant.

(*a*) I. 30⁵.   O.   Un *alta* originaria fonte
                  altra = 2, 6, 7, 8, 9, 11, 12, (14)
              F. 'a further spring', cf. Carew 'another'
F. is slightly ambiguous but perhaps nearer to 'altra'. It is
possible that he took his line from Carew who was himself not
following Osanna's text, although F.'s adjective is his own.

(*b*) I. 38⁸.   O.   squadrc
                  insegne = 1, 2, 3, 5, 7, (8), (9), (11), 12,
                  (14), (15)
              F. 38⁷.   standards
Oddly enough Carew's 'squadrons' uses the O. reading here:
he may have picked it up from a variant. F.'s 'standards' may
be a deliberate change.

(*c*) I. 63⁷.   O.   guardò
                  guido = 1, (8), (9), (11), (14), (15)
              F. guied (rhyme)

(*d*) I. 78⁶, ⁷.   O.   *che* le biade | Ogni isola
                  de = 6, 8, 9, 10, (11), 14, 15
Neil Dodge thinks F. is departing from O. here, but it is by
no means clear that he is.

(*e*) IV. 15⁷.   O.   Diede, che che si fosse, à lui vittoria.
                  Hebbero i pui felici alhor vittoria = 2, 4,
                  (8), 9, (11), 13, 14
Neil Dodge regards F.'s couplet as a departure from O. It is
possible, but it could be the result of an effective rhetorical
ambiguity.

(*f*) V 91¹.   O.   n'indirizza
                  v'indirizza = 1, 2, 6, 7, 8, 9, 11, 12, 14, 15
Neil Dodge notes F.'s 'you' as slightly nearer to the reading
'*v*' indirizza'. Carew has 'you' and F. might have picked it up
from his line or very easily misread 'n' for 'v'.

(*g*) VII. 85^3.   O.   Minaccia

Spaventa = 2, 4, 5

Neil Dodge notes F.'s 'affraid' as a trifle nearer to 'Spaventa', but it is very slight evidence.

(*h*) VIII. 1^7.   O.   Astagorre

Astragorre = 3, 6, 7, 8, 9, 11, 12, 14, 15

F. Astragor

(*i*) IX. 37^4.   O.   procurare

provocare = 1, 2, 3, 4, 5, 6, 7, 8, 9, 11, 12, 13, 14, 15

F. provoke

(*j*) IX. 68^3.   O.   Berlingier

Beringhier = 2, 4, 5

F. Berengario

(*k*) XI. 76^7.   O.   tremor

timor = 2, 4, 5

F. a chilling feare

This is perhaps slightly in favour of the reading of 'timor'.

(*l*) XIV. 37^2.   O.   sotto *quel* rio

del = 3, 4, 7, 8, 9, 11, 12, 14, 15

F. 'under the flood'

(*m*) XV. 45^7.   O.   e quando

Mà = 3, 6, 7, 8, 9, 11, (12), 14, 15

F. *But* at

(*n*) XV. 50^8.   O.   ogni nativo *ardire*

L'ira, e'l nativo *orgoglio*, = 3, 6, 7, (9), 11, 12, 14, 15

F. 'his native wrath'

By the context this could be arrived at via O.

(*o*) XVII. 14^4.   O.   al mare usurpò il *letto*.

lito = 2, 3, 4, 5, 7

F. salt sea side

This is too loose to be determinative, but F. does not pick up the 'bed' metaphor.

(*p*) XVII. 86^1.   O.   Taciti se ne gian per *l'aria nera*

van per l'ombra = 3, 4, (7), (8), 10, (13), (14)

> F. While silent so through nights dark shade
> they flie,

Very slight evidence.

(*q*) xx. 6[6].   O.   *a' suoi* liberator

> *al suo* = 2, 4, 5
> F. their deliverer

Very slight evidence.

From this analysis it would seem that if Fairfax had access to numbers 9 or 14 he could have found the readings he appears to have preferred in all except five cases (instances g, j, k, o, q); for these five readings he could have been served by numbers 2 or 4 or 5. That is, in addition to the staple Osanna text, 1584, it looks as though he knew of Venice, Francesco de' Francheschi Senese, 1583 (such as the Holkham copy now in the Bodleian) or Venice, Altobello Salicato, 1589, with a possible use of Venice, Gratioso Perchacino, 1581 or A. Canacci and Erasmo Viotto, Casalmaggiore and Parma, 1581 or Lyons, Alessandro Marsilii, 1581.

TEXT OF
GODFREY OF BULLOIGNE

To her High Maiestie

WIts *rich triumph*, Wisdomes *glorie*,
Arts *chronicle*, Learnings *storie*,
Towre *of goodnes, vertue, bewtie:*
Forgiue me, that presume to lay
My labours in your cleere eies ray:
This boldnes springs fro faith, zeal, dewtie.

Her hand, her lap, her vestures hem,
Muse touch not for polluting them,
All that is hers is pure, cleere, holie,
Before her footstoole humble lie,
So may she blesse thee with her eie,
The sunne shines not on good things solie.

Oliue *of peace,* Angell *of pleasure,*
What line of praise can your worth measure?
Calme sea of blisse which no shore boundeth,
Fame *fils the world no more with lies,*
But busied in your histories
Her trumpet those true wonders soundeth:

O Fame, *say all the good thou maist,*
Too little is that all thou saist,
What if her selfe her selfe commended?
Should we then know nere knowne before,
Whether her wit or worth were more?
Ah no! that booke would nere be ended.

Your Maiesties humble subject,

EDWARD FAIREFAX.

The Allegorie of the
Poem

Heroicall Poetrie (as a liuing Creature, wherein two natures are conioined) is compounded of *Imitation* and *Allegorie*: with the one she allureth vnto her the mindes and eares of men, and maruellously delighteth them; with the other, either in vertue or knowledge, she instructeth them. And as the heroically written *Imitation* of an *Other*, is nothing else, but the patterne and image of humane action: so the *Allegorie* of an Heroicall Poeme is none other than the glasse and figure of humane life. But *Imitation* regardeth the *Actions* of man subiected to the outward senses, and about them being principally imployed, seeketh to represent them with effectuall and expressiue phrases, such as liuely set before our corporall eies the things represented: It doth not consider the customes, affections, or discourses of the *Minde*, as they be inward, but onely as they come forth thence, and being manifested in words, in deedes, or working, doe accompanie the *Action*. On the other side, *Allegorie* respecteth the passions, the opinions and customes, not onely as they doe appeare, but principally in their being hidden & inward; and more obscurely doth expresse them with notes (as a man may say) misticall, such as only the vnderstanders of the nature of things can fully comprehend. Now leauing *Imitation* apart, we will according to our purpose speake of *Allegorie*: which, as the life of man is compound, so it represents to vs, sometime the figure of the one, sometime the figure of the other: yet because that commonly by *Man*, we vnderstand this compound of the bodie, soule, or minde, and then mans life, is said to be that, which of such compound is proper, in the operations whereof euerie part thereof concurres, and by working gets that perfection, of the which by her nature she is capable: sometime (although more seldome) by *Man* is vnderstood, not the compound, but the most noble part, namely the *Minde*; According to this last signification, it may be said, that the life of man is *Contemplatiue*, and to worke simplie with the *Vnderstanding*, forasmuch as this life doth seeme much to participate of heauen, and as it were changde from humanitie, to become angelicall. Of the life of the *Contemplatiue Man*, the Comedie of *Dantes* and the *Odyssees* are (as it were) in euerie part thereof a figure: but the ciuill life is seene to be shadowed throughout the *Iliads*, and *Æneids* also, although in this

6 *Other* < *Other*

there be rather set out a mixture of *Action* and *Contemplation*. But since the *Contemplatiue Man* is solitarie; and the *Man* of *Action* liueth in ciuill companie, thence it commeth that *Dantes* & *Ulysses* in their departure from *Calipso* are fained not to be accompanied of the armie, or of a multitude of soldiers, but to depart alone; whereas *Agamemnon* 5 and *Achilles* are described, the one Generall of the *Grecian* Armie, the other leader of many troupes of *Mirmidons*, and *Æneas* is seene to be accompanied when he fighteth, or doth other ciuill actes; but when he goeth to hell and the Elisian fields, he leaues his followers, accompanied onely with his most faithfull friend *Achates*, who neuer de- 10 parted from his side. Neither doth the Poet at randon faine that he went alone, for that in his voiage there is signified this onely *Contemplation* of these paines and rewardes which in another world are reserued for good or guiltie soules. Moreouer, the operation of the *Vnderstanding speculatiue*, which is the working of one only power, 15 is commodiously figured vnto vs by the action of one alone: but the *Operation Politicall*, which proceedeth together from the other powers of the minde (which are as citizens vnited in one commonwealth) cannot so commodiously be shadowed of *Action*, wherein many together and to one end working, doe not concurre. To these reasons, 20 and to these examples I hauing regarde, haue made the *Allegorie* of my *Poem* such, as now shall be manifested.

The *Army* compounded of diuers Princes, and of other Christian souldiers, signifieth *Man*, compounded of soule and bodie, and of a soule not simple, but diuided into many and diuers powers. *Ierusalem* 25 the strong citie placed in a rough and hilly countrey, whereunto as to the last ende, are directed all the enterprises of the faithfull armie, doth here signifie the *Ciuill happines*, which may come to a Christian man (as hereafter shall be declared) which is a good, verie difficult to attaine vnto, and situated vpon the top of the Alpine and wearisome 30 hill of virtue; and vnto this are turned (as vnto the last marke) all the Actions of the politicke man. *Godfrey*, which of all the assembly is chosen Chieftaine, stands for *Vnderstanding*, & particularly for that vnderstanding, which considereth not the things necessarie, but the mutable and which may diuersly happen, & those by the wil of God. 35 And of *Princes* he is chosen Captaine of this enterprise, because vnderstanding is of God, and of Nature made Lord ouer the other virtues of the soule and bodie, and commaunds these, one with ciuill power, the other with roiall command. *Rinaldo*, *Tancredie*, and the other Princes are in lieu of the other powers of the soule; and the *Bodie* 40 here becomes notified by the souldiers lesse noble. And because that through the imperfection of humane nature, and by the deceits of his enemy, man attaines not this felicitie without many inward difficulties, and without finding by the way many outward impediments,

all these are noted vnto vs by Poeticall figures. As the death of
Sweno, and his companions, not being ioined to the campe, but
slaine farre off, may here shew the losses, which a ciuill man hath of
his friends, followers, and other externall goods, instruments of
5   vertue, & aids to the attaining of true felicitie. The armies of Affricke,
Asia, and vnlucky battels, are none other than his enemies, his losses,
and the accidents of contrarie fortune. But comming to the inward
impediments, loue, which maketh *Tancredie* and the other woorthies
to dote, and disioine them from *Godfrey*, and the disdaine which
10 entiseth *Rinaldo* from the enterprise, doe signifie the conflict and
rebellion which the *Concupiscent* and *Irefull* powers doe make with the
Reasonable. The *Diuels* which doe consult to hinder the conquest of
Ierusalem, are both a figure, and a thing figured, and doe here repre-
sent the verie same euils, which doe oppose themselues against our
15 ciuill happines, so that it may not be to vs a ladder of Christian
blessednes. The two Magitians *Ismen* and *Armida*, seruants of the
diuell, which indeuour to remooue the Christians from making war,
are two deuilish temptations which doe lay snares for two powers of
the soule, from whence all other sinnes doe proceed. *Ismen* doth
20 signifie that temptation, which seeketh to deceiue with false beliefe
the vertue (as a man may call it) Opinatiue: *Armida* is that tempta-
tion which laieth siege to the power of our desires, so from that
proceed the errours of *Opinion*; from this, those of the *Appetite*. The
inchantments of *Ismen* in the wood, deceiuing with illusions, signifie
25 no other thing than the falsitie of the reasons and perswasions which
are ingendred in the wood; that is, in the varietie and multitude of
opinions and discourses of men. And since that man followeth vice
and flieth vertue, either thinking that trauels and dangers are euils
most greeuous and insupportable, or iudging (as did the Epicure and
30 his followers) that in pleasure and idlenesse consisted chiefest
felicitie; by this, double is the inchantment and illusion. The *Fier*,
the *Whirlewinde*, the *Darkenes*, the *Monsters*, and other faigned sem-
blances, are the deceiuing allurements which doe shew vs honest
trauels and honorable danger vnder the shape of *Euill*. The *Flowers*,
35 the *Fountains*, the *Riuers*, the *Musicall* instruments, the *Nymphes*, are
the deceitfull inticements, which do here set downe before vs the
pleasures and delights of the sense, vnder the shew of *Good*. So let
it suffice to haue saide thus much of the impediments which a man
findes as well within as without himselfe: yet if the Allegorie of
40 anything be not well expressed, with these beginnings euerie man
by himselfe may easily finde it out. Now let vs passe to the out-
ward and inward helpes; with which the *Ciuill man* ouercomming all

2 *Syrenus*, < *Sweno, see note*   6 unluckly < unlucky   11 powers, <
powers

difficultie, is brought to this desired happines. The target of *Diamond* which *Raimond* recouereth, and afterward is shewed readie in the defence of *Godfrey*, ought to be vnderstood for the special safegard of the Lord God. The *Angels* doe signifie somtime *Heauenly helpe*, and somtime *Inspiration*, the which are here shadowed in the dream of *Godfrey*, & in the records of the *Hermite*. The *Hermite*, who for the deliuerance of *Rinaldo* did sende the two messengers to the wiseman, doth shewe vnto vs the supernaturall knowledge receiued by Gods grace, as the wise man doth humane wisdome, forasmuch as of humane wisedome & of the knowledge of the workes of Nature, & the mysteries thereof, is bred & established in our minds, *Justice*, *temperance*, despising of *death* and mortall pleasures, *magnanimite*, and euery other morall vertue. And great aid may a ciuill man receiue in euery action he attempteth, by *contemplation*. It is fained, that this wise man was by birth a Pagan, but being by the *Hermite* conuerted to the true faith, becommeth a Christian, and despising his first arrogancie, he doth not much presume of his owne wisedome, but yeeldeth himselfe to the iudgment of his master, albeit that *Philosophie* be borne & nourished amongst the Gentiles in Ægypt and Greece, and from thence hath passed ouer vnto us, presumptious of herselfe, a miscreant bold and proud aboue measure: but of *Saint Thomas* and the other *holy Doctors* she is made the disciple and handmaid of Diuinitie, and is become by their indeuour more modest, and more religious, nothing daring rashly to affirme against that which is reuealed to her *Maistres*. Neither in vaine is the person of the wise man brought in, (*Rinaldo* being able by the onely counsel of the *Hermite* to be found & brought backe againe) for that, it is brought in shew, that the grace of God doth not worke alwaies in men immediately, or by extraordinarie waies, but many times worketh by naturall meanes. And it is verie reasonable that *Godfrey* which in holines and religion doth excell all other, and is (as hath bin said) the figure of *Vnderstanding*, be specially graced and priuiledged with fauours not communicated to any other. This humane wisedome, when it is directed of the superior or more high vertue, doth deliuer the sensible soule from vice, & therein placeth morall vertue. But bicause this sufficeth not, *Peter* the *Hermite* first confesseth *Godfrey* & *Rinaldo*, and conuerted *Tancredie*. *Godfrey* & *Rinaldo* being two persons, which in our *Poem* do hold the principall place, it can not be but pleasing to the Reader, that I repeating some of the already spoken things, do particularly lay open the allegoricall sense, which vnder the vaile of their actions, lie hidden. *Godfrey* which holdeth the principall place in this storie, is no other in the Allegorie but the

26 in, *Rinaldo* < in, (*Rinaldo*

Vnderstanding, which is signified in many places of the *Poeme* as in
that verse,

> By thee the counsell giuen is, by thee the scepter rul'd.

And more plainly in that other:

5   *Thy soule is of the campe both minde and life.*

And *Life* is added, bicause in the powers more noble, the lesse noble
are contained: therefore *Rinaldo*, which in action is in the second
degree of honour, ought also to be placed in the Allegorie in the
answerable degree: but what this power of the mind, holding the
10 second degree of dignitie is, shall be nowe manifested. The *Irefull*
vertue is that, which amongst all the powers of the minde, is lesse
estranged from the nobility of the soule, insomuch that *Plato* (doubt-
ing) seeketh whether it differeth from reason or no. And such is it
in the minde, as the chiefetaine in an assemblie of souldiours: for
15 as of these the office is to obey their princes, which do giue directions
and commandements to fight against their enimies: so is it the dutie
of the irefull, warlike, and soueraigne part of the minde, to be armed
with reason against concupiscence, and with that vehemencie and
fiercenes (which is proper vnto it) to resist and driue awaie whatsoeuer
20 impediment to felicitie. But when it doth not obey Reason, but
suffers itselfe to be carried of her owne violence, it falleth out, that
it fighteth not against concupiscence, but by concupiscence, like a
dogge that biteth not the theeues, but the cattle committed to his
keeping. This violent, fierce, and vnbridled furie, as it can not be
25 fully noted by one *man of warre*, is neuertheles principally signified
by *Rinaldo*, where it is said of him, that being

> *—A right warrelike knight*
> *Did scorne by reasons rule to fight.*

Wherin (whilest fighting against *Gernando*, he did passe the bounds
30 of ciuill reuenge, and whilest he serued *Armida*) may be noted vnto
vs, *Anger*, not gouerned by reason: whilest hee disinchanteth the
wood, entreth the citie, breaketh the enemies array, *Anger*, directed
by reason. His returne and reconciliation to *Godfrey*, noteth *Obedi-
ence*, causing the *Irefull* power to yeelde to the *Reasonable*. In these
35 Reconciliations two things are signified, first, *Godfrey* with ciuill
moderation is acknowledged to be superior to *Rinaldo*, teaching vs,
that Reason commandeth Anger, not imperiously, but curteouslie
and ciuillie: contrariwise in that, by imprisoning *Argillanus* imperi-
ously, the sedition is quieted; it is giuen vs to vnderstand, the
40 power of the *Minde*, to be ouer the bodie, regall and predominate:
Secondly, that as the reasonable part ought not (for heerein the

Stoiks were very much deceiued) to exclude the *Irefull* from actions,
nor *vsurpe* the offices thereof, for this vsurpation shoulde bee against
nature and iustice, but it ought to make her her companion and
handmaid: So ought not *Godfrey* to attempt the adventure of the
wood himselfe, thereby arrogating to himselfe the other offices
belonging to *Reinaldo*. Lesse skill should then be shewed, and lesse
regard had to the profite, which the Poet, as subiected to policie,
ought to haue for his aime, if it had been fained, that by *Godfrey*
onlie, all was wrought, which was necessarie for the conquering of
Ierusalem. Neither is there contrarietie or difference from that which
hath been said, in putting downe *Rinaldo* and *Godfrey* for that figure
of the *Reasonable* and of the *Irefull* vertue, which *Hugo* speakes of in
his dreame, whereas he compareth the one to the *Head*, the other to
the *right Hand* of the army, bicause the *Head* (if we believe *Plato*) is
the seat of Reason, and the *right Hand*, if it be not the seat of wrath,
it is at least her most principall instrument. Finally, to come to the
conclusion, the army wherein *Rinaldo* and the other Woorthies by
the grace of God and aduise of Man, are returned and obedient to
their chieftaine, signifieth man brought againe into the state of
naturall Iustice and heauenly obedience: where the superior powers
do command, as they ought, and the inferior do obey, as they should.
Then the wood is easily disinchanted, the citty vanquished, the
enimies armie discomfited, that is, all externall impediments being
easily ouercome, man attaineth the politike happines. But for that
this *Politike blessednes*, ought not to be the last marke of a Christian
man, but he ought to looke more high, that is, to *Euerlasting felicitie*,
for this cause *Godfrey* doth not desire to win the earthly Ierusalem,
to haue therein onely temporall dominion, but bicause heerein may
be celebrated the worship of God, and that the Holy sepulchre may
be the more freely visited of godly strangers and deuout Pilgrims;
and the Poem is shut vp in the praiers of *Godfrey*, it is shewed vnto vs,
that the *Vnderstanding* being trauelled and wearied in ciuill actions
ought in the ende to rest in deuotion and in the contemplation of
the eternall blessednes of the other most happie and immortall life.

FINIS.

The first Booke of Godfrey *of Bulloigne*

God sends his Angell to Tortosa downe,
Godfrey vnites the Christian peeres and knights,
And all the Lords and Princes of renowne
Choose him their Duke, to rule the wars and fights,
He mustreth all his host, whose number knowne,
He sends them to the fort that Sion hights,
*   The aged Tyrant* Iudaes *land that guides*
*   In feare and trouble to resist prouides.*

I

I Sing the warre made in the Holy land,
    And the Great Chiefe that Christs great tombe did free:
Much wrought he with his wit, much with his hand,
Much in that braue atchieument suffred hee:
In vaine doth hell that Man of God withstand,
In vaine the worlds great Princes armed bee;
    For heau'n him fauour'd; and he brought againe
    Vnder one standard all his scatt'red traine.

2

O heauenly muse, that not with fading baies
Deckest thy brow by th'Heliconian spring,
But sittest crownd with stars immortal raies,
In heauen where legions of bright Angels sing,
Inspire life in my wit, my thoughts vpraise,
My verse ennoble, and forgiue the thing,
    If fictions light I mixe with truth diuine,
    And fill these lines with others praise then thine.

3

Thither thou know'st the world is best inclinde
Where luring Parnase most his sweete imparts,

2⁵ wit < wit,

And truth conuay'd in verse of gentle kinde,
To reade perhaps will moue the dullest harts:
So we (if children yong diseas'd we finde)
Annoint with sweets the vessels formost parts,
　To make them taste the potions sharpe we giue;
　They drinke deceiu'd; and so deceiued, they liue.

4

Ye noble Princes, that protect and save
The pilgrim muses, and their ship defend
From rocke of ignorance, and errors waue,
Your gracious eies vpon this labour bend:
To you these tales of loue and conquests braue
I dedicate, to you this worke I send,
　My muse hereafter shall perhaps vnfold
　Your fights, your battailes, and your combats bold.

5

For if the Christian Princes euer striue
To win faire Greece out of the tyrants hands,
And those vsurping Ismalites depriue
Of wofull Thrace, which now captiued stands,
You must from realmes and seas the Turkes forth driue,
As *Godfrey* chased them from Iudais lands,
　And in this legend, all that glorious deede
　Read, whil'st you arme you; arme you, whil'st you reed.

6

Sixe yeeres were ronne since first in martiall guize
The Christian Lords warraid the eastren land,
Nice by assault, and Antioch by surprize,
Both faire, both rich, both wonne, both conquer'd stand,
And this defended they in noblest wize
Gainst Persian knights and many a valiant band,
　Tortosa wonne, (least winter might them shend)
　They drew to holds, and comming spring attend.

7

The sullen season now was come and gone,
That forst them late cease from their noble war,

When God almightie from his loftie throne,
Set in those parts of heau'n that purest ar,
(As far aboue the cleere stars euery one,
As it is hence vp to the highest star)
   Look'd downe, and all at once this world behield,
   Each land, each citie, countrie, towne and field:

8

All things he view'd, at last in Syria stai'd
Vpon the Christian Lords, his gracious eie,
That wondrous looke wherewith he oft suruai'd
Mens secret thoughts that most concealed lie,
He cast on puissant *Godfrey*, that assai'd
To driue the Turks from Sions bulwarks hie,
   And (full of zeale and faith) esteemed light
   All worldly honour, empire, treasure, might.

9

In *Baldwine* next, he spide another thought,
Whom spirits proud to vaine ambition moue,
Tancred he saw his liues ioy set at nought,
So woe begon was he with paines of loue:
Boemond the conquer'd folke of Antioch brought
The gentle yoke of Christian rule to proue,
   He taught them lawes, statutes, and customes new,
   Arts, craftes, obedience, and religion trew.

10

And with such care his busie worke he plied
That to nought els his acting thoughts he bent,
In yong *Rinaldo* fierce desires he spied,
And noble hart, of rest impatient,
To wealth or soueraigne powre he nought applied
His wits, but all to vertue excellent,
   Patternes and rules of skill and courage bolde
   He tooke from *Guelpho*, and his fathers olde.

11

Thus, when the Lord discouer'd had and seene
The hidden secrets of each worthies brest,

Out of the Hierarchies of Angels sheene
The gentle *Gabriell* call'd he from the rest,
Twixt God and soules of men that righteous beene
Ambassador is he, for euer blest,
 The iust commaunds of heau'ns eternall king
 Twixt skies and earth, he vp and downe doth bring.

12

To whom the Lord thus spake, '*Godfredo* finde
And in my name aske him, why doth he rest?
Why be his armes to ease and peace resignde?
Why frees he not Hierusalem distrest?
His Peeres to counsell call, each baser minde
Let him stir vp; for, chieftaine of the rest
 I chose him heere, the earth shall him allow,
 His fellowes late, shall be his subiects now.'

13

This said, the Angell swift himselfe preparde
To execute the charge impos'd aright,
In forme of airie members faire imbarde,
His spirits pure were subject to our fight,
Like to a man in shew and shape he farde,
But full of heau'nly maiestie and might,
 A stripling seem'd he thrice fiue winters olde,
 And radiant beames adorn'd his locks of golde.

14

Of siluer wings he tooke a shining paire,
Fringed with gold, vnwearied, nimble, swift,
With these he parts the windes, the clouds, the aire,
And ouerseas and earth himselfe doth lift,
Thus clad he cut the spheares and circles faire
And the pure skies with sacred feathers clift,
 On Libanon at first his foote he set,
 And shooke his wings with roarie May-dewes wet.

15

Then to Tortosas confines swiftly sped
The sacred messenger, with headlong flight;

Aboue the eastern waue appeered red
The rising sunne, yet scantly halfe in sight,
Godfrey euen then his morne deuotions fed,
(As was his custome) when with Titan bright
   Appeer'd the Angell, in his shape diuine,
   Whose glorie far obscured Phebus shine.

16

'*Godfrey* (quoth he) behold the season fit
To war, for which thou waited hast so long,
Now serues the time (if thou oreslip not it)
To free Hierusalem, from thrall and wrong:
Thou with thy Lords in counsell quickly sit,
Comfort the feeble and confirme the strong,
   The Lord of hosts their Generall doth make thee,
   And for their chieftaine they shall gladly take thee.

17

'I messenger from euerlasting Ioue
In his great name thus his behests doe tell,
Oh what sure hope of conquest ought thee moue?
What zeale, what loue should in thy bosome dwell?'
This said, he vanisht to those seats aboue,
In height and cleerenes which the rest excell,
   Downe fell the Duke, his ioints dissolu'd asunder,
   Blinde with the light, and stroken dead with wonder.

18

But when recou'red, he consid'red more
The man, his maner, and his message, saide.
If earst he wished, now he longed sore
To end that war, whereof he Lord was made,
Nor sweld his brest with vncouth pride therefore,
That heau'n on him aboue this charge had laide,
   But for his great Creator would the same,
   His will encreast; so fire augmenteth flame.

19

The captaines cald foorthwith from euery tent,
Vnto the Rende-vous he them inuites,

Letter on letter, post on post he sent,
Entreatance faire with counsell he vnites,
All, what a noble courage could augment,
The sleeping sparke of valour what incites,
 He vs'd, that all their thoughts to honour reased,
 Some prais'd, some prai'd, some counselled, all pleased.

20

The captaines, soldiers, all, (saue *Boemound*) came,
And pitcht their tents, some in the fields without,
Some of greene boughes their slender cabbins frame,
Some lodged were Tortosas streetes about,
Of all the host the chiefe of worth and name
Assembled beene, a senate graue and stout;
 Then *Godfrey* (after silence kept a space)
 Lift vp his voice, and spake with princely grace.

21

'Warriors (whom God himselfe elected hath
His worship true in Sion to restore,
And still preseru'd from danger, harme and scath,
By many a sea and many an vnknowne shore)
You haue subiected lately to his faith
Some prouinces rebellious long before:
 And after conquests great, haue in the same
 Erected trophies to his crosse and name,

22

'But not for this, our homes we first forsooke,
And from our natiue soile haue march'd so far:
Nor vs to dangrous seas haue we betooke,
Expos'd to hazard of so far sought war,
Of glorie vaine to gaine an idle smooke,
And lands possesse that wilde and barbrous ar:
 That for our conquests were too meane a pray,
 To shed our bloods, to worke our soules decay.

23

'But this the scope was of our former thought,
Of Sions fort to scale the noble wall,

The Christian folke from bondage to haue brought,
Wherein alas, they long haue liued thrall,
In Palestine an empire to haue wrought
Where godlines might raigne perpetuall,
    And none be left, that pilgrims might denay
    To see Christes tombe, and promis'd vowes to pay.

24

'What to this howre successiuely is donne
Was full of perill, to our honour small,
Nought to our first designment, if we shonne
The purpos'd end, or here lie fixed all,
What bootes it vs these wars to haue begonne?
Or Europe rais'd to make proud Asia thrall?
    If our beginnings haue this ending knowne,
    Not kingdoms rais'd, but armies ouerthrowne.

25

'Not as we list erect we empires new
On fraile foundations, laid in earthly molde,
Where of our faith and countrie be but few,
Among the thousands stout of Pagans bolde,
Where nought behooues vs trust to Greece vntrew,
And westren aide we far remou'd beholde,
    Who buildeth thus, me thinkes, so buildeth he,
    As if his worke should his sepulcher be.

26

'Turks, Persians conquer'd, Antiochia wonne,
Be glorious actes, and full of glorious praise,
By heau'ns meere grace, not by our prowesse, donne:
Those conquests were atchieu'd by wondrous waies,
If now from that directed course we ronne,
The God of battailes thus before vs laies,
    His louing kindness shall we loose I dout,
    And be a by-word to the lands about.

25³ Whereof < Where of   25⁵ no ught < nought

27

'Let not these blessings then sent from aboue
Abused be, or split in prophane wife,
But let the issue correspondent proue
To good beginnings of each enterprise,
The gentle season might our courage moue,
Now euery passage plaine and open lies:
    What lets vs than the great Hierusalem
    With valiant squadrons round about to hem?

28

'Lords, I protest, and harken all to it
Ye times and ages, future, present, past,
Heare all ye blessed in the heau'ns that sit,
The time for this atchieument hastneth fast:
The longer rest worse will the season fit,
Our suretie shall with doubts be ouercast,
    If we foreslowe the siege I well foresee
    From Egypt will the Pagans succour'd bee.'

29

This said, the hermite *Peter* rose and spake,
(Who sate in counsell those great Lords among)
'At my request this war was vndertake,
In priuate cell who earst liu'd closed long,
What *Godfrey* wils, of that no question make,
There cast no doubts where truth is plaine and strong,
    Your actes I trust will correspond his speach,
    Yet one thing more I would you gladly teach.

30

'These striues (vnles I far mistake the thing)
And discords rais'd, oft in disordred sort,
Your disobedience, and ill menaging
Of actions, lost, for want of due support,
Refer I iustly to a further spring,
Spring of sedition, strife, oppression, tort,
    I meane commanding powre to sundry giuen,
    In thought, opinion, worth, estate, vneuen.

31

'Where diuers Lords diuided empire holde,
Where causes be by gifts not iustice tride,
Where offices be falsly bought and solde,
Needes must the lordship there from vertue slide.
Of friendly parts one bodie then vpholde,
Create one head the rest to rule and guide,
   To one the regall powre and scepter giue,
   That henceforth may your king and soueraigne liue.'

32

And therewith staide his speech. O gratious muse,
What kindling motions in their brests doe frie?
With grace diuine the hermits talke infuse
That in their harts his words may fructifie;
By this a vertuous concord they did chuse,
And all contentions then began to die;
   The princes with the multitude agree,
   That *Godfrey* ruler of those wars should bee.

33

This powre they gaue him, by his princely right
All to command, to iudge all, good and ill,
Lawes to impose to lands subdew'd by might,
To maken war both when and where he will,
To hold in due subiection euerie wight
Their valours to be guided by his skill;
   This done, report displaies her teltale wings,
   And to each eare the newes and tidings brings.

34

She told the soldiers, who allowed him meet
And well deseruing of that soueraigne place,
Their first salutes and acclamations sweet
Receiued he, with loue and gentle grace:
After their reuerence done with kinde regreet
Requited was, with milde and cheerefull face,
   He bids his armies should the following day
   On those faire plaines, their standards proud display.

35

The golden sunne rose from the silver waue,
And with his beames ennameld euery greene,
When vp arose each warrior bold and braue,
Glistring in filed steele and armours sheene,
With iolly plumes their crests adorn'd they haue,
And all tofore their chieftaine mustred beene:
 He from a mountaine, cast his curious sight
 On euery footeman, and on euery knight.

36

My minde, times enimie, obliuions foe,
Disposer true of each note-worthie thing,
O let thy vertuous might auaile me soe,
That I each troupe and captaine great may sing
That in this glorious war did famous groe,
Forgot till now, by times euill handling:
 This worke (deriued from thy treasures deare)
 Let all times harken, neuer age outweare.

37

The French came foremost battailous and bold,
Late led by *Hugo* brother to their king,
From France the isle that riuers fower enfold
With rolling streames descending from their spring,
But *Hugo* dead, the Lillie faire of gold
Their wonted ensigne, they tofore them bring
 Vnder *Clotharius* great, a captaine good,
 And hardie knight, isprong of princes blood,

38

A thousand were they in strong armours clad,
Next whome there marched foorth another band,
That number, nature and instruction had
Like them, to fight far off, or charge at hand,
All valiant Normans, by Lord *Robert* lad,
The natiue Duke of that renowmed land,
 Two Bishops next their standards proud vpbare
 Call'd reuerend *William*, and good *Ademare*.

39

Their iollie notes they chanted lowd and cleare,
On merrie mornings, at the masse diuine,
And horrid helmes high on their heads they beare,
When their fierce courage they to war incline,
The first fowre hundreth horsemen gathred neare
To Orange towne, and lands that it confine:
    But *Ademare* the Poggian youth brought out,
    In number like, in hard assaies, as stout.

40

Baldwine his ensigne faire did next despreed
Among his Bulloyners of noble fame,
His brother gaue him all his troopes to leed
When he commander of the field became,
The Count *Carinto* did him straight succeed,
Graue in aduise, well skild in *Mars* his game,
    Fowre hundreth brought he, but so many thrice
    Led *Baldwine*, clad in gilden armes of price:

41

Guelpho next them the land and place possest,
Whose fortunes good with his great actes agree,
By his Italian Sire, fro th'house of *Est*
Well could he bring his noble pedegree,
A German borne, with rich possessions blest,
A worthie branch sprong from the *Guelphian* tree.
    Twixt Rhene and Danubie the land contain'd
    He rul'd, where Swaues and Rhetians whilome raign'd,

42

His mothers heritage was this and right,
To which he added more by conquest got,
From thence approoued men of passing might
He brought, that death or danger feared not;
It was their wont in feasts to spend the night,
And passe cold daies in bathes and houses hot,
    Fiue thousand late, of which now scantly ar
    The third part left, such is the chance of war.

43

The nation than with crisped lockes and faire,
That dwell betweene the seas and Arden wood,
Where Mosell streames and Rhene the meadowes weare,
A battle soile for graine, for pasture good,
Their Islanders with them, who oft repaire
Their earthen bulwarks gainst the Ocean flood,
　　The flood, elsewhere that ships and barks deuowres,
　　But there drownes cities, countries, townes and towres.

44

Both in one troope, and but a thousand all,
Vnder another *Robert* fierce they ronne,
Then th'English squadron, soldiers stout and tall,
By *William* led their Soueraignes yonger sonne,
These Archers be, and with them come withall,
A people neere the northren pole that wonne,
　　Whom Ireland sent from loughes and forrests hore,
　　Diuided far by sea from Europes shore.

45

Tancredie next, nor mongst them all was one
Rinald except, a prince of greater might,
With maiestie his noble count'nance shone,
Hie were his thoughts, his hart was bold in fight,
No shamefull vice his worth had ouergone,
His fault was loue, by vnaduised sight;
　　Bred in the dangers of aduentrous armes,
　　And nurst with grieues, with sorrowes, woes, & harmes.

46

Fame tels, that on that euer-blessed day,
When Christian swords with Persian blood were dide,
The furious prince *Tancredie* from that fray
His coward foes chased through forrests wide,
Till tired with the fight, the heate, the way,
He sought some place to rest his wearie side,
　　And drew him neare a silver streame, that plade
　　Among wilde herbes, vnder the greene-wood shade.

45⁶ sight < sight;

47

A Pagan damsell there vnwares he met,
In shining steele, all save her visage faire,
Her haire vnbound she made a wanton net
To catch sweete breathing, from the cooling aire.
On her at gaze his longing lookes he set,
Sight, wonder; wonder, loue; loue bred his caire,
   O loue, O wonder; loue new borne, new bred,
    Now growne, now arm'd, this champion captiue led.

48

Her helme the virgin don'd, and but some wight
She fear'd might come to aide him as they fought,
Her courage earn'd to haue assail'd the knight,
Yet thence she fled, vncompaned, vnsought,
And left her image in his hart ipight,
Her sweete Idea wandred through his thought.
   Her shape, her gesture and her place in minde
    He kept, and blew loues fire with that winde.

49

Well might you read his sicknes in his eies,
Their banks were full, their tide was at the flow,
His helpe far off, his hurt within him lies,
His hopes vnsprong, his cares were fit to mowe,
Eight hundreth horse (from Champaine came) he guies,
Champaine a land where wealth, ease, pleasure growe,
   Rich natures pompe and pride, the Tirrhene maine
    There wowes the hils, hils wowe the valleis plaine.

50

Two hundred Greekes came next, in fight well tride,
Not surely arm'd, in steele or iron strong,
But each a glaue had pendant by his side,
Their bowes and quiuers at their shoulders hong,
Their horses well enur'd to chace and ride,
In diet spare, vntir'd with labour long,
   Readie to charge and to retire at will,
    Though broken, scattred, fled, they skirmish still.

51

Tatine their guide, and except *Tatine*, none
Of all the Greekes went with the Christian host,
O sinne, O shame, O Greece accurst alone!
Did not this fatall war affront thy coast?
Yet sattest thou an idle looker on,
And glad attendest which side wonne or lost:
    Now if thou be a bond slave vile become
    No wrong is that, but Gods most righteous dome.

52

In order last, but first in worth and fame,
Vnfear'd in fight, vntir'd with hurt or wound,
The noble squadron of aduentrers came,
Terrors to all that tread on Asian ground,
Cease *Orpheus* of thy *Minois*, *Arthur* shame
To boast of *Launcelot*, or thy table round,
    For these whom antique times with laurell drest,
    These far exceed, them, thee, and all the rest.

53

Dudon of Consa was their guide and Lord,
And for of worth and birth alike they beene,
They chose him captaine, by their free accord,
For he most actes had done, most battails seene,
Graue was the man in yeeres, in lookes, in word,
His locks were gray, yet was his courage greene,
    Of worth and might the noble badge he bore,
    Old scarres of greeuous wounds, receiu'd of yore.

54

After came *Eustace*, well ysteemed man
For *Godfreyes* sake his brother, and his owne,
The king of Norwaies heire *Gernando* than,
Proud of his fathers titles, scepter, crowne,
Roger of Balnauill, and *Engerlan*
For hardie knights approoued were and knowne,
    Besides were numbred in that warlike traine
    Rambald, *Gentonio*, and the *Gerards* twaine.

55

Vbaldo than, and puissant *Rosimond*
Of Lancaster the heire, in ranke succeed,
Let none forget *Obizo* of Tuscaine lond,
Well worthie praise for many a worthie deed,
Nor those three brethren, Lombards fierce and yond,
Achilles, Sforza, and sterne *Palameed,*
 Nor *Ottons* shield he conqu'red in those stowres,
 In which a snake a naked childe deuoures.

56

Guascher and *Raiphe* in valour like there was,
The one and other *Guido,* famous both,
Gernier and *Eberard* to ouerpas
In foule obliuion would my muse be loth,
With his *Gildippes* deere, *Edward* alas,
A louing paire, to war among them go'th
 In bond of vertuous loue together tied,
 Together seru'd they and together died.

57

In schoole of loue are all things taught we see,
There learn'd this maide of armes the irefull guise,
Still by his side a faithfull garde went shee,
One trueloue knot their liues together ties,
No wound to one alone could dang'rous bee,
But each the smart of others anguish tries,
 If one were hurt, the other felt the sore,
 She lost her blood, he spent his life therefore.

58

But these and all, *Rinaldo* far exceedes,
Star of this spheare, the dimond of this ring,
The nest, where courage with sweete mercie breedes:
A comet, worthie each eies wondering,
His yeeres are fewer than his noble deedes,
His fruit is ripe soone as his blossoms spring,
 Armed, a *Mars* might coyest *Venus* moue,
 And if disarm'd, then God himselfe of loue.

56³ Germer < Gernier

59

Sophia by Adige flowrie banke him bore,
Sophia the faire, spouse to *Bertoldo* great,
Fit mother for that pearle, and before
The tender impe was wained from the teat,
The Princesse *Maud* him tooke, in vertues lore
She brought him vp, fit for each worthie feat,
　　Till of these wars the golden trumpe he heares
　　That soundeth glorie, fame, praise in his eares.

60

And then (though scantly three times fiue yeeres old)
He fled alone, by many an vnknowne coast,
Ore Aegean seas, by many a Greekish hold,
Till he arriued at the Christian hoast;
A noble flight, aduentrous, braue and bold,
Whereon a valiant Prince might iustly boast,
　　Three yeeres he seru'd in field, when scant begin
　　Few golden haires to decke his Iuorie chin.

61

The horsemen past, their void left stations fill
The bands on foote, and *Reymond* them beforne,
Of Tholouse Lord, from lands neere Piraene hill,
By Garound streames, and salt sea billowes worne,
Fowre thousand foote he brought, well arm'd, and skill
Had they all paines and trauell to haue borne,
　　Stout men of armes, and with their guide of powre
　　Like Troyes old towne, defenst with Ilions towre.

62

Next *Stephen* of Amboise did fiue thousand leed,
The men he prest from Toures and Blois but late,
To hard assaies vnfit, vnsure at need,
Yet arm'd to point in well attempted plate,
The land did like itselfe the people breed,
The soile is gentle, smooth, soft, delicate;
　　Boldly they charge, but soone retire for dout,
　　Like fire of straw soone kindled, soone burnt out.

63

The third *Alcasto* marched, and with him
The Boaster brought sixe thousand Switzers bold,
Audacious were their lookes, their faces grim,
Strong castles on the Alpine clifts they hold,
Their shares and culters broke, to armours trim
They change that mettall, cast in warlike mold,
    And with this band late heards and flocks that guied,
    Now kings and realmes he threat'ned and defied.

64

The glorious standard last to heau'n they sprad,
With *Peters* keyes ennobled, and his crowne,
With it seuen thousand stout *Camillo* had,
Embattailed in wals of iron browne,
In this aduenture and occasion, glad
So to reuiue the Romaines old renowne,
    Or proue at least to all of wiser thought
    Their harts were fertill land, although vnwrought.

65

But now was passed euery regiment,
Each band, each troope, each person worth regard,
When *Godfrey* with his Lords to counsell went,
And thus the Duke his princely will declar'd:
'I will when day next cleeres the firmament,
Our readie host in haste be all prepar'd,
    Closely to march to Sions noble wall,
    Vnseene, vnheard; or vndescride at all.

66

'Prepare you then, for trauaile strong and light,
Fierce to the combat, glad to victorie:'
And with that word and warning soone was dight
Each soldier, longing for neere comming glorie,
Impatient be they of the morning bright,
Of honour so them prickt the memorie.
    But yet their chieftaine had conceau'd a feare
    Within his hart, but kept it secret theare:

67

For he by faithfull spiall was assured,
That Egypts king was forward on his way,
And to arriue at Gaza old procured,
A fort, that on the Sirian frontiers lay,
Nor thinkes he that a man to wars enured
Will ought forslow, or in his iourney stay,
   For well he knew him for a dang'rous foe,
   An herald cald he then, and spake him soe.

68

'A pinnesse take thee swift as shaft from bowe,
And speede thee (*Henrie*) to the Greekish maine,
There should arriue (as I by letters knowe
From one that neuer ought reports in vaine)
A valiant youth, in whom all vertues flowe,
To helpe vs this great conquest to obtaine,
   The Prince of Danes he is, and brings to war
   A troope with him from vnder th'Artick star.

69

'And for I doubt the Greekish monarch slie,
Will vse with him some of his woonted craft,
To stay his passage, or diuert awrie
Elsewhere his forces, his first iournay last,
My herald good, and messenger well trie,
See that these succours be not vs berast,
   But send him thence with such conuenient speed,
   As with his honour stands, and with our need.

70

'Returne not thou, but legier stay behinde,
And mooue the Greekish Prince to send vs aide,
Tell him his kingly promise doth him binde
To giue vs succours, by his couenant maide;'
This said, and thus instruct, his letters signde
The trustie herald tooke, nor longer staid,
   But sped him thence to done his Lords behest,
   And thus the Duke redus'd his thoughts to rest.

71

Aurora bright her cristall gates vnbard,
And bride-groome-like forth stept the glorious sunne,
When trumpets lowd and clarions shrill were hard,
And euery one to rowse him fierce begunne,
Sweete musicke to each hart for war prepar'd,
The soldiers glad by heapes to harnesse runne;
　　So if with drought endang'red be their graine,
　　Poore plowmen ioy, when thunders promise raine.

72

Some shirts of maile, some coates of plate put on,
Some dond a curace, some a corslet bright,
An hawberke some, and some a haberion,
So eu'rie one in armes was quickly dight,
His woonted guide each soldiers tends vpon,
Loose in the winde waued their banners light,
　　Their standard royall towards heau'n they spread,
　　The crosse triumphant on the Pagans dead.

73

Meanewhile the carre that beares the light'ning brand,
Vpon the eastren hill was mounted hie,
And smote the glistring armies as they stand,
With quiu'ring beames which daz'd the wondring eie,
That Phaeton-like it fiered sea and land,
The sparkles seem'd vp to the skies to flie,
　　The horses ney, and clattring armours sowne,
　　Pursue the Eccho ouer dale and downe.

74

Their generall did with due care prouide
To saue his men from ambush and from traine,
Some troopes of horse (that lightly armed ride)
He sent to scoure the woods and forrests maine,
His pioners their busie worke applide,
To eeuen the paths and make the hy-waies plaine,
　　They fild the pits, and smooth'd the rougher ground,
　　And open'd euery strait they closed found.

71³ clarious < clarions

75

They meet no forces gath'red by their foe,
No towres, defenst with rampire, mote or wall,
No streame, no wood, no mountaine could forsloe
Their hastie pace, or stop their march at all:
So when his banks the prince of riuers, Poe
Doth ouerswell, he breakes with hideous fall,
    The mossie rocks and trees oregrowne with age,
    Nor ought withstands his furie and his rage.

76

The king of Tripolie in euery hold
Shut vp his men, munition and his treasure,
The straggling troopes sometimes assaile he wold,
Saue that he durst not moue them to displeasure,
He staid their rage with presents, gifts and gold,
And led them through his land at ease and leasure,
    To keepe his realme in peace and rest he chose,
    With what conditions *Godfrey* list impose.

77

Those of mount Seir (that neighboreth by east
The holie citie) faithfull folke each one,
Downe from the hill descended most and least,
And to the Christian Duke by heapes they gone,
And welcome him and his with ioy and feast,
On him they smile, on him they gaze alone,
    And were his guides, (as faithfull from that day
    As Hesperus, that leads the sunne his way.)

78

Along the sands his armies safe they guide,
By waies secure, to them well knowne before,
Vpon the tumbling billowes fraughted ride
The armed ships, coasting along the shore,
Which for the campe might euery day prouide
To bring munition good, and victuals store,
    The Isles of Greece sent in prouision meete,
    And store of wine from Scios came and Creete.

79

Great *Neptune* grieued vnderneath the load
Of ships, hulks, gallies, barks and brigandines,
In all the mid-earth seas was left no road
Wherein the Pagan his bold sailes vntwines,
Spred was the huge Armado wide and broad,
From Venice, Genes, and townes which them confines,
 From Holland, England, France and Scicill sent,
 And all for *Iuda* readie bound and bent,

80

All these together were combin'd, and knit
With surest bonds of loue and friendship strong,
Together sail'd they, fraught with all things fit
To seruice done by land that might belong,
And when occasion seru'd disbarked it,
Then sail'd the Asian coasts and isles along,
 Thither with speede their hastie course they plied,
 Where Christ the Lord for our offences died.

81

The brasen trumpe of iron winged fame,
(That mingleth faithfull troath with forged lies)
Foretold the Heathen how the Christians came,
How thitherward the conqu'ring armie hies,
Of euery knight it sounds the worth and name,
Each troope, each band, each squadron it descries,
 And threat'neth death to those, fire, sword and slaughter,
 Who held captiued *Israels* fairest daughter.

82

The feare of ill exceedes the euill we feare,
For so our present harmes still most annoy vs,
Each minde is prest, and open euery eare
To heare new tidings, though they no way ioy vs.
This secret rumor whisp'red euery where
About the towne, these Christians will destroy vs,
 The aged king his comming euill that knew,
 Did cursed thoughts, in his false hart renew.

83

This aged Prince ycleped *Aladine*,
Ruled in care, new soueraigne of this state,
A Tyrant earst, but now his fell ingine
His grauer age did somewhat mitigate,
He heard the westren Lords would vndermine
His cities wall, and lay his towres prostrate,
    To former feare he addes a newcome dout,
    Treason he feares within, and force without.

84

For nations twaine inhabite there and dwell
Of sundry faith, together in that towne,
The lesser part on Christ beleeued well,
On *Termagant* the more and on *Mahowne*.
But when this king had made his conquest fell,
And brought that region subiect to his crowne,
    Of burdens all he set the Paynims large,
    And on poore Christians laid the double charge.

85

His natiue wrath reuiu'd with this new thought,
With age and yeeres that weak'ned was of yore,
Such madnes in his cruell bosome wrought,
That now than euer, blood he thirsteth more;
So stings a snake that to the fire is brought,
Which harmelesse lay benumm'd with cold before,
    A lion so his rage renewed hath
    (Though tame before) if he be moou'd to wrath.

86

'I see (quoth he) some expectation vaine
In these false Christians, and some new content,
Our common losse they trust will be their gaine,
They laugh, we weepe; they ioy while we lament,
And more, perchance by treason or by traine
To murder vs they secretly consent,
    Or otherwise to worke vs harme and woe,
    To ope the gates, and so let in our foe.

87

'But least they should effect their cursed will,
Let vs destroy this serpent on his nest,
Both yoong and old let vs this people kill,
The tender infants at their mothers brest,
Their houses burne, their holy temples fill
With bodies slaine, of those that lou'd them best,
    And on that tombe they hold so much in price,
    Lets offer vp their priests in sacrifice.'

88

Thus thought the tyrant in his trait'rous minde,
But durst not follow what he had decreed,
Yet if the innocents some mercie finde,
From cowardise, not ruth, did that proceed.
His noble foes durst not his crauen kinde
Exasperate, by such a bloody deed,
    For if he need what grace could then be got,
    If thus of peace he broke or loos'd the knot?

89

His villaine hart his cursed rage restrained,
To other thoughts he bent his fierce desire,
The suburbs first flat with the earth he plained,
And burnt their buildings with deuouring fire,
Loth was the wretch the Frenchmen should haue gained
Or helpe or ease, by finding ought intire,
    Cedron, Bethsaida, and each watring els
    Empoison'd he, both fountains, springs and wels.

90

So warie wise, this childe of darknes was,
The cities selfe he strongly fortifies,
Three sides by scite it well defensed has,
That's onely weake that to the northward lies,
With mightie barres of long enduring bras,
The steele-bound doores, and iron gates he ties,
    And lastly legions armed well, prouides
    Of subiects borne, and hired aide besides.

The Second Booke of Godfrey of Bulloigne

The argument.

Ismeno *coniures, but his charmes are vaine:*
Aladine *will kill the Christians in his ire:*
Sophronia *and* Olindo *would be slaine*
To save the rest, the king grants their desire;
Clorinda *heares their fact and fortunes plaine*
Their pardon gets and keepes them from the fire:
Argantes, *when* Aletes *speeches ar*
Despis'd, defies the Duke to mortall war.

1

WHile thus the Tyrant bends his thoughts to armes,
  Ismeno gan tofore his sight appeare,
Ismen dead bones laid in cold graues that warmes
And makes them speake, smell, taste, touch, see and heere;
Ismen (with terrour of his mightie charmes)
That makes great Dis in deepest hell to feare,
  That bindes and looseth soules condemn'd to woe,
  And sends the diuels on errands to and froe.

2

A Christian once, *Macon* he now adores,
Nor could he quite his wonted faith forsake,
But in his wicked arts both oft implores
Helpe from the Lord, and aide from *Pluto* blake;
He, from deepe caues by *Acherons* darke shores,
(Where circles vaine and spels he vs'd to make)
  T'aduise his king in these extremes is come,
  Achitophell so counsell'd *Absalome,*

3

'My liege (he saies) the campe fast hither mooues,
The axe is laid vnto this Cedars rout,
But let vs worke as valiant men behooues,
For boldest harts good fortune helpeth out:

Your princely care your kingly wisdome prooues,
Well haue you labour'd, well foreseene about,
  If each performe his charge and dutie so,
  Nought but his graue here conquer shall your foe:

4

'From surest castell of my secret cell
I come, partaker of your good and ill,
What counsell sage or magikes sacred spell
May profit vs, all that performe I will:
The sprites impure from blisse that whilome fell
Shall to your seruice bow, constrain'd by skill;
  But how we must begin this enterprise,
  I will your highnes thus in breefe aduise.

5

'Within the Christians Church, from light of skies,
An hidden Altar stands, far out of sight,
On which the image consecrated lies
Of Christes deere mother, call'd a virgin bright,
An hundreth lampes aie burne before her eies,
She in a slender vaile of tinsell dight,
  On euery side great plentie doth behold
  Of offrings brought, myrrhe, frankincense and gold.

6

'This idoll would I have remoou'd away
From thence, and by your princely hand transport
In *Macons* sacred temple safe it lay,
Which then I will enchant in wondrous sort,
That while the image in that church doth stay,
No strength of armes shall win this noble fort,
  Or shake this puissant wall, such passing might
  Haue spels and charmes, if they be said aright.'

7

Aduised thus, the king impatient
Flew in his furie to the house of God,
The image tooke, with words vnreuerent
Abus'd the prelates, who that deed forbod,

Swift with his pray away the tyrant went,
Of Gods sharpe iustice nought he fear'd the rod,
    But in his chappell vile the image laid,
    On which th'enchanter charmes and witchcrafts said.

8

When Phebus next vnclos'd his wakefull eie,
Vprose the Sexten of that place prophaine,
And mist the image where it vs'd to lie,
Each where he sought in greefe, in feare, in vaine;
Then to the king his losse he gan descrie,
Who sore enraged kild him for his paine,
    And straight conceiu'd in his malitious wit,
    Some Christian bad this great offence commit.

9

But whether this were act of mortall hand,
Or else the Prince of heau'ns eternall pleasure,
That of his mercie would this wretch withstand,
Nor let so vile a chest, hold such a treasure,
As yet coniecture hath not fully scand;
By godlines let vs this action measure,
    And truth of purest faith will fitly proue,
    That this rare grace came downe from heau'n aboue.

10

With busie search the tyrant gan inuade
Each house, each hold, each temple and each tent,
To them the fault or faultie one bewrai'd
Or hid, he promist gifts or punishment,
His idle charmes the false enchanter said,
But in this maze still wandred and miswent,
    For heauen decreed to conceale the same,
    To make the miscreant more to feele his shame.

11

But when the angrie king discouer'd not
What guiltie hand this sacrilege had wrought,
His irefull courage boild in vengeance hot
Against the Christians, whom he faulters thought,

All ruth, compassion, mercie he forgot,
A staffe to beate that dog he long had sought,
　'Let them all die,' quoth he, 'kill great and small,
　So shall th'offender perish sure withall.

12

'To spill the wine with poison mixt who spares?
Slay then the righteous, with the faultie one,
Destroy this field, that yeeldeth nought but tares,
With thornes this vineyard all is ouergone,
Among these wretches is not one, that cares
For vs, our lawes, or our religion,
　Vp, vp, deere subiects, fire and weapon take,
　Burne, murder, kill, these traitors, for my sake.'

13

This *Herod* thus would Bethlems infants kill,
The Christians soone these direfull newes recaue,
The trumpe of death sounds in their hearing shrill,
Their weapon, faith; their fortresse, was the graue;
They had no courage, time, deuise, or will,
To fight, to flie, excuse, or pardon craue,
　But stood prepar'd to die, yet helpe they finde
　Whence least they hope, such knots can heau'n vnbind.

14

Among them dwelt (her parents ioy and pleasure)
A maide, whose fruit was ripe, not oueryeared,
Her beautie was her not esteemed, treasure;
The field of loue, with plow of vertue eared,
Her labour goodnes; godlines her leasure,
Her house the heau'n by this full moone aye cleared,
　For there, from louers eies withdrawne, alone
　With virgin beames this spotlesse *Cinthia* shone.

15

But what avail'd her resolution chaste,
Whose sobrest lookes were whetstones to desire?

13⁸ vnbind, < vnbind.

Nor loue consents that beauties field lie waste,
Her visage set *Olindoes* hart on fire,
O subtile loue, a thousand wiles thou hast
By humble suit, by seruice, or by hire,
　To win a maidens hold, a thing soone donne,
　For nature fram'd all women to be wonne.

16

Sophronia she, *Olindo* hight the yuth,
Both of one towne, both in one faith were taught,
She faire, he full of bashfulnes and truth,
Lou'd much, hop'd little, and desired nought,
He durst not speake, by suit to purchase ruth,
She saw not, markt not, wist not what he sought,
　Thus lou'd, thus seru'd he long, but not regarded,
　Vnseene, vnmarkt, vnpitied, vnrewarded.

17

To her came message of the murderment,
Wherein her guiltlesse friends, should hopelesse sterue,
She that was noble wise, as faire and gent,
Cast how the might their harmlesse liues preserue,
Zeale was the spring whence flow'd her hardiment,
From maidens shame yet was she loth to swerue:
　Yet had her courage tane so sure a hold,
　That boldnes, shamefast; shame had made her bold.

18

And foorth she went, a shop for merchandise
Full of rich stuffe, but none for sale exposed,
A vaile obscur'd the sunshine of her eies,
The rose within her selfe her sweetnes closed,
Each ornament about her seemely lies,
By curious chance, or careless art, composed;
　For what she most neglects, most curious proue,
　So beautie's helpt by nature, heau'n and loue.

18⁷ the < she

19

Admir'd of all on went this noble maid
Vntill the presence of the king she gained,
Nor for he sweld with ire was she affraid,
But his fierce wrath with fearlesse grace sustained,
'I come,' quoth she, '(but be thine anger staid,
And causelesse rage gainst faultlesse soules restrained)
   I come to shew thee and to bring thee both
    The wight, whose fact hath made thy hart so wroth.'

20

Her modest boldnes, and that light'ning ray
Which her sweete beautie streamed on his face,
Had strooke the Prince with wonder and dismay,
Changed his cheere and cleer'd his moodie grace,
That had her eies dispos'd their lookes to play,
The king had snared been in loues strong lace,
   But wayward beautie doth not fancie moue,
    A frowne forbids, a smile engendreth loue.

21

It was amazement, wonder and delight,
(Although not loue) that mou'd his cruell sense,
'Tell on,' quoth he, 'vnfold the chance aright,
Thy peoples liues I grant for recompence.'
Then she, 'behold the faulter here in fight,
This hand committed that suppos'd offence,
   I tooke the image, mine that fault, that fact,
    Mine be the glorie of that vertuous act.'

22

This spotlesse lambe thus offred vp her blood
To save the rest of Christs selected fold,
O noble lie! was euer truth so good?
Blest be the lips that such a leasing told,
Thoughtfull awhile remain'd the tyrant wood,
His natiue wrath he gan a space withold
   And said, 'that thou discouer soone I will,
    What aide? what counsell hadst thou in that ill?'

23

My loftie thoughts (she answer'd him) enuide
Anothers hand should worke my high desire,
The thirst of glorie can no partner bide,
With mine owne selfe I did alone conspire.'
'On thee alone (the tyrant then replide)
Shall fall the vengeance of my wrath and ire.'
   'Tis iust and right (quoth she) I yeeld consent,
   Mine be the honour, mine the punishment.'

24

The wretch of new enraged at the same
Askt where she hid the image so conuai'd:
'Not hid (quoth she) but quite consum'd with flame,
The idoll is of that eternall maid,
For so at least I haue preseru'd the same
With hands profane from being eft betraid.
   My Lord, the thing thus stolne demaund no more;
   Here see the theefe, that scorneth death therefore.

25

'And yet no theft was this, yours was the sin,
I brought againe what you vniustly tooke;'
This heard, the tyrant did for rage begin
To whet his teeth, and bend his frowning looke,
No pitie, youth; fairenesse, no grace could win;
Ioy, comfort, hope, the virgin all forsooke;
   Wrath kill'd remorse, vengeance stopt mercies breath,
   Loue's thrall to hate, and beautie slaue to death.

26

Tane was the damsell, and without remorse,
The king condemn'd her (guiltlesse) to the fire,
Her vaile and mantle pluckt they off by force,
And bound her tender arms in twisted wire:
Dumbe was this siluer doue, while from her corse
These hungrie kites pluckt off her rich attire,
   And for some-deale perplexed was her sprite,
   Her damaske late, now chang'd to purest white.

27

The newes of this mishap spred far and neare,
The people ran, both yong and old, to gace;
Olindo also ran, and gan to feare
His Ladie was some partner in this cace;
But when he found her bound, stript from her geare,
And vile tormentors ready saw in place,
    He broke the throng, and into presence brast,
    And thus bespake the king in rage and haste.

28

'Not so, not so this girle shall beare away
From me the honour of so noble feat,
She durst not, did not, could not so conuay
The massie substance of that Idoll great,
What sleight had she the wardens to betray?
What strength to heaue the goddesse from her seat?
    No, no, my Lord, she sailes, but with my winde,'
    (Ah thus he lou'd, yet was his loue vnkinde.)

29

He added further, 'where the shining glasse
Lets in the light amid your temples side,
By broken by-waies did I inward passe,
And in that window made a postren wide,
Nor shall therefore this ill-aduised lasse
Vsurpe the glorie should this fact betide,
    Mine be these bonds, mine be these flames so pure,
    O glorious death, more glorious sepulture.'

30

Sophronia rais'd her modest lookes from ground,
And on her louer bent her eie-sight milde,
'Tell me, what furie? what conceit vnsound
Presenteth here to death so sweet a childe?
Is not in me sufficient courage found
To beare the anger of this tyrant wilde?
    Or hath fond loue thy hart so ouergone?
    Would'st thou not liue, nor let me die alone?'

31

Thus spake the Nimph, yet spake but to the winde,
She could not alter his well setled thought:
O miracle! O strife of wondrous kinde!
Where loue and vertue such contention wrought,
Where death the victor had for meed assignde,
Their owne neglect, each others safetie sought;
    But thus the king was more prouoakt to ire,
    Their strife for bellowes seru'd to angers fire.

32

He thinkes (such thoughts selfe-guiltinesse findes out)
They scorn'd his powre, and therefore scorn'd the paine:
'Nay, nay,' quoth he, 'let be your strife and dout,
You both shall win, and fit reward obtaine.'
With that the sargeants hent the yong man stout,
And bound him likewise in a worthlesse chaine;
    Then backe to backe fast to a stake both ties,
    Two harmlesse turtles, dight for sacrifies.

33

About the pile of fagots, sticks and hay,
The bellowes rais'd the newly kindled flame,
When thus *Olindo*, in a dolefull lay,
Begun too late his bootlesse plaints to frame:
'Be these the bonds? Is this the hopt-for day
Should ioyne me to this long desired dame?
    Is this the fire alike should burne our harts?
    Ah hard reward for louers kinde desarts!

34

'Far other flames and bonds kinde louers proue,
But thus our fortune casts the haplesse die,
Death hath exchang'd againe his shafts with loue,
And *Cupid* thus lets borrow'd arrowes flie.
O *Hymen* say, what furie doth thee moue
To lend thy lampes to light a tragedie?
    Yet this contents me that I die for thee,
    Thy flames, not mine, my death and torment bee.

35

'Yet happie were my death, mine ending blest,
My torments easie, full of sweet delight,
If this I could obtaine, that brest to brest
Thy bosome might receiue my yeelded spright;
And thine with it in heau'ns pure clothing drest,
Through cleerest skies might take vnited flight.'
 Thus he complain'd, whom gently she reproued,
 And sweetly spake him thus, that so her loued.

36

'Far other plaints (deere friend) teares and laments
The time, the place, and our estates require,
Thinke on thy sinnes, which mans old foe presents
Before that iudge that quites each soule his hire,
For his name suffer, for no paine torments
Him, whose iust prayers to his throne aspire:
 Behold the heau'ns, thither thine eie-sight bend,
 Thy lookes, sighes, teares, for intercessors send:'

37

The Pagans lowd cride out to God and man,
The Christians mourn'd in silent lamentation,
The tyrants selfe (a thing vnus'd) began
To feele his hart relent, with meere compassion,
But not dispos'd to ruth or mercie than,
He sped him thence, home to his habitation:
 Sophronia stood not greeu'd, nor discontented,
 By all that saw her (but her selfe) lamented.

38

The louers standing in this dolefull wise,
A warriour bold vnwares approched neare,
In vncouth armes yclad and strange disguise,
From countries far but new arriued theare,
A sauage tygresse on her helmet lies,
The famous badge *Clorinda* vs'd to beare,
 That woonts in euerie warlike stowre to winne,
 By which bright signe well knowne was that faire Inne.

39

She scorn'd the artes these seelie women vse,
Another thought her nobler humour fed,
Her loftie hand would of it selfe refuse
To touch the daintie needle, or nice thred,
She hated chambers, closets, secret mewes,
And in broad fields preseru'd her maidenhed:
    Proud were her lookes, yet sweet, though stern and stout,
    Her dame a doue, thus brought an eagle out.

40

While she was yong, she vs'd with tender hand
The foming steed with froarie bit to steare,
To tilt and tournay, wrestle in the sand,
To leaue with speed *Atlanta* swift arreare,
Through forrests wilde and vnfrequented land
To chase the Lion, boare or rugged beare,
    The Satyres rough, the Fawnes and Fairies wilde,
    She chased oft, oft tooke, and oft beguilde.

41

This lustie Ladie came from Persia late,
She with the Christians had encountred eft,
And in their flesh had opened many a gate
By which their faithfull soules their bodies left,
Her eie at first presented her the state
Of these poore soules, of hope and helpe bereft,
    Greedie to know (as is the minde of man:)
    Their cause of death, swift to the fire she ran.

42

The people made her roome, and on them twaine
Her pearcing eies their fierie weapons dart,
Silent she saw the one, the other plaine,
The weaker bodie lodg'd the nobler hart:
Yet him she saw lament, as if his paine
Were griefe and sorrow for anothers smart,
    And her keepe silence so, as if her eies
    Dumbe orators were to intreat the skies.

43

Clorinda chang'd to ruth her warlike mood,
Few siluer drops her vermile cheeks depaint,
Her sorrow was for her that speechlesse stood,
Her silence more preuail'd then his complaint,
She askt an aged man, seem'd graue and good,
'Come say me sire (quoth she) what hard constraint
 Would murder here loues queene, and beauties king?
 What fault or fate doth to this death them bring?'

44

Thus she enquir'd, and answer short he gaue,
But such as all the chance at large disclosed,
She wondred at the case, the virgin braue
That both were guiltlesse of the fault supposed,
Her noble thought cast how she might them saue,
The meanes on suit or battell she reposed,
 Quicke to the fire she ran, and quencht it out,
 And thus bespake the sargeants and the rout:

45

'Be there not one among you all that dare
In this your hatefull office ought proceed,
Till I returne from court, nor take you care
To reape displeasure for not making speed:'
To doe her will the men themselues prepare,
In their faint harts her lookes such terror breed,
 To court she went, their pardon would she get,
 But on the way the courteous king she met.

46

'Sir king, quoth she, my name *Clorinda* hight,
My fame perchance hath pearst your eares ere now,
I come to trie my woonted power and might,
And will defend this land, this towne, and yow,
All hard assaies esteeme I eath and light,
Great actes I reach to, to small things I bow,
 To fight in field, or to defend this wall,
 Point what you list, I nought refuse at all.'

47

To whom the king, 'what land so far remot
From Asias coastes, or Phebus glistring raies,
(O glorious virgin) that recordeth not
Thy fame, thine honour, worth, renowne and praise?
Since on my side I haue thy succours got,
I need not feare in these mine aged daies,
    For in thine aid more hope, more trust I haue,
    Than in whole armies of these soldiers braue.

48

'Now *Godfrey* staies too long, he feares I weene,
Thy courage great keepes all our foes in awe,
For thee all actions far vnwoorthie beene
But such as greatest danger with them drawe,
Be you commaundresse therefore, Princesse, queene
Of all our forces, be thy word a lawe.'
    This said, the virgin gan her beauoir vale,
    And thankt him first, and thus began her tale.

49

'A thing vnus'd (great monarch) may it seeme,
To aske reward for seruice, yet to come;
But so your vertuous bountie I esteeme,
That I presume for to entreat, this grome
And seelie maid from danger to redeeme,
Condemn'd to burne by your vnpartiall dome,
    I not excuse, but pitie much their yuth,
    And come to you for mercie and for ruth.

50

'Yet giue me leaue to tell your highnes this,
You blame the Christians, them my thoughts acquite,
Nor be displeas'd, I say you iudge amis,
At euerie shot looke not to hit the white,
All what th'enchantour did perswade you, is
Against the lore of *Macons* sacred rite,
    For vs commaundeth mightie *Mahomet*
    No idols in his temples pure to set.

51

'To him therefore this wonder done refar,
Giue him the praise and honour of the thing,
Of vs the Gods benigne so carefull ar
Least customes strange into their church we bring,
Let *Ismen* with his squares and trigons war,
His weapons be the staffe, the glasse, the ring;
    But let vs menage war with blowes, like knights,
    Our praise in armes, our honour lies in fights.'

52

The virgin held her peace when this was said:
And though to pitie neuer fram'd his thought,
Yet for the king admir'd the noble maid,
His purpose was not to denie her ought,
'I grant them life (quoth he) your promist aid
Against these Frenchmen, hath their pardon bought:
    Nor further seeke what their offences bee,
    Guiltlesse I quite; guiltie, I set them free.'

53

Thus were they loos'd, happiest of humane kinde
Olindo, blessed be this act of thine,
True witnes of thy great and heau'nly minde,
Where sunne, moone, stars, of loue, faith, vertue, shine.
So foorth they went and left pale death behinde,
To ioy the blisse of marriage rites diuine,
    With her he would haue dide, with him content
    Was she to liue, that would with her haue brent.

54

The king (as wicked thoughts are most suspitious)
Suppos'd too fast this tree of vertue grew,
O blessed Lord! why should this *Pharoe* vicious,
Thus tyrannize vpon thy Hebrewes trew?
Who to performe his will, vile and malitious,
Exiled these, and all the faithfull crew,
    All that were strong of body, stout of minde,
    But kept their wiues and children pledge behinde.

55

A hard diuision, when the harmlesse sheepe
Must leaue their lambes to hungrie wolues in charge,
But labour's vertue's watching, ease her sleepe,
Trouble best winde that driues saluations barge,
The Christians fled, whither they tooke no keepe,
Some straied wilde among the forrests large,
  Some to Emmaus to the Christian host,
  And conquer would againe their houses lost.

56

Emmaus is a citie small, that lies
From Sions wals distant a little way,
A man that early on the morne doth rise,
May thither walke ere third howre of the day.
Oh, when the Christian Lords this towne espies
How merie were their harts? how fresh? how gay?
  But for the sunne enclined fast to west,
  That night there would their chieftaine take his rest.

57

Their canuas castles vp they quickly reare,
And build a citie in an howres space,
When loe (disguised in vnusuall geare)
Two Barons bold approchen gan the place,
Their semblance kinde, and milde their gestures weare,
Peace in their hands and friendship in their face,
  From Egypts king ambassadours they come,
  Them many a squire attends, and many a grome.

58

The first *Aletes*, borne in lowly shed
Of parents base, a rose, sprong from a brier,
That now his branches ouer Egypt spred,
No plant in *Pharoes* garden prospred hier,
With pleasing tales his Lords vaine eares he fed,
A flatterer, a pickthanke, and a lier,
  Curst be estate got with so many a crime,
  Yet this is oft the staire by which men clime.

55³ labour and vertues < labour's vertue's *see commentary*

59

Argantes called is that other knight,
A stranger came he late to Egypt land,
And there aduanced was to honours hight,
For he was stout of courage, strong of hand,
Bold was his hart, and restlesse was his spright,
Fierce, sterne, outragious, keene as sharp'ned brand,
    Scorner of God, scant to himselfe a frend,
    And prickt his reason on his weapons end.

60

These two entreatance made they might be hard,
Nor was their iust petition long denide;
The gallants quickly made their court of gard,
And brought them in where sate their famous guide,
Whose kingly looke his princely minde declar'd,
Where noblesse, vertue, troth and valour bide,
    A slender courtsie made *Argantes* bold,
    So as one prince salute another wold.

61

Aletes laid his right hand on his hart,
Bent downe his head, and cast his eies full low,
And reu'rence made with courtly grace and art,
For all that humble lore to him was know,
His sober lips then did he softly part,
Whence of pure rhetorike, whole streames out flow,
    And thus he said, (while on the Christian Lords
    Downe fell the mildew of his sugred words.)

62

'O only worthy, whom the earth all feares,
High God defend thee, with his heau'nly sheeld,
And humble so the harts of all thy peares,
That their stiffe necks to thy sweete yoke may yeeld:
These be the sheaues that honours haruest beares,
The feed thy valiant actes, the world the feeld,
    Egypt the headland is, where heaped lies
    Thy fame, worth, iustice, wisedome, victories.

59[8] end, < end.

63

'These all together, doth our soueraigne hide
In secret storehouse of his princely thought,
And praies he may in long accordance bide
With that great Worthie, which such wonders wrought,
Nor that oppose against the comming tide
Of profred loue, for that he is not tought
   Your Christian faith, for though of diuers kinde,
   The louing vine about her elme is twin'd.

64

'Receiue therefore in that vnconquered hand
The pretious handle of this cup of loue,
If not religion, vertue be the band
Twixt you to fasten friendship, not to moue:
But for our mightie king doth vnderstand,
You meane your powre gainst Iuda land to proue,
   He would, before this threat'ned tempest fell,
   I should his minde and princely will first tell.

65

'His minde is this, he praies thee be contented
To ioy in peace, the conquests thou hast got,
Be not thy death, or Sions fall lamented,
Forbeare this land, Iudea trouble not,
Things done in haste at leasure be repented:
Withdraw thine armes, trust not vncertaine lot,
   For oft we see what least we thinke betide,
   He is thy friend gainst all the world beside.

66

'True labour in the vineyard of thy Lord,
Ere prime thou hast th'imposed day-worke donne,
What armies conquered, perisht with thy sword?
What cities sackt? what kingdomes hast thou wonne?
All eares are maz'de, while toongs thine acts record,
Hands quake for feare, all feete for dread doe ronne,
   And though no realmes you may to thraldome bring,
   No higher can your praise, your glorie spring.

63⁵ that? *read* yet *see note*

67

'Thy sunne in his Apogæon placed,
And when it moueth next, must needes descend,
Chance is vncertaine, fortune double faced,
Smiling at first, she frowneth in the end,
Beware thine honour be not then disgraced,
Take heed thou marre not, when thou think'st to mend,
    For this the follie is of fortunes play,
      Gainst doubtfull, certaine; much, gainst small, to lay.

68

'Yet still we saile while prosp'rous blowes the winde,
Till on some secret rocke vnwares we light,
The sea of glorie hath no bankes assignde,
They who are wont to win in euerie fight,
Still feed the fire, that so enflames thy minde
To bring mo nations subject to thy might;
    This makes thee blessed peace so light to hold,
    Like sommers flies that feare not winters cold.

69

'They bid thee follow on the path, now made
So plaine and easie, enter fortunes gate,
Nor in thy scabberd sheath that famous blade
Till setled be thy kingdome, and estate,
Till *Macons* sacred doctrine fall and fade,
Till wofull Asia, all lie desolate.
    Sweet words I grant, baits and allurements sweet,
    But greatest hopes oft greatest crosses meet.

70

'For, if thy courage doe not blinde thine eies,
If cloudes of furie hide not reasons beames,
Then maist thou see this desp'rate enterpries,
The field of death, watred with dangers streames,
High state the bed is where misfortune lies,
Mars most vnfriendly, when most kind he seames,
    Who climeth hie, on earth he hardest lights,
    And lowest falles, attend the highest flights.

67[1] sinne < sunne *see note*

71

'Tell me, if great in counsell, armes and gold,
The Prince of Egypt, war gainst you prepare?
What if the valiant Turkes and Persians bold,
Vnite their forces with *Cassanoes* haire?
O then, what marble pillar shall vphold
The falling trophies of your conquests faire?
   Trust you the monarch of the Greekish land?
   That reed will breake; and breaking, wound your hand.

72

'The Greekish faith is like that halfe cut tree,
By which men take wilde Elephants in Inde,
A thousand times it hath beguiled thee,
As firme as waues in seas, or leaues in winde.
Will they, who earst denide you passage free,
(Passage to all men free, by vfe and kinde)
   Fight for your sake? or on them doe you trust
   To spend their blood, that could scarce spare their dust?

73

'But all your hope and trust perchance is laid
In these strong troopes, which thee enuiron round;
Yet foes vnite are not so soone dismaid,
As when their strength you earst diuided found:
Besides, each howre thy bands are weaker maid
With hunger, slaughter, lodging on cold ground,
   Meane-while the Turkes seeke succours from our king,
   Thus fade thy helps, and thus thy cumbers spring.

74

'Suppose no weapon can thy valours pride
Subdue, that by no force thou maist be wonne,
Admit no steele can hurt or wound thy side,
And be it heau'n hath thee such fauour donne;
Gainst famine yet what shield canst thou prouide?
What strength resist? what sleight her wrath can shonne?
   Goe shake thy speare, and draw thy flaming blade,
   And trie if hunger so be weaker made.

73[8] spring, < spring.   74[4] fauout < fauour (*cf. 1624*)

75

'Th'inhabitants each pasture and each plaine
Destroied haue, each field to waste is lade,
In fensed towres bestowed is their graine,
Before thou cam'st this kingdome to inuade,
These horse and foote, how canst thou then sustaine?
Whence comes thy store? whence thy prouision made?
  Thy ships to bring it are (perchance) assignde,
  O that you liue so long as please the winde!

76

'Perhaps thy fortune doth controull the winde,
Doth loose or binde their blastes in secret caue,
The sea (pardie) cruell and deafe by kinde,
Will heare thy call, and still her raging waue:
But if our armed gallies be assignde
To aide those ships, which Turks and Persians haue,
  Say then, what hope is left thy slender fleet?
  Dare flockes of crowes, a flight of Eagles meet?

77

'My Lord, a double conquest must you make,
If you atchieue renowne by this empries:
For if our fleet your nauie chase or take,
For want of victails all your campe then dies;
Or if by land the field you once forsake,
Then vaine by sea were hope of victories.
  Nor could your ships restore your lost estate:
  For steed once stolne, we shut the doore too late.

78

'In this estate, if thou esteemest light
The profred kindnesse of th'Egyptian king,
Then giue me leaue to say, this ouersight
Beseemes thee not, in whom such vertues spring:
But heau'ns vouchsafe to guide thy minde aright
To gentle thoughts, that peace and quiet bring,
  So that poore Asia her complaints may ceace,
  And you enioy your conquest got, in peace.

79

'Nor ye that part in these aduentures haue,
Part in his glorie, partners in his harmes,
Let not blinde fortune so your mindes desaue,
To stir him more to trie these fierce alarmes,
But like the sailer (scaped from the waue)
From further perill, that his person armes,
    By staying safe at home, so stay you all,
    Better sit still (men say) than rise to fall.'

80

This said *Aletes*: and a murmur rose
That shew'd dislike among the Christian Peares,
Their angrie gestures with mislike disclose,
How much his speech offends their noble eares.
Lord *Godfreyes* eie three times enuiron goes,
To view what count'nance euerie warriour beares,
    And lastly on th'Egyptian Baron staid,
    To whom the Duke thus (for his answer) said.

81

'Ambassador, full both of threates and praise,
Thy doubtfull message hast thou wisely told,
And if thy soueraigne loue vs (as he saies)
Tell him he sowes, to reape an hundreth fold,
But where thy talke the comming storme displaies
Of threat'ned warfare, from the Pagans bold:
    To that I answer (as my custome is)
    In plainest phrase, least mine intent thou mis.

82

'Know, that till now we suffred haue much paine,
By lands and seas, where stormes and tempests fall,
To make the passage easie, safe and plaine
That leades vs to this venerable wall,
That so we might reward from heau'n obtaine,
And free this towne, from being longer thrall;
    Nor is it greeuous to so good an end
    Our honours, kingdoms, liues and goods to spend.

83

'Not hope of praise, nor thirst of worldly good,
Entised vs to follow this emprise,
The heau'nly father keepe his sacred brood
From foule infection of so great a vice:
But by our zeale aye be that plague withstood,
Let not those pleasures vs to sinne entise.
    His grace, his mercie, and his powrefull hand
    Will keepe vs safe from hurt, by sea and land.

84

'This is the spurre, that makes our coursers run;
This is our harbour, safe from dangers floods:
This is our beild, the blustring windes to shun:
This is our guide, through desarts, forrests, woods,
This is our sommers shade, our winters sun:
This is our wealth, our treasure, and our goods:
    This is our engin, towres that ouerthroes,
    Our speare that hurts, our sword that wounds our foes.

85

'Our courage hence, our hope, our valour springs,
Not from the trust we haue in shield or speare,
Not from the succours France or Grecia brings,
On such weake postes we list no buildings reare:
He can defend vs from the powre of kings,
From chance of war, that makes weake harts to feare,
    He can these hungrie troopes, with Manna feed,
    And make the seas, land; if we passage need.

86

'But if our sinnes vs of his helpe depriue,
Or his high iustice let no mercie fall;
Yet should our deaths vs some contentment giue,
To die, where Christ receiu'd his buriall,
So might we die, not enuying them that liue;
So would we die, not vnreuenged all:
    Nor Turkes, nor Christians (if we perish such)
    Haue cause to ioy, or to complaine too much.

87

'Thinke not that wars we loue, and strife affect,
Or that we hate sweet peace, or rest denay,
Thinke not your soueraignes friendship we reiect,
Bicause we list not in our conquests stay:
But for it seemes he would the Iewes protect,
Pray him from vs that thought aside to lay,
   Nor vs forbid this towne and realme to gaine,
   And he in peace, rest, ioy, long mote he raine,'

88

This answer giuen, *Argantes* wilde drew nar,
Trembling for ire, and waxing pale for rage,
Nor could he hold, his wrath encreast so far,
But thus (enflam'd) bespake the captaine sage:
'Who scorneth peace, shall haue his fill of war,
I thought thy wisdome should thy furie swage,
   But well you shew what ioy you take in fight,
   Which makes you prise our loue and friendship light.'

89

This said, he tooke his mantles formost part,
And gan the same together fold and wrap;
Then spake againe with fell and spitefull hart,
(So lions rore enclos'd in traine or trap)
'Thou proud despiser of inconstant *Mart*,
I bring thee war and peace clos'd in this lap,
   Take quickly one, thou hast no time to muse;
   If peace, we rest; we fight, if war thou chuse.'

90

His semblant fierce and speeches proud, prouoke
The soldiers all, 'war, war,' at once to crie,
Nor could they tarie till their chieftaine spoke,
But for the knight was more enflam'd hereby,
His lap he opened and spred foorth his cloke:
'To mortall wars (he saies) I you defie;'
   And this he vttred with fell rage and hate,
   And seemed of *Ianus* church t'vndoe the gate.

91

It seemed furie, discord, madnes fell
Flew from his lap, when he vnfolds the same,
His glaring eies with angers venome swell,
And like the brand of foule *Alecto* flame,
He lookt like huge *Tiphoius* loos'd from hell
Againe to shake heau'ns euerlasting frame,
　　Or him that built the towre on Shinaar,
　　Which threat'neth battell gainst the morning star.

92

Godfredo than; 'depart, and bid your king
Haste hitherward, or else within short while,
(For gladly we accept the war you bring)
Let him expect vs on the banks of Nile.'
He entertain'd them then with bancketting,
And gifts presented to those Pagans vile;
　　Aletes had a helmet, rich and gay,
　　Late found at Nice, among the conqu'red pray;

93

Argant a sword, whereof the web was steele,
Pommell, rich stone; hilts, gold, approu'd by tuch,
With rarest workmanship all forged weele,
The curious art exceld the substance much:
Thus faire, rich, sharpe; to see, to haue, to feele,
Glad was the Painim to enjoy it such,
　　And said, 'how I this gift can vse and wield,
　　Soone shall you see, when first we meet in feild.'

94

Thus tooke they congee, and the angrie knight
Thus to his fellow parled on their way,
'Goe thou by day, but let me walke by night,
Goe thou to Egypt, I at Sion stay,
The answer giuen thou canst vnfold aright,
No need of me what I can doe or say,
　　Among these armes I will goe wreake my spight,
　　Let *Paris* court it, *Hector* lou'd to fight.'

95

Thus he, who late arriu'd a messengar,
Departs a foe, in act, in word, in thought,
The law of nations, or the lore of war,
If he transgresse, or no, he reaketh nought.
Thus parted they, and ere he wandred far
The friendly star-light to the walles him brought:
    Yet his fell hart thought long that little way,
    Greeu'd with each stop, tormented with each stay.

96

Now spred the night her spangled canopie,
And sommon'd euery restlesse eie to sleepe:
On beds of tender grasse the beastes downe lie,
The fishes slumbred in the silent deepe,
Vnheard was serpents hisse, and dragons crie,
Birds left to sing, and Philomene to weepe,
    Onely that noice heau'ns rolling circles kest,
    Sung lullabie, to bring the world to rest.

97

Yet neither sleepe, nor ease, nor shadowes darke,
Could make the faithfull campe or captaine rest,
They long'd to see the day, to heare the larke
Record her hymnes and chant her carols blest,
They earnd to view the wals, the wished marke
To which their iourneies long they had addrest,
    Each hart attends, each longing eie beholds
    What beame the eastren window first vnfolds.

The third Booke of Godfrey *of Bulloigne*

The argument.

The campe at great Hierusalem arriues:
Clorinda *giues them battell, in the brest*
Of faire Erminia Tancreds *loue reuiues,*
He iusts with her vnknowne whom he lou'd best,
Argant *th' aduentrers of their guide depriues,*
With stately pompe they lay their Lord in chest:
Godfrey *commands to cut the forrest downe,*
And make strong engins to assault the towne.

1

THe purple morning left her crimsen bed,
　And dond her robes of pure vermilion hew,
Her amber locks she crown'd with roses red,
In Edens flowrie gardens gathred new.
When through the campe a murmur shrill was spred,
'Arme, arme,' they cride; 'arme, arme,' the trumpets blew,
　　Their merrie noise preuents the ioyfull blast,
　　So humme small bees, before their swarmes they cast.

2

Their captaine rules their courage, guides their heate,
Their forwardnes he staid with gentle raine;
And yet more easie (haply) were the feat
To stop the currant neere Charybdis maine,
Or calme the blustring windes on mountaines great,
Than fierce desires of warlike harts restraine;
　　He rules them yet, and rankes them in their haste,
　　For well he knowes disordred speed, makes waste.

3

Feath'red their thoughts, their feet in wings were dight,
Swiftly they marcht, yet were not tir'd thereby,
For willing mindes make heauiest burdens light.
But when the gliding sunne was mounted hie,

Hierusalem (behold) appeer'd in sight,
Hierusalem they view, they see, they spie,
   Hierusalem with merrie noise they greet,
   With ioyfull shouts, and acclamations sweet:

4

As when a troope of iolly sailers row
Some new-found land, and countrie to descrie,
Through dang'rous seas and vnder stars vnknow,
Thrall to the faithlesse waues, and trothlesse skie,
If once the wished shore begin to show,
They all salute it with a ioyfull crie,
   And each to other shew the land in hast,
   Forgetting quite their paines and perils past.

5

To that delight which their first sight did breed,
That pleased so the secret of their thought,
A deepe repentance did foorthwith succeed,
That reu'rend feare and trembling with it brought.
Scantly they durst their feeble eies despreed
Vpon that towne, where Christ was sold and bought,
   Where for our sinnes he faultlesse suffred paine,
   There where he dide and where he liu'd againe:

6

Soft words, low speech, deepe sobs, sweete sighes, salt teares
   Rose from their brests, with ioy and pleasure mixt;
   For thus fares he the Lord aright that feares,
   Feare on deuotion, ioy on faith is fixt:
   Such noice their passions make, as when one heares
   The hoarse sea waues, rore hollow rocks betwixt;
      Or as the winde in houltes and shadie greaues,
      A murmur makes, among the boughes and leaues.

7

Their naked feet troad on the dustie way,
Following th'ensample of their zealous guide,
Their scarffes, their crests, their plumes, and feathers gay,
They quickly doft, and willing laid aside,

Their moulten harts their woonted pride allay,
Along their watrie cheekes warme teares downe slide,
   And then such secret speech as this, they vsed,
   While to himselfe, each one himselfe accused.

8

'Flower of goodnes, root of lasting blisse,
Thou well of life, whose streames were purple blood
That flowed here, to clense the fowle amisse
Of sinfull man, behold this brinish flood,
That from my melting hart distilled is,
Receiue in grce these teares (O Lord so good)
   For neuer wretch with sinne so ouergone,
   Had fitter time, or greater cause to mone.

9

This while the warie watchman looked ouer
(From tops of Sions towres) the hils and dales,
And saw the dust the fields and pastures couer,
As when thicke mistes arise from moorie vales.
At last the sun-bright shieldes he gan discouer,
And glistring helmes for violence none that fales,
   The mettall shone like lightning bright in skies,
   And man and horse amid the dust descries.

10

'Then lowd he cries, O what a dust ariseth?
Oh how it shines with shields and targets cleere?
Vp, vp, to armes, for valiant hart despiseth
The threat'ned storme of death, and danger neere,
Behold your foes; then further thus deuiseth,
Haste, haste, for vaine delay encreaseth feare,
   These horrid cloudes of dust that yonder flie,
   Your comming foes doth hide, and hide the skie.'

11

The tender children, and the fathers old,
The aged matrons, and the virgin chast,
That durst not shake the speare, nor target hold,
Themselues deuoutly in their temples plast,

The rest, of members strong and courage bold;
On hardie brestes their harnesse dond in haste,
  Some to the walles, some to the gates them dight,
  Their king meane-while directs them all aright.

12

All things well ordred, he withdrew with speed
Vp to a turret high, two ports betweene,
That so he might be neare at euerie need,
And ouerlooke the lands and furrowes greene,
Thither he did the sweet *Erminia* leed,
That in his court had entertained beene
  Since Christians Antioch did to bondage bring,
  And slew her father, who thereof was king.

13

Against their foes *Clorinda* sallied out,
And many a Baron bold was by her side,
Within the postern stood *Argantes* stout
To rescue her, if ill mote her betide:
With speeches braue she cheer'd her warlike rout,
And with bold words them hart'ned as they ride,
  'Let vs some braue act (quoth she) this day
  Of Asias hopes the ground-worke found and lay.'

14

While to her folke thus spake the virgin braue,
Thereby behold foorth past a Christian band,
Towards the campe that herds of cattell draue,
For they that morne had forraid all the land,
The fierce Virago would that bootie saue,
Whom their commander singled hand for hand,
  A mightie man at armes, who *Guardo* hight,
  But far too weake to match with her in fight.

15

They met, and low in dust was *Guardo* laid,
Twixt either armie, from his cell downe kest,
The Pagans shout for ioy, and hopefull said,
Those good beginnings would haue endings blest:

Against the rest on went the noble maid,
She broke the helme, and pearst the armed brest,
   Her men the paths rode through made by her sword,
   They passe the streame where she had found the ford.

16

Soone was the pray out of their hands recou'red,
By step and step the Frenchmen gan retire,
Till on a little hill at last they hou'red,
Whose strength preseru'd them from *Clorindas* ire:
When, as a tempest that hath long been cou'red
In watrie cloudes, breakes out with sparkling fire.
   With his strong squadron Lord *Tancredie* came,
   His hart with rage, his eies with courage flame:

17

Mast great the speare was which the gallant bore,
That in his warlike pride he made to shake,
As windes tall Cedars tosse on mountaines hore;
The king, that wondred at his brau'rie, spake
To her, that neere him seated was before,
Who felt her hart with loues hot feuer quake,
   'Well should'st thou know (quoth he) each Christian knight
   By long aquaintance, though in armour dight.

18

'Say, who is he showes so great worthinesse,
That rides so ranke, and bends his lance so fell?'
To this the Princesse said nor more nor lesse,
Her hart, with sighes; her eies, with teares did swell;
But sighes and teares she wisely could suppresse,
Her loue and passion she dissembled well,
   And stroue her loue and hot desire to couer,
   Till hart with sighes, and eies with teares ron ouer.

19

At last she spake, and with a craftie slight
Her secret loue disguis'd in clothes of hate,
'Alas too well (she saies) I know that knight,
I saw his force and courage prooued late,

Too late I view'd when his powre and might
Shooke downe the pillar of *Cassanoes* state,
 Alas what wounds he giues? how fierce, how fell?
 No phisicke helpes them cure, nor magicks spell.

20

'*Tancred* he hight, O *Macon* would he weare
My thrall, ere fates him of this life depriue,
For to his hatefull head such spite I beare,
I would him reaue his cruell hart on liue.'
Thus said she, they that her complainings heare
In other sense her wishes credit giue.
 She sigh'd withall, they constred all amisse,
 And thought she wisht to kill, who long'd to kisse.

21

This while foorth prickt *Clorinda* from the throng,
And gainst *Tancredie* set her speare in rest,
Vpon their helmes they crackt their lances long,
And from her head her guilden caske he kest,
For euery lace he broke and euery thong,
And in the dust threw downe her plumed crest,
 About her shoulders shone her golden locks,
 Like sunnie beames, on Alablaster rocks.

22

Her lookes with fire, her eies with lightning blaze,
Sweet was her wrath, what then would be her smile?
Tancred whereon think'st thou? what dost thou gaze?
Hast thou forgot her in so short a while?
The same is she, the shape of whose sweet face
The god of loue did in thy hart compile,
 The same that left thee by the cooling streame,
 Safe from sunnes heat, but scorcht with beauties beame.

23

The Prince well knew her, though her painted shield
And golden helme he had not markt before,

21 71 < 21 (*cf.* 1624)

She sau'd her head, and with her axe (well stield,)
Assail'd the knight: but her the knight forbore,
Gainst other foes he prou'd him through the field,
Yet she for that refrained nere the more,
    But following 'turne thee' cride, in irefull wise,
    And so at once she threats to kill him twice.

24

Not once the Baron lift his armed hand
To strike the maide, but gazing on her eies,
Where lordly *Cupid* seem'd in armes to stand,
No way to ward or shun her blowes he trics;
But softly sayes, 'no stroke of thy strong hand
Can vanquish *Tancred*, but thy conquest lies
    In those faire eies, which fierie weapons dart,
    That finde no lighting place except this hart.'

25

At last resolu'd, although he hopt small grace,
Yet ere he dide to tell how much he loued,
For pleasing words in womens eare finde place,
And gentle harts with humble suit are moued:
'O thou (quoth he) withhold thy wrath a space,
For if thou long to see my valour proued,
    Were it not better, from this warlike rout
    Withdrawne, somewhere, alone to fight it out?

26

'So singled, may we both our courage trie:'
Clorinda to that motion yeelded glad,
And helmlesse to the forrestward gan hie,
Whither the Prince right pensiue went and sad,
And there the virgin gan him soone defie,
One blow she strooken and he warded had,
    When he cride 'hold, and ere we proue our might,
    First heare thou some conditions of the fight.'

27

She staid, and desprate loue had made him bold,
'Since from the fight thou wilt no respite giue,

The cou'nants be (he said) that thou vnfold
This wretched bosome, and my hart out riue,
Giuen thee long since, and if thou cruell would,
I should be dead, let me no longer liue,
    But pearse this brest, that all the world may say
    The Eagle made the turtle doue her pray.

28

'Saue with thy grace, or let thine anger kill,
Loue hath disarm'd my life of all defence;
An easie labour harmlesse blood to spill,
Strike then, and punish where is none offence.'
This said the Prince, and more perchance had will
To haue declar'd, to moue her cruell sense.
    But in ill time of Pagans thither came
    A troope, and Christians that pursu'd the same.

29

The Pagans fled before their valiant foes,
For dread or craft, it skils not that we knew,
A soldier wilde, carelesse to win or loes,
Saw where her locks about the damsell flew,
And at her backe he profreth (as he goes)
'To strike where her he did disarmed view:
    But *Tancred* cride, 'oh stay thy cursed hand,'
    And for to ward the blow lift vp his brand.

30

But yet the cutting steele arriued theare,
Where her faire necke adioin'd her noble head,
Light was the wound, but through her amber heare
The purple drops downe railed bloodie read,
So rubies set in flaming gold appeare:
But Lord *Tancredie* pale with rage as lead,
    Flew on the villaine, who to flight him bound;
    The smart was his, though she receiu'd the wound:

29² know < knew *as corrected in B*

31

The villaine flies, he, full of rage and ire
Pursues, she stood and wondred on them both,
But yet to follow them shew'd no desire,
To stray so far she would perchance be loth,
But quickly turn'd her, fierce as flaming fire,
And on her foes wreaked her anger wroth,
    On euerie side she kils them downe amaine,
    And now she flies, and now she turnes againe:

32

As the swift Vre by Volgaes rolling flood
Chas'd through the plaines the mastiuc currcs toforne,
Flies to the succour of some neighbor wood,
And often turnes againe his dreadfull horne
Against the dogs imbru'd in sweat and blood,
That bite not, till the beast to flight retorne;
    Or as the Moores at their strange tennise run
    Defenst, the flying balles vnhurt to shun:

33

So ronne *Clorinda*, so her foes pursewed,
Vntill they both approcht the cities wall,
When loe the Pagans their fierce wrath renewed,
Cast in a ring about they wheeled all,
And gainst the Christians backes and sides they shewed
Their courage fierce, and to new combat fall,
    When downe the hill *Argantes* came to fight
    Like angrie *Mars* to aide the Troian knight,

34

Furious, tofore the formost of his ranke,
In sturdie steele foorth stept the warriour bold,
The first he smote downe from his saddle sanke,
The next vnder his steed lay on the mold,
Vnder the Sarsens speare the worthies shranke,
No brest-plare could that cursed tree out-hold,
    When that was broke his pretious sword he drew,
    And whom he hit, he felled, hurt or slew.

35

Clorinda slue *Ardelio* aged knight,
Whose grauer yeeres would for no labour yield,
His age was full of puissance and might,
Two sonnes he had to guard his noble eild,
The first (far from his fathers care and sight)
Cald *Alicandro* wounded lay in feild,
   And *Poliphern* the yonger by his side,
   Had he not nobly fought had surely dide.

36

Tancred by this, that stroue to ouertake
The villaine that had hurt his only deare,
From vaine pursuite at last returned bake,
And his braue troope discomfite saw welneare,
Thither he spurd, and gan huge slaughter make,
His shocke no steed, his blow no knight could beare.
   For dead he strikes him whom he lights vpon,
   So thunders breake high trees on Libanon.

37

Dudon his squadron of aduentrers brings,
To aide the worthie and his tired crew,
Before the res'due yong *Rinaldo* flings
As swift, as firie light'ning kindled new,
His Argent Eagle with her siluer wings
In field of Azure, faire *Erminia* knew,
   'See there sir king, (she sayes) a knight as bold
   And braue, as was the sonne of *Peleus* old.

38

'He winnes the prise in Iust and Turnament,
His actes are numberlesse, though few his yeares,
If Europe sixe like him to war had sent
Among these thousands, strong of Christian Peares,
Syria were lost, lost were the Orient,
And all the lands the southren Ocean weares,
   Conquer'd were all hot Affrikes tawnie kings,
   And all that dwell by Nilus vnknowne springs.

39

'*Rinaldo* is his name, his armed fist
Breakes downe stone walles, when rams and engins faile;
But turne your eies because I would you wist
What Lord that is, in greene and golden maile,
Dudon he hight who guideth as him list
Th'aduentrers troope, whose prowesse seld doth faile,
     High birth, graue yeeres and practise long in war,
     And fearlesse hart, make him renowmed far.

40

'See that big man, that all in browne is bound,
Gernando call'd, the king of Norwaies sonne,
A prouder knight treads not on grasse or ground,
His pride hath lost the praise, his prowesse wonne,
And that kinde paire in white all armed round,
Is *Edward* and *Gildippes*, who begonne
     Through loue the hazard of fierce war to proue,
     Famous for armes, but famous more for loue.'

41

While thus they tell their foemens worthinesse,
The slaughter rageth in the plaine at large,
Tancred and yong *Rinaldo* breake the presse,
They bruise the helme, and pearse the seuenfold targe,
The troope by *Dudon* led perform'd no lesse,
But in they come and giue a furious charge:
     Argantes selfe, feld at one single blow,
     Inglorious, bleeding lay, on earth full low:

42

Nor had the boaster euer risen more,
But that *Rinaldoes* horse eu'n then downe fell,
And with the fall his leg opprest so sore,
That for a space there must he algates dwell.
Meane-while the Pagan troopes were nie forlore,
Swiftly they fled, glad they escapt so well,
     Argantes and with him *Clorinda* stout,
     For banke and bulwarke seru'd to saue the rout.

43

These fled the last, and with their force sustained
The Christians rage, that follow'd them so neare,
Their scattred troopes to safetie well they trained,
And while the res'due fled, the brunt these beare,
Dudon pursu'd the victorie he gained,
And on *Tigranes* nobly broke his speare,
 Then with his sword headlesse to ground him cast,
 So gard'ners branches lop, that spring too fast.

44

Algazers breast-plate, of fine temper made,
Nor *Corbans* helmet, forg'd by magike art,
Could saue their owners, for Lord *Dudons* blade
Cleft *Corbans* head, and pearst *Algazers* hart,
And their proud soules downe to th'infernall shade,
From *Amurath* and *Mahomet* depart,
 Nor strong *Argantes* thought his life was sure,
 He could not safely flie, nor fight secure.

45

The angrie Pagan bit his lips for teene,
He ran, he staid, he fled, he turn'd againe,
Vntill at last vnmarkt, vnuiew'd, vnseene,
(When *Dudon* had *Almansor* newly slaine)
Within his side he sheath'd his weapon keene,
Downe fell the Worthie on the dustie plaine,
 And lifted vp his feeble eies vneath,
 Opprest with leaden sleepe, of iron death.

46

Three times he stroue to view heau'ns golden ray,
And rais'd him on his feeble elbow thries,
And thrise he tumbled on the lowly lay,
And three times clos'd againe his dying eies,
He speakes no word, yet makes he signes to pray,
He sighes, he faints, he grones and then he dies:
 Argantes proud to spoile the corps disdain'd,
 But shooke his sword with blood of *Dudon* stain'd.

47

And turning to the Christian knights, he cride
'Lordings, behold, this bloodie reeking blade,
Last night was giuen me by your noble guide,
Tell him what proofe thereof this day is made,
Needs must this please him well that is betide,
That I so well can vse this martiall trade,
     To whom so rare a gift he did present,
     Tell him the workman fits the instrument.

48

'If further proofe hereof he long to see,
Say it still thirsts, and would his hart blood drinke;
And if he haste not to encounter mee,
Say I will finde him when he least doth thinke:'
The Christians at his words enraged bee,
But he to shun their ire doth safely shrinke
     Vnder the shelter of the neighbour wall,
     Well guarded with his troopes and soldiers all.

49

Like stormes of haile the stones fell downe from hie,
Cast from the bulwarks, flankers, ports and towres,
The shafts and quarries from their engins flie,
As thicke as falling drops in Aprill showres:
The French withdrew, they list not prease too nie,
The Sarrasins escaped all the powres.
     But now *Rinaldo* from the earth vp lept,
     Where by the leg his steed had long him kept;

50

He came and breathed vengeance from his brest
Gainst him that noble *Dudon* late had slaine,
And being come, thus spake he to the rest,
'Warriours, why stand you gazing here in vaine?
Pale death our valiant leader hath opprest,
Come wreake his losse, whom bootlesse you complaine.
     These walles are weake, they keepe but cowards out,
     No rampier can withstand a courage stout.

48⁷ shelter, < shelter

51

'Of double iron, brasse or adamant,
Or if this wall were built of flaming fire,
Yet should the Pagan vile a fortresse want
To shrowd his coward head safe from mine ire;
Come follow then and bid base feare auant,
The harder worke deserues the greater hire:'
   And with that word close to the walles he starts,
   Nor feares he arrowes, quarries, stones or darts.

52

Aboue the waues as *Neptune* lift his eies
To chide the windes, that Troian ships opprest,
And with his count'nance calm'd seas, windes and skies;
So lookt *Rinaldo*, when he shooke his crest
Before those walles, each Pagan feares and flies
His dreadfull sight, or trembling staid at lest:
   Such dread his awfull visage on them cast,
   So seeme poore doues at goshaukes sight agast.

53

The herald *Sigiere* now from *Godfrey* came,
To will them stay and calme their courage hot,
'Retire, quoth he, *Godfrey* commands the same,
To wreake your ire this season fitteth not:
Though loth *Rinaldo* staid, and stopt the flame
That boyled in his hardie stomacke hot;
   His bridled furie grew thereby more fell,
   So riuers stopt, aboue their banks doe swell.

54

The bands retire, not dang'red by their foes
In their retrait, so wise were they and warie,
To murdred *Dudon* each lamenting goes,
From wonted vse of ruth they list not varie,
Vpon their friendly armes they soft impose
The noble burden of his corps to carie:
   Meane-while *Godfredo* from a mountaine great
   Beheld the sacred cittie and her seat.

55

Hierusalem is seated on two hils
Of height vnlike, and turned side to side,
The space betweene a gentle valley fils,
From mount to mount expansed faire and wide.
Three sides are sure imbard, with crags and hils,
The rest is easie, scant to rise espide:
    But mightie bulwarks fence that plainer part,
    So art helpes nature, nature strength'neth art.

56

The towne is stor'd of troughes and cestrens, made
To keepe fresh water, but the countrie seames
Deuoid of grasse, vnfit, for plowmens trade,
Not fertill, moist with riuers, wels and streames.
There grow few trees, to make the sommers shade,
To shield the parched land from scorching beames,
    Saue that a wood stands sixe mile from the towne,
    With aged Cedars darke, and shadowes browne.

57

By East, among the dustie valleis, glide
The siluer streames of Iordans christall flood;
By West, the midland sea, with bounders tide
Of sandie shores, where Ioppa whilome stood;
By North Samaria stands, and on that side
The golden calfe was rear'd in Bethel wood;
    Bethleem by South, where Christ incarnate was,
    A pearle in steele, a diamond set in brasse,

58

While thus the Duke on euery side descried
The cities strength, the walles and gates about,
And saw where least the same was fortified,
Where weakest seem'd the walles to keepe him out;
Erminia as he armed rode, him spied
And thus bespake the heathen tyrant stout,
    'See *Godfrey* there, in purple clad and gold,
    His stately port, and princely looke behold:

59

'Well seemes he borne to be with honour crown'd,
So well the lore he knowes of regiment,
Peerelesse in fight, in counsell graue and sound,
The double gift of glorie excellent,
Among these armies is no warriour found
Grauer in speech, bolder in Turnament.
    Raimond pardie in counsell match him might;
    Tancred and yong *Rinaldo* like in fight.'

60

To whom the king; 'he likes me well therefore,
I knew him whilome in the court of France,
When I from Egypt went Ambassadore,
I saw him there breake many a sturdie lance,
And yet his chinne no signe of manhood bore,
His youth was forward, but with gouernance,
    His words, his actions, and his portance braue,
    Of future vertue, timely tokens gaue.

61

'Presages ah too true:' with that a space
He sigh'd for griefe, then said, 'faine would I know
The man in red, with such a knightly grace,
A worthie Lord he seemeth by his show,
How like to *Godfrey* lookes he in the face?
How like in person? but some-deale more low.'
    '*Baldwine* (quoth she) that noble Baron hight,
    By birth his brother, and his match in might.

62

'Next looke on him that seemes for counsell fit,
Whose siluer locks bewray his store of daies,
Raimond he hight, a man of wondrous wit,
Of Tholouse Lord, his wisdome is his praise,
What he forethinkes doth (as he lookes for) hit,
His stratagems haue good successe alwaies:
    With guilden helme beyond him rides the milde
    And good Prince *William*, Englands kings deere childe.

63

'With him is *Guelpho* as his noble mate,
In birth, in actes, in armes alike the rest,
I know him well, since I beheld him late,
By his broad shoulders and his squared brest:
But my proud foe that quite hath ruinate
My high estate, and Antioch opprest,
   I see not, *Boemond*, that to death did bring
   Mine aged Lord, my father and my king.'

64

Thus talked they; meane-while *Godfredo* went
Downe to the troopes, that in the valley staid,
And for in vaine he thought the labour spent,
T'assaile those partes that to the mountaines laid,
Against the northren gate his force he bent,
Gainst it he campt, gainst it his engins plaid,
   All felt the furie of his angrie powre,
   That from those gates lies to the corner towre.

65

The townes third part was this, or little lesse,
Fore which the Duke his glorious ensignes spred,
For so great compasse had that forteresse,
That round it could not be enuironed
With narrow siege, (nor Babels king I gesse
That whilome tooke it, such an armie led)
   But all the waies he kept, by which his foe
   Might to or from the citie, come or goe.

66

His care was next, to cast the trenches deepe,
So to preserue his resting campe by night,
Least from the citie (while his soldiers sleepe)
They might assaile them with vntimely fight.
This donne, he went where Lords and Princes weepe,
With dire complaints, about the murdred knight,
   Where *Dudon* dead, lay slaughtred on the ground,
   And all the soldiers sate lamenting round.

63 37 < 63 (*cf. 1624*)

67

His wayling friends adorn'd the mournfull beare
With wofull pompe, whereon his corpes they laid,
And when they saw the Bulloigne Prince draw neare,
All felt new greefe, and each new sorrow maid,
But he, withouten shew or change of cheare,
His springing teares within their fountaines staid,
  His ruefull lookes vpon the coarse he cast
  Awhile, and thus bespake the same at last.

68

'We need not mourne for thee, here laid to rest,
Earth is thy bed, and not thy graue, the skies
Are for thy soule the cradle and the nest,
There liue, for here thy glorie neuer dies:
For like a Christian knight and champion blest
Thou didst both liue and die, now feed thine eies
  With thy redeemers sight, where crown'd with blis
  Thy faith, zeale, merit, well-deseruing is,

69

'Our losse, not thine, prouokes these plaints and teares,
For when we lost thee, then our ship her mast,
Our chariot lost her wheeles, their points our spears,
The bird of conquest her chiefe feather cast:
But though thy death, far from our armie beares
Her chiefest earthlie aide, in heau'n yet plast
  Thou wilt procure vs helpe diuine, so reapes
  He, that sowes godly sorrow, ioy by heapes.

70

'For if our God the Lord Armipotent
Those armed Angels in our aide downe send,
That were at Dothan to his Prophet sent,
Thou wilt come downe with them, and well defend
Our host, and with thy sacred weapons bent
Gainst Sions fort, these gates and bulwarks rend,
  That so thy hand may win this hold, and wee
  May in these temples praise our Christ for thee.'

71

Thus he complain'd; but now the sable shade
Icleped night, had thicke enueloped
The sun, in vaile of double darknes made,
Sleepe, eased care; rest, brought complaint to bed:
All night the warie Duke deuising laide
How that high wall should best be battered,
    How his strong engins he might aptly frame,
    And whence get timber, fit to build the same.

72

Vp with the larke the sorrowfull Duke arose,
A mourner chiefe at *Dudons* buriall,
Of Cipresse sad a pile his friends compose
Vnder a hill, oregrowne with Cedars tall,
Beside the hearce a fruitfull palme tree groes,
(Ennobled since by this great funerall)
    Where *Dudons* corpes they softly laid in ground,
    The priestes sung hymnes, the soldiers wept around.

73

Among the boughes, they here and there bestowe
Ensignes and armes, as witnes of his praise,
Which he from Pagan Lords, that did them owe,
Had wonne in prosprous fights, and happie fraies
His shield they fixed on the bole belowe,
And there this distich vnder-writ, which saies,
    This palme with stretched armes, doth ouerspread
    The champion *Dudons* glorious carkasse dead.

74

This worke performed with aduisement good,
Godfrey his carpenters, and men of skill
In all the campe, sent to an aged wood,
(With conuoy meet to garde them safe from ill)
Within a valley deepe this forrest stood,
To Christian eies vnseene, vnknowne, vntill
    A Syrian told the Duke, who thither sent
    Those chosen workmen, that for timber went.

75

And now the axe rag'd in the forrest wilde,
The Eccho sighed in the groues vnseene,
The weeping Nymphes fled from their bowres exilde,
Downe fell the shadie tops of shaking treene,
Downe came the sacred palmes, the ashes wilde,
The funerall Cipresse, Hollie euer greene,
   The weeping Firre, thicke Beech, and sailing Pine,
   The maried Elme fell with his fruitfull vine.

76

The showter Eugh, the broad-leau'd Sicamore,
The barraine Platane, and the Wall-nut sound,
The Myrrhe, that her foule sinne doth still deplore,
The Alder owner of all watrish ground,
Sweet Iuniper, whose shadow hurteth sore,
Proud Cedar, Oake, the king of forrests crown'd,
   Thus fell the trees, with noice the desarts rore,
   The beastes, their caues; the birds, their nests forlore.

The fourth Booke of Godfrey *of Bulloigne*

The argument.

Sathan his feends and sprites assembleth all,
And sends them foorth to worke the Christians woe,
False Hidraort *their aide from hell doth call,*
And sends Armida *to entrap his foe:*
She telles her birth, her fortune and her fall,
Askes aide, allures and winnes the worthies soe,
That they consent her enterprize to proue;
She winnes them with deceit, craft, beautie, loue.

I

WHile thus their worke went on with luckie speed,
    And reared rammes their horned fronts aduance,
The ancient foe to man, and mortall seed,
His wannish eies vpon them bent askance;
And when he saw their labours well succeed,
He wept for rage, and threat'ned dire mischance,
    He chokt his curses, to himselfe he spake,
    Such noise wilde buls, that softly bellow make.

2

At last resoluing in his damned thought,
To finde some let, to stop their warlike feat,
He gaue command his princes should be brought
Before the throne of his infernall seat,
O foole! as if it were a thing of nought
God to resist, or change his purpose great,
    Who on his foes doth thunder in his ire,
    Whose arrowes hailestones be, and coles of fire.

3

The drearie trumpet blew a dreadfull blast,
And rombled through the lands and kingdomes vnder,
Through wastnes wide it roard, and hollowes vast,
And fild the deepe, with horror, feare and wonder,

Not halfe so dreadfull noise the tempests cast,
That fall from skies, with storms of haile and thunder,
   Nor halfe so lowd the whistling winds doe sing,
   Broke from the earthen prisons of their king.

4

The Peeres of *Plutoes* realme assembled beene
Amid the pallace of their angrie king,
In hideous formes and shapes, to fore vnseene,
That feare, death, terror and amasement bring,
With ouglie pawes some trample on the greene,
Some gnaw the snakes that on their shoulders hing,
   And some their forked tailes stretch forth on hie,
   And teare the twinkling stars from trembling skie.

5

There were *Cilenos* foule and loathsome rout,
There Sphinges, Centaures, there were *Gorgons* fell,
There howling Scillaes, yawling round about,
There serpents hisse, there seu'n-mouth'd Hydraes yell,
Chimera there spues fire and brimstone out,
And *Poliphemus* blinde supporteth hell,
   Besides ten thousand monsters therein dwels
   Mis-shapt, vnlike themselues, and like nought els.

6

About their Prince each tooke his wonted seat
On thrones red hot, ibuilt of burning brasse,
Pluto in middest heau'd his trident great,
Of rustie iron huge that forged was,
The rockes, on which the salt sea billowes beat,
And Atlas tops, the clouds in height that passe,
   Compar'd to his huge person, mole-hils be,
   So his rough front, his hornes so lifted he.

7

The tyrant proud frown'd from his loftie cell,
And with his lookes made all his monsters tremble,
His eies, that full of rage and venome swell,
Two beacons seeme, that men to armes assemble,

His feltred lockes, that on his bosome fell,
On rugged mountaines briers and thornes resemble,
  His yawning mouth, that fomed clotted blood,
  Gapte like a whirlepoole wide in Stygian flood.

8

And as mount Etna vomits sulphur out,
With clifts of burning crags, and fire and smoke,
So from his mouth flew kindled coales about,
Hot sparks and smels, that man and beast would choke,
The gnarring porter durst not whine for dout,
Still werc thc Furics, while their soueraigne spoke,
  And swift *Cocytus* staid his murmur shrill,
  While thus the murdrer thundred out his will.

9

'Ye powres infernall, worthier far to sit
Aboue the sunne, whence you your ofspring take,
With me that whilome, through the welkin flit,
Downe tombled headlong to this emptie lake,
Our former glorie, still remember it,
Our bold attemptes and war we once did make
  Gainst him, that rules aboue the starrie sphere,
  For which like traitors we lie damned here.

10

'And now in stead of cleere and gladsome skie,
Of *Titans* brightnes, that so glorious is,
In this deepe darknes loe we helplesse lie,
Hopelesse againe to ioy our former blis,
And more (which makes my grieues to multiplie)
That sinfull creature man, elected is,
  And in our place, the heauens possesse he must,
  Vile man, begot of clay, and borne of dust.

11

'Nor this suffis'd, but that he also gaue
His only sonne, his darling to be slaine,
To conquer so, hell, death, sinne and the graue,
And man condemned to restore againe,

He brake our prisons and would algates saue
The soules that here should dwell in woe and paine,
 And now in heau'n with him they liue alwaies
 With endlesse glorie crown'd, and lasting praise.

12

'But why recount I thus our passed harmes?
Remembrance fresh makes weak'ned sorrowes strong,
Expulsed were we with iniurious armes
From those due honours, vs of right belong.
But let vs leaue to speake of these alarmes,
And bend our forces gainst our present wrong,
 Ah see you not, how he attempted hath
 To bring all lands, all nations to his faith?

13

'Then, let vs carelesse spend the day and night,
Without regard what haps, what comes or goes.
Let Asia subject be to Christians might,
A pray be Sion to her conquering foes,
Let her adore againe her Christ aright,
Who her before all nations whilome choes,
 In brasen tables be his lore iwrit,
 And let all tongues and lands acknowledge it.

14

'So shall our sacred altars all be his,
Our holie Idols tombled in the mold,
To him the wretched man, that sinfull is,
Shall pray, and offer incense, myrrhe and gold;
Our temples shall their costly deckings mis,
With naked walles and pillars freezing cold,
 Tribute of soules shall end, and our estate,
 Or *Pluto* raigne in kingdoms desolate.

15

'Oh, be not than the courage perisht cleene,
That whilome dwelt within your haughtie thought,
When, arm'd with shining fire and weapons keene,
Against the Angels of proud heau'n we fought,

I grant we fell on the Phlegrean greene,
Yet good our cause was, though our fortune nought;
    For chance assisteth oft th'ignobler part,
    We lost the field, yet lost we not our hart.

16

'Goe then my strength, my hope, my spirits, goe,
These westren rebels, with your power withstand,
Plucke vp these weedes, before they ouergroe
The gentle garden of the Hebrewes land,
Quench out this sparke, before it kindle soe
That Asia burne, consumed with the brand.
    Vse open force, or secret guile vnspied;
    For craft is vertue gainst a foe defied.

17

'Among the knights and worthies of their traine,
Let some like out-lawes wander vncouth waies,
Let some be slaine in field, let some againe
Make oracles of womens yeaes and naies,
And pine in foolish loue, let some complaine
On *Godfreyes* rule, and mutines gainst him raise,
    Turne each ones sword, against his fellowes hart,
    Thus kill them all, or spoile the greatest part.'

18

Before his words the tyrant ended had,
The lesser deuils arose with gastlie rore,
And thronged foorth about the world to gad,
Each land they filled, riuer, streame and shore,
The Goblins, Fairies, Feends and Furies mad,
Ranged in flowrie dales, and mountaines hore,
    And vnder euerie trembling leafe they sit,
    Betweene the solid earth and welkin flit.

19

About the world they spread both far and wide,
Filling the thoughts of each vngodly hart,
With secret mischiefe, anger, hate and pride,
Wounding lost soules with sinnes impoyson'd dart.

But say (my muse) recount whence first they tride
To hurt the Christian Lords, and from what part,
   Thou know'st of things perform'd so long agone,
   This later age heares little troath or none.

20

The towne Damascus and the lands about
Rul'd *Hidraort*, a wisard graue and sage,
Acquainted well with all the damned rout
Of *Plutoes* raigne, eu'n from his tender age;
Yet of this war he could not figure out
The wished ending, or successe presage;
   For neither stars aboue, nor powres of hell,
   Nor skill, nor art, nor charme, nor deuill could tell.

21

And yet he thought (O vaine conceit of man!
Which as thou wishest, iudgest things to come)
That the French host to sure destruction ran,
Condemned quite by heau'ns eternall dome:
He thinkes no force withstand or vanquish can
Th'Egyptian strength, and therefore would that some,
   Both of the pray and glorie of the fight,
   Vpon his Syrian folke should haply light.

22

But for he held the French mens worth in prise,
And fear'd the doubtfull gaine of bloodie war,
He, that was closely false and slilie wise,
Cast how he might annoy them most from far:
And as he gan vpon this point deuise,
(As counsellers in ill still neerest ar)
   At hand was *Sathan*, readie ere men need,
   It once they thinke to make them doe the deed.

23

He counseld him how best to hunt his game,
What dart to cast, what net, what toile to pitch,
A neece he had, a nice and tender dame,
Peerelesse in wit, in natures blessings ritch,

To all deceit she could her beautie frame,
False, faire and yong, a virgin and a witch;
   To her he told the summe of this emprise,
   And prais'd her thus, for she was faire and wise.

24

'My deere, who vnderneath these lockes of gold,
And natiue brightnesse of thy louely hew,
Hidest graue thoughts, ripe wit, and wisedome old,
More skill than I, in all mine artes untrew
To thee my purpose great I must vnfold,
This enterprise thy cunning must pursew,
   Weaue thou to end this web which I begin,
   I will the distaffe hold, come thou and spin.

25

'Goe to the Christians host, and there assay
All subtile sleights that women vse in loue,
Shed brinish teares, sob, sigh, entreat and pray,
Wring thy faire hands, cast vp thine eies aboue,
(For mourning beautie hath much powre (men say)
The stubbron harts with pitie fraile to moue)
   Looke pale for dread, and blush sometime for shame,
   In seeming troath thy lies will soonest frame.

26

'Take with the baite Lord *Godfrey*, if thou maste,
Frame snares, of lookes; traines, of alluring speach;
For if he loue, the conquest than thou hast,
Thus purpos'd war thou maist with ease impeach,
Else lead the other Lords to desarts wast,
And hold them slaues far from their leaders reach:'
   Thus taught he her, and for conclusion, saith,
   All things are lawfull for our lands and faith.'

27

The sweet *Armida* tooke this charge on hand,
A tender peece, for beautie, sexe and age,
The sunne was sunken vnderneath the land
When she began her wanton pilgrimage,

In silken weedes she trusteth to withstand,
And conquer knights, in warlike equipage,
   Of their night ambling dame, the Syrians prated
   Some good, some bad, as they her lou'd or hated.

28

Within few daies, the Nymph arriued theare
Where puissant *Godfrey* had his tents ipight;
Vpon her strange attire, and visage cleare,
Gazed each soldier, gazed euerie knight,
As when a comet doth in skies appeare,
The people stand amazed at the light,
   So wondred they, and each at other sought,
   What mister wight she was, and whence ibrought.

29

Yet neuer eie to *Cupids* seruice vow'd
Beheld a face of such a louely pride,
A tinsell vaile her amber locks did shrowd,
That stroue to couer what it could not hide,
The golden sunne, behinde a siluer cloud,
So streameth out his beames on euerie side,
   The marble goddesse, set at *Gnidos*, naked,
   She seem'd, were she vncloath'd, or that awaked.

30

The gamesome winde among her tresses plaies,
And curleth vp, those growing riches, short;
Her sparefull eie to spread his beames denaies,
But keepes his shot, where *Cupid* keepes his fort;
The rose and lillie on her cheeke, assaies
To paint true fairenesse out, in brauest sort,
   Her lips, where bloomes nought but the single rose,
   Still blush, for still they kisse, while still they close.

31

Her brests, two hils orespred with purest snow,
Sweet, smooth and supple, soft and gently swelling,

29⁷ *Guidos,* < *Gnidos,* (*see note*)

Betweene them lies a milken dale below,
Where loue, youth, gladnes, whitenes make their dwelling,
Her brests halfe hid, and halfe were laid to show;
Her enuious vesture greedie sight repelling,
  So was the wanton clad, as if thus much
  Should please the eie, the rest vnseene, the tuch.

32

As when the sun-beames diue through Tagus waue,
To spie the store-house of his springing gold,
Loue pearsing thought so through her mantle draue,
And in her gentle bosome wandred bold:
It view'd the wondrous beautie virgins haue,
And all to fond desire (with vantage) told,
  Alas what hope is left, to quench his fire
  That kindled is, by sight; blowne, by desire.

33

Thus past she, praised, wisht, and wondred at,
Among the troopes, who there encamped lay,
She smil'd for ioy, but well dissembled that
Her greedie eie chose out her wished pray;
On all her gestures, seeming vertue sat,
Towards th'imperiall tent she asked the way:
  With that she met a bold and louesome knight,
  Lord *Godfreys* yongest brother, *Eustace* hight.

34

This was the foule that first fell in the snare,
He saw her faire, and hopte to finde her kinde;
The throne of *Cupid* hath an easie staire,
His barke is fit to saile with euerie winde,
The breach he makes no wisdome can repaire:
With reu'rence meet the Baron low enclinde,
  And thus his purpose to the virgin told,
  For youth, vse, nature, all had made him bold.

33⁵ gestnres < gestures (*cf. 1624*)

35

'Ladie, if thee beseeme a stile so low,
In whose sweet lookes such sacred beauties shine,
(For neuer yet did heau'n such grace bestow
On any daughter borne of *Adams* line)
Thy name let vs (though far vnworthie) knoe,
Vnfold thy will, and whence thou art in fine,
 Least my audacious boldness learne, too late,
 What honors due become thy high estate.'

36

'Sir knight (quoth she) your praises reach too hie
Aboue her merit you commenden soe,
A haplesse maid I am, both borne to die,
And dead to ioy, that liue in care and woe,
A virgin helplesse, fugitiue pardie,
My natiue soile and kingdome thus foregoe
 To seeke Duke *Godfreys* aide, such store men tell
 Of vertuous ruth doth in his bosome dwell.

37

'Conduct me than that mightie Duke before,
If you be courteous, sir, as well you seeme.'
'Content (quoth he) since of one wombe ibore,
We brothers are, your fortune good esteeme
T'encounter me, whose word preuaileth more
In *Godfreys* hearing, than you haply deeme,
 Mine aide I grant, and his I promise too,
 All that his scepter, or my sword, can doo.'

38

He led her easly foorth when this was said,
Where *Godfrey* sate among his Lords and peares,
She reu'rence did, then blusht, as one dismaid
To speake, for secret wants and inward feares,
It seem'd a bashfull shame her speeches staid,
At last the courteous Duke her gently cheares;
 Silence was made, and she began her tale,
 They fit to heare, thus sung this nightingale.

39

'Victorious Prince, whose honorable name
Is held so great among our Pagan kings,
That to those lands thou dost by conquest tame,
That thou hast wonne them, some content it brings;
Well knowne to all is thy immortal fame,
The earth, thy worth; thy foe, thy praises sings,
   And Painims wronged come to seeke thine aide,
   So doth thy vertue, so thy powre perswaide.

40

'And I though bred in *Macons* heath'nish lore,
Which thou oppressest with thy puissant might,
Yet trust thou wilt an helplesse maide restore,
And repossesse her in her fathers right:
Others in their distresse doe aide implore
Of kinne and friends; but I in this sad plight
   Inuoke thy helpe, my kingdome to inuade,
   So doth thy vertue, so my need perswade.

41

'In thee I hope, thy succours I inuoke,
To win the crowne whence I am dispossest;
For like renowne awaiteth on the stroke
To cast the haughtie downe, or raise th'opprest;
Nor greater glorie brings a scepter broke,
Than doth deliu'rance of a maid distrest:
   And since thou canst at will performe the thing,
   More is thy praise to make, than kill a king.

42

'But if thou would'st thy succours due excuse,
Bicause in Christ I haue no hope nor trust,
Ah yet for vertues sake, thy vertue vse!
Who scorneth gold because it lies in dust?
Be witnes heau'n, if thou to grant refuse,
Thou dost forsake a maid in cause most iust,
   And for thou shalt at large my fortunes know,
   I will my wrongs, and their great treasons show.

43

'Prince *Arbilan* that raigned in his life
On faire Damascus, was my noble sire,
Borne of meane race he was, yet got to wife
The Queene *Chariclia*, such was the fire
Of her hot loue, but soone the fatall knife
Had cut the threed that kept their ioyes intire,
    For so mishap her cruell lot had cast,
    My birth, her death; my first day, was her last.

44

'And ere fiue yeeres were fully come and gone,
Since his deere spouse to hastie death did yeild,
My father also dide, consum'd with mone,
And sought his loue amid th'Elisian feild,
His crowne and me (poore orphan) left alone,
Mine vncle gouern'd in my tender eild;
    For well he thought, if mortall men haue faith,
    In brothers brest true loue his mansion haith.

45

'He tooke the charge of me, and of the crowne,
And with kinde shewes of loue so brought to passe,
That through Damascus great report was blowne
How good, how iust, how kinde mine vncle was;
Whether he kept his wicked hate vnknowne,
And hid the serpent in the flowring grasse,
    Or that true faith did in his bosome wonne,
    Bicause he ment to match me with his sonne.

46

'Which sonne, within short while, did vndertake
Degree of knighthood, as beseem'd him well,
Yet neuer durst he for his Ladies sake
Breake sword or lance, aduanst in loftie cell:
As faire he was, as *Cithereas* make,
As proud as he, that signoriseth hell,
    In fashions way-ward, and in loue vnkinde,
    For *Cupid* deignes not wound, a currish minde.

47

'This Paragon should Queene *Armida* wed,
A goodly swaine to be a Princesse pheare,
A louely partner of a Ladies bed,
A noble head, a golden crowne to weare:
His glosing sire his errand daily fed,
And sugred speeches whispred in mine eare,
　　To make me take this darling in mine armes,
　　But still the adder stopt her eares from charmes.

48

'At last he left me with a troubled grace,
Through which transparent was his inward spight,
Me thought I red the storie in his face
Of these mishaps, that on me since haue light,
Since that foule spirits haunt my resting place,
And gastly visions breake my sleepe by night,
　　Greefe, horror, feare my fainting soule did kill,
　　For so my minde foreshew'd my comming ill.

49

'Three times the shape of my deere mother came,
Pale, sad, dismaid, to warne me in my dreame,
Alas, how far transformed from the same,
Whose eies shone earst, like *Titans* glorious beame:
"Daughter, she saies, flie, flie, behold thy dame
Foreshowes the treasons of thy wretched eame,
　　Who poyson gainst thy harmlesse life prouides,"
　　This said, to shapelesse aire vnseene, she glides.

50

'But what auailes high walles or bulwarks strong,
Where fainting cowards haue the peece to gard?
My fexe too weake, mine age was all too yong,
To vndertake alone, a worke so hard,
To wander wilde, the desart woods among,
A banisht maid, of wonted ease debard,
　　So grieuous seem'd, that leifer were my death,
　　And there t'expire where first I drew my breath.

51

'I fear'd deadly euill, if long I staid,
And yet to flie had neither will nor powre,
Nor durst my hart declare it waxt affraid,
Least so I hasten might my dying howre:
Thus restlesse waited I (vnhappie maid)
What hand should first plucke vp my springing flowre,
 Euen as the wretch condemn'd to lose his life,
 Awaites the falling of the murdring knife.

52

'In these extremes (for so my fortune would,
Perchance preserve me to my further ill)
One of my noble fathers seruants ould,
That for his goodnes bore his childe good will,
With store of teares this treason gan vnfould,
And said; my guardian would his pupill kill,
 And that himselfe, if promise made he kept,
 Should giue me poison dire ere next I slept.

53

'And further told me, if I wisht to liue,
I must conuay my selfe by secret flight,
And offred than all succours he could giue
To aide his mistris, banisht from her right,
His words of comfort feare to exile driue,
The dread of death made lesser dangers light:
 So we concluded when the shadowes dim,
 Obscur'd the earth, I should depart with him.

54

'Of close escapes the aged patronesse,
Blacker than earst, her sable mantle spred,
When with two trustie maides in great distresse,
Both from mine vncle and my realme I fled;
Oft lookt I backe, but hardly could suppresse
Those streames of teares, mine eies vncessant shed,
 For when I looked on my kingdome lost,
 It was a griefe, a death, an hell almost.

55

'My steeds drew on the burden of my limmes,
But still my lookes, my thoughts, drew backe as fast,
So fare the men, that from the hauens brims,
Far out to sea, by sudden storme are cast,
Swift ore the grasse the rolling chariot swims,
Through waies vnknowne, all night, all day we hast,
   At last (nie tir'd) a castle strong we fand,
   The vtmost border of my natiue land.

56

'The fort *Arontes* was, for so the knight
Was call'd, that my delu'rance thus had wrought.
But when the tyrant saw, by mature flight
I had escapt the treasons of his thought,
The rage encreased in the cursed wight
Gainst me, and him, that me to safetie brought,
   And vs accus'd, we would haue poysoned
   Him, but descride to saue our liues we fled.

57

'And that in lew of his approued truth,
To poison him I hired had my guide,
That he dispatched, mine vnbridled yuth
Might range at will, in no subiection tide,
And that each night I slept (O foule vntruth!)
(Mine honor lost) by this *Arontes* side:
   But heau'n I pray send downe reuenging fire,
   When so base loue shall change my chaste desire.

58

'Not that he sitteth on my regall throne,
Nor that he thirst to drinke my lukewarme blood,
So greeueth me, as this despite alone,
That my renowne, which euer blamelesse stood,
Hath lost the light wherewith it alwaies shone:
With forged lies he makes his tale so good,
   And holds my subiects harts in such suspence,
   That none takes armour for their Queenes defence.

59

'And though he doe my regall throne possesse,
Cloathed in purple, crown'd with burnisht gold;
Yet is his hate, his rancour, nere the lesse,
Since nought asswageth malice when tis old:
He threats to burne *Arontes* forteresse,
And murder him vnlesse he yeeld the hold,
 And me and mine threates (not with war, but death)
 Thus causelesse hatred, endlesse is vneath.

60

'And so he trusts to wash away the staine,
And hide his shamefull fact with mine offence,
And saith he will restore the throne againe
To his late honour, and due excellence,
And therefore would I should be algates slaine,
For while I liue, his rights is in suspence.
 This is the cause my guiltlesse life is sought,
 For on my ruine is his safetie wrought.

61

'And let the tyrant haue his harts desire,
Let him performe the crueltie he ment,
My guiltlesse blood must quench the ceaslesse fire,
On which my endlesse teares were bootlesse spent,
Vnlesse thou helpe; to thee renowned sire,
I flie, a virgin, orphan, innocent,
 And let these teares that on thy feet distill,
 Redeeme the drops of blood, he thirsts to spill.

62

'By these thy glorious feet, that tread secure
On necks of tyrants, by thy conquests braue,
By that right hand, and by those temples pure,
Thou seekes to free from *Macons* lore, I craue
Helpe for this sicknes, none but thou canst cure,
My life and kingdome let thy mercie saue
 From death and ruine: but in vaine I proue thee,
 If right, if truth, if iustice cannot moue thee.

63

'Thou, who dost all thou wishest, as thy will,
And neuer willest ought, but what is right,
Preserue this guiltlesse blood they seeke to spill,
Thine be my kingdome, saue it with thy might:
Among these captains, Lords, and knights of skill,
Appoint me ten, approued most in fight,
 Who with assistance of my friends and kin
 May serue, my kingdome lost, againe to win.

64

'For loe a knight, that hath a gate to ward,
(A man of chifest trust about his king)
Hath promised so to beguile the gard,
That me and mine he vndertakes to bring
Safe, where the tyrant haply sleepeth hard:
He counseld me to vndertake this thing,
 Of thee some little succour to intreat,
 Whose name alone accomplish can the feat.'

65

This said, his answer did the Nymph attend,
Her lookes, her sighes, her gestures all did pray him:
But *Godfrey* wisely did his grant suspend,
He doubts the worst, and that awhile did stay him,
He knowes, who feares no God, he loues no frend,
He feares the heathen false would thus betray him:
 But yet such ruth dwelt in his princely minde,
 That gainst his wisdome, pitie made him kinde.

66

Besides the kindnes of his gentle thought,
Readie to comfort each distressed wight,
The maidens offer profit with it brought;
For if the Syrian kingdome were her right,
That wonne, the way were easie, which he sought
To bring all Asia subiect to his might,
 There might he raise munition, armes and treasure,
 To worke th'Egyptian king and his displeasure.

67

Thus was his noble hart long time betwixt
Feare and remorse, not granting nor denaying,
Vpon his eies the dame her lookings fixt,
As if her life and death lay on his saying,
Some teares she shed, with sighes and sobbings mixt,
As if her hope were dead through his delaying;
    At last her earnest suit the Duke denaid,
    But with sweet words thus would content the maid.

68

'If not in service of our God we fought,
In meaner quarrell if this sword were shaken,
Well might thou gather in thy gentle thought,
So faire a Princesse should not be forsaken;
But since these armies, from the worlds end brought,
To free this sacred towne haue vndertaken,
    It were vnfit we turn'd our strength away,
    And victorie, euen in her comming, stay.

69

'I promise thee, and on my princely word
The burden of thy wish and hope repose,
That when this chosen temple of the Lord,
Her holy doores shall to his saints vnclose
In rest and peace; then this victorious sword
Shall execute due vengeance on thy foes:
    But if for pitie of a worldlie dame
    I left this worke, such pitie, were my shame.'

70

At this the Princesse bent her eies to ground,
And stood vnmou'd, though not vnmarkt, a space,
The secret bleeding of her inward wound
Shed heau'nly dew, vpon her angels face.
'Poore wretch' (quoth she) in teares and sorrowes drown'd,
'Death be thy peace, the graue thy resting place,
    Since such thy hap, that least thou mercie finde,
    The gentlest hart on earth is proou'd vnkind.

71

'Where none attends, what bootes it to complaine?
Mens froward harts are mou'd with womens teares,
As marble stones are pearst with drops of raine,
No plaints finde passage through vnwilling eares:
The tyrant (haply) would his wrath restraine
Heard he these praiers, ruthlesse *Godfrey* heares,
　　Yet not thy fault is this, my chance (I see)
　　Hath made eu'n pitie, pitilesse in thee.

72

'So both thy goodnes, and good hap, denaid me,
Griefe, sorrow, mischiefe, care, hath ouerthrowne me,
The star that rul'd my birth-day hath betraid me,
My Genius sees his charge, but dares not owne me,
Of Queene-like state, my flight hath disarraid me,
My father dide, ere he fiue yeeres had knowne me,
　　My kingdome lost, and lastly resteth now,
　　Downe with the tree, sith broke is euery bow.

73

'And for the modest lore of maidenhood,
Bids me not soiourne with these armed men,
Oh whither shall I flie? what secret wood
Shall hide me from the tyrant? or what den,
What rocke, what vault, what caue can doe me good?
No, no, where death is sure, it resteth then
　　To scorne his powre, and be it therefore seene,
　　Armida liu'd, and dide, both like a Queene.'

74

With that she lookt, as if a proud disdaine
Kindled displeasure in her noble minde,
The way she came she turn'd her steps againe,
With gestures sad, but in disdainfulle kinde,
A tempest railed downe her cheekes amaine,
With teares of woe, and sighes of angers winde;
　　The drops her footsteps wash, whereon she treads,
　　And seemes to step on pearles, or christall beads.

75

Her cheekes on which this streaming Nectar fell,
Still'd through the limbecke of her diamond eies,
The roses white and red resembled well,
Whereon the roarie May-deaw sprinkled lies,
When the faire morne first blusheth from her cell,
And breatheth balme from opened paradies;
 Thus sigh'd, thus mourn'd, thus wept, this louely queene,
 And in each drop, bathed a grace vnseene.

76

Thrice twenty *Cupids* vnperceiued flew
To gather vp this licour, ere it fall,
And of each drop an arrow forged new,
Else, as it came, snatcht vp the christall ball,
And at rebellious harts for wilde fire threw,
O wondrous loue! thou makest gaine of all;
 For if she weeping sit, or smiling stand,
 She bends thy bow, or kindleth else thy brand.

77

This forged plaint drew forth vnfained teares
From many eies, and pearst each worthies hart,
Each one condoleth with her that her heares,
And of her griefe would helpe her beare the smart:
If *Godfrey* aide her not, not one but sweares
Some tygresse gaue him sucke, on roughest part
 Midst the rude crags, on Alpine cliffes aloft:
 Hard is that hart which beautie makes not soft.

78

But iollie *Eustace*, in whose brest the brand
Of loue and pitie, kindled had the flame,
While other softly whispred vnderhand
Before the Duke, with comely boldnes, came:
Brother and Lord (quoth he) too long you stand
In your first purpose, yet vouchsafe to frame
 Your thoughts to ours, and lend this virgin aid:
 Thanks are halfe lost, when good turnes are delaid.

79

'And thinke not that *Eustaces* talke assaies
To turne these forces from this present war,
Or that I wish you should your armies raise
From Sions walles, my speech tends not so far:
But we that venter all, for fame and praise,
That to no charge nor seruice bounden ar,
    Foorth of our troope may ten well spared bee
    To succour her, which nought can weaken thee.

80

'And know, they shall in Gods high seruice fight,
That virgins innocent, saue and defend:
Deere will the spoiles be in the heavens sight,
That from a tyrants hatefull head we rend:
Nor seem'd I forward in this Ladies right,
With hope of gaine or profit in the end;
    But for I know he armes vnwoorthie beares,
    To helpe a maidens cause, that shunnes or feares.

81

'Ah! be it not pardie declar'd in France,
Or elsewhere told where courtsie is in prise,
That we forsooke so faire a cheuisance,
For doubt or feare that might from fight arise;
Else, here surrender I both sword and lance,
And sweare no more to vse this martiall guise;
    For ill deserues he to be term'd a knight,
    That beares a blunt sword, in a Ladies right.'

82

Thus parled he: and with confused sound,
The rest approued what the gallant said.
Their Generall the knights encompast round,
With humble grace, and earnest suit they praid:
'I yeeld (quoth he) and be it happie found,
What I haue granted, let her haue your aid:
    Yours be the thanks, for yours the danger is,
    If ought succeed (as much I feare) amis.

83

'But if with you my words may credit finde,
O temper then this heat misguides you soe!'
Thus much he said: but they, with fancie blinde,
Accept his grant, and let his counsell goe.
What works not beautie, mans relenting minde,
Is eath to moue with plaints and shewes of woe:
  Her lips cast forth a chaine of sugred words,
  That captiue led most of the Christian Lords.

84

Eustace recall'd her, and bespake her thus:
'Beauties chiefe darling, let these sorrowes bee,
For such assistance shall you finde in vs,
As with your need, or will, may best agree;
With that she cheer'd her forehead dolorous,
And smil'd for ioy, that *Phebus* blusht to see,
  And had she daign'd her vaile for to remoue,
  The god himselfe, once more, had falne in loue.

85

With that she broke the silence once againe,
And gaue the knight great thanks in little speach,
She said she would his handmaid poore remaine,
So far as honours lawes receiu'd no breach.
Her humble gestures made the res'due plaine,
Dumbe eloquence, perswading more, than speach:
  Thus women know, and thus they vse the guise,
  T'enchant the valiant, and beguile the wise.

86

And when she saw her enterprise had got
Some wished meane, of quicke and good proceeding,
She thought to strike the iron that was hot;
For euerie action hath his howre of speeding:
Medea or false *Circe* changed not,
So far the shapes of men, as her eies spreeding
  Altred their harts, and with her *Sirens* found
  In lust, their minds; their harts, in loue she drown'd.

87

All wilie sleights, that subtile women know,
Howrely she vs'd, to catch some louer new.
None kend the bent of her vnstedfast bow,
For with the time her thoughts her lookes renew,
From some she cast her modest eies below,
At some her gazing glances roauing flew,
 And while she thus pursewd her wanton sport,
 She spurd the slow, and rain'd the forward short.

88

If some, as hopelesse that she would be wonne,
Forbore to loue, because they durst not moue her,
On them her gentle lookes to smile begonne,
As who say, she is kinde, if you dare proue her:
On euerie hart thus shone this lustfull sonne,
All stroue to serue, to please, to wowe, to loue her,
 And in their harts that chaste and bashfull weare,
 Her eies hot glance dissolu'd the frost of feare.

89

On them, who durst with fingring bold assay
To touch the softnes of her tender skin,
She lookt as coy, as if she list not play,
And made as things of worth were hard to win;
Yet tempred so her deignfull lookes alway,
That outward scorne shew'd store of grace within:
 Thus with false hope their longing harts she fired,
 For hardest gotten things, are most desired.

90

Alone sometimes she walkt in secret where,
To ruminate vpon her discontent,
Within her eie-lids sat the swelling teare,
Not powred forth, though sprong from sad lament;
And with this craft a thousand soules welneare,
In snares of foolish ruth and loue she hent,
 And kept as slaues, by which we fitly proue,
 That witlesse pitie, breedeth fruitlesse loue.

91

Sometimes, as if her hope vnloosed had
The chaines of griefe, wherein her thoughts lay fettered,
Vpon her minions lookt she blithe and glad,
In that deceitfull lore so was she lettered;
Not glorious *Titan*, in his brightnes clad,
The sun-shine of her face in luster bettered:
 For when she list to cheare her beauties so,
 She smil'd away the cloudes of griefe and wo.

92

Her double charme of smiles and sugred words,
Lulled on sleepe the vertue of their sences,
Reason small aide gainst those assaults affords,
Wisedome no warrant from those sweet offences,
Cupids deepe riuers, haue their shallow fordes,
His griefes, bring ioyes; his losses recompences;
 He breedes the sore, and cures vs of the paine:
 Achilles lance that wounds and heales againe.

93

While thus she them torments twixt frost and fier,
Twixt ioy and griefe, twixt hope and restlesse feare,
The slie enchantresse, felt her gaine the nier,
These were her flockes that golden fleeces beare:
But if some one durst vtter his desier,
And by complaining make his grieues appeare,
 He labored hard rocks with plaints to moue,
 She had not learn'd the Gamut then of loue.

94

For downe she bent her bashfull eies to ground,
And dond the weede of womens modest grace,
Downe from her eies welled the pearles round,
Vpon the bright Ennamell of her face;
Such honie drops on springing flowres are found,
When *Phebus* holds the crimsen morne in chace;
 Full seem'd her lookes of anger, and of shame;
 Yet pitie shone transparent through the same.

95

If she perceiued by his outward cheare,
That any would his loue by talke bewray,
Sometimes she heard him, sometimes stopt her eare,
And played fast and loose the liue-long day:
Thus all her louers kinde deluded weare,
Their earnest suit got neither yea nor nay;
   But like the sort of wearie huntsmen fare,
   That hunt all day, and lose at night the hare.

96

These were the artes by which she captiued
A thousand soules, of yong and lustie knights;
These were the armes wherewith loue conquered
Their feeble harts, subdew'd in wanton fights:
What wonder if *Achilles* were mis-led,
Or great *Alcides* at their Ladies sights,
   Since these true champions of the Lord aboue
   Were thralles to beautie, yeelden slaues to loue.

The fifth Booke of Godfrey of Bulloigne

The argument.

Gernando *scornes* Rinaldo *should aspire*
To rule that charge, for which he seekes and striues,
And slanders him so far, that in his ire
The wronged knight his foe of life depriues:
Far from the campe the slayer doth retire,
Nor lets himselfe be bound in chaines or giues:
Armide *departs content, and from the seas*
Godfrey *heares newes, which him and his displeas.*

I

WHile thus *Armida* false the knights misled
  In wandring errours of deceitfull loue,
And thought, besides the champions promised,
The other Lordings in her aide to moue,
In *Godfreys* thought a strong contention bred,
Who fittest were this hazard great to proue;
  For all the worthies of th'aduentrers band
  Were like in birth, in powre, in strength of hand.

2

But first the Prince (by graue aduise) decreed
They should some knight chuse (at their owne election)
That in his charge Lord *Dudon* might succeed,
And of that glorious troope should take protection;
So none should grieue, displeased with the deed,
Nor blame the causer of their new subiection:
  Besides *Godfredo* shew'd by this deuice,
  How much he held that regiment in price.

3

He call'd the worthies than, and spake them soe,
'Lordings, you know I yeelded to your will,
And gaue you licence with this Dame to goe,
To win her kingdome, and that tyrant kill:

But now againe I let you further knoe,
In following her it may betide you ill;
   Refraine therefore, and change this forward thought,
   For death vnsent for, danger comes vnsought.

4

'But if to shun these perils, sought so far,
May seem disgracefull to the place you hold;
If graue aduise and prudent counsell, ar
Esteem'd detractors from your courage bold;
Then knowe, I none against his will debar,
Nor what I granted earst I now withhold;
   But be mine empire (as it ought of right)
   Sweet, easie, pleasant, gentle, meeke and light.

5

'Goe than or tarrie, each as likes him best,
Free powre I grant you on this enterprise;
But first in *Dudons* place (now laid in chest)
Chuse you some other captaine, stout and wise:
Then ten appoint among the worthiest,
But let no moe attempt this hard emprise,
   In this my will content you that I haue,
   For powre constrain'd is but a glorious slaue.'

6

Thus *Godfrey* said, and thus his brother spake,
And answer'd for himselfe and all his Peares;
'My Lord, as well it fitteth thee to make
These wise delaies, and cast these doubts and feares:
So tis our part at first to vndertake,
Courage and haste beseemes our might and yeares;
   And this proceeding with so graue aduise,
   Wisedome, in you; in vs, were cowardise.

7

'Since than the feat is easie, danger none,
All set in battell and in hardie fight,
Doe thou permit the chosen ten to gone
And aide the damsell:' thus deuis'd the knight,

To make men thinke the sunne of honour shone,
There where the lampe of *Cupid* gaue the light:
　The rest perceiue his guile, and it approue,
　And call that knighthood, which was childish loue.

8

But louing *Eustace*, that with iealous eie
Beheld the worth of *Sophias* noble childe,
And his faire shape did secretly enuie,
Beside the vertues in his brest compilde,
(And for in loue he would no companie)
He stor'd his mouth with speeches smoothly filde,
　Drawing his riuall to attend his word,
　Thus with faire sleight he laid the knight abord.

9

'Of great *Bertoldo* thou far greater haire,
Thou star of knighthood, flowre of chiualrie,
Tell me, who now shall lead this squadron faire,
Since our late guide in marble cold doth lie?
I, that with famous *Dudon* might compaire
In all, but yeeres, hoare locks, and grauitie,
　To whom should I, Duke *Godfreys* brother, yeeld,
　Vnlesse to thee, the Christian armies sheeld?

10

'Thee (whom high birth makes equall with the best)
Thine actes prefer both me and all beforne,
Nor that in fight thou both surpasse the rest
And *Godfreys* worthie selfe, I hold in scorne,
Thee to obey then am I only prest,
Before these worthies be thine eagle borne,
　This honour haply thou esteemest light,
　Whose day of glorie neuer yet found night.

11

'Yet maist thou further (by this means) display
The spreading wings of thy immortall fame,
I will procure it, if thou saist not nay,
And all their wils to thine election frame:

But for I scantly am resolu'd which way
To bend my force, or where imploy the same,
  Leaue me (I pray) at my discretion, free
  To helpe *Armida*, or serue here with thee.'

12

This last request (for loue is euill to hide)
Empurpled both his cheekes with scarlet read,
Rinaldo soone his passions had describe,
And gently smiling turn'd aside his head,
And, for weake *Cupid* was too feeble eide
To strike him sure, the fire in him was dead;
  So that of riualls was he nought affraid,
  Nor car'd he for the iourney or the maid:

13

But in his noble thought reuolu'd he oft
Dudons high prowesse, death and buriall,
And how *Argantes* bore his plumes aloft,
Praising his fortune for that worthies fall;
Besides, the knights sweet words and praises soft
To his due honour did him fitly call,
  And made his hart reioice, for well he knew
  (Though much he prais'd him) all his words were trew.

14

'Degrees (quoth he) of honours hie to hold,
I would them first deserue, and then desire;
And were my valour such as you haue told,
Would I for that to higher place aspire:
But if to honours due raise me you would,
I will not of my works refuse the hire;
  And much it glads me, that my powre and might
  Ipraised is by such a valiant knight.

15

'I neither seeke it, nor refuse the place,
Which if I get, the praise and thanks be thine.'
Eustace (this spoken) hied thence apace
To know which way his fellowes harts incline:

But Prince *Gernando* coueted the place,
Whom though *Armida* sought to vndermine,
  Gainst him yet vaine did all her engins proue,
  His pride was such, there was no place for loue.

16

Gernando was the king of Norwaies sonne,
That many a realme and region had to guide,
And for his elders lands and crownes had wonne,
His hart was puffed vp with endlesse pride:
The other boasts more what himselfe had donne
Than all his ancestors great actes beside;
  Yet his forefathers old before him weare
  Famous in war and peace, fiue hundreth yeare.

17

This barb'rous Prince, who only vainly thought
That blisse in wealth and kingly powre doth lie,
And in respect esteem'd all vertue nought,
Vnlesse it were adorn'd with titles hie,
Could not endure, that to the place he sought
A simple knight should dare to prease so nie;
  And in his brest so boiled fell despite,
  That ire and wrath exiled reason quite.

18

The hidden deuill, that lies in close awate
To win the fort of vnbeleeuing man,
Found entrie there, where ire vndid the gate,
And in his bosome vnperceiued ran,
It fild his hart with malice, strife and hate,
It made him rage, blaspheme, sweare, curse and ban,
  Inuisible it still attends him neare,
  And thus each minute whisp'reth in his eare.

19

'What, shall *Rinaldo* match thee? dares he tell
Those idle names of his vaine pedegree?
Then let him say (if thee he would excell)
What lands, what realmes his tributaries bee:

If his forefathers in the graues that dwell,
Were honored like thine that liue, let see,
   Oh how dares one so meane aspire so hie,
   Borne in that seruile countrie Italie?

20

'Now, if he win, or if he lose the day,
Yet is his praise and glorie hence derived,
For that the world will (to his credit) say,
Loe, this is he that with *Gernando* striued.
The charge some-deale thee haply honour may,
That noble *Dudon* had while here he liued;
   But laid on him, he would the office shame,
   Let it suffice, he durst desire the same.

21

'If when this breath from mans fraile bodie flies,
The soule take keepe, or know the things done heare,
Oh! how lookes *Dudon* from the glorious skies?
What wrath: what anger in his face appeare?
On this proud yongling while he bends his eies,
Marking how high he doth his feathers reare?
   Seeing his rash attempt, how soone he dare
   (Though but a boy) with his great worth compare.

22

'He dares not only, but he striues and proues,
Where chastisement were fit, there winnes he praise:
One counsels him, his speech, him forward moues;
Another foole approueth all he saies:
If *Godfrey* fauour him more than behoues,
Why then he wrongeth thee an hundreth waies;
   Nor let thy state so far disgraced bee,
   But what thou art and canst, let *Godfrey* see.'

23

With such false words the kindled fire began
To euerie vaine his pois'ned heat to reach,
It swell'd his scornefull hart, and forth it ran
At his proud lookes, and to audacious speach;

All that he thought blame-worthie in the man,
To his disgrace, that would he each-where preach;
   He term'd him proud and vaine, his worth in fight
   He call'd foole-hardice, rashnes, madnes, right.

24

All that in him was rare or excellent,
All that was good, all that was princely found,
With such sharpe words as malice could inuent,
He blam'd (such powre hath wicked tongue to wound)
The youth (for euerie where those rumours went)
Of these reproches heard sometimes the sound;
   Nor did for that his tongue the fault amend,
   Vntill it brought him to his wofull end.

25

The cursed feend that set his tongue at large,
Still bred moe fancies in his idle braine,
His hart with slanders new did ouercharge,
And soothed him still in his angrie vaine:
Amid the campe a place was broad and large,
Where one faire regiment might easly traine;
   And there, in Tilt and harmlesse Turnament
   Their daies of rest, the youthes and gallants spent.

26

There (as his fortune would it should betide)
Amid the prease *Gernando* gan retire,
To vomit out his venome vnespide,
Wherewith foule enuie did his hart inspire.
Rinaldo heard him as he stood beside,
And (as he could not bridle wrath and ire)
   'Thou liest', cride he lowd, and with that word
   About his head he tost his flaming sword.

27

Thunder his voice, and lightning seem'd his brand,
So fell his looke and furious was his cheare,
Gernando trembled, for he saw at hand
Pale death, and neither helpe nor comfort neare;

Yet for the soldiers all to witnes stand,
He made proud signe as though he nought did feare,
   But brauely drew his little helping blade,
   And valiant shew of strong resistance made.

28

With that a thousand blades of burnisht steele
Glistred on heaps, like flames of fire in sight,
Hundreds, that knew not yet the quarell weele,
Ranne thither, some to gaze and some to fight:
The emptie aire a sound confus'd did feele
Of murmurs low and outcries lowd on hight,
   Like rolling waues, and Boreas angrie blasts,
   When roaring seas against the rocks he casts.

29

But not for this the wronged warrior staid
His iust displeasure, and incensed ire,
He car'd not what the vulgar did or said,
To vengeance did his courage fierce aspire:
Among the thickest weapons way he maid,
His thundring sword made all on heapes retire,
   So that of nere a thousand staid not one,
   But prince *Gernando* bore the brunt alone.

30

His hand (too quicke to execute his wrath)
Performed all, as pleas'd his eie and hart,
At head and brest oft times he strooken hath,
Now at the right, now at the other part:
On euerie side thus did he harme and scath,
And oft beguil'd his sight with nimble art,
   That no defence the Prince of wounds acquits,
   Where least he thinkes, or feares, there most he hits.

31

Nor ceased he, till in *Gernandos* brest
He sheathed once or twice his furious blade;
Downe fell the haplesse Prince with death opprest,
A double way to his weake soule was made,

His bloodie sword the victor wipte and drest:
Nor longer by the slaughtred bodie staide,
  But sped him thence, and soone appeased hath
  His hate, his ire, his rancour and his wrath.

32

Call'd by the tumult, *Godfrey* drew him neare,
And there beheld a sad and rufull sight,
The signes of death vpon his face appeare,
With dust and blood his locks were loathly dight,
Sighes and complaints on each side might he heare,
Made for the sudden death of that great knight:
  Amaz'd, he askt who durst and did so much;
  For yet he knew not whom the fault would tuch.

33

Arnoldo, minion of the Prince thus slaine,
Augments the fault in telling it, and saith,
'This Prince is murdred, for a quarrell vaine,
By yong *Rinaldo*, in his desp'rate wraith,
And with that sword, that should Christs law maintaine,
One of Christs champions bold he killed haith,
  And this he did, in such a place and howre,
  As if he scorn'd your rule, despis'd your powre.'

34

And further ads, that he deserued death
By law, and law should be inuiolate,
That none offence could greater be vneath,
And yet the place the fault did aggrauate:
If he escapte, that mischiefe would take breath,
And flourish bold, in spite of rule and state;
  And that *Gernandos* friends would venge the wrong,
  Although to iustice that should first belong.

35

And by that meanes, should discord, hate and strife
Raise mutinies, and what thereof ensu'th:
Lastly he prais'd the dead, and still had rife
All words he thought could veng'ance moue or ruth.

Against him *Tancred* argued for life,
With honest reasons to excuse the yuth:
   The Duke heard all, but with such sober cheare,
   As banisht hope, and still encreased feare.

36

'Graue Prince (quoth *Tancred*) set before thine eies
Rinaldos worth and courage, what it is,
How much our hope of conquest in him lies;
Regard that princely house and race of his;
He that correcteth euerie fault he spies,
And iudgeth all alike, doth all amis;
   For faultes (you know) are greater thought or lesse,
   As is the persons selfe, that doth transgresse.'

37

Godfredo answer'd him, 'if high and low
Of soueraigne powre alike should feele the stroke,
Than *Tancred* ill you counsell vs (I trow)
If Lords should know no law as earst you spoke,
How vile and base our empire were you know,
If none but slaues and peasants beare the yoke;
   Weake is the scepter and the powre is small,
   That such prouisoes brings annext withall.

38

'But mine was freely giuen ere it was sought,
Nor that it lesned be, I now consent;
Right well know I both when and where I ought
To giue condigne reward, and punishment,
Since you are all in like subiection brought,
Both high and low obey, and be content.'
   This heard, *Tancredie* wisely staid his words,
   Such weight the sayings haue of kings and Lords.

39

Old *Raymond* prais'd his speech (for old men thinke
They euer wisest seeme when most seuere)

'Tis best (quoth he) to make these great ones shrinke,
The people loue him whom the nobles feare:
There must the rule to all disorders sinke,
Where pardons, more than punishment, appeare;
  For feeble is each kingdome, fraile and weake,
  Vnlesse his basis be this feare I speake.'

40

These words *Tancredie* heard and pondred well,
And by them wist how *Godfreys* thoughts were bent,
Nor list he longer with these old men dwell,
But turn'd his horse and to *Rinaldo* went,
Who when his noble foe death wounded fell,
Withdrew him softly to his gorgeous tent;
  There *Tancred* found him, and at large declar'd
  The words and speeches sharpe, which late you hard.

41

And said, 'although I wot the outward show
Is not true witnes of the secret thought,
For that some men so subtill are I trow,
That what they purpose most, appeereth nought;
Yet dare I say *Godfredo* meanes I know,
(Such knowledge hath his lookes and speeches wrought)
  You shall first prisner be, and then be tride,
  As he shall deeme it good, and law prouide.'

42

With that a bitter smile well might you see
Rinaldo cast, with scorne and hie disdaine,
'Let them in fetters plead their cause (quoth hee)
That are base peasants, borne of seruile straine,
I was free borne, I liue, and will die free,
Before these feet be fettred in a chaine:
  These hands were made to shake sharp spears & swords,
  Not to be tide in giues and twisted cords.

42² *Ridaldo* < *Rinaldo*

43

'If my good seruice reape this recompence,
To be clapt vp in close and secret mew,
And as a theefe be after dragd from thence,
To suffer punishment, as law findes dew;
Let *Godfrey* come or send, I will not hence,
Vntill we know who shall this bargaine rew,
  That of our tragedie the late done fact,
  May be the first, and this the second, act.

44

'Giue me mine armes' he cride; his squire them brings,
And clad his head and brest in iron strong,
About his necke his siluer shield he flings,
Downe by his side a cutting sword there hong;
Among this earthes braue Lords, and mightie kings,
Was none so stout, so fierce, so faire, so yong,
  God *Mars* he seem'd descending from his spheare,
  Or one whose lookes could make great *Mars* to feare.

45

Tancredie labour'd with some pleasing speach
His spirits fierce and courage to appease:
'Yong Prince, thy valour' (thus he gan to preach)
'Can chastise all that doe thee wrong, at ease,
I know your vertue can your enemies teach,
That you can venge you when and where you please:
  But God forbid this day you lift your arme,
  To doe this campe, and vs your friends, such harme.

46

'Tell me what will you doe? why would you staine
Your noble hands in our vnguiltie blood?
By wounding Christians will you againe
Pearse Christ, whose parts they are and members good?
Will you destroy vs for your glorie vaine,
Vnstaid as rolling waues in Ocean flood?
  Far be it from you so to proue your strength,
  And let your zeale appease your rage at length.

47

'For Gods loue stay your heat, and iust displeasure,
Appease your wrath, your courage fierce asswage,
Patience, a praise; forbearance, is a treasure;
Suffrance, an angell is; a monster, rage:
At least your actions by ensample measure,
And thinke how I in mine vnbridled age
   Was wronged, yet I nould reuengement take
   On all this campe, for one offenders sake.

48

'Cilicia conquer'd I, as all men wot,
And there the glorious crosse on hie I reared,
But *Baldwine* came, and what I nobly got
Bereft me falsly, when I least him feared;
He seem'd my friend, and I discouer'd not
His secret couetise which since appeered;
   Yet striue I not to get mine owne by fight,
   Or ciuill war, although perchance I might.

49

'If than you scorne to be in prison pent,
If bonds, as hie disgrace, your hands refuse;
Or if your thoughts still to maintaine are bent
Your libertie, as men of honour vse:
To Antioch what if forthwith you went?
And leaue me here your absence to excuse,
   There with Prince *Boemond* liue in ease and peace,
   Vntill this storme of *Godfreys* anger cease.

50

'For soone, if forces come from Egypt land,
Or other nations that vs here confine,
Godfrey will beaten be with his owne wand,
And feele he wants that valour great of thine,
Our campe may seeme an arme without a hand,
Amid our troopes vnlesse thy eagle shine:'
   With that came *Guelpho* and those words approued,
   And praid him goe, if him he fear'd or loued.

51

Their speeches soften much the warriors hart,
And make his wilfull thoughts at last relent,
So that he yeelds, and saith he will depart,
And leaue the Christian campe incontinent.
His friends, whose loue did neuer shrinke or start,
Profred their aide, what way so ere he went:
    He thankt them all, but left them all, besides
    Two bold and trustie squires, and so he rides.

52

He rides, reuoluing in his noble spright
Such hawtie thoughts, as fill the glorious minde;
On hard aduentures was his whole delight,
And now to wondrous actes his will inclinde;
Alone against the Pagans would he fight,
And kill their kings from Egypt vnto Inde,
    From Cinthias hils, and Nilus vnknowne spring,
    He would fetch praise and glorious conquest bring.

53

But *Guelpho* (when the Prince his leaue had take,
And now had spurr'd his courser on his way)
No longer tarriance with the rest would make,
But hastes to finde *Godfredo*, if he may:
Who seeing him approching, forthwith spake,
'*Guelpho* (quoth he) for thee I only stay,
    For thee I sent my heralds all about,
    In euerie tent to seeke and finde thee out.'

54

This said, he softly drew the knight aside
Where none might heare, and then bespake him thus:
'How chanceth it thy nephewes rage and pride,
Makes him so far forget himselfe and vs?
Hardly could I beleeue what is betide,
A murder done for cause so friuolous,
    How I haue lou'd him, thou and all can tell;
    But *Godfrey* lou'd him, but whil'st he did well.

55

'I must prouide that euerie one haue right,
That all be heard, each cause be well discust,
As far from partiall loue, as free from spight,
I heare complaints, yet nought but proues I trust:
Now if *Rinaldo* weigh our rule so light,
And haue the sacred lore of war so brust,
  Take you the charge that he before vs come,
  To cleare himselfe and heare our vpright dome.

56

'But let him come withouten bond or chaine,
For still my thoughts to doe him grace are framed:
But if our powre he haply shall disdaine,
(As well I know his courage yet vntamed)
To bring him by perswasion take some paine:
Else, if I proue seuere, both you be blamed,
  That force my gentle nature (gainst my thought)
  To rigor, least our lawes returne to nought.'

57

Lord *Guelpho* answered thus: what hart can beare
Such slanders false, deuis'd by hate and spight?
Or with staid patience, reproches heare,
And not reuenge by battaile and by fight?
The Norway Prince hath bought his follie deare,
But who with words could stay the angrie knight?
  A foole is he that comes to preach or prate,
  When men with swords their right and wrong debate.

58

'And where you wish he should himselfe submit
To heare the censure of your vpright lawes;
Alas, that cannot be, for he is flit
Out of this campe, withouten stay or pause.
There take my gage, behold I offer it
To him that first accus'd him in this cause,
  Or any else that dare, and will maintaine
  That for his pride the Prince was iustly slaine.

59

'I say with reason Lord *Gernandos* pride
He hath abated, if he haue offended
Gainst your commands, who are his Lord and guide,
Oh pardon him, that fault shall be amended.'
'If he be gone (quoth *Godfrey*) let him ride
And braule elsewhere, here let all strife be ended:
    And you Lord *Guelpho*, for your nephewes sake,
    Breed vs no new, nor quarrels old awake.'

60

This while, the faire and false *Armida* striued
To get her promist aide, in sure possession,
The day to end, with endlesse plaint, she driued;
Wit, beautie, craft for her made intercession:
But when the earth was once of light depriued,
And westren seas felt *Titans* hot impression,
    Twixt two old knights, and matrons twaine she went,
    Where pitched was her faire and curious tent.

61

But this false Queene of craft and slie inuention,
(Whose lookes, loues arrowes were; whose eies, his quiuers;
Whose beautie matchlesse, free from reprehension,
(A wonder left by heau'n to after liuers)
Among the Christian Lords had bred contention,
Who first should quench his flames in *Cupids* riuers,
    With all her weapons and her darts rehersed,
    Had not *Godfredos* constant bosome persed.

62

To change his modest thought the dame procureth,
And profreth heapes of loues entising treasure:
But as the faulcon newly gorg'd endureth
Her keeper lure her oft, but comes at leasure;
So he, whom fulnesse of delight assureth,
What long repentance comes of loues short pleasure,
    Her crafts, her artes, her selfe and all despiseth,
    So base affections fall, when vertue riseth.

63

And not one foot his stedfast foot was moued
Out of that heau'nly path, wherein he paced,
Yet thousand wiles, and thousand waies, she proued,
To haue that castle faire of goodnes raced:
She vs'd those lookes and smiles, that most behoued
To melt the frost which his hard hart imbraced,
   And gainst his brest a thousand shot she ventred,
   Yet was the fort so strong it was not entred.

64

The Dame who thought that one blinke of her eie,
Could make the chastest hart feele loues sweet paine,
Oh, how her pride abated was hereby!
When all her sleights were voide, her crafts were vaine,
Some other where she would her forces trie,
Where at more ease she might more vantage gaine,
   As tired soldiers whom some fort keepes out,
   Thence raise their siege, and spoile the townes about.

65

But yet al waies the wilie witch could finde,
Could not *Tancredies* hart to loue-ward moue,
His sailes were filled with another winde,
He list no blast of new affection proue;
For, as one poison doth exclude by kinde
Anothers force, so loue excludeth loue:
   These two alone nor more, nor lesse the Dame
   Could win, the rest all burnt in her sweet flame.

66

The Princesse (though her purpose would not frame,
As late she hoped, and as still she would)
Yet, for the Lords and knights of greatest name
Became her pray, as earst you heard it told;
She thought, ere truth-reuealing time, or fame
Bewraid her act, to lead them to some hold,
   Where chains & bands she meant to make them proue,
   Compos'd by *Vulcan*, not by gentle loue.

65¹ alwaies < al waies

67

The time prefixt at length was come and past,
Which *Godfrey* had set downe, to lend her aid,
When at his feet her selfe to earth she cast,
'The howre is come (my Lord)' she humbly said;
'And if the tyrant haply heare at last,
His banisht neece hath your assistance praid,
   He will in armes (to saue his kingdome) rise,
   So shall we harder make this enterprise.

68

'Before report can bring the tyrant newes,
Or his espials certifie their king,
O let thy goodnes these few champions chuse,
That to her kingdome should thy handmaid bring;
Who, except heauen to aide the right refuse,
Recouer shall her crowne, from whence shall spring
   Thy profit; for betide thee peace or war,
   Thine all her cities, all her subiects ar.'

69

The captaine sage the damsell faire assured,
His word was past, and should not be recanted,
And she with sweet and humble grace endured
To let him point those ten, which late he granted:
But to be one, each one sought and procured,
No suit, entreatie, intercession wanted;
   Their enuie each at others loue exceeded,
   And all importunate made, more than needed.

70

She (that well saw the secret of their harts)
And knew how best to warme them in their blood,
Against them threw the cursed poyson'd darts
Of iealousie, and griefe at others good,
For loue she wist was weake without those arts,
And slow; for iealousie, is *Cupids* food;
   For the swift steed runs not so fast alone,
   As when some straine, some striue him to outgone.

71

Her words in such alluring sort she framed,
Her lookes entising, and her wowing smiles,
That euerie one his fellowes fauours blamed,
That of their mistris he receiu'd erewhiles:
This foolish crew of louers, vnashamed,
Mad with the poyson of her secret wiles,
    Ran forward still, in this disordred sort,
    Nor could *Godfredoes* bridle raine them short.

72

He that would satisfie each good desire
(Withouten partiall loue) of euerie knight,
Although he sweld with shame, with griefe and ire,
To see these follies, and these fashions light;
Yet since by no aduice they would retire,
Another way he sought, to set them right:
    'Write all your names (quoth he) and see whom chance
    Of lot, to this exploit will first aduance.'

73

Their names were writ, and in a helmet shaken,
While each did fortunes grace and aid implore;
At last they drew them, and the formost taken
The Earle of Pembrooke was, *Artimidore*,
Doubtlesse the Countie thought his bread well baken;
Next *Gerrard* follow'd, then with tresses hore
    Old *Wenceslaus*, that felt *Cupids* rage
    Now in his doting, and his dying age.

74

Oh how contentment in their foreheads shined!
Their lookes with ioy; thoughts sweld with secret pleasure,
These three it seemed good successe desined
To make the Lords of loue, and beauties treasure:
Their doubtfull fellowes at their hap repined,
And with small patience wait fortunes leasure,
    Vpon his lips that red the scrowles attending,
    As if their liues were on his words depending.

75

Guascar the fourth, *Ridolpho* him succeedes,
Then *Vldericke* whom loue list so aduance,
Lord *William* of Ronciglion next he reedes,
Then *Eberard*, and *Henrie* borne in France,
Rambaldo last, whom wicked lust so leedes,
That he forsooke his Sauiour with mischance;
    This wretch the tenth was, who was thus deluded,
    The rest to their huge griefe were all excluded.

76

Orecome with enuie, wrath and iealousie,
The rest blinde fortune curse, and all her lawes,
And mad with loue, yet out on loue they crie,
That in his kingdome let her iudge their cause:
And for mans minde is such, that oft we trie
Things most forbidden, without stay or pause,
    In spite of fortune, purpos'd many a knight,
    To follow faire *Armida* when 'twas night.

77

To follow her, by night or else by day,
And in her quarell venture life and lim:
With sighes and teares she gan them softly pray
To keepe that promise, when the skies were dim,
To this and that knight, did she plaine, and say
What griefe she felt to part withouten him:
    Meane-while the ten had dond their armour best,
    And taken leaue of *Godfrey* and the rest.

78

The Duke aduis'd them euery one apart,
How light, how trustlesse was the Pagans faith,
And told what policie, what wit, what art,
Auoides deceit, which heedlesse men betrai'th;
His speeches pearse their eare, but not their hart,
Loue calles it follie, what so wisdome saith:
    Thus warn'd he leaues them to their wanton guide,
    Who parts that night; such haste had she to ride.

79

The conqueresse departs, and with her led
These prisoners, whom loue would captiue keepe,
The harts of those she left behinde her, bled,
With point of sorrowes arrow pearsed deepe.
But when the night her drousie mantle spred,
And fild the earth with silence, shade and sleepe,
   In secret sort then each forsooke his tent,
   And as blinde *Cupid* led them, blinde they went.

80

Eustatio first, who scantly could forbeare,
Till friendly night might hide his haste and shame,
He road in poste, and let his beast him beare
As his blinde fancie would his iourney frame,
All night he wandred and he wist not wheare;
But with the morning he espide the Dame,
   That with her gard vp from a village rode,
   Where she and they that night had made abode.

81

Thither he gallopt fast, and drawing nere
Rambaldo knew the knight, and lowdly cride,
'Whence comes yong *Eustace*, and what seekes he here?'
'I come (quoth he) to serue the Queene *Armide*,
If she accept me, would we all were there
Where my good-will and faith might best be tride.'
   'Who (quoth the other) chuseth thee to proue
   This hie exploit of hers?' he answered, 'loue.'

82

'Loue hath *Eustatio* chosen, fortune thee,
In thy conceit which is the best election?'
'Nay then these shiftes are vaine,' replied hee,
'These titles false serue thee for no protection,
Thou canst not here for this admitted bee
Our fellow seruant, in this sweete subiection.'
   'And who (quoth *Eustace* angrie) dares denie
   My fellowship?' *Rambaldo* answered, 'I.'

83

And with that word his cutting sword he drew,
That glistred bright and sparkled flaming fire,
Vpon his foe the other champion flew,
With equall courage and with equall ire.
The gentle Princesse (who the danger knew)
Betweene them stept and prai'd them both retire.
 '*Rambald* (quoth she) why should you grudge or plaine,
 If I a champion, you an helper gaine?

84

'If me you loue, why wish you me depriued
(In so great need) of such a puissant knight?
But welcome *Eustace*, in good time arriued,
Defender of my state, my life, my right,
I wish my haplesse selfe no longer liued,
When I esteeme such good assistance light:'
 Thus talkt they on and trauail'd on their way,
 Their fellowship encreasing euery day.

85

From euerie side they come, yet wist there none
Of others comming or of others minde,
She welcomes all, and telleth euerie one,
What ioy her thoughts in his arriuall finde.
But when Duke *Godfrey* wist his knights were gone,
Within his brest his wiser soule deuinde
 Some hard mishap vpon his friends should light,
 For which he sigh'd all day, and wept all night.

86

A messenger (while thus he mus'd) drew neare,
All soil'd with dust and sweat, quite out of breath,
It seem'd the man did heauie tidings beare,
Vpon his lookes sat newes of losse and death:
'My Lord (quoth he) so many ships appeare
At sea, that *Neptune* beares the load vneath,
 From Egypt come they all, this lets thee weete
 William Lord Amrall of the Genoa fleete.

83² sparled < sparkled *as corrected in* B

87

'Besides, a conuoy (comming from the shore
With vittaile for this noble campe of thine)
Surprised was, and lost is all that store,
Mules, horses, camels loden, corne and wine,
Thy seruants fought till they could fight no more;
For all were slaine or captiues made in fine:
   Th'Arabian outlawes them assail'd by night,
   When least they fear'd, and least they lookt for fight.

88

'Their franticke boldnes doth presume so far,
That many Christians haue they falsly slaine,
And like a raging flood they sparsed ar,
And ouerflow each countrie, field and plaine;
Send therefore some strong troopes of men of war,
To force them hence, and driue them home againe,
   And keepe the waies betweene these tents of thine,
   And those broad seas, the seas of Palestine.'

89

From mouth to mouth the heauie rumour spred
Of these misfortunes, which dispersed wide
Among the soldiers, great amasement bred,
Famine they doubt and new come foes beside:
The Duke (that saw their woonted courage fled,
And in the place thereof weake feare espide)
   With merrie lookes these cheerefull words he spake,
   To make them hart againe and courage take.

90

'You champions bold, with me that scaped haue
So many dangers, and such hard assaies,
Whom still your God did keepe, defend and saue,
In all your battailes, combats, fights and fraies,
You that subdew'd the Turks and Persians braue,
That thirst and hunger held in scorne alwaies,
   And vanquisht hils, and seas, with heat and cold,
   Shall vaine reports appall your courage bold?

91

'That Lord, who helpt you out at euerie need,
When ought befell this glorious campe amis,
Shall fortune all your actions well to speed,
On whom his mercie large extended is;
Tofore his tombe, when conquering hands you spreed,
With what delite will you remember this?
  Be strong therefore, and keepe your valours hie
  To honour, conquest, fame and victorie.'

92

Their hope's halfe dead and courage well-nie lost,
Reuiu'd, with these braue speeches of their guide;
But in his brest a thousand cares he tost,
Although his sorrowes he could wisely hide;
He studied how to feed that mightie host,
In so great scarcenesse; and what force prouide
  He should, against th'Egyptian warriors slie,
  And how subdue those theeues of Arabie.

The sixth Booke *of* Godfrey *of* Bulloigne

The argument.

Argantes *calles the Christians out to iust:*
Otho *not chosen doth his strength assay,*
But from his saddle tumbleth in the dust,
And captiue to the towne is sent away:
Tancred *begins new fight and when both trust*
To win the praise and palme, night ends the fray:
Erminia *hopes to cure her wounded knight,*
And from the citie armed rides by night.

I

BVt better hopes had them recomforted
 That lay besieged in the sacred towne;
With new supplie late were they vittailed,
When night obscur'd the earth with shadowes browne,
Their armes and engins on the walles they spred,
Their slings to cast and stones to tumble downe;
  And all that side which to the northward lies;
  High rampires and strong bulwarks fortifies.

2

Their warie king commands now here now there,
To build this towre, to make that bulwarke strong,
Whither the sunne, the moone, or stars appere,
To giue them light, to worke no time comes wrong:
In euerie street new weapons forged were,
By cunning smithes, sweating with labour long;
  While thus the carefull Prince prousion maide,
  To him *Argantes* came, and boasting said.

3

'How long shall we (like prisoners in chaines)
Captiued lie inclos'd within this wall?
I see your workmen taking endlesse paines
To make new weapons for no vse at all;

Meane-while these westren theeues destroy the plaines,
Your townes are burnt, your forts and castels fall,
　Yet none of vs dares at these gates out-peepe,
　Or sound one trumpet shrill to breake their sleepe.

4

'Their time in feasting and good cheere they spend,
Nor dare we once their bankets sweet molest,
The daies and nights they bring likewise to end,
In peace, assurance, quiet, ease and rest:
But we must yeeld, whom hunger soone will shend,
And make for peace (to saue our liues) request,
　Else (if th'Egyptian armie stay too long)
　Like cowards die within this fortresse strong.

5

'Yet neuer shall my courage great consent
So vile a death should end my noble daies,
Nor on mine armes, within these walles ipent,
To morrowes sun shall spread his timely raies:
Let sacred heau'ns dispose (as they are bent)
Of this fraile life, yet not withouten praise
　Of valour, prowesse, might, *Argantes* shall
　Inglorious die, or vnreuenged fall.

6

'But if the rootes of wonted chiualrie
Be not quite dead, your princely brest within,
Deuise not how with fame and praise to die,
But how to liue, to conquer and to win;
Let vs together at these gates out-flie,
And skirmish bold, and bloodie fight begin;
　For when last need to desperation driueth,
　Who dareth most, he wisest counsell giueth.

7

'But if in field your wisdome dare not venter
To hazard all your troopes to doubtfull fight,
Then binde your selfe to *Godfrey* by endenter,
To end your quarels, by one single knight:

And, for the Christian this accord shall enter
With better will, say such you know your right,
   That he the weapons, place and time, shall chuse,
   And let him for his best, that vantage vfe.

8

'For though your foe had hands, like *Hector* strong,
With hart vnfear'd, and courage sterne and stout,
Yet no misfortune can your iustice wrong,
And what that wanteth, shall this arme helpe out,
In spite of fate shall this right hand ere long,
Returne victorious: if hereof you dout,
   Take it for pledge, wherein if trust you haue,
   It shall your selfe defend and kingdome saue.'

9

'Bold youth' (the tyrant thus began to speake)
'Although I with'red seeme with age and yeares,
Yet are not these old armes so faint and weake,
Nor this hoare head so full of doubts and feares;
But when as death this vitall threed shall breake,
He shall my courage heare, my death who heares:
   And *Aladine* that liu'd a king and knight,
   To his faire morne will haue an euening bright.

10

'But that (which yet I would haue further blaised)
To thee in secret shall be told and spoken,
Great *Soliman* of Nice (so far ipraised,
To be reuenged, for his scepter broken)
The men of armes of Arabie hath raised,
From Inde to Afrike, and (when we giue token)
   Attends the fauour of the friendly night
   To vittaile vs, and with our foes to fight.

11

'Now though *Godfredo* hold by warlike feat
Some castles poore, and fortes in vile oppression,
Care not for that; for still our princely seat,
This stately towne, we keepe in our possession:

But thou appease and calme that courage great,
Which in thy bosome makes so hot impression;
   And stay fit time, which will betide ere long,
   T'encrease thy glorie, and reuenge our wrong.'

12

The Saracine at this was inly spited,
Who *Solimans* great worth had long enuied,
To heare him praised thus he nought delited,
Nor that the king vpon his aide relied:
'Within your powre (sir king) he saies, vnited
Are peace and war, nor shall that be denied;
   But for the Turke and his Arabian band,
   He lost his owne, shall he defend your land?

13

'Perchance he comes some heau'nly messengare,
Sent downe to set the Pagan people free,
Then let *Argantes* for himselfe take care:
This sword (I trust) shall well safeconduct mee:
But while you rest and all your forces spare,
That I goe foorth to war at least agree,
   Though not your champion, yet a priuate knight,
   I will some Christian proue in single fight.'

14

The king replied, 'though thy force and might
Should be reseru'd, to better time and vse;
Yet that thou challenge some renowned knight,
Among the Christians bold I not refuse.'
The warrior breathing out desire of fight,
An herald call'd, and said, 'go tell these newes
   To *Godfreys* selfe, and to the westren Lords,
   And in their hearings boldly say these words.

15

'Say that a knight (who holds in great disdaine
To be thus closed vp in secret mew)
Will with his sword in open field maintaine,
(If any dare denie his words for trew)

That no deuotion (as they falsly faine)
Hath mou'd the French these countries to subdew;
    But vile ambition, and prides hatefull vice,
    Desire of rule and spoile, and couetice.

16

'And that to fight I am not only prest
With one or two that dare defend the cause,
But come the fourth or fift, come all the rest,
Come all that will, and all that weapon drawes,
Let him that yeelds obey the victors hest,
As wils the lore of mightie *Mars* his lawes:'
    This was the challenge that fierce Pagan sent,
    The herald dond his coate of armes, and went.

17

And when the man before the presence came
Of princely *Godfrey*, and his captaines bold;
'My Lord (quoth he) may I withouten blame
Before your grace, my message braue vnfold?'
'Thou maist,' he answer'd, 'we approue the same,
Withouten feare, be thine ambassage told.'
    'Then (quoth the herald) shall your highnes see,
    If this ambassage sharpe or pleasing bee.'

18

The challenge gan he then at large expose,
With mightie threats, high termes and glorious words,
On euerie side an angrie murmur rose,
To wrath so moued were the knights and Lords.
Then *Godfrey* spake and said, 'the man hath chose
An hard exploit, but when he feeles our swords,
    I trust we shall so faire intreat the knight,
    As to excuse the fourth or fift of fight.

19

'But let him come and proue, the field I grant,
Nor wrong nor treason let him doubt or feare,
Some here shall pay him for his glorious vant,
Without or guile or vantage, that I sweare.'

The herald turn'd when he had ended scant,
And hasted backe the way he came whileare,
　　Nor staid he ought, nor once foreslow'd his pace,
　　Till he bespake *Argantes* face to face.

20

'Arme you, my Lord, he said, your bold defies
By your braue foes accepted boldly beene,
This combat neither high nor low denies,
Ten thousand wish to meete you on the greene;
A thousand frown'd with angrie flaming eies,
And shakt for rage their swords and weapons keene;
　　The field is safely granted by their guide,'
　　This said, the champion for his armour cride.

21

While he was arm'd, his hart for ire nie brake,
So earned his courage hot his foe to finde:
The king, to faire *Clorinda* present, spake;
'If he goe foorth, remaine not you behinde,
But of our soldiers best a thousand take,
To garde his person and your owne assignde;
　　Yet let him meete alone the Christian knight,
　　And stand yourselfe aloofe, while they two fight.'

22

Thus spake the king, and soone without aboad
The troope went forth in shining armour clad,
Before the rest the Pagan champion road,
His wonted armes and ensignes all he had:
A goodly plaine displayed wide and broad,
Betweene the citie and the campe was sprad,
　　A place like that wherein proud Rome beheild
　　Her forward yong men menage speare and shield.

23

There all alone *Argantes* tooke his stand,
Defying Christ, and all his seruants trew,

22⁸ He < Her

In stature, stomacke, and in strength of hand,
In pride, presumption, and in dreadfull shew,
Encelade like, on the Phlegrean strand,
Or that huge giant *Ishaies* infant slew;
   But his fierce semblant they esteemed light,
   For most not knew, or else not fear'd, his might.

24

As yet not one had *Godfrey* singled out
To vndertake this hardie enterpries,
But on prince *Tancred* saw he all the rout
Had fixt their wishes, and had cast their eies,
On him he spide them gazing round about,
As though their honour on his prowesse lies,
   And now they whispred lowder what they ment,
   Which *Godfrey* heard and saw, and was content.

25

The rest gaue place; for euerie one describe
To whom their chieftaines will did most incline,
'*Tancred* (quoth he) I pray thee calme the pride,
Abate the rage, of yonder Sarracine:'
No longer would the chosen champion bide,
His face with ioy, his eies with gladnes shine,
   His helme he tooke, and readie steed bestroad,
   And guarded with his trustie friends, forth road.

26

But scantly had he spurr'd his courser swift
Neere to that plaine, where proud *Argantes* staid,
When vnawares his eies he chanst to lift,
And on the hill beheld the warlike maid,
As white as snowe vpon the Alpine clift
The virgin shone, in siluer armes arraid,
   Her ventall vp so hie, that he describe
   Her goodly visage, and her beauties pride.

27

He saw not where the Pagan stood, and stared,
As if with lookes he would his foeman kill,

But full of other thoughts he forward fared,
And sent his lookes before him vp the hill,
His gesture such his troubled soule declared,
At last as marble rocke he standeth still,
    Stone-cold, without; within, burnt with loues flame,
    And quite forgot himselfe, and why he came.

28

The challenger, that yet sawe none appeare
That made or signe or shew he came to iust,
'How long (cride he) shall I attend you heare?
Dares none come forth? dares none his fortune trust?'
The other stood amaz'd, loue stopt his eare,
He thinks on *Cupid*, thinke of *Mars* who lust;
    But forth start *Otho* bold, and tooke the field,
    A gentle knight, whom God from danger shield.

29

This youth was one of those, who late desired
With that vaine-glorious boaster to haue fought,
But *Tancred* chosen, he and all retired:
Yet to the field the valiant Prince they brought,
Now when his slacknes he a while admired,
And saw else-where employed was his thought,
    Nor that to iust (though chosen) once he profred,
    He boldly tooke that fit occasion offred.

30

No tyger, panther, spotted leopard,
Runs halfe so swift, the forrests wilde among,
As this yong champion hasted thitherward,
Where he attending saw the Pagan strong:
Tancredie started with the noise he hard,
As wakt from sleepe, where he had dreamed long,
    'Oh stay he cride, to me belongs this war,'
    But cride too late, *Otho* was gone too far.

31

Then full of furie, anger and despite,
He staid his horse, and waxed red for shame,

The fight was his, but now disgraced quite
Himselfe he thought, another plaid his game;
Meane-while the Sarracine did hugely smite
On *Othoes* helme, who to requite the same,
 His foe quite through his seu'n-fold targe did beare,
 And in his brest-plate stucke and broke his speare.

32

Th'incounter such, vpon the tender gras,
Downe from his steed the Christian backwards fell;
Yet his proud foe so strong and sturdie was,
That he nor shooke, nor staggred in his cell,
But to the knight, that lay full lowe (alas)
In high disdaine his will thus gan he tell,
 'Yeeld thee my slaue, and this thine honour be,
 Thou maist report thou hast encountred me.'

33

'Not so (quoth he) pardie its not the guise
Of Christian knights, though falne, so soone to yeeld;
I can my fall excuse in better wise,
And will reuenge this shame, or die in feeld.'
The great Circassian bent his frowning eies,
Like that grim visage in *Mineruaes* sheeld,
 'Then learne (quoth he) what force *Argantes* vseth
 Against that foole, that profred grace refuseth.'

34

With that he spurr'd his horse with speed and haste,
(Forgetting what good knights to vertue owe)
Otho his furie shunn'd, and (as he past)
At his right side he reacht a noble blowe,
Wide was the wound, the blood outstreamed fast,
And from his side fell to his stirrup lowe:
 But what auailes to hurt, if wounds augment
 Our foes fierce courage, strength and hardiment?

35

Argantes nimbly turn'd his readie stead,
And ere his foe was wist or well aware,

Against his side he droue his coursers head,
What force could he gainst so great might prepare?
Weake were his feeble ioints, his courage dead,
His hart amaz'd, his palenesse shew'd his care,
  His tender side gainst the hard earth he cast,
  Sham'd, with the first fall; bruised, with the last.

36

The victor spurr'd againe his light-foot stead,
And made his passage ouer *Othos* hart,
And cride; these fooles thus vnder foot I tread,
That dare contend with me in equall mart.
Tancred for anger shooke his noble head,
So was he grieu'd with that vnknightly part;
  The fault was his, he was so slowe before,
  With double valour would he salue that sore.

37

Forward he gallopt fast, and lowdly cride:
'Villaine (quoth he) thy conquest is thy shame,
What praise, what honour shall this fact betide?
What gaine, what guerdon shall befall the same?
Among th'Arabian theeues thy face goe hide,
Far from resort of men of worth and same,
  Or else in woods and mountaines wilde, by night,
  On sauage beasts, imploy thy sauage might.'

38

The Pagan patience neuer knew, nor vsed,
Trembling for ire, his sandie locks he tore,
Out from his lips flew such a sound confused,
As lions make, in desarts thicke which rore;
Or as when clouds together crusht and brused,
Powre downe a tempest by the Caspian shore:
  So was his speech imperfect, stopt and broken,
  He roar'd and thund'red, when he should haue spoken.

38⁸ thrund'red < thund'red

39

But when with threats they both had whetted keene
Their eager rage, their furie, spite and ire,
They turn'd their steeds, and left large space betweene,
To make their forces greater, proaching nire,
With termes that warlike and that worthie beene:
(O sacred muse) my hawtie thoughts inspire,
  And make a trumpet of my slender quill,
  To thunder out this furious combat shrill.

40

These sonnes of *Mavors* bore (in stead of speares)
Two knottie masts, which none but they could lift,
Each foming steed so fast his master beares,
That neuer beast, bird, shaft flew halfe so swift;
Such was their furie, as when *Boreas* teares
The shattred crags from *Taurus* northren clift,
  Vpon their helmes their lances long they broke,
  And vp to heau'n flew splinters, sparks, and smoke.

41

The shocke made all the towres and turrets quake,
And woods and mountaines all nie-hand resound;
Yet could not all that force and furie shake
The valiant champions, nor their persons wound;
Together hurtled both their steedes, and brake
Each others necke, the riders lay on ground:
  But they (great masters of wars dreadfull art)
  Pluckt forth their swords and soone from earth vp start.

42

Close at his surest warde each warriour lieth,
He wisely guides his hand, his foot, his eie,
This blow he proueth, that defence he trieth,
He trauerseth, retireth, preaseth nie,
Now strikes he out, and now he falsifieth,
This blowe he wardeth, that he lets slip bie,
  And for aduantage oft he lets some part
  Discouer'd seeme, thus art deludeth art.

43

The Pagan ill defenst with sword or targe
Tancredies thigh (as he suppos'd) espide,
And reaching forth gainst it his weapon large,
Quite naked to his foe leaues his left side;
Tancred auoideth quicke his furious charge,
And gaue him eeke a wound deepe, sore and wide;
 That donne himselfe safe to his ward retired,
 His courage prais'd by all, his skill admired.

44

The proud Circassian saw his streaming blood,
Downe from his wound (as from a fountaine) running,
He sigh'd for rage, and trembled as he stood,
He blam'd his fortune, follie, want of cunning;
He lift his sword aloft, for ire nigh wood,
And forward rusht: *Tancred* his furie shunning,
 With a sharpe thrust once more the Pagan hit,
 To his broad shoulder where his arme is knit.

45

Like as a beare through pearsed with a dart,
Within the secret woods, no further flieth,
But bites the senselesse weapon mad with smart,
Seeking reuenge till vnreueng'd she dieth;
So mad *Argantes* far'd, when his proud hart
Wound vpon wound, and shame on shame espieth,
 Desire of veng'ance so orecame his senses,
 That he forgot all dangers, all defenses.

46

Vniting force extreme, with endlesse wrath,
Supporting both with youth and strength vntired,
His thundring blowes so fast about he la'th,
That skies and earth the flying sparkles fired:
His foe to strike one blow no leasure hath,
Scantly he breathed, though he oft desired,
 His warlike skill and cunning all was waste,
 Such was *Argantes* force, and such his haste.

47

Long time *Tancredie* had in vaine attended,
When this huge storme should ouerblow and pas,
Some blowes his mightie target well defended,
Some fell beside and wounded deepe the gras;
But when he saw the tempest neuer ended,
Nor that the Painims force ought weaker was,
    He high aduanst his cutting sword at length,
    And rage to rage oppos'd, and strength to strength.

48

Wrath bore the sway, both art and reason faile,
Furie new force and courage new supplies,
Their armours forged were of mettall fraile,
On euery side, thereof huge cantels flies,
The land was strowed all with plate and maile,
That, on the earth; on that, their warme blood lies,
    And at each rush and euery blowe they smote,
    Thunder, the noise; the sparks, seem'd lightning hote.

49

The Christian people and the Pagans gazed,
On this fierce combat, wishing oft the end,
Twixt hope and feare they stood long time amased,
To see the knights assaile and eeke defend:
Yet neither signe they made, nor noise they raised,
But for the issue of the fight attend,
    And stood as still, as life and sense they wanted,
    Saue that their harts within their bosoms panted.

50

Now were they tired both, and well-nie spent,
Their blowes shew'd greater will, then powre to wound:
But night her gentle daughter darknes, sent
With friendly shade, to ouerspread the ground,
Two heralds to the fighting champions went,
To part the fray, as law of armes them bound,
    Aridens borne in France, and wife *Pindore*,
    The man that brought the challenge proud before.

51

These men their scepters interpose, betweene
The doubtfull hazards of vncertaine fight;
For such their priuilege hath euer beene,
The law of nations doth defend their right;
'*Pindore* began, stay, stay, you warriors keene,
Equall your honour, equall is your might;
    Forbeare this combate, so we deeme it best,
    Giue night her due, and grant your persons rest.

52

'Man goeth forth to labour with the sunne,
But with the night, all creatures draw to sleepe,
Nor yet of hidden praise in darknes wonne,
The valiant hart of noble knight takes keepe.'
Argantes answer'd him, 'the fight begonne
Now to forbeare, doth wound my hart right deepe:
    Yet will I stay, so that this Christian sweare,
    (Before you both) againe to meet me heare.'

53

'I sweare (quoth *Tancred*) but sweare thou likewise,
To make returne, thy prisner eeke with thee;
Else for atchieuement of this enterprise,
None other time but this expect of mee:'
Thus sware they both; the heralds both deuise,
What time for this exploite should fittest bee:
    And for their wounds of rest and cure had need,
    To meet againe the sixt day was decreed.

54

This fight was deepe imprinted in their harts,
That saw this bloodie fray to ending brought,
An horror great possest their weaker parts,
Which made them shrinke who on this combat thought:
Much speech was of the praise and high desarts,
Of these braue champions, that so nobly fought;
    But which for knightly worth was most ipraised,
    Of that was doubt, and disputation raised.

55

All long to see them end this doubtfull fray,
And as they fauour, so they wish successe,
These hope true vertue shall obtaine the day,
Those trust on furie, strength and hardinesse;
But on *Erminia* most this burthen lay,
Whose lookes her trouble and her feare expresse;
    For on this dang'rous combats doubtfull end,
    Her ioy, her comfort, hope and life depend.

56

Her the sole daughter of that haplesse king,
That of proud Antioch late wore the crowne,
The Christian soldiers to *Tancredie* bring,
When they had sackt and spoil'd that glorious towne,
But he (in whom all good and vertue spring)
The virgins honour sau'd, and her renowne;
    And when her citie and her state was lost,
    Then was her person lou'd, and honour'd most.

57

He honour'd her, seru'd her, and leaue her gaue,
And will'd her goe whither, and when she list,
Her gold and iewels had he care to saue,
And them restored all, she nothing mist,
She (that beheld his youth and person braue)
When, by this deed, his noble minde she wist,
    Laid ope her hart for *Cupids* shaft to hit,
    Who neuer knots of loue more surer knit.

58

Her bodie free, captiued was her hart,
And loue the keies did of that prison beare,
Prepar'd to goe it was a death to part
From that kinde Lord, and from that prison deare:
But thou O honour which esteemed art,
The chiefest vesture noble Ladies weare,
    Enforcest her against her will, to wend
    To *Aladine*, her mothers dearest frend.

59

At Sion was this princesse entertained,
By that old tyrant and her mother deare,
Whose losse too soone the wofull damsell plained,
Her griefe was such, she liu'd not halfe the yeare,
Yet banishment, nor losse of friends constrained
The haplesse maid, her passions to forbeare,
    For though exceeding were her woe and griefe,
    Of all her sorrowes yet her loue was chiefe.

60

The seelie maide in secret longing pined,
Her hope a mote drawne vp by *Phebus* raics,
Her loue a mountaine seem'd, whereon bright shined
Fresh memorie of *Tancreds* worth and praise,
Within her closet if her selfe she shrined,
A hotter fire her tender hart assaies:
    Tancred at last, to raise her hope nigh dead,
    Before those wals did his broad ensigne spread.

61

The rest to vew the Christian armie feared,
Such seem'd their number, such their powre and might,
But she alone her troubled forehead cleared,
And on them spred her beautie shining bright;
In euerie squadron when it first appeared,
Her curious eie sought out her chosen knight;
    And euerie gallant that the rest excels,
    The same seemes him, so loue and fancie tels.

62

Within the kingly pallace, builded hie,
A turret standeth neere the cities wall,
From which *Erminia* might at ease descrie
The westren host, the plaines and mountaines all,
And there she stood all the long day to spie,
From *Phebus* rising to his euening fall,
    And with her thoughts disputed of his praise,
    And euerie thought a scalding sigh did raise.

63

From hence the furious combat she suruaid,
And felt her hart tremble with feare and paine,
Her secret thought thus to her fancie said,
Behold thy deere in danger to be slaine;
So with suspect, with feare and griefe dismaid,
Attended she her darlings losse or gaine,
   And euer when the Pagan lift his blade,
   The stroke a wound in her weake bosome made.

64

But when she saw the end, and wist withall
Their strong contention should eftsoones begin,
Amasement strange her courage did appall,
Her vitall blood was icie cold within;
Sometimes she sighed, sometimes teares let fall,
To witnes what distresse her hart was in,
   Hopelesse, dismai'd, pale, sad, astonished,
   Her loue, her feare; her feare, her torment bred.

65

Her idle braine vnto her soule presented
Death, in an hundred vglie fashions painted,
And if she slept, then was her greefe augmented,
With such sad visions were her thoughts acquainted;
She saw her Lord with wounds and hurts tormented,
How he complain'd, call'd for her helpe, and fainted,
   And found, awakt from that vnquiet sleeping,
   Her hart with panting, sore; eies, red with weeping.

66

Yet these presages of his comming ill,
Not greatest cause of her discomfort weare,
She saw his blood from his deepe wounds distill,
Nor what he suffred could she bide or beare:
Besides, report her longing care did fill,
Doubling his danger, doubling so her feare,
   That she concludes (so was her courage lost)
   Her wounded Lord was weake, faint, dead almost.

67

And for her mother had her taught before
The secret vertue of each herbe that springs,
Besides fit charmes for euerie wound or sore
Corruption breedeth, or misfortune brings,
(An art esteemed in those times of yore,
Beseeming daughters of great Lords and kings)
    She would herselfe, be surgeon to her knight,
    And heale him with her skill, or with her sight.

68

Thus would she cure her loue, and cure her foe
She must, that had her friends and kinsfolke slaine:
Some cursed weedes her cunning hand did knoe,
That could augment his harme, encrease his paine;
But she abhorr'd to be reuenged soe,
No treason should her spotlesse person staine,
    And vertuelesse she wisht all herbes and charmes,
    Wherewith false men encrease their patients harmes.

69

Nor feared she among the bands to stray
Of armed men, for often had she seene
The tragike end, of many a bloodie fray;
Her life had full of haps and hazards beene,
This made her bold in euerie hard assay,
More than her feeble sexe became, I weene,
    She feared not the shake of euerie reed,
    So cowards are couragious made through need.

70

Loue, fearelesse, hardie, and audacious loue,
Embold'ned had this tender damsell so,
That where wilde beasts and serpents glide and moue,
Through Afrikes desarts, durst she ride or goe,
Saue that her honour (she esteem'd aboue
Her life and bodies safetie) told her noe;
    For in the secret of her troubled thought,
    A doubtfull combat, loue and honour fought.

70⁷ seeret < secret

71

'O spotlesse virgin (honour thus begonne)
That my true lore obserued firmly hast,
When with thy foes thou didst in bondage wonne,
Remember then I kept thee pure and chast,
At libertie, now whither wouldst thou ronne,
To lay that field of princely vertue waste?
  Or lose that iewell Ladies hold so deare?
  Is maidenhood so great a load to beare.'

72

'Or deem'st thou it a praise of little prise,
The glorious title of a virgins name?
That thou wilt gad by night in giglet wise,
Amid thine armed foes, to seeke thy shame.
O foole, a woman conquers when she flies,
Refusall kindleth, profers quench the flame.
  Thy Lord will iudge thou sinnest beyond measure,
  If vainly thus thou waste so rich a treasure.'

73

The slie deceiuer *Cupid*, thus beguild
The simple damsell, with his filed tong;
'Thou wert not borne (quoth he) in desarts wilde
The cruell beares, and sauage beastes among,
That thou shouldst scorne faire *Cithereas* childe,
Or hate those pleasures that to youth belong,
  Nor did the gods thy hart of iron frame;
  To be in loue is neither sinne nor shame.

74

'Goe then, goe, whither sweet desire inuiteth,
How can thy gentle knight so cruell bee?
Loue in his hart thy greefes and sorrowes writeth,
For thy laments how he complaineth, see.
Oh cruell woman, whom no care exciteth
To saue his life, that sau'd and honour'd thee!
  He languisheth, one foote thou wilt not moue
  To succour him, yet saist thou art in loue.

75

'No, no, stay here *Argantes* wounds to cure,
And make him strong to shed thy darlings blood,
Of such reward he may himselfe assure,
That doth a thanklesse woman so much good:
Ah may it be thy patience can endure
To see the strength of this Circassion wood,
   And not with horror and amazement shrinke,
   When on their future fight thou hapst to thinke?

76

'Besides the thanks and praises for the deed,
Suppose what ioy, what comfort shalt thou winne,
When thy soft hand doth wholsome plaisters spreed,
Vpon the breaches in his iuorie skinne,
Thence to thy deerest Lord, may health succeed,
Strength to his lims, blood to his cheekes so thinne,
   And his rare beauties now halfe dead and more,
   Thou maist to him, him, to thy selfe restore.

77

'So shall some part of his aduentures bold,
And valiant actes, henceforth be held as thine;
His deere embracements shall thee strait enfold,
Together ioin'd in marriage rites diuine:
Lastly high place of honour shalt thou hold
Among the matrons sage, and dames Latine,
   In Italie, a land (as each one tels)
   Where valour true, and true religion dwels.'

78

With such vaine hopes the seelie maid abused,
Promist herselfe mountaines, and hils of gold;
Yet were her thoughts with doubts and feares confused,
How to escape vnseene out of that hold,
Because the watchmen euery minute vsed
To garde the walles, against the Christians bold,
   And in such furie and such heat of war,
   The gates or seld, or neuer, opened ar.

79

With strong *Clorinda* was *Erminia* sweet,
In surest linkes of deerest friendship bound,
With her she vs'd the rising sunne to greet,
And her (when *Phebus* glided vnder ground)
She made the louely partner of her sheet;
In both their harts one will, one thought was found;
　　Nor ought she hid from that Virago bold,
　　Except her loue, that tale to none she told.

80

That kept she secret, if *Clorinda* hard
Her make complaints, or secretly lament,
To other cause her sorrow she refard:
Matter enough she had of discontent,
Like as the bird that hauing close imbard
Her tender yong ones in the springing bent,
　　To draw the searcher further from her neast,
　　Cries and complaines most, where she needeth least.

81

Alone, within her chambers secret part,
Sitting one day vpon her heauie thought,
Deuising by what meanes, what sleight, what art,
Her close departure should be safest wrought,
Assembled in her vnresolued hart,
An hundreth passions stroue and ceaselesse fought;
　　At last she saw high hanging on the wall
　　Clorindaes siluer armes, and sigh'd withall:

82

And sighing, softly to herselfe she said,
'How blessed is this virgin in her might?
How I enuie the glorie of the maid,
Yet enuie not her shape or beauties light;
Her steps are not with trailing garments staid,
Nor chambers hide her valours shining bright;
　　But arm'd she rides, and breaketh sword and speare,
　　Nor is her strength restrain'd by shame or feare.

83

'Alas, why did not heau'n these members fraile,
With liuely force and vigor strengthen so?
That I this silken gowne, and slender vaile
Might for a brestplate, and an helme forgoe?
Then should not heat, nor cold, nor raine, nor haile,
Nor stormes that fall, nor blustring windes that bloe
    Withhold me, but I would both day and night,
    In pitched field, or priuate combat, fight.

84

'Nor haddest thou *Argantes*, first begonne
With my deare Lord, that fierce and cruell fight,
But I to that encounter would haue ronne,
And, haply tane him captiue by my might;
Yet should he finde (our furious combat donne)
His thraldome easie, and his bondage light;
    For fetters, mine embracements should he proue;
    For diet, kisses sweet; for keeper, loue:

85

'Or else my tender bosome opened wide,
And hart through pearsed with his cruell blade,
The bloodie weapon in my wounded side
Might cure the wound, which loue before had made;
Then should my soule in rest and quiet slide
Downe to the valleies of th'Elisian shade,
    And my mishap the knight perchance would moue,
    To shed some teares vpon his murdred loue.

86

'Alas! impossible are all these things,
Such wishes vaine afflict my woefull spright,
Why yeeld I thus to plaints and sorrowings,
As if all hope and helpe were perisht quight?
My hart dares much, it soares with *Cupids* wings,
Why vse I not for once these armours bright?
    I may sustaine a while this shield aloft,
    Though I be tender, feeble, weake and soft.

87

'Loue, strong, bold, mightie, neuer-tired loue,
Supplieth force to all his seruants trew;
The fearefull stags he doth to battaile moue,
Till each his hornes in others blood imbrew;
Yet meane not I the haps of war to proue,
A stratageme I haue deuised new,
   Clorinda like in this faire harnesse dight,
   I will escape out of the towne this night.

88

'I know the men that haue the gate to ward,
If she command dare not her will denie,
In what sort else could I beguile the gard?
This way is only left, this will I trie:
O gentle loue, in this aduenture hard
Thine handmaide guide, assist and fortifie!
   The time, the howre now fitteth best the thing,
   While stout *Clorinda* talketh with the king.'

89

Resolued thus without delay she went,
(As her strong passion did her rashly guide)
And those bright armes downe from the rafter hent,
Within her closet did she closely hide,
That might she doe vnseene; for she had sent
The rest, on sleeuelesse errands from her side,
   And night her stealthes brought to their wished end,
   Night, patronesse of theeues, and louers frend.

90

Some sparkling fires on heau'ns bright visage shone,
His azure robe the orient blewnesse lost,
When she (whose wit and reason both were gone)
Call'd for a squire she lou'd and trusted most,
To whom and to a maid (a faithfull one)
Part of her will she told, how that in post
   She would depart from Iudais king, and fain'd
   That other cause her sudden flight constrain'd.

89⁶ Sheeuelesse < sleevelesse (*cf. 1624*)

91

The trustie squire prouided needments meet,
As for their iourney fitting most should bee;
Meane-while her vesture (pendant to her feet)
Erminia doft, as earst determin'd shee,
Stript to her petticote the virgin sweet,
So slender was, that wonder was to see;
    Her handmaid readie at her mistresse will,
    To arme her helpt, though simple were her skill.

92

The rugged steele oppressed and offended
Her daintie necke, and locks of shining gold;
Her tender arme so feeble was, it bended
When that huge target it presum'de to hold,
The burnisht steele bright raies far off extended,
She faigned courage, and appeared bold;
    Fast by her side vnseene smil'd *Venus* sonne,
    As earst he laughed when *Alcides* sponne.

93

Oh, with what labour did her shoulders beare
That heauie burden, and how slow she went!
Her maid (to see that all the coasts were cleere)
Before her mistresse through the streetes was sent;
Loue gaue her courage, loue exiled feare,
Loue to her tired lims new vigor lent,
    Till she approched where the squire abode,
    There tooke they horse forthwith and forward rode.

94

Disguis'd they went, and by vnused waies,
And sccrct pathes they stroue vnseene to gone,
Vntill the watch they meet, which sore affraies
These soldiers new, when swords and weapons shone;
Yet none to stop their iourney once assaies,
But place and passage yeelded euery one;
    For that white armour and that helmet bright,
    Were knowne and feared, in the darkest night.

92⁸ sponne, < sponne.

95

Erminia (though some-deale she were dismaid)
Yet went she on, and goodly count'nance bore,
She doubted least her purpose were bewraid,
Her too much boldnes she repented sore;
But now the gate her feare and passage staid,
The heedlesse porter she beguil'd therefore,
   'I am *Clorinda*, ope the gates she cride,
   Where as the king commands, thus late I ride.'

96

Her womans voice and termes all framed beene,
Most like the speeches of the Princesse stout,
Who would haue thought on horsebacke to haue seene
That feeble damsell armed round about?
The porter her obei'd, and she (betweene
Her trustie squire and maiden) sallied out,
   And through the secret dales they silent pas,
   Where danger least, least feare, least perill was.

97

But when these faire aduentrers entred weare
Deepe in a vale, *Erminia* staid her hast,
To be recall'd she had no cause to feare,
This formost hazard had she trimly past,
But dangers new (tofore vnseene) appeare,
New perils she descride, new doubts she cast.
   The way that her desire to quiet brought,
   More difficult now seem'd than earth she thought.

98

Armed to ride among her angrie foes,
She now perceiu'd it were great ouersight,
Yet would she not (she thought) her selfe disclose,
Vntill she came before her chosen knight,
To him she purpos'd to present the rose
Pure, spotlesse, cleane, vntoucht of mortall wight,
   She staid therefore, and in her thoughts more wise,
   She call'd her squire, whom she thus gan aduise.

99

'Thou must (quoth she) be mine ambassadore,
Be wise, be carefull, true, and diligent,
Goe to the campe, present thy selfe before
The Prince *Tancredie*, wounded in his tent;
Tell him thy mistresse comes to cure his sore,
If he to grant her peace and rest consent,
 Gainst whom fierce loue such cruell war hath reased,
 So shall his wounds be cur'd, her torments eased.

100

'And say, in him such hope and trust she hath,
That in his powres she feares no shame nor scorne,
Tell him thus much, and what so ere he sath,
Vnfold no more, but make a quicke returne,
I (for this place is free from harme and scath)
Within this valley will meanewhile soiorne,'
 Thus spake the Princesse: and her seruant trew
 To execute the charge imposed, flew;

101

And was receiu'd (he so discreetly wrought)
First of the watch, that guarded in their place,
Before the wounded Prince, than was he brought:
Who heard his message kinde, with gentle grace,
Which told, he left him tossing in his thought
A thousand doubts, and turn'd his speedie pace
 To bring his Ladie and his mistresse word,
 She might be welcome to that courteous Lord.

102

But she, impatient, to whose desire
Greeuous and harmefull seem'd each little stay,
Recounts his steps, and thinks, now drawes he nire,
Now enters in, now speakes, now comes his way,
And that which greeu'd her most, the carefull squire
Lesse speedie seem'd, than ere before that day;
 Lastly she forward rode with loue to guide,
 Vntill the Christian tents at hand she spide.

103

Inuested in her starrie vaile, the night
In her kinde armes embraced all this round,
The siluer moone from sea vprising bright
Spred frostie pearle on the canded ground:
And *Cinthia* like for beauties glorious light,
The loue-sicke Nymph threw glistring beames around,
   And counsellors of her old loue, she made
   Those vallies dumbe, that silence, and that shade.

104

Beholding then the campe (quoth she) 'O faire
And castle-like pauilions, richly wrought!
From you how sweet me thinketh blowes the aire,
How comforts it my hart, my soule, my thought?
Through heau'ns faire grace from gulfe of sad despaire
My tossed barke, to port well nie is brought:
   In you I seeke redresse for all my harmes,
   Rest, midst your weapons; peace amongst your armes.

105

'Receiue me than and let me mercie finde,
As gentle loue assureth me I shall,
Among you had I entertainment kinde,
When first I was the Prince *Tancredies* thrall:
I couet not (led by ambition blinde)
You should me in my fathers throne enstall,
   Might I but serue in you my Lord so deare,
   That my content, my ioy, my comfort weare.'

106

Thus parled she (poore soule) and neuer feared
The sudden blow of fortunes cruell spight,
She stood where *Phebes* splendant beame appeared
Vpon her siluer armour double bright,
The place about her round the shining cleered,
Of that pure white wherein the Nymph was dight:
   The Tigresse great (that on her helmet laid)
   Bore witnes where she went, and where she staid.

107

(So as her fortune would) a Christian band
Their secret ambush there had closely framed,
Led by two brothers of Italia land,
Yong *Polipherne* and *Alicandro* named,
These with their forces watched to withstand
Those that brought vittailes to their foes vntamed,
    And kept that passage; them *Erminia* spide,
    And fled as fast as her swift steed could ride.

108

But *Polipherne* (before whose watrie eies,
His aged father strong *Clorinda* slew)
When that bright sheeld and siluer helme he spies,
The Championesse he thought he saw and knew;
Vpon his hidden mates for aide he cries,
Gainst his supposed foe, and forth he flew,
    As he was rash, and heedlesse in his wrath,
    Bending his lance, 'thou art but dead' he sath.

109

As when a chased hinde her course doth bend
To seeke by soile to finde some ease or good,
Whether from craggie rocke the spring descend,
Or softly glide within the shadie wood;
If there the dogs she meet, where late she wend
To comfort her weake lims in cooling flood,
    Againe she flies swift as she fled at first,
    Forgetting weaknesse, wearinesse, and thirst.

110

So she, that thought to rest her wearie spright,
And quench the endlesse thirst of ardent loue,
With deare embracements of her Lord and knight,
But such as marriage rites should first approue,
When she beheld her foe with weapon bright
Threat'ning her death, his hastie courser moue,
    Her loue, her Lord, her selfe abandoned,
    She spurr'd her speedie steed, and swift she fled.

111

Erminia fled, scantly the tender graffe
Her *Pegasus* with his light footesteps bent,
Her maidens beast for speed did likewise passe;
Yet diuers waies (such was their feare) they went:
The squire who all too late return'd (alas)
With tardie newes from Prince *Tancredies* tent,
   Fled likewise, when he saw his mistresse gone,
   It booted not to soiourne there alone.

112

But *Alicandro* wiser than the rest,
Who this suppos'd *Clorinda* saw likewise,
To follow her yet was he nothing prest,
But in his ambush still and close he lies,
A messenger to *Godfrey* he addrest,
That should him of this accident aduise,
   How that his brother chas'd with naked blade
   Clorindas selfe, or else *Clorindas* shade:

113

Yet that it was, or that it could be she,
He had small cause or reason to suppose,
Occasion great and weightie must it be,
Should make her ride by night among her foes:
What *Godfrey* willed that obserued he,
Aud with his soldiers lay in ambush close:
   These newes through all the Christian armie went,
   In euerie cabbin talkt, and euerie tent.

114

Tancred, whose thoughts the squire had fild with doubt,
By his sweet words, suppos'd now, hearing this,
'Alas, the virgin came to seeke me out,
And for my sake her life in danger is;'
Himselfe foorthwith he singled from the rout,
And rode in haste, though halfe his armes he mis,
   Among those sandie fields and valleis greene,
   To seeke his loue, he gallopte fast vnseene.

The argument.

A shepherd faire Erminia *entertaines,*
Whom whilst Tancredie *seekes in vaine to finde,*
He is entrapped in Armidaes *traines:*
Raimond *with strong* Argantes *is assignde*
To fight an Angell *to his aide he gaines:*
Sathan *that sees the Pagans furie blinde,*
   And hastie wrath turne to his losse and harme,
   Doth raise new tempest, vprore and allarme.

1

E Rminiaes steed (this while) his mistresse bore
  Through forrests thicke among the shadie treene,
Her feeble hand the bridle raines forlore,
Halfe in a swoune she was for feare I weene;
But her flit courser spared nere the more,
To beare her through the desart woods vnseene
  Of her strong foes, that chas'd her through the plaine,
  And still pursu'd, but still pursu'd in vaine.

2

Like as the wearie hounds at last retire,
Windlesse, displeased, from the fruitlesse chace,
When the slie beast Tapisht in bush and brire,
No art nor paines can rowse out of his place:
The Christian knights so full of shame and ire
Returned backe, with faint and wearie pace;
  Yet still the fearefull Dame fled, swift as winde,
  Nor euer staid, nor euer lookt behinde.

3

Through thicke and thinne, all night, all day, she driued,
Withouten comfort, companie or guide,

1⁸ vaiue. < vaine.

Her plaints and teares with euery thought reuiued,
She heard and saw her greefes, but nought beside:
But when the sunne his burning chariot diued
In *Thetis* waue, and wearie teame vntide,
 On Iordans sandie banks her course she staid
 At last, there downe she light, and downe she laid.

4

Her teares, her drinke; her food, her sorrowings,
This was her diet that vnhappie night:
But sleepe (that sweet repose and quiet brings)
To ease the greetes of discontented wight,
Spred foorth his tender, soft, and nimble wings,
In his dull armes foulding the virgin bright;
 And loue, his mother, and the graces kept
 Strong watch and warde, while this faire Ladie slept.

5

The birds awakte her with their morning song,
Their warbling musicke pearst her tender eare,
The murmuring brookes and whistling windes among
The ratling boughes, and leaues, their parts did beare;
Her eies vnclos'd beheld the groues along
Of swaines and shepherd groomes, that dwellings weare;
 And that sweet noise, birds, winds and waters sent,
 Prouokte againe the virgin to lament.

6

Her plaints were interrupted with a sound,
That seem'd from thickest bushes to proceed,
Some iolly shepherd sung a lustie round,
And to his voice had tun'd his oaten reed;
Thither she went, an old man there she found,
(At whose right hand his little flocke did feed)
 Set making baskets, his three sonnes among,
 That learn'd their fathers art, and learn'd his song.

7

Beholding one in shining armes appeare
The seelie man and his were sore dismaid;

But sweet *Erminia* comforted their feare,
Her ventall vp, her visage open laid,
'You happie folke, of heau'n beloued deare,
Worke on (quoth she) vpon your harmelesse traid,
 These dreadfull armes I beare no warfare bring
 To your sweet toile, nor those sweet tunes you sing.

8

'But father, since this land, these townes and towres,
Destroied are with sword, with fire and spoile,
How may it be vnhurt, that you and yours
In safetie thus, applie your harmelesse toile?'
'My sonne (quoth he) this poore estate of ours
Is euer safe from storme of warlike broile;
 This wildernesse doth vs in safetie keepe,
 No thundring drum, no trumpet breakes our sleepe.

9

'Haply iust heau'ns defence and shield of right,
Doth loue the innocence of simple swaines,
The thunderbolts on highest mountaines light,
And seld or neuer strike the lower plaines;
So kings haue cause to feare *Bellonaes* might,
Not they whose sweat and toile their dinner gaines,
 Nor euer greedie soldier was entised
 By pouertie, neglected and despised.

10

'O pouertie, chiefe of the heau'nly brood,
Dearer to me than wealth or kingly crowne!
No wish for honour, thirst of others good,
Can moue my hart, contented with mine owne:
We quench our thirst with water of this flood,
Nor feare we poison should therein be throwne;
 These little flocks of sheepe and tender goates
 Giue milke for food, and wooll to make vs coates.

11

'We little wish, we need but little wealth,
From cold and hunger vs to cloath and feed;

These are my sonnes, their care preserues from stealth
Their fathers flocks, nor seruants moe I need:
Amid these groues I walke oft for my health,
And to the fishes, birds and beastes giue heed,
How they are fed, in forrest, spring and lake,
And their contentment for ensample take.

12

'Time was (for each one hath his doting time)
(These siluer locks were golden tresses than)
That countrie life I hated as a crime,
And from the forrests sweet contentment ran,
To Memphis stately pallace would I clime,
And there became the mightie Caliphes man,
And though I but a simple gardner weare,
Yet could I marke abuses, see and heare.

13

'Entised on with hope of future gaine,
I suffred long what did my soule displease;
But when my youth was spent, my hope was vaine,
I felt my natiue strength at last decrease;
I gan my losse of lustie yeeres complaine,
And wisht I had enioy'd the countries peace;
I bod the court farewell, and with content
My later age here haue I quiet spent.'

14

While thus he spake, *Erminia* husht and still
His wise discourses heard, with great attention,
His speeches graue those idle fancies kill,
Which in her troubled soule bred such dissention;
After much thought reformed was her will,
Within those woods to dwell was her intention,
Till fortune should occasion new afford,
To turne her home to her desired Lord.

15

She said therefore, 'O shepherd fortunate!
That troubles some didst whilom feele and proue,

Yet liuest now in this contented state,
Let my mishap thy thoughts to pitie moue,
To entertaine me as a willing mate
In shepherds life, which I admire and loue;
　　Within these pleasant groues perchance my hart,
　　Of her discomforts, may vnload some part.

16

'If gold or wealth of most esteemed deare,
If iewels rich, thou diddest hold in prise,
Such store thereof, such plentie haue I heare,
As to a greedie minde might well suffice:'
With that downe trickled many a siluer teare,
Two christall streames fell from her watrie eies;
　　Part of her sad misfortunes than she told,
　　And wept, and with her wept that shepherd old.

17

With speeches kinde, he gan the virgin deare
Towards his cottage gently home to guide;
His aged wife there made her homely cheare,
Yet welcomde her, and plast her by her side.
The Princesse dond a poore pastoraes geare,
A kerchiefe course vpon her head she tide;
　　But yet her gestures and her lookes (I gesse)
　　Were such, as ill beseem'd a shepherdesse.

18

Not those rude garments could obscure, and hide,
The heau'nly beautie of her angels face,
Nor was her princely ofspring damnifide,
Or ought disparag'de, by those labours bace;
Her little flocks to pasture would she guide,
And milke her goates, and in their folds them place,
　　Both cheese and butter could she make, and frame
　　Herselfe to please the shepherd and his dame.

19

But oft, when vnderneath the greene-wood shade
Her flocks lay hid from *Phebus* scorching raies,

Vnto her knight she songs and sonnets made,
And them engrau'd in barke of beech and baies;
She told how *Cupid* did her first inuade,
How conquer'd her, and ends with *Tancreds* praise:
　And when her passions writ she ouer red,
　Againe she mourn'd, againe salt teares she shed.

20

'You happie trees for euer keepe (quoth shee)
This wofull storie in your tender rinde,
Another day vnder your shade may bee,
Will come to rest againe some louer kinde;
Who if these trophies of my greefes he see,
Shall feele deere pitie pearse his gentle minde;'
　With that she sigh'd and said, 'too late I prooue
　There is no troath in fortune, trust in loue.

21

'Yet may it be (if gracious heau'ns attend
The earnest suit of a distressed wight)
At my entreat they will vouchsafe to send
To these huge desarts that vnthankfull knight,
That when to earth the man his eies shall bend,
And sees my graue, my tombe, and ashes light,
　My wofull death, his stubborne hart may moue,
　With teares and sorrowes to reward my loue.

22

'So, though my life hath most vnhappie beene,
At least yet shall my spirit dead be blest,
My ashes cold shall buried on this greene,
Enioy that good this bodie nere possest.'
Thus she complained to the senselesse treene,
Floods in her eies and fires were in her brest;
　But he for whom these streames of teares she shed,
　Wandred far off (alas) as chance him led.

23

He follow'd on the footsteps he had traced,
Till in high woods and forrests old he came,

Where bushes, thornes and trees so thicke were placed,
And so obscure the shadowes of the same,
That soone he lost the tract wherein he paced;
Yet went he on, which way he could not ame,
    But still attentiue was his longing eare,
    If noise of horse, or noise of armes he heare.

24

If with the breathing of the gentle winde,
An aspen leafe but shaked on the tree,
If bird or beast stird in the bushes blinde,
Thither he spurr'd, thither he rode to see;
Out of the wood by *Cinthiaes* fauour kinde,
At last (with trauaile great and paines) got hee,
    And following on a little path, he hard
    A rumbling sound, and hasted thitherward.

25

It was a fountaine from the liuing stone,
That powred downe cleere streames, in noble store,
Whose conduit pipes (vnited all in one)
Throughout a rockie chanell gastly rore,
Here *Tancred* staid, and call'd, yet answer'd none,
Saue babbling Eccho, from the crooked shore;
    And there the wearie knight at last espies,
    The springing day-light red and white arise.

26

He sighed sore, and guiltlesse heau'n gan blame,
That wisht successe to his desires denide,
And sharpe reuenge protested for the same,
If ought but good his mistresse faire betide;
Than wisht he to returne the way he came,
Although he wist not by what path to ride,
    And time drew nere when he againe must fight,
    With proud *Argantes*, that vaine-glorious knight.

23⁷ are, < eare,
25² cleree < cleere

27

His stalworth steed the champion stout bestroad,
And pricked fast to finde the way he lost,
But through a valley as he musing road,
He saw a man, that seem'd for haste a post,
His horne was hung betweene his shoulders broad,
As is the guise with vs: *Tancredie* crost
  His way, and gently praid the man to say,
  To *Godfreys* campe how he should finde the way.

28

'Sir (in the Italian language) answer'd hee,
I ride where noble *Boemond* hath me sent:'
The Prince thought this his vncles man should bee,
And after him his course with speed he bent,
A fortresse stately built at last they see,
Bout which a muddie stinking lake there went,
  There they arriu'd, when *Titan* went to rest
  His wearie lims, in nights vntroubled nest.

29

The currer gaue the fort a warning blast;
The draw-bridge was let downe by them within:
'If thou a Christian be (quoth he) thou mast
Till *Phebus* shine againe, here take thine Inne,
The Countie of Cofenza (three daies past)
This castle from the Turks did nobly winne.'
  The Prince beheld the piece, which scite and art
  Impregnable had made on euery part.

30

He fear'd within a pile so fortified,
Some secret treason or enchantment lay,
But had he knowne euen there he should haue died,
Yet should his lookes no signe of feare bewray;
For where so euer will or chance him guied,
His strong victorious hand still made him way;
  Yet for the combat he must shortly make,
  No new aduentures list he vndertake.

27⁶ *Tacredie* < *Tancredie* (*cf. 1624*)

31

Before the castle, in a medow plaine
Beside the bridges end, he staid and stood,
Nor was entreated by the speeches vaine
Of his false guide, to passe beyond the flood.
Vpon the bridge appear'd a warlike swaine,
From top to toe all clad in armour good,
 Who brandishing a broad and cutting sword,
 Thus threat'ned death with many an idle word:

32

'O thou, whom chance or will brings to the soile,
Where faire *Armida* doth the scepter guide,
Thou canst not flie, of armes thy selfe despoile,
And let thy hands with iron chaines be tide;
Enter and rest thee from thy wearie toile,
Within this dungeon shalt thou safe abide,
 And neuer hope againe to see the day,
 Or that thy haire for age shall turne to gray,

33

'Except thou sweare her valiant knights to aid
Against those traitors of the Christian crew.'
Tancred at this discourse a little staid,
His armes, his gesture and his voice he knew;
It was *Rambaldo* who for that false maid,
Forsooke his countrie, and religion trew,
 And of that fort defender chiefe became,
 And those vile customes stablisht in the same.

34

The warrior answer'd (blushing red for shame)
'Cursed Apostate, and vngracious wight,
I am that *Tancred*, who defend the name
Of Christ, and haue beene ay his faithfull knight;
His rebell foes can I subdue and tame,
As thou shalt finde before we end this fight;
 And thy false hart cleft with this vengefull sword,
 Shall feele the ire of thy forsaken Lord.'

35

When that great name *Rambaldoes* eares did fill,
He shooke for feare, and looked pale for dread,
Yet proudly said, '*Tancred* thy hap was ill
To wander hither where thou art but dead,
Where nought can helpe, thy courage, strength and skill,
To *Godfrey* will I send thy cursed head,
    That he may see, how for *Armidaes* sake,
    Of him and of his Christ a scorne I make.'

36

This said; the day to sable night was turned,
That scant one could anothers armes descrie,
But soone an hundreth lampes and torches burned,
That cleared all the earth and all the skie;
The castell seem'd a stage with lights adorned,
On which men play some pompous tragedie;
    Within a tarras sat on high the Queene,
    And heard and saw, and kept her selfe vnseene.

37

The noble Baron whet his courage hot,
And buskt him boldly to the dreadfull fight;
Vpon his horse long while he taried not,
Bicause on foot he saw the Pagan knight,
Who vnderneath his trustie sheeld was got,
His sword was drawne, clos'd was his helmet bright;
    Gainst whom the Prince marcht on a stately pace,
    Wrath in his voice, rage in his eies and face.

38

His foe, his furious charge not well abiding,
Trauerst his ground, and started here and there,
But he (though faint and wearie both with riding)
Yet followed fast and still opprest him nere,
And on what side he felt *Rambaldo* sliding,
On that his forces most imployed were;
    Now at his helme, now at his hawberke bright,
    He thundred blowes, now at his face and sight.

39

Against those members battrie chiefe he maketh,
Wherein mans life keepes chiefest residence;
At his proud threats the Gascoigne warriour quaketh,
An vncouth feare appalled euery sence,
To nimble shifts the knight himselfe betaketh,
And skippeth here and there for his defence;
     Now with his targe, now with his trustie blade,
     Against his blowes he good resistance made.

40

Yet no such quicknesse for defence he vsed,
As did the Prince to worke him harme and scath;
His sheeld was cleft in twaine, his helmet brused,
And in his blood his other armes did bath;
On him he heaped blowes, with thrusts confused,
And more or lesse each stroke annoy'd him hath;
     He fear'd, and in his troubled bosome stroue,
     Remorse of conscience, shame, disdaine and loue.

41

At last so carelesse, foule despaire him made,
He ment to proue his fortune ill or good,
His shield cast downe, he tooke his helplesse blade
In both his hands, which yet had drawne no blood,
And with such force vpon the Prince he lade,
That neither plate nor maile the blow withstood,
     The wicked steele seaz'd deepe in his right side,
     And with his streaming blood his bases dide:

42

Another stroke he lent him on the brow,
So great that lowdly roong the sounding steele;
Yet pearst he not the helmet with the blow,
Although the owner twise or thrise did reele.
The Prince (whose lookes his sdainfull anger show)
Now meant to vse his puissance euery deele,
     He shakt his head and crasht his teeth for ire,
     His lips breath'd wrath, eies sparkled shining fire.

43

The Pagan wretch no longer could sustaine
The dreadfull terror of his fierce aspect,
Against the threat'ned blow he saw right plaine,
No tempred armour could his life protect,
He leapt aside, the stroke fell downe in vaine,
Against a pillour neere the bridge erect,
    Thence flaming fire and thousand sparks out start,
    And kill with feare the coward Pagans hart.

44

Toward the bridge the fearefull Painim fled,
And in swift flight, his hope of life reposed;
Himselfe fast after Lord *Tancredie* sped,
And now in equall pace almost they closed,
When all the burning lampes extinguished
The shining fort his goodly splendure losed,
    And all those stars on heau'ns blew face that shone,
    With *Cinthiaes* selfe, dispeared were and gone.

45

Amid those witchcrafts and that ouglie shade,
No further could the Prince pursue the chace,
Nothing he saw, yet forward still he made,
With doubtfull steps, and ill assured pace;
At last his foot vpon a threshold trade,
And ere he wist he entred had the place;
    With gastly noise the doore leaues shut behinde,
    And clos'd him fast in prison darke and blinde.

46

As in our seas in the Commachian bay,
A seelie fish (with streames enclosed) striueth,
To shun the furie and auoid the sway
Wherewith the currant, in that whirlepoole, driueth;
Yet seeketh all in vaine, but findes no way
Out of the watrie prison, where she diueth;
    For with such force there be the tides in brought,
    There entreth all that will, thence issueth nought:

47

This prison so entrapt that valiant knight,
Of which the gate was fram'd by subtile traine,
To close without the helpe of humane wight,
So sure, none could vndoe the leaues againe;
Against the doores he bended all his might,
But all his forces were imploy'd in vaine,
　　At last a voice gan to him lowdly call,
　　'Yeeld thee (quoth it) thou art *Armidaes* thrall.

48

'Within this dungeon buried shalt thou spend
The res'due of thy wofull daies and yeares;'
The champion list not more with words contend,
But in his hart kept close his griefes and feares,
He blamed loue, chance gan he reprehend,
And gainst enchantment huge complaints he reares.
　　'It were small losse, softly he thus begunne,
　　To lose the brightnes of the shining sunne;

49

'But I alas, the golden beame forgoe
Of my far brighter sunne; nor can I say
If these poore eies shall ere be blessed soe,
As once againe to vew that shining ray:'
Then thought he on his proud Circassian foe,
And said, 'ah! how shall I performe that fray?
　　He (and the world with him) will *Tancred* blame,
　　This is my griefe, my fault, mine endlesse shame.'

50

While those high spirits of this champion good,
With loue and honours care are thus opprest,
While he torments himselfe, *Argantes* wood,
Waxt wearie of his bed and of his rest,
Such hate of peace, and such desire of blood,
Such thirst of glorie, boiled in his brest;
　　That though he scant could stir or stand vpright,
　　Yet long'd he for th'appointed day to fight.

51

The night which that expected day fore-went,
Scantly the Pagan clos'd his eies to sleepe,
He told how night her sliding howers spent,
And rose ere springing day began to peepe;
He call'd for armour, which incontinent
Was brought, by him that vs'd the same to keepe,
   That harnesse rich, old *Aladine* him gaue,
   A worthie present for a champion braue:

52

He dond them on, nor long their riches eied,
Nor did he ought with so great weight incline,
His wonted sword vpon his thigh he tied,
The blade was old and tough, of temper fine.
As when a comet far and wide descried,
In scorne of *Phebus* midst bright heav'n doth shine,
   And tidings sad of death and mischiefe brings
   To mightie Lords, to monarches, and to kings:

53

So shone the Pagan in bright armour clad,
And roll'd his eies great swolne with ire and blood,
His dreadfull gestures threat'ned horror sad,
And ouglie death vpon his forehead stood;
Not one of all his squires the courage had
T'approch their maister in his angrie mood,
   Aboue his head he shooke his naked blade,
   And gainst the subtile aire vaine battaile made.

54

'That Christian theete (quoth he) that was so bold
To combat me in hard and single fight,
Shall wounded fall inglorious on the mold,
His locks with clods of blood and dust bedight,
And liuing shall with watrie eies behold
How from his backe I teare his harnesse bright,
   Nor shall his dying words me so entreat,
   But that Ile giue his flesh to dogs for meat.'

52⁶ heau'n < heav'n

55

Like as a bull when prickt with iealousie,
He spies the riuall of his hot desire,
Through all the fields doth bellow, rore and crie,
And with his thund'ring voice augments his ire,
And threat'ning battaile to the emptie skie,
Teares with his horne, each tree, plant, bush and brire,
    And with his foot casts vp the sand on hight,
    Defying his strong foe to deadly fight:

56

Such was the Pagans furie, such his crie,
An herald call'd he than, and thus he spake;
'Goe to the campe, and in my name, defie
The man that combats for his *Iesus* sake;'
This said, vpon his steed he mounted hie,
And with him did his noble pris'ner take,
    The towne he thus forsooke, and on the greene
    He ran, as mad or franticke he had beene.

57

A bugle small he winded lowd and shrill,
That made resound the fields and valleis neare,
Lowder than thunder from Olimpus hill
Seemed that dreadfull blast to all that heare:
The Christian Lords of prowesse, strength and skill,
Within th'imperiall tent assembled weare,
    The herald there in boasting termes defide
    Tancredie first, and all that durst beside.

58

With sober cheere *Godfredo* lookt about,
And view'd at leasure euery Lord and knight;
But yet for all his lookes not one stept out,
With courage bold, to vndertake the fight:
Absent were all the Christian champions stout,
No newes of *Tancred* since his secret flight;
    Boemond far off, and banisht from the crew,
    Was that strong Prince, who proud *Gernando* slew:

58⁵ champious < champions

59

And eeke those tenne which chosen were by lot,
And all the worthies of the campe beside,
After *Armida* false were follow'd hot,
When night was come their secret flight to hide;
The rest their hands and harts that trusted not,
Blushed for shame, yet silent still abide;
    For none there was that sought to purchase fame,
    In so great perill, feare exiled shame.

60

The angrie Duke their feare discouer'd plaine,
By their pale lookes and silence, from each part,
And as she mooued was with iust disdaine,
These words he said, and from his seat vpstart:
'Vnworthie life I iudge that coward swaine,
To hazard it euen now that wants the hart,
    When this vile Pagan with his glorious boast,
    Dishonours and defies Christs sacred hoast.

61

'But let my campe sit still in peace and rest,
And my liues hazard at their ease behold,
Come bring me here my fairest armes and best;'
And they were brought sooner than could be told.
But gentle *Raimond*, in his aged brest
Who had mature aduise, and counsell old,
    Than whom in all the campe were none or few
    Of greater might, before *Godfredo* drew,

62

And grauely said, 'Ah let it not betide,
On one mans hand to venture all this host!
No priuate soldier thou, thou art our guide,
If thou miscarrie all our hope were lost,
By thee must Babel fall and all her pride;
Of our true faith thou art the prop and post,
    Rule with thy scepter, conquer with thy word,
    Let other combats make with speare and sword.

63

'Let me this Pagans glorious pride asswage,
These aged armes can yet their weapons vse,
Let other shun *Bellonaes* dreadfull rage,
These siluer locks shall not *Raimondo* scuse:
Oh that I were in prime of lustie age,
Like you, that this aduenture braue refuse,
  And dare not once lift vp your coward eies,
  Gainst him that you and Christ himselfe defies!

64

'Or as I was, when all the Lords of fame
And Germaine Princes great stood by to vew,
In *Conrades* court (the second of that name)
When *Leopold* in single fight I slew;
A greater praise I reaped by the same,
So strong a foe in combat to subdue,
  Than he should doe, who all alone should chace,
  Or kill a thousand of these Pagans bace.

65

'Within these armes, had I that strength againe,
This boasting Painim had not liu'd till now,
Yet in this brest doth courage still remaine;
For age or yeeres these members shall not bow;
And if I be in this encounter slaine,
Scotfree *Argantes* shall not scape, I vow;
  Giue me mine armes, this battaile shall with praise
  Augment mine honour, got in yonger daies.'

66

The iolly Baron old thus brauely spake,
His words are spurres to vertue; euery knight
That seem'd before to tremble and to quake,
Now talked bold, ensample hath such might;
Each one the battaile fierce would vndertake,
Now stroue they all who should begin the fight;
  Baldwine and *Roger* both, would combat faine,
  Stephen, Guelpho, Gernier and the *Gerrards* twaine:

67

And *Pyrrhus*, who with helpe of *Boemonds* sword,
Proud Antioch by cunning sleight opprest;
The battaile eeke with many a lowly word,
Ralph, *Rosimond*, and *Eberard* request,
A Scotsh, an Irish, and an English Lord,
Whose lands the sea diuides far from the rest:
 And for the fight did likewise humbly sue,
 Edward and his *Gildippes*, louers true.

68

But *Raimond* more then all the rest doth sue,
Vpon that Pagan fierce to wreake his ire,
Now wants he nought of all his armours due
Except his helme, that shone like flaming fire.
To whom *Godfredo* thus; 'O mirrour true
Of antique worth! thy courage doth inspire
 New strength in vs, of *Mars* in thee doth shine
 The art, the honour and the discipline.

69

'If tenne like thee of valour and of age,
Among these legions I could haply finde,
I should the heat of Babels pride asswage,
And spread our faith from Thule to furthest Inde;
But now I pray thee calme thy valiant rage,
Reserue thyselfe till greater need vs binde,
 And let the rest each one write downe his name,
 And see whom fortune chooseth to this game,

70

'Or rather see whom Gods high iudgement taketh,
To whom is chance and fate and fortune slaue:'
Raimond his earnest suit not yet forsaketh,
His name writ with the res'due would he haue,
Godfrey himselfe in his bright helmet shaketh
The scroules, with names of all the champions braue,
 They drew, and red the first whereon they hit,
 Wherein was *Raimond* Earle of Tholouse writ.

71

His name with ioy and mightie shoutes they blis;
The rest allow his choise, and fortune praise,
New vigor blushed through those lookes of his:
It seem'd he now resum'd his youthfull daies,
Like to a snake whose slough new changed is,
That shines like gold against the sunnie raies:
    But *Godfrey* most approu'd his fortune hie,
    And wisht him honour, conquest, victorie.

72

Then from his side he tooke his noble brand,
And giuing it to *Raimond*, thus he spake;
'This is the sword wherewith in Saxon land,
The great *Rubello* battaile vs'd to make,
From him I tooke it fighting hand to hand,
And tooke his life with it, and many a lake
    Of blood with it I haue shed since that day,
    With thee God grant it proue as happie may.'

73

Of these delaies meane-while impatient,
Argantes threat'neth lowd and sternly cries,
'O glorious people of the Occident!
Behold him here that all your host defies:
Why comes not *Tancred*, whose great hardiment,
With you is pris'd so deere? pardie he lies
    Still on his pillow, and presumes the night
    Againe may shield him from my powre and might.

74

'Why than some other come, by band and band
Come all, come forth on horsebacke, come on foot,
If not one man dares combat hand to hand,
In all the thousands of so great a rout:
See where the tombe of *Maries* sonne doth stand,
March thither warriors bold, what makes you dout?
    Why run you not, there for your sinnes to weepe,
    Or to what greater need these forces keepe?'

75

Thus scorned by that heathen Sarracine,
Were all the soldiers of Christs sacred name:
Raimond (while others at his words repine)
Burst forth in rage, he could not beare this shame:
For fire of courage brighter far doth shine,
If challenges and threats augment the same;
  So that, vpon his steed he mounted light,
  Which *Aquilino* for his swiftnes hight.

76

This Iennet was by Tagus bred; for oft
The breeder of these beasts to war assinde,
When first on trees burgen the blossomes soft,
Prickt forward with the sting of fertile kinde,
Against the aire cast vp her head aloft,
And gath'reth seed so from the fruitfull winde,
  And thus conceauing of the gentle blast,
  (A wonder strange and rare) she foales at last.

77

And had you seene the beast, you would haue said
The light and subtill winde his father was;
For if his course vpon the sands he maid,
No signe was left what way the beast did pas;
Or if he menag'd were, or if he plaid,
He scantly bended downe the tender gras:
  Thus mounted rode the Earle, and as he went,
  Thus prai'd, to heau'n his zealous lookes vp bent,

78

'O Lord, that diddest saue, keepe and defend
Thy seruant *Dauid*, from *Golias* rage,
And broughtest that huge giant to his end,
Slaine by a faithfull childe, of tender age;
Like grace (O Lord) like mercie now extend,
Let me this vile blasphemous pride asswage,
  That all the world may to thy glorie know,
  Old men and babes thy foes can ouerthrow.'

79

Thus prai'd the Countie, and his praiers deare
Strength'ned with zeale, with godlines and faith,
Before the throne of that great Lord appeare,
In whose sweet grace is life, death in his wraith,
Among his armies bright and legions cleare,
The Lord an angell good selected haith,
　　To whom the charge was giuen to garde the knight,
　　And keepe him safe from that fierce Pagans might.

80

The angell good, appointed for the guard
Of noble *Raimond* from his tender eild,
That kept him than, and kept him afterward,
When speare and sword he able was to weild,
Now when his great creators will he hard,
That in this fight he should him chiefly sheild,
　　Vp to a towre set on a rocke he flies,
　　Where all the heau'nly armes and weapons lies:

81

There stands the lance wherewith great *Michael* slew
The aged dragon in a bloodie fight,
There are the dreadfull thunders forged new,
With stormes and plagues that on poore sinners light;
The massie trident maist thou pendant vew,
There on a golden pinne hung vp on hight,
　　Wherewith sometimes he smites this solid land,
　　And throwes down towns & towres theron which stand.

82

Among the blessed weapons there which stands
Vpon a diamond shield his lookes he bended,
So great that it might couer all the lands,
Twixt Caucasus and Atlas hils extended;
With it the Lords deere flocks and faithfull bands,
The holy kings and cities are defended,
　　The sacred Angell tooke this target sheene,
　　And by the Christian champion stood vnseene.

83

But now the walles and turrets round about,
Both yong and old with many thousands fill;
The king *Clorinda* sent and her braue rout,
To keepe the field, she staid vpon the hill:
Godfrey likewise some Christian bands sent out,
Which arm'd and rankt in good aray stood still,
   And to their champions emptie let remaine
   Twixt either troope a large and spacious plaine.

84

Argantes looked for *Tancredie* bold,
But saw an vncouth foe at last appeare,
Raimond rode on, and what he askt hem, told,
'Better thy chance, *Tancred* is now else-wheare,
Yet glorie not of that, my selfe behold
Am come prepar'd, and bid thee battaile heare,
   And in his place, or for myselfe, to fight,
   Loe here I am, who scorne thy heath'nish might.'

85

The Pagan cast a scornefull smile, and said,
'But where is *Tancred*, is he still in bed?
His lookes late seem'd to make high heau'n affraid,
But now for dread he is or dead or fled,
But were earthes center or the deepe sea maid
His lurking hole, it should not saue his hed.'
   'Thou liest', he saies, 'to say so braue a knight
   Is fled from thee, who thee exceedes in might.'

86

The angrie Pagan said, 'I haue not spilt
My labour then, if thou his place supplie,
Goe, take the field, and lets see how thou wilt
Maintaine thy foolish words and that braue lie;'
Thus parled they to meet in equall tilt,
Each tooke his aime at others helme on hie,
   Eu'n in the sight his foe good *Raimond* hit,
   But shakt him not, he did so firmely sit.

87

The fierce Circassian missed of his blowe,
A thing which seld befell the man before,
The angell by vnseene his force did knowe,
And far awrie the poinant weapon bore,
He burst his lance against the sand belowe,
And bit his lips for rage, and curst and swore,
    Against his foe return'd he swift as winde,
    Halfe mad in armes a second match to finde;

88

Like to a ram that buttes with horned head,
So spurr'd he forth his horse with desp'rate race:
Raimond at his right hand let slide his stead,
And as he past strooke at the Pagans face;
He turn'd againe the Earle nothing dread,
Yet stept aside and to his rage gaue place,
    And on his helme with all his strength gan smite,
    Which was so hard his courtlax could not bite.

89

The Sarracine imploi'd his art and force,
To gripe his foe within his mightie armes;
But he auoided nimbly with his horse,
He was no prentise in those fierce allarmes,
About him made he many a winding corse,
No strength, no sleight the subtile warriour harmes,
    His nimble steed obeid his ready hand,
    And where he stept no print left in the sand.

90

As when a captaine doth besiege some hold,
Set in a marish or high on a hill,
And trieth waies and wiles a thousand fold,
To bring the piece subiected to his will;
So far'd the Countie with the Pagan bold,
And when he did his head and brest none ill,
    His weaker partes he wisely gan assaile,
    And entrance searched oft twixt maile and maile;

91

At last he hit him on a place or twaine,
That on his armes the red blood trickled downe,
And yet himselfe vntouched did remaine,
No naile was broke, no plume cut from his crowne;
Argantes raging spent his strength in vaine,
Waste were his strokes, his thrusts were idle throwne,
    Yet preas'd he on, and doubled still his blowes,
    And where he hits he neither cares nor knowes.

92

Among a thousand blowes the Sarracine
At last stroake one, when *Raymond* was so neare,
That not the swiftnes of his Aquiline
Could his deere Lord from that huge danger beare:
But loe (at hand vnseene was helpe diuine,
Which saues when worldly comforts none appeare)
    The angell on his targe receiu'd that stroke,
    And on that shield *Argantes* sword was broke.

93

The sword was broke, therein no wonder lies,
If earthly tempred mettall could not hold,
Against that target forg'd aboue the skies,
Downe fell the blade in peeces on the mold,
The proud Circassian scant beleeu'd his eies,
Though nought were left him but the hilts of gold,
    And full of thoughts amaz'd a while he stood,
    Wondring the Christians armour was so good.

94

The brittle web of that rich sword he thought,
Was broke through hardnes of the Counties sheeld;
And so thought *Raimond*, who discou'red nought,
What succour heau'n did for his safetie yeeld:
But when he saw the man gainst whom he fought,
Vnweaponed, still stood he in the feeld;
    His noble hart esteem'd the glorie light,
    At such aduantage if he slew the knight.

95

'Goe fetch,' he would haue said, 'another blade,'
When in his hart a better thought arose,
How for Christes glorie he was champion made,
How *Godfrey* had him to this combat chose,
The armies honour on his shoulder lade,
To hazards new he list not that expose;
   While thus his thoughts debated on the cace,
   The hilts *Argantes* hurled at his face.

96

And forward spurr'd his mounture fierce withall,
Within his armes longing his foe to straine,
Vpon whose helme the heauie blowe did fall,
And bent well nie the mettall to his braine:
But he, whose courage was heroicall,
Leapt by and makes the Pagans onset vaine,
   And woundes his hand, which he outstretched saw,
   Fiercer than eagles talent, lions paw.

97

Now here now there on euery side he road,
With nimble speed, and spurr'd now out now in,
And as he went and came still laid on load
Where Lord *Argantes* armes were weake and thin,
All that huge force which in his armes aboad,
His wrath, his ire, his great desire to win,
   Against his foe together all he bent,
   And heau'n and fortune furthred his intent.

98

But he, whose courage for no perill failes,
Well arm'd and better harted, scornes his powre,
Like a tall ship when spent are all her sailes,
Which still resists the rage of storme and showre,
Whose mightie ribs fast bound with bands and nailes,
Withstands fierce *Neptunes* wrath, for many an howre,
   And yeelds not vp her brused keele to windes,
   In whose sterne blasts no ruth nor grace she findes.

99

Argantes such thy present danger was,
When Sathan stirr'd to aide thee at thy need,
In humane shape he forg'd an airie mas,
And made the shade a body seeme indeed;
Well might the spirit for *Clorinda* pas,
Like her it was, in armour and in weed,
  In stature, beautie, countenance and face,
  In lookes, in speech, in gesture and in pace.

100

And for the sprite should seeme the same indeed,
From where she was whose show and shape it had,
Towards the wall it road with faigned speed,
Where stood the people all dismaid and sad
To see their knight of helpe haue so great need,
And yet the law of armes all helpe forbad.
  There in a turret sat a soldier stout
  To watch, and at a loope-hole peeped out;

101

The spirit spake to him call'd *Oradine*,
The noblest archer then that handled bow,
'O *Oradin* (quoth she) who straight as line
Canst shoot, and hit each marke set high or low,
If yonder knight (alas) be slaine in fine,
As likest is, great ruth it were you know,
  And greater shame, if his victorious foe
  Should with his spoiles triumphant homeward goe.

102

'Now proue thy skill, thine arrowes sharpe head dip
In yonder theeuish French-mans guiltie blood,
I promise thee thy soueraigne shall not slip,
To giue thee large rewards for such a good;'
Thus said the sprite: the man did laugh and skip
For hope of future gaine, nor longer stood,
  But from his quiuer huge a shaft he hent,
  And set it in his mightie bowe new bent,

103

Twanged the string, out flew the quarell long,
And through the subtile aire did singing pas,
It hit the knight the buckles rich among,
Wherewith his pretious girdle fast'ned was,
It brused them and pearst his hawberke strong,
Some little blood downe trickled on the gras;
    Light was the wound; the angell by vnseene,
    The sharpe head blunted of the weapon keene.

104

Raimond drew forth the shaft (as much behoued)
And with the steele, his blood out streaming came,
With bitter words his foe he than reproued,
For breaking faith, to his eternall shame.
Godfrey whose carefull eies from his beloued
Were neuer turned, saw and markt the same,
    And when he vew'd the wounded Countie bleed,
    He sigh'd, and feared, more perchance than need;

105

And with his words and with his threat'ning eies,
He stirr'd his captaines to reuenge that wrong;
Forthwith the spurred courser forward hies,
Within their rests put were their lances long,
From either side a squadron braue out flies,
And boldly made a fierce encounter strong,
    The raised dust to ouerspread begunne
    Their shining armes, and far more shining sunne.

106

Of breaking speares, of ringing helme and shield,
A dreadfull rumour roard on euery side,
There lay an horse, another through the field
Ran masterlesse, dismounted was his guide;
Here one lay dead, there did another yeeld,
Some sigh'd, some sobb'd, some praied and some cride;
    Fierce was the fight, and longer still it lasted,
    Fiercer and fewer, still themselues they wasted.

Headline sixth < seuenth (*cf. 1624*)

107

Argantes nimbly leapt amid the throng,
And from a soldier wrung an iron mace,
And breaking through the ranks and ranges long,
Therewith he passage made himselfe and place,
Raimond he sought, the thickest prease among,
To take reuenge for late receiu'd disgrace,
    A greedie woolfe he seem'd, and would asswage
    With *Raimonds* blood his hunger and his rage.

108

The way he found not easie as he would,
But fierce encounters put him oft to paine,
He met *Ormanno* and *Rogero* bould,
Of Balnauile, *Guie*, and the *Gerards* twaine;
Yet nothing might his rage and haste withhould,
These worthies stroue to stop him, but in vaine,
    With these strong lets increased still his ire,
    Like riuers stopt, or closely smouldred fire.

109

He slew *Ormanno*, wounded *Guie*, and laid
Rogero lowe, among the people slaine,
On euery side new troopes the man inuaid,
Yet all their blowes were waste, their onsets vaine.
But while *Argantes* thus his prises plaid,
And seem'd alone this skirmish to sustaine,
    The Duke his brother call'd and thus he spake,
    'Goe with thy troope, fight for thy Sauiours sake;

110

'There enter in where hottest is the fight,
Thy force against the left wing strongly bend,'
This said, so braue an onset gaue the knight,
That many a Painim bold there made his end:
The Turks too weake seem'd to sustaine his might,
And could not from his powre their liues defend,
    Their ensignes rent and broke was their array,
    And men and horse on heapes together lay.

111

Orethrowne likewise away the right wing ran,
Nor was there one againe that turn'd his face,
Saue bold *Argantes*, else fled euery man,
Feare droue them thence on heapes, with headlong chace:
He staid alone, and battaile new began,
Fiue hundreth men, weapon'd with sword and mace,
 So great resistance neuer could haue made,
 As did *Argantes* with his single blade:

112

The strokes of swords and thrusts of many a speare,
The shocke of many a iust, he long sustained,
He seem'd of strength enough this charge to beare,
And time to strike now here now there he gained,
His armours broke, his members brused weare,
He sweat and bled, yet courage still he fained;
 But now his foes vpon him preas'd so fast,
 That with their weight they bore him backe at last.

113

His backe against this storme at length he turned,
Whose headlong furie bore him backward still,
Not like to one that fled, but one that murned
Bicause he did his foes no greater ill,
His threat'ning eies like flaming torches burned,
His courage thirsted yet more blood to spill,
 And euery way and euery meane he sought,
 To stay his flying mates, but all for nought.

114

This good he did, while thus he plaid his part,
His bands and troopes at ease, and safe, retired;
Yet coward dread lacks order, feare wants art,
Deafe to attend, commanded or desired.
But *Godfrey* that perceiu'd in his wise hart,
How his bold knights to victorie aspired,
 Fresh soldiers sent, to make more quicke pursuit,
 And helpe to gather conquests pretious fruit.

115

But this (alas) was not th'appointed day,
Set downe by heau'n to end this mortall war,
The westren Lords this time had borne away
The prise, for which they trauail'd had so far,
Had not the diuels (that saw the sure decay
Of their false kingdome by this bloodie war)
    At once made heau'n and earth with darknes blinde,
    And stird vp tempests, stormes and blustring winde.

116

Heau'ns glorious lampe wrapt in an ouglie vaile
Of shadowes darke, was hid from mortall eie,
And hels grim blacknes did bright skies assaile,
On euerie side the fierie light'nings flie,
The thunders roare, the streaming raine and haile
Powre downe, and make that sea which earst was drie,
    The tempests rend the Oakes and Cedars brake,
    And make not trees, but rocks and mountaines shake.

117

The raine, the lightning and the raging winde,
Bet in the French-mens eies, with hideous force,
The soldiers staid amaz'd in hart and minde,
The terror such stopped both man and horse,
Surprised with this euill no way they finde,
Whither for succour to direct their corse.
    But wise *Clorinda* soone th'aduantage spied,
    And spurring forth thus to her soldiers cried:

118

'You hardie men at armes behold (quoth shee)
How heau'n, how iustice in our aide doth fight,
Our visages are from this tempest free,
Our hands at will may weild our weapons bright,
The furie of this friendly storme you see
Vpon the foreheads of our foes doth light,
    And blindes their eies, then let vs take the tide,
    Come follow me, good fortune be our guide,'

116[8] bnt < but *corrected in B*

119

This said, against her foes on rode the Dame,
And turn's their backs against the winde and raine,
Vpon the French with furious rage she came,
And scorn'd those idle blowes they stroke in vaine;
Argantes at the instant did the same,
And them who chased him now chas'd againe,
   Nought but his fearefull backe, each Christian showes
   Against the tempest, and against their blowes.

120

The cruell haile and deadly wounding blade,
Vpon their shoulders smote them as they fled,
The blood new spilt while thus they slaughter made,
The water falne from skies had died red,
Among the murdred bodies *Pyrrhus* lade,
And valiant *Raiphe* his hart blood there out bled,
   The first subdu'd by strong *Argantes* might,
   The second conqu'red by that virgin knight.

121

Thus fled the French, and them pursu'd in chace
The wicked sprites and all the Syrian traine:
But gainst their force and gainst the fell menace
Of haile and winde, of tempest and of raine,
Godfrey alone turn'd his audacious face,
Blaming his Barons for their feare so vaine,
   Himselfe the campe gate boldly stood to keepe,
   And sau'd his men within his trenches deepe,

122

And twice vpon *Argantes* proud he flew,
And beat him backward maugre all his might,
And twice his thirstie sword he did imbrew
In Pagans blood where thickest was the fight;
At last himselfe with all his folke withdrew,
And that daies conquest gaue the virgin bright,
   Which got, she home retir'd and all her men,
   And thus she chas'd this lion to his den.

123

Yet ceased not the furie and the ire
Of these huge stormes, of winde, of raine and haile,
Now was it darke, now shone the light'ning fire,
The winde and water euery place assaile,
No banke was safe, no rampire left intire,
No tent could stand, when beame and cordage faile,
　Winde, thunder, raine, all gaue a dreadfull sound,
　And with that musicke deaft the trembling ground.

The eight Booke of Godfrey *of Bulloigne*

The argument.

A messenger to Godfrey *sage doth tell*
The Prince of Denmarks valour, death and end:
Th' Italians trusting signes vntrue too well,
Thinke their Rinaldo *slaine: the wicked fend*
Breedes furie in their brests, their bosomes swell
With ire and hate, and war and strife forth send:
    They threaten Godfrey, *he praies to the Lord,*
    And calmes their furie with his looke and word.

1

Now were the skies of stormes and tempests cleered,
  Lord *AEolus*, shut vp his windes in hold,
The siluer mantled morning fresh appeared,
With roses crown'd, and buskind high with gold:
The spiritis yet which had these tempests reared,
Their malice would still more and more vnfold;
  And one of them that *Astragor* was named,
  His speeches thus, to foule *Alecto* framed.

2

'*Alecto*, see, we could not stop nor stay.
The knight that to our foes new tidings brings,
Who from the hands escapt (with life away)
Of that great Prince, chiefe of all Pagan kings,
He comes, the fall of his slaine Lord to say,
Of death and losse he tels, and such sad things,
  Great newes he brings, and greatest danger is,
  Bertoldoes sonne shall be call'd home for this.

3

'Thou know'st what would befall, bestir thee than;
Preuent with craft, what force could not withstand,
Turne to their euill the speeches of the man,
With his owne weapon wound *Godfredoes* hand;

Kindle debate, infect with poyson wan
The English, Switzer and Italian band,
   Great tumults moue, make braules and quarrels rife,
   Set all the campe on vprore and at strife.

4

'This act beseemes thee well, and of the deed
Much maist thou boast, before our Lord and king,'
Thus said the sprite: perswasion small did need,
The monster grants to vndertake the thing.
Meane-while the knight whose comming thus they dreed,
Before the campe his wearie lims doth bring,
   And well nie breathlesse, 'warriors bold (he cride)
   Who shall conduct me to your famous guide?'

5

An hundreth stroue the strangers guide to bee,
To harken newes the knights by heapes assemble,
The man fell lowly downe vpon his knee,
And kist the hand that made proud Babel tremble;
'Right puissant Lord, whose valiant actes (quoth hee)
The sands and starres in number best resemble,
   Would God some gladder newes I might vnfold,'
   And there he paws'd, and sigh'd; then thus he told:

6

'*Sweno* the king of Denmarks only haire,
The stay and staffe of his declining eild,
Longed to be among these squadrons faire,
Who for Christes faith here serue with speare and shield,
No wearinesse, no stormes of sea or aire,
No such contents as crownes and scepters yeild,
   No deere entreaties of so kinde a sire,
   Could in his bosome quench that glorious fire.

7

'He thirsted sore to learne this warlike art
Of thee, great Lord and master of the same,
And was ashamed in his noble hart,
That neuer act he did deserued fame;

Besides, the newes and tidings from each part
Of yong *Rinaldoes* worth, and praises came;
  But that which most his courage stirred haith
  Is zeale, religion, godlinesse and faith.

8

'He hasted forward than without delay,
And with him tooke of knights a chosen band,
Directly toward Thrace we tooke the way,
To Bizance old, chiefe fortresse of that land,
There the Greeke monarch gently praid him stay,
And there an herald sent from you we fand,
  How Antioch was wonne, who first declar'd,
  And how defended nobly afterward.

9

Defended gainst *Corbana* valiant knight,
That all the Persian armies had to guide,
And brought so many soldiers bold to fight,
That void of men he left that kingdome wide,
He told thine actes, thy wisdome and thy might,
And told the deedes of many a Lord beside,
  His speech at length to yong *Rinaldo* past
  And told his great atchieuements, first and last:

10

'And how this noble campe of yours, of late
Besieged had this towne, and in what sort,
And how you praid him to participate
Of the last conquest, of this noble fort.
In hardie *Sweno* opened was the gate
Of worthie anger, by this braue report,
  So that each hower seemed fiue yeeres long,
  Till he were fighting, with these Pagans strong.

11

'And while the herald told your fights and fraies,
Himselfe of cowardise reprou'd he thought,
And him, to stay that counsels him, or praies,
He heares not, or (else heard) regardeth nought,

He feares no perils, but (whil'st he delaies)
Least this last worke without his helpe be wrought:
  In this his doubt, in this his danger lies,
  No hazard else he feares, no perill spies.

12

'Thus hasting on, he hasted on his death,
Death that to him and vs was fatall guide,
The rising morne appeared yet vneath,
When he and we were arm'd, and fit to ride,
The neerest way seem'd best, ore hoult and heath
We went, through desarts waste and forrests wide,
  The streetes and waies he openeth as he goes,
  And sets each land, free from intruding foes.

13

'Now want of food, now dang'rous waies we finde,
Now open war, now ambush closely laid;
Yet past we forth, all perils left behinde,
Our foes or dead, or run away affraid,
Of victorie so happie blew the winde,
That carelesse all, and heedlesse to it maid:
  Vntill one day his tents he hapt to reare,
  To Palestine when we approched neare,

14

'There did our scoutes returne, and bring vs newes
That dreadfull noise of horse and armes they heare,
And that they deem'd by sundrie signes and shewes,
There was some mightie host of Pagans neare.
At these sad tidings many chang'd their hewes,
Some looked pale for dread, some shooke for feare,
  Only our noble Lord was alterd nought,
  In looke, in face, in gesture or in thought.

15

'But said, a crowne prepare you to possesse
Of martyrdome, or happie victorie;
For this I hope, for that I wish no lesse,
Of greater merit, and of greater glorie.

Brethren, this campe will shortly be I gesse,
A temple, sacred to our memorie,
  To which the holy men of future age,
  To vew our graues shall come in pilgrimage.'

16

'This said, he set the watch in order right
To garde the campe, along the trenches deepe,
And as he armed was, so euery knight
He willed on his backe his armes to keepe.
Now had the stilnesse of the quiet night
Drown'd all the world in silence and in sleepe,
  When suddenly we heard a dreadfull sound,
  Which deaft the earth, and tremble made the ground:

17

"Arme, arme" they cride, Prince *Sweno* at the same,
Glistring in shining steele leapt formost out,
His visage shone, his noble lookes did flame,
With kindled brand of courage bold and stout,
When loe the Pagans to assault vs came,
And with huge numbers hemm'd vs round about,
  A forrest thicke of speares about vs grew,
  And ouer vs a cloud of arrowes flew:

18

'Vneuen the fight, vnequall was the fray,
Our enimies were twenty men to one,
On euery side the slaine and wounded lay,
Vnseene, where nought but glistring weapons shone:
The number of the dead could no man say,
So was the place with darknes ouergone,
  The night her mantle blacke vpon vs spreedes,
  Hiding our losses, and our valiant deedes.

19

'But hardie *Sweno*, midst the other traine,
By his great actes was well descride I wote,
No darknes could his valours day light staine,
Such wondrous blowes on euery side he smote;

A streame of blood, a banke of bodies slaine,
About him made a bulwarke and a mote,
  And when so ere he turn'd his fatall brand,
  Dread in his lookes, and death sat in his hand,

20

'Thus fought we till the morning bright appeared,
And strowed roses on the azure skie,
But when her lampe had nights thicke darknes cleared,
Wherein the bodies dead did buried lie,
Then our sad cries to heau'n for greefe we reared,
Our losse apparant was, for we descrie
  How all our campe destroied was almost,
  And all our people well nie slaine and lost.

21

'Of thousands twaine an hundreth scant suruiued,
When *Sweno* murdred saw each valiant knight,
I know not if his hart in sunder riued,
For deare compassion, of that wofull sight;
He shew'd no change, but said, "since so depriued
We are of all our friends by chance of fight,
  Come follow them, the path to heau'n their blood
  Marks out, now angels made, of martyrs good."

22

'This said, and glad I thinke of death at hand,
The signes of heau'nly ioy shone through his eies,
Of Sarracines against a mightie band,
With fearelesse hart, and constant brest he flies;
No steele could shield them from his cutting brand,
But whom he hits without recure he dies,
  He neuer stroke but feld or kild his foe,
  And wounded was himselfe from top to toe.

23

'Not strength, but courage now, preseru'd on liue
This hardie champion, fortresse of our faith,
Stroken he strikes, still stronger more they striue,
The more they hurt him, more he doth them scaith,

When towards him a furious knight can driue,
Of members huge, fierce lookes, and full of wraith,
  That with the aide of many a Pagan crew,
  After long fight, at last Prince *Sweno* slew.

24

'Ah heauie chance! downe fell the valiant yuth,
Nor mongst vs all did one so strong appeare,
As to reuenge his death, that this is truth,
By his deere blood and noble bones I sweare,
That of my life I had nor care nor ruth,
No wounds I shonn'd, no blowes I would off beare,
  And had not heau'n my wished end denied,
  Eu'n there I should, and willing should haue died.

25

'Aliue I fell among my fellowes slaine,
Yet wounded so that each one thought me dead,
Nor what our foes did since can I explaine,
So fore amazed was my hart and head;
But when I opened first mine eies againe,
Nights curtaine blacke vpon the earth was spread,
  And through the darknes to my feeble sight,
  Appear'd the twinkling of a slender light.

26

'Not so much force or iudgement in me lies,
As to discerne things, seene and not mistake,
I saw like them, who ope and shut their eies
By turnes, now halfe asleepe, now halfe awake,
My bodie eeke another torment tries,
My wounds began to smart, my hurtes to ake;
  For euery sore, each member pinched was,
  With nights sharpe aire, heau'ns frost, and earthes cold gras.

27

'But still the light approched neare and neare,
And with the same a whispring murmur ronne,
Till at my side arriued both they weare,
When I to spread my feeble eies begonne:

Two men behold in vestures long appeare,
With each a lampe in hand, who said, "O sonne
  In that deare Lord who helpes his seruants, trust,
  Who ere they aske grants all things to the iust.

28

'This said, each one his sacred blessing slings
Vpon my coarse, with broad outstretched hand,
And mumbled hymnes and psalmes and holy things,
Which I could neither heare, nor vnderstand;
"Arise" (quoth they) with that as I had wings,
All whole and sound I leapt vp from the land,
  O miracle, sweet, gentle, strange and trew!
  My lims new strength receiu'd, and vigour new.

29

'I gazde on them like one, whose hart denai'th
To thinke that donne, he sees so strangely wrought;
Till one said thus, "O thou of little faith,
What doubts perplex thy vnbeleeuing thought?
Each one of vs a liuing bodie haith,
We are Christes chosen seruants, feare vs nought,
  Who to auoid the worlds allurements vaine,
  In wilfull penance, hermits poore remaine.

30

' "Vs messengers to comfort thee elect
That Lord hath sent that rules both heau'n and hell;
Who often doth his blessed will effect,
By such weake meanes, as wonder is to tell;
He will not that this body lie neglect,
Wherein so noble soule did lately dwell,
  To which againe when it vprisen is,
  It shall vnited be, in lasting blis.

31

' "I say Lord *Swenoes* corpes, for which prepar'd
A tombe there is according to his worth,

29⁶ nouhht < nought *corrected in B*

By which his honour shall be far declar'd,
And his iust praises spred from south to north:
But lift thine eies vp to the heauens ward,
Marke yonder light that like the sunne shines forth,
   That shall direct thee with those beames so cleare,
   To finde the bodie of thy maister deare."

32

'With that I saw from *Cinthias* siluer face,
Like to a falling star a beame downe slide,
That bright as golden line markt out the place,
And lightned with cleere streames the forrest wide,
So *Latmos* shone when *Phebe* left the chace,
And laid her downe by her *Endimions* side;
   Such was the light, that well discerne I could
   His shape, his wounds, his face (though dead) yet bould.

33

'He lay not groueling now, but as a knight
That euer had to heauenly things desire,
So towards heau'n the Prince lay bolt vpright,
Like him, that vpward still sought to aspire,
His right hand closed held his weapon bright,
Readie to strike and execute his ire,
   His left vpon his brest was humbly laid,
   That men might know, that while he dide he praid.

34

'Whilst on his wounds with bootlesse teares I wept,
That neither helped him, nor eas'd my care,
One of those aged fathers to him stept,
And forst his hand that needlesse weapon spare:
"This sword (quoth he) hath yet good token kept,
That of the Pagans blood he drunke his share,
   And blusheth still, he could not saue his Lord,
   Rich, strong and sharpe, was neuer better sword.

35

' "Heau'n therefore will not, though the Prince be slaine,
Who vsed earst to weild this pretious brand,

That so braue blade vnused should remaine;
But that it passe from strong, to stronger hand,
Who with like force can wield the same againe,
And longer shall in grace of fortune stand,
  And with the same shall bitter vengeance take,
  On him that *Sweno* slew, for *Swenoes* sake.

36

' "Great *Soliman* kill'd *Sweno*, *Soliman*
For *Swenoes* sake, vpon this sword must die.
Here take the blade and with it haste thee than
Thither where *Godfrey* doth encamped lie,
And feare not thou that any shall or can
Or stop thy way, or lead thy steps awrie;
  For he that doth thee on this message send,
  Thee with his hand shall guide, keepe and defend.

37

' "Arriued there it is his blessed will,
With true report that thou declare and tell
The zeale, the strength, the courage, and the skill
In thy beloued Lord, that late did dwell,
How for Christes sake he came his blood to spill,
And sample left to all of doing well,
  That future ages may admire his deed,
  And courage take when his braue end they reed.

38

' "It resteth now, thou know that gentle knight,
That of this sword shall be thy masters haire,
It is *Rinaldo* yong, with whom in might
And martiall skill, no champion may compaire,
Giue it to him and say; the heauens bright
Of this reuenge to him commit the caire."
  While thus I list'ned what this old man said,
  A wonder new from further speech vs staid;

39

'For there whereas the wounded body lay,
A stately tombe with curious worke (behold)

And wond'rous art was built out of the clay,
Which rising round the carkas did enfold,
With works engrauen in the marble gray,
The warriours name, his worth and praise that told,
  On which I gazing stood, and often read
  That epitaph of my deere master dead.

40

' "Among his soldiers (quoth the hermit) heare
Must *Swenoes* corpes remaine in marble chest,
While vp to heau'n are flowne their spirits deare,
To liue in endlesse ioy for euer blest,
His funerall thou hast with many a teare
Accompaned, its now high time to rest,
  Come be my guest, vntill the morning ray
  Shall light the world againe, then take thy way."

41

'This said, he led me ouer holts and hags,
Through thornes and bushes scant my legs I drew,
Till vnderneath an heape of stones and crags
At last he brought me to a secret mew,
Among the beares, wilde boares, the wolues and stags,
There dwelt he safe with his disciple trew,
  And fear'd no treason, force, nor hurt at all,
  His guiltlesse conscience was his castels wall.

42

'My supper, rootes; my bed, was mosse and leaues;
But wearinesse in little rest found ease:
But when the purple morning night bereaues
Of late vsurped rule, on lands and seas,
His loathed couch each wakefull hermite leaues,
To pray rose they, and I, for so they please,
  I congee tooke when ended was the same,
  And hitherward, as they aduis'd me, came.'

43

The Dane his wofull tale had done, when thus
The good Prince *Godfrey* answer'd him, "sir knight,

Thou bringest tidings sad and dolorous,
For which our heauie campe laments of right,
Since so braue troopes and so deere friends to vs,
One howre hath spent, in one vnluckie fight;
    And so appeared hath thy maister stout,
    As lightning doth, now kindled, now quencht out.

44

'But such a death and end exceedeth all
The conquests vaine of realmes, or spoiles of gold,
Nor aged Romes proud stately capitall,
Did euer triumph yet like theirs behold,
They sit in heau'n on thrones celestiall,
Crowned with glorie, for their conquest bold,
    Where each his hurtes I thinke to other showes,
    And glorie in those bloodie wounds and blowes.

45

'But thou who hast part of thy race to ronne,
With haps and hazards of this world itost,
Reioice, for those high honours they haue wonne,
Which cannot be by chance or fortune crost:
But for thou askest for *Bertoldoes* sonne,
Know, that he wandreth, banisht from this host,
    And till of him new tidings some man tell,
    Within this campe I deeme it best thou dwell.'

46

These words of theirs in many a soule renewed
The sweet remembrance of faire *Sophias* childe,
Some with salt teares for him their cheekes bedewed,
Least euill betide him mongst the Pagans wilde,
And euery one his valiant prowesse shewed,
And of his battailes stories long compilde,
    Telling the Dane his actes and conquests past,
    Which made his eares amaz'd, his hart agast.

47

Now when remembrance of the youth had wrought
A tender pitie in each softned minde,

Behold returned home with all they cought,
The bands that were to forrage late assinde,
And with them in abundance great they brought
Both flockes and herds of euery sort and kinde,
And corne although not much, and hay to feed
   Their noble steads and coursers when they need.

48

They also brought of misaduenture sad
Tokens and signes, seem'd too apparant trew,
Rinaldoes armour frusht and hackt they had,
Oft pearsed through, with blood besmeared new,
About the campe, (for alwaies rumors bad,
Are furthest spred) these wofull tidings flew,
   Thither assembled straight both hie and low,
   Longing to see what they were loth to know.

49

His heauie hawberke was both seene and knowne,
And his broad shield, wherein displaied flies
The bird, that proues her chickens for her owne,
By looking gainst the sun with open eies,
That shield was to the Pagans often showne
In many a hard and hardie enterpries,
   But now with many a gash and many a stroke,
   They see (and sigh to see it) frusht and broke.

50

While all his soldiers whispred vnder hand,
And here and there the fault and cause doe lay,
Godfrey before him called *Aliprand*
Captaine of those that brought of late this pray,
A man who did on points of vertue stand,
Blamelesse in words, and true what ere he say,
   'Say (quoth the Duke) where you this armour had,
   Hide not the truth, but tell it good or bad.'

51

He answer'd him, 'as far from hence thinke I
As on two daies a speedie post well rideth,

To Gaza ward a little plaine doth lie,
It selfe among the steepie hils which hideth,
Through it slow falling from the mountaines hie,
A rolling brooke twixt bush and bramble glideth,
    Clad with thick shade of boughes of broad leau'd treene,
    Fit place for men to lie in wait vnseene.

52

'Thither, to seeke some flocks or heards, we went
Perchance close hid vnder the greene wood shaw,
And found the springing grasse with blood besprent,
A warriour tumbled in his blood we saw,
His armes though dustie, bloodie, hackt and rent,
Yet well we knew, when neere the coarse we draw;
    To which (to view his face) in vaine I started,
    For from his bodie his faire head was parted;

53

'His right hand wanted eeke, with many a wound
The trunke through pearsed was from backe to brest,
A little by his emptie helme we found
The siluer Eagle shining on his crest,
To spie at whom to aske we gazed round,
A churle towards vs his steps addrest,
    But when vs armed by the coarse he spide,
    He ran away his fearfull face to hide,

54

'But we pursu'd him, tooke him, spake him faire,
Till comforted at last he answere made,
How that the day before, he saw repaire
A band of soldiers from that forrests shade,
Of whom one caried by the golden haire
A head, but late cut off with murdring blade,
    The face was faire and yong, and on the chin
    No signe of beard to bud did yet begin.

55

'And how in sindall wrapt away he bore
That head with him hung at his saddle bow,

And how the murth'rers by the armes they wore,
For soldiers of our campe he well did know;
The carkasse I disarm'd and weeping sore,
Bicause I guest who should that harnesse owe;
    Away I brought it, but first order gaue,
    That noble body should be laid in graue.

56

'But if it be his trunke whom I beleeue,
A nobler tombe his worth deserueth well,'
This said good *Aliprando* tooke his leeue,
Of certaine troath he had no more to tell.
Sore sigh'd the Duke, so did these newes him greeue,
Feares in his hart, doubts in his bosome dwell,
    He earnd to know, to finde, and learne the truth,
    And punish would them that had slaine the yuth.

57

But now the night despred her lazie wings,
Ore the broad fields of heau'ns bright wildernesse,
Sleepe the soules rest, and ease of carefull things,
Buried in happie peace, both more and lesse,
Thou *Argillan* alone, whom sorrow stings
Still wakest, musing on great deedes I gesse,
    Nor suffrest in thy watchfull eies to creepe,
    The sweet repose, of milde and gentle sleepe.

58

This man was strong of lims, and all his saies
Were bold, of readie toong, and working spright,
Nere Trento borne, bred vp in braules and fraies,
In iarres, in quarrels, and in ciuill fight,
For which exil'd, the hils and publike waies
He fill'd with blood, and robb'ries day and night,
    Vntill to Asiaes wars at last he came,
    And boldly there he seru'd, and purchas'd fame.

59

He clos'd his eies at last when day drew neare,
Yet slept he not, but senselesse lay opprest,

With strange amazednes, and sodaine feare,
Which false *Alecto* breathed in his brest,
His working powres within deluded weare,
Stone still he quiet lay, yet tooke no rest,
   For to his thought the feend her selfe presented,
   And with strange visions his weake braine tormented.

60

A murdred bodie huge beside him stood,
Of head and right hand both, but lately spoiled,
His left hand bore the head, whose visage good,
Both pale and wan, with dust and gore defoiled,
Yet spake, though dead, with whose sad words, the blood
Forth at his lips, in huge abundance boiled,
   'Flie *Argillan* from this false campe flie far,
   Whose guide, a traitor; captaines, murdrers ar.

61

'*Godfrey* hath murdred me by treason vile,
What fauour than hope you my trustie frends?
His villaine hart is full of fraud and guile,
To your destruction all his thoughts he bends,
Yet if thou thirst, of praise for noble stile,
If in thy strength thou trust, thy strength that ends
   All hard assaies, flie not, first with his blood
   Appease my ghost wandring by *Lethe* flood;

62

'I will thy weapon whet, enflame thine ire,
Arme thy right hand, and strengthen euery part.'
This said; euen while she spake she did inspire
With furie, rage, and wrath his troubled hart:
The man awakte, and from his eies like fire
The poys'ned sparks of headstrong madnes start,
   And armed as he was forth is he gone,
   And gath'red all th'Italian bands in one.

63

He gath'red them where lay the armes that late
Were good *Rinaldoes*; then with semblance stout,

And furious words, his fore conceiued hate
In bitter speeches, thus he vomits out;
'Is not this people barb'rous and ingrate,
In whom troath findes no place, faith takes no rout?
   Whose thirst vnquenched is of blood and gold,
   Whom no yoke boweth, bridle none can hold.

64

'So much we suffred haue these seu'n yeeres long,
Vnder this seruile and vnworthie yoke,
That thorow Rome and Italie our wrong
A thousand yeeres hereafter shall be spoke:
I count not how Cilicias kingdome strong,
Subdued was by Prince *Tancredies* stroke,
   Nor how false *Baldwine* him that land bereaues
   Of vertues haruest, fraud there reapt the sheaues:

65

'Nor speake I how each howre, at euery need
Quicke, ready, resolute at all assaies,
With fire and sword we hasted forth with speed,
And bore the brunt of all their fights and fraies;
But when we had perform'd and done the deed,
At ease and leasure they diuide the praies,
   We reaped nought but trauaile for our toile,
   Their was the praise, the realmes, the gold, the spoile.

66

'Yet all this season were we willing blinde,
Offended, vnreueng'd, wrong'd, but vnwroken,
Light greefes could not prouoke our quiet minde,
But now (alas) the mortall blow in stroken,
Rinaldo haue they slaine, and law of kinde,
Of armes, of nations and of high heau'n broken,
   Why doth not heau'n kill them with fire and thunder?
   To swallow them why cleaues not earth asunder?

67

'They haue *Rinaldo* slaine the sword and sheeld
Of Christes true faith, and vnreueng'd he lies,

Still vnreuenged lieth in the feeld
His noble corpes, to feed the crowes and pies:
Who murdred him? who shall vs certaine yeeld?
Who sees not that although he wanted eies?
  Who knowes not how th'Italian chiualrie
  Proud *Godfrey*, and false *Baldwine* both enuie?

68

'What need we further proofe? heau'n, heau'n I sweare,
Will not consent herein we be beguiled,
This night I saw his murdred sprite appeare,
Pale, sad and wan, with wounds and blood defiled,
A spectacle full both of greefe and feare,
Godfrey for murdring him, the ghost reuiled.
  I saw it was no dreame, before mine eies,
  How ere I looke, still still me thinkes it flies.

69

'What shall we doe? shall we be gouern'd still,
By this false hand, contaminate with blood?
Or else depart and trauaile forth, vntill
To Euphrates we come, that sacred flood?
Where dwels a people voide of martiall skill,
Whose cities rich, whose land is fat and good,
  Where kingdoms great we may at ease prouide,
  Far from these French mens malice, from their pride.

70

'Than let vs goe, and no reuengement take
For this braue knight, though it lie in our power,
No, no, that courage rather newly wake,
Which neuer sleepes in feare and dread one hower,
And this pestifrous serpent, poys'ned snake,
Of all our knights that hath destroi'd the flower,
  First let vs slay, and his deserued end
  Ensample make to him that kils his frend.

71

'I will, I will, if your couragious force,
Dareth so much as it can well performe,

Teare out his cursed hart without remorse?
The neast of treason false and guile enorme.'
Thus spake the angrie knight, with headlong corse
The rest him followed like a furious storme,
   'Arme, arme,' they cride, to armes the soldiers ran,
   And as they ron, arme, arme', cride euery man.

72

Mongst them *Alecto* strowed wastefull fire,
Enuenoming the harts of most and least,
Follie, disdaine, madnes, strife, rancour, ire,
Thirst to shed blood, in euery brest encreast,
This ill spread far, and till it set-on fire
With rage, th'Italian lodgings neuer ceast,
   From thence vnto the Switzers campe it went,
   And last infected euery English tent.

73

Not publike losse of their beloued knight,
Alone stirr'd vp their rage and wrath vntamed,
But fore-conceiued greefes, and quarrels light,
Their ire still nourished, and still enflamed,
Awaked was each former cause of spight,
The Frenchmen cruell and vniust they named,
   And with bold threats they made their hatred knowne,
   Hate seeld kept close, and oft vnwisely showne:

74

Like boyling liquor in a seething pot,
That fumeth, swelleth hie, and bubbleth fast,
Till ore the brimmes among the embers hot,
Part of the broth and of the scum it cast,
Their rage and wrath those few appeased not,
In whom of wisdome yet remain'd some tast,
   Camillo, *William*, *Tancred* were away,
   And all whose greatnes might their madnes stay.

75

Now headlong ran to harnesse in this heat
These furious people, all on heapes confused,

73⁵ spright, < spight,

The roaring trumpets battaile gan to threat,
As it in time of mortall war is vsed,
The messengers ran to *Godfredo* great,
And bod him arme, while on this noise he mused,
　And *Baldwin* first well clad in iron hard,
　Stept to his side, a sure and faithfull gard.

76

Their murmurs heard, to heau'n he lift his eine
As was his wont, to God for aide he fled;
'O Lord, thou knowest this right hand of mine
Abhorred euer ciuill blood to shed,
Illumine their darke soules with light diuine,
Represse their rage, by hellish furie bred,
　The innocencie of my guiltlesse minde
　Thou know'st, and make these know, with furie blinde.'

77

This said, he felt infused in each vaine,
A sacred heat from heau'n aboue distilled,
A heat in man that courage could constraine,
That his graue looke with awfull boldnesse filled,
Well garded forth he went to meet the traine
Of those that would reuenge *Rinaldo* killed;
　And though their threats he heard, and saw them bent
　To armes on euery side, yet on he went.

78

Aboue his hawberke strong a cote he ware,
Embrodred faire with pearle and rich stone,
His hands were naked, and his face was bare,
Wherein a lampe of maiestie bright shone;
He shooke his golden mace wherewith he dare
Resist the force of his rebellious fone:
　Thus he appear'd, and thus he gan them teach
　In shape an angell, and a God in speach:

79

'What foolish words? what threats be these I heare?
What noise of armes? who dares these tumults moue?

Am I so honour'd? stand you so in feare?
Where is your late obedience? where your loue?
Of *Godfreys* falshood who can witnes beare?
Who dare or will these accusations proue?
  Perchance you looke I should entreaties bring,
  Sue for your fauours, or excuse the thing.

80

'Ah God forbid, these lands should heare or see
Him so disgrast, at whose great name they quake;
This scepter and my noble actes for mee,
A true defence before the world can make:
Yet for sharpe iustice gouerned shall bee
With clemencie, I will no veng'ance take
  For this offence, but for *Rinaldoes* loue,
  I pardon you, hereafter wiser proue.

81

'But *Argillanoes* guiltie blood shall wash
This staine away, who kindled this debate,
And led by hastie rage and furie rash,
To these disorders first vndid the gate:'
While thus he spoke the lightning beames did flash
Out of his eies of maiestie and state,
  That *Argillan* (who would haue thought it) shooke
  For feare and terrour, conqu'red with his looke.

82

The rest with vndiscreet and foolish wrath
Who threatned late, with words of shame and pride,
Whose hands so ready were to harme and scath,
And brandished bright swords on euery side;
Now husht and still attend what *Godfrey* sath,
With shame and feare their bashfull lookes they hide,
  And *Argillan* they let in chaines be bound,
  Although their weapons him enuiron'd round.

83

So when a lion shakes his dreadfull maine,
And beates his taile, with courage proud and wroth,

If his commander come, who first tooke paine
To tame his youth, his loftie crest downe go'th,
His threats he feareth and obaies the raine
Of thraldome base, and seruiceage, though loth,
   Nor can his sharpe teeth nor his armed pawes,
   Force him rebell against his rulers lawes.

84

Fame is a winged warriour they beheild,
With semblant fierce and furious looke that stood,
And in his left hand had a splendant shield,
Wherewith he couered safe their chieftaine good,
His other hand a naked sword did wield,
From which distilling fell the lukewarme blood,
   The blood pardie of many a realme and towne,
   Whereon the Lord his wrath had powred downe.

85

Thus was the tumult (without bloodshed) ended,
Their armes laid downe, strife into exile sent,
Godfrey his thoughts to greater actions bended,
And homeward to his rich pauilion went,
For to assault the fortresse he entended,
Before the second or third day were spent;
   Meane-while his timber wrought he oft suruaid,
   Whereof his rammes and engins great he maid.

The argument.

Alecto false great Soliman *doth moue*
By night the Christians in their tents to kill:
But God who their intents saw from aboue,
Sends Michael *downe from his sacred hill:*
The spirits foule to hell the angell droue;
The knights deliu'red from the witch at will
    Destroy the Pagans, scatter all their host:
    The Soldan flies when all his bands are lost.

1

THe grisly childe of *Herebus* the grim,
   Who saw these tumults done and tempests spent,
(Gainst streame of grace who euer stroue to swim,
And all her thoughts against heau'ns wisdome bent)
Departed now, bright *Titans* beames were dim,
And fruitfull lands waxt barren as she went,
   She sought the rest of her infernall crew,
   New stormes to raise, new broiles, and tumults new.

2

She (that well wist her sisters had entised,
By their false artes, far from the Christian host,
Tancred, *Rinaldo*, and the rest, best prised
For martiall skill, for might esteemed most)
Said, (of these discords and these strifes aduised)
Great *Soliman*, when day his light hath lost,
   These Christians shall assaile with sodaine war,
   And kill them all, while thus they striue and iar.

3

With that where *Soliman* remain'd she flew,
And found him out with his Arabian bands,

1² (Who < Who   1³ Gainst < (Gainst

Great *Soliman*, of all Christes foes vntrew,
Boldest of courage, mightiest of his hands,
Like him was none of all that earth-bred crew
That heaped mountaines on th'Aemonian sands,
  Of Turkes he soueraigne was, and Nice his seat,
  Where late he dwelt, and rul'd that kingdome great.

4

The lands forenenst the Greekish shore he held,
From Sangars mouth to crookt Meanders fall,
Where they of Phrygia, Misia, Lidia dweld,
Bythinias townes, and Pontus cities all:
But when the harts of Christian Princes sweld,
And rose in armes to make proud Asia thrall,
  Those lands were wonne where he did scepter weild,
  And he twise beaten was, in pitched feild.

5

When fortune oft he had in vaine assaid,
And spent his forces, which auaild him nought,
To Egypts king himselfe he close conuaid;
Who welcomd him as he could best haue thought,
Glad in his hart and inly well appaid,
That to his court so great a lord was brought:
  For he decreed his armies huge to bring,
  To succour Iuda land, and Iudaes king.

6

But (ere he open war proclaim'de) he would
That *Soliman* should kindle first the fire,
And with huge summes of false entising gould,
Th'Arabian theeues he sent him forth to hire,
While he the Asian Lords and Morians bould
Vnites; the Soldan wonne to his desire
  Those outlawes, ready aie for gold to fight:
  The hope of gaine hath such alluring might.

7

Thus made their captaine, to destroy and burne
In Iuda land he entred is so far,

That all the waies whereby he should returne,
By *Godfreys* people, kept and stopped ar,
And now he gan his former losses murne,
This wound had hit him on an elder scar,
  On great aduentures ronne his hardie thought,
  But not assur'de, he yet resolu'd on nought.

8

To him *Alecto* came, and semblant bore
Of one, whose age was great, whose lookes were graue,
Whose cheekes were bloodlesse, and whose locks were hore,
Mustachoes strouting long, and chin close shaue,
A steepled Turbant, on her head she wore,
Her garment side, and by her side, her glaue,
  Her guilden quiuer at her shoulders hong,
  And in her hand a bow was, stiffe and strong.

9

'We haue (quoth she) through wildernesses gone,
Through sterill sands, strange paths, and vncouth waies,
Yet spoile or bootie haue we gotten none,
Nor victorie, deseruing fame or praise.
Godfrey meane-while to ruine sticke and stone
Of this faire towne, with battrie sore, assaies;
  And if a while we rest, we shall behold
  This glorious citie smoking lie in mold.

10

'Are sheepe coates burnt, or praies of sheepe or kine,
The cause why *Soliman* these bands did arme?
Canst thou that kingdome lately lost of thine
Recouer thus, or thus redresse thy harme?
No, no, when heau'ns small candles next shall shine,
Within their tents giue them a bold allarme;
  Beleeue *Araspes* old, whose graue aduice
  Thou hast in exile prou'd, and prou'd in Nice.

11

'He feareth nought, he doubts no sodaine broile,
From these ill armed, and worse harted bands,

He thinks this people, vs'd to rob and spoile,
To such exploit dares not lift vp their hands;
Vp than and with thy courage put to foile
This fearelesse campe, while thus secure it stands.'
 This said, her poyson in his brest she hides,
 And than to shapelesse aire vnseene, she glides.

12

The Soldan cride, 'O thou, which in my thought
Encreased hast, my rage and furie so,
Nor seem'st a wight of mortall mettall wrought,
I follow thee, where so thee list to goe,
Mountaines of men by dint of sword downe brought
Thou shalt behold, and seas of red blood floe
 Where ere I goe; only be thou my guide,
 When sable night the azure skies shal hide.'

13

When this was said, he mustred all his crew,
Reprou'd the cowards, and allow'd the bould:
His forward campe, inspir'd with courage new,
Was readie dight to follow, where he would:
Alectoes selfe the warning trumpet blew,
And to the winde his standard great vnrould,
 Thus on they marched, and thus on they went,
 Of their approach their speed the newes preuent.

14

Alecto left them, and her person dight,
Like one, that came some tidings new to tell:
It was the time, when first the rising night
Her sparkling dimonds, powreth forth to sell,
When (into Sion come) she marched right
Where Iudais aged tyrant vs'd to dwell,
 To whom of *Solimans* designment bold,
 The place, the manner, and the time she told.

15

Their mantle darke the grisly shadowes spred,
Stained with spots of deepest sanguine hew,

Warme drops of blood, on earthes blacke visage shed,
Supplide the place of pure and pretious dew,
The moone and stars for feare of sprites were fled,
The shriking gobblings each where howling flew,
    The Furies roare, the ghosts and Fairies yell,
    The earth was fild with deuils, and emptie hell.

16

The Soldan fierce (through all this horror) went
Toward the campe of his redouted foes,
The night was more than halfe consum'd and spent;
Now headlong downe the westren hill she goes,
When distant scant a mile from *Godfreys* tent
He let his people there a while repose,
    And victail'd them, and then he boldly spoke
    These words, which rage and courage might prouoke:

17

'See there a campe, full stuft of spoiles and praies,
Not halfe so strong, as false report recordeth;
See there the store-house, where there captaine laies
Our treasures stolne, where Asiaes wealth he hordeth;
Now chance the ball vnto our racket plaies,
Take than the vantage which good lucke affordeth,
    For all their armes, their horses, gold and treasure
    Are ours, ours without losse, harme or displeasure.

18

'Nor is this campe that great victorious host
That slew the Persian Lords, and Nice hath wonne;
For those in this long war are spent and lost,
These are the dregs, the wine is all out ronne,
And these few left, are drown'd and dead almost
In heauie sleepe, the labour halfe is donne,
    To send them headlong to *Auernus* deepe,
    For little differs death and heauie sleepe.

19

'Come, come, this sword the passage open shall
Into their campe, and on their bodies slaine

We will passe ore their rampire and their wall;
This blade, as sithes cut downe the fields of graine,
Shall cut them so, Christes kingdome now shall fall,
Asia her freedome, you shall praise obtaine:'
  Thus he enflam'd his soldiers to the fight,
  And led them on through silence of the night.

20

The Sentinell by star light (loe) describe
This mightie Soldan, and his host draw neare,
Who found not as he hopte the Christians guide
Vnware, ne yet vnready was his geare:
The scout when this huge armie they describe
Ran backe, and gan with shoutes the larum reare,
  The watch start vp and drew their weapons bright,
  And buskt them bold to battaile and to fight.

21

Th'Arabians wist they could not come vnseene,
And therefore lowd their iarring trumpets sound,
Their yelling cries to heau'n vp heaued beene,
The horses thundred on the solid ground,
The mountaines roared, and the valleies greene,
The Eccho sighed from the caues around,
  Alecto with her brand (kindled in hell)
  Tokened to them, in *Dauids* towre that dwell.

22

Before the rest forth prickt the Soldan fast,
Against the watch, not yet in order iust,
As swift as hideous *Boreas* hastie blast
From hollow rocks when first his stormes outbrust,
The raging floods, that trees and rocks downe cast,
Thunders, that townes and towres driue to dust:
  Earthquakes, to teare the world in twaine that threat,
  Are nought, compared to his furie great.

23

He stroke no blow, but that his foe he hit;
And neuer hit, but made a greeuous wound:

And neuer wounded, but death followed it;
And yet no perill, hurt or harme he found,
No weapon on his hard'ned helmet bit,
No puissant stroke his senses once astound,
　　Yet like a bell his tinkling helmet rong,
　　And thence flew flames of fire and sparks among.

24

Himselfe well nie had put the watch to flight,
A iollie troope of Frenchmen strong and stout,
When his Arabians came by heapes to fight,
Couering (like raging floods) the fields about;
The beaten Christians ran away full light,
The Pagans (mingled with the flying rout)
　　Entred their campe, and filled (as they stood)
　　Their tents with ruine, slaughter, death and blood.

25

High on the Soldans helme enamel'd laid
An hideous dragon, arm'd with many a scaile,
With iron pawes, and leathren wings displaid,
Which twisted on a knot her forked taile,
With triple toong it seem'd she hist and braid,
About her iawes the froth and venome traile,
　　And as he stirr'd, and as his foes him hit,
　　So flames to cast, and fire she seem'd to spit.

26

With this strange light, the Soldan fierce appeared
Dreadfull to those that round about him beene,
As to poore sailers (when huge stormes are reared)
With lightning flash the raging seas are seene,
Some fled away, bicause his strength they feared,
Some bolder gainst him bent their weapons keene,
　　And froward night (in euils and mischiefes pleased)
　　Their dangers hid, and dangers still encreased.

27

Among the rest (that stroue to merite praise)
Was old *Latinus*, borne by Tibers banke,

To whose stout hart (in fights and bloodie fraies)
For all his eeld, base feare yet neuer sanke;
Fiue sonnes he had, the comforts of his daies,
That from his side in no aduenture shranke,
But long before their time, in iron strong
They clad their members, tender, soft and yong.

28

The bold ensample of their fathers might
Their weapons whetted, and their wrath encreast,
'Come let vs goe (quoth he) where yonder knight
Vpon our soldiers makes his bloodie feast,
Let not their slaughter once your harts affright,
Where danger most appeares, there feare it least;
For honour dwels in hard attemptes (my sonnes)
And greatest praise, in greatest perill, wonnes.'

29

Her tender brood the forrests sauage queene
(Ere on their crestes their rugged maines appeare,
Before their mouthes by nature armed beene,
Or pawes haue strength a seelie lambe to teare)
So leadeth forth to pray, and makes them keene,
And learnes by her ensample, nought to feare
The hunter, in those desart woods that takes
The lesser beastes, whereon his feast he makes.

30

The noble father and his hardie crew
Fierce *Soliman* on euery side inuade,
At once all sixe vpon the Soldan flew,
With lances sharpe, and strong encounters made,
His broken speare the eldest boy downe threw,
And boldly (ouer boldly) drew his blade,
Wherewith he stroue (but stroue therewith in vaine)
The Pagans stead (vnmarked) to haue slaine.

31

But as a mountaine or a cape of land
Assail'd with stormes and seas on euery side,
Doth vnremoued, stedfast, still withstand
Storme, thunder, lightning, tempest, winde and tide:
The Soldan so withstood *Latinus* band,
And vnremou'd did all their iustes abide,
   And of that haplesse youth (who hurt his stead)
   Downe to the chin he cleft in twaine the head.

32

Kinde *Aramante* (who saw his brother slaine)
To hold him vp stretcht forth his friendly arme,
O foolish kindnes, and O pitie vaine,
To adde our proper losse, to others harme!
The Prince let fall his sword and cut in twaine
(About his brother twinde) the childes weake arme,
   Downe from their saddles both together slide,
   Together mourn'd they, and together dide.

33

That done, *Sabinos* lance with nimble force
He cut in twaine, and gainst the stripling bold
He spurr'd his stead, that vnderneath his horse
The hardie infant tumbled on the mold,
Whose soule (out squeased from his brused corse)
With ougly painfulnes forsooke her hold,
   And deepely mourn'd, that of so sweet a cage
   She left the blisse, and ioyes of youthfull age.

34

But *Picus* yet and *Laurence* were on liue,
Whom at one birth their mother faire brought out,
A paire whose likenes made the parents striue
Oft which was which, and ioyed in their dout:
But what their birth did vndistinguisht giue,
The Soldans rage made knowne, for *Picus* stout
   Headlesse at one huge blow he laid in dust,
   And through the brest his gentle brother thrust.

Headline eight < ninth (*as corrected in M.*)

35

Their father, (but no father now, alas!
When all his noble sonnes at once were slaine)
In their fiue deathes so often murdred was,
I know not how his life could him sustaine,
Except his hart were forg'd of steele or bras,
Yet still he liu'd, pardie, he saw not plaine
   Their dying lookes, although their deathes he knoes,
   It is some ease, not to behold our woes.

36

He wept not, for the night her curtaine spred
Betweene his cause of weeping and his eies,
But still he mourn'd and on sharpe veng'ance fed,
And thinkes he conquers, if reueng'd he dies;
He thirstes the Soldans heath'nish blood to shed,
And yet his owne at lesse then nought doth prise,
   Nor can he tell whether he leifer would,
   Or die himselfe, or kill the Pagan bould.

37

'At last, is this right hand (quoth he) so weake,
That thou disdainst gainst me to vse thy might?
Can it nought doe? can this toong nothing speake
That may prouoke thine ire, thy wrath, and spight?'
With that he stroke (his anger great to wreake)
A blowe, that pearst the maile and mettall bright,
   And in his flanke set ope a flood-gate wide,
   Whereat the blood out streamed from his side.

38

Prouoked with his crie, and with that blowe
The Turke vpon him gan his blade discharge,
He cleft his brest-plate, hauing first pearst throwe
(Lined with seu'n bulles hides) his mightie targe,
And sheath'd his weapon in his guts belowe,
Wretched *Latinus* at that issue large,
   And at his mouth, powr'd out his vitall blood,
   And sprinkled with the same his murdred brood.

39

On Appenine like as a sturdie tree,
Against the windes that makes resistance stout,
If with a storme it ouerturned bee,
Falles downe and breakes the trees and plants about;
So *Latine* fell, and with him felled hee
And slew the nearest of the Pagans rout,
    A worthie end, fit for a man of fame,
     That dying, slew; and conqu'red, ouercame.

40

Meane-while the Soldan stroue his rage interne
To satisfie with blood of Christians spild,
Th'Arabians hartned by their captaine sterne,
With murder euery tent and cabbin fild,
Henry the English knight, and *Olipherne*,
O fierce *Draguto* by thy hands were kild!
    Gilbert and *Phillip* were by *Ariadene*
     Both slaine, both borne vpon the banks of Rhene.

41

Albazar with his mace *Ernesto* slew,
Vnder *Algazell Engerlan* downe fell,
But the huge murder of the meaner crew,
Or maner of their deathes, what toong can tell?
Godfrey, when first the heathen trumpets blew,
Awakt, which heard, no feare could make him dwell,
    But he and his were vp and arm'd ere long,
     And marched forward with a squadron strong,

42

He that well heard the rumour and the crie,
And markt the tumult still grow and more,
Th'Arabian theeues he iudged by and by
Against his soldiers made this battaile sore;
For that they forraid all the countries nie,
And spoil'd the fields, the Duke knew well before,
    Yet thought he not they had the hardiment
     So to assaile him in his armed tent.

43

'All sodainly he heard (while on he went)
How to the citie ward 'arme, arme,' they cride,
The noise vpreared to the firmament
With dreadfull howling fild the valleies wide:
This was *Clorinda*, whom the king forth sent
To battaile, and *Argantes* by her side.
   The Duke (this heard) to *Guelpho* turn'd, and prai'd
   Him, his lieutenant be, and to him said:

44

'You heare this new alarme from yonder part,
That from the towne breakes out with so much rage,
Vs needeth much your valour and your art
To calme their furie, and there heate to swage;
Goe thither then, and with you take some part
Of these braue soldiers of mine equipage,
   While with the res'due of my champions bold
   I driue these wolues againe out of our fold.'

45

They parted (this agreed on them betweene)
By diuers pathes, Lord *Guelpho* to the hill,
And *Godfrey* hasted where th'Arabians keene,
His men like seelie sheepe destroy and kill;
But as he went his troopes encreased beene,
From euery part the people flocked still,
   That now growne strong enough, he proched nie
   Where the fierce Turke caus'd many a Christian die.

46

So from the top of Vesulus the cold,
Downe to the sandie valleies, tumbleth Poe,
Whose streames the further from their fountaine rold
Still stronger wax, and with more puissance goe;
And horned like a bull his forehead bold
He liftes, and ore his broken banks doth floe,
   And with his hornes to pearse the sea assaies,
   To which he profreth war, not tribute paies.

47

The Duke his men fast flying did espie,
And thither ran, and thus (displeased) spake,
'What feare is this? O whither doe you flie?
See who they be that this pursuit doe make,
A hartlesse band, that dare no battell trie,
Who wounds before dare neither giue nor take,
 Against them turne your sterne eies threatning sight,
 An angrie looke will put them all to flight.'

48

This said, he spurred forth where *Soliman*
Destroi'd Christes vineyard like a sauage bore,
Through streames of blood, through dust and dirt, he ran,
Ore heapes of bodies wallowing in their gore,
The squadrons close his sword to ope began,
He brake their ranks, behinde, beside, before,
 And (where he goes) vnder his feet he treades
 The armed Sarracines, and barbed steades.

49

This slaughter-house of angrie *Mars* he past,
Where thousands dead, halfe dead, and dying weare.
The hardy Soldan saw him come in hast,
Yet neither stept aside not shrunke for feare,
But buskt him bold to fight, aloft he cast
His blade, prepar'd to strike, and stepped neare,
 These noble Princes twaine (so fortune wrought)
 From the worlds ends here met, and here they fought:

50

With vertue, furie; strength with courage stroue,
For Asias mightie empire, who can tell
With how strange force their cruell blowes they droue?
How sore their combat was, how fierce, how fell?
Great deedes they wrought, each others harnesse cloue;
Yet still in darknes (more the ruth) they dwell.
 The night their actes her blacke vaile couered vnder,
 Their actes whereat the sunne, the world might wonder.

51

The Christians (by their guides ensample) harted,
Of their best armed made a squadron strong,
And to defend their chieftaine forth they started:
The Pagans also sau'd their knight from wrong,
Fortune her fauours twixt them eu'nly parted,
Fierce was th'encounter bloodie, doubtfull, long,
 These wonne, those lost; these lost, those wonne againe,
 The losse was equall, eu'n the numbers slaine.

52

With equall rage as when the southren winde
Meeteth in battaile strong the northren blast,
The sea and aire to neither is refinde,
But cloud gainst cloud, and waue gainst waue they cast:
So from this skirmish neither part declinde,
But fought it out, and kept their footings fast,
 And oft with furious shocke together rush,
 And shield gainst shield, and helme gainst helme they crush.

53

The battaile eeke to Sion ward grew hot,
The soldiers slaine the hardie knights were kild,
Legions of sprites from Limboes prisons got,
The emptie aire the hils and valleies fild,
Harting the Pagans that they shrinked not,
Till where they stood their dearest blood they spild,
 And with new rage, *Argantes* they inspire,
 Whose heate no flames, whose burning need no fire.

54

Where he came in he put to shamefull flight
The fearefull watch, and ore the trenches leapt,
Eu'n with the ground he made the rampires hight,
And murdred bodies in the ditch vp heapt,
So that his greedie mates with labour light,
Amid the tents, a bloodie haruest reapt:
 Clorinda went the proud Circassian bie,
 So from a piece two chained bullets flie.

55

Now fled the Frenchmen, when in luckie howre
Arriued *Guelpho*, and his helping band,
He made them turne against this stormie showre,
And with bold face their wicked foes withstand.
Sternly they fought, that from their wounds downe powre
The streames of blood, and ronne on either hand:
    The Lord of heauen meane-while vpon this fight,
    From his hie throne bent downe his gracious sight.

56

From whence, with grace and goodnes compast round,
He ruleth, blesseth, keepeth all he wrought,
Aboue the aire, the fire, the sea and ground,
Our sense, our wit, our reason and our thought,
Where persons three (with powre and glorie crown'd)
Are all one God, who made all things of nought,
    Vnder whose feete (subiected to his grace)
    Sit nature, fortune, motion, time and place.

57

This is the place, from whence like smoke and dust
Of this fraile world the wealth, the pompe and powre,
He tosseth, tumbleth, turneth as he lust,
And guides our life, our death, our end and howre:
No eie (how euer vertuous, pure and iust)
Can vew the brightnes of that glorious bowre,
    On euery side the blessed spirits bee,
    Equall in ioies, though diffring in degree.

58

With harmonie of their celestiall song
The pallace ecchoed from the chambers pure,
At last he *Michael* call'd (in harnesse strong
Of neuer yeelding dimonds armed sure)
'Behold (quoth he) to doe despite and wrong
To that deere flocke my mercie hath in cure,
    How *Sathan* from hels lothsome prison sends
    His ghosts, his sprites, his furies and his fends.

59

'Goe bid them all depart, and leaue the caire
Of war to soldiers, as doth best pertaine:
Bid them forbeare t'infect the earth and aire,
To darken heau'ns faire light, bid them refraine;
Bid them to *Acherons* blacke flood repaire,
Fit house for them, the house of greefe and paine,
 There let their king himselfe and them torment,
 So I command, goe tell them mine intent.'

60

This said, the winged warriour lowe inclinde
At his creators feet with reu'rence dew;
Then spred his golden feathers to the winde,
And swift as thought away the angell flew,
He past the light, and shining fire assinde
The glorious seat of his selected crew,
 The mouer first and circle Christalline,
 The firmament, where fixed stars all shine.

61

Vnlike in working than, in shape and show,
At his left hand, *Saturne* he left and *Ioue*,
And those vntruly errant call'd I trow,
Since he erres not, who them doth guide and moue:
The fields he passed then, whence haile and snow,
Thunder and raine fall downe from cloudes aboue,
 Where heat and cold, drinesse and moisture striue,
 Whose wars all creatures kill, and slaine, reuiue.

62

The horrid darknes and the shadowes dunne
Dispersed he with his eternall wings,
The flames (which from his heau'nly eies outrunne)
Beguilde the earth, and all her sable things;
After a storme so spreadeth forth the sunne
His raies, and bindes the cloudes in golden strings,
 Or in the stilnesse of a moone-shine eauen,
 A falling star so glideth downe from heauen.

63

But when th'infernall troope he proched neare,
That still the Pagans ire and rage prouoke,
The angell on his wings himselfe did beare,
And shooke his lance, and thus at last he spoke;
'Haue you not learned yet to know and feare
The Lords iust wrath, and thunders dreadfull stroke?
    Or in the torments of your endlesse ill,
    Are you still fierce, still proud, rebellious still?

64

'The Lord hath sworne to breake the iron bands
The brasen gates of Sions fort which close,
Who is it that his sacred will withstands?
Against his wrath who dares himselfe oppose?
Goe hence you curst to your appointed lands,
The realmes of death, of torments, and of woes,
    And in the deepes of that infernall lake
    Your battailes fight, and there your triumphes make,

65

There tyrannise vpon the soules you finde
Condemn'd to woe, and double still their paines,
Where some complaine, where some their teeth doe grinde,
Some howle and weepe, some clinke their iron chaines:'
This said, they fled, and those that staid behinde
With his sharpe lance he driueth and constraines,
    They sighing left the lands, his siluer sheepe
    Where *Hesperus* doth lead, doth feed, doth keepe,

66

And towards hell their lazie wings display,
To wreake their malice on the damned gostes,
The birds that follow *Titans* hottest ray,
Passe not by so great flocks to warmer costes,
Nor leaues by so great numbers fall away,
When winter nips them with his new-come frostes,
    The earth (deliu'red from so foule annoy)
    Recall'd her beautie, and resum'd her ioy.

67

But not for this (in fierce *Argantes* brest)
Less'ned the rancour or decai'd the ire,
Although *Alecto* left him to infest,
With the hot brands of her infernall fire,
His armed head with his sharpe blade he blest,
And those thicke ranks which seemed most intire
 He broke, the strong, the weake, the high, the low,
 Were equallized by his murdring blow.

68

Not far from him, amid the blood and dust,
Heads, armes, and legs *Clorinda* strowed wide,
Her sword through *Berengarios* brest she thrust,
Quite through his hart where life doth chiefly bide,
And that fell blow she stroke so sure and iust,
That at his backe his blood and life forth glide,
 Euen in the mouth she smote *Albinus* than,
 And cut in twaine the visage of the man;

69

Gerniers right hand she from his arme deuided,
Whereof but late she had receiu'd a wound,
The hand his sword still held, although not guided,
The fingers (halfe on liue) stirr'd on the ground,
So from a serpent slaine the taile deuided
Moues in the grasse, rolleth and tumbleth round.
 The Championesse so wounded left the knight,
 And gainst *Achilles* turn'd her weapon bright:

70

Vpon his necke light that vnhappie blowe
And cut the sinewes and the throte in twaine,
The head fell downe vpon the earth belowe,
And soil'd with dust the visage on the plaine;
The headlesse trunke (a wofull thing to knowe)
Still in the saddle seated did remaine,
 Vntill his stead (that felt the raines at large)
 With leapes and flings that burden did discharge.

71

While thus this faire and fierce *Bellona* slew
The westren Lords, and put their troopes to flight,
Gildippes raged mongst the Pagan crew,
And low in dust laid many a worthie knight:
Like was their sexe, their beautie and their hew,
Like was their youth, their courage and their might;
    Yet fortune would they should the battaile trie, :
    Of mightier foes, for both were fram'd to die.

72

Yet wisht they oft, and stroue in vaine to meet,
So great betwixt them was the prease and throng.
But hardie *Guelpho* gainst *Clorinda* sweet
Ventred his sword, to worke her harme and wrong,
And with a cutting blow so did her greet,
That from her side the blood stream'd downe along;
    But with a thrust an answer sharpe she made,
    And twixt his ribs colour'd some-deale her blade.

73

Lord *Guelpho* stroke againe, but hit her not,
For strong *Osmida* haply passed bie,
And not meant him, anothers wound he got,
That cleft his front in twaine aboue his eie:
Neare *Guelpho* now the battaile waxed hot,
For all the troopes he led gan thither hie,
    And thither drew eeke many a Painim knight,
    That fierce, sterne, bloodie, deadly waxt the fight.

74

Meane-while the purple morning peeped ore
The eastren threshold, to our halfe of land,
And *Argillano* in this great vprore
From prison loosed was, and what he fand,
Those armes he hent, and to the field them bore,
Resolu'd to take his chance what came to hand,
    And with great actes amid the Pagan host
    Would winne againe his reputation lost.

75

As a fierce stead scapte from his stall at large,
Where he had long beene kept for warlike need,
Runnes through the fieldes vnto the flowrie marge
Of some greene forrest, where he vs'de to feed,
His curled maine his shoulders broad doth charge,
And from his loftie crest doth spring and spreed,
  Thunder his feet, his nostrels fire breath out,
  And with his neie the world resoundes about:

76

So *Argillan* rusht forth, sparkled his eies,
His front high lifted was, no feare therein,
Lightly he leapes and skips, it seemes he flies,
He left no signe in dust imprinted thin,
And comming nere his foes, he sternly cries,
(As one that forst not all their strength a pin,)
  'You outcasts of the world, you men of nought,
  What hath in you this boldnesse newly wrought?

77

'Too weake are you to beare an helme or sheild,
Vnfit to arme your brest in iron bright,
You runne halfe naked, trembling through the feild,
Your blowes are feeble and your hope in flight,
Your factes and all the actions that you weild,
The darknes hides, your bulwarke is the night,
  Now she is gone, how will your fights succeed?
  Now better armes and better harts you need.'

78

While thus he spoke he gaue a cruell stroke
Against *Algazells* throte with might and maine;
And as he would haue answer'd him, and spoke,
He stopt his words, and cut his iawes in twaine;
Vpon his eies death spred his mistie cloke,
A chilling frost congealed euery vaine,
  He fell, and with his teeth the earth he tore,
  Raging in death, and full of rage before.

76⁶ pin, < pin,)

79

Then by his puissance mightie *Saladine*,
Proud *Agricalt* and *Muleasses* dide,
And at one wondrous blow his weapon fine,
Did *Adiazell* in two parts deuide,
Then through the brest he wounded *Ariadine*,
Whom dying with sharpe taunts he gan deride,
　　He lifting vp vneath his feeble eies,
　　To his proud scornes thus answ'reth, ere he dies:

80

'Not thou (who ere thou art) shall glorie long
Thy happie conquest in my death, I trow,
Like chance awaites thee from a hand more strong,
Which by my side will shortly lay thee low:'
He smilde, and said, of mine howre short or long
Let heau'n take care; but here meane-while die thow,
　　Pasture for woolues and crowe, on him his fout
　　He set, and drew his sword and life both out.

81

Among this squadron rode a gentle page,
The Soldans minion, darling and delite,
On whose faire chin the spring-time of his age
Yet blossom'd out her flowres, small or lite;
The sweat (spred on his cheekes with heat and rage)
Seem'd pearles or morning dewes, on lillies white,
　　The dust therein vprold, adorn'd his haire,
　　His face seem'd fierce and sweet, wrathfull and faire.

82

His stead was white and white as purest snow
That falles on tops of aged Appenine,
Lightning and storme are not so swift I trow
As he, to run, to stop, to turne and twine,
A dart his right hand shaked, prest to throw,
His curtlax by his thigh, short, hooked, fine,
　　And brauing in his Turkish pompe he shone,
　　In purple robe, ore fret with gold and stone.

83

The hardie boy (while thirst of warlike praise
Bewitched so his vnaduised thought)
Gainst euery band his childish strength assaies,
And little danger found, though much he sought,
Till *Argillan* (that watcht fit time alwaies
In his swift turnes to strike him as he fought)
    Did vnawares his snowe-white courser slay,
    And vnder him his master tumbling lay:

84

And gainst his face (where loue and pitie stand,
To pray him that rich throne of beautie spare)
The cruell man stretcht forth his murdring hand,
To spoile those gifts, where of he had no share:
It seem'd remorse and sense was in his brand,
Which lighting flat, to hurt the lad forbare;
    But all for nought, gainst him the point he bent,
    That (what the edge had spared) pearst and rent.

85

Fierce *Soliman*, that with *Godfredo* striued
Who first should enter conquests glorious gate,
Left off the fray, and thither headlong driued,
When first he saw the lad in such estate;
He brake the prease and soone enough arriued
To take reuenge, but to his aide too late,
    Bicause he saw his *Lesbine* slaine and lost,
    Like a sweet flower nipt with vntimely frost:

86

He saw waxe dim the starre-light of his eies,
His iuorie necke vpon his shoulders fell,
In his pale lookes kinde pities image lies,
That death eu'n mourn'd, to heare his passing bell,
His marble hart such soft impression tries,
That midst his wrath, his manly teares outwell,
    Thou weepest *Soliman* thou that beheild
    Thy kingdoms lost, and not one teare couldst yeild.

86⁷ *Soliman*) < *Soliman*

87

But when the murdrers sword he hapt to vew
Dropping with blood of his *Lesbino* dead,
His pitie vanisht, ire and rage renew,
He had no leasure bootlesse teares to shead;
But with his blade on *Argillano* flew,
And cleft his shield, his helmet, and his head,
    Downe to his throte; and worthie was that blow
    Of *Soliman,* his strength and wrath to show:

88

And not content with this, downe from his horse
He light, and that dead carkas rent and tore,
Like a fierce dog that takes his angrie corse
To bite the stone, which had him hit before.
O comfort vaine! for greefe of so great force,
To wound the senselesse earth, that feels no sore.
    But mightie *Godfrey* gainst the Soldans traine
    Spent not (this while) his force and blowes in vaine.

89

A thousand hardie Turkes afront he had
In sturdie iron arm'd from head to fout,
Resolu'd in all aduentures good or bad,
In actions wise, in execution stout,
Who *Soliman* into Arabia lad
When from his kingdome he was first cast out,
    Where liuing wilde with their exiled guide,
    To him in all extremes they faithfull bide;

90

All these in thickest order sure vnite,
For *Godfreys* valour small or nothing shranke,
Corcutes first he on the face did smite,
Then wounded strong *Rosteno* in the flanke,
At one blowe *Selims* head he stroke off quite,
Then both *Rossanoes* armes, in euery ranke
    The boldest knights (of all that chosen crew)
    He felled, maimed, wounded, hurt and slew.

91

While thus he killed many a Sarracine,
And all their fierce assaults vnhurt sustained,
Ere fortune wholy from the Turks decline,
While still they hoped much, though small they gained,
Behold a cloud of dust, wherein doth shine
Lightning of war, in midst thereof contained,
   Whence vnawares burst forth a storme of swords,
   Which tremble made the Pagan knights and Lords.

92

These fiftie champions were, mongst whom there stands
(In siluer field) the ensigne of Christes death,
If I had mouthes and toongs as *Briareus* hands,
If voice as iron tough, if iron breath,
What harme this troope wrought to the heathen bands,
What knights they slew, I could recount vneath,
   In vaine the Turks resist, th'Arabians flie;
   For if they flie, th'are slaine; if fight, they die.

93

Feare, crueltie, griefe, horrour, sorrow, paine,
Ronne through the field, disguis'd in diuers shapes,
Death might you see triumphant on the plaine,
Drowning in blood him that from blowes escapes.
The king meane-while with parcell of his traine,
Comes hastly out, and for sure conquest gapes,
   And from a banke whereon he stood beheild,
   The doubtfull hazard of that bloodie feild.

94

But when he saw the Pagans shrinke away,
He sounded the retreat, and gan desire
His messengers in his behalfe to pray
Argantes and *Clorinda* to retire;
The furious couple both at once said nay,
Eu'n drunke with shedding blood, and mad with ire,
   At last they went and to recomfort thought,
   And stay their troopes from flight, but all for nought.

95

For who can gouerne cowardise or feare?
Their host already was begon to flie,
They cast their shields and cutting swords arreare,
As not defended, but made slow thereby,
A hollow dale the cities bulwarks neare,
From west to south out stretched long doth lie,
    Thither they fled, and in a mist of dust,
    Towards the walles they ronne, they throng, they thrust.

96

While downe the banke disordred thus they ran,
The Christian knights huge slaughter on them maide;
But when to clime the other hill they gan,
Old *Aladine* came fiercely to their aide:
On that steepe bray Lord *Guelpho* would not than
Hazard his folke, but there his soldiers staide,
    And safe within the cities walles the king
    The reliques small of that sharpe fight did bring:

97

Meane-while the Soldan in this latest charge
Had done as much, as humane force was able,
All sweat and blood appear'd his members large,
His breath was short, his courage waxt vnstable,
His arme grew weake, to beare his mightie targe,
His hand to rule his heauie sword vnable,
    Which bruis'd, not cut, so blunted was the blade,
    It lost the use for which a sword was made.

98

Feeling his weaknesse, he gan musing stand,
And in his troubled thought this question tost,
If he himselfe should murder with his hand,
(Bicause none else should of his conquest bost)
Or he should saue his life, when on the land
Lay slaine the pride of his subdued host,
    'At last to fortunes power (quoth he) I yield,
    And on my flight let her her trophies beild.

99

'Let *Godfrey* vew my flight, and smile to see
This mine vnworthie second banishment,
For arm'd againe soone shall he heare of mee,
From his proud head th'vnsetled crowne to rent,
For (as my wrongs) my wrath eterne, shall bee,
And euery howre (the bow of war new bent)
   I will arise againe, a foe, fierce, bold,
    Though dead, though slaine, though burnt to ashes cold.'

The tenth Booke of Godfrey of Bulloigne

The argument.

Ismen from sleepe awakes the Soldan great,
And into Sion brings the Prince by night,
Where the sad king sits fearfull on his seat,
Whom he embold'neth and excites to fight:
Godfredo *heares his Lords and knights repeat*
How they escapt Armidaes *wrath and spight:*
Rinaldo *knowne to liue,* Peter *fore saies*
His ofsprings vertue good desarts and praies.

I

A Gallant stead (while thus the Soldan said)
    Came trotting by him, without Lord or guide,
Quickly his hand vpon the raines he laid,
And weake and wearie climbed vp to ride;
The snake (that on his crest hot fire out braid,
Was quite cut off, his helme had lost the pride,
  His coate was rent, his harnesse hackt and cleft,
  And of his kingly pompe no signe was left.

2

As when a sauage woolfe chas'd from the fold
(To hide his head) runnes to some holt or wood,
Who though he filled haue while it might hold
His greedy panch, yet hungreth after food,
With sanguine toong forth of his lips out rold
About his iawes that lickes vp fome and blood;
  So from this bloodie fray the Soldan hied,
  His rage vnquencht, his wrath vnsatisfied.

3

And (as his fortune would) he scaped free
From thousand arrowes which about him flew,
From swords and lances, instruments that bee
Of certaine death, himselfe he safe withdrew,

Vnknowne, vnseene, disguised, trauail'd hee
By desart pathes, and waies but vs'd by few,
   And rode reuoluing in his troubled thought
   What course to take, and yet resolu'd on nought.

4

Thither at last he ment to take his way,
Where Egypts king assembled all his host,
To ioine with him, and once againe assay
To winne by fight, by which so oft he lost:
Determin'd thus he made no longer stay,
But thither ward spurr'd forth his steed in post,
   Nor need he guide, the way right well he could,
   That leades to sandie plaines of Gaza ould.

5

Nor though his smarting wounds torment him oft,
His body weake and wounded backe and side,
Yet rested he, nor once his armour doft,
But all day long ore hils and dales doth ride:
But when the night cast vp her shade aloft,
And all earthes colours strange in sables dide
   He light, and as he could his wounds vpbound,
   And shooke ripe dates downe from a palme he found.

6

On them he supped, and amid the feild
To rest his wearie lims a while he sought,
He made his pillow of his broken sheild,
To ease the griefes of his distempred thought,
But little ease could so hard lodging yeild,
His wounds so smarted that he slept right nought,
   And (in his brest) his proud hart rent in twaine,
   Two inward vultures, sorrow and disdaine.

7

At length when midnight with her silence deepe
Did heau'n and earth husht, still and quiet make,
Sore watcht and wearie, he began to steepe
His cares and sorrowes in obliuions lake,

And in a little, short, vnquiet sleepe
Some small repose his fainting spirits take,
   But (while he slept) a voice graue and seueare
   At vnawares thus thundred in his eare:

8

'O *Soliman*! thou far renowmed king
Till better season serue, forbeare thy rest;
A stranger doth thy lands in thraldome bring,
Nice is a slaue, by Christian yoke opprest,
Sleepest thou here, forgetfull of this thing,
That here thy friends lie slaine, not laid in chest?
   Whose bones beare witnes of thy shame and scorne,
   And wilt thou idly here attend the morne?'

9

The king awakt, and saw before his eies
A man whose presence seemed graue and old,
A writhen staffe his steps vnstable guies,
Which seru'd his feeble members to vphold,
'And what art thou? (the Prince in scorne replies)
What sprite to vexe poore passengers so bold,
   To breake their sleepe? or what to thee belongs
   My shame, my losse, my veng'ance, or my wrongs?'

10

'I am the man; of thine intent (quoth hee)
And purpose new, that sure coniecture hath,
And better than thou weenest know I thee,
I proffer thee my seruice and my faith,
My speeches therefore sharpe and biting bee,
Bicause quicke words the whetstones are of wrath,
   Accept in gree (my Lord) the words I spoke,
   As spurres thine ire and courage to prouoke.

11

'But now to visit Egypts mighty king,
Vnlesse my iudgement faile you are prepar'd,
I prophesie about a needlesse thing
You suffer shall a voiage long and hard:

For though you stay the monarch great will bring
His new assembled host to Iuda ward,
　No place of seruice there, no cause of fight,
　Nor gainst our foes to vse your force and might.

12

'But if you follow me, within this wall
(With Christian armes hemm'd in on euery side)
Withouten battaile, fight or stroke at all,
(Eu'n at noone day) I will you safely guide,
Where you delight, reioice and glorie shall
In perils great, to see your prowesse tride.
　That noble towne you may preserue and shield,
　Till Egypts host come to renue the field.'

13

While thus he parled of this aged guest,
The Turke the words and lookes did both admire,
And from his hautie eies and furious brest
He laid apart his pride, his rage and ire,
And humbly said, 'I willing am and prest
To follow where thou leadest (reuerend sire)
　And that aduise best fits my angrie vaine,
　That tels of greatest perill, greatest paine.'

14

The old man prais'd his words, and for the aire
His late receiued wounds to worse disposes,
A quintessence therein he powred faire,
That stops the bleeding, and incision closes:
Beholding than before *Apolloes* chaire
How fresh *Aurora* violets straw'd and roses,
　'Its time' he saies 'to wend, for *Titan* bright
　To wonted labour, sommons euery wight.'

15

And to a chariot (that beside did stand)
Ascended he, and with him *Soliman*,

13⁸ grearest < greatest

He tooke the raines, and with a maistring hand
Ruled his steades and whipt them now and than,
The wheeles or horses feet vpon the land
Had left no signe nor token where they ran,
   The coursers pant and smoke with lukewarme sweat,
   And (foming creame) their iron mouthfuls eat.

16

The aire about them round (a wondrous thing)
It selfe on heapes in solid thicknes drew,
The chariot hiding and enuironing
The subtile mist no mortall eie could vew,
And yet no stone from engin cast or sling
Could pearse the cloud, it was of proofe so trew;
   Yet seene it was to them within which ride,
   And heau'n and earth without, all cleere beside.

17

His beetle browes the Turke amazed bent,
He wrinkled vp his front, and wildly stared
Vpon the cloud and chariot, as it went,
For speed to *Cinthias* carre right well compared:
The other seeing his astonishment
How he bewondred was, and how he fared,
   All sodainly by name the Prince gan call,
   By which awaked thus he spoke withall.

18

'Who ere thou art aboue all worldly wit
That hast these high and wondrous maruailes wrought,
And know'st the deepe intents which hidden sit
In secret closet of mans priuate thought,
If in thy skilfull hart this lore be writ
To tell th'euent of things to end vnbrought;
   Then say, what issue and what end the starres
   Allot to Asias troubles, broiles and warres.

19

'But tell me first thy name, and by what art
Thou dost these wonders strange, aboue our skill;

For full of maruaile is my troubled hart,
Tell then and leaue me not amazed still.'
The wisard smil'd and answ'red, 'in some part
Easie it is to satisfie thy will,
    Ismen I hight, call'd an enchanter great,
    Such skill haue I in magikes secret feat.

20

'But that I should the sure euents vnfold
Of things to come, or destinies foretell,
Too rash is your desire, your wish too bold,
To mortall hart such knowledge neuer fell;
Our wit and strength on vs bestow'd I hold,
To shunne th'euils and harmes, mongst which we dwell,
    They make their fortune who are stout and wise,
    Wit rules the heau'ns, discretion guides the skies.

21

'That puissant arme of thine that well can rend
From *Godfreys* brow the new vsurped crowne,
And not alone protect, saue and defend
From his fierce people, this besieged towne,
Gainst fire and sword with strength and courage bend,
Aduenture, suffer, trust, tread perils downe,
    And to content and to encourage thee,
    Know this, which I as in a cloud foresee.

22

'I guesse (before the ouer-gliding sonne
Shall many yeeres meet out by weekes and daies)
A Prince that shall in fertill Egypt wonne
Shall fill all Asia with his prosp'rous fraies;
I speake not of his actes in quiet donne,
His policie, his rule, his wisdomes praise,
    Let this suffice, by him these Christians shall
    In fight subdued flie, and conquered fall.

23

'And their great empire and vsurped state
Shall ouerthrowne in dust and ashes lie,

Their wofull remnant in an angle strate
Compast with sea themselues shall fortifie,
From thee shall spring this Lord of war and fate,'
Whereto great *Soliman* gan thus replie;
   'O happie man to so great praise ibore,'
   Thus he reiois'd, but yet enuied more;

24

And said, 'let chance with good or bad aspect
Vpon me looke as sacred heau'ns decree,
This hart to her I neuer will subiect,
Nor euer conqu'red shall she looke on mee;
The moone her chariot shall awrie direct,
Ere from this course I will diuerted bee,'
   While thus he spake it seem'd he breathed fire,
   So fierce his courage was, so hot his ire.

25

Thus talked they, till they arriued beene
Nie to the place where *Godfreys* tents were reared,
There was a wofull spectacle iseene,
Death in a thousand ougly formes appeared,
The Soldan changed hew for greefe and teene,
On that sad booke his shame and losse he leared,
   Ah with what griefe his men, his friends he found,
   And standards proud, inglorious lie on ground!

26

And saw on visage of some well knowne frend
(In foule despite) a rascall French man tread,
And there another ragged peasant rend
The armes and garments from some champion dead,
And there with stately pompe by heapes they wend,
And Christians slaine rolle vp in webs of lead;
   Lastly the Turks and slaine Arabians (brought
   On heapes) he saw them burne with fire to nought.

27

Deepely he sighed, and with naked sword
Out of the coach he leaped in the mire,

But *Ismen* call'd againe the angrie Lord,
And with graue words appeas'd his foolish ire.
The Prince content remounted at his word,
Towards a hill on droue the aged sire,
   And hasting forward vp the banke they passe,
   Till far behinde the Christian leaguer was.

28

There they alight and tooke their way on fout,
The emptie chariot vanisht out of sight,
Yet still the cloud enuiron'd them about,
At their left hand downe went they from the hight
Of Sions hill, till they approcht the rout,
On that side where to west he looketh right,
   There *Ismen* staied and his eie-sight bent
   Vpon the bushie rocks, and thither went.

29

A hollow caue was in the craggie stone,
Wrought out by hand a number yeeres tofore,
And for of long that way had walked none,
The vault was hid with plants and bushes hore,
The wisard stooping in thereat to gone,
The thornes aside and scratching brambles bore,
   His right hand sought the passage through the cleft,
   And for his guide he gaue the Prince his left.

30

'What (quoth the Soldan) by what priuie mine?
What hidden vault behooues it me to creepe?
This sword can finde a better way than thine,
Although our foes the passage garde and keepe.'
'Let not (quoth he) thy princely foote repine
To tread this secret path, though darke and deepe;
   For great king *Herod* vs'd to tread the same,
   He that in armes had whilome so great fame.

30⁶ seeret < secret

31

'This passage made he, when he would suppresse
His subiects pride, and them in bondage hold;
By this he could from that small forteresse
Antonia call'd, of *Antonie* the bold,
Conuay his folke vnseene of more and lesse
Eu'n to the middest of the temple old,
　　Thence, hither; where these priuie waies begin,
　　And bring vnseene whole armies out and in.

32

'But now saue I in all this world liues none
That knowes the secret of this darksome place,
Come then where *Aladine* sits on his throne,
With Lords and princes set about his grace,
He feareth more then fitteth such an one,
Such signes of doubt shew in his cheere and face;
　　Fitly you come, heare, see, and keepe you still,
　　Till time and season serue, then speake your fill.'

33

This said, that narrow entrance past the knight,
(So creepes a camell through a needles eie)
And through the waies as black as darkest night
He followed him, that did him rule and guie;
Strait was the way at first, withouten light,
But further in did further amplifie;
　　So that vpright walked at ease the men
　　Ere they had passed halfe that secret den,

34

A priuie doore *Ismen* vnlockt at last,
And vp they clombe a little vsed staire,
Thereat the day a feeble beame in cast,
Dimme was the light, and nothing cleere the aire;
Out of the hollow caue at length they past,
Into a goodly hall, high, broad and faire,
　　Where crown'd with gold and all in purple clad
　　Sate the sad king, among his nobles sad.

35

The Turke (close in his hollow cloud imbard)
Vnseene, at will did all the prease behold,
These heauie speeches of the king he hard,
Who thus from loftie siege his pleasure told;
'My Lords, last day our state was much empard,
Our friends were slaine, kild were our soldiers bold,
   Great helpes and greater hopes are vs bereft,
   Nor ought but aide from Egypt land is left:

36

'And well you see far distant is that aid,
Vpon our heeles our danger treadeth still,
For your aduise was this assemblie maid,
Each what he thinketh speake, and what he will.'
A whisper soft arose when this was said,
As gentle winds the groues with murmur fill,
   But with bold face, high lookes and merrie cheare
   Argantes rose, the rest their talke forbeare.

37

'O worthie soueraigne' (thus began to say
The hardie yong man to the tyrant wise)
'What words be these? what feares doe you dismay?
Who knowes not this, you need not our aduise?
But on our hands your hope of conquest lay,
And, for no losse true vertue damnifies,
   Make her our shield, pray her vs succours giue,
   And without her let vs not wish to liue.

38

'Nor say I this for that I ought misdeeme
That Egypts promis'd succours faile vs might,
Doubtfull of my great maisters words to seeme,
To me were neither lawfull, iust, nor right:
I speake these words, for spurres I them esteeme
To waken vp each dull and fearfull spright,
   And make our harts resolu'd to all assaies,
   To winne with honour or to die with praise.'

39

Thus much *Argantes* said, and said no more,
(As if the case were cleere of which he spoke.)
Orcano rose, of princely stem ibore,
Whose presence mongst them bore a mightie stroke,
A man esteemed well in armes of yore;
But now was coupled new in marriage yoke,
 Yong babes he had, to fight which made him loth,
 He was a husband and a father both.

40

'My Lord (quoth he) I will not reprehend
The earnest zeale of this audacious speach,
From courage sprong, which seld is close i'pend
In swelling stomacke without violent breach;
And though to you our good Circassian frend,
In termes too bold and feruent oft doth preach,
 Yet hold I that for good, in warlike feat
 For his great deedes respond his speeches great.

41

'But if it you beseeme (whom grauer age
And long experience hath made wise and slie)
To rule the heat of youth and hardie rage,
Which somewhat haue misled this knight awrie,
In equall ballance ponder than and gage
Your hopes far distant, with your perils nie;
 This townes old walles and rampires new compare,
 With *Godfreys* forces, and his engins rare.

42

'But (if I may say what I thinke vnblamed)
This towne is strong, by nature, scite and art,
But engins huge and instruments are framed
Gainst these defences by our aduerse part,
Who thinkes him most secure is eathest shamed;
I hope the best, yet feare vnconstant *Mart*,
 And with this siege if we be long vp pent,
 Famine I doubt, our store will all be spent.

43

'For all that store of cattell and of graine
Which yesterday within these walles you brought,
While your proud foes triumphant through the plaine
On nought but shedding blood, and conquest thought,
Too little is this citie to sustaine,
To raise the siege, vnlesse some meanes be sought;
 And it must last, till the prefixed howre,
 That it be rais'd by Egypts aide and powre.

44

'But what if that appointed day they mis?
Or else (ere we expect) what if they came?
The victorie yet is not ours for this,
Oh saue this towne from ruine, vs from shame!
With that same *Godfrey* still our warfare is,
These armies, soldiers, captaines are the same,
 Who haue so oft amid the dustie plaine,
 Turks, Persians, Syrians and Arabians slaine:

45

'And thou *Argantes* wottest what they bee,
Oft hast thou fled from that victorious host,
Thy shoulders often hast thou let them see,
And in thy feet hath beene thy sauegard most,
Clorinda bright and I fled eeke with thee,
None than his fellowes had more cause to bost,
 Nor blame I any; for in euery fight
 We shewed courage, valour, strength and might:

46

'And though this hardie knight the certaine threat
Of neare approching death to heare disdaine;
Yet to this state of losse and danger great,
From this strong foe I see the tokens plaine;
No fort how strong so ere by art or feat,
Can hinder *Godfrey* why he should not raine:
 This makes me say (to witnes heau'n I bring)
 Zeale, to this state; loue, to my Lord and king.

47

'The king of Tripolie was well aduised
To purchase peace and so preserue his crowne:
But *Soliman* (who *Godfreys* loue despised)
Is either dead or deepe in prison throwne;
Else fearefull is he run away disguised,
And scant his life is left him for his owne,
   And yet with gifts, with tribute and with gold,
   He might in peace his empire still haue hold.'

48

Thus spake *Orcanes*, and some inkling gaue
In doubtfull words of that he would haue said,
To sue for peace or yeeld himselfe a slaue,
He durst not openly his king perswade:
But at those words the Soldan gan to raue,
And gainst his will wrapt in the cloud he staid,
   Whom *Ismen* thus bespake, 'how can you beare
   These words, my Lord? or these reproches heare?'

49

'Oh let me speake (quoth he) with ire and scorne
I burne, and gainst my will thus hid I stay!'
This said, the smokie cloud was cleft and torne,
Which like a vaile vpon them stretched lay,
And vp to open heau'n forthwith was borne,
And left the Prince in vew of lightsome day,
   With princely looke amid the prease he shin'de,
   And on a sodaine, thus declar'd his minde.

50

'Of whom you speake behold the Soldan here,
Neither affraid nor ron away for dread,
And that these slanders, lies and fables were,
This hand shall proue vpon that cowards head,
I, who haue shed a sea of blood well nere,
And heapt vp mountaines high of Christians dead,
   I in their campe who still maintain'd the fray,
   (My men all murdred) I that ron away.

51

'If this, or any coward vile beside,
False to his faith and countrie, dares replie;
And speake of concord with yond men of pride,
By your good leaue (sir king) here shall he die,
The lambes and wolues shall in one fold abide,
The doues and serpents in one nest shall lie,
    Before one towne vs and these Christians shall
    In peace and loue, vnite within one wall.'

52

While thus he spoke, his broad and trenchant sword
His hand held high aloft, in threatning guise;
Dombe stood the knights, so dreadfull was his word;
A storme was in his front, fire in his eies,
He turn'd at last to Sions aged Lord,
And calm'd his visage sterne in humbler wise:
    'Behold (quoth he) good Prince, what aide I bring,
    Since *Soliman* is ioyn'd with Iudaes king.'

53

King *Aladine* from his rich throne vpstart,
And said, 'oh how I ioy thy face to vew,
My noble friend! it less'neth in some part
My greefe, for slaughter of my subiects trew,
My weake estate to stablish come thou art,
And maist thine owne againe in time renew,
    If heau'ns consent:' with that the Soldan bold
    In deere embracements did he long enfold.

54

Their greetings done, the king resinde his throne
To *Solman*, and set himselfe beside,
In a rich seat adorn'd with gold and stone,
And *Ismen* sage did at his elbow bide,
Of whom he askt what way they two had gone,
And he declar'd all what had them betide:
    Clorinda bright to *Soliman* addrest
    Her salutations first, then all the rest.

55

Among them rose *Ormusses* valiant knight,
Whom late the Soldan with a conuoy sent,
And when most hot and bloodie was the fight,
By secret pathes and blinde by-waies he went,
Till aided by the silence and the night
Safe in the cities walles himselfe he pent,
    And there refresht with corne and cattell store
    The pined soldiers, famisht nie before.

56

With surly count'nance and disdainfull grace
Sullen and sad, sate the Circassian stout,
Like a fierce lion grombling in his place,
His firie eies that turnes and rolles about;
Nor durst *Orcanes* vew the Soldans face,
But still vpon the floore did pore and tout:
    Thus with his Lords and peeres in counselling,
    The Turkish monarch sate with Iudaes king.

57

Godfrey this while gaue victorie the raine,
And following her the streits he opened all;
Then for his soldiers and his captaines slaine,
He celebrates a stately funerall,
And told his campe within a day or twaine
He would assault the cities mightie wall,
    And all the heathen there enclos'd doth threat,
    With fire and sword, with death and danger great.

58

And for he had that noble squadron knowne,
In the last fight which brought him so great aid,
To be the Lords and Princes of his owne,
Who followed late the slie entising maid,
And with them *Tancred* (who had late beene throwne
In prison deepe, by that false witch betrai'd)
    Before the hermit and some priuate frends,
    For all those worthies, Lords and knights, he sends;

59

And thus he said, 'some one of you declare
Your fortunes, whether good or to be blamed,
And to assist vs with your valours rare,
(In so great need) how was your comming framed?'
They blush and on the ground amazed stare,
(For vertue is of little guilt ashamed)
    At last the English Prince with count'nance bold,
    The silence broke, and thus their errors told:

60

'We (not elect to that exploit by lot)
With secret flight from hence our selues withdrew,
Following false *Cupid*, I denie it not,
Entised forth by loue, and beauties hew,
A iealous fire burnt in our stomackes hot,
And by close waies we passed least in vew,
    Her words, her lookes (alas I know too late)
    Nursed our loue, our iealousie, our hate.

61

'At last we gan approach that wofull clime,
Where fire and brimstone downe from heau'n was sent,
To take reuenge for sinne and shamefull crime
Gainst kinde commit, by those who nould repent;
A lothsome lake of brimstone, pitch and lime,
Oregoes that land, earst sweet and redolent,
    And when it moues, thence stinch and smoke vp flies,
    Which dim the welkin, and infect the skies.

62

'This is the lake in which yet neuer might
Ought that hath weight sinke to the bottome downe,
But like to corke, to leaues or feathers light,
Stones, iron, men there fleet, and neuer drowne,
Therein a castle stands, to which by sight
But ore a narrow bridge no way is knowne,
    Hither vs brought, here welcomd vs the witch,
    The house within was stately, pleasant, ritch.

61[6] thar < that

63

'The heau'ns were cleere, and wholsome was the aire,
High trees, sweet medowes, waters pure and good;
For there in thickest shade of Mirtles faire
A christall spring powr'd out a siluer flood;
Amid the herbes, the grasse and flowres rare,
The falling leaues downe pattred from the wood;
  The birds sung hymnes of loue, yet speake I nought
  Of gold and marble rich, and richly wrought.

64

'Vnder the curtaine of the greene-wood shade,
Beside the brooke, vpon the veluet grasse,
In massie vessell of pure siluer made,
A banket rich and costly furnisht was,
All beastes, all birds beguil'd by fowlers trade,
All fish were there in floods or seas that passe,
  All dainties made by art, and at the table
  An hundreth virgins seru'd, for husbands able.

65

'She with sweet words and false entising smiles,
Infused loue among the dainties set,
And with empoys'ned cups our soules beguiles,
And made each knight himselfe, and God forget:
She rose, and turn'd againe within short whiles,
With changed lookes where wrath and anger met,
  A charming rod, a booke with her she brings,
  On which she mumbled strange and secret things.

66

'She red, and change I felt my will and thought,
I long'd to change my life, and place of biding,
That vertue strange in me no pleasure wrought,
I leapt into the flood my selfe there hiding,
My legs and feet both into one were brought,
Mine armes and hands into my shoulders sliding,
  My skin was full of scales, like shields of bras,
  Now made a fish, where late a knight I was.

67

'The rest with me like shape, like garments wore,
And diu'de with me in that quicksiluer streame,
Such minde (to my remembrance) then I bore,
As when on vaine and foolish things men dreame;
At last our shape it pleas'd her to restore,
Then full of wonder and of feare we seame,
   And with an irefull looke the angrie maid
   Thus threat'ned vs, and made vs thus affraid.

68

' "You see (quoth she) my sacred might and skill,
How you are subiect to my rule and powre,
In endlesse thraldome damned if I will,
I can torment and keepe you in this towre,
Or make you birdes, or trees on craggie hill,
To bide the bitter blastes of storme and showre;
   Or harden you to rocks on mountaines old,
   Or melt your flesh and bones to riuers cold:

69

' "Yet may you well auoid mine ire and wraith,
If to my will your yeelding harts you bend,
You must forsake your Christendome and faith,
And gainst *Godfredo* false my crowne defend."
We all refus'd, for speedie death each prai'th,
Saue false *Rambaldo*, he became her frend,
   We in a dungeon deepe were helplesse cast,
   In miserie and iron chained fast.

70

'Then (for alone they say falles no mishap)
Within short while Prince *Tancred* thither came,
And was vnwares, surprised in the trap:
But there short while we staid, the wilie dame
In other foldes our mischiefes would vpwrap.
From *Hidraort* an hundreth horsemen came,
   Whose guide a Baron bold to Egypts king
   Should vs disarm'd, and bound in fetters, bring:

71

'Now on our way the way to death we ride,
But prouidence diuine thus for vs wrought,
Rinaldo (whose high vertue is his guide
To great exploits, exceeding humane thought)
Met vs, and all at once our garde defide,
And ere he left the fight to earth them brought,
   And in their harnesse arm'd vs in the place,
   Which late were ours, before our late disgrace.

72

'I, and all these, the hardie champion knew,
We saw his valour, and his voice we hard;
Then is the rumor of his death vntrew,
His life is safe, good fortune long it gard,
Three times the golden sunne hath risen new,
Since vs he left and rode to Antioch ward;
   But first his armours broken, hackt and cleft,
   Vnfit for seruice there he doft and left.'

73

Thus spake the Briton prince, with humble cheare
The Hermit sage to heau'n cast vp his eine,
His colour and his count'nance changed weare,
With heauenly grace his lookes and visage shine,
Rauisht with zeale his soule approched neare
The seat of angels pure, and saints diuine,
   And there he learnd of things and haps to come
   To giue foreknowledge true, and certaine dome;

74

At last he spoke (in more then humane sound)
And told what things his wisedome great foresaw,
And at his thundring voice the folke around
Attentiue stood, with trembling and with awe:
'*Rinaldo* liues,' he said, 'the tokens found
From womens craft their false beginnings draw,
   He liues and heau'n will long preserue his daies,
   To greater glorie, and to greater praise.

75

'These are but trifles yet, though Asias kings
Shrinke at his name and tremble at his vew,
I well foresee he shall do greater things,
And wicked emprours conquer and subdew;
Vnder the shadow of his eagles wings,
Shall holie church preserue hir sacred crew,
  From *Cæsars* bird he shall the sable traine
  Plucke off, and breake her talons sharpe in twaine.

76

'His childrens children at his hardinesse,
And great attempts shall take ensample faire,
From emperours vniust in all distresse
They shall defend the state of *Peters* chaire,
To raise the humble vp, pride to suppresse,
To helpe the innocents shall be their caire.
  This bird of East, shall flie with conquest great,
  As farre as moone giues light, or sunne giues heat;

77

'Her eies behold the truth and purest light,
And thunders downe in *Peters* aide shee brings,
And where for Christ and christian faith men fight,
There foorth shee spreadeth hir victorious wings,
This vertue Nature giues hir and this might,
Then lure her home, for on her presence hings
  The happie end of this great enterpries,
  So heau'n decrees, and so command the skies.'

78

These words of his, of Prince *Rinaldoes* death
Out of their troubled harts, the feare had raced;
In all this ioy yet *Godfrey* smil'd vneath,
In his wise thought such care and heed was placed.
But now from deepes of regions vnderneath
Nights vaile arose, and sunnes bright luster chaced,
  When all full sweetly in their cabbins slept,
  Saue he, whose thoughts his eies still open kept.

The argument.

With graue procession, songs and psalmes deuout
Heau'ns sacred aide the Christian Lords inuoke;
That done, they scale the wall which kept them out;
The fort is almost wonne, the gates nie broke:
Godfrey *is wounded by* Clorinda *stout,*
And lost is that daies conquest by the stroke;
The Angell cures him, he returnes to fight,
But lost his labour for day lost his light.

I

THe Christian armies great and puissant guide,
  T'assault the towne that all his thoughts had bent,
Did ladders, rammes, and engins huge prouide,
When reuerent *Peter* to him grauely went,
And drawing him with sober grace aside,
With words seuere thus told his high intent;
  "Right wel (my Lord) these earthly strengthes you moue,
  But let vs first begin from heau'n aboue:

2

'With publike praier, zeale, and faith deuout,
The aide, assistance, and the helpe obtaine
Of all the blessed of the heau'nly rout,
With whose support you conquest sure may gaine;
First let the priestes before thine armies stout,
With sacred hymnes their holy voices straine,
  And thou and all thy Lords and peeres with thee,
  Of godlinesse and faith ensamples bee.'

3

Thus spake the hermit graue in words seueare:
Godfrey allow'd his counsell, sage and wise,
'Of Christ the Lord (quoth he) thou seruant deare,
I yeeld to follow thy diuine aduise,

And while the Princes I assemble heare,
The great procession, songs and sacrifice,
  With Bishop *William*, thou and *Ademare*,
  With sacred and with solemne pompe, prepare.'

4

Next morne the Bishops twaine, the heremite,
And all the clarks and priests of lesse estate,
Did in the middest of the campe vnite
Within a place for praier consecrate,
Each priest adorn'd was in a surplesse white,
The Bishops dond their albes and copes of state,
  Aboue their rockets button'd faire before,
  And miters on their heads, like crownes they wore.

5

Peter alone (before) spred to the winde
The glorious signe of our saluation great,
With easie pace the quire come all behinde,
And hymnes and psalmes in order true repeat,
With sweet respondence in harmonious kinde
Their humble song the yeelding aire doth beat;
  Lastly together went the reuerend pare
  Of prelates sage, *William* and *Ademare*:

6

The mighty Duke came next, as Princes do,
Without companion, marching all alone,
The Lords and captaines came by two and two,
The soldiers for their garde were arm'd each one;
With easie pace thus ordred, passing throw
The trench and rampire, to the fields they gone,
  No thundring drum, no trumpet shrill they heare,
  Their godly musicke psalmes and praiers weare.

7

To thee, O Father, Sonne and sacred Spright,
One true, eternall, euerlasting king,
To Christes deere mother *Marie* virgin bright,
Psalmes of thankesgiuing and of praise they sing,

To them that angels downe from heau'n to fight
Gainst the blasphemous beast and dragon bring,
　　To him also that of our Sauiour good,
　　Washed the sacred front in Iordans flood.

8

Him likewise they inuoke, called the rocke
Whereon the Lord (they say) his Church did reare,
Whose true successors close or else vnlocke
The blessed gates of grace and mercie deare,
And all th'elected twelue the chosen flocke,
Of his triumphant death who witnes beare,
　　And them by torment, slaughter, fire and sword
　　Who martyrs died, to confirme his word:

9

And them also whose bookes and writings tell
What certaine path to heau'nly blisse vs leades,
And hermits good, and ancresses that dwell,
Mewed vp in walles and mumble on their beades,
And virgin nunnes in close and priuate cell,
Where (but shrift fathers) neuer mankinde treades,
　　On these they called and on all the rout
　　Of angels, martyrs, and of saints deuout.

10

Singing and saying thus the campe deuout
Spred forth her zealous squadrons broad and wide,
Towards mount Oliuet went all this rout,
So call'd of Oliue trees the hill which hide,
A mountaine knowne by fame the world throughout,
Which riseth on the cities eastren side,
　　From it deuided by the valley greene
　　Of *Iosaphat*, that fils the space betweene.

11

Hither the armies went, and chanted shrill,
That all the deepe and hollow dales resound,
From hollow mounts and caues in euery hill,
A thousand Ecchoes also sung around,

It seem'd some quire (that sung with art and skill)
Dwelt in those sauage dennes and shadie ground,
 For oft resounded from the banks they heare,
 The name of Christ and of his mother deare.

12

Vpon the walles the Pagans old and yong
Stood husht and still, amated and amased,
At their graue order and their humble song,
At their strange pompe and customes new they gased:
But when the shew they had beholden long,
An hideous yell the wicked miscreants rased,
 That with vile blasphemies the mountaines hoare,
 The woods, the waters and the valleis roare.

13

But yet with sacred notes the hostes proceed,
Though blasphemies they heare and cursed things;
So with *Apolloes* harpe *Pan* tunes his reed,
So adders hisse, where Philomela sings,
Nor flying dartes nor stones the Christians dreed,
Nor arrowes shot, nor quarries cast from slings;
 But with assured faith as dreading nought
 The holy worke begun to end they brought.

14

A table set they on the mountaines hight
To minister thereon the Sacrament,
In golden candlesticks a hallowed light,
At either end of virgin waxe there brent:
In costly vestments sacred *William* dight,
With feare and trembling to the altar went,
 And praier there and seruice lowd beginnes,
 Both for his owne and all the armies sinnes;

15

Humbly they heard his words that stood him nie,
The rest far off vpon him bent their eies,
But when he ended had the seruice hie,
You seruants of the Lord depart he cries:

His hands he lifted than vp to the skie,
And blessed all those warlike companies;
    And they dismist return'd the way they came,
    Their order as before, their pompe the same.

16

Within their campe arriu'd, this voiage ended,
Towards his tent the Duke himselfe withdrew,
Vpon their guide by heapes the bands attended,
Till his pauilions stately doore they vew,
There to the Lord his welfare they commended,
And with him left the worthies of the crew,
    Whom at a costly and rich feast he placed,
    And with the highest roome old *Raimond* graced.

17

Now when the hungrie knights sufficed ar
With meat, with drinke, with spices of the best,
Quoth he, 'when next you see the morning star,
T'assault the towne be ready all and prest:
Tomorrow is a day of paines and war,
This of repose, of quiet, peace and rest;
    Goe, take your ease this euening, and this night,
    And make you strong against to morrowes fight.'

18

They tooke their leaue, and *Godfreys* haralds road
To intimate his will on euery side,
And publisht it through all the lodgings broad,
That gainst the morne each should himselfe prouide,
Meane-while they might their harts of cares vnload,
And rest their tired limmes that euening tide;
    Thus fared they till night their eies did close,
    Night frend to gentle rest and sweet repose.

19

With little signe as yet of springing day
Out peept, not well appear'd the rising morne,
The plough yet tore not vp the fertile lay,
Nor to their feed the sheepe from folds retorne.

The birds sate silent on the greene wood spray
Amid the groues, vnheard was hound and horne,
  When trumpets shrill true signes of hardie fights,
  Call'd vp to armes the soldiers, call'd the knights:

20

'Arme, arme' at once an hundreth squadrons cride,
And with their crie to arme them all begin,
Godfrey arose, that day he laid aside
His hawberke strong he wontes to combat in,
And dond a brestplate faire, of proofe vntride,
Such one as footmen vse, light, easie, thin:
  Scantly their Lord thus clothed had his gromes,
  When aged *Raimond* to his presence comes,

21

And furnisht thus when he the man beheild,
By his attire his secret thought he guest,
'Where is (quoth he) your sure and trustie shield?
Your helme, your hawberke strong? where all the rest?
Why be you halfe disarm'd? why to the feild
Approch you in these weake defences drest?
  I see this day you meane a course to ronne,
  Wherein may perill much, small praise be wonne.

22

'Alas, doe you that idle praise expect,
To set first foot this conquered wall aboue?
Of lesse account some knight thereto obiect,
Whose losse so great and harmfull cannot proue,
My Lord, your life with greater care protect,
And loue your selfe bicause all vs you loue,
  Your happie life is spirit, soule and breath
  Of all this campe, preserue it than from death.'

23

To this he answered thus, 'you know (he sade)
In Clarimont by mightie *Vrbans* hand
When I was girded with this noble blade,
For Christes true faith to fight in euery land,

To God eu'n than a secret vow I made,
Not as a captaine here this day to stand,
   And giue directions, but with shield and sword
   To fight, to winne or die for Christ my Lord.

24

'When all this campe in battaile strong shall bee
Ordain'd and ordred, well disposed all,
And all things done which to the high degree
And sacred place I hold, belongen shall;
Then reason is it, nor disswade thou mee,
That I likewise assault this sacred wall,
   Least from my vow to God late made I swerue,
   He shall this life defend, keepe and preserue.'

25

Thus he concludes, and euery hardie knight
His sample follow'd, and his brethren twaine,
The other Princes put on harnesse light,
As footemen vse: but all the Pagan traine
Towards that side bent their defensiue might,
That lies expos'd to vew of *Charles* waine,
   And *Zephirus* sweet blastes, for on that part
   The towne was weakest, both by scite and art.

26

On all parts else the fort was strong by scite,
With mighty hils defenst from forraine rage,
And to this part the tyrant gan vnite,
His subiects borne and bands that serue for wage,
From this exploit he spar'd nor great nor lite,
The aged men and boyes of tender age,
   To fire of angrie war, still brought new fewell,
   Stones, dartes, lime, brimstone and bitumen cruell.

27

All full of armes and weapons was the wall,
Vnder whose basis that faire plaine doth ronne,
There stood the Soldan like a giant tall,
(So stood at Rhodes the Coloss of the sonne)

Wast high *Argantes* shew'd himselfe withall,
At whose sterne lookes the French to quake begonne,
 Clorinda on the corner towre alone,
 In siluer armes like rising *Cinthia* shone.

28

Her ratling quiuer at her shoulders hong,
Therein a flash of arrowes feathered weele,
In her left hand her bow was bended strong,
Therein a shaft headed with mortall steele,
So fit to shoot she singled forth among
Her foes, who first her quarries strength should feele,
 So fit to shoot *Latonas* daughter stood,
 When *Niobe* she kill'd and all her brood.

29

The aged tyrant trotted on his feet
From gate to gate, from wall to wall he flew,
He comforts all his bands with speeches sweet,
And cucry fort and bastion doth reuew,
For euery need prepar'd in euery street
New regiments he plast, and weapons new.
 The matrons graue within their temples hie,
 To idols false for succours call and crie;

30

'O *Macon*, breake in twaine the steeled lance
Of wicked *Godfrey*, with thy righteous hands,
Against thy name he doth his arme aduance,
His rebell blood powre out vpon these sands,'
These cries within his eares no enterance
Could finde; for nought he heares, nought vnderstands.
 While thus the towne for her defence ordaines,
 His armies *Godfrey* ordreth on the plaines,

31

His forces first on foot he forward brought,
With goodly order, prouidence and art,
And gainst these towers which t'assaile he thought,
In battailes twaine his strength he doth depart,

Betweene them crosbowes stood and engins wrought
To cast a stone, a quarrie or a dart,
From whence like thunders dint or lightnings new,
Against the bulwarks stones and lances flew.

32

His men at armes did backe his bands on fout,
The light horse ride far off and serue for wings,
He gaue the signe, so mighty was the rout
Of those that shot with bowes and cast with slings,
Such stormes of shaftes and stones flew all about,
That many a Pagan proud to death it brings,
Some dide, some at the loopes durst scant out peepe,
Some fled and left the place they tooke to keepe.

33

The hardie Frenchmen (full of heat and hast)
Ran boldly forward to the ditches large,
And ore their heads an iron pentise vast
They built, by ioyning many a shield and targe,
Some with their engins ceaslesse shot and cast,
And vollies huge of arrowes sharpe discharge,
Vpon the ditches some emploi'd their paine,
To fill the mote and eu'n it with the plaine.

34

With slime or mud the ditches were not soft,
But drie and sandy, void of waters cleare,
Though large and deepe the Christians fill them oft,
With rubbish, faggots, stones and trees they beare:
Adrastus first aduanst his crest aloft,
And boldly gan a strong scalado reare,
And through the falling storme did vpward clime
Of stones, dartes, arrowes, fire, pitch and lime:

35

The hardie Switzer now so far was gone,
That halfe way vp with mickle paine he got,
A thousand weapons he sustain'd alone,
And his audacious climbing ceased not;

At last vpon him fell a mightie stone,
As from some engin great it had beene shot,
  It broke his helme, he tumbled from the height,
  The strong Circassian cast that wondrous weight;

36

Not mortall was the blow, yet with the fall
On earth sore brus'd the man lay in a swoune.
Argantes gan with boasting words to call,
Who commeth next? this first is tumbled downe,
Come hardie soldiers, come assault this wall,
I will not shrinke, nor flie, nor hide my crowne,
  If in your trench your selues for dread you hold,
  There shall you die, like sheepe kild in their fold.'

37

Thus boasted he, but in their trenches deepe
The hidden squadrons kept themselues from scath,
The curtaine made of shields did well off keepe
Both darts and shot, and scorned all their wrath.
But now the ramme vpon the rampires steepe
On mightie beames his head aduanced hath,
  With dreadfull hornes of iron tought tree-great,
  The walles and bulwarks trembled at his threat.

38

An hundred able men meane-while let fall
The weights behinde, the engin tumbled downe,
And battred flat the battlements and wall,
(So fell Taigetus hill on Sparta towne)
It crusht the steeled shield in peeces small,
And beat the helmet to the wearers crowne,
  And on the ruines of the walles and stones,
  Dispersed left their blood, their braines, and bones.

39

The fierce assailants kept no longer close
Vnder the shelter of their targets fine,
But their bold fronts to chance of war expose,
And gainst those towres let their vertue shine,

The scaling ladders vp to skies arose,
The groundworks deepe some closely vndermine,
   The walles before the Frenchmen shrinke and shake,
   And gaping signe of headlong falling make:

40

And falne they had, so far the strength extends
Of that fierce ramme and his redoubted stroke,
But that the Pagans care the place defends,
And sau'd by warlike skill the wall nie broke:
For to what part so ere the engin bends,
There sacks of wooll they place the blow to choke,
   Whose yeelding breakes the strokes theron which light,
   So weakenes oft subdues the greatest might.

41

While thus the worthies of the westren crew
Maintain'd their braue assault and skirmish hot,
Her mightie bow *Clorinda* often drew,
And many a sharpe and deadly arrow shot;
And from her bow no steeled shaft there flew,
But that some blood the cursed engin got,
   Blood of some valiant knight or man of fame,
   For that proud shootresse scorned weaker game.

42

The first she hit among the Christian Peeres,
Was the bold sonne of Englands noble king,
Aboue the trench himselfe he scantly reares,
But she an arrow loosed from the string,
The wicked steele his gantlet breakes and teares,
And through his right hand thrust the pearsing sting;
   Disabled thus from fight, he gan retire,
   Groning for paine, but fretting more for ire.

43

Lord *Stephen* of Amboise on the ditches brim,
And on a ladder high, *Clotharious* dide,
From backe to brest an arrow pearsed him,
The other was shot through from side to side:

42⁵ gantled < gantlet

Then as he menag'd braue his courser trim
On his left arme she hit the Flemmings guide,
 He stopt, and from the wound the reed out twinde,
 But left the iron in his flesh behinde.

44

As *Ademare* stood to behold the fight
High on a banke, withdrawne to breathe a space,
A fatall shaft vpon his forehead light,
His hand he lifted vp to feele the place,
Whereon a second arrow chanced right,
And nail'd his hand vnto his wounded face,
 He fell, and with his blood distain'd the land,
 His holy blood shed by a virgins hand.

45

While *Palamede* stood nere the battlement,
Despising perils all and all mishap,
And vpward still his hardie footings bent,
On his right eie he caught a deadly clap,
Through his right eie *Clorindaes* seu'nth shaft went,
And in his necke broke forth a bloodie gap;
 He vnderneath that bulwarke dying fell,
 Which late to scale and win he trusted well.

46

Thus shot the maide: the Duke with hard assay
And sharpe assault, meane-while the towne opprest,
Against that part which to his campe ward lay,
An engin huge and wondrous he addrest,
A towre of wood built for the townes decay,
As high as were the walles and bulwarks best,
 A turret full of men and weapons pent,
 And yet on wheeles it rolled, mou'd and went.

47

This rolling fort his nie approches made,
And dartes and arrowes spit against his foes,
As ships are wont in fight; so it assade
With the strong wall to grapple and to close:

The Pagans on each side the piece inuade,
And all their force against this masse oppose,
Sometimes the wheels, sometimes the battlement
With timber, logs and stones, they broke and rent.

48

So thicke flew stones and darts, that no man sees
The azure heauens, the sunne his brightnes lost,
The clouds of weapons, like two swarmes of bees,
Met in the aire, and there each other crost:
And looke how falling leaues drop downe from trees,
When the moist sap is nipt with timely frost,
Or apples in strong windes from branches fall;
The Saracines so tumbled from the wall.

49

For on their part the greatest slaughter light,
They had no shelter gainst so sharpe a shower,
Some left on liue betooke themselues to flight,
So feared they this deadly thundring tower:
But *Soliman* staide like a valiant knight,
And some with him, that trusted in his power,
Argantes with a long beach tree in hand,
Ran thither, this huge engin to withstand:

50

With this he pusht the towre and backe it driues
The length of all his tree, a woondrous way,
The hardie virgin by his side arriues,
To helpe *Argantes* in this hard assay:
The band that vs'd the ram, this season striues
To cut the cordes, wherein the woolpacks lay,
Which done, the sackes downe in the trenches fall,
And to the battrie naked left the wall.

51

The towre aboue, the ram beneath doth thunder,
What lime and stone such puissance could abide?
The wall began (now brus'd and crusht asunder)
Her wounded lappe to open broad and wide,

Godfrey himselfe and his brought safely vnder
The shattred wall, where greatest breach he spide,
   Himselfe he saues behinde his mightie targe,
   A shielde not vs'd but in some desp'rate charge.

52

From hence he sees where *Soliman* descends
Downe to the threshold of the gaping breach,
And there it seemes the mightie Prince entends
Godfredoes hoped entrance to impeach:
Argantes (and with him the maide) defends
The wals aboue, to which the towre doth reach,
   His noble hart, when *Godfrey* this beheld,
   With courage newe, with wrath and valour sweld.

53

He turnd about and to good *Sigiere* spake,
Who bare his greatest sheild and mightie bow,
'That sure and trustie target let me take,
Impenetrable is that sheild I know,
Ouer these ruines will I passage make,
And enter first, the way is eath and low,
   And time requires that by some noble feat
   I should make knowne my strength and puissance great:'

54

He scant had spoken, scant receiu'd the targe,
When on his legge a sudden shaft him hit,
And through that part a hole made wide and large,
Where his strong sinnewes fastned were and knit.
Clorinda, thou this arrow didst discharge,
And let the Pagans blesse thy hand for it,
   For by that shot thou sauedst them that day
   From bondage vile, from death and sure decay.

55

The wounded Duke, as though he felt no paine,
Still forward went, and mounted vp the breach,
His high attempt at first he nould refraine,
And after cald his Lords with cheerefull speach;

But when his legge could not his weight sustaine,
He saw his will did far his powre out reach,
  And more he stroue his griefe increast the more,
  The bold assault he left at length therefore:

56

And with his hand he beckned *Guelpho* neare,
And said, 'I must withdraw me to my tent,
My place and person in mine absence beare,
Supply my want, let not the fight relent,
I goe and will ere long againe be heare,
I goe and straight returne,' this said, he went,
  On a light stead he lept, and ore the greene
  He road, but road not (as he thought) vnseene.

57

When *Godfrey* parted, parted eeke the hart,
The strength and fortune of the Christian bands,
Courage increased in their aduerse part,
Wrath in their harts and vigor in their hands:
Valour, successe, strength, hardines, and art
Faild in the Princes of the Westren lands,
  Their swords were blunt, faint was their trumpets blast,
  Their sunne was set, or else with cloudes orecast.

58

Vpon the bulwarks now appeered bould
That fearefull band that late for dread was fled;
The women that *Clorindaes* strength behould,
Their countries loue to warre encouraged,
They weapons got and fight like men they would,
Their gownes tuckt vp, their lockes were loose and spred,
  Sharpe darts they cast, and without dread or feare
  Expos'd their brests to saue their fortresse deare.

59

But that which most dismaid the christian knights,
And added courage to the Pagans most,
Was *Guelphos* sodaine fall, in all mens sights
Who tumbled headlong downe, his footing lost,

A mightie stone vpon the woorthy lights,
But whence it came none wist, nor from what coast;
   And with like blow, which more their harts dismaid,
   Beside him low in dust old *Raimond* laid:

60

And *Eustace* eeke within the ditches large,
To narrow shifts and last extreames they driue,
Vpon their foes so fierce the Pagans charge,
And with good fortune so their blowes they giue,
That whom they hit, in spite of helme or targe,
They deepely wounde, or else of life depriue.
   At this their good successe *Argantes* proud,
   Waxing more fell, thus roard and cried loud:

61

'This is not Antioch, nor the euening darke,
Can helpe your priuie sleights with friendly shade,
The sunne yet shines, your falshood can we marke,
In other wise this bould assault is made,
Of praise and glorie quenched is the sparke
That made you first these easterne lands inuade,
   Why cease you now? why take you not this fort?
   What are you wearie for a charge so short?'

62

Thus raged he, and in such hellish sort
Encreast the furie in the brainsicke knight,
That he esteemed that large and ample fort
To strait a field, wherein to prooue his might,
There where the breach had fram'd a new made port,
Himselfe he plast, with nimble skips and light,
   He clear'd the passage out, and thus he cride
   To *Soliman*, that fought close by his side:

63

'Come *Soliman*, the time and place behould,
That of our valours well may iudge the doubt,
What staiest thou?' among these Christians bould,
First leape he foorth that houlds himselfe most stout:

While thus his will the mightie champion tould,
Both *Soliman* and he, at once leapt out,
   Furie the first prouokt, disdaine the last,
   Who scorn'd the chalenge ere his lips it past.

64

Vpon their foes vnlooked for they flew,
Each spited other for his vertues sake,
So many souldiers this fierce couple slew,
So many shieldes they cleft and helmes they brake,
So many ladders to the earth they threw,
That well they seem'd a mount thereof to make,
   Or else some vamure fit to saue the towne,
   In stead of that the Christians late bet downe.

65

The folke that stroue with rage and haste before
Who first the wall and rampire should ascend,
Retire, and for that honour striue no more,
Scantly they could their limmes and liues defend,
They fled, their engins lost the Pagans tore
In peeces small, their rams to nought they rend,
   And all vnfit for further seruice make,
   With so great force and rage their beames they brake.

66

The Pagans ran transported with their ire,
Now heere now there, and wofull slaughters wrought,
At last they called for deuouring fire,
Two burning pines against the towre they brought,
So from the pallace of their hellish Sire
(When all this world they would consume to nought)
   The furie sisters come with fire in hands,
   Shaking their snakie lockes and sparkling brands.

67

But noble *Tancred*, who this while applied
Graue exhortations to his bould Latines,
When of these knights the wondrous acts he spied,
And sawe the champions with their burning pines,

He left his talke and thither foorthwith hied,
To stop the rage of those fell Saracines,
   And with such force the fight he there renewed,
   That now they fled and lost, who late pursewed.

68

Thus chang'd the state and fortune of the fray,
Meane-while the wounded Duke in griefe and teene,
Within his great pauilion rich and gay,
Good *Sigiere* and *Baldwine* stood betweene;
His other friends whom his mishap dismay,
With griefe and teares about assembled beene:
   He stroue in haste the weapon out to winde,
   And broke the reed, but left the head behinde.

69

He bod them take the speediest way they might,
Of that vnluckie hurt to make him sound,
And to lay ope the depth thereof to sight,
He will'd them open, search and launce the wound,
'Send me againe (quoth he) to end this fight,
Before the sunne be sunken vnder ground,'
   And leaning on a broken speare, he thrust
   His leg straight out, to him that cure it must.

70

Erotimus, borne on the banks of Poe,
Was he that vndertooke to cure the knight,
All what greene herbes or waters pure could doe,
He knew their powre, their vertue and their might,
A noble poët was the man also;
But in this science had a more delight,
   He could restore to health death wounded men,
   And make their names immortall with his pen.

71

The mightie Duke yet neuer changed cheare,
But greeu'd to see his friends lamenting stand;
The leach prepar'd his clothes and clensing geare,
And with a belt his gowne about him band,

Now with his herbes the steelie head to teare
Out of the flesh he prou'd, now with his hand,
  Now with his hand, now with his instrument
  He shakt and pluckt it, yet not forth it went;

72

His labour vaine, his art preuailed nought,
His lucke was ill, although his skill were good,
To such extremes the wounded Prince he brought,
That with fell paine he swouned as he stood:
But th'angell pure (that kept him) went and sought
Diuine Dictamnum, out of Ida wood,
  This herbe is rough and beares a purple flowre,
  And in his budding leaues lies all his powre.

73

Kinde nature first vpon the craggie clift
Bewrai'd this herbe vnto the mountaine goate,
That when her sides a cruell shaft hath rift,
With it she shakes the reed out of her cote,
This in a moment fetcht the angell swift,
And brought from Ida hill, though far remote,
  The iuice whereof in a prepared bath
  Vnseene the blessed spirit powred hath:

74

Pure Nectar from that spring of Lidia than,
And Panaces diuine therein he threw,
The cunning leach to bathe the wound began,
And of it selfe the steelie head out flew,
The bleeding stancht, no vermile drop out-ran,
The leg againe waxt strong with vigor new:
  Erotimus cride out, this hurt and wound
  No humane art, or hand so soone makes sound;

75

Some angell good I thinke come downe from skies
Thy surgeon is, for here plaine tokens ar
Of grace diuine, which to thy helpe applies,
Thy weapon take and haste againe to war;

In pretious clothes his leg the chieftaine ties,
Nought could the man from blood and fight debar,
  A sturdie lance in his right hand he braced,
  His shield he tooke, and on his helmet laced:

76

And with a thousand knights and Barons bold,
Towards the towne he hasted from his campe,
In cloudes of dust was *Titans* face enrold,
Trembled the earth whereon the worthies stampe,
His foes far off his dreadfull lookes behold,
Which in their harts of courage quencht the lampe,
  A chilling feare ran cold through euery vaine,
  Lord *Godfrey* showted thrice and all his traine:

77

Their soueraignes voice his hardie people knew,
And his lowd cries, that chear'd each fearfull hart,
Thereat new strength they tooke and courage new,
And to the fierce assault againe they start.
The Pagans twaine this while themselues withdrew
Within the breach, to saue that battred part,
  And with great losse a skirmish hot they hold,
  Against *Tancredie* and his squadron bold.

78

Thither came *Godfrey* armed round about
In trustie plate, with fierce and dreadfull looke,
At first approch against *Argantes* stout
Headed with poinant steele a lance he shooke,
No casting engin with such force throwes out
A knottie speare, and as the way it tooke,
  It whistled in the aire, the fearelesse knight
  Oppos'd his shield against that weapons might,

79

The dreadfull blow quite through his target droue,
And bored through his brestplate strong and thicke,
The tender skin it in his bosome roue,
The purple bloud outstreamed from the quicke,

To wrest it out the wounded Pagan stroue,
And little leasure gaue it there to sticke;
　At *Godfreys* head the launce againe he cast,
　And said, 'lo there againe thy dart thou hast:'

80

The speare flew backe the way it lately came,
And would reuenge the harme it selfe had done,
But mist the marke whereat the man did ame,
He stept aside the furious blow to shunne:
But *Sigiere* in his throate receau'd the same,
The murdring weapon at his necke outrunne,
　Nor ought it greeu'd the man to loose his breath,
　Since in his Princes stead he suffred death.

81

Eu'n then the Souldan strooke with monstrous maine
The noble leader of the Norman band,
He reeld a while and staggred with the paine,
And wheeling round fell groueling on the sand:
Godfrey no longer could the greefe sustaine
Of these displeasures, but with flaming brand,
　Vp to the breach in heat and hast he goes,
　And hand to hand there combats with his foes,

82

And there great wonders surely wrought he had,
Mortall the fight, and fierce had beene the fray,
But that darke night, from her pauilion sad,
Her cloudy wings did on the earth display,
Her quiet shades she interposed glad,
To cause the knights their armes aside to lay;
　Godfrey withdrew, and to their tents they wend,
　And thus this bloudie day was brought to end.

83

The weake and wounded ere he left the feild
The godly Duke to safetie thence conuaid,
Nor to his foes his engins would he yeild,
In them his hope to win the fortresse laid;

Then to the towre he went, and it beheild,
The towre that late the Pagan Lords dismaid,
But now stood brused, broken, crackt and shiuered,
From some sharpe storme as it were late deliuered,

84

From dangers great escapt but late it was,
And now to safetie brought welnie it seames,
But as a ship that vnder saile doth pas
The roaring billowes and the raging streames,
And drawing nie the wished port (alas)
Breakes on some hidden rocke her ribs and beames;
Or as a stead rough waies that well hath past,
Before his Inne stumbleth, and fals at last:

85

Such hap befell that towre, for on that side
Gainst which the Pagans force and battrie bend,
Two wheeles were broke whereon the peece should ride,
The maymed engin could no further wend,
The troupe that guarded it that part prouide
To vnderprop, with posts, and it defend,
Till carpenters and cunning workemen came,
Whose skill should helpe and reare againe the same.

86

Thus *Godfrey* bids, and that ere springing day
The cracks and bruses all amend they should,
Each open passage and each priuie way
About the piece, he kept with souldiers bould:
But the loud rumour both of that they say,
And that they do, is heard within the hould,
A thousand lights about the towre they vew,
And what they wrought all night both saw and knew.

The argument.

Clorinda *heares her Eunuch old report*
Her birth her ofspring, and her natiue land;
Disguis'd she fireth Godfreys *rolling fort,*
The burned peece falles smoking on the sand:
With Tancred *long vnknowne in desp'rate sort*
She fights, and falles through pearsed with his brand:
    Christned she dies: with sighes, with plaints, and teares,
    He wailes her death; Argant *reuengement sweares.*

1

NOw in darke night was all the world imbard;
    But yet the tired armies tooke no rest,
The carefull French kept heedfull watch and ward,
While their high towre the workemen newly drest,
The Pagan crew to reinforce prepar'd
The weak'ned bulwarks, late to earth downe kest,
    Their rampires broke and brused walles to mend,
    Lastly their hurts the wounded knights attend.

2

Their wounds were drest; part of the worke was brought
To wished end, part left to other daies,
A dull desire to rest deepe midnight wrought,
His heauie rod sleepe on their eye-lids laies:
Yet rested not *Clorindaes* working thought,
Which thirsted still for fame and warlike praise,
    Argantes eeke accompaned the maid,
    From place to place, which to her selfe thus said:

3

'This day *Argantes* strong and *Soliman*
Strange things haue done, and purchast great renowne,
Among our foes out of the walles they ran,
Their rammes they broke and rent their engins downe;

I vs'd my bow, of nought else boast I can,
My selfe stood safe meane-while within this towne,
  And happie was my shot and prosprous too,
  But that was all a womans hand could doo.

4

'On birds and beastes in forrests wilde that feed,
It were more fit mine arrowes to bestow,
Than for a feeble maid in warlike deed,
With strong and hardie knights her selfe to show,
Why take I not againe my virgins weed?
And spend my daies in secret cell vnknow?'
  Thus thought, thus mused, thus deuis'd the maid,
  And turning to the knight, at last thus said:

5

'My thoughts are full (my Lord) of strange desire,
Some high attempt of warre to vndertake,
Whether high God my minde therewith inspire,
Or of his will his God mankind doth make,
Among our foes behold the light and fire,
I will among them wend and burne or brake
  The towre, God grant therein I haue my will,
  And that perform'd, betide me good or ill.

6

'But if it fortune such my chance should bee,
That to this towne I neuer turne againe,
Mine Eunuch (whom I deerely loue) with thee
I leaue, my faithfull maides, and all my traine,
To Egypt then conducted safely see
Those wofull damsels, and that aged swaine,
  Helpe them (my Lord) in that distressed case,
  Their feeble sex, his age deserueth grace.'

7

Argantes wondring stood, and felt th'effect
Of true renowne peirce through his glorious minde,
'And wilt thou go (quoth he) and me neglect,
Disgras'd, despis'd, leaue in this fort behind?

Shall I while these strong wals my life protect,
Behold thy flames and fires tost in the wind,
  No, no, thy fellow haue I beene in armes,
  And will be still, in praise, in death, in harmes:

8

'This hart of mine deaths bitter stroke despiseth,
For praise this life, for glory take this breath',
'My soule the more (quoth she) thy friendship priseth,
For this thy profer'd aid requir'd vneath,
I but a woman am, no losse ariseth
To this besieged citie by my death,
  But if (as Gods forbid) this night thou fall,
  Ah who shall then, who can, defend this wall?'

9

'Too late these scuses vaine (the knight replide)
You bring, my will is firme, my minde is set,
I follow you where so you list me guide,
Or go before if you my purpose let.'
This said, they hasted to the pallace wide
About their prince where all his Lords were met,
  Clorinda spoke for both, and said, 'sir king,
  Attend my words, heare; and allow the thing:

10

'*Argantes* here this bold and hardie knight,
Will vndertake to burne the wondrous towre,
And I with him, only we stay till night
Burie in sleepe our foes at deadest howre.'
The king with that cast vp his hands on hight,
The teares for ioy vpon his cheekes downe powre,
  'Praised (quoth he) be *Macon* whom we serue,
  This land I see he keepes and will preserue:

11

'Nor shall so soone this shaken kingdome fall,
While such vnconquer'd harts my state defend:
But for this act what praise or guerdon shall
I giue your vertues, which so far extend?

Let fame your praises sound through nations all,
And fill the world therewith to either end,
    Take halfe my wealth and kingdome for your meed?
    You are rewarded halfe eu'n with the deed.'

12

Thus spake the Prince, and gently gan distraine
Now him, now her, betweene his friendly armes:
The Soldan by, no longer could refraine
That noble enuie which his bosome warmes,
'Nor I (quoth he) beare this broad sword in vaine,
Nor yet vnexpert am in night alarmes,
    Take me with you:' 'ah (quoth *Clorinda*) noe!
    Whom leane we here of prowesse if you goe?'

13

This spoken, readie with a proud refuse
Argantes was his proffred aid to scorne,
Whom *Aladine* preuents, and with excuse
To *Soliman* thus gan his speeches torne:
'Right noble Prince, as aie hath beene your use,
Your selfe so still you beare and long haue borne,
    Bold in all actes, no danger can affright
    Your hart, nor tired is your strength with fight:

14

'If you went forth great things performe you would,
In my conceit yet far vnfit it seames,
That you (who most excell in courage bould)
At once should leaue this towne in these extreames,
Nor would I that these twaine should leaue this hould,
My hart their noble liues far worthier deames,
    If this attempt of lesse importance weare,
    Or weaker postes so great a weight could beare.

15

'But for well garded is the mightie towre
With hardie troupes and squadrons round about,
And cannot harmed be with little powre,
Nor fits the time to send whole armies out,

This paire, who past haue many a dreadfull stowre,
And proffer now to proue this venture stout,
   Alone to this attempt let them goe forth,
   Alone then thousands of more price and worth.

16

'Thou (as it best beseemes a mightie king)
With readie bands beside the gate attend,
That when this couple haue perform'd the thing,
And shall againe their footsteps homeward bend,
From their strong foes vpon them following
Thou maist them keepe, preserue, saue and defend:'
   Thus said the king, the Soldan must consent,
   Silent remain'd the Turke, and discontent.

17

Then *Ismen* said, 'you twaine that vndertake
This hard attempt, a while I pray you stay,
Till I a wilde-fire of fine temper make,
That this great engin burne to ashes may;
Haply the garde that now doth watch and wake,
Will then lie tumbled sleeping on the lay;'
   Thus they conclude, and in their chambers sit,
   To wait the time for this aduenture fit.

18

Clorinda there her siluer armes off rent
Her helme, her shield, her hawberke shining bright,
An armour blacke as ieat or cole she hent,
Wherein withouten plume her selfe she dight;
For thus disguis'd amid her foes she ment
To passe vnseene, by helpe of friendly night,
   To whom her Eunuch old *Arsetes* came,
   That from her cradle nurst and kept the Dame.

19

This aged sire had follow'd far and neare
(Through lands and seas) the strong and hardie maid,
He saw her leaue her armes and wonted geare,
Her danger nie that sodaine change foresaid:

By his white lockes from blacke that changed weare
In following her, the wofull man her praid,
  By all his seruice and his taken paine,
  To leaue that fond attempt, but praid in vaine.

20

'At last (quoth he) since hardn'd to thine ill,
Thy cruell hart is to thy losse prepar'd,
That my weake age, nor tearcs that downe distill,
Nor humble suit, nor plaint, thou list regard;
Attend a while, strange things vnfold I will,
Heare both thy birth and high estate declar'd;
  Follow my counsell or thy will, that donne,'
  She fit to heare, the Eunuch thus begonne:

21

'*Senapus* rul'd, and yet perchance doth raine
In mightie Ethiope and her desarts waste,
The lore of Christ both he and all his traine
Of people blacke, hath kept and long imbraste,
To him a Pagan was I sold for gaine,
And with his queene (as her cheefe Eunuch) plaste;
  Blacke was this queene as ieat, yet on her eies
  Sweet louelinesse (in blacke attired) lies.

22

'The fire of loue and frost of iealousie
Her husbands troubled soule alike torment,
The tide of fond suspition flowed hie,
The foe to loue and plague to sweet content,
He mew'd her vp from sight of mortall eie,
Nor day he would his beames on her had bent:
  She (wise and lowly) by her husbands pleasure,
  Her ioy, her peace, her will, her wish did measure.

23

'Her prison was a chamber, painted round
With goodly purtraites and with stories old,
As white as snow there stood a virgin bound,
Besides a dragon fierce, a champion bold

The monster did with poinant speare through wound,
The gored beast lay dead vpon the mold;
   The gentle queene before this image laid,
   She plain'd, she mourn'd, she wept, she sigh'd, she praid:

24

'At last with childe she prou'd, and forth she brought
(And thou art she) a daughter faire and bright,
In her thy colour white new terrour wrought,
She wondred on thy face with strange affright;
But yet she purpos'd in her fearefull thought
To hide thee from the king thy fathers sight,
   Least thy bright hew should his suspect approue,
   For seld a crow begets a siluer doue.

25

'And to her spouse to shew she was dispos'd
A Negrose babe, late borne, in roome of thee,
And for the towre wherein she lay enclos'd,
Was with her damsels onely wond and mee,
To me, on whose true faith she most repos'd,
Shee gaue thee, ere thou couldest christned bee,
   Nor could I since finde meanes thee to baptise,
   In Pagan lands thou know'st its not the guise.

26

'To me she gaue thee, and she wept withall,
To foster thee in some far distant place,
Who can her griefes and plaints to reck'ning call,
How oft she swouned at the last imbrace?
Her streaming teares amid her kisses fall,
Her sighes, her dire complaints did enterlace:
   And looking vp at last, "O God (quoth shee)
   Who dost my hart and inward mourning see,

27

' "If minde and bodie spotlesse to this day,
If I haue kept my bed still vndefilde,
(Not for my selfe a sinfull wretch I pray,
That in thy presence am an abiect vilde)

Preserue this babe, whose mother must denay
To nourish it, preserue this harmelesse childe,
   Oh let it liue, and chast like me it make,
   But for good fortune elsewhere sample take.

28

' "Thou heau'nly souldier which deliu'red hast
That sacred virgin from the serpent old,
If on thine Altars I haue offrings plast,
And sacrifis'd Myrrhe, Frankinscence and gold,
On this poore childe thy heau'nly lookes downe cast,
With gratious eie this seelie babe behold,"
   This said, her strength and liuing sprite was fled,
   She sigh'd, she groan'd, she swouned in her bed.

29

'Weeping I tooke thee, in a little chest,
Cou'red with herbes and leaues, I brought thee out
So secretly, that none of all the rest
Of such an acte suspition had or dout,
To wildernesse my steps I first addrest,
Where horride shades enclos'd me round about,
   A tygresse there I met, in whose fierce eies
   Furie and wrath, rage, death and terrour lies:

30

'Vp to a tree I leapt, and on the grasse
(Such was my sodaine feare) I left thee lying,
To thee the beast with furious course did passe,
With curious lookes vpon thy visage prying,
All sodainly both meeke and milde she was,
With friendly cheere thy tender body eying,
   At last she lickt thee, and with gesture milde
   About thee plai'd, and thou vpon her smilde.

31

'Her fearefull muzle full of dreadfull threat
In thy weake hand thou took'st withouten dreed,
The gentle beast with milke out stretched teat;
(As nurses custome) proffred thee to feed,

As one that wondreth on some maruaile great,
I stood this while amazed at the deed,
   When thee she saw well fild and satisfied
   Vnto the woods againe the tygresse hied.

32

'She gone, downe from the tree I came in hast,
And tooke thee vp and on my iourney wend,
Within a little thorpe I staid at last,
And to a nurse the charge of thee commend,
And sporting with thee there long time I past
Till terme of sixteene monthes were brought to end,
   And thou begonne (as little children doe)
   With halfe clipt words to prattle, and to goe.

33

'But hauing past the August of mine age,
When more than halfe my tap of life was ronne,
Rich by rewards giuen by your mother sage
For merits past, and seruice yet vndonne,
I long'd to leaue this wandring pilgrimage,
And in my natiue soile againe to wonne,
   To get some seely home I had desire,
   Loth still to warme me at anothers fire:

34

'To Egypt ward (where I was borne) I went,
And bore thee with me, by a rolling flood
Till I with sauage theeues well nie was hent,
Before, the brooke: the theeues, behinde me stood:
Thee to forsake I neuer could consent,
And gladly would I scape those outlawes wood,
   Into the flood I leapt far from the brim,
   My left hand bore thee, with the right I swim.

35

'Swift was the currant, in the middle streame
A whirlpoole gaped with deuouring iawes,
The gulph (on such mishap ere I could dreame)
Into his deepe abysse my carkasse drawes,

There I forsooke thee, the wilde waters seame
To pitie thee, a gentle winde there blowes,
  Whose friendly puffes safe to the shore thee driue,
  Where wet and wearie I at last arriue:

36

'I tooke thee vp and in my dreame that night
(When buried was the world in sleepe and shade)
I saw a champion clad in armour bright,
That ore my head shaked a flaming blade,
He said "I charge thee execute aright
That charge this enfants mother on thee laid,
  Baptise the childe, high heau'n esteemes her deare,
  And I her keeper will attend her neare:

37

' "I will her keepe, defend, saue and protect,
I made the waters milde, the tygresse tame,
O wretch that heau'nly warnings dost reiect!"
The warriour vanisht hauing said the same.
I rose and iournayd on my way direct,
When blushing morne from *Tithons* bed foorth came,
  But for my faith is true and sure I weene,
  And dreames are false, you still vnchristened beene.

38

'A Pagan therefore thee I fostred haue,
Nor of thy birth the truth did euer tell,
Since you encreased are in courage braue,
Your sexe and natures selfe you both excell,
Full many a realme haue you made bond and slaue,
Your fortunes last your selfe remember well,
  And how in peace and warre, in ioy and teene,
  I haue your seruant, and your tutor beene.

39

'Last morne, from skies erre stars exiled weare,
In deepe and deathlike sleepe my senses dround,
The selfesame vision did againe appeare,
With stormy wrathfull lookes, and thundring sound,

37⁶ morne < morne from

"Villaine (quoth he) within short while thy deare
Must change her life, and leaue this sinfull ground,
   Thine be the losse, the torment and the caire,"
    This said, he fled through skies, through cloudes & aire.

40

'Heare then my ioy, my hope, my darling, heare
High heau'n some dire misfortune threatned hath,
Displeasd pardie, because I did thee leare
A lore, repugnant to thy parents faith;
Ah, for my sake, this bold attempt forbeare;
Put off these sable armes, appease thy wrath.'
   This said, he wept, she pensiue stood and sad,
   Because like dreame her selfe but lately had.

41

With cheerefull smile she answer'd him at last,
'I will this faith obserue, it seemes me true,
Which from my cradle age thou taught me hast;
I will not change it for religion new,
Nor with vaine shewes of feare and dreed agast,
This enterprise forbeare I to pursew,
   No, not if death in his most dreadfull face
   Wherewith he scareth mankind, kept the place.'

42

Approchen gan the time (while thus she spake)
Wherein they ought that dreadfull hazard trie,
She to *Argantes* went, who should partake
Of her renowne and praise, or with her die.
Ismen with words more hastie still did make
Their vertue great, which by it selfe did flie,
   Two balles he gaue them made of hollow bras,
   Wherein enclos'd fire, pitch and brimston was.

43

And foorth they went, and ouer dale and hill
They hasted forward with a speedie pace,
Vnseene, vnmarked, vndescride, vntill
Beside the engine close themselues they place,

New courage there their swelling harts did fill,
Rage in their breasts, furie shone in their face,
  They earnd to blow the fire, and draw the sword,
  The watch descride them both, and gaue the word.

44

Silent they passed on, the watch begonne
To reare a huge alarme with hideous cries,
Therewith the hardie couple forward ronne
To execute their valiant enterpries;
So from a cannon or a roaring gonne
At once the noise, the flame and bullet flies,
  They runne, they giue the charge, begin the fray,
  And all at once their foes breake, spoile and slay.

45

They passed first through thousand thousand blowes,
And then performed their designment bould,
A firie ball each on the engin throwes,
The stuffe was drie, the fire tooke quickely hould,
Furious vpon the timber worke it growes,
How it encreased cannot well be tould,
  How it crept vp the peice, and how to skies
  The burning sparkes, and towring smoake vp-flies.

46

A masse of sollid fier burning bright
Roll'd vp in smouldring fumes there brusteth out,
And there the blustring winds adde strength and might,
And gather close the sparsed flames about:
The Frenchmen trembled at the dreadfull light,
To armes in haste and feare ran all the rout,
  Downe fell the peice dreaded so much in warre,
  Thus, what long daies doth make, one houre doth marre.

47

Two christian bands, this while came to the place
With speedie haste, where they beheld the fire,
Argantes to them cride, with scornfull grace,
'Your bloud shall quench these flames and quench mine ire:'

This said, the maide and he with sober pace
Drew backe, and to the banke themselues retire,
    Faster then brookes which falling showres encrease,
    Their foes augment, and faster on them prease.

48

The guilden port was opened, and foorth stept
With all his souldiers bould, the Turkish king,
Readie to aide them two his force he kept,
When Fortune should them home with conquest bring,
Ouer the barres the hardie couple lept,
And after them a band of Christians fling,
    Whom *Soliman* droue backe with courage stout,
    And shut the gate but shut *Clorinda* out.

49

Alone was she shut foorth, for in that howre
Wherein they clos'd the port, the virgin went
And full of heat and wrath, her strength and powre
Gainst *Arimon* (that stroake her earst) shee bent,
Shee slew the knight, nor *Argant* in that stowre
Wist of her parting, or her fierce entent,
    The fight, the prease, the night and darksome skies,
    Care from his hart had tane, sight from his eies.

50

But when appeased was her angrie moode,
Her furie calm'd, and setled was her head,
She saw the gates were shut, and how shee stoode
Amid her foes, she held her selfe for dead;
While none her markt, at last she thought it good
To saue her life some other path to tread,
    She feign'd her one of them, and close her drew
    Amid the prease that none her sawe nor knew:

51

Then as a wolfe guiltie of some misdeed
Flies to some groue to hide himselfe from vew,
So fauour'd with the night, with secret speed
Disseuered from the prease the damsell flew:

Tancred alone of her escape tooke heed,
He on that quarter was arriued new,
   When *Arimon* she kild, he thither came,
   He sawe it, markt it, and pursu'd the dame,

52

He deem'd she was some man of mickle might,
And on her person would he worship win,
Ouer the hilles the nimph her iourney dight
Towards another port, there to get in:
With hideous noise fast after spurr'd the knight,
She heard and staide, and thus her words begin,
   'What haste hast thou? ride softly, take thy breath,
   What bringest thou?' he answerd, 'warre and death.'

53

'And warre and death (quoth she) heere maist thou get
If thou for battle come,' with that she staid:
Tancred to ground his foote in haste downe set,
And left his stead, on foote he saw the maid,
Their courage hot, their ire and wrath they whet,
And either champion drew a trenchant blaid,
   Togither ran they, and togither stroke,
   Like two fierce buls, whom rage and loue prouoke.

54

Woorthie of royal listes and brightest day,
Woorthie a golden trompe and lawrell crowne,
The actions were and woonders of that fray,
Which sable night did in darke bosome drowne:
Yet night, consent that I their actes display,
And make their deeds to future ages knowne,
   And in records of long enduring storie,
   Enroll their praise, their fame, their woorth & glorie.

55

They neither shrunke, nor vantage sought of ground,
They trauerst not, nor skipt from part to part,
Their blowes were neither false nor faigned found,
The night, their rage, would let them vse no art,

Their swords togither clash with dreadfull sound,
Their feete stand fast, and neither stir nor start,
   They moue their hands, stedfast their feete remaine,
   Nor blow nor foine they stroake or thrust in vaine.

56

Shame bred desire a sharpe reuenge to take,
And veng'ance taken gaue new cause of shame:
So that with haste and little heed they strake,
Fuell enough they had to feed the flame,
At last so close their battell fierce they make,
They could not weild their swords, so nie they came,
   They vs'd the hilts, and each on other rusht,
   And helme to helme, and shield to shield they crusht.

57

Thrice his strong armes he fouldes about her waste,
And thrice was forst to let the virgine goe,
For she disdained to be so embraste,
No louer would haue strain'd his mistresse soe:
They tooke their swords againe, and each enchaste
Deepe wounds in the soft flesh of his strong foe,
   Till weake and wearie, faint, aliue vneath,
   They both retirde at once, at once tooke breath;

58

Each other long beheild, and leaning stood
Vpon their swords, whose points in earth were pight,
When day breake rising from the Eastren flood
Put forth the thousand eies of blindfold night,
Tancred beheild his foes out streaming blood,
And gaping wounds, and waxt proud with the sight,
   O vanitie of mans vnstable minde,
   Puft vp with euerie blast of friendly winde!

59

Why ioi'st thou wretch? O what shall be thy gaine?
What trophie for this conquest ist, thou reares?
Thine eies shall shed (in case thou be not slaine)
For euerie drop of blood a sea of teares:

59 95 < 59 (*cf. 1624*)   59³ ease < case (*cf. 1624*)

The bleeding warriours leaning thus remaine,
Each one to speake one word long time forbeares,
  Tancred the silence broake at last, and said,
  (For he would know with whom this fight he maid:)

60

'Euill is our chance, and hard our fortune is,
Who here in silence and in shade debate,
Where light of sunne and witnes all we mis,
That should our prowesse and our praise dilate:
If words in armes finde place, yet grant me this,
Tell me thy name, thy countrey and estate,
  That I may know (this dang'rous combate donne)
  Whom I haue conquerd, or who hath me wonne.'

61

'What I nill tell, you aske (quoth she) in vaine,
Nor mou'd by praier, nor constraind by powre,
But thus much know, I am one of those twaine
Which late with kindled fire destroi'd the towre.'
Tancred at her proud words sweld with disdaine,
'That hast thou said (quoth he) in euill howre,
  Thy vaunting speeches, and thy silence both,
  (Vnciuill wretch) hath made my hart more wroth.'

62

Ire in their chafed breasts renew'd the fray,
Fierce was the fight, though feeble were their might,
Their strength was gone, their cunning was away,
And furie in their stead maintain'd the fight,
Their swords both points and edges sharpe embay
In purple bloud, where so they hit or light,
  And if weake life yet in their bosomes lie,
  They liu'd bicause they both disdain'd to die.

63

As Egeans seas when stormes be calm'd againe,
That roll'd their tumbling waues with troublous blasts,
Do yet of tempests past some shewes retaine
And here and there their swelling billowes casts;

So, though their strength were gone, and might were vaine,
Of their first fiercenes still the furie lasts,
    Wherewith sustain'd, they to their tackling stood,
    And heaped wound on wound, and blood on blood.

64

But now alas, the fatall howre arriues,
That her sweete life must leaue that tender hold,
His sword into her bosome deepe he driues,
And bath'd in lukewarme blood his iron cold,
Betweene her brests the cruell weapon riues
Her curious square, embost with swelling gold,
    Her knees grow weake, the paines of death she feeles,
    And like a falling Cedar bends and reeles.

65

The Prince his hand vpon her shield doth streach,
And low on earth the wounded damsell laith,
And while she fell, with weake and woefull speach,
Her praiers last, and last complaints she saith,
A spirit new did her those praiers teach,
Spirit of hope, of charitie, and faith;
    And though her life to Christ rebellious weare,
    Yet died she his childe and handmaide deare.

66

'Friend thou hast wonne, I pardon thee, nor saue
This bodie, that all torments can endure,
But saue my soule, baptisme I dying craue,
Come wash away my sinnes with waters pure:'
His hart relenting nigh insunder raue,
With woefull speech of that sweete creature,
    So that his rage, his wrath and anger dide,
    And on his cheekes salt teares for ruthe downe slide.

67

With murmur lowd downe from the mountaines side
A little runnell tumbled neere the place,
Thither he ran and fild his helmet wide,
And quicke return'd to do that worke of grace,

With trembling hands her beauer he vntide,
Which done he saw, and seeing, knew her face,
   And lost therewith his speech and moouing quight,
   O woefull knowledge, ah vnhappie sight!

68

He died not, but all his strength vnites,
And to his vertues gaue his hart in gard,
Brideling his greefe, with water he requites
The life, that he bereft with iron hard;
And while the sacred words the knight recites,
The Nymphe to heau'n with ioy her selfe prepard;
   And as her life decaies, her ioyes encrease,
   She smild and said, 'farewell, I die in peace.'

69

As Violets blew mongst Lillies pure men throw,
So palenes midst her natiue white begonne.
Her lookes to heau'n she cast, their eies I trow
Downeward for pitie bent both heau'n and sunne,
Her naked hand she gaue the knight, in show
Of loue and peace, her speech (alas) was donne,
   And thus the virgin fell on endlesse sleepe,
   Loue, beautie, vertue, for your darling weepe.

70

But when he saw her gentle soule was went,
His manly courage to relent began,
Greefe, sorrow, anguish, sadnes, discontent,
Free empire got, and lordship on the man,
His life within his hart they close vp pent,
Death through his senses and his visage ran:
   Like his dead Ladie, dead seem'd *Tancred* good,
   In palenesse, stilnesse, wounds and streames of blood.

71

And his weake sprite (to be vnbodied
From fleshly prison free that ceaselesse striued)
Had follow'd her faire soule but lately fled,
Had not a Christian squadron there arriued,

To seeke fresh water thither haply led,
And found the Princesse dead, and him depriued
    Of signes of life, yet did the knight remaine
    On liue, nigh dead, for her himselfe had slaine.

72

Their guide far off the Prince knew by his shield,
And thither hasted full of greefe and feare,
Her dead, him seeming so, he there beheild,
And for that strange mishap shed many a teare;
He would not leaue the corses faire in field
For food to wolues, though she a Pagan weare,
    But in their armes the soldiers both vphent,
    And both lamenting brought to *Tancreds* tent:

73

With those deere burthens to their campe they passe,
Yet would not that dead seeming knight awake,
At last he deepely groan'd, which token was
His feeble soule had not her flight yet take:
The other lay a still and heauie masse,
Her spirit had that earthen cage forsake,
    Thus were they brought, and thus they placed weare
    In sundry roomes, yet both adioyning neare.

74

All skill and art his carefull seruants vsed
To life againe their dying Lord to bring,
At last his eies vnclos'd, with teares suffused,
He felt their hands and heard their whispering,
But how he thither came long time he mused,
His minde astonisht was with euery thing;
    He gaz'd about, his squires in fine he knew,
    Then weake and wofull thus his plaints out threw:

75

'What liue I yet? and doe I breathe and see
Of this accursed day the hatefull light?
This spitefull ray which still vpbraideth mee
With that accursed deed, I did this night,

Ah coward hand! affraid why shouldst thou bee?
(Thou instrument of death, shame and despite)
　　Why shouldst thou feare, with sharp & trenchant knife,
　　To cut the threed of this blood-guiltie life?

76

'Pierce through this bosome, and my cruell hart
In peeces cleaue, breake euery string and vaine;
But thou to slaughters vile which vsed art,
Think'st it were pitie so to ease my paine:
Of lucklesse loue therefore in torments smart,
A sad example must I still remaine,
　　A wofull monster of vnhappie loue,
　　Who still must liue, least death his comfort proue:

77

'Still must I liue in anguish, griefe and caire,
Furies my guiltie conscience that torment,
The ougly shades, darke night, and troubled aire
In grisly formes her slaughter still present,
Madnes and death about my bed repaire,
Hell gapeth wide to swallow vp this tent;
　　Swift from my selfe I ronne, my selfe I feare,
　　Yet still my hell within my selfe I beare:

78

'But where (alas) where be those reliques sweet,
Wherein dwelt late all loue, all ioy, all good?
My furie left them cast in open street,
Some beast hath torne her flesh and lickt her blood,
Ah noble pray! for sauage beast vnmeet,
Ah sweet! too sweet, and far too pretious food,
　　Ah seely Nymph! whom night and darksome shade
　　To beasts, and me (far worse than beasts) betrade.

79

'But where you be, if still you be, I wend
To gather vp those reliques deere at least,
But if some beast hath from the hils descend,
And on her tender bowels made his feast,

Let that selfe monster me in peeces rend,
And deepe entombe me in his hollow cheast:
  For where she buried is, there shall I haue
  A stately tombe, a rich and costly graue.'

80

Thus mourn'd the knight, his squires him told at last,
They had her there for whom those teares he shed;
A beame of comfort his dim eies out cast,
Like lightning through thicke cloudes of darknes spred,
The heauie burthen of his lims in hast
With mickle paine, he drew forth of his bed,
  And scant of strength to stand, to moue or goe,
  Thither he staggred, reeling to and froe:

81

When he came there, and in her brest espide
(His handiworke) that deepe and cruell wound,
And her sweet face with leaden palenesse dide,
Where beautie late spred forth her beames around,
He trembled so, that nere his squires beside
To hold him vp, he had sunke downe to ground,
  And said, 'O face in death still sweet and faire!
  Thou canst not sweeten yet my greefe and caire:

82

'O faire right hand, the pledge of faith and loue!
Giuen me but late, too late, in signe of peace,
How haps it now thou canst not stir nor moue?
And you deere lims now laid in rest and ease,
Through which my cruell blade this flood-gate roue,
Your paines haue end, my torments neuer cease,
  O hands! O cruell eies accurst alike!
  You gaue the wound, you gaue them light to strike.

83

'But thither now ronne forth my guiltie blood,
Whither my plaints, my sorrowes cannot wend,'
He said no more, but, as his passion wood
Enforced him, he gan to teare and rend

His haire, his face, his wounds, a purple flood
Did from each side in rolling streames descend,
  He had beene slaine, but that his paine and woe
  Bereft his senses, and preseru'd him soe.

84

Cast on his bed his squires recall'd his spright,
To execute againe her hatefull charge,
But tattling fame the sorrowes of the knight,
And hard mischance had told this while at large:
Godfrey and all his Lords of worth and might,
Ran thither, and the dutie would discharge
  Of friendship true, and with sweet words the rage
  Of bitter greefe and woe, they would asswage.

85

But as a mortall wound the more doth smart
The more it searched is, handled or sought;
So their sweete words to his afflicted hart
More griefe, more anguish, paine and torment brought:
But reuerend *Peter* that nould set apart
Care of his sheepe, as a good sheepheard ought,
  His vanitie with graue aduise reprooued,
  And told what mourning Christian knights behooued:

86

'O *Tancred, Tancred,* how farre different
From thy beginnings good these follies bee?
What makes thee deafe? what hath thy eiesight blent?
What mist, what cloud thus ouershadeth thee?
This is a warning good from heau'n downe sent,
(Yet his aduise thou canst not heare nor see)
  Who calleth and conducts thee to the way,
  From which thou willing dost and witting stray:

87

'To woorthie actions and atchiuements fit
For Christian knights, he would thee home recall;
But thou hast left that course and changed it,
To make thy selfe a heathen damsels thrall;

But see, thy griefe and sorrowes painefull fit
Is made the rod to scourge thy sinnes withall,
   Of thine owne good thy selfe the meanes he makes,
   But thou his mercy, goodnes, grace forsakes.

88

'Thou dost refuse of heau'n the profred grace,
And gainst it still rebell with sinfull ire,
O wretch! O whither doth thy rage thee chace?
Refraine thy griefe, bridle thy fond desire,
At hels wide gate vaine sorrow doth thee place,
Sorrow, misfortunes sonne, despaires foule sire:
   O see thine euill, thy plaint and woe refraine,
   The guides to death, to hell, and endlesse paine.'

89

This said, his will to die the patient
Abandoned, that second death he feared,
These words of comfort to his hart downe went,
And that darke night of sorrow somewhat cleared;
Yet now and then his griefe deepe sighes foorth sent,
His voice shrill plaints and sad laments oft reared,
   Now to himselfe, now to his murdred loue,
   He spoke, who heard perchance from heau'n aboue.

90

Till *Phœbus* rising from his euening fall
To her, for her, he mournes, he cals, he cries;
The nightingall so when her children small
Some churle takes before their parents eies,
Alone, dismaid, quite bare of comforts all,
Tires with complaints the seas, the shores, the skies,
   Till in sweete sleepe against the morning bright
   She fall at last; so mourn'd, so slept the knight.

91

And clad in starrie vale amid his dreame,
(For whose sweete sake he mourn'd) appeard the maid,
Fairer than earst, yet with that heau'nly beame,
Not out of knowledge was her louely shaid,

With lookes of ruth, her eies celestiall seame
To pitie his sad plight, and thus she said,
   'Behold how faire, how glad thy loue appeares,
   And for my sake (my deare) forbeare these teares.

92

'Thine be the thankes, my soule thou madest flit
At vnawares out of her earthly nest,
Thine be the thankes thou hast aduanced it
In *Abrahams* deare bosome long to rest,
There still I loue thee, there for *Tancred* fit
A seat prepared is, among the blest;
   There in eternall ioy eternall light,
   Thou shalt thy loue enioy, and she her knight:

93

'Vnlesse thy selfe, thy selfe heau'ns ioies enuie,
And thy vaine sorrow thee of blisse depriue,
Liue, know I loue thee, that I nill denie,
As angels, men; as saints may wights on liue:'
This said, of zeale and loue foorth of her eie
An hundreth glorious beames bright shining driue,
   Amid which raies her selfe she clos'd from sight,
   And with new ioy, new comfort left her knight.

94

Thus comforted he wakt, and men discreet
In surgerie to cure his wounds were sought,
Meane-while of his deare loue the reliques sweet
(As best he could) to graue with pompe he brought:
Her tombe was not of viride Spartane greet,
Nor yet by cunning hand of *Scopas* wrought,
   But built of polisht stone, and thereon laid
   The liuely shape and purtrait of the maid.

95

With sacred burning lamps in order long
And mournfull pompe the corps were brought to ground,
Her armes vpon a leauelesse pine were hong,
The herse, with cypresse; armes, with lawrell crown'd:

Next day the Prince (whose loue and courage strong
Drew foorth his limmes, weake, feeble and vnsound)
  To visite went, with care and reu'rence meet,
  The buried ashes of his mistresse sweet:

96

Before her new made tombe at last arriued,
The wofull prison of his liuing spright,
Pale, cold, sad, comfortlesse; of sense depriued,
Vpon the marble gray he fixt his sight,
Two streames of teares were from his eies deriued:
Thus with a sad alas, began the knight,
  'Oh marble deare on my deare mistresse plast!
  My flames within, without my teares thou hast.

97

'Not of dead bones art thou the mournfull graue,
But of quicke loue the fortresse and the hold,
Still in my hart thy woonted brands I haue
More bitter farre (alas) but not more cold,
Receaue these sighes, these kisses sweete recaue,
In liquid drops of melting teares enrold,
  And giue them to that bodie pure and chast
  Which in thy bosome cold entombd thou hast.

98

'For if her happie soule her eie doth bend
On that sweet body which it lately drest,
My loue, thy pittie, cannot her offend,
Anger and wrath is not in angels blest,
She pardon will the trespasse of her frend,
That hope relieues me with these griefes opprest,
  This hand she knowes hath onely sinn'd, not I,
  Who liuing lou'd her, and for loue now die:

99

'And louing will I die, O happie day
When ere it chanceth! but O farre more blest
If as about thy polisht sides I stray,
My bones within thy hollow graue might rest,

Togither should in heau'n our spirits stay,
Togither should our bodies lie in chest;
    So happie death should ioyne, what life doth seuer,
    O death, O life! sweete both, both blessed euer.'

100

Meanewhile the newes in that besieged towne
Of this mishap was whispred here and there,
Foorthwith it spred, and for too true was knowne,
Her wofull losse was talked euery where,
Mingled with cries and plaints to heau'n vp throwne,
As if the cities selfe new taken were
    With conqu'ring foes, or as if flame and fire,
    Nor house nor church, nor streete had left intire.

101

But all mens eies were on *Arsetes* bent,
His sighes were deepe, his lookes full of despaire,
Out of his wofull eies no teare there went,
His hart was hardned with his too much care,
His siluer locks with dust he foule besprent,
He knockt his breast, his face he rent and tare,
    And while the prease flockt to the Eunuch ould,
    Thus to the people spake *Argantes* bould,

102

'I would, when first I knew the hardie maid
Excluded was among her Christian foes,
Haue follow'd her to giue her timely aid,
Or by her side this breath and life to lose,
What did I not, or what left I vnsaid
To make the king the gates againe vnclose?
    But he denide, his powre did aie restraine
    My will, my suit was waste, my speech was vaine:

103

'Ah, had I gone, I would from danger free
Haue brought to Sion that sweete nymph againe,
Or in the bloudie fight, where kild was shee,
In her defence there noblie haue beene slaine:

But what could I do more? the counsels bee
Of God and man gainst my designments plaine,
   Dead is *Clorinda* faire, laid in colde graue,
   Let me reuenge her whom I could not saue.

104

'Hierusalem, heare what *Argantes* saith,
Heare heau'n (and if he breake his oath and word,
Vpon this head cast thunder in thy wrath)
I will destroy and kill that Christian Lord,
Who this faire dame by night thus murdred hath,
Nor from my side I will vngird this sword,
   Till *Tancreds* hart it cleaue and shed his blood,
   And leaue his corse to wolues and crowes for food.'

105

This said, the people with a ioyfull shoute
Applaud his speeches and his words approue,
And calm'd their griefe in hope the boaster stoute
Would kill the Prince, who late had slaine his loue.
O promise vaine! it otherwise fell out:
Men purpose, but high Gods dispose aboue,
   For vnderneath his sword this boaster dide,
   Whom thus he scorn'd and threat'ned in his pride.

The thirteenth Booke of Godfrey of Bulloigne.

The argument.

Ismeno sets to garde the forrest ould
The wicked sprites, whose ougly shapes affray
And put to flight the men, whose labour would
To their darke shades let in heau'ns golden ray:
Thither goes Tancred *hardie, faithfull, bould,*
But foolish pitie lets him not assay
  His strength and courage: heat the Christian powre
  Annoies, whom to refresh Gods sends a showre.

1

BVt scant dissolued into ashes cold
  The smoking towre fell on the scorched grasse,
When new deuise found out th'enchanter old,
By which the towne besieg'd, secured was,
Of timber fit his foes depriue he wold:
Such terrour bred that late consumed masse,
  So that the strength of Sions walles to shake,
  They should no turrets, rammes, nor engins make.

2

From *Godfreyes* campe a groue a little way
Amid the vallies deepe growes out of sight,
Thicke with old trees whose horrid armes display
An ougly shade, like euerlasting night;
There when the sunne spreads forth his clearest ray,
Dim, thicke, vncertaine, gloomie seemes the light;
  As when in eu'ning day and darknes striue,
  Which should his foe from our horizon driue.

3

But when the sunne his chaire in seas doth steepe,
Night, horrour, darknes thicke, the place inuade,
Which vaile the mortall eies with blindnes deepe,
And with sad terrour make weake harts affraide,

Thither no groome driues forth his tender sheepe
To brouze, or ease their faint in cooling shade,
   Nor trauellor, nor pilgrime there to enter
   (So awfull seemes that forrest old) dare venter.

4

Vnited there the ghostes and gobblins meet
To frolicke with their mates in silent night,
With dragons wings some cleaue the welkin fleet,
Some nimbly ronne ore hils and vallies light,
A wicked troupe, that with allurement sweet
Drawes sinfull man from that is good and right,
   And there with hellish pompe, their bankets brought
   They solemnise, thus the vaine Pagans thought.

5

No twist, no twig, no bough nor branch therefore,
The Saracines cut from that sacred spring;
But yet the Christians spared nere the more,
The trees to earth with cutting steele to bring:
Thither went *Ismen* old with tresses hore,
When night on all this earth spred forth her wing,
   And there in silence deafe and mirksome shade,
   His characters and circles vaine he made:

6

He in the circle set one foot vnshod,
And whispred dreadfull charmes in gastly wise,
Three times (for witchcraft loueth numbers od)
Toward the east he gaped, westward thrise,
He stroke the earth thrise with his charmed rod,
Wherewith dead bones he makes from graues to rise,
   And thrise the ground with naked foote he smote,
   And thus he cried lowd, with thundring note.

7

'Heare, heare, you spirits all that whilome fell,
Cast downe from heau'n with dint of roaring thunder;
Heare, you amid the emptie aire that dwell,
And stormes and showres powre on these kingdoms vnder;

Heare, all you deuils that lie in deepest hell,
And rend with torments damned ghostes asunder,
And of those lands of death, of paine and feare,
Thou monarch great, great Dis, great *Pluto*, heare.

8

'Keepe you this forrest well, keepe euery tree,
Numbred I giue you them and truly tould;
As soules of men in bodies cloathed be,
So euerie plant a sprite shall hide and hould,
With trembling feare make all the Christians flee,
When they presume to cut these Cedars ould:'
This said, his charmes he gan againe repeat,
Which none can say but they that vse like feat.

9

At those strange speeches, still nights splendant fires
Quenched their lights, and shrunke away for doubt,
The feeble moone her siluer beames retires,
And wrapt her hornes with foulding cloudes about,
Ismen his sprites to come with speed requires,
'Why come you not you euer damned rout?
Why tarrie you so long? pardie you stay
Till stronger charmes and greater words I say.

10

'I haue not yet forgot for want of vse,
What dreadfull tearmes belong this sacred feat,
My toong (if still your stubburne harts refuse)
That so much dreaded name can well repeat,
Which heard great *Dis* cannot himselfe excuse,
But hither runne from his eternall seat,'
O great and fearfull! more he would haue said,
But that he saw the sturdie sprites obaid.

11

Legions of deuills by thousands thither come,
Such as in sparsed aire their biding make,
And thousands also which by heauenly dome
Condemned lie in deepe Auernus lake,

But slow they came, displeased all and some,
Bicause those woods they should in keeping take,
  Yet they obai'd and tooke the charge in hand,
  And vnder euerie branch and leafe they stand.

12

When thus his cursed worke performed was,
The wisard to his king declar'd the feat,
'My Lord, let feare, let doubt and sorrow pas,
Henceforth in safetie stands your regall seat,
Your foe (as he suppos'd) no meane now has
To build againe his rams and engins great:'
  And then he told at large from part to part,
  All what he late perform'd by wondrous art.

13

'Besides this helpe, another hap (quoth hee)
Will shortly chance that brings not profit small,
Within few daies *Mars* and the *Sunne* I see
Their firie beames vnite in *Leo* shall;
And then extreme the scorching heat will bee;
Which neither raine can quench, nor dewes that fall,
  So placed are the Planets high and low,
  That heat, fire, burning all the heau'ns forshow:

14

'So great with vs will be the warmth therefore,
As with the Garamantes or those of Inde;
Yet nill it grieue vs in this towne so sore,
We haue sweet shade and waters cold by kinde:
Our foes abroad will be tormented more,
What shield can they or what refreshing finde?
  Heau'n will them vanquish first, then Egypts crew
  Destroy them quite, weake, wearie, faint and few;

15

'Thou shalt sit still and conquer, proue no more
The doubtfull hazard of vncertaine fight.
But if *Argantes* bold (that hates so sore
All cause of quiet peace, though iust and right)

Prouoke thee forth to battaile (as before)
Finde meanes to calme the rage of that fierce knight,
  For shortly heau'n will send thee ease and peace,
  And war and trouble mongst thy foes encrease.'

16

The king assured by these speeches faire,
Held *Godfreyes* powre, his might and strength in scorne,
And now the walles he gan in part repaire,
Which late the ram had brus'd with iron horne,
With wise foresight and well aduised caire,
He fortifide each breach and bulwarke torne,
  And all his folke, men, women, children small,
  With endlesse toile againe repair'd the wall.

17

But *Godfrey* nould this while bring forth his powre
To giue assault against that fort in vaine,
Till he had builded new his dreadfull towre,
And reared high his downe-falne rammes againe:
His workmen therefore he dispatcht that howre,
To hew the trees out of the forrest maine,
  They went, and scant the wood appear'd in sight,
  When wonders new their fearfull harts affright:

18

As seely children dare not bend their eie
Where they are told strange Bugbeares haunt the place,
Or as new monsters while in bed they lie,
Their fearefull thoughts present before their face;
So feared they, and fled, yet wist not why,
Nor what pursu'd them in that fearefull chace,
  Except their feare perchance while thus they fled,
  New Chimeres, Sphinges, or like monsters bred;

19

Swift to the campe they turned backe dismai'd,
With words confus'd vncertaine tales they told,
That all which heard them scorned what they said,
And those reportes for lies and fables hold.

A chosen crew in shining armes arrai'd
Duke *Godfrey* thither sent of soldiers bold,
   To garde the men, and their faint armes prouoke
   To cut the dreadfull trees with hardie stroke:

20

These drawing neere the wood, where close ipent
The wicked sprites in syluan pinfoldes weare,
Their eies vpon those shades no sooner bent,
But frosen dread pearst through their entrals deare;
Yet on they stalked still, and on they went,
Vnder bold semblance hiding coward feare,
   And so far wandred forth with trembling pace,
   Till they approcht nigh that inchanted place:

21

When from the groue a fearefull sound out brakes,
As if some earthquake hill and mountaine tore,
Wherein the southren winde a rumbling makes,
Or like sea waues against the craggie shore,
There lions gromble, there hisse scalie snakes,
There howle the woolues, the rugged beares there rore,
   There trumpets shrill are heard and thunders fell,
   And all these sounds one sound expressed well:

22

Vpon their faces pale well might you note
A thousand signes of hart amating feare,
Their reason gone, by no deuise they wote
How to prease nie, or stay still where they weare,
Against that sodaine dread their brests which smote,
Their courage weake no shield of proofe could beare,
   At last they fled, and one than all more bold,
   Excus'd their flight, and thus the wonders told.

23

'My Lord, not one of vs there is, I grant,
That dares cut downe one branch in yonder spring,
I thinke there dwels a sprite in euerie plant,
There keepes his court great *Dis* infernall king,

He hath a hart of hardned Adamant
That without trembling dares attempt the thing,
  And sense he wanteth who so hardie is,
  To heare the forrest thunder, roare and his.'

24

This said, *Alcasto* to his words gaue heed,
Alcasto leader of the Switzers grim,
A man both voide of wit, and voide of dreed,
Who fear'd not losse of life, nor losse of lim,
No sauage beastes in desarts wilde that feed,
Nor ougly monster could disharten him,
  Nor whirle winde, thunder, earthquake, storme, or ought
  That in this world is strange or fearfull thought:

25

He shooke his head, and smiling thus gan say,
'The hardinesse haue I that wood to fell,
And those proud trees low in the dust to lay,
Wherein such grislie feends and monsters dwell,
No roaring goast my courage can dismay,
No shrike of birdes, beasts roare, or dragons yell;
  But through and through that forrest will I wend,
  Although to deepest hell the pathes descend.'

26

Thus boasted he, and leaue to goe desired,
And forward went with ioyfull cheare and will,
He view'd the wood and those thicke shades admired,
He heard the wondrous noise and rumbling shrill;
Yet not one foote th'audacious man retired,
He scorn'd the perill preasing forward still,
  Till on the forrests outmost marge he stept,
  A flaming fire from entrance there him kept.

27

The fire encreast, and built a stately wall
Of burning coales, quicke sparkes, and embers hot,
And with bright flames the wood enuiron'd all,
That there no tree nor twist *Alcasto* got,

24⁷ oug < ought

The higher stretched flames seem'd bulwarkes tall,
Castles and turrets full of firie shot,
    With slinges and engins strong of euerie sort,
    What mortall wight durst scale so strange a fort?

28

O what strange monsters on the battlement
In loathsome formes stood to defend the place?
Their frowning lookes vpon the knight they bent,
And threatned death with shot, with sword and mace:
At last he fled, and though but slow he went,
As lyons doe whom iolly hunters chace;
    Yet fled the man and with sad feare withdrew,
    Though feare till then he neuer felt nor knew.

29

That he had fled long time he neuer wist,
But when far ronne he had discou'red it,
Himselfe for wonder with his hand he blist,
A bitter sorrow by the hart him bit,
Amas'd, asham'd, disgras'd, sad, silent, trist,
Alone he would all day in darknes sit,
    Nor durst he looke on man of worth or fame,
    His pride late-great, now greater made his shame.

30

Godfredo call'd him, but he found delaies
And causes why he should his cabben keepe,
At length perforce he comes, but nought he saies,
Or talkes like those that babble in their sleepe.
His shamefastnes to *Godfrey* plaine bewraies
His flight, so doth his sighes and sadnes deepe:
    Whereat amas'd, 'what chance is this (quoth he?)
    These witchcrafts strange or natures wonders be.

31

'But if his courage any champion moue
To trie the hazard of this dreedfull spring,
I giue him leaue th'aduenture great to proue,
Some newes he may report vs of the thing:'

This said, his Lords attempt the charmed groue,
Yet nothing backe but feare and flight they bring,
 For them enforst with trembling to retire
 The sight, the sound, the monsters and the fire.

32

This hapt when woefull *Tancred* left his bed,
To lay in marble cold his mistresse deare,
The liuely colour from his cheeke was fled,
His limmes were weake, his helme or targe to beare;
Nathlesse when need to heigh attempts him led,
No labour would he shunne, no danger feare,
 His valour, boldnesse, hart and courage braue,
 To his faint body strength and vigor gaue.

33

To this exploit forth went the ventrous knight,
Fearlesse, yet heedfull; silent, well aduised,
The terrours of that forrests dreadfull sight,
Stormes, earthquakes, thunders, cries, he all despised,
He feared nothing, yet a motion light
(That quickly vanisht) in his hart arised,
 When loe betweene him and the charmed wood,
 A firie citie high as heau'n vp stood:

34

The knight stept backe and tooke a sodaine pause,
And to himselfe, 'what helpe these armes, (quoth he?)
If in this fire or monsters gaping iawes
I headlong cast my selfe, what bootes it me?
For common profit or my countries cause,
To hazard life before me none should be:
 But this exploit of no such weight I hold,
 For it to lose a Prince or champion bold.

35

'But if I flie, what will the Pagans say?
If I retire, who shall cut downe this spring?
Godfredo will attempt it euery day.
What if some other knight performe the thing?

32⁵ attemps < attempts (*cf. 1624*)

These flames vprisen to forestall my way,
Perchance more terrour far than danger bring,
  But hap what shall,' this said, he forward stept,
  And through the fire (O wondrous boldnes) lept!

36

He boulted through, but neither warmth nor heat
He felt, nor signe of fire or scorching flame;
Yet wist he not in his dismai'd conceat,
If that were fire or no, through which he came;
For at first touch vanisht those monsters great,
And in their steed the cloudes blacke night did frame,
  And hideous stormes and showres of haile and raine,
  Yet stormes and tempests vanisht straight againe,

37

Amaz'd, but not affraid the champion good
Stood still, but when the tempest past he spied,
He entred boldly that forbidden wood,
And of the forrest all the secrets eied,
In all his walke no sprite or fantasme stood,
That stopt his way or passage free denied,
  Saue that the growing trees so thicke were set,
  That oft his sight, and passage oft they let.

38

At length a faire and spatious greene he spide,
Like calmest waters, plaine, like veluet, soft,
Wherein a Cipresse clad in sommers pride
Pyramide wise, lift vp his tops aloft;
In whose smooth barke vpon the eeuenest side,
Strange characters he found and view'd them oft,
  Like those which priests of Egypt earst in stead
  Of letters vs'd, which none but they could read,

39

Mongst them he picked out these words at last,
(Writ in the Syriake toong, which well he could)
'O hardie knight, who through these woods hast past!
Where death his pallace and his court doth hould!

O trouble not these soules in quiet plast,
O be not cruell as thy hart is bould,
  Pardon these ghoasts depriu'd of heau'nly light,
  With spirits dead why should men liuing fight?'

40

This found he grauen in the tender rinde,
And while he mused on this vncouth writ,
Him thought he heard the softly whistling winde,
His blastes amid the leaues and branches knit,
And frame a sound like speech of humaine kinde,
But full of sorrow, griefe and woe was it,
  Whereby his gentle thoughts all filled weare
  With pitie, sadnes, greefe, compassion, feare:

41

He drew his sword at last and gaue the tree
A mightie blow, that made a gaping wound,
Out of the rift red streames he trickling see
That all bebled the verdant plaine around,
His haire start vp, yet once againe stroake he,
He nould giue ouer till the end he found
  Of this aduenture, when with plaint and mone,
  (As from some hollow graue) he heard one grone.

42

'Enough enough' the voice lamenting said,
'*Tancred* thou hast me hurt, thou didst me driue
Out of the bodie of a noble maid,
Who with me liu'd, whom late I kept on liue,
And now within this woefull Cipresse laid,
My tender rinde thy weapon sharpe doth riue,
  Cruell, ist not enough thy foes to kill,
  But in their graues wilt thou torment them still?

43

'I was *Clorinda*, now imprison'd heere,
(Yet not alone) within this plant I dwell,
For euerie Pagan Lord and Christian peere,
Before the cities walles last day that fell,

(In bodies new or graues I wote not cleere)
But here they are confin'd by magikes spell,
    So that each tree hath life, and sense each bou,
    A murdrer if thou cut one twist art thou.'

44

As the sicke man that in his sleepe doth see
Some oughly dragon or some chimere new,
Though he suspect or halfe perswaded bee,
It is an idle dreame, no monster trew,
Yet still he feares, he quakes, and striues to flee,
So fearefull is that wondrous forme to vew;
    So feard the knight, yet he both knew and thought
    All were illusions false by witchcraft wrought:

45

But cold and trembling waxt his frozen hart,
Such strange affects, such passions it torment,
Out of his feeble hand his weapon start,
Himselfe out of his wits nigh, after went:
Wounded he saw (he thought) for paine and smart
His Ladie weepe, complaine, mourne and lament,
    Nor could he suffer her deere blood to see,
    Or heare her sighes that deepe far fetched be.

46

Thus his fierce hart which death had scorned oft,
Whom no strange shape, or monster could dismay,
With faigned showes of tender loue made soft,
A spirit false did with vaine plaints betray,
A whirling winde his sword heau'd vp aloft,
And through the forrest bare it quite away,
    Orecome retir'd the Prince, and as he came
    His sword he found and repossest the same:

47

Yet nould returne, he had no minde to trie
His courage further in those forrests greene,
But when to *Godfreyes* tent he proched nie,
His spirits wakte, his thoughts composed beene,

'My Lord (quoth he) a witnesse true am I
Of woonders strange, beleeued scant though seene,
What of the fire, the shades, the dreadfull sound,
You heard, all true by proofe my selfe haue found,

48

'A burning fire (so are those desarts charmed)
Built like a batled wall to heau'n was reared,
Whereon with dartes and dreadfull weapons armed,
Of monsters foule mishapt whole bands appeared;
But through them all I past, vnhurt, vnharmed,
No flame or threatned blow I felt or feared,
Then raine and night I found, but straight againe
To day, the night; to sunshine turnd the raine,

49

'What would you more? each tree through all that wood
Hath sense, hath life, hath speech, like humaine kind,
I heard their words, as in that groue I stood,
That mournfull voice still, still I beare in minde:
And (as they were of flesh) the purple blood,
At euery blow streames from the wounded rind,
No, no, not I, nor any else (I trow)
Hath powre to cut one leafe, one branch, one bow.

50

While thus he said; the Christians noble guide
Felt vncouth strife in his contentious thought,
He thought, what if himselfe in person tride
Those witchcrafts strange, and bring those charmes to nought,
For such he deem'd them, or elsewhere prouide
For timber easier got though further sought,
But from his studie he at last abraid,
Call'd by the Hermit old that to him said,

51

'Leaue off thy hardie thought, an others hands
Of these her plants the wood dispoilen shall,
Now, now the fatall ship of conquest lands,
Her sailes are strucke, her siluer anchores fall,

49[8] brow < bow

Our champion broken hath his worthlesse bands,
And looseth from the soile which held him thrall,
 The time drawes nie when our proud foes in field
 Shall slaughtred lie, and Sions fort shall yield.'

52

This said, his visage shone with beames diuine
And more than mortall was his voices sound,
Godfredos thought to other actes encline,
His working braine was neuer idle found.
But in the Crabbe now did bright *Titan* shine,
And scorcht with scalding beames the parched ground,
 And made vnfit for toile or warlike feat,
 His souldiers, weake with labour, faint with sweat:

53

The Planets milde their lamps benigne quencht out,
And cruell starres in heau'n did signories,
Whose influence cast fierie flames about,
And hot impressions through the earth and skies,
The growing heat still gathred deeper rout,
The noisome warmth through lands and kingdomes flies,
 A harmefull night a hurtfull day succeeds,
 And woorse than both next morne her light outspreeds.

54

When *Phœbus* rose he left his golden weed,
And dond a gite in deepest purple dide,
His sanguine beames about his forhead spreed
A sad presage of ill that should betide,
With vermile drops at eau'n his tresses bleed,
Fore showes of future heat, from th'Ocean wide
 When next he rose, and thus encreased still,
 Their present harmes with dread of future ill.

55

While thus he bent gainst earth his scorching raies,
He burnt the flowrets, burnt his *Clitie* deare,
The leaues grew wan vpon the withred spraies,
The grasse and growing hearbs all parched weare,

Earth cleft in riftes, in floods their streames decaies,
The barren cloudes with lightning bright appeare,
  And mankind feard least *Climenes* childe againe,
  Had driuen awry his sires il-guided waine;

56

As from a furnace, flew the smoake to skies,
Such smoake as that when damned Sodome brent,
Within his caues sweete *Zephire* silent lies,
Still was the aire, the racke nor came nor went,
But ore the lands with lukewarme breathing flies
The southren winde, from sunburnt Africke sent,
  Which thicke and warme his interrupted blasts
  Vpon their bosomes, throates and faces casts.

57

Nor yet more comfort brought the gloomie night,
In her thicke shades was burning heat vprold,
Her sable mantle was embrodred bright,
With blazing starres, and gliding fires for gold,
Nor to refresh (sad earth) thy thirstie spright,
The niggard Moone let fall her May-dewes cold,
  And dried vp the vitall moisture was,
  In trees, in plants, in herbes, in flowres, in grasse.

58

Sleepe to his quiet dales exiled fled,
From these vnquiet nights, and oft in vaine
The souldiers restlesse sought the god in bed,
But most for thirst they mourn'd and most complaine;
For *Iudais* tyrant had strong poison shed,
(Poison that breedes more woe and deadly paine,
  Than *Acheron* or *Stigian* waters bring)
  In euerie fountaine, cestern, well, and spring.

59

And little *Siloe* that his store bestowes
Of purest Chrystall on the Christian bands,
The peebles naked in his chanell showes,
And scantly glides aboue the scorched sands;

Nor Poe in May when ore his bankes he flowes,
Nor Ganges, watrer of the Indian lands,
   Nor seu'n mouth'd Nile that yeelds all Egypt drinke,
   To quench their thirst the men sufficient thinke.

60

He that the gilding riuers earst had seene,
Adowne their verdant chanels gently rold,
Or falling streames which to the valleies greene
Distill'd from tops of Alpine mountaines cold,
Those he desir'd in vaine, new torments beene,
Augmented thus, with wish of comforts old,
   Those waters coole he dranke in vaine conceit,
   Which more encreast his thirst, encreast his heat.

61

The sturdie bodies of the warriours strong,
Whom neither marching far, nor tedious way,
Nor weightie armes which on their shoulders hong,
Could wearie make, nor death it selfe dismay;
Now weake and feeble cast their limmes along,
Vnweildie burthens, on the burned clay,
   And in each vaine a smouldring fire there dwelt,
   Which dride their flesh, and sollid bones did melt.

62

Languisht the stead late fierce, and profred gras,
His fodder earst, despis'd, and from him kest,
Each step he stumbled, and which loftie was
And heigh aduanst before, now fell his crest,
His conquests gotten all forgotten pas,
Nor with desire of glorie sweld his brest,
   The spoiles wonne from his foe, his late rewards,
   He now neglects, despiseth, nought regards.

63

Languisht the faithfull dog, and wonted caire
Of his deare Lord and cabben both forgot,
Panting he laid, and gathred fresher aire
To coole the burning in his entrals hot:

59⁶ ganges < Ganges *as in other copies*

But breathing (which wise Nature did prepare
To swage the stomackes heat) now booted not,
   For little ease (alas) small helpe they win,
    That breath foorth aire, and scalding fire sucke in.

64

Thus languished the earth, in this estate
Lay woefull thousands of the Christians stout,
The faithfull people grew nie desperate
Of hoped conquest, shamefull death they dout,
Of their distresse they talke and oft debate,
These sad complaints were heard the campe throughout,
   'What hope hath *Godfrey*? Shall we still here lie,
    Till all his souldiers, all our armies die?

65

'Alas, with what deuice, what strength, thinkes he
To scale these walles, or this strong fort to get?
Whence hath he engins new? doth he not see,
How wrathfull heau'n gainst vs his sword doth whet?
These tokens showne true signes and witnesse be,
Our angrie God our proud attempts doth let,
   And scorching sunne so hot his beames outspreeds,
    That not more cooling Inde nor Æthiop needs:

66

'Or thinkes he it an eath or little thing,
That vs despis'd, neglected, and disdain'd,
Like abiects vile to death he thus should bring?
That so his Empire may be still maintain'd?
Is it so great a blisse to be a king,
When he that weares the crowne with blood is stain'd,
   And buies his scepter with his peoples liues?
    See whither glorie vaine, fond mankinde driues.

67

'See, see the man, call'd holy, iust and good,
That curteous, meeke, and humble would be thought,
Yct neuer car'd in what distresse we stood,
If his vaine honour were diminisht nought,

When dried vp from vs is spring and flood,
His water must from Iordan streames be brought,
  And now he sits at feastes and bankets sweet,
  And mingleth waters fresh, with wines of Creet.'

68

The French thus murmour'd, but the Greekish knight
Tatine, that of this war was wearie growne,
'Why die we here (quoth he) slaine without fight,
Kild, not subdu'd? murdred, not ouerthrowne?
Vpon the Frenchmen let the penance light
Of *Godfreyes* follie, let me saue mine owne,'
  And as he said, without farewell, the knight
  And all his cornet stole away by night:

69

His bad example many a troupe prepares
To imitate, when his escape they know,
Clotharius his band, and *Ademares*,
And all, whose guides in dust were buried low,
Discharg'd of duties chaines and bondage snares,
Free from their oath, to none they seruice owe,
  But now concluded all on secret flight,
  And shrunke away by thousands euery night.

70

Godfredo this both heard and saw, and knew,
Yet nould with death them chastise though he mought,
But with that faith wherewith he could remew
The stedfast hils, and seas drie vp to nought,
He praid the Lord vpon his flocke to rew,
To ope the springs of grace, and ease this drought,
  Out of his lookes shone zeale, deuotion, faith,
  His hands and eies to heau'n he heaues, and saith;

71

'Father and Lord, if in the desarts wast
Thou hadst compassion on thy children deare,
The craggie rocke when *Moses* cleft and brast,
And drew forth flowing streames of waters cleare,

Like mercie (Lord) like grace, on vs downe cast;
And though our merits lesse than theirs appeare,
  Thy grace supply that want, for though they be
  Thy first borne sonne, thy children yet are we.'

72

These praiers iust from humble hart forth sent,
Were nothing slow to climbe the starrie skie,
But swift as winged bird themselues present
Before the father of the heauens hie:
The Lord accepted them and gently bent
Vpon the faithfull host his gracious eie,
  And in what paine and what distresse it laid,
  He saw, and greeu'd to see, and thus he said:

73

'Mine armies deere till now haue suffred woe,
Distresse and danger, hels infernall powre
Their enimie hath beene, the world their foe,
But happie be their actions from this howre,
What they begin to blessed end shall goe,
I will refresh them with a gentle showre;
  Rinaldo shall returne, th'Egyptian crew
  They shall encounter, conquer and subdew.'

74

At these high words great heau'n began to shake,
The fixed stars, the planets wandring still,
Trembled the aire, the earth and Ocean quake,
Spring, fountaine, riuer, forrest, dale and hill,
From north to east a lightning flash out-brake,
And comming drops presag'd with thunders shrill:
  With ioyfull shoutes the soldiers on the plaine,
  These tokens blesse of long desired raine,

75

A sodaine cloud, as when *Helias* praid,
(Not from drie earth exhail'd by *Phebus* beames)
Arose, moist heau'n his windowes open laid,
Whence cloudes by heapes out-rush, and watrie streames,

The world ore spred was with a gloomie shade,
That like a darke and mirksome eu'n it seames;
  The dashing raine, from molten skies downe fell,
  And ore their banks the brookes and fountaines swell.

76

In sommer season, when the cloudie skie
Vpon the parched ground doth raine downe send,
As ducke and mallard in the furrowes drie,
With merrie noise the promist showres attend,
And spreading broad their wings displaied lie
To keepe the drops that on their plumes descend,
  And where the streames swell to a gathred lake
  Therein they diue, and sweet refreshing take:

77

So they the streaming showres with showtes and cries
Salute, which heau'n shed on the thirstie lands,
The falling liquor from the dropping skies
He catcheth in his lap, he barehead stands,
And his bright helme to drinke therein vnties,
In the fresh streames he diues his sweatie hands,
  Their faces some, and some their temples wet,
  And some to keepe the drops large vessels set.

78

Nor man alone to ease his burning sore,
Herein doth diue and wash, and hereof drinks,
But earth itselfe weake, feeble, faint before,
Whose solid limmes were cleft with rifts and chinks,
Receiu'd the falling showres and gathred store
Of liquour sweet, that through her vaines downe sinks,
  And moisture new infused largely was
  In trees, in plants, in herbes, in flowres, in gras.

79

Earth, like the patient was, whose liuely blood
Hath ouercome at last some sicknes strong,
Whose feeble limmes had been the bait and food,
Whereon his strange disease depastred long,

But now restor'd, in health and welfare stood,
As sound as earst, as fresh, as faire, as yong;
　So that forgetting all his griefe and paine,
　His pleasant robes, and crownes he takes againe.

80

Ceased the raine, the sunne began to shine,
With fruitfull, sweet, benigne, and gentle ray,
Full of strong powre and vigour masculine,
As be his beames in Aprill or in May.
O happy zeale, who trusts in helpe diuine,
The worlds afflictions thus can driue away,
　Can stormes appease, and times and seasons change,
　And conquer fortune, fate and dest'nie strange.

The fourteenth Booke of Godfrey *of Bulloigne*

The argument.

The Lord to Godfrey *in a dreame doth shew*
His will; Rinaldo *must returne at last;*
They haue their asking who for pardon sew:
Two knights to finde the Prince are sent in hast,
But Peter *who by vision all foreknew*
Sendeth the searchers to a wisard, plast
   Deepe in a vault, who first at large declares
   Armidaes *traines, then how to shun those snares.*

1

NOw from the fresh, the soft and tender bed
   Of her still mother, gentle night out flew,
The fleeting baulme on hils and dales she shed,
With honie drops of pure and pretious dew,
And on the verdure of greene forrests spred
The virgin primrose and the violet blew,
   And sweet breath'd Zephire on his spreading wings
   Sleepe, ease, repose, rest, peace and quiet brings.

2

The thoughts and troubles of broad-waking day
They softly dipt in milde obliuions lake;
But he, whose Godhead heau'n and earth doth sway,
In his eternall light did watch and wake,
And bent on *Godfrey* downe the gracious ray
Of his bright eie, still ope for *Godfreyes* sake,
   To whom a silent dreame the Lord downe sent,
   Which told his will, his pleasure and intent.

3

Far in the east (the golden gate beside
Whence *Phebus* comes) a christall port there is,
And ere the sunne his broad doores open wide,
The beame of springing day vncloseth this,

Hence come the dreames, by which heau'ns sacred guide
Reueales to man those high decrees of his,
  Hence towards *Godfrey* ere he left his bed
  A vision strange his golden plumes bespred:

4

Such semblances, such shapes, such purtraites faire
Did neuer yet in dreame or sleepe appeare,
For all the formes in sea, in earth, or aire,
The signes in heau'n, the stars in euery spheare,
All what was wondrous, vncouth, and strange raire,
All in that vision well presented weare,
  His dreame had plast him in a christall wide,
  Beset with golden fires, top, bottom, side.

5

There while he wondreth on the circles vast,
The stars, their motions, course and harmonie,
A knight (with shining raies and fire embrast)
Presents himselfe vnwares before his eie,
Who with a voice that far for sweetnes past
All humaine speech, thus said approching nie,
  'What *Godfrey* know'st thou not thy *Hugo* heere?
  Come and imbrace thy friend and fellow deere:'

6

He answ'red him, 'that glorious shining light
Which in thine eies his glistring beames doth place,
Estranged hath from my foreknowledge quight
Thy countenance, thy fauour, and thy face:'
This said, three times he stretch his hands outright,
And would in friendly armes the knight embrace,
  And thrice the spirit fled, that thrice he twinde
  Nought in his folded armes, but aire and winde.

7

Lord *Hugo* smil'd, 'not as you thinke (quoth hee)
I clothed am in flesh and earthly mould,
My spirite pure and naked soule you see,
A Citizen of this celestiall hould,

This place is heau'n, and heere a roome for thee
Prepared is, among Christs champions bould:'
  'Ah when (quoth he) (these mortall bonds vnknit)
  Shall I in peace, in ease, and rest there sit?'

8

Hugo replide, 'ere many yeeres shall ronne,
Amid the saints in blisse here shalt thou raine;
But first great wars must by thy hand be donne,
Much blood be shed, and many Pagans slaine,
The holy citie by assault be wonne,
The land set free from seruile yoke againe,
  Wherein thou shalt a Christian Empire frame,
  And after thee shall *Baldwine* rule the same.

9

'But to encrease thy loue and great desire
To heauen ward, this blessed place behould,
These shining lampes, these globes of liuing fire,
How they are turned, guided, moou'd and rould,
The Angels singing here and all their quire;
Then bend thine eies on yonder earth and mould,
  All in that masse, that globe, and compasse see,
  Land, sea, spring, fountaine, man, beast, grasse and tree,

10

'How vile, how small, and of how slender price,
Is there reward of goodnesse, vertues gaine;
A narrow roome our glorie vaine vp-ties,
A little circle doth our pride containe,
Earth like an Isle amid the water lies,
Which sea sometime is call'd, sometime the maine,
  Yet nought therein responds a name so great,
  Its but a lake, a pond, a marrish streat.'

11

Thus said the one, the other bended downe
His lookes to ground, and halfe in scorne he smilde,
He sawe at once earth, sea, floud, castell, towne,
Strangely deuided, strangely all compilde,

And wondred follie man so farre should drowne,
To set his hart on things so base and vilde,
  That seruile empire searcheth and dombe fame,
  And scornes heau'ns blisse, yet profreth heau'n the same.

12

Wherefore he answered, 'since the Lord not yet
Will free my spirit from this cage of clay,
Least worldly errour vaine my voiage let,
Teach me to heau'n the best and surest way:'
Hugo replide, 'thy happy foote is set
In the true path, nor from this passage stray,
  Onely from exile yoong *Rinaldo* call,
  This giue I thee in charge, else nought at all.

13

'For as the Lord of hoastes, the king of blis,
Hath chosen thee to rule the faithfull band;
So he thy stratagems appointed is
To execute, so both shall winne this land,
The first is thine, the second place is his,
Thou art this armies head, and he the hand,
  No other champion can his place supplie,
  And that thou do it doth thy state denie.

14

'Th'inchanted forrest, and her charmed treene
With cutting steele shall he to earth downe hew,
And thy weake armies which too feeble beene
To scale againe these wals r'inforced new,
And fainting lie dispersed on the greene,
Shall take newe strength, newe courage at his vew,
  The heigh built towres, the eastren squadrons all
  Shall conquerd be, shall flie, shall die, shall fall,'

15

He held his peace: and *Godfrey* answred so,
'O how his presence would recomfort mee,
You that mans hidden thoughts perceaue and kno,
(If I say truth, or if I loue him) see,

14⁶ strenght, < strength,

But say, what messengers shall for him go?
What shall their speeches, what their errand bee?
  Shall I entreat or else command the man?
  With credit neither well performe I can.'

16

'Th'eternall Lord (the other knight replide)
That with so many graces hath thee blest,
Will, that among the troupes thou hast to guide,
Thou honour'd be and fear'd of most and lest:
Then speake not thou least blemish some betide
Thy sacred Empire, if thou make request;
  But when by suit thou mooued art to ruth,
  Then yeeld, forgiue, and home recall the youth.

17

'*Guelpho* shall pray thee (God shall him inspire)
To pardon this offence, this fault commit
By hastie wrath, by rash and headstrong ire,
To call the knight againe, yeeld thou to it:
And though the youth (enwrapt in fond desire)
Farre hence in loue and loosenes idle sit,
  Yet feare it not he shall returne with speed,
  When most you wish him, and when most you need.

18

'Your hermit *Peter*, to whose sapient hart
High heau'n his secrets opens, tels, and shewes,
Your messengers direct can to that part,
Where of the Prince they shall heare certaine newes,
And learne the way, the manner, and the art
To bring him backe to these thy warlike crewes,
  That all thy souldiours wandred and misgone,
  Heau'n may vnite againe and ioine in one.

19

'But this conclusion shall my speeches end,
Know that his blood shall mixed be with thine.
Whence Barons bold and Worthies shall descend,
That many great exploits shall bring to fine.'

This said, he vanisht from his sleeping friend,
Like smoake in winde, or mist in *Titans* shine;
  Sleepe fled likewise, and in his troubled thought,
  With woonder, pleasure; ioy, with maruell fought.

20

The Duke lookt vp, and saw the Azure skie
With Argent beames of siluer morning spred,
And started vp, for praise and vertue lie
In toile and trauell, sinne and shame in bed:
His armes he tooke, his sword girt to his thie,
To his pauilion all his Lords them sped,
  And there in counsell graue the Princes sit,
  For strength by wisedome, warre is rul'd by wit.

21

Lord *Guelpho* there (within whose gentle brest
Heau'n had infus'd that new and sudden thought)
His pleasing words thus to the Duke addrest;
'Good prince, milde, though vnaskt, kinde, vnbesought,
O let thy mercie grant my iust request,
Pardon this fault by rage, not malice, wrought;
  For great offence, I grant, so late commit,
  My suit too hastie is, perchance vnfit.

22

'But since to *Godfrey* meeke, benigne and kinde,
For Prince *Rinaldo* bold, I humbly sue,
And that the sutors selfe is not behinde
Thy greatest friends, in state, or friendship true;
I trust I shall thy grace and mercie finde
Acceptable to me and all this crue;
  Oh call him home, this trespasse to amend,
  He shall his blood in *Godfreyes* seruice spend:

23

'And if not he, who els dares vndertake
Of this enchanted wood to cut one tree?
Gainst death and danger who dares battell make,
With so bould face, so fearlesse hart, as he?

Beat downe these walles, these gates in pieces breake,
Leape ore these rampires heigh, thou shalt him see:
    Restore therefore to this desirous band
      Their wish, their hope, their strength, their sheild, their hand;

24

'To me my nephew, to thy selfe restore
A trustie helpe, when strength of hand thou needs,
In idlenesse let him consume no more,
Recall him to his noble acts and deeds.
Knowne be his worth as was his strength of yore,
Where ere thy standard broad her crosse outspreeds,
    O let his fame and praise, spread far and wide,
      Be thou his Lord, his teacher, and his guide.'

25

Thus he entreated, and the rest approue
His words, with friendly murmures whispred low,
Godfrey as though their suite his minde did moue
To that, whereon he neuer thought till now,
'How can my hart (quoth he) if you I loue
To your request and suit but bend and bow?
    Let rigor goe, that right and iustice bee,
      Wherein you all consent, and all agree.

26

'*Rinaldo* shall returne, let him restraine
Henceforth his headstrong wrath and hastie ire,
And with his hardie deedes let him take paine
To correspond your hope, and my desire:
Guelpho thou must call home the knight againe,
See that with speed he to these tents retire,
    The messengers appoint as likes thy minde,
      And teach them where they should the yongman finde.'

27

Vpstart the Dane that bore Prince *Swenos* brand,
'I will (quoth he) that message vndertake,
I will refuse no paines by sea or land
To giue the knight this sword, kept for his sake,'

This man was bold of courage, strong of hand,
Guelpho was glad he did the proffer make,
  'Thou shalt (quoth he) *Vbaldo* shalt thou haue
  To goe with thee, a knight, stout, wise, and graue.'

28

Vbaldo in his youth had knowne and seene
The fashions strange of many an vncouth land,
And trauell'd ouer all the Realmes, betweene
The Articke circle and hot Meroes strand,
And as a man whose wit his guide had beene,
Their customes vse he could, toongs vnderstand,
  For thy when spent his youthfull seasons weare
  Lord *Guelpho* entertain'd and held him deare.

29

To these committed was the charge and caire
To finde, and bring againe the champion bold,
Guelpho commaunds them to the fort repaire
Where *Boemond* doth his seat and scepter hold,
For publike fame said that *Bertoldoes* haire
There liu'd, there dwelt, there stai'd, the hermit old
  (That knew they were misled by false report)
  Among them came, and parled in this fort:

30

'Sir knights (quoth he) if you entend to ride,
And follow each report fond people say,
You follow but a rash and trothlesse guide,
That leades vaine men amisse, and makes them stray,
Neere Ascalon goe to the salt sea side,
Where a swift brooke fals in with hideous sway,
  An aged sire, our friend, there shall you finde,
  All what he saith that doe, that keepe in minde,

31

'Of this great voyage which you vndertake,
Much by his skill, and much by mine aduise
Hath he foreknowne, and welcome for my sake
You both shall be, the man is kinde and wise;'

Instructed thus no further question make
The twaine, elected for this enterprise,
But humblie yeelded to obey his word,
For what the Hermit said, that said the Lord.

32

They tooke their leaue, and on their iourney went,
Their will could brooke no stay, their zeale, no let;
To Ascalon their voyage straight they bent,
Whose broken shores with brackish waues are wet,
And there they heard how gainst the cliftes (besprent
With bitter fome) the roaring surges bet,
A tumbling brooke their passage stopt and staid,
Which late falne raine had proud and puissant maid,

33

So proud that ouer all his bankes he grew,
And through the fieldes ran swift as shaft from bow,
While here they stopt and stood, before them drew
An aged sire, graue and benigne in show,
Crown'd with a beechen garland gathred new,
Clad in a linnen roabe that raught downe low,
In his right hand a rod, and on the flood
Against the streame he marcht, and drieshod yood.

34

As on the Rhene (when winters freesing cold
Congeales the streames to thicke and hardned glas)
The beauies faire of Shepheards daughters bold,
With wanton winde laies ronne, turne, play and pas;
So on this riuer past the wisard old,
Although vnfrosen, soft, and swift it was,
And thither stalked where the warriours staid,
To whom (their greetings done) he spoke, and said:

35

'Great paines, great trauaile (Lords) you haue begonne,
And of a cunning guide great need you stand,
Farre off (alas) is great *Bertoldoes* sonne,
Imprison'd in a waste and desart land,

34⁷ warrious < warriours (1624)

What soile remaines by which you must not ronne?
What promontorie, rocke, sea, shore or sand?
   Your search must stretch before the prince be found,
   Beyond our world, beyond our halfe of ground.

36

'But yet vouchsafe to see my cell I pray,
In hidden caues and vaults though builded low,
Great wonders there, strange things I will bewray,
Things good for you to heare, and fit to know:'
This said, he bids the riuer make them way,
The floud retirde, and backward gan to flow,
   And here and there two christall mountaines rise,
   So fled the red sea once, and Iordan thrise.

37

He tooke their hands and led them headlong downe
Vnder the flood, through vast and hollow deepes,
Such light they had as when through shadowes browne
Of thickest desarts feeble *Cinthia* peepes,
There spacious caues they sawe all ouerflowne,
There all his waters pure great *Neptune* keepes,
   And thence to moisten all the earth, he brings
   Seas, riuers, flouds, lakes, fountaines, wels and springs:

38

Whence Ganges, Indus, Volga, Ister, Poe,
Whence Euphrates, whence Tygresse spring they vew,
Whence Tanais, whence Nilus comes alsoe,
(Although his head till then no creature knew)
But vnder these a wealthie streame doth goe
That Sulphur yeelds and Oare, rich, quicke and new,
   Which the sunbeames doth polish, purge and fine,
   And makes it siluer pure, and gold diuine.

39

And all his bankes the rich and wealthie streame
Hath faire beset, with pearle and precious stone,
Like stars in skie, or lampes on stage that seame,
The darknes there was day, the night was gone,

There sparkled (clothed in his azure beame)
The heau'nly Zaphire, there the Iacinth shone,
 The Carbuncle there flamde, the Dimond sheene,
 There glistred bright, there smilde the Emrauld greene.

40

Amas'd the knights amid these woonders past,
And fixt so deepe the marueiles in their thought,
That not one word they vttred, till at last
Vbaldo spake, and thus his guide besought,
'O father tell me, by what skill thou hast
These wonders donne? and to what place vs brought?
 For well I know not if I wake or sleepe,
 My hart is drownd in such amazement deepe.'

41

'You are within the hollow wombe (quoth he)
Of fertill earth, the nurse of all things made,
And but you brought and guided are by me,
Her sacred entrals could no wight inuade,
My pallace shortly shall you splendant see
With glorious light, though built in night and shade,
 A Pagan was I borne, but yet the Lord
 To grace (by baptisme) hath my soule restor'd.

42

'Nor yet by helpe of deuill, or aide from hell
I doe this vncouth worke and woondrous feat,
The Lord forbid, I vse or charme or spell
To raise foule *Dis* from his infernall seat,
But of all herbes, of euery spring and well,
The hidden powre I know and vertue great,
 And all that kinde hath hid from mortall sight,
 And all the starres, their motions and their might,

43

'For in these caues I dwell not buried still
From sight of heau'n, but often I resort
To tops of Libanon or Carmell hill,
And there in liquid aire my selfe disport,

There *Mars* and *Venus* I behold at will,
As bare, as earst when *Vulcan* tooke them short,
   And how the rest roule, glide and moue, I see,
   How their aspects benigne or froward bee.

44

'And vnderneath my feet the cloudes I view,
Now thicke, now thin, now bright with *Iris* bow,
The frost and snow, the raine, the haile, the dew,
The windes from whence they come, and whence they blow,
How *Ioue* his thunder makes, and lightning new,
How with the boult he strikes the earth below,
   How comate, crinite, caudate starres are fram'd
   I knew, my skill with pride my hart enflam'd.

45

'So learned, cunning, wise, my selfe I thought,
That I suppos'd my wit so high might clime
To know all things that God had fram'd or wrought,
Fire, aire, sea, earth, man, beast, sprite, place, and time:
But when your hermit me to baptisme brought,
And from my soule had washt the sinne and crime,
   Then I perceiu'd my sight was blindnes still,
   My wit, was follie; ignorance, my skill.

46

'Then saw I, that like owles in shining sonne,
So gainst the beames of truth, our soules are blinde,
And at my selfe to smile I then begonne,
And at my hart, puft vp with follies winde,
Yet still these artes as I before had donne
I practised, such was the hermits minde:
   Thus hath he chang'd my thoughts, my hart, my will,
   And rules mine art, my knowledge, and my skill.

47

'In him I rest, on him my thoughts depend,
My Lord, my teacher, and my guide is he,
This noble worke he striues to bring to end,
He is the Architect, the workmen we;

The hardie youth home to this campe to send
From prison strong, my care, my charge shall be,
   So he commands, and me ere this foretold
    Your comming oft, to seeke the champion bold.'

48

While this he said, he brought the champions twaine
Downe to a vault, wherein he dwels and lies,
It was a caue high, wide, large, ample, plaine,
With goodly roomes, halles, chambers, galleries,
All what is bred in rich and pretious vaine
Of wealthie earth, and hid from mortall eies,
   There shines, and faire adorn'd was euery part,
    With riches growne by kinde, not fram'd by art:

49

An hundreth groomes, quicke, diligent and neat,
Attendance gaue about these strangers bold,
Against the wall there stood a cupboord great
Of massie plate, of siluer, christall, gold.
But when with pretious wines and costly meat
They filled were, thus spake the wisard old,
   'Now fits the time (sir knights) I tell and show
    What you desire to heare, and long to know;

50

'*Armidaes* craft, her sleight and hidden guile
You partly wote, her actes and artes vntrew,
How to your campe she came, and by what wile
The greatest Lords and Princes thence she drew,
You know she turn'd them first to monsters vile,
And kept them since clos'd vp in secret mew,
   Lastly to Gaza ward in bonds them sent,
    Whom yoong *Rinaldo* rescude as they went.

51

'What chanced since I will at large declare,
(To you vnknowne) a storie strange and trew,
When first her pray (got with such paine and care.)
Escapte and gone, the witch perceiu'd and knew,

Her hands she wroong for griefe, her clothes she tare,
And full of woe these heauie words out threw:
    "Alas, my knights are slaine, my pris'ners free,
    Yet of that conquest neuer boast shall hee;

52

' "He in their place shall serue me, and sustaine
Their plagues, their torments suffer, sorrowes beare,
And they his absence shall lament in vaine,
And waile his losse and theirs, with many a teare:"
Thus talking to her selfe she did ordaine
A false and wicked guile, as you shall heare,
    Thither she hasted, where the valiant knight
    Had ouercome and slaine her men in fight.

53

'*Rinaldo* there had doft and left his owne,
And on his backe a Pagans harnesse tide,
Perchance he deemed so to passe vnknowne,
And in those armes lesse noted safe to ride,
A headlesse corse in fight late ouerthrowne,
The Witch in his forsaken armes did hide,
    And by a brooke expos'd it on the sand
    Whither she wisht would come a Christian band:

54

'Their comming might the dame foreknow right well,
For secret spies she sent foorth thousand waies,
Which euery day newes from the campe might tell,
Who parted thence, booties to search or praies:
Beside, the sprights coniur'd by sacred spell,
All what she askes or doubts, reueales and saies,
    The bodie therefore plast she in that part,
    That furthred best her sleight, her craft, and art;

55

'And neere the corpes a varlet false and slie
She left, attirde in shepheards homely weed,
And taught him how to counterfeit, and lie
As time requir'd, and he perform'd the deed,

With him your souldiers spoke, of iealousie
And false suspect mongst them he strow'd the seede,
 That since brought foorth the fruit of strife and iarre,
 Of ciuill brawles, contention, discord, warre.

56

'And as she wished so the soldiers thought,
By *Godfreyes* practise that the Prince was slaine,
Yet vanisht that suspicion false to nought,
When truth spred forth her siluer wings againe:
Her false deuises thus *Armida* wrought,
This was her first deceit, her formost traine,
 What next she practis'd (shall you heare me tell)
 Against our knight, and what thereof befell.

57

'*Armida* hunted him through wood and plaine,
Till on Orontes flowrie banks he staid,
There, where the streame did part and meet againe,
And in the midst a gentle Island maid,
A pillour faire was pight beside the maine,
Nere which a little frigot floting laid,
 The marble white the Prince did long behold,
 And this inscription read, there writ in gold:

58

' "Who so thou art whom will or chance doth bring
With happie steps to flood Orontes sides,
Know, that the world hath not so strange a thing,
(Twixt east and west) as this small Island hides,
Then passe and see, without more tarrying."
The hastie youth to passe the streame prouides,
 And for the cogge was narrow, small and strait,
 Alone he row'd, and bod his squires there wait;

59

'Landed he stalkes about, yet nought he sees
But verdant groues, sweet shades, and mossie rockes,
With caues and fountaines, flowers, herbes and trees,
So that the words he red he takes for mockes:

But that greene Isle was sweet at all degrees,
Wherewith entis'd downe sits he and vnlockes
  His closed helme, and bares his visage faire,
  To take sweet breath from coole and gentle aire.

60

'A rumbling sound amid the waters deepe
Meanewhile he heard, and thither turn'd his sight,
And tumbling in the troubled streame tooke keepe,
How the strong waues together rush and fight,
Whence first he saw (with golden tresses) peepe
The rising visage of a virgin bright,
  And then her necke, her brests, and all, as low
  As he for shame could see, or she could show.

61

'So in the twylight doth sometimes appeare
A Nymph, a Goddesse, or a Fairie queene,
And though no Siren but a sprite this weare;
Yet by her beautie seem'd it she had beene
One of those sisters false, which haunted neare
The Tirrhene shores, and kept those waters sheene,
  Like theirs her face, her voice was and her sound,
  And thus she sung, and pleas'd both skies and ground.

62

' "Ye happy youthes, whom Aprill fresh and May
Attire in flowring greene of lustie age,
For glorie vaine, or vertues idle ray,
Doe not your tender limmes to toile engage,
In calme streames, fishes; birds, in sunshine play,
Who followeth pleasure he is onely sage,
  So nature saith, yet gainst her sacred will
  Why still rebell you, and why striue you still?

63

' "O fooles who youth possesse, yet scorne the same,
A pretious, but a short abiding, treasure,
Vertue it selfe is but an idle name,
Priz'd by the world boue reason all and measure,

And honour, glorie, praise, renowme and fame,
That mens proud harts bewitch with tickling pleasure,
　　An Eccho is, a shade, a dreame, a flowre
　　With each winde blasted, spoil'd with euery showre.

64

' "But let your happie soules in ioy possesse
The Iuorie castels of your bodies faire,
Your passed harmes salue with forgetfulnesse,
Haste not your comming euils with thought and caire,
Regard no blazing star with burning tresse,
Nor storme, nor threatning skie, nor thundring aire,
　　This wisdome is, good life, and worldly blis,
　　Kinde teacheth vs, nature commands vs this."

65

'Thus sung the spirit false, and stealing sleepe
(To which her tunes entis'd his heauie eies)
By step and step did on his senses creepe,
Still euery limme therein vnmoued lies,
Not thunders lowd could from this slumber deepe
(Of quiet death true image) make him rise:
　　Then from her ambush forth *Armida* start,
　　Swearing reuenge, and threatning torments smart.

66

'But when shee looked on his face a while,
And saw how sweet he breath'd, how still he lay,
How his faire eies though closed seeme to smile,
At first she staid, astound with great dismay,
Then sat her downe, so loue can arte beguile,
And as she sate and lookt fled fast away
　　Her wrath, that on his forehead gazde the maid,
　　As in his spring *Narcissus* tooting laid;

67

'And with a vaile she wiped now and than
From his faire cheeke, the globes of siluer sweat,
And coole aire gathred with a trembling fan,
To mittigate the rage of melting heat,

Thus (who would thinke it) his hot eie-glance can
Of that cold frost dissolue the hardnesse great,
   Which late congeald the hart of that faire dame,
   Who late a foe, a louer now became.

68

'Of woodbines, lillies, and of roses sweete,
Which proudly flowred through that wanton plaine,
All pletted fast, well knit, and ioyned meete,
She fram'd a soft, but surely holding chaine,
Wherewith she bound his necke, his hands, and feete;
Thus bound, thus taken did the prince remaine,
   And in a coach which two old dragons drew,
   She laid the sleeping knight, and thence she flew:

69

'Nor turnd she to Damascus kingdomes large,
Nor to the fort built in Asphaltes lake,
But iealous of her deare and precious charge,
And of her loue asham'd, the way did take
To the wide Ocean, whither skiffe or barge
From vs doth selde or neuer voiage make,
   And there to frolike with her loue awhile,
   She chose a waste, a sole and desart ile.

70

'An Isle that with her fellowes beares the name
Of fortunate, for temperate aire and mould,
There in a mountaine high alight the dame,
A hill obscur'd with shades of forrests ould,
Vpon whose sides the witch by arte did frame
Continuall snow, sharpe frost and winter could,
   But on the top, fresh, pleasant, sweete and greene,
   Beside a lake a pallace built this queene.

71

'There in perpetuall, sweet and flowring spring
She liues at ease, and ioies her Lord at will;
The hardie youth from this strange prison bring
Your valours must, directed by my skill,

67⁵ eieglance < eie-glance (*cf. 1624*)

And ouercome each monster and each thing,
That guardes the pallace, or that keepes the hill,
 Nor shall you want a guide, or engins fit,
  To bring you to the mount, or conquer it.

72

'Beside the streame, Iparted shall you finde
A dame, in visage yoong, but old in yeeres,
Her curled lockes about her front are twinde,
A partie colour'd roabe of silke she weares:
This shall conduct you swift as aire or winde,
Or that flit birde that *Ioues* hot weapon beares,
 A faithfull Pilot, cunning, trustie, sure,
  As *Tiphis* was, or skilfull *Palinure*.

73

'At the hils foot, whereon the Witch doth dwell
The serpents hisse, and cast their poyson vilde,
The ouglie bores doe reare their bristles fell,
There gape the beares, and roare the lyons wilde;
But yet a rod I haue can easlie quell
Their rage and wrath, and make them meeke and milde.
 Yet on the top and height of all the hill,
  The greatest danger lies, and greatest ill:

74

'There welleth out a faire, cleere, bubbling spring,
Whose waters pure the thirstie guests entise,
But in those liquors cold the secret sting
Of strange and deadly poyson closed lies,
One suppe thereof the drinkers hart doth bring
To sudden ioy, whence laughter vaine doth rise,
 Nor that strange meriment once stops or staies
  Till, with his laughters end, he end his daies:

75

'Then from those deadly, wicked streames refraine
Your thirstie lippes, despise the daintie cheare
You finde expos'd vpon the grassie plaine,
Nor those false damsels once vouchsafe to heare,

That in melodious tunes their voices straine,
Whose faces louely, smiling, sweet, appeare;
    But you their lookes, their voice, their songs despise,
    And enter faire *Armidaes* Paradise.

76

'The house is builded like a maze within,
With turning staires, false doores and winding waies,
The shape whereof plotted in velam thin
I will you giue, that all those sleights bewraies,
In midst a garden lies, where many a gin
And net to catch fraile harts, false *Cupid* laies;
    There in the verdure of the herbours greene,
    With your braue champion lies the wanton queene.

77

'But when she haply riseth from the knight,
And hath withdrawne her presence from the place,
Then take a shield I haue of dimonds bright,
And hold the same before the yongmans face,
That he may glasse therein his garments light,
And wanton soft attire, and vew his case,
    That with the sight, shame and disdaine may moue
    His hart to leaue that base and seruile loue.

78

'Now resteth nought that needfull is to tell,
But that you goe secure, safe, sure and bold,
Vnseene the pallace may you enter well,
And passe the dangers all I haue foretold,
For neither art, nor charme, nor magicke spell
Can stop your passage or your steps withhold,
    Nor shall *Armida* (so you garded bee)
    Your comming ought foreknow, or once foresee:

79

'And eeke as safe from that enchanted fort
You shall returne, and scape vnhurt away;
But now the time doth vs to rest exhort,
And you must rise by peepe of springing day.'

This said, he led them through a narrow port,
Into a lodging faire wherein they lay,
   There glad and full of thoughts he left his ghests,
   And in his wonted bed the old man rests.

The fifteenth Booke of Godfrey *of Bulloigne*

I

THE rosie fingred morne with gladsome ray,
 Rose to her taske from old *Tithonus* lap,
When their graue host came where the warriours lay,
And with him brought the sheild, the rod, the map,
'Arise (quoth he) ere lately broken day,
In his bright armes the round world fold or wrap,
 All what I promist here, I haue them brought,
 Enough to bring *Armidas* charmes to nought.'

2

They started vp, and euerie tender lim
In sturdie steele and stubburne plate they dight,
Before the old man stalkt, they follow'd him
Through gloomie shades of sad and sable night,
Through vaults obscure againe and entries dim,
The way they came their steps remeasurde right,
 But at the flood arriu'd, 'farewell (quoth hee)
 Good lucke your aide, your guide good fortune bee.'

3

The flood receiu'd them in his bottome low,
And lift them vp, aboue his billowes thin;
The waters so cast vp a branch or bow,
By violence first plung'd and diu'd therein:

But when vpon the shore the waues them throw,
The knights for their faire guide to looke begin,
 And gasing round, a little barke they spide,
 Wherein a damsell sate the sterne to guide;

4

Vpon her front her lockes were curled new,
Her eies were curteous, full of peace and loue;
In looke a saint, an Angell bright in shew,
So in her visage grace and vertue stroue;
Her roabe seem'd sometimes red, and sometimes blew,
And changed still as shee did stirre or moue;
 That looke how oft mans eie beheild the same,
 So oft the colours changed, went and came.

5

The feathers so (that tender, soft and plaine,
About the doues smooth necke close couched beene)
Doe in one colour neuer long remaine,
But change their hew, gainst glimse of *Phœbus* sheene;
And now of rubies bright a vermile chaine,
Now make a Carknet rich of Emrauldes greene;
 Now mingle both, now alter, turne and change
 To thousand colours, rich, pure, faire and strange.

6

'Enter this boate, you happie men (she saies)
Wherein through raging waues secure I ride,
To which all tempest, storme, and winde obaies,
All burdens light, benigne is streame and tide:
My Lord (that rules your iourneies and your waies)
Hath sent me heere, your seruant and your guide,'
 This said, her Shallop droue she gainst the sand,
 And anchor cast amid the stedfast land.

7

They entred in, her anchors she vpwound,
And lanched foorth to sea her pinnesse flit,
Spred to the winde her sailes she broad vnbound,
And at the helme sate downe to gouerne it,

Swelled the floud that all his banks he drownd,
To beare the greatest ship of burthen fit;
   Yet was her Frigot, little, swift and light,
   That at his lowest ebbe beare it he might.

8

Swifter than thought the friendly winde foorth bore
The sliding boate, vpon the rowling waue,
With crudded fome, and froth the billowes hore
About the cable murmur, rore and raue;
At last they came where all his watrie store,
The floud in one deepe chanell did engraue,
   And foorth to greedie seas his streames he sent,
   And so his waues, his name, himselfe, he spent.

9

The wondrous boate scant toucht the troubled maine,
But all the sea still, husht, and quiet was,
Vanisht the clouds, ceased the winde and raine,
The tempests threatned ouerblow and pas,
A gentle breathing aire made eu'n and plaine
The azure face of heau'ns smooth looking glas,
   And heau'n it selfe, smild from the skies aboue,
   (With a calme cleernesse) on the earth his loue.

10

By Ascalon they sailed, and foorth driued,
Towards the west their speedie course they frame,
In sight of Gaza till the barke arriued,
A little port when first it tooke that name;
But since by others losse so well it thriued,
A citie great and rich that it became,
   And there the shores and borders of the land
   They found as full of armed men, as sand.

11

The passengers to landward turnd their sight,
And there sawe pitched many a stately tent,
Souldiour and footman, captaine, lord and knight,
Betweene the shore and cittie, came and went:

Huge elephants, strong camels, coursers light,
With horned hoofes the sandie waies out rent,
   And in the hauen many a ship and boate,
   (With mightie anchores fastned) swim and floate;

12

Some spred their sailes, some with strong owers sweepe
The waters smooth, and brush the buxome waue,
Their breasts in sunder cleaue the yeelding deepe,
The broken seas for anger fome and raue,
When thus their guide began, 'sir knights take keepe
How all these shores are spred with squadrons braue,
   And troupes of hardie knights, yet on these sands
   The monarch scant hath gathred halfe his bands.

13

'Of Egypt onely these the forces are,
And aid from other lands they here attend,
For twixt the nooneday sun and morning starre,
All realmes at his command do bowe and bend;
So that I trust we shall returne from farre,
And bring our iourney long to wished end,
   Before this (king or his lieutenant) shall
   These armies bring, to Sions conquerd wall.'

14

While thus she said, as soaring eagles flie
Mongst other birdes, securely through the aire,
And mounting vp behold with wakefull eie,
The radiant beames of old *Hiperions* haire,
Her gondelay so passed swiftly bie
Twixt ship and ship, withouten feare, or caire
   Who should her follow, trouble, stop or stay,
   And foorth to sea made luckie speed and way.

15

Themselues forenenst old *Raphias* towne they fand,
A towne that first to sailers doth appeere,
As they from Syria passe to Egypt land,
The sterill coastes of barren Rinoceere

11⁸ floate;) < floate;   14⁴ Hiperious < *Hiperions*

They past, and seas where Casius hill doth stand,
That with his trees orespreads the waters neere,
   Against whose rootes breaketh the brackish waue,
   Where *Ioue* his temple; *Pompeie* hath his graue.

16

Then Damiata next, where they behold
How to the sea his tribute Nilus paies,
By his seu'n mouthes renown'd in stories old,
And by an hundreth more ignoble waies
They past the towne built by the Grecian bold,
Of him call'd Alexandria till our daies,
   And *Pharos* towre and isle, remou'd of yore
   Far from the land, now ioyned to the shoer:

17

Both Creet and Rhodes they left by North vnseene,
And sail'd along the coastes of Africke lands,
Whose sea townes faire, but realmes more inward beene
All full of monsters and of desart sands,
With her fiue cities then they left Cireene,
Where that old temple of false *Hammon* stands:
   Next Ptolemais, and that sacred wood
   Whence spring the silent streames of Lethe flood.

18

The greater Sirtes (that sailers often cast
In perill great of death and losse extreame)
They compast round about, and safely past,
Then Cape Iudeca and flood Magras streame;
Then Tripolie, gainst which is Malta plast,
That low and hid, to lurke in seas doth seame:
   The little Sirtes then, and Alzerbes ile,
   Where dwelt the folke that Lotos eate erewhile.

19

Next Tunis on the crooked shore they spide,
Whose bay a rocke on either side defends,
Tunis all townes in beautie, wealth and pride,
Aboue, as far as Libias bounds extends;

Gainst which (from faire Scicilias fertile side)
His rugged front great Lilebenni bends,
  The Dame there pointed out where sometimes stoud,
  (Romes stately riuall whilome) Carthage proud,

20

Great Carthage lowe in ashes cold doth lie,
Her ruines poore the herbes in height scant passe,
So cities fall, so perish kingdomes hie,
Their pride and pompe lies hid in sand and grasse:
Then why should mortall man repine to die,
Whose life, is aire; breath, winde; and bodie, glasse?
  From thence the seas next Biserts walles they cleft,
  And far Sardignia on their right hand left.

21

Numidias mightie plaines they coasted then,
Where wandring shepherds vs'd their flockes to feed,
Then Bugia and Argiere, th'infamous den
Of Pirates false, Oran they left with speed,
All Tingitan they swiftly ouer-ren,
Where Elephants and angrie Lyons breed,
  Where now the Realmes of Fesse and Marocke bee,
  Gainst which Granadoes shores and coastes they see.

22

Now are they there, where first the sea brake in
By great *Alcides* helpe (as stories faine)
True may it be that where those floodes begin
It whilome was a firme and solid maine,
Before the sea there through did passage win,
And parted Africke from the land of Spaine,
  Abila hence, thence Calpe great vp springs,
  Such powre hath time to change the face of things.

23

Foure times the sunne had spred his morning ray,
Since first the Dame launcht foorth her wondrous barge,
And neuer yet tooke port in creeke or bay,
But fairely forward bore the knights her charge,

23² wandrous < wondrous

Now through the strait her iolly ship made way,
And boldly sail'd vpon the Ocean large;
  But if the sea in midst of earth was great,
  O what was this, wherein earth hath her seat?

24

Now deepe engulphed in the mightie flood
They saw not Gades, nor the mountaines neare,
Fled was the land, and townes on lande that stood,
Heau'n cou'red sea, sea seem'd the heau'ns to beare,
'At last, faire Ladie (quoth *Vbaldo* good)
That in this endlesse maine dost guide vs heare,
  If euer man before here sailed, tell,
  Or other landes here be wherein men dwell.'

25

'Great *Hercules* (quoth she) when he had quaild
The monsters fierce in Affricke and in Spaine,
And all along your coastes and countries saild,
Yet durst he not assay the Ocean maine,
Within his pillours would he haue impaild
The ouerdaring wit of mankinde vaine,
  Till Lord *Vlysses* did those bounders pas,
  To see and know he so desirous was.

26

'He past those pillours, and in open waue
Of the broad sea first his bould sailes vntwind,
But yet the greedie Ocean was his graue,
Nought helped him his skill gainst tide and wind,
With him all witnesse of his voyage braue
Lies buried there, no truth thereof we find,
  And they whom storme hath forced that way sence,
  Are drowned all, or vnreturn'd from thence:

27

'So that this mightie sea is yet vnsought,
Where thousand Isles and kingdomes lie vnknowne,
Not voide of men as some haue vainely thought,
But peopled well, and wonned like your owne,

The land is fertill ground, but scant well wrought,
Aire, wholesome; temp'rate sunne; grasse proudly growne.'
   'But (quoth *Vbaldo*) dame, I pray thee teach
   Of that hid world, what be the lawes and speach.'

28

'As diuers be their nations (answred shee)
Their toongs, their rites, their lawes so diffrent arre,
Some pray to beasts, some to a stone or tree,
Some to the earth, the sunne, or morning starre;
Their meates vnwholsome, vile and hatefull bee,
Some eate mans flesh, and captiues tane in warre,
   And all from Calpes mountaine west that dwell,
   In faith profane, in life are rude and fell.'

29

'But will our gracious God (the knight replide)
(That with his bloud all sinfull men hath bought)
His truth foreuer and his Gospell hide
From all those lands, as yet vnknowne, vnsought?'
'O no (quoth she) his name both farre and wide
Shall there be knowne, all learning thither brought,
   Nor shall these long and tedious waies for euer
   Your world and theirs, their lands, your kingdoms seuer.

30

'The time shall come that saylers shall disdaine
To talke or argue of *Alcides* streat,
And landes and seas that namelesse yet remaine,
Shall well be knowne, their bounders, scite and seat,
The ships encompasse shall the sollid maine,
As farre as seas outstretch their waters great,
   And measure all the world, and with the sunne
   About this earth, this globe, this compasse, runne.

31

'A knight of Genes shall haue the hardiment
Vpon this wondrous voyage first to wend,
Nor windes nor waues, that ships insunder rent,
Nor seas vnus'd, strange clime or poole vnkend,

Nor other perill, nor astonishment
That makes fraile harts of men to bow and bend,
  Within Abilas strait shall keepe and hold,
  The noble spirit of this saylor bold.

32

'Thy ship (*Columbus*) shall her canuasse wing
Spread ore that world, that yet concealed lies,
That scant swift fame her lookes shall after bring,
Though thousand plumes she haue, and thousand eies,
Let her of *Bacchus* and *Alcides* sing,
Of thee to future age let this suffies,
  That of thine actes she some forewarning giue,
  Which shall in verse and noble storie liue.'

33

Thus talking, swift twixt South and West they runne,
And sliced out twixt froth and fome their way;
At once they saw before, the setting sunne;
Behind, the rising beame of springing day;
And when the morne her drops and dewes begunne
To scatter broad vpon the flowring lay,
  Farre off a hill and mountaine high they spide,
  Whose top the cloudes enuiron, cloath and hide;

34

And drawing neere, the hill at ease they vew,
When all the cloudes were molten, falne and fled,
Whose top Pyramide wise did pointed shew,
High, narrow, sharpe, the sides yet more outspred,
Thence now and than fire, flame and smoake out flew,
As from that hill, where vnder lies in bed
  Enceladus, whence with imperious sway
  Bright fire breakes out by night, blacke smoake by day.

35

About the hill lay other Islands small,
Where other rockes, crags, clifts, and mountaines stood,
Th'isles fortunate these elder time did call,
To which high heau'n they fain'd so kinde and good,

And of his blessings ritch so liberall,
That without tillage earth giues corne for food,
    And grapes that swell with sweete and pretious wine,
    There without pruning yeelds the fertill vine.

36

The Oliue fat there euer buds and flowres,
The honie drops from hollow okes distill,
The falling brooke her siluer streames downe powres,
With gentle murmur from their natiue hill,
The westren blast tempreth with deawes and showres
The sunnie rayes, least heat the blossoms kill,
    The fields Elisian (as fond heathen taine)
    Were there, where soules of men in blisse remaine.

37

To these their pilot steard, and now (quoth shee)
Your voyage long to end is brought well neare,
The happie isles of fortune now you see,
Of which great fame, and little truth, you heare,
Sweet, wholsome, pleasant, fertile, fat they bee,
Yet not so rich as fame reports they weare.
    This said, towards an island fresh she bore,
    The first of ten, that lies next Africkes shore;

38

When *Charles* thus, 'if (worthie gouernesse)
To our good speed such tariance be no let,
Vpon this isle that heau'n so faire doth blesse,
(To view the place) on land a while vs set,
To know the folke, and what God they confesse,
And all whereby mans hart may knowledge get,
    That I may tell the wonders therein seene
    Another day, and say, there haue I beene.'

39

She answ'red him, 'well fits this high desire
Thy noble hart, yet cannot I consent,
For heau'ns decree, firme, stable and intire,
Thy wish repugnes, and gainst thy will is bent,

Nor yet the time hath *Titans* gliding fire
Met forth, prefixt for this discouerment,
   Nor is it lawfull of the Ocean maine
   That you the secrets know, or knowne explaine.

40

'To you withouten needle, map or card
Its giuen to passe these seas, and there arriue
Where in strong prison lies your knight imbard,
And of her pray you must the witch depriue:
If further to aspire you be prepar'd,
In vaine gainst fate and heau'ns decree you striue,'
   While thus she said, the first seene isle gaue place,
   And high and rough the second show'd his face.

41

They saw how Eastward stretcht in order long,
The happie islands sweetly flowring lay;
And how the seas betwixt those Isles inthrong,
And how they shouldred land from land away:
In seuen of them the people rude among
The shadie trees, their sheds had built of clay,
   The rest lay waste, vnlesse wilde beastes vnseene,
   Or wanton Nymphes, roam'd on the moutaines greene.

42

A secret place they found in one of those,
Where the cleft shore, sea in his bosome takes,
And twixt his stretched armes doth fold and close
An ample Bay, a rocke the hauen makes,
Which to the maine doth his broad backe oppose,
Whereon the roaring billow cleaues and brakes,
   And here and there two crags like turrets hie,
   Point forth a port, to all that saile thereby:

43

The quiet seas below lie safe and still,
The greenewood like a garland growes aloft,
Sweete caues within, coole shades and waters shrill,
Where lie the Nymphes on Mosse and Iuie soft;

No anchor there needes hold her frigot still,
Nor cabble twisted sure, though breaking oft:
　　Into this desart, silent, quiet glade,
　　Entred the dame, and there her hauen made.

44

'The pallace proudly built (quoth she) behold,
That sits on top of yonder mountaines hight,
Of Christes true faith there lies the champion bold
In idlenesse, loue, fancie, folly light;
When *Phœbus* shall his rising beames vnfold,
Prepare you gainst the hill to mount vpright,
　　Nor let this stay in your bold harts breed care,
　　For, saue that one, all howres vnluckie are;

45

'But yet this euening (if you make good speed)
To that hils foote with day-light might you passe.'
Thus said the Dame their guide, and they agreed,
And tooke their leaue, and leapt forth on the grasse,
They found the way that to the hill doth leed,
And softly went that neither tired was,
　　But at the mountaines foot they both arriued,
　　Before the sunne his teame in waters diued.

46

They saw how from the crags and cliftes below
His proud and stately pleasant top grew out,
And how his sides were clad with frost and snow,
The height was greene with herbes and flowrets sout,
Like hairie lockes the trees about him grow,
The rocks of ice keepe watch and warde about,
　　The tender roses and the lillies new,
　　Thus art can nature change, and kinde subdew.

47

Within a thicke, a darke and shadie plot,
At the hils foote that night the warriours dwell,
But when the sunne his rayes bright shining, hot,
Dispred, of golden light th' eternall well,

44⁴ folly, < folly　　45³ said, < said

'Vp, vp,' they cride, and fiercely vp they got,
And climed boldly gainst the mountaine fell;
   But forth there crept (from whence I cannot say)
   An ougly serpent, which forestall'd their way,

48

Armed with golden scales his head and crest
He lifted high, his necke sweld great with ire,
Flamed his eies, and hiding with his brest
All the broad path, he poyson breath'd and fire,
Now reacht he forth in foldes and forward prest,
Now would he backe in rowles and heapes retire,
   Thus he presents himselfe to garde the place,
   The knights preas'd forward with assured pace:

49

Charles drew forth his brand to strike the snake;
Vbaldo cride, 'stay my companion deare,
Will you with sword or weapon battaile make
Against this monster that affronts vs heare?'
This said, he gan his charmed rod to shake,
So that the serpent durst not hisse for feare,
   But fled, and dead for dread, fell on the gras,
   And so the passage plaine, eath, open was.

50

A little higher on the way they met
A lion fierce, that hugely roard and cride,
His crest he reared hie, and open set
Of his broad gaping iawes the fornace wide,
His sterne his backe ofts mote his rage to whet;
But when the sacred staffe he once espide,
   A trembling feare through his bold hart was spred,
   His natiue wrath was gone, and swift he fled.

51

The hardie couple on their way forth wend,
And met an host that on them rore and gape,
Of sauage beastes, tofore vnseene, vnkend,
Diffring in voice, in semblance and in shape;

All monsters which hot Affricke doth forth send,
Twixt Nilus, Atlas, and the southren cape,
　　Were all there met, and all wilde beastes besides,
　　Hircania breedes, or Hircane forrests hides.

52

But yet that fierce, that strange and sauage host,
Could not in presence of those worthies stand,
But fled away, their hart and courage lost,
When Lord *Vbaldo* shooke his charming wand,
No other let their passage stopt or crost,
Till on the mountaines top themselues they fand,
　　Saue that the ice, the frost, and drifted snow,
　　Oft made them feeble, wearie, faint and slow,

53

But hauing passed all that frosen ground,
And ouergone that winter sharpe and keene,
A warme, milde, pleasant, gentle skie they found,
That ouerspred a large and ample greene,
The windes breath'd Spikenard, Myrrhe and balme around,
The blastes there firme, vnchanged, stable beene,
　　Nor as elsewhere the windes now rise now fall,
　　And *Phebus* there aie shines, sets not at all.

54

Not as elsewhere now sunshine bright, now showres,
Now heat, now cold, there enterchanged weare,
But euerlasting spring milde heau'n downe powres,
In which nor raine, nor storme, nor cloudes appeare,
Nursing to fields, their grasse; to grasse, his flowres;
To flowres, their smell; to trees, the leaues they beare;
　　There by a lake a stately pallace stands,
　　That ouerlookes all mountaines, seas and lands:

55

The passage hard against the mountaine steepe,
These trauailers had faint and wearie maide,
That through those grassie plaines they scantly creepe,
They walkt, they rested oft; they went, they staide,

When from the rocks that seem'd for ioy to weepe,
Before their feete a dropping christall plaide,
  Entising them to drinke, and on the flowres
  The plentious spring a thousand streams downe powres.

56

All which vnited in the springing grasse,
Eate foorth a chanell through the tender greene,
And vnderneath eternall shade did passe,
With murmur shrill, colde, pure, and scantly seene;
Yet so transparent that perceiued was
The bottome rich, and sands that golden beene,
  And on the brimmes the silken grasse aloft
  Proffred them seates, swccte, easie, fresh and soft.

57

'See heare the streame of laughter, see the spring'
(Quoth they) 'of danger and of deadly paine,
Heere fond desire must by faire gouerning
Be rulde, our lust bridled with wisedomes raine,
Our eares be stopped while these Syrens sing,
Their notes entising man to pleasure vaine.'
  Thus past they forward where the streame did make
  An ample pond, a large and spatious lake;

58

There on a table was all daintie food
That sea, that earth, or liquid aire could giue,
And in the cristall of the laughing flood,
They sawe two naked virgins bathe and diue,
That sometimes toying, sometimes wrastling stood,
Sometimes for speed and skill in swimming striue,
  Now vnderneath they diude, now rose aboue,
  And tising baites laid foorth of lust and loue.

59

These naked wantons, tender, faire and white,
Mooued so farre the warriours stubborne harts,
That on their shapes they gazed with delite;
The Nymphes applide their sweete alluring artes,

And one of them aboue the waters quite,
Lift vp her head, her brests, and higher partes,
   And all that might weake eies subdew and take,
   Her lower beauties vaild the gentle lake.

60

As when the morning starre escapt and fled,
From greedie waues with dewie beames vp flies,
Or as the Queene of loue, new borne and bred
Of th' Oceans fruitfull froth, did first arise:
So vented she, her golden lockes foorth shed
Round pearles and cristall moist therein which lies:
   But when her eies vpon the knights she cast
   She start, and fain'd her of their sight agast.

61

And her faire lockes, that on a knot were tide
High on her crowne, she gan at large vnfold;
Which falling long and thicke, and spreading wide,
The iuorie soft and white, mantled in gold:
Thus her faire skin the dame would cloath and hide,
And that which hid it no lesse faire was hold;
   Thus clad in waues and lockes, her eies diuine
   From them ashamed did she turne and twine.

62

With all she smiled, and she blusht withall,
Her blush, her smiling; smiles, her blushing graced:
Ouer her face her amber tresses fall,
Where vnder loue himselfe in ambush placed:
At last she warbled forth a treble small,
And with sweet lookes, her sweet songs enterlaced;
   'O happie men! that haue the grace (quoth shee)
   This blisse, this heau'n, this paradise to see.

63

'This is the place wherein you may asswage
Your sorrowes past, here is that ioy and blis,
That florisht in the antique golden age,
Here needes no law, here none doth ought amis,

Put off those armes and feare not *Mars* his rage,
Your sword, your shield, your helmet needlesse is:
　　Then consecrate them here to endlesse rest,
　　You shall loues champions be, and soldiers blest.

64

'The fields for combat here are beds of downe,
Or heaped lillies vnder shadie brakes;
But come and see our queene with golden crowne,
That all her seruants blest and happie makes,
She will admit you gently for her owne,
Numbred with those that of her ioy partakes:
　　But first within this lake your dust and sweat
　　Wash off, and at that table sit and eat.'

65

While thus she sung, her sister lur'de them nie
With many a gesture kinde and louing show,
To musicks sound as dames in court applie
Their cunning feet, and dance now swift now slow;
But still the knights vnmoued passed bie,
These vaine delights for wicked charmes they know,
　　Nor could their heau'nly voice or angels looke
　　Surprise their harts, if eie or eare they tooke.

66

For if that sweetnes once but toucht their harts,
And profred there to kindle *Cupids* fire,
Straight armed reason to his charge vpstarts,
And quencheth lust, and killeth fond desire;
Thus scorned were the dames, their wiles and arts:
And to the pallace gates the knights retire,
　　While in their streames the damsels diued sad,
　　Asham'd, disgraste, for that repulse they had.

The sixteenth Booke *of* Godfrey *of* Bulloigne

The argument.

The searchers passe through all the pallace bright,
Where in sweet prison lies Rinaldo *pent,*
And doe so much, that full of rage and spight,
With them he goes sad, shamed, discontent.
With plaints and prayers to retaine her knight
Armida *striues; he heares, but thence he went,*
    And she forlorne her pallace great and faire
    Destroies for griefe, and flies thence through the aire.

1

THE pallace great is builded rich and round,
    And in the center of the inmost hold,
There lies a garden sweet, on fertile ground,
Fairer than that where grew the trees of gold:
The cunning sprites had buildings rear'd around,
With doores and entries false a thousand fold,
    A labyrinth they made that fortresse braue,
    Like *Dedals* prison or *Porsennaes* graue.

2

The knights past through the castles largest gate,
(Though round about an hundreth ports there shine)
The doore leaues fram'd of carued siluer plate,
Vpon their golden hinges turne and twine,
They staid to view this worke of wit and state,
The workmanship excell'd the substance fine,
    For all the shapes in that rich mettall wrought,
    Saue speech, of liuing bodies wanted nought.

3

Alcides there sate telling tales, and sponne
Among the feeble troupes of damsels milde,
He that the firie gates of hell had wonne,
And heau'n vpheld; false loue stood by and smild:

Armed with his club faire *Iolee* foorth ronne,
His club with bloud of monsters foule defilde,
    And on her backe his lions skin had shee,
    Too rough a barke for such a tender tree.

4

Beyond, was made a sea, whose azure flood
The hoarie froth crusht from the surges blew,
Wherein two nauies great well ranged stood
Of warlike ships, fire from their armes out flew,
The waters burnt about their vessels good,
Such flames the gold therein enchased threw,
    Cæsar his Romaines hence, the Asian kings
    Thence *Antonie*, and Indian princes brings.

5

The Ciclades seem'd to swim amid the maine,
And hill gainst hill, and mount gainst mountaine smote,
With such great furie met those armies twaine,
Here burnt a ship, there sunke a barke or bote,
Here darts and wildefire flew, there drown'd or slaine
Of princes dead, the bodies fleete and flote;
    Here *Cæsar* wins, and yonder conquerd beene
    The eastren ships, there fled th' Egyptian queene:

6

Antonius eeke himselfe to flight betooke,
The Empire lost to which he would aspire,
Yet fled not he, nor fight for feare forsooke,
But follow'd her, drawne on by fond desire:
Well might you see within his troubled looke,
Striue and contend, loue, courage, shame and ire;
    Oft lookt he backt, oft gaz'de he on the fight,
    But oftner on his mistresse and her flight:

7

Then in the secret creekes of fruitfull Nile,
Cast in her lappe, he would sadde death awate,
And in the pleasure of her louely smile,
Sweeten the bitter stroake of cursed fate,

All this did art with curious hand compile
In the rich mettall of that princely gate.
    The knights these stories viewed first and last,
    Which seene, they forward preas'd, and in they past:

8

As through his chanell crookt *Meander* glides
With turnes and twines, and rowles now to now fro,
Whose streames run foorth there to the salt sea sides,
Here backe returne, and to their springward go:
Such crooked pathes, such waies this pallace hides;
Yet all the maze their mappe described so,
    That through the labyrinth they got in fine,
    As *Theseus* did by *Ariadnaies* line.

9

When they had passed all those troubled waies,
The garden sweete spred foorth her greene to shew,
The moouing christall from the fountaines plaies,
Faire trees, high plants, strange herbes and flowrets new,
Sunshinie hils, dales hid from *Phœbus* raies,
Groues, arbours, mossie caues at once they vew,
    And that which beautie most, most woonder brought,
    No where appeard the arte which all this wrought.

10

So with the rude the polisht mingled was,
That naturall seemd all, and euery part,
Nature would craft in counterfaiting pas,
And imitate her imitator art:
Milde was the aire, the skies were cleere as glas,
The trees no whirlewind felt, nor tempest smart,
    But ere their fruit drop off, the blossome comes,
    This springs, that fals, that ripeneth, and this blomes.

11

The leues vpon the selfesame bow did hide,
Beside the yoong the old and ripened figge,
Here fruit was greene, there ripe with vermile side,
The apples new and old grew on one twigge,

The fruitfull vine her armes spred high and wide,
That bended vnderneath their clusters bigge,
   The grapes were tender here, hard, yoong and sowre,
   There purple, ripe, and nectar sweete foorth powre.

12

The ioyous birds, hid vnder greenewood shade,
Sung merrie notes on euery branch and bow,
The winde (that in the leaues and waters plaid)
With murmur sweete, now song, and whistled now,
Ceased the birds, the winde loud answere made:
And while they sung, it rumbled soft and low;
   Thus, were it happe or cunning, chance or art,
   The winde in this strange musicke bore his part.

13

With partie coloured plumes and purple bill,
A woondrous bird among the rest there flew,
That in plaine speech sung louelaies loud and shrill,
Her leden was like humaine language trew,
So much she talkt and with such wit and skill,
That strange it seemed how much good she knew,
   Her feathred fellowes all stood husht to heare,
   Dombe was the winde, the waters silent weare.

14

'The gentlie budding rose (quoth she) behold,
That first scant peeping foorth with virgin beames,
Halfe ope, halfe shut, her beauties doth vpfold
In their deare leaues, and lesse seene, fairer seames,
And after spreeds them foorth more broad and bold,
Then languisheth and dies in last extreames,
   Nor seemes the same, that decked bed and boure
   Of many a ladie late, and paramoure:

15

'So, in the passing of a day, doth pas
The bud and blossome of the life of man,
Nor ere doth flourish more, but like the gras
Cut downe, becommeth withred, pale and wan:

O gather then the rose while time thou has,
Short is the day, done when it scant began,
   Gather the rose of loue, while yet thou mast
   Louing, be lou'd; embrasing, be embrast.'

16

She ceast, and as approouing all she spoke,
The quire of birds their heau'nly tunes renew,
The turtles sigh'd, and sighes with kisses broke,
The foules to shades vnseene, by paires, withdrew;
It seemd the laurell chast, and stubborne oke,
And all the gentle trees on earth that grew,
   It seemd the land, the sea, and heau'n aboue,
   All breath'd out fancie sweete, and sigh'd out loue.

17

Through all this musicke rare, and stronge consent
Of strange allurements, sweete boue meane and measure,
Seuere, firme, constant, still the knights foorth went,
Hardning their harts gainst false entising pleasure,
Twixt leafe and leafe, their sight before they sent,
And after crept themselues at ease and leasure,
   Till they beheld the Queene, set with their knight
   Besides the lake, shaded with bowes from sight:

18

Her breasts were naked, for the day was hot,
Her lockes vnbound, wau'd in the wanton winde;
Somedeale she swet (tir'd with the game you wot)
Her sweat-drops bright, white, round, like pearles of Inde,
Her humide eies a firie smile foorth shot,
That like sunne-beames in siluer fountaines shinde,
   Ore him her lookes she hung, and her soft breast
   The pillow was, where he and loue tooke rest.

19

His hungrie eies vpon her face he fed,
And feeding them so, pinde himselfe away;
And she, declining often downe her hed,
His lippes, his cheekes, his eies kist, as he lay,

16[1] He ... he < She ... she

Wherewith he sigh'd, as if his soule had fled
From his fraile breast to hers, and there would stay
  With her beloued sprite, the armed pare
  These follies all beheld and this hot fare.

20

Downe by the louers side there pendant was
A Christall mirrour, bright, pure, smooth and neat,
He rose and to his mistresse held the glas,
(A noble Page, grac'd with that seruice great)
She, with glad lookes; he with enflam'd (alas)
Beautie and loue beheld, both in one seat;
  Yet them in sundrie obiects each espies,
  She, in the glasse; he, saw them in her eies:

21

Her, to commaund; to serue, it pleas'd the knight;
He proud of bondage; of her Empire, shee;
'My deare (she said) that blessest with thy sight
Euen blessed Angels, turne thine eies to me,
For painted in my hart and purtrai'd right
Thy woorth, thy beauties, and perfections bee,
  Of which the forme, the shape, and fashion best,
  Not in this glas is seene, but in my brest.

22

'And if thou me disdaine, yet be content
At least so to behold thy louely hew,
That while thereon thy lookes are fixt and bent,
Thy happie eies themselues may see and vew;
So rare a shape, no Christall can present,
No glas containe that heau'n of beauties trew;
  O let the skies thy woorthie mirrour bee!
  And in cleere starres thy shape and image see.'

23

And with that word she smil'd, and nerethelesse
Her loue-toies still she vs'd, and pleasures bold:
Her haire that donne she twisted vp in tresse,
And looser lockes in silken laces roll'd,

Her curles garland wise she did vpdresse,
Wherein (like ritch ennamell laid on gold.)
   The twisted flowrets smil'd, and her white brest
   The Lillies (there that spring) with Roses drest.

24

The iolly Peacocke spreeds not halfe so faire,
The eied feathers of his pompous traine;
Nor golden *Iris* so bendes in the aire
Her twentie colour'd bow, through cloudes of raine:
Yet all her ornaments, strange, rich and raire,
Her girdle did in price and beautie staine,
   Not that (with scorne) which *Tuscane Guilla* lost;
   Nor *Venus* Ceston, could match this for cost.

25

Of milde denaies, of tender scornes, of sweet
Repulses, warre, peace, hope, despaire, ioy, feare,
Of smiles, ieastes, mirth, woe, griefe, and sad regreet;
Sighes, sorrowes, teares, embracements, kisses deare,
That mixed first by weight and measure meet,
Then at an easie fire attempred weare;
   This wondrous girdle did *Armida* frame,
   And (when she would be loued) wore the same.

26

But when her wooing fit was brought to end,
Shee congee tooke, kist him, and went her way;
For once she vsed euery day to wend
Bout her affaires, her spels and charmes to say:
The youth remain'd, yet had no powre to bend
One step from thence, but vsed there to stray
   Mongst the sweete birds, through euerie walke & groue,
   Alone, saue for an hermit false call'd *Loue*.

27

And when the silence deepe and friendly shaide
Recall'd the louers to their wonted sport,
In a faire roome, for pleasure built, they laide,
And longest nights with ioies made sweet and short.

Now while the queene her houshold things suruaide,
And left her Lord, her garden, and disport,
  The twaine that hidden in the bushes weare,
  Before the Prince in glistring armes appeare:

28

As the fierce stead for age withdrawne from warre,
Wherein the glorious beast had alwaies wonne,
That in vile rest from fight sequestred farre,
Feedes with the mares at large, his seruice donne,
If armes he see, or heare the trumpets iarre,
He neieth lowd, and thither fast doth ronne,
  And wisheth on his backe the armed knight,
  Longing for iustes, for turnament and fight:

29

So farde *Rinaldo* when the glorious light
Of their bright harnesse glistred in his eies,
His noble sprite awaked at that sight,
His bloud began to warme, his hart to rise,
Though drunke with ease deuoid of wonted might,
On sleepe till then his weakned vertue lies,
  Vbaldo forward stept, and to him heild
  Of dimonds cleere, that pure and pretious sheild.

30

Vpon the targe his lookes amas'd he bent,
And therein all his wanton habite spide,
His ciuet, baulme, and perfumes redolent,
How from his lockes they smoakt, and mantle wide,
His sword that many a Pagan stout had shent,
Bewrapt with flowres, hung idlie by his side,
  So nicely decked, that it seemd the knight
  Wore it for fashion sake, but not for fight.

. 31

As when from sleepe and idle dreames abraid
A man awakt, cals home his wits againe;
So in beholding his attire he plaid,
But yet to view himselfe could not sustaine,

His lookes he downward cast, and nought he said,
Grieu'd, shamed, sad, he would haue died faine,
   And oft he wisht the earth or Ocean wide
   Would swallow him, and so his errours hide.

32

Vbaldo tooke the time, and thus begonne,
'All Europe now and Asia be in warre,
And all that Christ adore, and fame haue wonne,
In battaile strong, in Syria fighting arre;
But thee alone (*Bertoldoes* noble sonne)
This little corner keepes, exiled farre
   From all the world, buried in sloth and shame,
   A carpet champion for a wanton dame.

33

'What letharge hath in drowsinesse vp pend
Thy courage thus? what sloth doth thee infect?
Vp, vp, our campe and *Godfrey* for thee send,
Thee fortune, praise, and victorie expect,
Come fatall champion, bring to happie end
This enterprise begonne, and all that sect,
   (Which oft thou shaken hast) to earth full low
   With thy sharpe brand, strike downe, kill, ouerthrow.'

34

This said, the noble infant stood a space
Confused, speechlesse, senslesse, ill ashamed;
But when that shame to iust disdaine gaue place,
To fierce disdaine, from courage sprung vntamed,
Another rednesse blushed through his face,
Whence worthie anger shone, displeasure flamed,
   His nice attire in scorne he rent and tore,
   For of his bondage vile that witnes bore;

35 ◆

That donne, he hasted from the charmed fort,
And through the maze past with his searchers twaine.
Armida of her mount and chiefest port
Wondred to finde the furious keeper slaine,

33¹ vppend < vp pend

A while she feared, but she knew in short
That her deare Lord was fled, then saw she plaine
  (Ah wofull sight!) how from her gates the man
  In haste, in feare, in wrath, in anger ran.

36

'Whither O cruell, leau'st thou me alone?'
She would haue cride, her griefe her speeches staid,
So that her wofull words are backward gone,
And in her hart a bitter Eccho maide,
Poore soule, of greater skill than she was one
Whose knowledge from her thus her ioy conuaid,
  This wist she well, yet had desire to proue
  If art could keepe, if charmes recall her loue.

37

All what the witches of Thessalia land
With lips vnpure yet euer said or spake,
Words that could make heau'ns rolling circles stand,
And draw the damned ghostes from Limbo lake,
All well she knew, but yet no time she fand
To vse her knowledge, or her charmes to make,
  But left her artes, and forth she ran to proue,
  If single beautie were best charme for loue.

38

She ran, nor of her honour tooke regarde,
Oh where be all her vants and triumphes now?
Loues Empire great of late she made or marde,
To her his subiects humbly bend and bow,
And with her pride mixt was a scorne so harde,
That to be lou'd, she lou'd, yet whilst they wow
  Her louers all she hates, that pleas'd her will,
  To conquer men, and conqu'red so, to kill.

39

But now her selfe, disdain'd, abandoned,
Ran after him, that from her fled in scorne,
And her despised beautie laboured,
With humble plaints and praiers, to adorne;

She ran, and hasted after him that fled,
Through frost and snow, through brier, bush, and thorne,
　　And sent her cries on message her before,
　　That reacht not him, till he had reacht the shore:

40

'O thou that leau'st but halfe behinde (quoth shee)
Of my poore hart, and halfe with thee dost carrie,
O take this part, or render that to mee,
Else kill them both at once, ah tarrie, tarrie:
Heare my last words, no parting kisse of thee
I craue, for some more fit with thee to marrie
　　Keepe them (vnkinde) what fear'st thou if thou stay?
　　Thou mai'st denie, as well as runne away.'

41

At this *Rinaldo* stopt, stood still, and staid,
She came, sad, breathlesse, wearie, faint, and weake,
So woe begone was neuer Nymph or maid;
And yet her beauties pride griefe could not breake,
On him she lookt, shee gas'd, but nought she said,
She would not, could not, or she durst not speake,
　　At her he lookt not, glanst not, if he did,
　　Those glances shamefaste were, close, secret, hid.

42

As cunning singers, ere they straine on hie,
In loud melodious tunes, their gentle voice,
Prepare the hearers eares to harmonie,
With fainings sweet, low notes, and warbles choice:
So she, not hauing yet forgot pardie
Her woonted shifts and sleights in *Cupides* toies,
　　A sequence first of sighes and sobbes foorth cast,
　　To breed compassion deere, than spake at last.

43

'Suppose not (cruell) that I come to wow,
Or pray, as Ladies doe their loues and Lords;
Such were we late, if thou disdaine it now,
Or scorne to grant such grace as loue affords,

At least yet as an enmie listen thow:
Sworne foes sometime will talke, and chaffer words,
   For what I aske thee, maist thou grant right well,
   And lessen nought thy wrath and anger fell.

44

'If me thou hate, and in that hate delight,
I come not to appease thee, hate me still,
Its like for like; I bore great hate and spight
Gainst Christians all, chiefly I wisht thee ill:
I was a Pagan borne, and all my might
Against *Godfredo* bent, mine art and skill,
   I follow'd thee, tooke thee, and bore thee far
   To this strange isle, and kept thee safe from war:

45

'And more, which more thy hate may iustly moue,
More to thy losse, more to thy shame and griefe,
I thee enchanted and allur'd to loue,
Wicked deceit, craft worthie sharpe repriefe,
Mine honor gaue I thee all gifts aboue,
And of my beauties made thee Lord and chiefe,
   And to my sutors old what I denaid,
   That gaue I thee (my louer new) vnpraid.

46

'But reckon that among my faultes, and let
Those many wrongs prouoke thee so to wrath,
That hence thou ronne, and that at naught thou set
This pleasant house, so many ioyes which hath;
Goe, trauaile, passe the seas, fight, conquest get,
Destroy our faith, what shall I say our fath?
   Ah no! no longer ours, before thy shrine
   Alone I pray, thou cruell saint of mine,

47

'All only let me goe with thee (vnkinde)
A small request although I were thy foe,
The spoiler seldome leaues the praie behinde,
Who triumphes lets his captiues with him goe,

Among thy pris'ners poore *Armida* binde,
And let the campe encrease thy praises soe,
  That thy beguiler so thou couldst beguile,
  And point at me, thy thrall and bondslaue vile.

48

'Despised bondslaue, since my Lord doth hate
These lockes, why keepe I them or hold them deare?
Come cut them off, that to my seruile state
My habit answere may, and all my geare:
I follow thee in spite of death and fate
Through battles fierce where dangers most appeare,
  Courage I haue and strength enough (perchance)
  To lead thy courser spare, and beare thy lance:

49

'I will or beare, or be my selfe, thy shield,
And to defend thy life, will loose mine owne:
This breast, this bosome soft, shall be thy bield
Gainst stormes of arrowes, darts and weapons throwne;
Thy foes pardie encountring thee in field,
Will spare to strike thee (mine affection knowne)
  Least me they wound, nor will sharpe veng'ance take
  On thee, for this despised beauties sake.

50

'O wretch! dare I still vant, or helpe inuoake
From this poore beautie, scorned and disdained?'
She said no more, her teares her speeches broake,
Which from her eies like streames from springs down rained:
She would haue caught him by the hand or cloake,
But he stept backward, and himselfe restrained,
  Conquer'd his will, his hart ruth soft'ned not,
  There plaintes no ishue; loue, no entrance got.

51

Loue entred not to kindle in his brest
(Which reason late had quencht) his wonted flame;
Yet entred pitie in the place at lest:
Loues sister, but a chast and sober dame,

And stirr'd him so, that hardly he supprest
The springing teares that to his eies vp came;
But yet euen there his plaints repressed weare,
And (as he could) he lookte, and fained cheare.

52

'Madame (quoth he) for your distresse I grieue,
And would amend it, if I might or could,
From your wise hart that fond affection driue:
I cannot hate nor scorne you though I would,
I seeke no veng'ance, wrongs I all forgiue,
Nor you my seruant, nor my foe I hould,
Truth is, you err'de, and your estate forgot,
Too great your hate was, and your loue too hot.

53

'But those are common faultes, and faults of kind,
Excus'd by nature, by your sexe and yeares;
I erred likewise, if I pardon find,
None can condemne you, that our trespasse heares,
Your deare remembrance will I keepe in minde,
In ioies, in woes, in comforts, hopes and feares,
Call me your souldiour and your knight, as farre
As Christian faith permits, and Asias warre.

54

'Ah let our faults and follies here take end,
And let our errours past you satisfie,
And in this Angle of the world ipend,
Let both the fame and shame thereof, now die,
From all the earth where I am knowne and kend
I wish this fact should still concealed lie:
Nor yet in following me poore knight, disgrace
Your woorth; your beautie, and your princely race.

55

'Stay here in peace, I goe, nor wend you may
With me, my guide your fellowship denies,
Stay here or hence depart some better way,
And calme your thoughts, you are both sage and wise.'

53⁶ ioes < ioies *cf. 1624*, ioyes)

While thus he spoke, her passions found no stay,
But here and there she turn'd and roll'd her eies,
   And staring on his face a while, at last
   Thus in foule termes, her bitter wrath forth brast.

56

'Of Sophia faire thou neuer wert the childe,
Nor of the Azzaine race isprong thou art,
The mad sea waues thee bore, some Tigresse wilde
On Caucasus cold crags, nurst thee apart;
Ah cruell man! in whom no token milde
Appeeres, of pitie, ruth, or tender hart,
   Could not my griefes, my woes, my plaints and all
   One sigh straine from thy breast, one teare make fall?

57

'What shall I say, or how renew my speach?
He scornes me, leaues me, bids me call him mine:
The victor hath his foe within his reach;
Yet pardons her, that merits death and pine;
Heare how he counsels me, how he gan preach
(Like chast *Xenocrates*) gainst loue diuine;
   Oh heau'ns, oh gods! why doe these men of shame,
   Thus spoile your Temples, and blaspheme your name?

58

'Go cruell, go, go with such peace, such rest,
Such ioy, such comfort, as thou leau'st me heare:
My angrie soule discharg'd from this weake brest,
Shall haunt thee euer and attend thee neare,
And furie like in snakes and fire brands drest,
Shall aie torment thee, whom it late held deare:
   And if thou scape the seas, the rockes and sands,
   And come to fight amid the Pagan bands,

59

'There lying wounded, mongst the hurt and slaine,
Of these my wrongs thou shalt the vengeance beare,
And oft *Armida* shalt thou call in vaine,
At thy last gaspe; this hope I soone to heare:'

Heare fainted she, with sorrow griefe and paine,
Her latest words scant well expressed were,
   But in aswoune on earth outstretcht she lies,
   Stiffe were her frozen limmes, clos'd were her eies.

60

Thou clos'd thine eies (*Armida*) heau'n enuide
Ease to thy griefe, or comfort to thy woe;
Ah, open them againe, see teares downe slide
From his kinde eies, whom thou esteemes thy foe,
If thou hadst heard, his sighes had mollifide
Thine anger hard, he sigh'd and mourned soe;
   And as he could with sad and rufull looke
   His leaue of thee, and last farewell he tooke.

61

What should he do? leaue on the naked sand
This wofull ladie halfe aliue, halfe dead?
Kindnesse forbod, pittie did that withstand;
But hard constraint (alas) did thence him lead;
Away he went, the west winde blew from land
Mongst the rich tresses of their pilots head,
   And with that golden saile the waues she cleft,
   To land he lookt, till land vnseene he left.

62

Wakt from her traunce, forsaken, speechlesse sad,
Armida wildly star'd, and gas'd about,
'And is he gone (quoth she) nor pittie had
To leaue me thus twixt life and death in doubt?
Could he not stay? could not the traitor lad
From this last trance helpe or recall me out?
   And do I loue him still, and on this sand
   Still vnreuengde, still mourne, still weeping stand?

63

'Fie no, complaintes farewell, with armes and art
I will pursue to death this spitefull knight,
Not earthes low center, nor seas deepest part,
Nor heau'n, nor hell, can shield him from my might,

I will oretake him, take him, cleaue his hart,
Such veng'ance fits a wronged louers spight,
　　In crueltie that cruell knight surpasse
　　I will, but what auaile vaine words, alasse?

64

'O foole! thou shouldest haue beene cruell than,
(For than this cruell well deseru'd thine ire)
When thou in prison hadst entrapt the man,
Now dead with cold, too late thou askest fire;
But though my wit, my cunning nothing can,
Some other meanes shall worke my harts desire,
　　To thee (my beautie) thine be all these wrongs,
　　Veng'ance to thee, to thee reuenge belongs.

65

'Thou shalt be his reward, with murdring brand
That dare this traitor of his head depriue,
O you my louers, on this rocke doth stand
The castle of her loue, for whom you striue,
I, thee sole heire of all Damascus land,
For this reuenge my selfe and kingdome giue,
　　If by this price my will I cannot gaine,
　　Nature, giues beautie; fortune, wealth in vaine.

66

'But thee vaine gift (vaine beautie) thee I scorne,
I hate the kingdome, which I haue to giue,
I hate my selfe, and rue that I was borne,
Onely in hope of sweet reuenge I liue,'
Thus raging with fell ire she gan returne
From that bare shore in haste, and homeward driue,
　　And as true witnesse of her franticke ire,
　　Her lockes wau'd loose, face shone, eies sparkled fire.

67

When she came home, she call'd with outcries shrill,
A thousand deuils in Limbo deepe that wonne,
Blacke cloudes the skies with horrid darknes fill,
And pale for dread became th'eclipsed sonne,

The whirlewinde blustred big on euerie hill,
And hell to roare vnder her feet begonne,
  You might haue heard how through the pallace wide,
  Some spirits howld, some barkt, some hist, some cride.

68

A shadow, blacker than the mirkest night,
Enuiron'd all the place, with darknes sad,
Wherein a firebrand gaue a dreadfull light,
Kindled in hell by *Tisiphone* the mad;
Vanisht the shade, the sun appeard in sight,
Pale were his beames, the aire was nothing glad,
  And all the pallace vanisht was and gone,
  Nor of so great a worke was left one stone.

69

As oft the clouds frame shapes of castles great
Amid the aire, that little time do last,
But are dissolu'd by winde or *Titans* heat;
Or like vaine dreames soone made, and sooner past:
The pallace vanisht so, nor in his seat
Left ought, but rockes and crags, by kind there plast;
  She in her coach which two old serpents drew,
  Sat downe, and as she vs'd, away she flew.

70

She broake the clouds, and cleft the yeelding skie,
And bout her gathred tempest, storme, and winde,
The lands that view the south pole flew she bie,
And left those vnknowne countries farre behinde,
The straites of *Hercules* she past, which lie
Twixt Spaine and Africke, nor her flight enclinde
  To north or south, but still did forward ride
  Ore seas and streames, till Syrias coasts she spide:

71

Nor went she forward to Damascus faire,
But of her countrie deare she fled the sight,
And guided to Asphaltes lake her chaire,
Where stood her castle, there she ends her flight,

And from her damsels farre, she made repaire
To a deepe vault, far from resort and light,
 Where in sad thoughts a thousand doubtes she cast,
 Till griefe and shame, to wrath gaue place at last.

72

'I will not hence (quoth she) till Egypts lord
In aide of Sions king, his host shall moue;
Then will I vse all helps that charmes afford,
And change my shape, or sexe if so behoue:
Well can I handle bowe, or launce, or sword,
The worthies all will aide me, for my loue:
 I seeke reuenge, and to obtaine the same,
 Farewell regard of honour, farewell shame.

73

'Nor let mine vncle and protector me
Reproue for this, he most deserues the blame,
My hart and sex (that weake and tender be)
He bent to deedes, that maidens euill became;
His neece a wandring damsell first made he,
He spurr'd my youth, and I cast off my shame,
 His be the fault, if ought gainst mine estate
 did for loue, or shall commit for hate.'

74

This said, her knights, her ladies, pages, squires
She all assembleth, and for iourney fit,
In such faire armes and vestures them attires,
As shew'd her wealth, and well declar'd her wit;
And forward marched, full of strange desires,
Nor rested she by day or night one whit,
 Till she came there, where all the eastren bands,
 Their kings and princes, lay on Gazaes sands.

71⁸ -t last < at last

The seuenteenth Booke *of* Godfrey *of* Bulloigne

The argument.

Egypts great host in battaile ray forth brought,
The Caliph sends with Godfreyes *powre to fight;*
Armida who Rinaldoes *ruine sought,*
To them adioynes her selfe and Sirias might,
To satisfie her cruell will and thought,
She giues her selfe to him that kils her knight:
 He takes his fatall armes, and in his sheild
 His ancestors and their great deedes beheild.

1

GAZA the citie on the frontire stands
 Of Iudaes realme, as men to Egypt ride,
Built neare the sea, beside it of drie sands
Huge wildernesses lie, and desarts wide,
Which the strong windes lift from the parched lands,
And tosse like roring waues in roughest tide,
 That from those stormes poore passengers almost
 No refuge finde, but there are down'd and lost.

2

Within this towne (wonne from the Turkes of yore)
Strong garrison the king of Egypt plast,
And for it neerer was, and fitted more
That high emprise, to which his thoughts he cast,
He left great Memphis, and to Gaza bore
His regall throne, and there, from countries vast
 Of his huge Empire, all the puissant hoast
 Assembled he, and mustred on the coast.

3

Come say (my muse) what manner times these weare,
And in those times how stood the state of things,

What powre this monarch had, what armes they beare,
What nations subiect and what friends he brings;
For from all landes the Southren Ocean neare,
Or morning starre, came Princes, Dukes and Kings,
    And onely thou of halfe the world welnie
      The armies, Lords, and Captaines, canst descrie.

4

When Egypt from the Greekish Emperour
Rebelled first, and Christes true faith denide,
Of *Mahomets* descent, a warriour
There set his throne, and rulde that kingdome wide,
Caliph he hight, and *Caliphes* since that houre
Are his successors named all beside:
    So *Nilus* old his kings long time had seene
      That *Ptolemies* and *Pharoes* call'd had beene.

5

Establisht was that kingdome in short while,
And grew so great, that ouer Asias landes
And Libias Realmes, it stretched many a mile,
From Syrias coastes as far as Cirene sandes,
And Southward passed gainst the course of Nile,
Through the hot clime where burnt Siene standes,
    Hence bounded in with sandie desartes waft,
      And thence with *Euphrates* ritch flood embrast.

6

Maremma, Myrrhe and spices that doth bring,
And all the ritch red sea it comprehends,
And to those landes, toward the morning spring
That lie beyond that gulph, it farre extends:
Great is that Empire, greater by the king
That rules it now, whose worth the land amends,
    And makes more famous, Lord thereof by blood,
      By wisedome, valour, and all vertues good.

7

With Turkes and Persians war he oft did wage,
And oft he wonne, and sometime lost the feild,

Nor could his aduerse fortune ought asswage
His valours heat, or make his proud hart yeild,
But when he grew vnfit for war through age,
He sheath'd his sword, and laid aside his sheild:
    But yet his warlike minde he laid not downe,
    Nor his great thirst of rule, praise, and renowne,

8

But by his knights still cruell wars maintain'd.
So wise his words, so quicke his wit appeares,
That of the kingdome large ore which he rain'd,
The charge seem'd not too weightie for his yeares;
His greatnes Africks lesser kings constrain'd
To tremble at his name, all Inde him feares,
    And other realmes that would his friendship hold,
    Some armed soldiers sent, some gifts, some gold.

9

This mightie Prince assembled had the flowre
Of all his realmes, against the French men stout,
To breake their rising empire and their powre,
Nor of sure conquest had he feare or dout:
To him *Armida* came, eu'n at the howre
When in the plaines (old Gazaes walles without)
    The Lords and leaders all their armies bring
    In battaile ray, mustred before their king.

10

He on his throne was set, to which on hight
Who clombe, an hundred iuorie staires first told,
Vnder a pentise wrought of siluer bright,
And troade on carpets made of silke and gold;
His robes were such as best beseemen might
A king, so great, so graue, so rich, so old,
    And twin'd of sixtie elles of lawne and more,
    A Turbant strange, adorn'd his tresses hore.

11

His right hand did his pretious scepter weild,
His beard was gray, his lookes seuere and graue,

And from his eies (not yet made dim with eild)
Sparkled his former worth and vigor braue,
His gestures all the maiestie vpheild
And state, as his old age and empire craue,
  So *Phidias* caru'd, *Apelles* so (pardie)
  Earst painted *Ioue*, *Ioue* thundring downe from skie.

12

On either side him stood a noble lord,
Whereof the first held in his vpright hand,
Of seuere iustice the vnpartiall sword;
The other bore the seale and causes scand,
Keeping his folke in peace and good accord,
And termed was Lord Chancelour of the land;
  But Marshall was the first, and vs'd to leed
  His armies foorth to warre, oft with good speed.

13

Of bould Circassians with their halberds long,
(About his throne) his guard stood in a ring,
All richly armd in guilden corslets strong,
And by their sides their crooked swords downe hing:
Thus set, thus seated, his graue lords among,
His hoasts and armies great beheld the king,
  And euery band as by his throne it went,
  Their ensignes low enclind, and armes downe bent:

14

Their squadrons first the men of Egypt show,
In fowre troopes, and each his feu'rall guide,
Of the hie countrie two, two of the low,
Which Nile had wonne out of the salt sea side,
His fertile slime first stopt the waters flow,
Then hardned to firme land the plough to bide,
  So Egypt still encreast, within farre plast
  That part is now, where ships earst anchor cast.

15

The formost band the people were that dwell'd
In Alexandrias rich and fertile plaine,

Along the westren shore, whence Nile expell'd
The greedie billowes of the swelling maine;
Araspes was their guide, who more excell'd
In wit and craft, than strength or warlike paine,
  To place an ambush close, or to deuise
  A treason false, was none so slie, so wise.

16

The people next that gainst the morning raies
Along the coasts of Asia haue their seat,
Arontes led them, whom no warlike praise
Ennobled, but high birth and titles great,
His helme nere made him sweat in toilsome fraies,
Nor was his sleepe ere broake with trumpets threat,
  But from soft ease to trie the toile of fight,
  His fond ambition brought this carpet knight.

17

The third seem'd not a troupe or squadron small,
But an huge hoast; nor seem'd it so much graine
In Egypt grew, as to sustaine them all;
Yet from one towne thereof came all that traine,
A towne in people to huge shires equall,
That did a thousand streetes and more containe,
  Great Caire it hight, whose Commons from each side
  Came swarming out to war, *Campson* their guide.

18

Next vnder *Gazell* martched they that plow
The fertill landes aboue that towne which lie,
Vp to the place where *Nilus* tumbling low,
Falles from his second Catarrackt from hie:
Th'Egyptians weap'ned were with sword and bow,
No weight of helme or hawberke list they trie,
  And ritchly arm'd in their strong foes no dreed
  Of death, but great desire of spoile, they breed.

19

The naked folke of Barca these succeed,
Vnarmed halfe, *Alarcon* led that band,

That long in desarts liu'd (in extreme need)
On spoiles and praies, purchast by strength of hand,
To battell strong vnfit, their king did leed
His armie next brought from Zumara land;
    Then he of Tripolie, for sudden fight
    And skirmish short, both readie, bold and light.

20

Two Captaines next brought foorth their bandes to show,
Whom stonie sent and happie Arabie,
Which neuer felt the cold of frost and snow,
Or force of burning heat, vnlesse fame lie,
Where incense pure and all sweete odours grow,
Where the sole Phœnix, doth reuiue, not die,
    And midst the perfumes ritch and flowrets braue,
    Both birth, and buriall, cradle hath, and graue.

21

Their cloathes not ritch, their garments were not gay,
But weapons like th'Egyptian troupes they had;
Th'Arabians next that haue no certaine stay,
No house, no home, no mansion good or bad,
But euer (as the Scythian Hordas stray)
From place to place their wandring cities gad:
    These haue both voice and stature feminine,
    Haire, long and blacke; blacke face, and firie eine.

22

Long Indian Canes (with iron arm'd) they beare,
And as vpon their nimble steedes they ride,
Like a swift storme their speedie troupes appeare,
If windes so fast bring stormes from heauens wide:
By *Siphax* led the first Arabians weare;
Aldine the second squadron had to guide,
    And *Abiazer* proud, brought to the fight
    The third, a theefe, a murdrer, not a knight.

23

The Islanders came than their Prince before,
Whose landes Arabias gulph enclos'd about,

Wherein they fish and gather oisters store,
Whose shels great pearles ritch and round powre out;
The red sea sent with them from his left shore,
Of Negroes grim a blacke and ougly rout;
   These *Agricalt* and those *Osmida* brought,
    A man that set law, faith and truth at nought.

24

The Ethiops next which Meroe doth breed,
That sweet and gentle isle of Meroee,
Twixt Nile and Astrabore that far doth spreed,
Where two religions are, and kingdomes three,
These *Assamiro* and *Canario* leed,
Both kings, both Pagans, and both subiects bee
   To the great *Caliph*, but the third king kept
    Christes sacred faith, nor to these warres out stept.

25

After two kings (both subiects also) ride,
And of two bandes of archers had the charge,
The first Soldan of Orms plast in the wide
Huge Persian bay, a towne ritch, faire and large:
The last of Boecan, which at euerie tide
The sea cuts off from Persias Southren marge,
   And makes an isle; but when it ebs againe,
    The passage there is sandie, drie and plaine.

26

Nor thee (great *Altamore*) in her chastbed
Thy louing Queene kept with her deare embrace,
Shee tore her lockes, she smote her breast, and shed
Salt teares to make thee stay in that sweet place,
Seeme the rough seas more calme, cruell, she sed,
Than the milde lookes of thy kind spouses face?
   Or is thy shield, with blood and dust defilde,
    A dearer armefull than thy tender childe?

27

This was the mightie king of Sarmachand,
A captaine wise, well skill'd in feates of warre,

In courage fierce, matchlesse for strength of hand,
Great was his praise, his force was noised farre;
His worth rightwell the Frenchmen vnderstand,
By whom his vertues fear'd and loued arre:
   His men were arm'd with helmes and hawberks strong,
   And by their sides broad swords and mases hong.

28

Then from the mansions bright of fresh Aurore,
Adrastus came, the glorious king of Inde,
A snakes greene skinne spotted with blacke he wore,
That was made ritch by art and hard by kinde,
An Elephant this furious Giant bore,
He fierce as fire, his mounture swift as winde:
   Mutch people brought he from his kingdomes wide,
   Twixt Indus, Ganges, and the salt sea side.

29

The kings owne troupe came next, a chosen crew,
Of all the campe the strength, the crowne, the flowre,
Wherein each souldiours had with honours dew
Rewarded beene, for seruice, ere that howre;
Their armes were strong for need, and faire for shew,
Vpon fierce steeds well mounted roade this powre,
   And heau'n itselfe with the cleare splendure shone
   Of their bright armour, purple, gold and stone.

30

Mongst these *Alarco* fierce, and *Odemare*
The muster maister was, and *Hidraort*,
And *Rimedon*, whose rashnesse tooke no care
To shunne deathes bitter stroake, in field or fort,
Tigranes, *Rapold* sterne, the men that fare
By sea, that robbed in each creeke and port;
   Ormond, and *Marlabust* th'Arabian nam'd,
   Because that land rebellious he reclam'd.

31

There *Pirga*, *Arimon*, *Orindo* arre,
Brimarte the scaler, and with him *Swifant*

The breaker of wilde horses brought from farre;
Then the great wrastler strong *Aridamante*,
And *Tisipherne*, the thunderbolt of warre,
Whom none surpast, whom none to match durst vante
 At tilt, at turnay, or in combate braue,
  With speare or lance, with sword, with mase or glaue.

32

A false *Armenian* did this squadron guide,
That in his youth from Christes true faith and light,
To the blinde lore of Paganisme did slide,
That *Clement* late, now *Emireno*, hight;
Yet to his king he faithfull was, and tride
True in all causes, his in wrong and right:
 A cunning leader and a souldiour bold,
  For strength and courage, yoong; for wisedome, old.

33

When all these regiments were past and gone,
Appear'd *Armide*, and came her troupe to show,
Set in a chariot bright with pretious stone,
Her gowne tuckt vp, and in her hand a bow;
In her sweete face her new displeasures shone,
Mixt with the natiue beauties there which grow,
 And quickned so her lookes, that in sharpe wise
  It seemes she threats, and yet her threats entise.

34

Her chariot like *Auroraes* glorious waine,
With Carbuncles and Iacinthes glistred round:
Her coachman guided with the golden raine
Foure Vnicornes, by couples yoakte and bound;
Of Squires and louely Ladies hundreths twaine,
(Whose ratling quiuers at their backes resound)
 On milke white steedes, waite on the chariot bright,
  Their steeds to menage, readie; swift, to flight:

35

Follow'd her troupe led foorth by *Aradin*,
Which *Hidraort* from Syrias kingdome sent,
As when the new borne Phœnix doth begin
To flie to Ethiope ward, at the faire bent
Of her ritch wings strange plumes and feathers thin,
Her crownes and chaines, with natiue gold besprent,
    The world amazed stands, and with her flie
    An hoste of wondring birdes, that sing and crie:

36

So past *Armida*, lookt on, gaz'd on, soe,
A woondrous dame in habite, gesture, face;
There liu'd no wight to loue so great a foe,
But wisht and long'd those beauties to imbrace,
Scant seene, with anger sullen, sad for woe,
She conquer'd all the Lords and knights in place,
    What would shee doe (her sorowes past) thinke you,
    When her faire eies, her lookes and smiles shall wowe?

37

She past, the king commaunded *Emiren*
Of his ritch throne to mount the loftie stage,
To whom his hoste, his armie and his men,
He would commit, now in his grauer age.
With stately grace the man approched then;
His lookes, his comming honour did presage:
    The guard asunder cleft, and passage maide,
    He to the throne vp went, and there he staide;

38

To earth he cast his eies and bent his knee:
To whom the king thus gan his will explaine,
'To thee this scepter (*Emiren*) to thee
These armies I commit, my place sustaine
Mongst them goe set the king of Iuda free,
And let the Frenchmen feele my iust disdaine,
    Goe, meete them, conquer them, leaue none on liue,
    Or those that scape from battell, bring captiue.'

35⁷ stands; < stands,

39

Thus spake the tyrant, and the scepter laid
With all his soueraigne powre vpon the knight:
'I take this scepter at your hand (he said)
And with your happie fortune goe to fight,
And trust (my Lord) in your great vertues aid,
To venge all Asias harmes, her wrongs to right,
   Nor ere but victor will I see your face,
    Our ouerthrow shall bring death, not disgrace:

40

'Heau'ns grant if euill (yet no mishap I dread)
Or harme, they threaten gainst this campe of thine,
That all that mischiefe fall vpon my head,
Theirs be the conquest, and the danger mine;
And let them safe, bring home their captaine dead,
Buried in pompe of triumphes glorious shine.'
   He ceas'd, and then a murmur lowd vp went,
    With noise of ioy and sound of instrument;

41

Amid the noise and shout, vprose the king,
Enuironed with many a noble peere,
That to his royall tent the monarch bring,
And there he feasted them and made them cheere,
To him and him he talkt, and caru'd each thing,
The greatest honour'd, meanest graced weere.
   And while this mirth, this ioy and feast doth last,
    Armida found fit time her nets to cast:

42

But when the feast was done, she (that espide
All eies on her faire visage fixt and bent,
And by true notes and certaine signes descride,
How loues impoisned fire their entrals brent)
Arose, and where the king sate in his pride,
With stately pace and humble gestures, went;
   And as she could in lookes in voice she stroue
    Fierce, sterne, bould, angrie, and seuere to proue.

43

'Great Emperour, behold me heere (she said)
For thee, my countrey, and my faith to fight,
A dame, a virgin, but a royall maid,
And worthie seemes this warre a princesse hight,
For by the sword, the scepter is vpstaid,
This hand can use them both, with skill and might,
    This hand of mine can strike, and at each blow
    Thy foes and ours kill, wound, and ouerthrow.

44

'Nor yet suppose this is the formost day
Wherein to warre I bent my noble thought,
But for the suretie of thy realmes, and stay
Of our religion true, ere this I wrought:
Your selfe best known if this be true I say,
Or if my former deeds reiois'd you ought,
    When *Godfreyes* hardie knights and princes strong
    I captiue tooke, and held in bondage long:

45

'I tooke them, bound them, and so sent them bound
To thee, a noble gift, with whom they had
Condemned low in dungeon vnder ground
For euer dwelt, in woe and torment sad:
So might thine hoast an easie way haue found
To end this doubtfull warre, with conquest glad,
    Had not *Rinaldo* fierce my knights all slaine,
    And set those lords his friends, at large againe.

46

'*Rinaldo* is well knowne,' (and there a longe
And true rehearsall made she of his deeds)
'This is the knight that since hath done me wrong,
Wrong yet vntold, that sharpe reuengement needs:
Displeasure therefore, mixt with reason strong,
This thirst of warre in me, this courage breedes;
    Nor how hee iniur'd me time serues to tell,
    Let this suffice, I seeke reuengement fell,

47

'And will procure it, for all shaftes that flie
Light not in vaine, some worke the shooters will,
And *Ioues* right hand with thunders cast from skie,
Takes open vengeance oft for secret ill:
But if some champion dare this knight defie
To mortall battaile, and by fight him kill,
   And with his hatefull head will me present,
   That gift my soule shall please, my hart content:

48

'So please, that for reward enioy he shall,
(The greatest gift, I can or may afford)
My selfe, my beautie, wealth and kingdomes all,
To marrie him, and take him for my lord,
This promise will I keepe what ere befall,
And thereto binde my selfe by oath and word:
   Now he that deemes this purchase woorth his paine,
   Let him step foorth and speake, I none disdaine.'

49

While thus the Princesse said, his hungrie eine
Adrastus fed on her sweete beauties light,
'The gods forbid (quoth he) one shaft of thine
Should be dischargd gainst that discourteous knight,
His hart vnwoorthie is (shootresse diuine)
Of thine artillerie to feele the might;
   To wreake thine ire behold me prest and fit,
   I will his head cut off, and bring thee it:

50

'I will his hart with this sharpe sword diuide,
And to the vultures cast his carkasse out.'
Thus threatned he, but *Tisipherne* enuide
To heare his glorious vaunt and boasting stout,
And said, 'but who art thou, that so great pride
Thou shew'st before the king, me, and this rout?
   Pardie heere are some such, whose woorth exceeds
   Thy vaunting much, yet boast not of their deeds.'

51

The Indian fierce replide, 'I am the man
Whose acts his words and boasts haue aie surpast;
But if elsewhere the words thou now began
Had vttred beene, that speech had beene thy last.,
Thus quarrell'd they, the monarch staid them than,
And twixt the angrie knights his scepter cast;
    Then to *Armida* said, 'faire Queene, I see
    Thy hart is stout, thy thoughts couragious bee:

52

'Thou worthy art that their disdaine and ire
At thy commaunds these knights should both appease,
That gainst thy foe their courage hot as fire
Thou maist imploy, both when and where thou please,
There all their powre and force, and what desire
They haue to serue thee, may they shew at ease.,
    The monarch held his peace when this was said,
    And they new proffer of their seruice maid:

53

Nor they alone, but all that famous weare
In feates of armes, boast that he shall be dead,
All offer her their aid, all say and sweare
To take reuenge, on his condemned head:
So many armes mou'd she against her deare,
And swore her darling vnder foote to tread.
    But he, since first th'inchanted isle he left,
    Safe in his barge the roaring waues still cleft.

54

By the same way return'd the well taught bote
By which it came, and made like haste, like speed;
The friendly winde (vpon her saile that smote)
So turn'd, as to returne her ship had need:
The youth sometime the pole or beare did note,
Or wandring starres, which cleerest nights forth spreed:
    Sometimes the floods, the hils, or mountaines steepe,
    Whose woodie frontes oreshade the silent deepe:

51⁵ they < the

55

Now of the campe the man the state enquires;
Now askes the customes strange of sundrie landes,
And sail'd, till clad in beames and bright attires
The fourth daies sunne on th'Eastren threshold standes:
But when the Western seas had quencht those fires,
Their frigot stroake against the shore and sandes;
　　Then spoke their guide, 'the lande of Palestine
　　This is, here must your iourney end and mine;'

56

The Knights she set vpon the shore all three,
And vanish thence in twinkling of an eie.
Vprose the night in whose deepe blacknes bee
All colours hid of things, in earth or skie,
Nor could they house, or hold, or harbour see,
Or in that desart signe of dwelling spie,
　　Nor trackt of man or horse, or ought that might
　　Enforme them of some path or passage right.

57

When they had mus'd what way they trauaile should,
From the waste shore their steps at last they twinde,
And loe far off at last their eies behould
Something (they wist not what) that cleerely shinde,
With raies of siluer and with beames of gould,
Which the darke foulds of nights blacke mantle linde,
　　Forward they went and marched gainst the light,
　　To see and finde the thing, that shone so bright:

58

High on a tree they saw an armour new,
That glistred bright gainst *Cinthias* silver ray,
Therein (like stars in skies) the dimonds shew,
Fret in the gilden helme and harberke gay;
The mightie shield all scored full they vew
Of pictures faire, ranged in meet array;
　　To keepe them sate an aged man beside,
　　Who to salute them rose, when them he spide.

59

The twaine, who first were sent in this pursute,
Of their wise friend well knew the aged face:
But when the wisard sage their first salute
Receiu'd, and quited had, with kinde embrace,
To the yong Prince (that silent stood and mute,)
He turn'd his speech: in this vnused place
   'For you alone I waite (my Lord)' quoth he,
   'My chiefest care your state and welfare be;

60

'For (though you wote it not) I am your frend,
And for your profit worke, as these can tell,
I taught them how *Armidaes* charmes to end,
And bring you hither from loues hatefull cell,
Now to my words (though sharpe perchance) attend,
Nor be aggreu'd although they seeme too fell,
   But keepe them well in minde, till in the truth
   A wise and holier man instruct thy yuth.

61

'Not vnderneath sweete shades and fountaines shrill,
Among the nymphes, the fairies, leaues and flours;
But on the steepe, the rough and craggie hill
Of vertue, standes this blis, this good of ours:
By toile and trauaile, not by sitting still
In pleasures lap, we come to honors bours;
   Why will you thus in sloathes deepe valley lie?
   The royall Eagles on high mountaines flie.

62

'Nature liftes vp thy forehead to the skies,
And fils thy hart with high and noble thought,
That thou to heau'nward aie should'st lift thine eies,
And purchase fame by deedes well donne and wrought,
She giues thee ire, by which hot courage flies
To conquest, not through braules and battailes (fought
   For ciuill iarres) nor that thereby you might
   Your wicked malice wreake and cursed spight:

63

'But that your strength spurr'd forth with noble wraith,
With greater furie might Christes foes assault,
And that you bridle should with lesser scaith
Each secret vice, and kill each inward fault;
For so his godly anger ruled haith
Each righteous man, beneath heau'ns starrie vault,
    And at his will makes it now hot, now cold,
    Now lets it ronne, now doth it fettred hold.'

64

Thus parled he; *Rinaldo* husht and still
Great wisdome heard in those few words compilde,
He markt his speech, a purple blush did fill
His guiltie cheekes, downe went his eie-sight milde.
The hermit by his bashfull lookes his will
Well vnderstood, and said, 'looke vp my childe,
    And painted in this pretious shield behold
    The glorious deeds of thy forefathers old:

65

'Thine elders glorie herein see and know,
In vertues path how they troade all their daies,
Whom thou art farre behind, a runner slow
In this true course of honour, fame and praies:
Vp, vp, thy selfe incite by the faire show
Of Knightly worth, which this bright shield bewraies,
    That be thy spurre, to praise:' at last the knight
    Lookt vp, and on those purtraites bent his sight.

66

The cunning workeman had in little space
Infinite shapes of men there well exprest,
For there described was the worthie race,
And pedegree of all the house of *Est*:
Come from a Romaine spring ore all the place
Flowed pure streames of Christall East and West,
    With Laurell crowned stood the Princes old,
    Their warres the Hermit and their battailes told.

65⁶ Knigtly < Knightly

67

He show'd him *Caius* first, when first in pray
To people strange the falling empire went,
First Prince of Est, that did the scepter sway
Ore such as chose him Lord by free consent,
His weaker neighbours to his rule obey,
Need made them stoupe, constraint doth force content;
    After, (when Lord *Honorius* call'd the traine,
    Of sauage Gothes into his land againe,)

68

And when all Italie did burne and flame
With bloodie war, by this fierce people maid,
When Rome a captiue and slaue became,
And to be quite destroi'd was most affraid,
Aurelius (to his euerlasting fame)
Preferu'd in peace the folke that him obai'd:
    Next whom was *Forrest*, who the rage withstood
    Of the bold Hunnes, and of their tyrant prood.

69

Knowne by his looke was *Attila* the fell,
Whose dragon eies shone bright with angers sparke,
Worse faced than a dog, who vew'd him well,
Suppos'd they saw him grin, and heard him barke;
But when in single fight he lost the bell,
How through his troupes he fled there might you marke,
    And how Lord *Forrest* after fortified
    Aquilias towne, and how for it he died;

70

For there was wrought the fatall end and fine,
Both of himselfe and of the towne he kept:
But his great sonne renowned *Acarine*,
Into his fathers place and honour stept:
To cruell fate, not to the Hunnes, *Altine*
Gaue place, and when time seru'd againe forth lept,
    And in the vale of Poe built for his seat
    Of many a village small, a citie great,

71

Against the swelling flood he bankt it strong,
And thence vprose the faire and noble towne,
Where they of Est should by succession long
Command, and rule in blisse and high renowne:
Gainst *Odoacer* then he fought, but wrong
Oft spoileth right, fortune treads courage downe,
    For there he dide for his deere countries fake,
    And of his fathers praise did so partake:

72

With him dide *Alphorisio*, *Azzo* was
With his deere brother into exile sent,
But homewards they in armes againe repas,
(The Herule king opprest) from banishment
His front through pierced with a dart (alas:)
Next them of *Est* th'Epaminondas went,
    That smiling seemd to cruell death to yeild,
    When *Totila* was fled, and safe his sheild.

73

Of *Boniface* I speake, *Valerian*
His sonne in praise and powre succeeded him,
Who durst sustaine (in yeeres though scant a man)
Of the proud Gothes an hundreth squadrons trim:
Then he that gainst the Sclaues much honour wan,
Ernesto threatning stood with visage grim,
    Before him *Aldoard*, the Lombard stout
    Who from Monscelces bouldly earst shut out.

74

There *Henrie* was and *Berengare* the bould,
That seru'd great *Charles* in his conquests hie,
Who in each battle giue the onset would,
A hardie souldiour and a captaine slie;
After, prince *Lewes* did he well vphould
Against his nephew, king of Italie,
    He wonne the fielde and tooke that king on liue:
    Next him stood *Otho* with his children fiue.

75

Of *Almerike* the image next they vew,
Lord Marques of Ferrara first create,
Founder of many churches, that vpthrew
His eies, like one that vs'd to contemplate.
Gainst him the second *Azzo* stood in rew,
With *Berengarious* that did long debate,
 Till after often change of fortunes stroake,
 He wonne, and on all Itaile laid the yoake.

76

Albert his sonne the Germaines warde among,
And there his praise and fame was spred so wide,
That hauing foil'd the Danes in battaile strong,
His daughter yoong became great *Othoes* bride.
Behinde him *Hugo* stood with warfare long,
That broake the horne of all the Romaines pride,
 Who of all Italy the Marques hight,
 And Tuscane whole, possessed as his right.

77

After *Tedaldo*, puissant *Boniface*
And *Beatrice* his deere possest the stage;
Nor was there left heire male of that great race,
T'enioy the scepter, state and heritage;
The Princesse *Maude* alone supplide the place,
Supplide the want in number, sexe and age;
 For far aboue each scepter, throne and crowne,
 The noble Dame aduanst her vaile and gowne:

78

With manlike vigor shone her noble looke,
And more than manlike wrath her face orespred,
There the fell Normans, *Guichard* there forsooke
The field, till than who neuer fear'd nor fled;
Henrie the fourth she beat, and from him tooke
His standard, and in church it offered;
 Which donne, the Pope backe to the Vaticane
 She brought, and plast in *Peters* chaire againe.

79

As he that honour'd her, and held her deare
Azzo the fifth stood by her louely side;
But the fourth *Azzos* ofspring far and neare
Spred forth, and through Germania fructifide,
Sprong from that branch did *Guelpho* hold appeare,
Guelpho his sonne by *Cunigond* his bride,
    And in Bauarias field transplanted new
    This Romane grift florisht, encreast and grew.

80

A branch of Est there in the *Guelfian* tree
Engraffed was, which of it selfe was old,
Whereon you might the *Guelfoes* fairer see,
Renew their scepters and their crownes of gold,
On which heau'ns good aspectes so bended bee,
That high and broad it spred, and florisht bold,
    Till vnderneath his glorious branches lade
    Halfe Germanie, and all vnder his shade.

81

This regall plant from his Italian rout
Sprong vp as hie, and blossom'd faire aboue,
For nenst Lord *Guelpho*, *Bertold* issued out,
With the fixt *Azzo* whom all vertues loue;
This was the pedegree of worthies stout,
Who seem'd in that bright shield to liue and moue.
    Rinaldo waked vp and chear'd his face,
    To see these worthies of his house and race.

82

To doe like actes his courage wisht and sought,
And with that wish transported him so farre,
That all those deedes which filled aie his thought,
(Townes wonne, fortes taken, armies kild in warre)
As if they were things donne indeed and wrought,
Before his eies he thinks they present arre,
    He hastly armes him, and with hope and hast,
    Sure conquest met, preuented and imbrast.

83

But *Charles*, who had told the death and fall
Of the yong Prince of Danes his late deere Lord,
Gaue him the fatall weapon, and withall,
'Yong knight (quoth he) take with good lucke this sword,
Your iust, strong, valiant hand in battaile shall
Employ it long, for Christes true faith and word,
    And of his former Lord reuenge the wrongs,
    Who lou'd you so, that deed to you belongs.'

84

He answered, 'God for his mercie sake,
Grant that this hand which holds this weapon good,
For thy deere maister may sharpe veng'ance take,
May cleaue the Pagans hart, and shed his blood.'
To this but short replie did *Charles* make,
And thankt him much, nor more on termes they stood:
    For loe the wisard sage that was their guide
    On their darke iourney hastes them forth to ride,

85

'High time it is (quoth he) for you to wend
Where *Godfrey* you awaits, and many a knight,
There may we well arriue ere night doth end,
And through this darknesse can I guide you right.'
This said, vp to his coach they all ascend,
On his swift wheeles forth roll'd the chariot light,
    He gaue his coursers flit the rod and raine,
    And gallopt forth and eastward droue amaine;

86

While silent so through nights darke shade they flie,
The Hermit thus bespake the yong man stout,
'Of thy great house, thy race, thine ofspring hie,
Here hast thou seene the branch, the bole, the rout,
And as these worthies borne to chiualrie,
And deedes of armes, it hath tofore brought out;
    So is it, so it shall be fertile still,
    Nor time shall end, nor age that seed shall kill.

87

'Would God, as drawne from the forgetfull lap
Of antique time, I haue thine elders showne;
That so I could the Catalogue vnwrap
Of thy great nephewes yet vnborne, vnknowne,
That ere this light they vew, their fate and hap
I might foretell, and how their chance is throwne,
   That like thine elders so thou mightst behold
   Thy children many, famous, stout and bold.

88

'But not by art or skill, of things future
Can the plaine troath reueaeled be and told,
Although some knowledge doubtfull, darke, obscure
We haue of comming haps in cloudes vprold;
Nor all which in this cause I know for sure
Dare I foretell: for of that father old
   The hermit *Peter*, learn'd I much, and hee
   Withouten vaile heau'ns secrets great doth see.

89

'But this (to him reueal'd by grace diuine)
By him to me declar'd, to thee I say,
Was neuer race Greeke, Barb'rous, or Latine,
Great in times past, or famous at this day,
Richer in hardie knights than this of thine;
Such blessings heau'n shall on thy children lay,
   That they in fame shall passe, in praise orecome
   The worthies old of Sparta, Carthage, Rome.

90

'But mongst the rest I chose *Alphonsus* bould,
In vertue first, second in place and name,
He shall be borne when this fraile world growes ould,
Corrupted, poore, and bare of men of fame,
Better than he none shall, none can, or could
The sword or scepter use, or guide the same,
   To rule in peace, or to command in fight,
   Thine ofsprings glorie and thy houses light.

91

'His yonger age foretokens true shall yeild
Of future valour, puissance, force and might,
From him no rocke the sauage beast shall sheild;
At tilt or turnay match him shall no knight:
After he conquer shall in pitched feild
Great armies, and win spoiles in single fight,
    And on his locks (rewards for knightly praise)
    Shall garlands weare of grasse, of oke, of baies.

92

'His grauer age, as well that eild it fits,
Shall happie peace preserue, and quiet blest,
And from his neighbours strong mongst whom he sits,
Shall keepe his cities safe, in wealth and rest,
Shall nourish artes, and cherish pregnant wits,
Make triumphes great, and feast his subiects best,
    Reward the good, the euill with paines torment,
    Shall dangers all foresee; and seene, preuent.

93

'But if it hap against those wicked bands
That sea and earth infest with blood and warre,
And in these wretched times to noble lands
Giue lawes of peace, false and vniust that arre,
That he be sent, to driue their guiltie hands
From Christes pure altars, and high temples farre,
    O what reuenge? what veng'ance shall he bring
    On that false sect, and their accursed king?

94

'Too late the Moores, too late the Turkish king,
Gainst him should arme their troupes and legions bold;
For he beyond great Euphrates should bring,
Beyond the frozen tops of Taurus cold,
Beyond the land where is perpetual spring,
The crosse, the Eagle white, the lillie of gold,
    And by baptising of the Ethiops browne,
    Of aged Nile reueale the springs vnknowne.'

95

Thus said the hermit, and his prophesie
The Prince accepted with content and pleasure,
The secret thought of his posteritie,
Of his concealed ioyes heapt vp the measure.
Meane-while the morning bright was mounted hie,
And chang'd heau'ns siluer wealth to golden treasure,
   And high aboue the Christian tents they vew,
   How the broad ensignes trembled, wau'd and blew;

96

When thus againe their leader sage begonne,
'See how bright *Phebus* cleeres the darksome skies,
See how with gentle beames the friendly sonne
The tents, the townes, the hils and dales descries,
Through my well guiding is your voiage donne,
From danger safe, in trauaile oft which lies,
   Hence without feare of harme or doubt of foe,
   March to the campe, I may no neerer goe.'

97

Thus tooke he leaue, and made a quicke returne,
And forward went the champions three on fout,
And marching right against the rising morne,
A readie passage to the campe found out,
Mean-while had speedie fame the tidings borne
That to the tents approacht these Barons stout,
   And starting from his throne and kingly seat
   To entertaine them, rose *Godfredo* great.

The eighteenth Booke of Godfrey of Bulloigne

The argument.

The charmes and spirits false therein which lie,
Rinaldo *chaseth from the forrest old;*
The host of Egypt comes; Vafrine *the spie*
Entreth their campe, stout, craftie, wise and bold,
Sharpe is the fight about the bulwarks hie
And ports of Zion, to assault the hold:
  Godfrey *hath aide from heau'n, by force the towne*
  Is wonne, the Pagans slaine, walles beaten downe.

1

ARriu'd, where *Godfrey* to imbrace him stood,
  My soueraigne Lord, *Rinaldo* meekely said,
'To venge my wrongs against *Gernando* prood,
My honours care prouokt my wrath vnstaid;
But that I you displeasd my chieftaine good,
My thoughts yet grieue, my hart is still dismai'd,
  And here I come, prest all exploits to trie,
  To make me gracious in your gracious eie.'

2

To him that kneel'd (folding his friendly armes
About his necke) the Duke this answere gaue:
'Let passe such speeches sad, of passed harmes,
Remembrance is the life of griefe; his graue,
Forgetfulnes; and for amends, in armes
Your wonted valour use and courage braue;
  For you alone to happie end must bring,
  The strong enchantments of the charmed spring.

3

'That aged wood whence heretofore we got
(To build our scaling engins) timber fit,

Is now the fearfull seat (but how none wot)
Where ougly feends and damned spirits sit;
To cut one twist there of aduentreth not
The boldest knight we haue, nor without it
   This wall can battred be, where others dout
   There venter thou, and show thy courage stout.'

4

Thus said he, and the knight in speeches few
Profred his seruice to attempt the thing,
To hard assaies his courage willing flew,
To him praise was no spur, words were no sting:
Of his deare friends then he embrast the crew,
To welcome him which came; for in a ring
   About him *Guelfo*, *Tancred* and the rest
   Stood, of the campe the greatest, chiefe and best:

5

When with the Prince these Lords had iterate
Their welcomes oft, and oft their deare embrace;
Towards the rest of lesser woorth and state,
He turn'd, and them receiu'd with gentle grace,
The merrie souldiours bout him shout and prate,
With cries as ioyful and as cheerefull face,
   As if in triumphes chariot bright as sunne,
   He had return'd, Affricke or Asia wonne.

6

Thus marched to his tent the champion good,
And there sate downe with all his friends around;
Now of the warre he askt, now of the wood,
And answer'd each demaund they list propound.
But when they left him to his ease, vpstood
The Hermit, and fit time to speake once found,
   'My Lord he said, your trauels woondrous arre,
   Farre haue you straied, erred, wandred farre;

7

'Mutch are you bound to God aboue, who brought
You safe from false *Armidas* charmed hold;

And thee a straying sheepe whom once he bought,
Hath now againe reduced to his fold,
And against his heathen foes these men of nought,
Hath chosen thee in place next *Godfrey* bold;
   Yet mai'st thou not polluted thus with sinne,
   In his high seruice, warre or fight beginne:

8

'The world, the flesh with their infection vile,
Pollute the thoughts impure, thy spirit staine;
Not Poe, not Ganges, not seu'n mouthed Nile,
Not the wide seas can wash thee cleane againe,
Onely to purge all faults which thee defile,
His blood hath powre who for thy sinnes was slaine:
   His helpe therefore inuoake, to him bewray
   Thy secret faultes, mourne, weepe, complaine and pray.'

9

This said, the knight first with the Witch vnchast,
His idle loues and follies vaine lamented;
Then kneeling low with heauie lookes downe cast,
His other sinnes confest and all repented,
And meekely pardon crau'd for first and last.
The Hermit with his zeale was well contented,
   And said, on yonder hill next morne goe pray
   That turnes his forehead gainst the morning ray:

10

That done, march to the wood, whence each one brings
Such newes of furies, gobblings, feends, and sprites,
The Giants, monsters, and all dreedfull things
Thou shalt subdue, which that darke groue vnites:
Let no strange voice, that mournes or sweetly sings;
Nor beautie, whose glad smile fraile harts delites,
   Within thy breast make ruth or pitie rise,
   But their false lookes and praiers false despise.

11

Thus he aduis'd him, and the hardie knight
Prepar'd him gladly to this enterprise,

Thoughtfull he past the day, and sad the night;
And ere the siluer morne began to rise,
His armes he tooke, and in a coate him dight
Of colour strange, cut in the warlike guise;
  And on his way sole, silent, forth he went
  Alone, and left his friends, and left his tent.

12

It was the time when gainst the breaking day
Rebellious night yet stroue, and still repined;
For in the East appear'd the morning gray,
And yet some lampes in *Ioues* high pallace shined,
When to mount Oliuet he tooke his way,
And saw (as round about his eies he twined)
  Nights shadowes hence, from thence the mornings shine
  This bright, that darke; that earthly, this diuine:

13

Thus to himselfe he thought, 'how many bright
And splendant lamps shine in heau'ns temple hie,
Day hath his golden sun, her moone the night,
Her fixt and wandring stars the azure skie,
So framed all by their creators might,
That still they liue and shine, and nere shall die,
  Till (in a moment) with the last daies brand
  They burne, and with them burnes sea, aire and land.'

14

Thus as he mused, to the top he went,
And there kneeld downe with reuerence and feare,
His eies vpon heau'ns eastren face he bent,
His thoughts aboue all heau'ns vplifted weare,
'The sinnes and errours (which I now repent)
Of mine vnbridled youth, O father deare
  Remember not, but let thy mercy fall,
  And purge my faults, and mine offences all.'

15

Thus praied he, with purple wings vpflew
In golden weed the mornings lustie queene,

Begilding (with the radiant beames she threw)
His helme, his harnesse and the mountaine greene,
Vpon his brest and forehead gently blew
The aire, that balme and nardus breath'd vnseene,
   And ore his head let downe from cleerest skies
   A cloud of pure and precious dew there flies,

16

The heau'nly dew was on his garments spred,
To which compar'd, his clothes pale ashes seame,
And sprinkled so, that all that palenesse fled,
And thence of purest white bright raies outstreame:
So cheered are the flowres late withered,
With the sweete comfort of the morning beame;
   And so returnd to youth, a serpent old
   Adornes her selfe in new and natiue gold.

17

The louely whitenesse of his changed weed
The prince perceiued well, and long admirde,
Toward the forrest marcht he on with speed,
Resolu'd, as such aduentures great requir'de,
Thither he came whence shrinking backe, for dreed
Of that strange desarts sight, the first retir'de,
   But not to him fearefull or loathsome made
   That forrest was, but sweete with pleasant shade:

18

Forward he past, and in the groue before
He heard a sound that strange, sweete, pleasing was;
There roll'd a christall brooke with gentle rore,
There sigh'd the windes as through the leaues they pas,
There did the Nightingale her wrongs deplore,
There sung the swan, and singing dide (alas)
   There lute, harpe, cittren, humaine voice he hard,
   And all these sounds one sound right well declard.

16³ spinkled < sprinkled

19

A dreedfull thunderclap at last he hard,
The aged trees and plants wel nie that rent;
Yet heard he Nymphes and Sirens afterward,
Birdes, windes, and waters sing, with sweete consent:
Whereat amazd he staid, and well prepard
For his defence, heedfull and slow foorthwent:
 Nor in his way his passage ought withstood,
 Except a quiet, still, transparent flood,

20

On the greene banks which that faire streame inbound,
Flowers and odours sweetely smilde and smeld,
Which reaching out his stretched armes around,
All the large desart in his bosome held,
And through the groue one chanell passage found,
That, in the wood; in that, the forrest dweld:
 Trees, clad the streames; streames, greene those trees aie made,
 And so exchangd their moisture and their shade.

21

The knight some way sought out the floud to pas,
And as he sought a wondrous bridge appeard,
A bridge of golde, a huge and weightie mas,
On arches great of that rich mettall reard;
When through that golden way he entred was,
Downe fell the bridge, swelled the streame, and weard
 The worke away, not signe left where it stood,
 And of a riuer calme became a flood:

22

He turnd, amasd to see it troubled soe,
Like sodaine brookes encreast with molten snow,
The billowes fierce that tossed to and froe,
The whirlpooles suckt downe to their bosoms low;
But on he went to search for wonders moe,
Through the thicke trees, there high and broad which grow,
 And in that forrest huge and desart wide,
 The more he sought, more wonders still he spide.

23

Whereso he stept, it seem'd the ioyfull ground
Renew'd the verdure of her flowrie weed,
A fountaine here, a welspring there he found;
Here bud the Roses, there the Lillies spreed;
The aged wood ore and about him round
Flourisht with blossomes new, new leaues, new seed,
 And on the boughes and branches of those treene,
 The barke was softned, and renew'd the greene.

24

The Manna on each leafe did pearled lie,
The hony stilled from the tender rinde.
Againe he heard that woondrous harmonie,
Of songs and sweete complaints of louers kinde,
The humaine voices sung a triple hie,
To which respond the birdes, the streames, the winde,
 But yet vnseene those Nymphes, those fingers weare,
 Vnseene the lutes, harpes, viols which they beare.

25

He lookte, he listned, yet his thoughts denide
To thinke that true which he both heard and see,
A Mirtle in an ample plaine he spide,
And thither by a beaten path went hee:
The Mirtle spred her mightie branches wide,
Higher than Pine, or Palme, or Cipresse tree:
 And farre aboue all other plants was seene,
 That forrests Ladie, and that desarts queene.

26

Vpon the tree his eies *Rinaldo* bent,
And there a maruell great and strange began;
An aged Oake beside him cleft and rent,
And from his fertill hollow wombe forth ran,
(Clad in rare weedes and strange habiliment)
A Nymph, for age able to goe to man,
 An hundreth plants beside (euen in his sight)
 Childed an hundreth Nymphes, so great, so dight:

27

Such as on stages play, such as we see
The Dryads painted, whom wilde Satires loue,
Whose armes, halfe naked; lockes vntrussed bee,
With buskins laced on their legs aboue
And silken roabes tuckt short aboue their knee;
Such seem'd the *Siluan* daughters of this groue,
  Saue that in stead of shafts and boughes of tree,
  She bore a lute, a harpe or cittern shee.

28

And wantonly they cast them in a ring,
And sung and danst to moue her weaker sense,
Rinaldo round about enuironing,
As centers are with their circumference;
The tree they compast eeke, and gan to sing,
That woods and streames admir'd their excellence;
  'Welcome deere Lord, welcome to this sweet groue,
  Welcome our Ladies hope, welcome her loue;

29

'Thou com'st to cure our Princesse, faint and sicke
For loue, for loue of thee, faint, sicke, distressed;
Late blacke, late dreadfull was this forrest thicke,
Fit dwelling for sad folke with griefe oppressed,
See with thy comming how the branches quicke
Reuiued are, and in new blossoms dressed:'
  This was their song, and after, from it went
  First a sweet sound, and then the myrtle rent.

30

If antique times admir'd *Silenus* old,
That oft appeer'd set on his lasie asse,
How would they wonder if they had behold
Such sights as from the myrtle high did passe?
Thence came a Ladie faire with lockes of gold,
That like in shape, in face and beautie was
  To sweet *Armida*; *Rinald* thinkes he spies
  Her gestures, smiles and glances of her eies.

31

On him a sad and smiling looke she cast,
Which twenty passions strange at once bewraies,
'And art thou come (quoth she) return'd at last
To her, from whom but late thou ranst thy waies?
Comst thou to comfort me for sorrowes past?
To ease my widow nights, and carefull daies?
　Or comest thou to worke me griefe and harme?
　Why nilt thou speake? Why not thy face disarme?

32

'Comst thou a friend or foe? I did not frame
That golden bridge to entertaine my foe,
Nor op'ned flowres and fountaines as you came,
To welcome him with ioy that brings me woe:
Put off thy helme, reioice me with the flame
Of thy bright eies, whence first my fires did groe:
　Kisse me, embrace me, if you further venter,
　Loue keepes the gate, the fort is eath to enter.'

33

Thus as she wowes, she rowles her ruefull eies,
With pitious looke, and changeth oft her cheare,
An hundreth sighes from her false hart vpflies,
She sobbes, she mournes, it is great ruth to heare,
The hardest brest sweete pitie mollifies,
What stonie hart resists a womans teare?
　But yet the knight, wise, warie, not vnkind,
　Drew foorth his sword and from her carelesse twind.

34

Towards the tree he marcht, she thither start,
Before him stept, embrast the plant and cride,
'Ah, neuer do me such a spitefull part,
To cut my tree, this forrests ioy and pride,
Put vp thy sword, else pierce therewith the hart
Of thy forsaken and despis'd *Armide*;
　For through this brest, and through this hart (vnkind)
　To this faire tree thy sword shall passage find.'

35

He lift his brand, nor car'd though oft she praid,
And she her forme to other shape did change;
Such monsters huge, when men in dreames are laid,
Oft in their idle fancies roame and range:
Her bodie sweld, her face obscure was maid,
Vanisht her garments rich, and vestures strange,
   A giantesse before him high she stands,
    Like *Briareus* armd with an hundreth hands:

36

With fiftie swords, and fiftie targets bright,
She threatned death, she roared, cride and fought,
Each other nymph in armour likewise dight,
A Cyclops great became: he feard them nought,
But on the myrtle smote with all his might,
That groand like liuing soules to death nie brought,
   The skie seemd *Plutoes* court, the aire seemd hell,
    Therein such monsters roare, such spirits yell:

37

Lightned the heau'n aboue, the earth below
Roared aloud, that thundred, and this shooke;
Blustred the tempests strong, the whirlwinds blow,
The bitter storme droue hailestones in his looke;
But yet his arme grew neither weake nor slow,
Nor of that furie heed or care he tooke,
   Till low to earth, the wounded tree downe bended,
    Then fled the spirits all, the charmes all ended.

38

The heau'ns grew cleere, the aire waxt calme and still,
The wood returned to his wonted state,
Of witchcrafts free, quite void of spirits ill,
Of horrour full, but horrour there innate;
He further prou'd if ought withstood his will
To cut those trees, as did the charmes of late,
   And finding nought to stop him, smilde, and said,
    'O shadowes vaine! O fooles of shades affraid!'

39

From thence home to the campward turn'd the knight,
The hermit cride vpstarting from his seat,
'Now of the wood the charmes haue lost their might,
The sprites are conquer'd, ended is the feat,
See where he comes,' in glistring white all dight
Appear'd the man, bold, stately, high and great,
    His eagles siluer wings to shine begunne,
      With wondrous splendure gainst the golden sunne.

40

The campe receiu'd him with a ioyfull crie,
A crie the dales and hils about that fild;
Then *Godfrey* welcomd him with honours hie,
His glorie quencht all spite, all enuie kild:
'To yonder dreadfull groue (quoth he) went I,
And from the fearfull wood (as me you wild)
    Haue driuen the sprites away, thither let bee
      Your people sent, the way is safe and free.'

41

Sent were the workmen thither, thence they brought
Timber enough, by good aduise select,
And though, by skillesse builders fram'd and wrought,
Their engins rude and rammes were late erect,
Yet now the forts and towres (from whence they fought)
Were framed by a cunning architect.
    William, of all the Genoas Lord and guide,
      Which late rul'd all the seas from side to side;

42

But forced to retire from him at last,
The Pagan fleet the seas moist empire wunne,
His men with all their stuffe and store in hast
Home to the campe with their commander runne,
In skill, in wit, in cunning him surpast
Yet neuer enginer beneath the sunne,
    Of Carpenters an hundreth large he brought,
      That what their Lord deuised made and wrought.

41⁴ elect, < erect,

43

This man begunne with woondrous arte to make,
Not rammes, not mightie brakes, not slings alone,
Wherewith the firme and solid walles to shake,
To cast a dart or throw a shaft or stone;
But fram'd of Pines and Firres, did vndertake
To build a fortresse huge, to which was none
   Yet euer like, whereof he cloath'd the sides
   Against the balles of fire, with raw bulles hides,

44

In mortesses and sockets framed iust,
The beames, the studdes and punchions ioyn'd he fast;
To beat the cities wall, beneath forth brust
A ramme with horned front, about her wast
A bridge the engine from her side out thrust,
Which on the wall when need requir'd she cast;
   And from her top a turret small vpstood,
   Strong, surely arm'd, and builded of like wood:

45

Set on an hundreth wheeles the rolling mas,
On the smoothe landes went nimbly vp and downe,
Though full of armes and armed men it was;
Yet with small paines it ran, as it had flowne,
Woondred the campe so quicke to see it pas,
They prais'd the workmen, and their skill vnknowne,
   And on that day two towres they builded more,
   Like that which sweet *Clorinda* burnt before.

46

Yet wholy were not from the Saracines
Their workes concealed, and their labours hid,
Vpon that wall which next the campe confines,
They placed spies who marked all they did:
They saw the ashes wilde and squared Pines
How to the tents (trail'd from the groue) they slid;
   And engins huge they saw, yet could not tell
   How they were built, their formes they saw not well,

47

Their engins eeke they reard, and with great art
Repair'd each bulwarke, turret, port and towre,
And fortifide the plaine and easie part,
To bide the storme of euerie warlike stowre,
Till as they thought no sleight, or force of mart,
To vndermine or scale the same had powre:
    And false *Ismeno* gan new balles prepare
    Of wicked fire, wilde, wondrous, strange and rare.

48

He mingled brimstone with Bitumen fell
Fetch from that lake where Sodome earst did sinke,
And from that flood which nine times compast hell,
Some of the liquor whot he brought, I thinke,
Wherewith the quenchlesse fire he tempred well,
To make it smoake and flame and deadly stinke;
    And for his wood cut downe the aged sire
    Would thus reuengement take, with flame and fire.

49

While thus the campe, and thus the towne were bent,
These to assault, these to defend the wall,
A speedie doue through the cleare welkin went,
Straight ore the tents, seene by the souldiers all
With nimble fannes the yeilding aire she rent,
Not seemd it that she would alight or fall,
    Till she arriu'd neere that besieged towne,
    Then from the clouds at last she stouped downe;

50

But loe (from whence I nolte) a falcon came,
Armed with crooked bill and talons long,
And twixt the campe and citie crost her game,
That durst not bide her foes encounter strong;
But right vpon the royall tent downe came,
And there the lordes and princes great among,
    (When the sharpe hauke nie toucht her tender head)
    In *Godfreyes* lappe she fell, with feare halfe dead:

51

The Duke receiu'd her, saued her, and spide,
As he beheld the bird, a wondrous thing,
About her necke a letter close was tide,
By a small thred, and trust vnder her winge,
He loosed foorth the writ and spred it wide,
And read th'intent thereof, 'To Iudaies king,
    (Thus said the scedule) honors high encrease
      Th'Egyptian chiefetaine wisheth, health and peace:

52

'Feare not (renowned prince) resist, endure
Till the third day, or till the fourth at most,
I come and your deliuerance will procure,
And kill your coward foes and all their host.'
This secret in that briefe was clos'd vp sure,
Writ in strange language, to the winged post
    Giu'n to transport; for in their warlike need
      The East such message vs'd, oft with good speed.'

53

The Duke let goe the captiue doue at large,
And she that had his counsell close bewraid,
Traitresse to her great Lord toucht not the marge
Of Salems towne, but fled farre thence afraid;
The Duke before all those, which had or charge
Or office high, the letter red, and said;
    'See how the goodnes of the Lord foreshoes
      The secret purpose of our craftie foes.

54

'No longer then let vs protract the time,
But scale the bulwarke of this fortresse hie,
Through sweat and labour gainst those rockes sublime
Let vs ascend, which to the Southward lie;
Hard will it be that way in armes to clime,
But yet the place and passage both know I,
    And that high wall by scite strong on that part,
      Is least defenst by armes, by worke and art.

55

'Thou *Raimond*, on this side with all thy might
Assault the wall, and by those cragges ascend,
My squadrons with mine engins huge shall fight,
And gainst the Northren gate my puissance bend;
That so our foes beguiled with the sight,
Our greatest force and powre shall there attend,
 While my great towre from thence shall nimbly slide,
 And batter downe some worse defended side;

56

'*Camillo* thou not farre from me shalt reare
Another towre, close to the walles ibrought.'
This spoken, *Raimond* old that sate him neare,
(And while he talkte great things tost in his thought)
Said, 'To *Godfredoes* counsell giuen vs heare,
Nought can be added, from it taken nought:
 Yet this I further wish that some were sent
 To spie their campe, their secret and entent;

57

'That may their number and their squadrons braue
Describe, and through their tents disguised maske:'
Quoth *Tancred*, 'loe, a subtle squire I haue,
A person fit to vndertake this taske,
A man, quicke, readie, bold, slie to deceaue,
To answere, wise, and well aduisde to aske;
 Well languaged, and that with time and place
 Can change his looke, his voice, his gate, his grace.'

58

Sent for he came, and when his lord him tould
What *Godfreyes* pleasure was, and what his owne;
He smilde, and said foorthwith he gladly would,
'I goe quoth he, 'carelesse what chance be throwne,
And where encamped be these Pagans bould,
Will walke, in euery tent a spie vnknowne,
 Their campe euen at noone day I enter shall,
 And number all their horse and footemen all;

56⁵ to < 'To

59

'How great, how strong, how arm'd this army is,
And what their guide entendes, I will declare,
To me the secrets of that hart of his,
And hidden thoughts shall open lie and bare.'
Thus *Vafrine* spoke, nor longer staid on this,
But for a mantle changd the cote he ware,
   Nakte was his necke, and bout his forehead bould,
   Of linnen white full twentie yeards he rould;

60

His weapons were a Syrian bow and quiuer,
His gestures barb'rous, like the Turkish traine,
Wondred all they that heard his toong deliuer
Of euery land the language true and plaine,
In Tire, a borne Phenician, by the riuer
Of Nile, a knight bred in th'Egyptian maine,
   Both people would haue thought him, foorth he rides
   On a swift stead, ore hils and dales that glides.

61

But ere the third day came the French foorth sent
Their pioners to eeu'n the rougher waies,
And readie made each warlike instrument,
Nor ought their labour interrupts or staies;
The nights in busie toile they likewise spent,
And with long eueninges lengthned foorth short daies,
   Till nought was left the hosts that hinder might,
   To use their vtmost powre, and strength in fight.

62

That day, which of th'assault the day foreronne,
The godly Duke in praier spent welnie,
And all the rest, bicause they had misdonne,
The Sacrament receiue, and mercie crie;
Then oft the Duke his engins great begonne
To shew, where least he would their strength applie;
   His foes reiois'd, deluded in that sort,
   To see them bent against their surest port:

61[6] lenghtned < lengthned

63

But after aided by the friendly night
His greatest engin to that side he brought,
Where plainest seem'd the wall, where with their might
The flankers least could hurt them as they fought,
And to the Southern mountaines greatest hight
To raise his turret old *Raimondo* sought;
    And thou *Camillo* on that part hadst thine,
    Where from the North the wals did Westward twine.

64

But when amid the Estren heau'n appear'd
The rising morning bright as shining glas,
The troubled Pagans saw, and seeing fear'd,
How the great towre stood not where late it was,
And here and there tofore vnseene was rear'd,
Of timber strong a huge and fearfull mas,
    And numberlesse with beames, with roapes and strings
    They view the iron rammes, the brakes and slings.

65

The Syrian people now were no whit slow,
Their best defences to that side to beare,
Where *Godfrey* did his greatest engin show,
From thence where late in vaine they placed weare;
But he who at his backe right well did know,
The hoste of Egypt to be proaching neare,
    To him call'd *Guelfo*, and the *Roberts* twaine,
    And said, 'on horsebacke looke you still remaine,

66

'And haue regard while all our people striue
To scale this wall, where weake it seemes and thin,
Least vnawares some sudden hoste arriue,
And at our backes vnlookte for warre begin.'
This said, three fierce assaults at once they giue,
The hardie souldiours all would die or win,
    And on three parts resistance makes the king,
    And rage gainst strength, despaire gainst hope doth bring,

65⁵ rightwell < right well (*cf. 1624*)

67

Himselfe vpon his limmes with feeble eild
That shooke, (vnweildie with their proper weight,)
His armour laid and long vnused sheild,
And marcht gainst *Raimond* to the mountaines height:
Great *Soliman* gainst *Godfrey* tooke the feild,
Forenenst *Camillo* stood *Argantes* streight
  Where *Tancred* strong he found, so fortune will,
That this good Prince his wonted foe shall kill.

68

The archers shot their arrowes sharpe and keene
Dipt in the bitter iuice of poyson strong,
The shadie face of heau'n was scantly seene,
Hid with the cloudes of shaftes and quarries long;
Yet weapons sharpe with greater furie beene,
Cast from the towres the Pagan troupes among,
  For thence flew stones and clifts of marble rockes,
  Trees shod with iron, timber, logges and blockes.

69

A thunderbolt seem'd euerie stone, it brake
His lims and armours so on whom it light,
That life and soule it did not onely take,
But all his shape and face disfigur'd quight;
The launces stai'd not in the wounds they make,
But through the gored bodie tooke their flight,
  From side to side, through flesh, through skin and rinde
  They flew, and flying, left sad death behinde.

70

But yet not all this force and furie droue
The Pagan people to forsake the wall,
But to reuenge these deadly blowes they stroue,
With dartes that flie, with stones and trees that fall;
For need so cowards oft couragious proue,
For libertie they fight, for life and all,
  And oft with arrowes shaftes and stones that flie,
  Giue bitter answere to a sharpe replie.

71

This while the fierce assailants neuer cease,
But sternly still maintaine a threefold charge,
And gainst the cloudes of shaftes draw nie at ease,
Vnder a pentise made of many a targe,
The armed towres close to the bulwarks prease,
And striue to grapple with the battled marge,
 And lanch their bridges out, meane-while below
 With iron fronts the rammes the walles downe throw.

72

Yet still *Rinaldo* vnresolued went,
And far vnworthie him this seruice thought,
If mongst the common sort his paines he spent;
Renowne so got the Prince esteemed nought:
His angrie lookes on euerie side he bent,
And where most harme, most danger was he fought,
 And where the wall high, strong and surest was,
 That part would he assault, and that way pas.

73

And turning to the worthies him behind,
All hardie knights, whom *Dudon* late did guide,
'O shame (quoth he) this wall no warre doth find,
When battred is elsewhere each part, each side;
All paine is safetie to a valiant mind,
Each way is eath to him that dares abide,
 Come let vs scale this wall, though strong and hie,
 And with your shieldes keepe off the darts that flie:'

74

With him vnited all while thus he spake,
Their targets hard aboue their heads they threw,
Which ioynd in one an iron pentise make,
That from the dreadfull storme preseru'd the crew,
Defended thus their speedie course they take,
And to the wall without resistance drew,
 For that strong penticle protected well
 The knights, from all that flew and all that fell.

75

Against the fort *Rinaldo* gan vpreare
A ladder huge, an hundreth steps of hight,
And in his arme the same did easlie beare,
And mooue, as windes do reeds or rushes light,
Sometimes a tree, a rocke, a dart, or speare,
Fell from aboue, yet forward clombe the knight,
    And vpward fearelesse preased, careless still,
    Though mount Olympus fell or Ossa hill:

76

A mount of ruines, and of shaftes a wood
Vpon his shoulders and his shield he bore,
One hand the ladder held whereon he stood,
The other bare his targe his face before;
His hardie troupe, by his ensample good
Prouokt, with him the place assaulted sore,
    And ladders long against the wall they clappe,
    Vnlike in courage yet, vnlike in happe:

77

One dide, an other fell, he forward went,
And these he comforts, and he threatneth those,
Now with his hand outstrecht the battlement
Welnie he reacht, when all his armed foes
Ran thither, and their force and furie bent
To throw him headlong downe, yet vp he goes,
    A wondrous thing, one knight whole armed bands
    Alone, and hanging in the aire, withstands:

78

Withstands, and forceth his great strength so farre,
That like a palme whereon huge weight doth rest,
His forces so resisted stronger arre,
His vertues higher rise the more opprest,
Till all that would his entrance bould debarre
He backewarde droue, vpleaped, and possest
    The wall, and safe and easie with his blade,
    To all that after came, the passage made,

79

There killing such as durst and did withstand,
To noble *Eustace* that was like to fall,
He reached foorth his friendly conqu'ring hand,
And next himselfe helpt him to mount the wall.
This while *Godfredo* and his people fand
Their liues to greater harmes and dangers thrall,
  For there not man with man, nor knight with knight
  Contend, but engins there with engins fight.

80

For in that place the Paynims rear'd a post,
Which late had seru'd some gallant ship for mast,
And ouer it another beame they crost,
Pointed with iron sharpe, to it made fast
With ropes, which as men would the dormant tost,
Now out, now in, now backe, now forward cast,
  In his swift pullies oft the men withdrew
  The tree, and oft the riding balke foorth threw:

81

The mightie beame redoubled oft his blowes,
And with such force the engine smote and hit,
That her broad side the towre wide open throwes,
Her ioints were broke, her rafters cleft and split;
But yet gainst euery hap whence mischiefe growes
Prepard, the piece (gainst such extreames made fit)
  Lanch foorth two sithes, sharpe, cutting, long & broad,
  And cut the ropes whereon the engin road:

82

As an oulde rocke, which age or stormie wind
Teares from some craggie hill or mountaine steepe,
Doth breake, doth bruse, and into dust doth grind
Woods, houses, hamlets, herds, and fould of sheepe;
So fell the beame, and downe with it all kind
Of armes, of weapons, and of men did sweepe,
  Wherewith the towres once or twise did shake,
  Trembled the wals, the hils and mountaines quake.

83

Victorious *Godfrey* boldly forward came,
And had great hope euen then the place to win;
But loe a fire, with stinch, with smoake, and flame,
Withstood his passage, stopt his entrance in:
Such burnings *Etna* yet could neuer frame,
When from her entrals hot her fires begin,
  Nor yet in sommer on the Indian plaine
  Such vapours warme, from scorching aire, downe raine.

84

There balles of wilde fire, there flie burning speares,
This flame was blacke, that blew; this red as blood;
Stinch welnie choaketh them, noise deafes their eares,
Smoake blindes their eies, fire kindleth on the wood;
Nor those raw hides which for defence it weares,
Could saue the towre, in such distresse it stood;
  For now they wrinkle, now it sweates and fries,
  Now burnes, vnlesse some helpe come down from skies.

85

The hardie Duke before his folke abides,
Nor chang'd he colour, countenance or place,
But comforts those that from the scaldred hides,
With water stroue th'approching flames to chace:
In these extremes the Prince and those he guides
Halfe roasted stood before fierce *Vulcans* face,
  When loe a sudden and vnlookt for blast,
  The flames against the kindlers backward cast:

86

The windes droue backe the fire where heaped lie
The Pagans weapons, where their engins weare,
Which kindling quickly in that substance drie,
Burnt all their store and all their warlike geare:
O glorious captaine! whom the Lord from hie
Defends, whom God preserues, and holds so deare;
  For thee heau'n fights, to thee the windes (from farre,
  Call'd with thy trumpets blast) obedient arre.

87

But wicked *Ismen* to his harme that saw,
How the fierce blast droue backe the fire and flame,
By art would nature change, and thence withdraw
Those noisome windes, else calme and still the same;
Twixt two false Wizards without feare or aw
Vpon the walles in open fight he came,
  Blacke, grisly, loathsome, grim and ougly faced,
  Like *Pluto* old, betwixt two furies placed;

88

And now the wretch those dreadfull words begunne,
Which tremble make deepe hell and all her flocke,
Now troubled is the aire, the golden sunne
His fearefull beames in cloudes did close and locke,
When from the towre (which *Ismen* could not shunne)
Out flew a mightie stone, late halfe a rocke,
  Which light so iust vpon the Wizards three,
  That driu'n to dust their bones and bodies bee.

89

To lesse than nought their members old were torne,
And shiuer'd were their heads to pieces small,
As small, as are the brused graines of corne,
When from the mill resolu'd to meale they fall;
Their damned soules to deepest hell downe borne
(Far from the ioy and light celestiall)
  The furies plunged in th'infernall lake,
  O mankinde! at their ends ensample take.

90

This while the engin which the tempest could,
Had sau'd from burning with his friendly blast,
Approched had so neere the battred hould,
That on the walles her bridge at ease she cast:
But *Soliman* ran thither fierce and bould,
To cut the planke whereon the Christians past,
  And had perform'd his will, saue that vpreard
  High in the skies a turret new appeard;

91

Farre in the aire vp clombe the fortresse tall
Higher than house, then steeple, church or towre;
The Pagans trembled to behold the wall,
And citie subiect to her shot and powre;
Yet kept the Turke his stand, though on him fall
Of stones and dartes a sharpe and deadly showre,
   And still to cut the bridge, he hopes and striues,
   And those that feare, with cheerfull speech reuiues.

92

The Angell *Michaell* to all the rest
Vnseene, appear'd before *Godfredoes* eies,
In pure and heau'nly armour ritchly drest,
Brighter than *Titans* raies in cleerest skies;
'*Godfrey* (quoth he) this is the moment blest
To free this towne that long in bondage lies,
   See, see what legions in thine aide I bring,
   For heau'n assists thee, and heau'ns glorious king:

93

'Lift vp thine eies and in the aire behold
The sacred armies, how they mustred bee,
That cloud of flesh in which from times of old
All mankinde wrapped is, I take from thee,
And from thy senses their thicke mist vnfold,
That face to face thou maist these spirits see,
   And for a little space, right well sustaine
   Their glorious light, and vew those angels plaine.

94

'Behold the soules of euery Lord and knight
That late bore armes and dide for Christes deare sake,
How on thy side against this towne they fight,
And of thy ioy and conquest will partake:
There where the dust and smoke blinde all mens sight,
Where stones and ruines such an heape doe make,
   There *Hugo* fights, in thickest cloude imbard,
   And vndermines that bulwarks groundworke hard.

95

'See *Dudon* yonder, who with sword and fire
Assailes and helpes to scale the northren port,
That with bold courage doth thy folke inspire,
And reares their ladders gainst th'assaulted fort:
He that high on the mount in graue attire
Is clad, and crowned stands in kingly sort,
   Is Bishop *Ademare*, a blessed spirite,
   Blest for his faith, crown'd for his death and merite.

96

'But higher lift thy happie eies, and vew
Where all the sacred hosts of heau'n appeare.'
He lookt, and saw where winged armies flew,
Innumerable, pure, diuine, and cleare;
A battaile round of squadrons three they shew,
And all by threes those squadrons ranged weare,
   Which spreading wide in rings, still wider goe,
   Mou'd with a stone, calme water circleth soe.

97

With that he winkte, and vanisht was and gone
That wondrous vision when he lookt againe,
His worthies fighting vew'd he one by one,
And on each side saw signes of conquest plaine,
For with *Rinaldo* gainst his yeelding fone,
His knights were entred and the Pagans slaine.
   This seene, the Duke no longer stay could brooke,
   But from the bearer bold his ensigne tooke:

98

And on the bridge he stept, but there was staid
By *Soliman*, who entrance all denide,
That narrow tree to vertue great was maid,
The field as in few blowes right soone was tride,
'Here will I giue my life for Sions aid,
Here will I end my daies', the Soldan cride,
   'Behinde me cut, or breake this bridge, that I
   May kill a thousand Christians first, then die.'

96² appeare; < appeare.   97¹ winkte < winkte, (*cf.* wink'd and, M)

99

But thither fierce *Rinaldo* threat'ning went,
And at his sight fled all the Soldans traine,
'What shall I doe? if here my life be spent,
I spend and spill (quoth he) my blood in vaine:'
With that his steps from *Godfrey* backe he bent,
And to him let the passage free remaine,
　　Who threat'ning follow'd as the Soldan fled,
　　And on the walles the purple crosse dispred,

100

About his head he tost, he turn'd, he cast
That glorious ensigne, with a thousand twines,
Thereon the winde breathes with his sweetest blast,
Thereon with golden raies glad *Phebus* shines,
Earth laughes for ioy, the streames forbeare their hast,
Floods clap their hands, on mountaines dance the pines,
　　And Sions towres and sacred temples smile,
　　For their deliu'rance from that bondage vile.

101

And now the armies rear'd the happie crie
Of victorie, glad, ioyfull, lowd and shrill,
The hils resound, the Eccho showteth hie,
And *Tancred* bold that fights and combats still,
With proud *Argantes*, brought his towre so nie,
That on the wall, against the boasters will,
　　In his despite, his bridge he also laid,
　　And wonne the place, and there the crosse displaid.

102

But on the southren hill (where *Raimond* fought,
Against the townesmen and their aged king)
His hardie Gascoignes gained small or nought;
Their engin to the walles they could not bring,
For thither all his strength the Prince had brought,
For life and safetie sternly combatting,
　　And for the wall was feeblest on that cost,
　　There were his soldiers best, and engins most.

103

Besides, the towre vpon that quarter found
Vnsure, vneasie, and vneeu'n the way,
Not art could helpe, but that the rougher ground
The rolling masse did often stop and stay;
But now of victorie the ioyfull sound
The king and *Raimond* heard, amid their fray;
   And by the showte they and their soldiers know,
   The towne was entred on the plaine below.

104

Which heard, *Raimondo* thus bespake this crew,
'The towne is wonne (my friends) and doth it yet
Resist? are we kept out still by these few?
Shall we no share in this high conquest get?'
But from that part the king at last withdrew,
He stroue in vaine their entrance there to let,
   And to a stronger place his folke he brought,
   Where to sustaine th'assault a while he thought.

105

The conquerours at once now entred all,
The walles were wonne, the gates were op'ned wide,
Now brused, broken downe, destroyed fall
The portes, and towres, that battrie durst abide;
Rageth the sword, death murdreth great and small,
And proud twixt woe and horrour sad doth ride,
   Here ronnes the blood, in ponds there stands the gore,
   And drownes the knights in whom it liu'd before.

The argument.

Tancred *in single combat killes his foe*
Argantes *strong: the king and Soldan flie*
To Dauids *towre and saue their persons soe*:
Erminia *well instructs* Vafrine *the spie*,
With him she rides away, and as they goe
Findes where her Lord for dead on earth doth lie,
   First she laments, then cures him: Godfrey *heares*
   Ormondoes *treason and what marks he beares.*

I

NOW death, or feare, or care to saue their liues,
   From their forsaken walles the Pagans chace:
Yet neither force, nor feare, nor wisdome driues
The constant knight *Argantes*, from his place;
Alone, against ten thousand foes he striues,
Yet dreedlesse, doubtlesse, carelesse seem'd his face,
   Not death, not danger, but disgrace he feares,
   And still vnconquer'd (though oreset) appeares.

2

But mongst the rest vpon his helmet gay
With his broad sword *Tancredie* came and smote:
The Pagan knew the Prince by his array,
By his strong blowes, his armour and his cote;
For once they fought, and when night staid that fray,
New time they chose to end their combat hote,
   But *Tancred* fail'd, wherefore the Pagan knight
   Cride, '(*Tancred*) com'st thou thus, thus late to fight?

3

'Too late thou com'st and not alone to warre,
But yet the fight I neither shun nor feare,
Although from knighthood true thou errest farre,
Since like an enginer thou dost appeare,

That towre, that troupe, thy shield and safetie arre,
Strange kinde of armes in single fight to beare;
    Yet shalt thou not escape (O conqu'rer strong
    Of Ladies faire) sharpe death, to venge that wrong.'

4

Lord *Tancred* smiled, with disdaine and scorne,
And answer'd thus, 'to end our strife (quoth hee)
Behold at last I come, and my retorne
(Though late) perchance will be too soone for thee;
For thou shalt wish (of hope and helpe forlorne)
Some sea or mountaine plast twixt thee and mee,
    And well shalt know before we end this fray,
    No feare or cowardise hath caus'd my stay.

5

'But come aside thou, by whose prowesse dies
The monsters, knights and giants in all lands,
The killer of weake women thee defies.'
This said, he turned to his fighting bands
And bids them all retire, 'forbeare' he cries
'To strike this knight, on him let none lay hands;
    For mine he is (more than a common fo)
    By challenge new and promise old also.'

6

'Descend' (the fierce *Circassian* gan replie)
'Alone, or all this troupe for succour take
To desarts waste, or place frequented hie,
For vantage none I will the fight forsake:'
Thus giuen and taken was the bold defie,
And through the prease (agreed so) they brake,
    Their hatred made them one, and as they wend
    Each knight his foe did for despite defend.

7

Great was his thirst of praise, great the desire
That *Tancred* had the Pagans blood to spill,
Nor could that quench his wrath, or calme his ire,
If other hand his foe should foile or kill,

He sau'd him with his shield, and cride 'retire'
To all he met, 'and doe this knight none ill:'
    And thus defending gainst his friends his foe,
    Through thousand angrie weapons safe they goe.

8

They left the citie, and they left behind
Godfredoes campe, and far beyond it past,
And came where into creekes and bosomes blinde
A winding hill his corners turn'd and cast,
A valley small and shadie dale they finde,
Amid the mountaines steepe so laid and plast,
    As it some Theatre or closed place
    Had beene, for men to fight, or beasts to chace,

9

There stai'd the champions both, with ruefull eies
Argantes gan the fortresse wonne to vew;
Tancred his foe withouten shield espies,
And farre away his target therefore threw,
And said, 'whereon doth thy sad hart deuies?
Thinkst thou this howre must end thy life vntrew?
    If this thou feare, and dost foresee thy fate,
    Thy feare is vaine, thy foresight comes too late.'

10

'I thinke (quoth he) on this distressed towne,
The aged Queene of Iudaies ancient land,
Now lost, now sacked, spoil'd and troden downe,
Whose fall in vaine I striued to withstand,
A small reuenge for Sions fort orethrowne
That head can be cut off by my strong hand;'
    This said, togither with great heed they flew,
    For each his foe for bold and hardie knew:

11

Tancred of bodie actiue was and light,
Quicke, nimble, ready both of hand and fout:

10⁵ orethrnowne < orethrowne (*1624*)

But higher by the head the Pagan knight,
Of limmes farre greater was, of hart as stout:
Tancred laid low and trauerst in his fight,
Now to his ward retired, now strucke out,
    Oft with his sword his foes fierce blowes he broake,
    And rather chose to warde, then beare his stroake.

12

But bould, and boult vpright *Argantes* fought,
Vnlike in gesture, like in skill and art,
His sword out stretcht before him farre he brought;
Nor would his weapon touch, but pierce his hart,
To catch his point prince *Tancred* stroue and sought,
But at his breast or helmes vnclosed part
    He threatned death, and would with stretcht out brand
    His entrance close, and fierce assaults withstand.

13

With a tall ship so doth a gallie fight,
When the still windes stirre not th'vnstable maine,
Where this in nimblenesse, as that in might,
Excels; that stands, this goes and comes againe,
And shifts from prow to poope with turnings light;
Meanwhile the other doth vnmou'd remaine,
    And on her nimble foe approcheth nie,
    Her weightie engins tumbleth downe from hie:

14

The christian sought to enter on his foe,
Voiding his point, which at his brest was bent;
Argantes at his face a thrust did throe,
Which while the prince awards, and doth preuent,
His ready hand the Pagan turned soe,
That all defence his quickenes farre orewent,
    And pierst his side, which done he said and smilde,
    'The craftsman is in his owne craft beguilde:'

12⁴ put < but

15

Tancredie bit his lips for scorne and shame,
Nor longer stood on points of fence and skill,
But to reuenge so fierce and fast he came,
As if his hand could not oretake his will,
And at his visour aiming iust, gan frame
To his proud boast an answere sharpe, but still
 Argantes broake the thrust; and at halfe sword,
 Swift, hardie, bould, in stept the christian lord.

16

With his left foote fast forward gan he stride,
And with his left the Pagans right arme hent,
With his right hand meanewhile the mans right side
He cut, he wounded, mangled, tore, and rent,
'To his victorious teacher (*Tancred* cride)
His conquerd scholler hath this answer sent;'
 Argantes chased, struggled, turnd and twind,
 Yet could not so his captiue arme vnbind:

17

His sword at last he let hang by the chaine,
And gripte his hardie foe in both his hands,
In his strong armes *Tancred* caught him againe,
And thus each other held and wrapt in bands.
With greater might *Alcides* did not straine,
The giant *Antheus* on the Libian sands,
 On holdfast knots their brawnie armes they cast,
 And whom he hateth most, each held embrast:

18

Such was their wrestling, such their shockes and throwes,:
That downe at once they tumbled both to ground,
Argantes (were it hap or skill who knowes)
His better hand loose and in freedome found;
But the good prince his hand more fit for blowes
With his huge weight the Pagan vnderbound;
 But he, his disaduantage great that knew,
 Let go his hold, and on his feete vpflew:

19

Farre slower rose th'vnweldie Saracine,
And caught a rappe ere he was reard vpright.
But as against the blustring windes a pine
Now bends his toppe, now lifts his head on hight,
His courage so (when it gan most decline)
The man r'enforced, and aduanst his might,
    And with fierce change of blowes renewed the fray,
    Where rage, for skill: horrour, for art bore sway.

20

The purple drops from *Tancreds* sides downe railed,
But from the Pagan ran whole streames of blood,
Wherewith his force grew weake, his courage quailed,
As fiers die which fuell want or food.
Tancred that saw his feeble arme now failed
To strike his blowes, that scant he stirr'd or stood,
    Asswagd his anger and his wrath alaid,
    And stepping backe, thus gently spoke and said.

21

'Yeeld hardie knight, and chance of warre, or mee
Confesse to haue subdew'd thee in this fight,
I will no trophee, triumph, spoile of thee,
Nor glorie wish, nor seeke a victors right:'
More terrible than earst, herewith grew hee,
And all awakt, his furie, rage and might,
    And said, 'dar'st thou of vantage speake or thinke?
    Or moue *Argantes* once to yeeld or shrinke?

22

'Vse, vse, thy vantage, thee and fortune both
I scorne, and punish will thy foolish pride:
As a hot brand flames most ere it forth go'th,
And dying blazeth bright on euery side;'
So he (when blood was lost) with anger wroth,
Reuiu'd his courage, when his puissance dide,
    And would his latest howre which now drew nie
    Illustrate with his end, and nobly die;

23

He ioin'd his left hand to her sister strong,
And with them both let fall his weightie blade.
Tancred to warde his blow his sword vp flong,
But that it smote aside, nor there it stade,
But from his shoulder to his side along
It glanst, and many wounds at once it made:
    Yet *Tancred* feared nought, for in his hart,
    Found coward dread no place, feare had no part.

24

His fearefull blow he doubled, but he spent
His force in wast, and all his strength in vaine:
For *Tancred* from the blow against him bent
Leaped aside, the stroke fell on the plaine,
With thine owne weight orethrowne to earth thou went
(*Argantes* stout) nor could'st thy selfe sustaine,
    Thy selfe thou threwest downe, O happie man!
    Vpon whose fall none boast, or triumph can:

25

His gaping wounds the fall set open wide,
The streames of blood about him made a lake,
Helpt with his left hand on one knee he tride
To reare himselfe, and new defence to make:
The curteous Prince stept backe, and 'yeeld thee,' cride,
No hurt he profred him, no blow he strake.
    Mean while by stealth the Pagan false him gaue
    A sodaine wound, threat'ning with speeches braue:

26

Herewith *Tancredie* furious grew, and saide,
'Villaine, dost thou my mercie so despies?'
Therewith he thrust and thrust againe his blade,
And through his ventall pierst his dazeled eies:
Argantes dide, yet no complaint he made,
But as he furious liu'd, he carelesse dies;
    Bold, proud, disdainfull, fierce and voide of feare;
    His motions last, last lookes, last speeches weare.

27

Tancred put vp his sword, and praises glad
Gaue to his God, that sau'd him in this fight;
But yet this bloodie conquest feebled had
So much the conquerours force, strength, and might,
That through the way he fear'd which homeward lad
He had not strength enough to walke vpright;
    Yet as he could his steps from thence he bent,
    And foote by foot a heauie pace foorth went;

28

His legges could beare him but a little stound,
And more he hastes (more tirde) lesse was his speed,
On his right hand, at last, laid on the ground
He lean'd, his hand weake like a shaking reed,
Daz'led his eies, the world on wheeles ran round;
Day wrapt her brightnesse vp in sable weed;
    At length he swouned, and the victor knight
    Nought diffred from his conquer'd foe in sight.

29

But while these Lords their priuate fight pursue,
Made fierce and cruell through their secret hate,
The victors ire destroi'd the faithlesse crue
From street to street, and chas'd from gate to gate.
But of the sacked towne the image true
Who can describe? or paint the woefull state?
    Or with fit words this spectacle expresse
    Who can? or tell the cities great distresse?

30

Blood, murder, death, each streete, house, church defilde,
There heaps of slaine appeare, there mountaines hie;
There vnderneath th'vnburied hils vp-pilde
Of bodies dead, the liuing buried lie;
There the sad mother with her tender childe
Doth teare her tresses, loose, complaine, and flie,
    And there the spoiler (by her Amber haire)
    Drawes to his lust the virgin chast and faire.

30³ vppilde < vp-pilde (*cf. 1624*)

31

But through the way that to the West hill yood,
Whereon the old and stately temple stands,
All soild with gore, and wet with lukewarme blood
Rinaldo ronne, and chas'd the Pagan bands,
Aboue their heads he heau'd his curtlax good,
Life in his grace, and death lay in his hands;
   Nor helme nor target strong his blowes off beares,
   Best armed there seem'd he, no armes that weares;

32

For gainst his armed foes he onely bends
His force, and scornes the naked folke to wound;
Them whom no courage armes, no armes defends,
He chased with his lookes, and dreedfull sound:
Oh, who can tell how farre his force extends?
How these he scornes, threats those, laies them on ground?
   How with vnequall harme, with equall feare
   Fled all, all that well arm'd or naked weare,

33

Fast fled the people weake, and with the same
A squadron strong is to the temple gone,
Which burnt and builded oft, still keepes the name
Of the first founder, wise king *Salomone,*
That Prince this stately house did whilome frame
Of Cedar trees of gold and marble stone;
   Now not so ritch, yet strong and sure it was,
   With turrets hie, thicke wals, and doores of bras.

34

The knight arriued where in warlike sort
The men that ample church had fortified,
And closed found each wicket, gate and port,
And on the top defences readie spied,
He lift his frowning lookes and twise that fort
From his high top downe to the groundworke eied,
   And entrance sought, and twise with his swift fout
   The mightie place he measured about.

35

Like as a Wolfe about the closed fold
Rangeth by night his hoped pray to get,
Enrag'd with hunger, and with malice old,
Which kinde twixt him and harmelesse sheepe hath set.
So searcht he high and low about that hold,
Where he might enter without stop or let,
    In the great court he stai'd, his foes aboue
    Attend th'assault, and would their fortune proue.

36

There lay by chance a posted tree therebie,
Kept for some needfull use, what ere it were,
The armed gallies not so thicke nor hie
Their tail and loftie masts at Genes vpreare;
This beame the knight against the gates made flie
From his strong hands, all weights which lift and beare,
    Like a light lance the tree he shooke and tost,
    And brus'd the gate, the threshold, and the post.

37

No marble stone, no mettall strong outbore
The wondrous might, of that redoubled blow,
The brasen henges from the walles it tore,
It broke the lockes, and laid the dores downe low,
No iron ramme, no engin could do more,
Nor cannons great that thunderbolts forth throw,
    His people like a flowing streame inthrong,
    And after them entred the victor strong;

38

The wofull slaughter blacke and loathsome maid
That house, sometime the sacred house of God,
O heau'nly iustice! if thou be delaid
On wretched sinners sharper fals thy rod,
In them this place profaned which inuaid
Thou kindled ire, and mercy all forbod,
    Vntill with their hart blouds the Pagans vile
    This temple washt, which they did late defile.

37⁴ breoke < broke (*corrected in Ch Ch*)

39

But *Soliman* this while himselfe fast sped
Vp to the fort, which *Dauids* towre is named,
And with him all the souldiers left he led,
And gainst each entrance new defences framed:
The tyrant *Aladine* eeke thither fled,
To whom the Soldan thus (farre off) exclamed,
   'Come, come, renowned king, vp to this rocke,
   Thy selfe, within this fortresse safe vplocke:

40

'For well this fortresse shall thee and thy crowne
Defend, awhile heere may we safe remaine.'
'Alas (quoth he) alas, for this faire towne,
Which cruell warre beates downe eeu'n with the plaine,
My life is done, mine empire troden downe,
I raind, I liu'd, but now nor liue nor raine;
   For now (alas) behold the fatall howre,
   That ends our liues, and ends our kingly powre.'

41

'Where is your vertue, where your wisedome graue,
And courage stout?' the angrie Soldan said,
'Let chance our kingdomes take which earst she gaue;
Yet in our harts our kingly worth is laid;
But come and in this fort your person saue,
Refresh your wearie limmes and strength decaid:'
   Thus counseld he and did to saftie bring,
   Within that fort the weake and aged king.

42

His iron mace in both his hands he hent,
And on his thigh his trustie sword he tide,
And to the entrance fierce and fearlesse went,
And kept the strait, and all the French deside:
The blowes were mortall which he gaue or lent,
For whom he hit he slew, else by his side
   Laid low on earth, that all fled from the place
   Where they beheld that great and dreedfull mace.

43

But old *Raimondo* with his hardie crew
By chance came thither, to his great mishap,
To that defended path the old man flew,
And scorn'd his blowes and him that kept the gap,
He stroake his foe, his blow no blood foorth drew,
But on the front with that he caught a rap,
    Which in a swoune, low in the dust him laid,
    Wide open, trembling, with his armes displaid.

44

The Pagans gathred hart at last, though feare
Their courage weake had put to flight but late,
So that the conquerours repulsed weare,
And beaten backe, else slaine before the gate:
The Soldan (mongst the dead beside him neare
That saw Lord *Raimond* lie in such estate)
    Cride to his men, within these barres (quoth he)
    'Come draw this knight, and let him captiue be.'

45

Forward they rusht to execute his word,
But hard and dang'rous that emprise they found,
For none of *Raimonds* men forsooke their Lord,
But to their guides defence they flocked round,
Thence furie fights, hence pitie drawes the sword,
Nor striue they for vile cause, or on light ground,
    The life and freedome of that champion braue,
    Those spoile, these would preserue, those kill, these saue.

46

But yet at last (if they had longer fought)
The hardie Soldane would haue wonne the field;
For gainst his thundring mace auailed nought
Or helme of temper fine, or seu'nfold shield:
But from each side great succour now was brought
To his weake foes, now fit to faint and yield,
    And both at once to aide and helpe the same
    The souereigne Duke and yoong *Rinaldo* came.

47

As when a shepherd, raging round about
That fees a storme with winde, haile, thunder, raine,
(When gloomy cloudes haue daies bright eie put out)
His tender flockes driues from the open plaine,
To some thicke groue or mountaines shadie fout,
Where heau'ns fierce wrath they may vnhurt sustaine,
　　And with his hooke, his whistle and his cries
　　Driues foorth his fleecie charge, and with them flies:

48

So fled the Soldan, when he gan descrie
This tempest come from angrie warre foorth cast,
The armours clashte and lightned gainst the skie,
And from each side swords, weapons, fire out brast:
He sent his folke vp to the fortresse hie,
To shunne the furious storme, himselfe staid last,
　　Yet to the danger he gaue place at length,
　　For wit, his courage; wisedome, rulde his strength.

49

But scant the knight was safe the gate within,
Scant closed were the doores, when hauing broake
The barres, *Rinaldo* doth assault begin
Against the port, and on the wicket stroake
His matchlesse might, his great desire to win,
His oath and promise, doth his wrath prouoake,
　　For he had sworne (nor should his word be vaine)
　　To kill the man that had Prince *Sweno* slaine.

50

And now his armed hand that castle great
Would haue assaulted, and had shortly wonne,
Nor safe pardie the Soldan there a seat
Had found his fatall foes sharpe wrath to shonne,
Had not *Godfredo* sounded the retreat;
For now darke shades to shrowd the earth begonne,
　　Within the towne the Duke would lodge that night
　　And with the morne renew th'assault and fight.

51

With cheerefull looke thus to his folke he said,
'High God hath holpen well his children deare,
This worke is donne, the rest this night delai'd
Doth little labour bring, lesse doubt, no feare,
This towre (our foes weake hope and latest aid)
We conquer will, when sunne shall next appeare:
　　Meane-while with loue and tender ruth goe see
　　And comfort those which hurt and wounded bee;

52

'Goe cure their wounds which boldly ventured
Their liues, and spilt their bloods to get this hold,
That fitteth more this host for Christ forth led,
Then thirst of veng'ance, or desire of gold;
Too much (ah) too much blood this day is shed!
In some we too much haste to spoile behold,
　　But I command no more you spoile and kill,
　　And let a trumpet publish forth my will;'

53

This said, he went where *Raimond* panting lay,
Wakt from the swoune wherein he late had beene.
Nor *Soliman* with countenance lesse gay
Bespake his troupes, and kept his griefe vnseene;
'My friends, you are vnconquered this day,
In spite of fortune, still our hope is greene,
　　For vnderneath great showes of harme and feare,
　　Our dangers small, our losses little weare:

54

'Burnt are your houses, and your people slaine,
Yet safe your towne is, though your walles be gone,
For in your selues and in your souereigne
Consists your citie, not in lime and stone;
Your king is safe, and safe is all his traine,
In this strong fort defended from their fone,
　　And on this emptie conquest let them bost,
　　Till with this towne againe, their liues be lost;

55

'And on their heads the losse at last will light,
For with for goodtune proud and insolent,
In spoile and murder spend they day and night,
In riot, drinking, lust and rauishment,
And may amid their prayes with little fight
At ease be ouerthrowne, kild, slaine and spent,
 If in this carelesnesse th'Egyptian hoast
 Vpon them fall, which now drawes neere this coast.

56

'Mean-while the highest buildings of this towne
We may shake downe with stones, about their eares,
And with our dartes and speares from engins throwne,
Commaund that hill Christs sepulchre that beares:'
Thus comforts he their hopes and harts cast downe,
Awakes their valours, and exiles their feares.
 But while these things hapt thus, *Vafrino* goes
 Vnknowne, amid ten thousand armed foes.

57

The sunne nie set had brought to ende the day,
When *Vafrine* went the Pagan hoste to spie,
He past vnknowne a close and secret way;
A traueller, false, cunning, craftie, slie,
Past Ascalon he saw the morning gray
Step ore the threshold of the Estren skie,
 And ere bright Titan, halfe his course had runne,
 That campe, that mightie hoste to show begunne.

58

Tents infinite and standards broad he spies,
This red, that white, that blew, this purple was,
And heares strange toongs, and stranger harmonies
Of trumpets, clarions, and well sounding bras:
The Elephant there braies, the Camell cries;
The horses neigh as to and fro they pas:
 Which seene and heard, he said within his thought,
 'Hither all Asia is, all Affricke, brought.'

58³ harmornies < harmonies (*cf. 1624*)

59

He view'd the campe awhile, her scite and seat,
What ditch, what trench it had, what rampire strong,
Nor close, nor secret waies to worke his feat
He longer sought, nor hid him from the throng;
But entred through the gates, broad, roiall, great,
And oft he askt, and answer'd oft among,
    In questions wise, in answeres short and slie;
    Bold was his looke, eies quicke, front lifted hie:

60

On euerie side he pried here and theare,
And markt each way, each passage and each tent:
The knights he notes, their steads, and armes they beare;
Their names, their armours and their gouerment,
And greater secrets hopes to learne, and heare
Their hidden purpose, and their close entent:
    So long he walkt and wandred, till he spide
    The way t'approch the great Pauilions side;

61

There as he lookte, he saw the canuasse rent,
Through which the voice found eath and open way,
From the close lodgings of the regall tent,
And inmost closet, where the captaine lay;
So that if *Emireno* spake, forth went
The sound to them that listen what they say,
    There *Vafrine* watcht, and those that saw him thought
    To mend the breach, that there he stood and wrought.

62

The captaine great within bare headed stood,
His bodie arm'd and clad in purple weed;
Two Pages bore his shield and helmet good,
He leaning on a bending launce, gaue heed
To a bigge man, whose lookes were fierce and prood,
With whom he parled of some haughtie deed,
    Godfredoes name as *Vafrine* watcht he hard,
    Which made him giue more heed, take more regard:

61⁶ They < The

63

Thus spake the Chieftaine to that surly sire,
'Art thou so sure that *Godfrey* shall be slaine?'
'I am (quoth he) and sweare nere to retire
(Except he first be kill'd) to court againe,
I will preuent those that with me conspire:
Nor other guerdon aske I for my paine,
　　But that I may hang vp his harnesse braue
　　At Caire, and vnder them these words engraue,

64

'"These armes *Ormondo* tooke in noble fight
From *Godfrey* proud, that spoil'd all Asias lands,
And with them tooke his life, and here on hight
(In memorie thereof) this trophie stands." '
The Duke replide, 'nere shall that deed (bold knight)
Passe vnrewarded at our sou'raignes hands,
　　What thou demaundest shall he gladly grant,
　　Nor gold nor guerdon shalt thou wish, or want.

65

'Those counterfeited armours than prepare,
Bicause the day of fight approacheth fast,'
'They readie are' (quoth he:) then both forbare
From further talke, these speeches were the last.
Vafrine (these great things heard) with griefe and care
Remain'd astound, and in his thoughts oft cast
　　What treason false this was, how feigned weare
　　Those armes, but yet that doubt he could not cleare.

66

From thence he parted, and broad waking lay
All that long night, nor slumbred once nor slept:
But when the campe by peepe of springing day
Their banners spred, and knights on horsebacke lept,
With them he marched foorth in meete array,
And where they pitched, lodg'd, and with them kept,
　　And then from tent to tent he stalkt about,
　　To heare and see, and learne this secret out;

67

Searching about on a ritch throne he fand
Armida set, with dames and knights around,
Sullen she sate, and sigh'd, it seemd she scand
Some weightie matters in her thoughts profound,
Her rosie cheeke leand on her lillie hand,
Her eies (loues twinckling stars) she bent to ground,
  Weepe she, or no, he knowes not, yet appeares
  Her humid eies eu'n great with childe with teares.

68

He sawe before her set *Adrastus* grim,
That seemed scant to liue, mooue, or respire,
So was he fixed on his mistres trim,
So gazed he, and fed his fond desire;
But *Tisiperne* beheld now her, now him,
And quakte, sometime for loue, sometime for ire,
  And in his cheekes the colour went and came,
  For their wrathes fire now burnt, now shone loues flame.

69

Then from the garland faire of virgins bright,
(Mongst whom he lay enclosd rose), *Altamore*,
His hot desire he hid and kept from sight,
His lookes were ruld by *Cupids* craftie lore,
His left eie viewd her hand, her face; his right
Both watcht her beauties hid, and secret store,
  And entrance found where her thin vaile bewraid
  The milken way betweene her breasts that laid.

70

Her eies *Armida* lift from earth at last,
And cleard againe her front and visage sad,
Midst clouds of woe her lookes which ouercast
She lightned foorth a smile, sweete, pleasant, glad;
'My Lord (quoth she) your oath and promise past,
Hath freed my hart of all the griefes it had,
  That now in hope of sweete reuenge it liues,
  Such ioy, such ease, desired vengeance giues.'

71

'Cheare vp thy lookes (answer'd the Indian king)
And for sweete beauties sake, appease thy woe,
Cast at your feete ere you expect the thing,
I will present the head of thy strong foe;
Else shall this hand his person captiue bring
And cast in prison deepe, he boasted soe.'
　　His riuall heard him well, yet answerd nought,
　　But bit his lips, and grieu'd in secret thought.

72

To *Tisiphern* the damsell turning right,
'And what say you, my noble lord?' (quoth she)
He taunting said, 'I, that am slow to fight
Will follow farre behinde, the worth to see
Of this your terrible and puissant knight,'
In scornefull words this bitter scoffe gaue hee.
　　'Good reason (quoth the king) thou come behinde,
　　Nor ere compare thee with the prince of Inde.'

73

Lord *Tisiphernes* shooke his head, and said,
'Oh had my powre free like my courage beene,
Or had I libertie to use this blade,
Who slow, who weakest is, soone should be seene,
Nor thou, nor thy great vants make me affraid,
But cruell loue I feare, and this faire queene.'
　　This said, to chalenge him the king foorth lept,
　　But vp their mistresse start and twixt them stept:

74

'Will you thus robbe me of that gift (quoth shee)
Which each hath vowd to giue by word and oth?
You are my champions, let that title bee
The bond of loue and peace, betweene you both;
He that displeasd is, is displeasd with mee
For which of you is grieud, and I not wroth?'
　　Thus warnd she them, their harts (for ire nie broake)
　　In forced peace and rest, thus bore loues yoake.

75

All this heard *Vafrine* as he stood beside,
And hauing learn'd the troth, he left the tent,
That treason was against the christians guide
Contriud, he wist, yet wist not how it went,
By words, and questions farre off, he tride
To finde the truth, more difficult, more bent
   Was he to know it, and resolued to die,
   Or of that secret close th'entent to spie.

76

Of slie intelligence he prou'd all waies,
All crafts, all wiles, that in his thoughts abid,
Yet all in vaine the man by wit assaies,
To know that false compact and practise hid:
But chance (what wisdome could not tell) bewraies,
Fortune of all his doubt the knots vndid,
   So that prepard for *Godfreies* last mishappe
   (At ease) he found the net, and spide the trappe.

77

Thither he turnd againe, where seated was
The angrie louer, twixt her friends and lords,
For in that troupe much talke he thought would pas,
Each great assemblie store of newes affords,
He sided there a lustie louely las,
And with some courtly tearmes the wench he bords,
   He faines acquaintance, and as bold appeares
   As he had knowne that virgin twentie yeares:

78

He said, 'would some sweete ladie grace me soe,
To chuse me for her champion, friend, and knight,
Proud *Godfreies* or *Rinaldoes* head (I troe)
Should feele the sharpnes of my curtlax bright;
Aske me the head (faire mistresse) of some foe,
For to your beautie vowed is my might,'
   So he began, and ment in speeches wise
   Further to wade, but thus he brake the ise:

79

Therewith he smild, and smiling gan to frame
His lookes, so to their ould and natiue grace,
That towards him another virgin came,
Heard him, beheld him, and with bashfull face
Said, 'for thy mistresse chuse no other dame
But me, on me thy loue and seruice place,
   I take thee for my champion, and apart
   Would reason with thee, if my knight thou art.'

80

Withdrawne, she thus began, '*Vafrine* (pardie)
I know thee well, and me thou knowst of old,'
To his last trumpe this droue the subtile spie,
But smiling towards her he turnd him bold,
'Nere that I wote I saw thee earst with eie,
Yet for thy worth all eies should thee behold,
   Thus much I know right well, for from the same
   Which earst you gaue me diffrent is my name.

81

'My mother bore me neere *Bisertas* wall,
Her name was *Lesbine*, mine is *Almansore*:'
'I knew long since (quoth she) what men thee call,
And thine estate, dissemble it no more,
From me thy friend hide not thy selfe at all,
If I bewraie thee let me die therefore,
   I am *Erminia*, daughter to a prince,
   But *Tancreds* slaue, thy fellow seruant since;

82

Two happie months within that prison kind,
Vnder thy guard, reioiced I to dwell,
And thee a keeper meeke and good did find,
The same, the same I am; behould me well.'
The squire her louely beautie call'd to mind,
And markt her visage faire: 'from thee expell
   All feare (she saies) for me liue safe and sure,
   I will thy safetie, not thy harme procure.

83

'But yet I praie thee (when thou dost retorne)
To my deare prison lead me home againe;
For in this hatefull freedome eau'n and morne
I sigh for forrow, mourne and weepe for paine:
But if to spie perchance thou here soiorne,
Great hap thou hast, to know their secrets plaine,
   For I their treasons false, false traines, can say,
   Which fewe beside can tell, none will bewray.'

84

On her he gazd, and silent stood this while,
Armidas sleights he knew, and traines vniust,
Women haue toongs of craft, and harts of guile,
They will, they will not, fooles that on them trust,
For in their speech, is death; hell, in their smile;
At last he said, 'if hence depart you lust,
   I will you guide, on this conclude we heare,
   And further speech, till fitter time, forbeare.'

85

Forthwith (ere thence the campe remooue) to ride
They were resolu'd, their flight that season fits,
Vafrine departs, she to the dames beside
Returnes, and there on thornes awhile she sits,
Of her new knight she talkes, till time and tide
To scape vnmarkt she finde, then forth she gits,
   Thither where *Vafrine* her vnseene abode,
   There tooke shee horse, and from the campe they rode.

86

And now in desarts waste and wilde arriued,
Farre from the campe, farre from resort and sight,
Vafrine began, gainst *Godfreies* life contriued
The false compacts and traines vnfould aright:
Then she those treasons (from their spring deriued)
Repeats, and brings their hid deceits to light,
   'Eight knights' she saies, '(all courtiers braue) there arre,
   (But *Ormond* strong, the rest surpasseth farre)

87

'These (whether hate or hope of gaine them moue)
Conspired haue, and fram'd their treason soe,
That day when *Emiren* by fight shall proue
To winne lost Asia from his christian foe,
These, with the crosse scor'd on their armes aboue,
And armd like Frenchmen, will disguised goe,
   Like *Godfreies* guard that gould and white do weare,
   Such shall their habite be, and such their geare:

88

'Yet each will beare a token in his crest,
That so their friends for Pagans may them know:
But in close fight when all the souldiours best
Shall mingled be, to giue the fatall blow,
They will creepe neere, and pierce *Godfredoes* brest,
While of his faithfull guard they beare false show,
   And all their swords are dipt in poison strong,
   Bicause each wound shall bring sad death ere long.

89

'And for their chiefetaine wist I knew your guize,
What garments, ensignes, and what armes you carrie,
Those feigned armes he forst me to deuize,
So that from yours but small or nought they varrie:
But these vniust commands my thoughts despize,
Within their campe therefore I list not tarrie,
   My hart abhorres I should this hand defile
   With spot of treason, or with act of guile.

90

'This is the cause, but not the cause alone:'
And there she ceast, and blusht, and on the maine
Cast downe her eies, these last words scant outgone,
She would haue stopt, nor durst pronounce them plaine.
The squire, what she conceald, would know, as one
That from her breast her secret thoughts could straine,
   'Of little faith (quoth he) why wouldst thou hide
   Those causes true, from me thy squire and guide?'

91

With that she fecht a sigh, sad, sore, and deepe,
And from her lips her words slow, trembling came,
'Fruitlesse (she said) vntimely, hard to keepe,
Vaine modestie farewell, and farewell shame,
Why hope you restlesse loue to bring on sleepe?
Why striue your fires to quench sweete *Cupids* flame?
　　No, no, such cares, and such respects beseeme
　　Great Ladies, wandring maides them nought esteeme.

92

'That night, fatall to me and Antioch towne,
Then made a praie to her commaunding foe,
My losse was greater than was seene or knowne,
There ended not, but thence began my woe:
Light was the losse of friends, of Realme or crowne;
But with my state, I lost my selfe alsoe,
　　Nere to be found againe, for then I lost
　　My wit, my sense, my hart, my soule almost.

93

'Through fire and sword, through blood and death (*Vafrine*)
(Which all my friends did burne, did kill, did chace)
Thou know'st I ronne to thy deere Lord and mine,
When first he entred had my fathers place,
And kneeling with salt teares in my swolne eine;
"Great Prince (quoth I) grant mercie, pitie, grace,
　　Saue not my kingdome, not my life I saide,
　　But saue mine honour, let me die a maide." '

94

'He lift me by the trembling hand from ground,
Nor staide he till my humble speech was donne;
But said, "a friend and keeper hast thou found
(Faire virgin) nor to me in vaine you ronne:"
A sweetnesse strange from that sweet voices sound
Pierced my hart, my brests weake fortresse wonne,
　　Which creeping through my bosome soft, became
　　A wound, a sickenes, and a quenchlesse flame.

95

'He visits me, with speeches kinde and graue
He sought to ease my griefes, and sorrowes smart:
He said, I giue thee libertie, recaue
All that is thine, and at thy will depart:
Alas, he robb'd me when he thought he gaue,
Free was *Erminia*: but captiu'd her hart,
 Mine was the bodie, his the soule and minde,
 He gaue the cage, but kept the birde behinde.

96

'But who can hide desire, or loue suppresse?
Oft of his worth with thee in talke I stroue,
Thou (by my trembling fit that well couldst guesse
What feauer held me) saidst, thou art in loue;
But I denaid for what can maids doe lesse?
And yet my sighes thy sayings true did proue,
 In stead of speech, my lookes, my teares, mine eies,
 Told in what flame, what fire, thy mistresse fries.

97

'Vnhappie silence, well I might haue told
My woes, and for my harmes haue sought reliefe,
Since now my paines and plaints I vtter bold,
Where none that heares can helpe or ease my griefe:
From him I parted, and did close vpfold
My wounds within my bosome, death was chiefe
 Of all my hopes and helpes, till loues sweet flame
 Pluckt off the bridle of respect and shame,

98

'And caus'd me ride to seeke my Lord and knight,
For he that made me sicke could make me sound:
But on an ambush I mischanst to light
Of cruell men, in armour clothed round,
Hardly I scapt their hands by mature flight,
And fled to wildernesse and desart ground,
 And there I liu'd in groues and forrests wilde,
 With gentle groomes and shepheards daughters milde.

99

'But when hot loue, which feare had late supprest,
Reuiu'd againe, there nould I longer fit,
But rode the way I came, not ere tooke rest,
Till on like danger, like mishap I hit,
A troupe to forrage and to spoile addrest.
Encountred me, nor could I flie from it:
    Thus was I tane, and those that had me cought
    Egyptians were, and me to Gaza brought,

100

'And for a present to their captaine gaue,
Whom I entreated and besought so well,
That he mine honour had great care to saue,
And since with faire *Armida* let me dwell.
Thus taken oft, escaped oft I haue,
Ah, see what haps I past, what dangers fell,
    So often captiue, free so oft againe,
    Still my first bandes I keepe, still my first chaine.

101

'And he that did this chaine so surely binde
About my hart, which none can loose but hee,
Let him not say, goe (wandring damsell) finde
Some other home, thou shalt not bide with mee,
But let him welcome me with speeches kinde,
And in my wonted prison set me free:'
    Thus spake the Princesse, thus she and her guide
    Talkt day and night, and on their iourney ride.

102

Through the high waies *Vafrino* would not pas,
A path more secret, safe and short, he knew,
And now close by the cities wall he was,
When sunne was set, night in the East vpflew,
With drops of blood besmeerd he found the gras,
And saw where lay a warriour murdred new,
    That all bebled the ground, his face to skies
    He turnes, and seemes to threat, though dead he lies:

101⁸ ride, < ride.

103

His harnesse and his habit both bewraid
He was a Pagan, forward went the squire,
And saw whereas another champion laid
Dead on the land, all soild with blood and mire,
This was some Christian knight *Vafrino* said;
And marking well his armes and ritch attire,
   He loos'd his helme, and saw his visage plaine,
   And cride, alas, here lies *Tancredie* slaine!

104

The woefull virgin tarried, and gaue heed
To the fierce lookes of that proud Saracine,
Till that high crie (full of sad feare and dreed)
Pierst through her hart with sorrow, griefe and pine,
At *Tancreds* name thither she ranne with speed,
Like one halfe mad, or drunke with too much wine,
   And when she sawe his face, pale, bloodlesse, dead,
   She lighted, nay, she tumbled from her stead:

105

Her springs of teares she looseth foorth, and cries
'Hither why bringst thou me, ah fortune blinde?
Where dead (for whom I liu'd) my comfort lies,
Where warre, for peace; trauell for rest I finde;
Tancred, I haue thee, see thee, yet thine eies
Lookte not vpon thy loue and handmaide kinde,
   Vndoe their doores, their lids fast closed seuer,
   Alas, I finde thee for to lose thee euer.

106

'I neuer thought that to mine eies (my deare)
Thou could'st haue greeuous or vnpleasant beene;
But now would blinde or rather dead I weare,
That thy sad plight might be vnknowne, vnseene,
Alas, where is thy mirth and smiling cheare?
Where are thine eies cleere beames and sparkles sheene?
   Of thy faire cheeke where is the purple read,
   And foreheads whitnes? are all gone, all dead?

107

'Though gone, though dead, I loue thee still behold;
Death wounds, but kils not loue; yet if thou liue
Sweete soule, still in his brest, my follies bold
Ah, pardon, loues, desires and stealthes forgiue;
Grant me from his pale mouth some kisses cold,
Since death doth loue of iust reward depriue;
   And of thy spoiles sad death affoord me this,
   Let me his mouth pale, cold and bloodlesse kis;

108

'O gentle mouth! with speeches kinde and sweete,
Thou didst relieue my griefe, my woe and paine,
Ere my weake soule from this fraile bodie fleete,
Ah, comfort me with one deare kisse or twaine,
Perchance if we aliue had hapt to meete,
They had beene giu'n which now are stolne, O vaine,
   O feeble life, betwixt his lips out flie,
   O let me kisse thee first, then let me die!

109

'Receiue my yeilded spirit, and with thine
Guide it to heau'n, where all true loue hath place:'
This saide, she sigh'd, and tore her tresses fine,
And from her eies two streames powrde on his face,
The man reuiued with those showres diuine,
Awakt, and opened his lips a space:
   His lips were open; but fast shut his eies,
   And with her sighes, one sigh from him vpflies.

110

The dame perceiu'd that *Tancred* breath'd and sight,
Which calm'd her griues somedeale and eas'd her feares:
'Vnclose thine eies she saies) my Lord and knight,
See my last seruices, my plaints and teares,
See her that dies to see thy woefull plight,
That of thy paine her part and portion beares,
   Once looke on me, small is the gift I craue,
   The last which thou canst giue, or I can haue.'

111

Tancred lookt vp, and clos'd his eies againe,
Heauie and dim, and she renew'd her woe:
Quoth *Vafrine*, 'cure him first, and then complaine,
Med'cine is lifes chiefe friend; plaint her most foe,'
They pluckt his armour off, and she each vaine,
Each ioint, and sinew felt, and handled soe,
    And searcht so well, each thrust, each cut and wound,
    That hope of life her loue and skill soone found.

112

From wearinesse and losse of blood she spide
His greatest paines and anguish most proceede,
Nought but her vaile amid those desarts wide
She had to binde his wounds, in so great neede,
But loue could other bands (though strange) prouide,
And pitie wept for ioy to see that deede,
    For with her amber lockes cut off each wound
    She tide: O happie man, so cur'd, so bound!

113

For why her vaile was short and thin, those deepe
And cruell hurtes to fasten, rowle, and binde,
Nor salue, nor simple had she, yet to keepe
Her knight on liue, strong charmes of wondrous kinde
She said, and from him droue that deadly sleepe,
That now his eies he lifted, turn'd and twinde,
    And saw his squire, and saw that curteous dame
    In habit strange, and wondred whence she came.

114

He said, 'O *Vafrine*, tell me, whence com'st thow?
And who this gentle surgeon is, disclose;'
She smil'd, she sigh'd, she lookt she wist not how,
She wept, reioist, she blusht as red as rose,
'You shall know all (she saies) your surgeon now
Commands you silence, rest, and soft repose,
    You shall be sound, prepare my guerdon meete,'
    His head then laid she in her bosome sweete.

115

Vafrine deuis'd this while how he might beare
His maister home, ere night obscur'd the land,
When loe a troupe of soldiers did appeare,
Whom he descride to be *Tancredies* band,
With him when he and *Argant* met they weare;
But when they went to combat hand for hand,
 He bod them stay behinde, and they obaid,
 But came to seeke him now, so long he staid.

116

Besides them, many follow'd that enquest,
But these alone found out the rightest way,
Vpon their friendly armes the men addrest
A seat, whereon he sate, he lean'd, he lay:
(Quoth *Tancred*) 'shall the strong Circassian rest
In this broad field, for wolues and crowes a pray?
 Ah no, defraud not you that champion braue
 Of his iust praise, of his due tombe and graue,

117

'With his dead bones no longer warre haue I,
Boldly he dide, and noblie was he slaine,
Then let vs not that honour him denie,
Which after death alonely doth remaine:'
The Pagan dead they lifted vp on hie,
And after *Tancred* bore him through the plaine.
 Close by the virgin chast did *Vafrine* ride,
 As he that was her squire, her guard, her guide.

118

'Not home (quoth *Tancred*) to my wonted tent,
But beare me to this roiall towne, I pray,
That if cut short by humaine accident
I die, there I may see my latest day,
The place where Christ vpon his crosse was rent,
To heau'n perchance may easier make the way,
 And ere I yeeld to deathes and fortunes rage,
 Perform'd shall be my vow and pilgrimage.'

118⁸ pilgririage, < pilgrimage. (*cf. 1624*)

119

Thus to the cittie was *Tancredie* borne,
And fell on sleepe, laid on a bed of downe.
Vafrino where the damsell might soiorne,
A chamber got, close, secret, neere his owne:
That done he came the mightie Duke beforne,
And entrance found, for till his newes were knowne
　　Nought was concluded mongst those knights & Lords,
　　Their counsell hung on his report and words.

120

Where weake and wearie wounded *Raimond* laid,
Godfrey was set vpon his couches side,
And round about the man a ring was maid
Of lords and knights, that fild the chamber wide;
There while the squire his late discou'rie said,
To breake his talke none answerd, none replide,
　　'My lord (he said) at your command I went
　　And vew'd their campe, each cabbin, booth and tent;

121

'But of that mightie hoast the number trew
Expect not that I can, or should descrie,
All couerd with their armies might you vew
The fieldes, the plaines, the dales and mountaines hie,
I saw what way so ere they went and drew,
They spoild the land, drunke flouds and fountaines drie,
　　For not whole Iordan could haue giu'n them drinke,
　　Nor all the graine in Syria, bread, I thinke.

122

'But yet amongst them many bands are found
Both horse and foote, of little force and might,
That keep no order, know no trumpets found,
That draw no sword, but farre off shoot and fight,
But yet the Persian army doth abound
With many a footeman strong, and hardie knight,
　　So doth the kings owne troupe which all is framed
　　Of souldiours old, th'immortall squadron named.

123

'Immortall called is that band of right,
For of that number neuer wanteth one,
But in his emptie place some other knight
Steps in, when any man is dead or gone:
This armies leader *Emireno* hight,
Like whom in wit and strength are fewe or none,
    Who hath in charge in plaine and pitched feild,
    To fight with you, to make you flie or yeild.

124

'And well I know their armie and their host,
Within a day or two, will here arriue:
But thee, *Rinaldo*, it behooueth most
To keepe thy noble head, for which they striue,
For all the chiefe in armes or courage, bost
They will the same to queene *Armida* giue,
    And for the same she giues her selfe in price,
    Such hire will many hands to worke entice.

125

'The chiefe of these (that haue thy murder sworne)
Is *Altamore*, the king of Sarmachand;
Adrastus then, whose realme lies neere the morne,
A hardie giant, bould, and strong of hand,
This king vpon an elephant is borne,
For vnder him no horse can stirre or stand;
    The third is *Tisipherne*, as braue a lord
    As euer put on helme, or guirt on sword.'

126

This said, from yong *Rinaldoes* angrie eies
Flew sparks of wrath, flames in his visage shinde,
He long'd to be amid those enimies,
Nor rest nor reason in his hart could finde.
But to the Duke *Vafrine* his talke applies,
'The greatest newes (my Lord) are yet behinde,
    For all their thoughts, their crafts and counsels tend
    By treason false to bring thy life to end:'

127

Then all from point to point he gan expose
The false compact, how it was made and wrought,
The armes and ensignes fained, poison close,
Ormondos vant, what praise, what thanke he sought,
And what reward, and satisfide all those
That would demaund, enquire, or aske of ought,
  Silence was made a while, when *Godfrey* thus,
  '*Raimondo* say, what counsell giu'st thou vs?'

128

'Not as we purpos'd late, next morne (quoth hee)
Let vs not scale, but round besiege this towre,
That those within may haue no issue free
To sallie out, and hurt vs with their powre,
Our campe well rested and refreshed see,
Prouided well gainst this last storme and showre,
  And then in pitched field, fight, if you will;
  If not, delay, and keepe this fortresse still:

129

'But least you be endangred, hurt or slaine,
Of all your cares take care your selfe to saue,
By you this campe doth liue, doth winne, doth raine,
Who else can rule or guide these squadrons braue?
And for the traitors shall be noted plaine,
Command your garde to change the armes they haue,
  So shall their guile be knowne, in their owne net
  So shall they fall, caught in the snare they set.'

130

'As it hath euer (thus the Duke begonne)
Thy counsell shewes thy wisdome and thy loue,
And what you left in doubt, shall thus be donne,
We will their force in pitched battell proue;
Clos'd in this wall and trench, the fight to shonne,
Doth ill this campe beseeme, and worse behoue,
  But we their strength and manhood will assay,
  And trie, in open field and open day.

131

'The fame of our great conquests to sustaine,
Or bide our lookes and threates, they are not able,
And when this armie is subdu'd and slaine,
Then is our empire setled, firme and stable,
The towre shall yeeld, or but resist in vaine,
For feare her anchor is, despaire her cable,'
    Thus he concludes, and rowling downe the west
    Fast set the starres, and call'd them all to rest.

The twentieth Booke of Godfrey of Bulloigne

The argument.

The Pagan host arriues, and cruell fight
Makes with the Christians, and their faithfull powre;
The Soldan longs in field to proue his might,
With the old king quits the besieged towre;
Yet both are slaine and in eternall night
A famous hand giues each his fatall howre;
Rinald appeast Armida; first the feild
The Christians winne; then praise to God they yeild.

1

THe sunne call'd vp the world from idle sleepe,
   And of the day ten howres were gone and past,
When the bould troupe that had the towre to keepe,
Espide a sodaine mist, that ouercast
The earth, with mirksome clouds and darknes deepe,
And sawe it was th'Egyptian campe at last,
   Which rais'd the dust, for hils and valleies broad
   That hoast did ouerspread and ouerload:

2

Therewith a merrie shout and ioyfull crie
The Pagans reard, from their besieged hold;
The cranes from Thrace with such a rumour flie,
His hoarie frost and snow when Hyems old
Powres downe, and fast to warmer regions hie,
From the sharpe winds, fierce stormes and tempests cold,
   And quicke and readie this new hope and aid,
   Their hands, to shoot; their toongs to threaten maid.

3

From whence their ire, their wrath and hardie threat
Proceeds, the French well knew, and plaine espide,

3⁴ strenght, < strength,

For from the wals and ports the army great
They saw, her strength, her number, pompe and pride,
Swelled their brests with valours noble heat,
Battaile and fight they wisht, 'arme, arme', they cride,
  The youth to giue the signe of fight all praid
  Their Duke, and were displeasd, bicause delaid,

4

Till morning next for he refusd to fight,
Their haste and heat he bridled, but not brake,
Nor yet with sodaine fray or skirmish light,
Of these new foes would he vaine triall make,
'After so many warres (he saies) good right
It is, that one daies rest at least you take,'
  For thus in his vaine foes he cherish would
  The hope, which in their strength they haue and hould.

5

To see Auroras gentle beame appeare,
The souldiers armed, prest and ready lay,
The skies were neuer halfe so faire and cleare,
As in the breaking of that blessed day,
The merrie morning smild, and seemed to weare
Vpon her siluer crowne, suns golden ray,
  And without cloud, heau'n his redoubled light
  Bent downe, to see this field, this fray, this fight.

6

When first he sawe the day breake, shew and shine,
Godfrey his hoast in good array brought out,
And to besiege the tyrant *Aladine*
Raimond he left, and all the faithfull rout,
That from the townes was come of Palestine,
To serue and succour their deliuerer stout,
  And with them left a hardie troupe beside
  Of Gascoignes strong; in armes well prou'd, oft tride.

7

Such was *Godfredoes* count'nance, such his cheare,
That from his eie sure conquest flames and streames,

Heau'ns gracious fauours in his lookes appeare,
And great and goodly more than earst he seames,
His face and forehead full of noblesse weare,
And on his cheeke smiled youthes purple beames
    And in his gate, his grace, his actes, his eies
    Somewhat (farre more than mortall) liues and lies.

8

He had not marched farre, ere he espied
Of his proud foes the mightie hoast draw nie,
A hill at first he tooke, and fortified
At his left hand which stood his armie bie,
Broad in the front, behinde more straite vp tied,
His armie readie stoode the fight to trie,
    And to the middle ward well armed he brings
    His footemen strong, his horsemen serud for wings;

9

To the left wing, spred vnderneath the bent
Of the steepe hill, that sau'd their flanke and side,
The *Roberts* twaine, two leaders good, he sent;
His brother had the middle ward to guide;
To the right wing himselfe in person went,
Downe, where the plaine was dangrous, broad and wide,
    And where his foes with their great numbers, would
    Perchance enuiron round his squadrons bould.

10

There all his Lorreners and men of might,
All his best armd he plast, and chosen bands,
And with those horse some footemen armed light,
That archers were, (vsd to that seruice stands,
Th'aduentrers then, in battaile and in fight
Well tride, a squadron famous through all lands,
    On the right hand he set, somedeale aside,
    Rinaldo was their leader, lord, and guide.

11

To whom the Duke, 'in thee our hope is laid
Of victorie, thou must the conquest gaine,

Behinde this mightie wing, so farre displaid,
Thou with thy noble squadron close remaine;
And when the Pagans would our backs inuaide,
Assaile them then, and make their onset vaine;
    For if I gesse aright, they haue in minde
    To compasse vs, and charge our troupes behinde.'

12

Then through his hoast, that tooke so large a scope,
He road, and vewd them all, both horse and fout,
His face was bare, his helme vnclos'd and ope,
Lightned his eies, his lookes bright fire shot out,
He cheers the fearefull, comforts them that hope,
And to the bould recounts his boasting stout,
    And to the valiant his aduentures hard,
    These bids he looke for praise, those for reward.

13

At last he staid, whereof his squadrons bold,
And noblest troupes, assembled was best part,
There from a rising banke his will he told,
And all that heard his speech thereat tooke hart:
And as the molten snow from mountaines cold
Runs downe in streames, with eloquence and art,
    So from his lips his words and speeches fell,
    Shrill, speedie, pleasant, sweete, and placed well.

14

'My hardie host, you conqu'rours of the East,
You scourge, wherewith Christ whips his heathen fone,
Of victorie, behould the latest feast,
See the last day, for which you wisht alone;
Not without cause the Sarzens most and least,
Our gracious Lord hath gathred here in one,
    For all your foes and his, assembled arre,
    That one daies fight may end seaune yeares of warre.

15

'This fight shall bring vs many victories,
The danger none, the labour will be small,

Let not the number of your enimies
Dismay your harts, grant feare no place at all;
For strife and discord through their armie flies,
Their bands ill rankt themselues entangle shall,
   And fewe of them to strike or fight shall come,
   For some want strength, some hart, some elbow rome.

16

'This host, with whom you must encounter now,
Are men halfe naked, without strength or skill,
From idlenes, or following the plow,
Late pressed foorth to warre, against their will,
Their swordes are blunt, shieldes thinne, soone pierced throw,
Their banners shake, their bearers shrinke, for ill
   Their leaders heard, obaid, or follow'd bee,
   Their losse, their flight, their death I well foresee:

17

'Their captaine, clad in purple, armd in gould,
That seemes so fierce, so hardie, stout and strong,
The Moores or weake Arabians vanquish could,
Yet can he not resist your valours long,
What can he do, (though wise, though sage, though bould)
In that confusion, trouble, thrust and throng?
   Ill knowne he is, and woorse he knowes his host,
   Strange lords ill feard are, ill obaid of most.

18

'But I am captaine of this chosen crew,
With whom I oft haue conquer'd, triumpht oft,
Your lands and linages long since I knew,
Each knight obaies my rule, milde, easie, soft,
I know each sword, each dart, each shaft I vew,
Although the quarrell flie in skies aloft,
   Whether the same of Ireland be or France,
   And from what bowe it comes, what hand perchance.

19

'I aske an easie, and an vsuall thing,
As you haue oft, this day, so winne the feild,

Let zeale and honour be your vertues sting,
Your liues, my fame, Christs faith, defend and sheild,
To earth these Pagans slaine and wounded bring,
Tread on their necks, make them all die or yeild,
   What need I more exhort you? from your eies
   I see how victorie, how conquest flies.'

20

Vpon the captaine (when his speech was donne)
It seemed a lampe and golden light downe came,
As from nights azure mantle oft doth ronne
Or fall, a sliding starre, or shining flame;
But from the bosome of the burning sonne
Proceeded this, and garland wise the same
   Godfredoes noble head encompast round,
   And (as some thought) foreshewd he should be cround:

21

Perchance (if mans proud thought, or saucie tong,
Haue leaue to iudge, or guesse at heau'nly things)
This was the angell which had kept him long,
That now came downe, and hid him with his wings.
While thus the Duke bespeakes his armies stronge,
And euerie troupe and band in order brings,
   Lord *Emiren* his hoast disposed well,
   And with bould words whet on their courage fell;

22

The man brought foorth his armie great with speed,
In order good, his foes at hand he spide,
Like the newe moone his hoast two hornes did spreed,
In midst the foote, the horse were on each side,
The right wing kept he for himselfe to leed,
Great *Altamore* receau'd the left to guide,
   The middle ward led *Muleasses* prood,
   And in that battaile faire, *Armida* stood.

23

On the right quarter stood the Indian grim,
With *Tisipherne* and all the kings owne band;

But where the left winge spred her squadrons trim
Ore the large plaine, did *Altamoro* stand,
With Aphrican and Persian kings with him,
And two that came from Meroes hot sand,
   And all his crosbowes and his slinges he plast,
   Where roome best seru'd to shoot, to throw, to cast.

24

Thus *Emiren* his host put in array,
And road from band to band, from ranke to ranke,
His Truchmen now, and now himselfe doth say,
What spoile his folke shall gaine, what praise, what thanke,
To him that feard, looke vp, ours is the day
He saies, vile feare to bould harts neuer sanke,
   How dareth one against an hundreth fight?
   Our crie, our shade, will put them all to fight.

25

But to the bould, 'go hardie knight (he saies,)
His praie out of this lions pawes go teare,'
To some before his thoughts the shape he laies,
And makes therein the image true appeare,
How his sad countrie him entreats and praies,
His house, his louing wife, and children deare,
   'Suppose (quoth he) thy countrie doth beseech
   And pray thee thus, suppose this is her speech:

26

'Defend my lawes, vphold my temples braue,
My blood, from washing of my streetes, withhold,
From rauishing my virgins keepe, and saue
Thine auncestors dead bones and ashes cold,
To thee thy fathers deare, and parents graue
Shew their vncoured heads, white, hoarie, old,
   To thee thy wife her brests with teares orespred
   Thy sonnes, their cradles, shewes, thy mariage bed.

27

'To all the rest, you for her honours sake,
Whom Asia makes her champions, by your might

Vpon these theeues, weake, feeble, fewe, must take
A sharpe reuenge, yet iust, deserued and right,'
Thus many words in seu'rall toongs he spake,
And all his sundry nations to sharpe fight
  Encouraged, but now the Dukes had donne
  Their speeches all, the hoasts togither ronne.

28

It was a great, a strange, and wondrous fight,
When front to front those noble armies met,
How euerie troupe, how in each troupe each knight
Stood prest to moue, to fight, and praise to get,
Loose in the winde waued their ensignes light,
Trembled the plumes that on their crests were set;
  Their armes impreses, colours, gold and stone
  Gainst the sunne beames, smild, flamed, sparkled, shone,

29

Of drie topt Oakes, they seemd two forrests thicke:
So did each hoste with speares and pikes abound,
Bent were their bowes, in rests their launces sticke,
Their hands shooke swords, their slings held cobles round:
Each stead to runne was readie, prest and quicke
At his commaunders spurre, his hand, his sound;
  He chafes, he stampes, careers, and turnes about,
  He fomes, snorts, neies, and fire and smoake breaths out.

30

Horrour, it selfe in that faire sight seem'd faire,
And pleasure flew amid sad dreed and feare:
The trumpets shrill, that thundred in the aire,
Were musicke milde and sweete to euerie eare:
The faithfull campe (though lesse) yet seem'd more raire
In that strange noice, more warlike, shrill and cleare,
  In notes more sweete, the Pagan trumpets iarre,
  These sung, their armours shin'd, these glistred farre.

31

The Christian trumpets giue the deadly call,
The Pagans answere, and the fight accept;

The godly Frenchmen on their knees downe fall
To pray, and kist the earth, and then vplept
To fight, the land betweene was vanisht all,
In combat close each hoste to other stept;
  For now the wings had skirmish hot begonne,
  And with their battels forth the footmen ronne.

32

But who was first of all the Christian traine,
That gaue the onset first, first wonne renowne?
Gildippes thou wert she, for (by thee slaine)
The king of Orms, *Hircano*, tumbled downe,
The mans brest bone thou clou'st and rent in twaine,
So heau'n with honour would thee blesse and crowne:
  Pierst through he fell, and falling hard withall,
  His foe prais'd for her strength, and for his fall.

33

Her launce thus broake, the hardie dame forth drew
(With her strong hand) a fine and trenchant blade,
And gainst the Persians fierce and bold she flew,
And in their troupe wide streets and lanes she made,
Euen in the girdling stead deuided new
In peeces twaine, *Zopire* on earth she lade;
  And then *Alarcos* head she swapt off cleene,
  Which like a football tumbled on the greene.

34

A blow feld *Artaxerxes*, with a thrust
Was *Argeus* slaine, the first lay in a trance,
Ismaels left hand cut off fell in the dust;
For on his wrest her sword fell downe by chance:
The hand let goe the bridle where it lust,
The blow vpon the coursers eares did glance,
  Who felt the raines at large, and with the stroake
  Halfe mad, the rankes disordred, troubled, broake:

33¹ lannce < launce (*cf. 1624*)

35

All these, and many moe, by time forgot,
She slew and wounded, when against her came
The angrie Persians all, cast on a knot,
For on her person would they purchace fame:
But her deare spouse and husband wanted not
(In so great need) to aide the noble dame;
 Thus ioin'd, the haps of warre vnhurt they proue,
 Their strength was double, double was their loue.

36

The noble louers use well might you see,
A woundrous guise, till then vnseene, vnhard,
To saue themselues forgot both he and shee,
Each others life did keepe, defend and guard;
The stroakes that gainst her Lord discharged bee,
The dame had care to beare, to breake, to ward,
 His shield kept off the blowes bent on his deare,
 Which (if need be) his naked head should beare.

37

So each sau'd other, each for others wrong
Would veng'ance take, but not reuenge their owne:
The valiant Soldan *Artabano* strong
Of Boecan isle, by her was ouerthrowne,
And by his hand (the bodies dead among)
Aluante (that durst his mistresse wound) fell downe,
 And she betweene the eies hit *Arimonte*,
 (Who hurt her Lord) and cleft in twaine his fronte.

38

But *Altamore* who had that wing to lead
Farre greater slaughter on the Christians made;
For where he turn'd his sword, or twinde his stead,
He slew, or man and beast on earth downe lade,
Happie was he that was at first strucke dead,
That fell not downe on liue, for whom his blade
 Had spar'd, the same cast in the dustie streete
 His horse tore with his teeth, brus'd with his feete.

39

By this braue Persians valour kild and slaine
Were strong *Brunello*, and *Ardonio* great;
The first his head and helme had cleft in twaine,
The last in stranger wise he did entreat,
For through his hart he pierst, and through the vaine
Where laughter hath his fountaine and his seat,
  So that (a dreedfull thing, beleeu'd vneath)
  He laught for paine, and laught himselfe to death.

40

Nor these alone with that accursed knife
Of this sweete light and breath depriued lie;
But with that cruell weapon lost their life
Gentonio, *Guascar*, *Rosimond* and *Guie*;
Who knowes how many in that fatall strife
He slew? What knights his courser fierce made die?
  The names and countries of the people slaine
  Who tels? their wounds and deaths who can explaine?

41

With this fierce king encounter durst not one,
Not one durst combat him in equall field,
Gildippes vndertooke that taske alone;
No doubt could make her shrinke, no danger, yield,
By *Thermodonte* was neuer *Amazone*,
('That menag'd steeled axe, or caried shield)
  That seem'd so bold as she, so stronge, so light,
  When foorth she ronne to meet that dreadfull knight:

42

She hit him, where with gold and ritch anmaile,
His Diademe did on his helmet flame,
She broake and cleft the crowne, and caus'd him vaile
His proud and loftie top, his crest downe came,
Strong seem'd her arme that could so well assaile:
The Pagan shooke for spite, and blusht for shame,
  Forward he rusht, and would at once requite
  Shame, with disgrace; and with reuenge, despite.

43

Right on the front he gaue that Ladie kinde
A blow, so huge, so strong, so great, so sore,
That out of sense and feeling, downe she twinde:
But her deare knight his loue from ground vpbore,
Were it their fortune, or his noble minde,
He staid his hand, and stroake the dame no more:
   A Lion so stalkes by, and with proud eies
   Beholds, but scornes to hurt, a man that lies.

44

This while *Ormondo* false, whose cruell hand
Was arm'd, and prest to giue the traitrous blow,
With all his fellowes mongst *Godfredoes* band
Entred vnseene, disguis'd that few them know:
The theeuish Wolfes (when night oreshades the land)
That seeme like faithfull dogs in shape and show,
   So to the closed folds in secret creepe,
   And entrance seeke, to kill some harmlesse sheepe.

45

He proched nie, and to *Godfredoes* side
The bloodie Pagan now was placed neare;
But when his colours gold and white he spide,
And saw the other signes that forged weare,
'See see, this traitor false (the captaine cride)
That like a Frenchman would in show appeare,
   Behold how neere his mates and he are crept.'
   This said, vpon the villaine foorth he lept,

46

Deadly he wounded him, and that false knight
Nor strikes, nor wards, nor striueth to be gone;
But (as *Medusas* head ware in his sight)
Stood like a man new turn'd to marble stone,
All lances broke, vnsheath'd all weapons bright,
All quiuers emptied were, on them alone,
   In parts so many were the traitours cleft,
   That those dead men, had no dead bodies left.

47

When *Godfrey* was with Pagan blood bespred
He entred then the fight, and that was past,
Where the bold Persian fought and combatted,
Where the close rankes he op'ned, cleft and brast;
Before the knight the troupes and squadrons fled,
As Affricke dust before the Southren blast,
   The Duke recall'd them, in array them placed,
   Staid those that fled, and him assail'd that chaced.

48

The champions strong there fought a battell stout,
Troie neuer saw the like by *Xanthus* old:
A conflict sharpe there was meane-while on fout
Twixt *Baldwine* good and *Muleasses* bold:
The horsemen also (neare the mountaines rout,
And in both wings) a furious skirmish hold,
   And where the barb'rous Duke in person stood,
   Twixt *Tisiphernes* and *Adrastus* prood;

49

With *Emiren Robert* the Norman stroue,
Long time they fought, yet neither lost nor wonne;
The other *Roberts* helme the Indian cloue,
And broke his armes, their fight would soone be donne:
From place to place did *Tisiphernes* roue,
And found no match, against him none durst ronne,
   But where the prease was thickest thither flew
   The knight, and at each stroke feld, hurt or slew.

50

Thus fought they long, yet neither shrinke nor yeild,
In equall ballance hung their hope and feare:
All full of broken lances lay the feild,
All full of armes that clou'n and shattred weare,
Of swords, some to the body naile the sheild,
Some cut mens throtes, and some their bellies teare,
   Of bodies, some vpright, some groueling lay,
   And for themselues eat graues out of the clay:

51

Beside his lord slaine lay the noble stead,
There friend with friend lay kild, like louers trew,
There foe with foe, the liue vnder the dead,
The victor vnder him whom late he slew:
A hoarse vnperfect sound did each where spread,
Whence neither silence, nor plaine outcries flew,
    There furie roares, ire threats, and woe complaines,
    One weepes, another cries, he sighes for paines.

52

The armes that late so faire and glorious seame,
Now soild and slubbred, sad and sullen grow,
The steele his brightnes lost; the gould his beame;
The colours had no pride, nor beauties show;
The plumes and feathers on their crests that streame,
Are strowed wide vpon the earth below:
    The hosts both clad in blood, in dust and mire,
    Had changd their cheare, their pride, their rich attire.

53

But now the Moores, Arabians, Ethiops blacke,
(Of the left wing that held the vtmost marge)
Spread forth their troupes and purpos'd at the backe
And side, their heedlesse foes t'assaile and charge:
Slingers and Archers were not slow, nor slacke
To shoot and cast, when with his battell large
    Rinaldo came, whose furie, haste, and ire,
    Seem'd earthquake, thunder, tempest, storme and fire.

54

The first he met was *Asimere* his throne
That set in *Meroës* hot, sunne-burnt, land,
He cut his necke in twaine, flesh, skin and bone,
The sable head downe tumbled on the sand;
But when by death of this blacke Prince alone,
The taste of blood and conquest once he fand,
    Whole squadrons then, whole troupes to earth he brought,
    Things wondrous, strange, incredible, he wrought;

53³ Rpread < Spread (*as corrected in other copies*)

55

He gaue moe deaths than stroakes, and yet his blowes
Vpon his feeble foes fell oft and thicke,
To mooue three toongs as a fierce serpent showes,
Which rolles the one she hath swift, speedie, quicke;
So thinkes each Pagan, each Arabian trowes,
He weilds three swords, all in one hilt that sticke,
　His readinesse their eies so blinded hath,
　Their dreed that wounder bred, feare gaue it fath,

56

The Affricke tyrants and the Negro kings
Fell downe on heapes, drown'd each in others blood,
Vpon their people ranne the knights he brings,
Prickt forward by their guides ensample good,
Kild were the Pagans, broake their bowes and slings:
Some dide, some fell; some yeelded, none withstood:
　A massacre was this, no fight; these put
　Their foes to death; those hold their throates to cut.

57

Small while they stood, with hart and hardie face
On their bold brests deepe wounds and hurts to beare,
But fled away, and troubled in the chace
Their rankes disordred be with too much feare:
Rinaldo follow'd them from place to place,
Till quite discomfit and disperst they weare,
　That done he staies, and all his knights recalles,
　And scornes to strike his foe that flies or falles.

58

Like as the winde stopt by some wood or hill,
Growes strong and fierce, teares boughes and trees in twaine,
But with milde blasts, more temprate, gentle, still,
Blowes through the ample field, or spatious plaine;
Against the rockes as sea-waues murmur shrill,
But silent passe amid the open maine:
　Rinaldo so, when none his force withstood,
　Asswagd his furie, calmd his angrie mood,

59

He scornd vpon their fearefull backes that fled
To wreake his ire, and spend his force in vaine,
But gainst the footemen strong his troupes he led,
Whose side the Moores had open left and plaine,
The Affricanes, that should haue succoured
That battaile, all were ronne away or slaine,
    Vpon their flanke with force and courage stout,
    His men at armes assaild the bands on fout:

60

He brake their pikes, and brake their close array,
Entred their battaile, feld them downe around,
So winde or tempest with impetious sway
The eares of ripened corne strikes flat to ground:
With blood, armes, bodies dead, the hardned clay
Plastred the earth, no grasse nor greene was found,
    The horsemen running through & through their bands,
    Kill, murder, stay, few scape, not one withstands.

61

Rinaldo came where his forlorne *Armide*
Sate on her golden chariot mounted hie,
A noble guard she had on euery side
Of lords, of louers, and much chiualrie:
She knew the man when first his armes she spide,
Loue, hate, wrath, sweet desire, stroue in her eie,
    He changd some deale, his looke & countnance bold,
    She changd from frost, to fire; from heat, to cold:

62

The prince past by the chariot of his deare,
Like one that did his thoughts elsewhere bestow,
Yet suffred not her knights and louers neare
Their riuall so to scape withouten blow,
One drew his sword, another coucht his speare,
Herselfe an arrow sharpe set in her bow,
    Disdaine her ire new sharpt and kindled hath,
    But loue appeasd her, loue asswagd her wrath.

63

Loue brideled furie, and reuiu'd of new
His fire, not dead, though buried in displeasure,
Three times her angrie hand the bow vp drew,
And thrice againe let slacke the string at leasure;
But wrath preuail'd at last, the reed out flew,
For loue findes meane, but hatred knowes no measure,
　Out flew the shaft, but with the shaft, this charme,
　This wish she sent: heau'ns grant it doe no harme:

64

She bids the reed returne the way it went,
And pearse her hart which so vnkinde could proue,
Such force had loue, though lost and vainly spent,
What strength hath happie, kinde and mutuall loue?
But she that gentle thought did straight repent,
Wrath, furie, kindnes, in her bosome stroue,
　She would, she would not, that it mist or hit,
　Her eies, her hart, her wishes followed it.

65

But yet in vaine the quarrell lighted not,
For on his hawberke hard the knight it hit,
Too hard for womans shaft or womans shot,
In stead of pearsing there it broke and split;
He turn'd away, she burnt with furie hot,
And thought he scorn'd her powre, and in that fit
　Shot oft and oft, her shaftes no entrance found,
　And while she shot, loue gaue her wound on wound.

66

'And is he then vnpearceable (quoth shee)
That neither force nor foe he needes regard?
His lims (perchance) arm'd with that hardnes bee,
Which makes his hart so cruell and so hard,
No shot that flies from eie or hand I see,
Hurtes him, such rigor doth his person gard,
　Arm'd, or disarm'd; his foe, or mistresse kinde,
　Despis'd alike, like hate, like scorne I finde.

67

'But what new forme is left, deuise, or art,
By which, to which exchang'd, I might finde grace?
For in my knights and all that take my part
I see no helpe, no hope, no trust I place,
To his great prowesse, might, and valiant hart,
All strength is weake, all courage vile and bace.'
   This said she, for she saw, how, through the feild,
   Her champions flie, faint, tremble, fall and yeild.

68

Nor left alone can she her person saue,
But to be slaine or taken stands in feare,
Though with her bow a iauelin long she haue,
Yet weake was *Phebes* bow, blunt *Pallas* speare.
But, as the swan, that sees the Eagle braue,
Threatning her flesh and siluer plumes to teare,
   Falles downe, to hide her mongst the shadie brookes;
   Such were her fearfull motions, such her lookes.

69

But *Altamore*, this while that stroue and sought
From shamefull flight his Persian host to stay,
That was discomfit and destroi'd to nought,
Whilst he alone mantain'd the fight and fray,
Seeing distrest the goddesse of his thought,
To aide her ran, nay flew, and laid away
   All care, both of his honour and his host,
   If she were safe, let all the world be lost.

70

To the ilguarded chariot swift he flew,
His weapon made him way with bloodie warre:
Mean-while Lord *Godfrey* and *Rinaldo* slew
His feeble bands, his people murdred arre,
He saw their losse, but aided not his crew,
A better louer than a leader farre,
   He set *Armida* safe, then turn'd againe
   With tardie succour, for his folke were slaine.

71

And on that side the woefull Prince behield
The battell lost, no helpe nor hope remain'd;
But on the other wing the Christians yield,
And flie, such vantage there th'Egyptians gain'd,
One of the *Roberts* was nigh slaine in field;
The other by the Indian strong constrain'd
 To yeeld himselfe, his captiue and his slaue;
 Thus equall losse and equall foile they haue.

72

Godfredo tooke the time and season, fit
To bring againe his squadrons in array,
And either campe well ordred, rang'd and knit,
Renew'd the furious battel, fight and fray,
New streames of blood were shed, new swords them hit;
New combats fought, new spoiles were borne away,
 And vnresolu'd and doubtfull (on each side)
 Did praise and conquest, *Mars* and *Fortune* ride.

73

Betweene the armies twaine while thus the fight
Waxt sharpe, hot, cruell, though renewd but late,
The *Soldan* clombe vp to the towers hight,
And sawe farre off their strife and fell debate,
As from some stage or theatre the knight
Saw plaid the tragedie of humaine state,
 Sawe death, blood, murder, woe and horrour strange,
 And the great acts of fortune, chance and change:

74

At first astonisht and amazd he stood,
Then burnt with wrath, and selfe consuming ire,
Swelled his bosome like a raging flood,
To be amid that battaile, such desire.
Such haste he had, he dond his helmet good,
His other armes he had before entire,
 'Vp, vp, he cride, no more, no more, within
 This fortresse stay, come follow, die or win.'

75

Whether the same were prouidence diuine,
That made him leaue the fortresse he possest,
For that the empire proud of Palestine
This day should fall, to rise againe more blest;
Or that he breaking felt the fatall line
Of life, and would meete death with constant brest,
    Furious and fierce he did the gates vnbarre,
    And sodaine rage brought foorth, and sodaine warre;

76

Nor staide he till the folke on whom he cride
Assemble might, but out alone he flies,
A thousand foes the man alone defide,
And ronne among a thousand enimies:
But with his furie cald from euery side,
The rest ronne out, and *Aladine* foorth hies,
    The cowards had no feare, the wise no caire,
    This was not hope, nor courage, but despaire.

77

The dreadfull Turke with sodaine blowes downe cast,
The first he met, nor gaue them time to plaine,
Or pray, in murdring them he made such haste,
That dead they fell, ere one could see them slaine;
From mouth to mouth, from eie to eie foorth past
The feare and terrour, that the faithfull traine
    Of Syrian folke, not vsd to dangrous fight,
    Were broken, scattred, and nigh put to flight.

78

But with lesse terrour and disorder lesse,
The Gascoignes kept array, and kept their ground,
Though most the losse and perill them oppresse,
Vnwares assaild they were, vnreadie found:
No rav'ning tooth or tallon hard I guesse
Of beast, or eager hauke, doth stay and wound
    So many sheepe, or foules weake, feeble, small,
    As his sharpe sword kild knights and souldiour tall:

78⁵ rauning < rav'ning

79

It seemd his thirst and hunger swage he would
With their slaine bodies, and their blood powrd out,
With him his troupes and *Aladino* ould
Slew their besiegers, kild the Gascoigne rout:
But *Raimond* ranne to meete the *Soldan* bould,
Nor to encounter him had feare or dout,
   Though his right hand by proofe too well he know,
   Which laid him late for dead, at one huge blow,

80

They met and *Raimond* fell amid the feild,
This blow againe vpon his forehead light,
It was the fault and weakenes of his eild,
Age is not fit to beare stroakes of such might,
Each one lift vp his sword, aduanst his sheild,
Those would destroy, and these defend the knight,
   On went the *Soldan*, for the man he thought
   Was slaine, or easie might be captiue brought.

81

Among the rest he ranne, he ragd, he smote,
And in small space, small time, great wonders wrought;
And as his rage him led and furie hote,
To kill and murder matter new he sought:
As from his supper poore, with hungrie throte,
A peasant hasts to a rich feast ibrought,
   So from this skirmish to the battaile great
   He ranne, and quencht with blood his furies heat.

82

Where battred was the wall he sallied out,
And to the field in haste and heat he goes,
With him went rage and furie, feare and dout
Remaind behind, among his scattred foes:
To win the conquest, stroue his squadron stout,
Which he vnperfect left, yet loth to loes
   The day: the Christians fight, resist and die,
   And readie were to yeeld, retire and flie.

83

The Gascoigne bands retir'd, but kept array,
The Syrian people ran away outright,
The fight was neere the place where *Tancred* lay,
His house was full of noise, and great affright,
He rose and looked foorth to see the fray,
Though euery limme were weake, faint, voide of might,
   He sawe the countie lie, his men orethrowne,
   Some beaten backe, some kild, some felled downe:

84

Courage in noble harts that nere is spent,
Yet fainted not, though faint were euery lim,
But reinforst each member cleft and rent,
And want of blood and strength supplide in him,
In his left hand his heauie shield he hent,
Nor seemd the weight too great, his curtlax trim
   His right hand drew, nor for more armes he stood,
   Or staid, he needs no more, whose hart is good:

85

But comming foorth, cride, 'whither will you ronne,
And leaue your leader to his foes in pray?
What? shall these heathen of his armour wonne,
(In their vile temples) hang vp trophies gay?
Go home to Gascoigne then, and tell his sonne,
That where his father dide you ran away,'
   This said, against a thousand armed foes,
   He did his brest weake, naked, sicke, oppoes,

86

And with his heauie, stronge, and mightie targe,
(That with feau'n hard buls hides was surely lind)
And strengthned with a couer thicke and large,
Of stiffe and well attempred steele behind,
He shielded *Raimond* from the furious charge,
From swords, from darts, from weapons of each kind,
   And all his foes droue backe with his sharpe blade,
   That sure and safe he lay, as in a shade.

84⁴ strenght < strength (*cf. 1624*)

87

Thus sau'd, thus shielded *Raimond* gan respire,
He rose and reard himselfe in little space,
And in his bosome burnt the double fire
Of vengeance; wrath his hart, shame fill'd his face;
He lookt around to spie, (such was his ire)
The man, whose stroake had laid him in that place,
   Whom when he sees not, for disdaine he quakes,
   And on his people sharpe reuengement takes.

88

The Gascoines turne againe, their Lord in haste
To venge their losse his band reordred brings,
The troupe that durst so much now stood agast,
For where sad feare grew late, now boldnes springs,
Now follow'd, they that fled; fled, they that chast;
So in one howre altreth the state of things,
   Raimond requites his losse, shame, hurt and all,
   And with an hundreth deathes reueng'd one fall.

89

Whil'st *Raimond* wreaked thus his iust disdaine
On the proud heads of captaines, Lords and peares,
He spies great Sions king amid the traine,
And to him leapes, and high his sword he reares,
And on his forehead strikes, and strikes againe,
Till helme and head he breakes, he cleaues, he teares,
   Downe fell the king, the guiltlesse land he bit,
   That now keepes him, bicause he kept not it.

90

Their guides one murdred thus, the other gone,
The troupes diuided were in diuers thought,
Despaire made some ronne headlong gainst their fone,
To seeke sharpe death, that comes vncall'd, vnsought;
And some (that laid their hope on flight alone)
Fled to their fort againe; yet chance so wrought,
   That (with the fliers) in the victors pas,
   And so the fortresse wonne, and conquer'd was.

87⁴ vengeance, wrath, his hart; < vengeance; wrath his hart,

91

The hold was wonne, slaine were the men that fled,
In courtes, halles, chambers high; aboue, below,
Old *Raimond* fast vp to the leads him sped,
And there (of victorie true signe and show)
His glorious standard to the winde he spred,
That so both armies his successe might know.
    But *Soliman* saw not the towne was lost,
    For far from thence he was, and neere the host;

92

Into the field he came, the lukewarme blood
Did smoke, and flow through all the purple feild,
There of sad death the court and pallace stood,
There did he triumphes lead, and trophies beild,
An armed stead fast by the Soldan yood,
That had no guide, nor lord the raines to weild,
    The tyrant tooke the bridle, and bestroad
    The coursers emptie backe, and foorth he road.

93

Great, yet but short and sodaine, was the aid,
That to the Pagans, faint and weake he brought,
A thunderbolt he was, you would haue said,
Great, yet that comes and goes as swift as thought,
And of his comming swift, and flight vnstaid
Eternall signes in hardest rockes hath wrought,
    For by his hand an hundreth knights were slaine,
    But time forgot hath all their names, but twaine;

94

Gildippes faire, and *Edward* thy deare lord,
Your noble death, sad end, and woefull fate,
(If so much powre our vulgar toong afford)
To all strange wits, strange eares let me dilate,
That ages all your loue, and sweete accord,
Your vertue, prowesse, worth, may imitate,
    And some kind seruant of true loue (that heares)
    May grace your death, my verses, with some teares.

95

The noble ladie thither boldly flew,
Where the fierce *Soldan* fought, and him defide,
Two mightie blowes she gaue the Turke vntrew,
One cleft his shield, the other pierst his side;
The prince the damsell by her habite knew,
'See, see, this mankind strumpet, see (he cride)
     This shamelesse whore, for thee fit weapons weare
     Thy neeld and spindle, not a sword and speare.'

96

This said, full of disdaine, rage, and despite,
A strong, a fierce, a deadly stroake he gaue,
And pierst her armour, pierst her bosome white,
Worthie no blowes, but blowes of loue, to haue,
Her dying hand let goe the bridle quite,
She faints, she falles, twixt life and death she straue,
     Her lord to helpe her came, but came too late,
     Yet was not that his fault, it was his fate.

97

What should he do? to diuers parts him call
Iust ire and pittie kind, one bids him goe,
And succour his deare ladie, like to fall;
The other cals for vengeance on his foe,
Loue biddeth both, loue saies he must doe all,
And with his ire, ioines griefe; with pittie, woe.
     What did he then? with his left hand the knight
     Would hould her vp, reuenge her with his right.

98

But to resist against a knight so bold
Too weake his will and powre deuided, weare;
So that he could not his faire loue vphold,
Nor kill the cruell man that slew his deare,
His arme, that did his mistres kind enfold
The Turke cut off, pale grew his lookes and cheare,
     He let her fall, himselfe fell by her side,
     And for he could not saue her, with her dide.

U

99

As the high elme (whom his deare vine hath twind
Fast in her hundred armes, and houlds embrast,)
Beares downe to earth his spouse and darling kind,
If storme or cruell steele the tree downe cast,
And her full grapes to nought doth bruze and grind,
Spoiles his owne leaues, withers, dies at last,
    And seemes to mourne and die, not for his owne
    But for her death, with him that lies orethrowne:

100

So fell he mourning, mourning for the dame,
Whom life and death had made for euer his;
They would haue spoke, but not one word could frame,
Deepe sobs their speech, sweete sighes their language is,
Each gazd on others eies, and, while the same
Is lawfull, ioine their hands, embrace and kis:
    And thus sharpe death, their knot of life vntied,
    Togither fainted they, togither died.

101

But now swift fame her nimble wings dispred,
And told each where their chance, their fate, their fall,
Rinaldo heard the case, by one that fled
From the fierce Turke, and brought him newes of all,
Disdaine, goodwill, woe, wrath the champion led
To take reuenge, shame, griefe, for vengeance call.
    But as he went *Adrastus* with his blade,
    Forestall'd the way, and shew of combate made.

102

The giant cride, 'by sundrie signes I note,
That whom I wish, I search, thou, thou art hee,
I markt each woorthies sheild, his helme, his cote,
And all this day haue call'd and cride for thee,
To my sweete saint I haue thy head deuote,
Thou must my sacrifice, my offring bee,
    Come let vs heere our strength and courage trie,
    Thou art *Armidas* foe, her champion I.'

103

Thus he defide him, on his front before,
And on his throat he stroke him, yet the blow
His helmet neither brused, cleft nor tore,
But in his saddle made him bend and bow;
Rinaldo hit him on the flanke so sore,
That neither art nor hearbe could helpe him now;
 Downe fell the Giant strong, one blow such powre,
 Such puissance had; so falles a thundred towre.

104

With horrour, feare, amazednesse and dreed,
Cold were the harts of all that saw the fray,
And *Soliman* (that view'd that noble deed)
Trembled, his palenesse did his feare bewray;
For in that stroake he did his ende arreed,
He wist not what to thinke, to doe, to say,
 A thing in him vnused, rare and strange,
 But so doth heau'n mens harts turne, alter, change.

105

As when the sicke or frantike men oft dreame
In their vnquiet sleepe, and slumber short,
And thinke they ronne some speedie course, and seame
To mooue their legs and feete in hastie sort;
Yet feele their limmes farre slower than the streame
Of their vaine thoughts, that beares them in this sport,
 And oft would speake, would crie, would call or shout,
 Yet neither sound, nor voice, nor word send out:

106

So runne to fight the angrie Soldan would,
And did enforce his strength, his might, his ire,
Yet felt not in himselfe his courage ould,
His woonted force, his rage and hot desire,
His eies (that sparkled wrath and furie bould)
Grew dim and feeble, feare had quencht that fire,
 And in his hart an hundreth passions fought,
 Yet not on feare or base retire he thought.

107

While vnresolu'd he stood, the victor knight
Arriu'd, and seem'd in quicknesse, haste and speed,
In boldnesse, greatnes, goodlines and might,
Aboue all Princes borne of humaine seed:
The Turke small while resists, not death, nor fight
Made him forget his state, or race, through dreed,
 He fled no stroakes, he fetcht no groane nor sigh,
 Bold were his motions last, proud, stately, high.

108

Now when the Soldan (in these battels past
That *Antheus* like oft fell, oft rose againe,
Euer more fierce, more fell) fell downe at last
To lie for euer, when this Prince was slaine:
Fortune, that seld is stable, firme, or fast,
No longer durst resist the Christian traine,
 But rang'd her selfe in row with *Godfreies* knights,
 With them she serues, she ronnes, she rides, she fights.

109

The Pagan troupes, the kings owne squadron fled,
Of all the East the strength, the pride, the flowre,
Late call'd immortall, now discomfited,
It lost that title proud, and lost all powre:
To him that with the royall standard fled,
Thus *Emireno* said, with speeches sowre,
 'Art not thou he to whom to beare I gaue
 My kings great banner, and his standard braue?

110

'This ensigne (*Rimedon*) I gaue not thee
To be the witnesse of thy feare and flight,
Coward, dost thou thy Lord and Captaine see
In battell strong, and ronn'st thy selfe from fight?
What seek'st thou? saftie? come, returne with mee,
The way to death, is path to vertue right,
 Here let him fight that would escape; for this
 The way to honour, way to saftie is.'

111

The man return'd, and sweld with scorne and shame,
The Duke with speeches graue exhorts the rest;
He threates, he strikes sometime, till backe they came,
And rage gainst force, despaire gainst death addrest.
Thus of his broken armies gan he frame
A battell now, some hope dwelt in his brest,
    But *Tisiphernes* bold reuiu'd him most,
    Who fought, and seem'd to winne, when all was lost;

112

Wonders that day wrought noble *Tisipherne*,
The hardie Normans all he ouerthrew;
The Flemmings fled before the champion sterne,
Gernier, *Rogero*, *Gerard* bold he slew;
His glorious deeds to praise and fame eterne
His liues short date prolong'd, enlarg'd and drew,
    And then (as he that set sweete life at nought)
    The greatest perill, danger most he sought.

113

He spide *Rinaldo*, and although his feild
Of azure, purple now and sanguine showes,
And though the siluer bird amid his sheild
Were armed gules; yet he the champion knowes,
And saies, 'here greatest perill is, heau'ns yeild
Strength to my courage, fortune to my blowes,
    That faire *Armida* her reuenge may see,
    Helpe *Macon*, for his armes I vow to thee.'

114

Thus praied he, but all his vowes were vaine,
Mahound was deafe, or slept in heauens aboue,
And as a lion strikes him with his traine,
His natiue wrath to quicken and to moue;
So he awakte his furie and disdaine,
And sharpt his courage on the whetstone loue,
    Himselfe he sau'd behinde his mightier targe,
    And forward spurr'd his stead, and gaue the charge.

115

The Christian saw the hardie warriour come,
And leaped forth to vndertake the fight,
The people round about gaue place and rome,
And wondred on that fierce and cruell sight,
Some prais'd their strength, their skill, and courage some,
Such and so desp'rate blowes strooke either knight,
    That all that saw forgot both ire and strife,
    Their wounds, their hurts, forgot both death and life:

116

One stroke, the other did both strike and wound,
His armes were surer, and his strength was more;
From *Tisipherne* the blood stream'd downe around,
His shield was cleft, his helme was rent and tore.
The dame (that saw his blood besmeare the ground,
His armour broke, limmes weake, wounds deepe and sore,
    And all her garde dead, fled, and ouerthrowne)
    Thought, now her field lay wast, her hedge lay downe:

117

Enuiron'd with so braue a troupe but late,
Now stood she in her chariot all alone,
She feared bondage, and her life did hate,
All hope of conquest and reuenge was gone,
Halfe mad and halfe amas'd, from where she sate,
She leaped downe, and fled from friends and fone,
    On a swift horse she mounts, and forth she rides
    Alone, saue for disdaine and loue, her guides.

118

In daies of old, Queene *Cleopatra* soe
Alone fled from the fight and cruell fray,
Against *Augustus* great his happie foe,
Leauing her Lord, to losse, and sure decay.
And as that Lord for loue let honour goe,
Follow'd her flying sailes, and lost the day:
    So *Tisipherne* the faire and fearfull dame
    Would follow, but his foe forbids the same.

119

But when the Pagans ioy and comfort fled,
It seem'd the sunne was set, the day was night,
Gainst the braue Prince with whom he combatted
He turn'd, and on the forehead stroake the knight:
When thunders forg'd are in *Tiphoius* bed,
Not *Brontes* hammer falles so swift, so right;
    The furious stroake fell on *Rinaldoes* crest,
    And made him bend his head downe to his brest.

120

The champion in his stirrups high vpstart,
And cleft his hawberke hard and tender side,
And sheath'd his weapon in the Pagans hart,
The castle where mans life and soule do bide;
The cruell sword his brest and hinder part
With double wound vnclos'd, and op'ned wide;
    And two large doores made for his life and breath,
    Which past, and curde hot loue, with frosen death.

121

This done, *Rinaldo* staid, and lookte around,
Where he should harme his foes, or helpe his friends;
Nor of the Pagans saw he squadron sound:
Each standard falles, ensigne to earth descends;
His furie quiet than and calme he found,
There all his wrath, his rage and rancour ends.
    He call'd to minde, how (farre from helpe or aid)
    Armida fled, alone, amas'd, affraid:

122

Well sawe he when she fled, and with that sight
The Prince had pitie, curtesie and care;
He promist her to be her friend and knight,
When earst he left her in the island bare:
The way she fled he ranne and road aright,
Her palfraies feete signes in the grasse out ware:
    But she this while found out an ougly shade,
    Fit place for death, where nought could life perswade.

123

Well pleased was she with those shadowes browne,
And yet displeasd with lucke, with life, with loue,
There from her stead she lighted, there laid downe
Her bowe and shafts, her armes that helpelesse proue,
'There lie with shame (she saies) disgrast, orethrowne,
Blunt are the weapons, blunt the armes I moue,
    Weake to reuenge my harmes, or harme my foe,
    My shafts are blunt, ah loue, would thine were soe!

124

'Alas, among so many, could not one,
Not one draw blood, one wound or rend his skin?
All other brests to you are marble stone,
Dare you than pierce a womans bosome thin?
See, see, my naked hart, on this alone,
Imploy your force, this fort is eath to win,
    And loue will shoote you from his mightie bow,
    Weake is the shot that dripile falles in snow.

125

'I pardon will your feare and weakenes past,
Be strong (mine arrowes) cruell, sharpe gainst mee,
Ah wretch, how is thy chance and fortune cast,
If plast in these, thy good and comfort bee?
But since all hope is vaine, all helpe is wast,
Since hurts ease hurts, wounds must cure wounds in thee;
    Then with thine arrowes stroake cure stroakes of loue,
    Death for thy hart must salue, and surgeon proue.

126

'And happie me, if being dead and slaine,
I beare not with me this strange plague to hell,
Loue, staie behind, come thou with me disdaine,
And with my wronged soule for euer dwell;
Or else with it turne to the world againe,
And vexe that knight with dreames and visions fell,
    And tell him (when twixt life and death I stroue)
    My last wish, was reuenge; last word, was loue.'

123⁴ proue < proue,

127

And with that word halfe mad, halfe dead, she seames,
An arrow, poignant, strong and sharpe she tooke,
When her deare knight found her in these extreames,
Now fit to die, and passe the Stygian brooke,
Now prest to quench her owne and beauties, beames;
Now death sate on her eies, death in her looke,
   When to her backe he stept, and staid her arme
   Stretcht foorth, to doe that seruice last, last harme.

128

She turnes, and (ere she knowes) her Lord she spies,
Whose comming was vnwisht, vnthought, vnknowne,
She shrikes, and twines away her sdeignfull eies
From his sweete face, she falles dead in a swoune,
Falles as a flowre halfe cut, that bending lies:
He held her vp, and least she tumble downe,
   Vnder her tender side his arme he plast,
   His hand her girdle loos'd, her gowne vnlast;

129

And her faire face, faire bosome he bedewes
With teares, teares of remorse, of ruth, of sorrow.
As the pale Rose her colour lost renewes,
With the fresh drops falne from the siluer morrow;
So she reuiues, and cheekes empurpled shewes,
Moist with their owne teares, and with teares they borrow;
   Thrice lookte she vp, her eies thrice closed shee,
   As who say, 'let me die, ere looke on thee.'

130

And his strong arme, with weake and feeble hand,
She would haue thrust away, loos'd, and vntwined:
Oft stroue she (but in vaine) to breake that band,
For he the hold he got not yet resined,
Her selfe fast bound in those deare knots she fand,
Deare, though she faigned scorne, stroue and repined:
   At last she speakes, she weepes, complaines and cries;
   Yet durst not, did not, would not see his eies.

131

'Cruell at thy departure, at retorne
As cruell, say, what chance thee hither guideth,
Would'st thou preuent her death, whose hart forlorne
For thee, for thee deathes stroakes each howre deuideth?
Comst thou to saue my life? alas, what scorne,
What torment for *Armida* poore abideth?
   No, no, thy crafts and sleights I well descrie,
   But she can little doe that cannot die.

132

'Thy triumph is not great, nor well arrai'd,
Vnlesse in chaines thou lead a captiue dame;
A dame now tane by force, before betrai'd,
This is thy greatest glorie, greatest fame:
Time was that thee of loue and life I prai'd,
Let death now end my loue, my life, my shame,
   Yet let not thy false hand bereaue this breath,
   For if it were thy guift, hatefull were death.

133

'Cruell, my selfe an hundreth waies can finde,
To rid me from thy malice, from thy hate,
If weapons sharpe, if poisons of all kinde,
If fire, if strangling faile, in that estate;
Yet waies enough I know to stop this winde:
A thousand entries hath the house of fate.
   Ah, leaue these flattries, leaue weake hope to moue,
   Cease, cease, my hope is dead, dead is my loue.'

134

Thus mourned shee, and from her watrie eies,
Disdaine and loue dropt downe, roll'd vp in teares;
From his pure fountaines ranne two streames likewise,
Wherein chast pitie and milde ruth appeares:
Thus with sweete words the Queene he pacifies,
'Madame, appease your griefe, your wrath, your feares,
   For to be crown'd, not scorn'd, your life I saue;
   Your foe, nay but your friend, your knight, your slaue.

135

'But if you trust no speech, no oath, no word;
Yet in mine eies, my zeale, my truth, behold:
For to that throne (whereof thy sire was Lord)
I will restore thee, crowne thee with that gold,
And if high heau'n would so much grace afford,
As from thy hart this cloude, this vaile vnfold
    Of Paganisme, in all the East no dame
    Should equalize thy fortune, state and fame.'

136

Thus plaineth he, thus praies, and his desire
Endeares with sighes that flie, and teares that fall;
That as against the warm'th of *Titans* fire,
Snow drifts consume on tops of mountaines tall:
So melts her wrath, but loue remaines entire.
'Behold (she saies) your handmaid and your thrall;
    My life, my crowne, my wealth use at your pleasure:'
    Thus death her life became, losse prou'd her treasure.

137

This while the Captaine of th'Egyptian host,
That saw his roiall standard laid on ground,
Saw *Rimedon*, that ensignes prop and post,
By *Godfreies* noble hand, kild with one wound,
And all his folke discomfit, slaine and lost,
No coward was in this last battell found,
    But road about and sought (not sought in vaine)
    Some famous hand of which he might be slaine:

138

Against lord *Godfrey* bouldly out he flew,
For nobler foe he wisht not, could not spie,
Of desprate courage shew'd he tokens trew,
Where ere he ioind, or staid, or passed bie,
And cried to the Duke as neere he drew,
'Behold of thy strong hand I come to die,
    Yet trust to ouerthrow thee with my fall,
    My castles ruines shall breake downe thy wall.'

139

This said, foorth spurr'd they both, both high aduance
Their swords aloft, both stroake at once, both hit,
His left arme wounded had the knight of France,
His shield was pierst, his vantbrace cleft and split,
The Pagan backward fell, halfe in a trance,
On his left eare his foe so hugely smit,
   And as he sought to rise, *Godfredoes* sword
   Pierced him through, so dide that armies Lord.

140

Of his great host when *Emiren* was dead,
Fled the small remnant that aliue remained;
Godfrey espied as he turnd his stead,
Great *Altamore* on foote, with blood all stained,
With half a sword, halfe helme vpon his head,
Gainst whom an hundreth fought, yet not one gained,
   'Cease, cease this strife,' he cride: 'and thou braue knight,
   Yeeld, I am *Godfrey*, yeeld thee to my might.'

141

He that till then his proud and haughtie hart
To act of humblenes did neuer bend,
When that great name he heard, from the north part
Of our wide world, renown'd to Aethiops end,
Answer'd, 'I yeeld to thee, thou worthy art,
I am thy pris'ner, fortune is thy frend:
   On *Altamoro* great thy conquest bold
   Of glorie shall be rich, and rich of gold:

142

'My louing queene, my wife and Lady kinde
Shall ransome me with iewels, gold and treasure.'
'God shield (quoth *Godfrey*) that my noble minde
Should praise and vertue so by profit measure,
All that thou hast from Persia and from Inde
Enioy it still, therein I take no pleasure,
   I set no rent on life, no price on blood,
   I fight, and sell not warre for gold or good.'

143

This said, he gave him to his knights to keepe,
And after those that fled his course he bent;
They to their rampires fled and trenches deepe,
Yet could not so deathes cruell stroke preuent,
The campe was wonne, and all in blood doth steepe,
The blood in riuers stream'd from tent to tent,
   It soil'd, defilde, defaced all the pray,
   Shields, helmets, armours, plumes and feathers gay.

144

Thus conquer'd *Godfrey*, and as yet the sonne
Diu'd not in siluer waues his golden waine,
But day-light seru'd him to the fortresse wonne
With his victorious host to turne againe,
His bloodie cote he put not off, but ronne
To the high Temple with his noble traine,
   And there hung vp his armes, and there he bowes
   His knees, there prai'd, and there perform'd his vowes.

FINIS.

ADDENDA

*John Bill's dedication of the second edition (1624)
to Prince Charles*

SIR,

THe command of his Maiestie, seconded by your Highnesse, hath caused mee to renew the impression of this booke. The former edition had the honour to bee dedicated to the late Queene *Elizabeth*, of famous memorie, as appeareth by a worthy Elogie, here preserved. I could not leave this second birth of so excellent an Author, without a living Patron; and none could be found fitter, than your Princely selfe, who as you have highly commended it, so it is to be presumed, you will take it into your safe and Princely protection. For the Author *Torquato Tasso*, I may say of him, that as *Plato* hath of some beene called *Moses Ethnicus*; so this may bee stiled *Homerus Christianus*: and this will bee as fit to bee found in the hand of a Christian Prince, as *Homer* was to lie under the pillow of that Macedonian Emperor. All the ornament I could adde to this edition, was to illustrate the chiefe subject of the booke, that is, *Godfrey* of *Bullen*, the great Champion of Christendome; which I have done as well as I could, by prefixing his pourtraict, as it was brought from Hierusalem, and by a briefe description of his life, out of the best writers. Here is an example of pietie and valour ioyned together, to redeeme one countrey to the honour of Christ, who redeemed the whole world for the benefit of man. Though *Godfrey* were the first in this Holy band,

Robert of *Normandie* was not the last, a noble branch of your royall tree: and it were to bee wished, that the same spirit would in this latter age inflame all Christian Princes to the like designe, that the Theater of *Mars* might be erected in the gates of Hierusalem and Constantinople, which now is too much frequented in the territories of Christendome. A parallel to this enterprise cannot more fitly be given, than that of *Lepanto*, toward which though our Northerne Princes gave no aid, yet your Royall Father, our Soveraigne, hath given a perpetuall memorie, by his learned and religious Poeme, worthily imitated in the French, by *Du Bartas*: wherein *Don Juan d'Austria* doth not better follow the example of *Godfrey*, in the acting, than his Maiestie doth *Tasso* in describing the conquest, which the Christians obtained against the Turkes. They that have not abilitie in the Tuscan language, (in which it was first penned very curiously) may delight themselves with this translation: which will be so much the more worthy to bee read, because beside the story, (which must needs bee acceptable to all Christians) and the celebration of so many *Heroës*, the art of the Poet is admirable, both for the imitation, which is the life of Poetrie, and for Allegorie: For it doth not only containe the truth of an historicall narration, sweetned with some Poeticall fictions; but doth also secretly expresse a morall sense; shewing the Practicke part of vertue, leading to the consummation of felicitie: So that at once the understanding may be informed by the storie, the fancy delighted with the colours of Poetrie, and the will rectified with the examples of morality. Such ends have been aimed at in other Epicke Poemes, but never more happily attained, than in this; which offers it selfe, at the feet of your Highnesse, presenting to you a view of all the happy successe, in your Noble and Heroicall enterprises, which these great and memorable names are celebrated for: together with the humble service of him, who hath published this worke anew,

At your Highnesse command,

as

Your most humble and devoted servant,

JOHN BILL.

The Life of Godfrey of Boulogne (*1624*)

That Expedition of the Argonautes, who went into *Asia* to fetch the Golden fleece, is much celebrated by Poets; but the Expedition

of the Christian Princes, into the said countrie, to redeeme the
Golden Fleece & Patrimony of the Lambe of God, is much more
to be solemnized; who not for gaine, nor ambition, but for the
propagation of Christian Religion, and vindication of the Holy
Land, vndertooke this long, difficult, and dangerous enterprise:
of whom the Poet seemes long before to haue conceiued a Pro-
phesie: when he writes,

> *Alter erit tum Typhis, & altera quæ vehat Argo*
> *Delectos Heroas.——*

In the yeare therefore 1096. Pope *Vrban* the second, desirous to
enlarge the Christian faith, caused to be proclaimed a Voyage
against the Infidels and Saracens, which possessed the Holy Land,
called *Palestine*; and this, at the instance of one *Peter* the Heremite,
chiefe Author and Abettor of this voyage, called the Croysade,
because such as entred their names for this enterprise, were marked
with a red crosse, vpon the right shoulder; making this vow,
either to die, or returne Conquerors. The number of them that
were gathered together, for this purpose, was almost infinite; for
of all Nations, men of all qualities, assembled together, drawne
on with an emulation of pietie, and honour.

When the Armie was met at *Chalcedon* in *Asia*, it was mustered
to be six hundred thousand footmen, and one hundred thousand
horsemen; all which went voluntarily vpon their owne charge, for
the honour of Christian Religion.

Of the French, (that I may say nothing of other Nations) there
went *Hugh* the Great, brother to *Philip* King of France; two *Roberts*,
the one Duke of *Normandie*, and the other Earle of *Flandres*; *Stephen*
Earle of *Chartres*, *Godfrey*, *Eustace*, and *Balduin*, the sons of *Eustace*,
Earle of *Boulogne*, a sea towne in *Picardie*. The receiued opinion
is, that *Godfrey* was Captaine Generall of this Armie: it is ques-
tioned whether he was Duke of *Lorraine*: but this is for certaine,
that hee was descended of the ancient and Illustrious house of
Lorraine, that he was Duke of *Bouillon*, and Earle of *Boulogne* afore-
said; the memorable notes of which are vpon record as yet, in that
he sold *Mets* (a chiefe towne in *Lorraine*) to the inhabitants thereof:
and the Duchie of *Bouillon*, to *Hubert* Bishop of *Liege*, to furnish
himselfe with money for this holy Expedition.

And here we may obserue the error of some, about the name and
title of *Godfrey*, growne vpon the likenesse of the word: for there

is *Bologne*, a Citie in Italie, commonly called *Bononia*, with which, in this place, we haue nothing to doe: and there is *Boulogne* a Sea Towne in *Picardie*, famous amongst vs for being besieged by H. the eight, of which our *Godfrey* seemeth to haue been Earle; and thirdly there is *Bouillon*, adioyning to the Bishopricke of *Liege* of which *Godfrey* was stiled Duke.

The first enterprise that the Chriftians vndertooke, in their entrance into *Asia*, was the siege of *Nicea*, a citie in *Bithynia*, which is yet famous for the *Nicene* Councell; and that they wonne from the Turkes, in the space of 26. daies: after which they subdued other prouinces in *Asia*, as *Lycaonia*, *Cilicia*, *Syria*, *Mesopotamia*, and *Comagena*. In the yeere 1098. they won the citie *Antiochia*, vpon the riuer *Orontes*, after a difficult siege of nine moneths. At last they came to *Hierusalem*, which at that time the *Saracens* held, hauing newly recouered it from the Turkes, after the Turkes had possessed it eight yeeres. The Christians wonne this holie citie from the *Saracens*, after thirtie eight daies siege in the yeere 1099. in which they found so much difficulty, that they were about to leaue the siege, had they not beene animated to a new assault, by a prodigious and miraculous sight, which appeared from mount *Oliuet*, which by the shaking of a glittering shield, gaue them hope of victorious successe.

The chiefe honour of this conquest was giuen to *Godfrey*, because hee of all others, had raised a tower of wood, neere the wall of the citie, and from thence cast a bridge vpon the wall, by which the Christian souldiers made themselues masters of the Rampire, and so entred the towne. Hereupon by the consent of all the Princes *Godfrey* of *Bouillon* was chosen King of Hierusalem: who (shewing himselfe as full of Piety as valour) refused to be crowned with a crowne of gold, saying that it was not fit that any man should weare a crowne of gold in that citie, where Christ the King of Kings had worne a crowne of thornes: and thereupon made a vow to hold the kingdome of *Hierusalem*, and *Syria*, of the Pope, as a feudatarie Prince to the Church of *Rome*. But this perhaps was, to make some honourable amends for a fault he had committed, when being in the seruice of *Henry* the Emperour, in his warres against the Pope, he was the first that scaled the walls of *Rome*, and there planted his victorious Ensigne. So that he may be famous amongst Christian Princes, in that he conquered both Turke and Pope.

The Prouinces were diuided amongst the chiefe Princes; *Balduin* brother to *Godfrey* possessed *Cilicia, Comagena,* and *Mesopotamia,* and had the title of Count of *Edessa,* a citie in *Comagena,* which is the same that in the storie of *Tobias,* is called *Rages: Tancred* obtained the gouernment of *Tiberia,* and *Boemund* of *Antioche.*

Godfrey after he had enlarged his victories, with the conquest of diuers cities and places, in the land of *Palestine,* reigned one yeere King of *Hierusalem,* and then passed to the heauenly Hierusalem.

His Brother *Balduin* succeeded him, who increased the kingdome by the conquest of diuers famous cities; as *Antipatris, Cæsarea, Ptolemais, Tripolis, Laodicea,* and *Car* of *Mesopotamia:* and the *Iland Pharos* in *Egypt:* he reigned 18. yeeres, and left his successour *Balduin de Burgo,* his cousin German. In the reigne of this King was instituted the order of the Knights of *Hierusalem,* who commonly were called Knights of Saint *John,* and afterwards Knights of *Rhodes:* who for many yeeres defended Christendome against the Turkes and Saracens, and wonne many Ilands in the Mediterranean sea: but since that time the power of the Turke preuailing, and those countries being lost, these Knights hardly maintaine themselues within the straights of the Iland *Malta.* About this time also was the order of the *Templers* instituted, to be Champions for the holy war: but their riot brought them into contempt, and so they were dissolued. This second *Balduin* had great conquests against the Turkes and Saracens of Ægypt; winning from them *Damascus* and *Tirus.* He died in the yeare 1131. when he had reigned thirteene yeeres: after him grew dissentions amongst the Christian Princes, so that the kings of Hierusalem fell from their wonted pietie and prosperitie together; till at last in the yeare 1188, the Sultan of Ægypt recouered it wholly againe, and expelled or destroyed the Christians, when they had enioyed it 88. yeeres, after the first conquest.

So *Godfrey* died, in the yeeare 1100, the 15. of Iuly, and was buried in the Church of the Holy Sepulchre; vpon whose Tombe this is found written,

HIC IACET INCLYTVS DVX, GODFREY DVX DE BVILLON; QVI TOTAM ISTAM TERRAM ACQVISIVIT CVLTVI CHRISTIANO; CVIVS ANIMA REGNAT CVM CHRISTO. AMEN.

Verses: The Genius of Godfrey. To Prince Charles,
found in certain copies of the second edition,
e.g. Bodleian Library, Vet. A2.d.56

1624

The / Genius of Godfrey / To / Prince Charles

Nymphes of CALEDON, *happy are your bowres,*
Platted with wood-bine, Gessemine, and Bayes,
By which a silver streame so gently plaies,
And deckes the bancke on either side with flowres:
But far more happy were you in those dayes,
When as you waited in the stately towres,
Where CHARLES *was borne; & in his younger howres,*
Did give him suck & luld him with your layes.

You shepheards on the downes your flocks that keepe,
Happie you were, while your ELISA *daign'd*
To dwell amongst you; who so wisely raign'd
That never wolfe into your foulde durst peepe:
But now a better fortune have you gain'd,
For PAN *himselfe is carefull of your sheepe,*
And CHARLES *amidst your cottages doth sleepe,*
As PHOEBUS *did, when he a shepheard faign'd.*

You nymphs HESPERIDES, *you happy were,*
While in your power you had the trees of gold,
For none but HERCULES *that victor bold,*
Could put your fruit in danger, you in feare:
But you HESPERIAN *nymphs (could you have told)*
Were far more happie, while your shore did beare
Our noble CHARLES, *his like was never there;*
Who found your climate hot, your love but cold.

You NAIADES *that bathe you in the* SEINE
What triumphs did you make, what feasts, what games?
When TAGUS *sent a nymph among your Dames,*
Whom they with LILLIES *crownd to be their Queene:*
But you with greater ioy, shall send to IAMES
Your ÆGLE *faire; whom* CHARLES *shall take betweene*

His princely armes, and crowne with garlands greene;
And then for pompe TAGUS *shall yeeld to* THAMES.

You captive groves, and you polluted stones,
How welcome was to you, that warlike GROOME,
Who from wilde SATYRS *freed the sacred tombe,*
Where for three daies, our SHEPHERD *laid his bones?*
But yet you may expect a better doome,
When CHARLES *shall pitie take of all your grones,*
And leade an armie to expell those drones,
That doe usurpe HIERUSALEM *and* ROME.

COMMENTARY

THE ALLEGORY

A3^r, l. 25. Godfrey is chosen by the will of God and of the Princes: '. . . e che possono variamente avvenire, ed egli per voler d'Iddio e de' Principi . . .'

    F. repunctuates and mistakes the relation of clauses: '. . . which may diversely happen, and those by the will of God. And of Princes he is chosen Captain.'

A3^r, l. 35. 'Sweno' emends a slip for 'Syrenus': cf. VIII. 6, 'Sweno'. This is an easy misreading of 'Sueno', if indeed the error is F.'s and not the printer's.

A3^v, l. 19. F.'s 'inticements' for 'fallaci sillogismi' is perhaps too weak.

THE POEM

The first stanza exists in three forms, and the Argument in two. The case for the reconstruction of the stages of revision is given above in the Textual Introduction, Section I, 'Press Variants in 1600'.

The Argument: State a

God sends his angell to Tortosa downe:
Godfrey to counsell cals the Christian Peeres,
Where all the Lords and Princes of renowne
Chuse him their Generall, he straight appeeres,
Mustring his royall hoast, and in that stowne
Sends them to Sion, and then heart upcheeres.
The aged tyrant Iudaies land that guides
In feare and trouble to resist provides.

Stanza 1: State α

I sing the sacred armies and the knight
That Christs great tombe enfranchis'd and set free,
Much wrought he by his witte, much by his might,
Much in that glorious conquest suffred hee;
Hell hindred him in vaine, in vaine to fight
Asias and Affricks people armed bee;
Heav'n favour him, his lords and knights misgone
Under his Ensigne he reduc'd in one.

This is now known to be found only in two copies, one in the possession of Lady Fairfax and one in the Huntington Library.

The Argument: State b

God sends his Angell to Tortosa downe,
Godfrey unites the Christian peeres and knights,
And all the Lords and Princes of renowne
Choose him their Duke, to rule the wars and fights,

He mustreth all his host, whose number knowne,
He sends them to the fort that Sion hights,
    The aged Tyrant *Iudaes* land that guides
In feare and trouble to resist provides.

Stanza 1: State β

The sacred Armies, and the godly Knight
That the great Sepulcher of Christ did free,
I sing; much wrought his Valour and foresight,
And in that glorious warre much suffred he:
In vaine gainst him did Hell oppose her might,
In vaine the Turkes and Morians armed bee,
His souldiers wilde (to braules and mutines prest)
Reduced he to peace, so heav'n him blest.

The Argument as in b.

Stanza 1: State γ

I sing the warre made in the Holyland,
And the Great Chiefe that Christs great tombe did free:
Much wrought he with his wit, much with his hand,
Much in that brave atchievment suffred hee:
In vaine doth hell the Man of God withstand,
In vaine the worlds great princes armed bee;
For heav'n him favour'd; and he brought againe
Under one standard all his scatt'red traine.

This is supplied on a slip pasted over st. 1 following the Argument as in
State b.

Collier at one time[1] supposed that Fairfax had altered what he took to be
the first draft (i.e. b, above) because he had been accused of copying Carew
whose rendering is:

I sing the godly armes and that Chieftaine,
Who great Sepulchre of our Lord did free,
Much with his hande, much wrought he with his braine:
Much in his glorious conquest suffred hee:
And hell in vaine hit selfe opposde, in vaine
The mixed troopes, *Asian* and *Libick* flee
To armes; for heaven him favour'd, and he drew
To sacred ensignes his straid mates anew.

On the revised ordering, though not for Collier's reason, this seems feasible,
since line 4 of a, but for one word, corresponds exactly with the earlier
translation, as Koeppel once pointed out. Otherwise it is hard to detect
a more precise motive than a perfectionist at work.

The fact that the second edition (1624) prints version b has led some to
suppose that after all Fairfax preferred it; but it could equally well be argued

[1] J. Payne Collier, *A Bibliographical and Critical Account of the rarest books in the
English Language*, 2 vols. (London, 1865), i. 106.

that it was because he had little or nothing to do with this edition and the printer had available a copy without the pasted slip.

The five accidentals noted between a and b are of no authorial significance.

I

4. Tasso's dedication first to Alfonso II of Ferrara (nephew of Clement VIII), and later to Cinzio Aldobrandini (1533–97), is simplified to 'Noble Princes'. Fairfax supplies the allegorical hint in l. 3.

Waller echoes Fairfax in '*A Panegyric to my Lord Protector*', ll. 173–6:

> Then let the Muses, with such notes as these,
> Instruct us what belongs unto our peace;
> Your battles they hereafter shall indite,
> And draw the image of our Mars in fight.

5. Fairfax makes Tasso's general reference particular by naming Greece.

7. Cf. *Paradise Lost*, III. 542–3:

[Satan] Looks down with wonder at the sudden view
    Of all this world at once.

The use of a list in the last line becomes only too common a device. If examples are needed, see: I. 14, 30, 43, 79; II. 16, 47, 62; III. 49; IV. 25; V. 4, 18; VI. 4, 64, 87; VII. 55; VIII. 7; IX. 58, 73, 90; X. 3; XI. 57; XII. 29, 43; XIII. 29, 32; XIV. 1, 9, 23, 37, 45, 55; XVI. 25, 41; XIX. 16; XX. 13, 53, 73, 108.

11⁴. Fairfax omits Gabriel's precise status, 'ne' primi era secondo'. The sense of the couplet is a little blurred; Tasso's angel is said to carry the commands of God down, and the prayers of mortals up.

13. Cf. *Paradise Lost*, III. 636–42:

> And now a stripling cherub he appears,
> Not of the prime, yet such as in his face
> Youth smiled celestial, and to every limb
> Suitable grace diffused, so well he feigned;
> Under a coronet his flowing hair
> In curls on either cheek played, wings he wore
> Of many a coloured plume sprinkled with gold,

14. Fairfax takes his own way with the last line ('e si librò su l'adeguate penne') and supplies the reference to 'may dews' with the attractive, though tautologous, adjective 'roarie' which he appears to have coined; he uses it again in IV. 75.

Cf. *Paradise Lost*, V. 285–7:

> Like Maia's son he stood,
> And shook his plumes, that heavenly fragrance filled
> The circuit wide.

15⁷. Cf. *Paradise Lost*, VIII. 295:

> One came, methought, of shape divine,

16⁶. There is a faint echo of Isaiah 35: 3, 'strengthen the weak hands, and comfort the feeble knees' (Genevan version, 1560).

17⁷. Fairfax gives a ludicrous turn to Tasso's tactful phrasing:

> Resta Goffredo a i detti, a lo splendore,
> d'occhi abbagliato, attonito di core.

20. Fairfax makes the sense more vivid by supplying details; the third line is his own invention.

29. The looseness of Fairfax's rendering is reproved in *Retrospective Review*, iii (1821), 32–50, and contrasted with Carew's translation:

> He spake, his speech a muttring short befell,
> Next after solitarie *Peter* rose,
> Though private, mongst the princes at counsell,
> As he from whom that voyage chiefly groes,
> What *Godfrey* doth exhort, I say aswell,
> No doubt here fals, the truth so certaine shoes,
> It skryes hit selfe, he plaine demonstrance gave,
> Th' allowance longs to you, sole t'adde I have.

31¹. Cf. *Paradise Lost*, IV. 111:

> Divided empire with heaven's king I hold / By thee.

32. *Retrospective Review*, iii (1821), 38 notes Carew's superior accuracy. Fairfax slides over the condensed expression in ll. 5–6:

> Sgombri gl'inserti, anzi gl'innati affetti / di sovrastar, di libertà, d'onore,

and omits precise reference to Guglielmo and Guelfo; this is, perhaps, odd, since this William was said to be the son of William Rufus. Carew reads:

> The olde man silenst here. What thoughts? what breasts?
> Are shut from thee breath sacred! heat divine!
> Thou in the Hermite dost enspire these heasts,
> And in the Knights harts thou the same dost shrine,
> Th'ingraft, th'inborne affections thou outwrests
> Of rule, of libertie, of honours signe.
>   So as both Gwelfe and Guillam chiefe in place,
>   Did *Godfrey* first with name of Chieftaine grace.

34⁵. Cf. *Paradise Lost*, IX. 835: 'But first low reverence done'.

37. Carew and Fairfax make the same mistake. Tasso says that Clotareo was *not* of royal blood. 'France the Isle' = Île de France.

38. For the list of trees, which has a long history, Bell refers back to Chaucer, *The Parlement of Foules*, 176–82. See also below, III. 76.

40–1. Fairfax mistakes Tasso's 'Carnuti' (i.e. Stephen Earl of Chartres, Blois, and Tours) for 'Carinto', and omits to mention Carinthia as the region ruled by Guelfo (st. 41).

42. The baths are added by Fairfax.

44. See M. Drayton, 'The Legend of Robert, Duke of Normande', ll. 722–42, ed. Hebel and Hudson, ii. 403.

44.[7] Sir G(ilbert) T(albot), in a note in the manuscript translation in the Bodleian MSS. Rawlinson Poet. I and 4, objects that Tasso's reference to Guglielmo is faulty: it should be to Roberto. See below, III. 62.

Fairfax leaves out 'irsuti' in describing the Irish. Carew has 'locks shaggy'.

45[4]. Cf. *Paradise Regained*, I. 229: 'High are thy thoughts / O son.'

47[4]. Fairfax adds the detail of her hair in the breeze, and makes his own patterning in the sixth line.

49. Fairfax adds the metaphors of the tide and the crop; the wooing metaphor and the final antithesis are his also.

To some there is an echo in l. 6 of *Paradise Regained*, IV. 305:

Wealth, pleasure, pain or torment, death and life.

52. Fairfax adds Lancelot and substitutes Orpheus for Argo, presumably because a poem upon the Argonauts was attributed to Orpheus. Tasso's Mini = Minyae = Thessalians = Argonauts.

58. Fairfax takes this description very boldly and Philip Doyne objects. Carew is conservative:

But youth *Rinaldo* farre surpasseth these,
And passeth all that to the muster went,
Most sweetly fierce, up should you see him rayse
His royal looke and all lookes on it spent:
He hope oregoes, he overgrowes his dayes,
When bud was thought but bloome, out fruit he sent.

60[3]. The accentuation of Aegéan indicated by the metre is to be noted again in *Paradise Lost*, I. 746: 'On Lemnos the Aegaean isle.'

61. *Piraene*: Pyrenees. Fairfax adds the reference to Troy.

62[8]. Fairfax adds the simile. For the proverb see Tilley, F.270.

64. Fairfax recasts the couplet with his own metaphor. Cf.:

o mostri almen ch'a la virtù latina
o nulla manca, o sol la disciplina.

71. The second line incorporates an echo from Psalm 19: 5, and may be compared with *Faerie Queene*, I. v. 2.

73. Fairfax has an additional description of the horses and includes Phaeton, the son of Helios, who perished while attempting to drive the chariot of the sun.

75⁶. Cf. *Paradise Lost*, II. 177: 'Impendent horrors, threatening hideous fall . . .'.

77. *Mount seir*: Edom. Cf. l. 5 with *Comus*, l. 102:

> Meanwhile, welcome joy, and feast.

Fairfax adds the allusion to the evening star, Hesperus. Cf. *Paradise Lost*, IV. 605–6: 'Hesperus that led / The starry host.'

81. It is Fairfax who supplies the epithets for Fame.

82. 'Evil' is evidently monosyllabic.

84. Fairfax adds Termagant. Koeppel compares *Faerie Queene*, VI. vii. 47.

85. Tasso has summer warming the snake: Fairfax brings it to the fire.

89. Fairfax supplies the proper names for the wells.

90. The details in ll. 5–6 are Fairfax's expansion of Tasso's:

> ma da' primi sospetti ei le munia
> d'alti ripari il suo men forte canto,

II

1⁴. Cf. *Paradise Lost*, V. 410–11:

> Within them every lower faculty
> Of sense, whereby they hear, see, smell, touch, taste

2. Fairfax adds the reference to Acheron, the river flowing down into Hades, and also the mention of Achitophel and Absalom (2 Samuel 15–17).

A MS. note in the Dyce copy in the Victoria and Albert Museum runs: 'quote this (with the Italian) in a note on *Macbeth*.'

3². The scriptural echo of Matthew 3: 10 or Luke 3: 9 is contributed by Fairfax. Cf. with l. 6, *Paradise Lost*, II. 390:

> Well have ye judged, well ended long debate.

4⁵. Cf. *Paradise Lost*, III. 630:

> Glad was the spirit impure as now in hope . . .

5. Fairfax adds 'slender', 'an hundred', and substitutes 'myrrhe', etc. for the votive offerings. He misses the scorn of Ismen's reference to the credulous devotees.

8. Fairfax goes further than Tasso in making Aladine *kill* the watchmen.

9. The reference to the Virgin as 'regina e diva' is left out, and a padding third line supplied.

11. For the proverbial phrase added in l. 6, cf. Tilley, T.138,

12–13. The translation here is free, and coloured by scriptural allusions (to Isaiah 5: 6 and Matthew 13: 25–30) which are not in keeping with the pagan Aladine.

13³. Bell remarks a possible echo from Gower's *Confessio Amantis*, I. 2128–9:

> A trompe with a sterne breth
> Which was cleped the trompe of deth.

14. Doyne objects to Fairfax's free way with this stanza. Cf. Carew:

> Amongst them was a mayd of maidenhed
> To ripenesse growne, of high and noble thought:
> Of bewtie rare, but bewtie valewed,
> Or nought or sole, for it to vertue brought
> Accompt, most priz'd because straight cabyned,
> Twixt wals her prices great to hide she sought.
>   And of her wooers unbepranct and sole,
>   Both from the laud, and from the lookes she stole.

15. Fairfax skirts Tasso's allusion to love as now blind, now sighted like Argos, and uses the proverbial 'a woman to be won' as a conclusion: see Tilley, W.681. Cf. Carew:

> But guard is none that wholy can conceale,
> Bewtie of worth likt and admirde to be,
> Nor love consent will give, but it reveale
> Unto a young mans hote desires doth hee,
> Love that now blinde, now *Argos*, now with vaile
> Dost blind thine eyes, now open wide dost see,
>   Thou through a thousand watches into chast
>   Maides lodgings others sight conveyed hast.

18. Doyne and the writer in *Retrospective Review*, iii. 39 object to Fairfax's freedom, and contrast Carew:

> This maide alone through preace of vulgar went,
> Bewty she covers not, nor sets to sight,
> Shadow'd her eyes, in vayle her bodie pent,
> With manner coy, yet coy in noble plight,
> I note where car'de, or carelesse ornament,
> Where chance, or art her fairest countnance dight,
>   Friended by heav'ns, by nature, and by love,
>   Her meere neglects most artificiall prove.

In Fairfax's favour one may remark the felicity of the fourth line and cf. Keats:

> As though a rose should shut, and be a bud again.
> *The Eve of St. Agnes* (, stanza xxvii.)

22. Fairfax substitutes 'this spotlesse lamb' for 'cape altero'. Cf. Carew: 'hautie hed'.

26. Fairfax coarsens a little: 'Aspre ritorte' (Carew's 'hard wythes') becomes,

for rhyme's sake, 'twisted wires'. He addresses Sophronia as 'silver dove' and works in the kite metaphor. He misses a nice contrast caught by Carew's 'not a palenesse, but a whitnesse', and is content with 'damaske late, now changed to purest white'.

27⁵⁻⁶. Fairfax's concreteness avoids a harder distinction in Tasso:

> Come la bella prigionera in atto
> non pur di rea, ma di dannata ei scorse,

Cf. Carew:

> When as the prisner faire he founde in act
> Not of accusde, but cast to be the same.

28. Fairfax's rhetoric is vigorous; he slips a sailing metaphor into the couplet and simplifies Tasso's play upon 'amore':

> Ahi! tanto amò la non amante amata.

Cf. Carew 'So love not loving loved he alas.'

29. Fairfax elaborates the broken window and invents the last line.

31⁸. The bellows metaphor is Fairfax's.

32. Fairfax moralizes in the first line and supplies the adjective 'worthlesse'; he adds the 'two harmlesse turtles'.

34. Fairfax amplifies the reference to the gods of marriage and love, Hymen and Cupid. He has his own rhetoric in l. 6.

35. This passage seems to have been in William Browne's mind when telling the story of Coelia and Philocel in *Britannia's Pastorals*, Bk. II, Song 5, ll. 739–44.

36. The quieter style of Tasso's couplet is more telling:

> Mira 'l ciel com'e bello, e mira il sole
> ch'a sé par che n'inviti e ne console.

Cf. Carew:

> Behold how faire heav'n showes, the sunne behold
> You seemes t'invite, and comforts to unfold.

38. Fairfax adds the inn-sign metaphor.

39. Fairfax works in the dove/eagle contrast but omits Arachne. It is possible that he echoes Spenser's 'fine needle and nice thread' in a parallel passage, *Faerie Queene*, III. ii. 6.

40. Fairfax draws in the reference to Atlanta who outdistanced all suitors until she was tempted aside by the golden apples thrown in her way by Melanion. He takes the description of Clorinda's upbringing so freely that

Doyne suspects him of not understanding. Bell prefers to believe that he is deliberately avoiding awkward literalness such as Carew's. Singer suggests an eye-error of 'fera' as 'fairy' when glancing at Tasso's lines:

> Seguì le guerre, e'n esse e fra le selve
> fèra a gli uomini parve, uomo a le belve.

Fairfax's couplet is quite new. Cf. Carew's:

> She warre ensewes, in which, and in forreasts,
> Men savage her, man her deeme savage beasts.

41. Fairfax intrudes the parenthesis in l. 7 and leaves out the reference to Clorinda on horseback.

45. Fairfax adds 'courteous'.

48. Fairfax evades Tasso's sense in ll. 2–3, 'or tu dimandi / ch'impieghi io te'.
Cf. Carew:

> [Now, now, me seemes, *Godfrey* beyond his dew
> Protractes the time], and where you please, demaund
> Employd to be, [sole fit I deeme for you
> Exploytes, where hazard hath most honour pawnd,]

49. Fairfax simplifies Tasso's couplet:

> ma taccio questo, e taccio i segni espressi
> onde argomento l'innocenza in essi.

Carew has:

> But this I silence, and I silence signes
> Expresse, through which their innocency shines.

50⁴. For the proverb see Tilley, F.516.

51⁵⁻⁶. Fairfax adds terms which give precision.

52⁶. The reference to 'these Frenchmen' is an English interpolation.

53. The pattern in l. 4 is not uncommon in Elizabethan lyric poetry: Koeppel refers to Sidney's use, and an instance might be found in *Astrophil and Stella*, sonnet 32. A perfect parallel occurs rather later in *Antony and Cleopatra*, III. ii. 16–17:

> Hearts, tongues, figures, scribes, bards, poets cannot
> Think, speak, cast, write, sing, number . . .

54. Fairfax works in the parenthesis and the reference to Pharaoh.

55. The freedom of this stanza has frequently been censured: Fairfax intrudes the reference to sheep and tries to work in a proverbial expression (see Tilley, T.535); he reverts to Tasso in the couplet. The vexation of l. 3

is eased by adopting the reading 'labour's vertues', found in two copies B and M (see above), and further helped by the punctuation suggested by Singer:

> But labour's vertue's watching, ease her sleep,
> Trouble best wind that drives salvation's barge.

These lines are Fairfax's insertion, but seem to derive remotely from Tasso's:

> altri rubelli
> fèrsi, e più che 'l timor potè lo sdegno.

translated by Carew as:

> Many went wandring, some the redets play,
> Whom more then feare could quench, anger doth tind.

57. Fairfax intrudes descriptive details into the simpler reference to the dawn:

> L'avean già tese, e poco remota
> l'alma luce del sol da l'oceano,

58. Fairfax works in a rose metaphor and a moralizing couplet. Cf. Carew:

> A biter at the backe by such quaint wayes,
> As when he carpeth most, he seemes to prayse.

60. The reference to the humbleness of Godfrey's court is omitted.

61. Fairfax skips the reason why Alete's Syrian speech was easily understood by the French:

> e perché i Franchi han già il sermone appreso
> de la Soria, fu ciò ch'ei disso inteso.

62. Fairfax evades an allusion to Alcides and works to a softer, more general sense involving a harvest metaphor: Doyne objects. Cf. Carew:

> Within *Alcides* boundes your name to stay
> Brookes not, but ev'n mongst us takes farder flight,
> And fame hath through ech part of *Egypt* spred
> The tidings cleare of your great manlihed.

63. Fairfax's free rhetoric compares not unfavourably with Carew's endeavour to follow exactly, with the result that without the Italian alongside his English is hardly intelligible:

> Nor of so many any one not lent,
> (As men to marvailes use) hath listning eare,
> But them, my king, not with astonishment
> Alone, but with like great delight doth heare,
> And glad in their report oft time hath spent,
> Loving in you, what they envy and feare.
> He loves your valure, and doth free elect
> With you to ioyne in love, if not in sect.

Ne v'è fra tanti alcun che non le ascolte
come egli suol le meraviglie estreme,
ma dal mio re con istupore accolte
sono non sol, ma con diletto insieme;
e s'appaga in narrarle anco a le volte,
amando in te ciò ch'altri invia e teme.
    ama il valore, e volontario elegge
    teco unirsi d'amor, se non di legge.

It is tempting to read 'yet' for 'that' in Fairfax's l. 5, but it is not strictly necessary.

65. Fairfax substitutes a general sense with a proverbial ring in l. 5 (cf. Tilley, H.196) for Tasso's precise reference to danger from Persians and Turks.

66. Fairfax begins with a scriptural allusion to Matthew 3: 20 hardly appropriate for the Pagan speaker.

67[1]. 'Sinne' (1600 and 1624); 'sun' (1749); 'sonne' (Singer); 'sign' has also been conjectured. *O.E.D.* under 'apogee' uses the reading 'sunne'.

67–8. These stanzas are loosely translated, but the general sense is conveyed. The sea metaphor in st. 68 is Fairfax's own. He may be indebted to the *Shepheardes Calender*, February, l. 39 for his last line:

    Tho gynne you, fond flyes, the cold to scorne.

70. Fairfax adds a metaphorical touch in l. 4 and brings in the allusion to Mars, god of war.

71[8]. The Biblical echo of 2 Kings 18: 21 is of Fairfax's providing.

72. Fairfax reworks the first four lines introducing a simile and an ironic double comparison showing a touch of his learning.
    Cf. Tasso:

    La fede greca a chi non è palese?
    Tu da un sol tradimento ogni altro impara
    anzi da mille, perché mille ha tese
    insidie a voi la gente infida, avara.

73[2]. Cf. *Paradise Lost*, IX. 635–6:

    Compact of unctuous vapour, which the night
    Condenses, and the cold environs round,

77[8]. Compare Tilley, R.136 for this proverb.

89. Fairfax inserts his own comparison in the parenthesis.

91. Fairfax's handling of the last four lines is very free. He leaves out the second Fury, Megara, but gives to Tasso's giant the proper name of Tiphoeus, the hundred-handed monster who warred against Zeus and was at last

confined under Etna. Tasso's allusion to Nimrod and the Tower of Babel occupies four lines, Fairfax has to reduce it to the couplet to make room for the extra giant from Genesis 10: 10. *Paradise Lost*, II. 539 may echo the English addition:

> Others with vast Typhoean rage more fell . . .'.

93⁵. The pattern repeats one used in st. 53.

94. Fairfax makes room for the allusion to Paris, as the lover, and to Hector, as the warrior, among the sons of Priam, king of Troy; this sharpens Tasso's contrast.

96. The couplet is Fairfax's invention. It was remarked by Rymer, with some satisfaction, that the English poet salvaged the one detail (l. 524) that the Italian had omitted when he reworked the famous lines in Virgil's *Aeneid*, IV. 522–7:

> Nox erat, et placidum carpebant fessa soporem
> corpora per terras, silvaeque et saeva quierant
> aequora, *cum medio volvuntur sidera lapsu* [our italics],
> cum tacet omnis ager, pecudes pictaeque volucres,
> quaeque lacus late liquidos, quaeque aspera dumis
> rura tenent, somno positae sub nocte silenti.

(See J. E. Spingarn, *Critical Essays of the Seventeenth Century*, ii (1908), 176.)
The fanciful expression in the final line is changed by the 1749 editor to:

> Sooth'd mortal cares, and lull'd the world to rest.

97. Fairfax brings in the lark.

III

1. Fairfax adds the bee simile and gives the colours of the dawn.

4. Fairfax may have chosen 'iolly' for Tasso's 'audace' from a broadly comparable stanza in *Faerie Queene*, I. xii. 42. For l. 2 cf. *Paradise Lost*, I. 290:

> Or in Valdarno, to descry new lands.

For l. 8 cf. *Paradise Lost*, I. 208: '. . . and wished morn delays'.

6. Fairfax intrudes the moralizing in ll. 3 and 6. For l. 6 cf. *Paradise Lost*, II. 285–7:

>   as when hollow rocks retain
> The sound of blustering winds, which all night long
> Had roused the sea,

8. Fairfax recasts this stanza in the style of a medieval lyric.

9⁴. Fairfax makes the fourth line his own and gives it an English character; cf. Tasso, 'sì che par che gran nube in aria stampi'.

15–16. The final metaphors are Fairfax's own.

17. Fairfax introduces the nautical suggestion by his initial 'mast'; he supplies the simile in l. 3. The comparison with *Paradise Lost*, I. 292–4 is irresistible:

> His spear, to equal which the tallest pine
> Hewn on Norwegian hills, to be the mast
> Of some great ammiral, were but a wand,

19[6]. Fairfax supplies the proper name.

21. Fairfax adds the final simile.

22[4]. Cf. *Paradise Lost*, II. 747: 'Hast thou forgot me then . . .'.

22[8]. Fairfax completes the antithesis. There is perhaps an echo heard at the end of Pope's pastoral, *Summer*:

> On me love's fiercer flames for ever prey
> By night he scorches, as he burns by day.

23[3]. Fairfax adds the reference to the axe.

28. Cf. *Paradise Lost*, III. 227–37, esp. the sentences:

> Father, thy word is past, man shall find grace;
> . . . .
> . . . life for life
> I offer, on me let thine anger fall;

29[7]. Fairfax adds 'O stay thy cursed hand'.

31. The word-play of Tasso's couplet is simplified:

> or si volge o rivolge, or fugge o fuga,
> né si può dir la sua caccia né fuga.

32. The notorious freedom of this stanza may spring from an initial misunderstanding both of the simile of the bull in the arena and the reference to the Moorish games. Once started, Fairfax becomes so involved with his substituted comparison that he cuts out the two lines (5–6) which refer back to Clorinda. The reference to 'tennise' perhaps covers ignorance of the game popularly called 'caroselli' which is what is here intended. A full description is provided in the note in Caretti's edition (*Tutte le Poesie di Torquato Tasso*, i (1957), 679).

Cf. Carew's faithful, though awkward rendering:

> Right so fierce Bull sometimes in market-place,
> If hornes to dogges he turne, from whence he fled,
> They there retire, and if to flight he pace,
> Ech makes returne to chace emboldened:
> At backe *Clorinda* (whiles she flight doth trace)
> High holds her shield, and guards thereby her hed:
> Defenced in *Monseo* pastimes so,
> From balles against them throwne, the flyers go.

33[8]. Fairfax adds the allusion to Hector (cf. *Iliad*, V).

34. Fairfax fashions this line to suit himself. Cf. Tasso, 'molti cadendo compagnia gli fèro'.

36. Fairfax substitutes his own couplet. Cf. Carew:

> Nor he alone brought succour to his band,
> But eke that troupe which made for neede a stand.

37[8]. Fairfax tucks in the reference to Achilles, son of Peleus.

43[8]. The comparison that Fairfax adds suggests a recollection of *Faerie Queene*, V. xi. 11.

45[4]. Fairfax adds the explanatory parenthesis.

46. Fairfax elaborates the details of Dudon's death, but not to advantage! Cf. Tasso:

> Gli aprì tre volte, e i dolci rai del cielo
> cercò fruire e sovra un braccio alzarsi,
> e tre volte ricadde, e fosco velo
> gli occhi adombrò, che stanchi al fin serràrsi.
> Si dissolvono i membri, e 'l mortal gelo
> inrigiditi e di sudor gli ha sparsi.

49[4]. The inappropriate simile is Fairfax's responsibility.

51[6]. The *sententia* is Fairfax's providing.

62. Fairfax interpolates the reference to Neptune and the doves/goshawk simile, making room for them by transferring the mention of Sigier to st. 53. There may well be a memory of one of several uses that Spenser makes of this comparison, e.g. *Faerie Queene*, III. iv. 40; V. xii. 5; VI. viii. 49. Cf. Waller, *A Panegyric to my Lord Protector*, ll. 9–11:

> Above the waves as Neptune showed his face
> To chide the winds, and save the Trojan race,
> So has your Highness . . .

53[8]. The last line is Fairfax's own and may carry a memory of a Spenserian simile in *Faerie Queene*, II. iv. 11 or III. vii. 34.

57. The couplet is freely rendered. Cf. Tasso:

> Austro portar le suol piovoso nembo,
> Betelèm che 'l gran parto ascose in grembo.

62[4]. Fairfax supplies a detail about Raimond to fill in. Sir G(ilbert) T(albot) substitutes Robert for William. See above, I. 44.

65. The allusion in parenthesis is Fairfax's own.

69. The lament is freely taken with the addition of the metaphors in ll. 2–3.

Some compression was needed to make room for a new last line with its echo of Psalm 126: 5.

70. This stanza is boldly recast to work in the allusion to Dothan (2 Kings 6: 13 ff.).

71³. Cf. *Samson Agonistes*, l. 593: 'But yield to double darkness nigh at hand'.

72. The parenthesis is Fairfax's.

75–6. These two stanzas are freely translated with effective vigour. Fairfax supplies the echo and the nymphs and may have had in mind some of the many descriptions of the kind, e.g. Ovid, *Metamorphoses* X. 90; Lucan, *Pharsalia*, III. 440; Statius, *Thebaid*, VI. 98; Chaucer, *Parlement of Foules*, ll. 232–8; Spenser, *Faerie Queene*, I. i. 8/9 (Bell).

75³. Cf. Milton, *Ode on the Morning of Christ's Nativity*, ll. 187–8:

> With flower-inwoven tresses torn
> The nymphs in twilight shade of tangled thickets mourn.

I V

2. Fairfax expands the last line with a faintly scriptural echo, cf. Proverbs 25: 22 and Romans 12: 20.

Cf. the second half of the stanza with *Paradise Lost*, VI, 135–9:

> fool, not to think how vain
> Against the omnipotent to rise in arms;
> Who out of smallest things could without end
> Have raised incessant armies to defeat
> Thy folly;

3. Fairfax evades some of Tasso's harder turns which Carew follows with laboured accuracy:

> The dwellers of th'eternall shades he calles,
> By hellish trumpet of hoarse iarring sound,
> At such a dynne the wide darke vaulted walles,
> All quake the misty thicke aire gan rebound:
> Nor whistling so the flash downe ever falles
> From upper regions of the sky to ground,
> Nor shogged earth so ever bideth throwes,
> When bigge in wombe she doth the vapours close.

4⁸. Fairfax is not content with Tasso's comparison to a whip, but provides his own hyperbole in the last line:

> e lor s'aggira dietro immensa coda
> che quasi sferza si ripiega e snoda.

5. The translation is free. Fairfax omits the reference to Dante's monster,

Geryon (*Inferno*, XVII), and adds the reference to the Cyclops blinded by Odysseus, Polyphemus, who 'Blinde supporteth hell'. It is left ambiguous whether 'support' means 'endure' or 'hold up'. The allusion to 'Cilenos rout' for the Harpies may be an echo from *Faerie Queene*, II. vii. 23.

7. Fairfax changes Tasso's comet into 'two beacons', and adds the detai. in l. 6. He may be remembering *Faerie Queene*, I. xi. 14 and VI. vii. 42.
     Cf. *Paradise Lost*, I. 239:

> Both glorying to have scaped the Stygian flood . . .

9⁴. Fairfax changes Tasso's 'orribil chiostra' into 'emptie lake': Carew has 'ghastly denne'.

10. Fairfax misses the rhetorical force of the parenthesis in l. 5 which Carew contrives to convey:

> Then (ah this thought how heavie doth it way:)
> This tis which sharpely wounds a new my skarres.

11. Fairfax's stanza is more lyrical and stresses the joy of the redeemed souls rather than the implication of the victor's scorn of the defeated devils. Cf. Tasso:

> e riportarne al Ciel sì ricche prede,
> vincitor trionfando, e in nostro scherno
> l'insegne ivi spiegar del vinto Inferno.

     Cf. *Paradise Lost*, II. 695:

> To waste eternal days in woe and pain?

15⁵⁻⁸. Cf. *Paradise Lost*, I. 576–7:

> though all the Giant brood
> Of Phlegra with heroic race were joined . . .

16. Fairfax introduces the metaphor of weeds and works up to the sententious l. 8.
     Cf. *Paradise Lost*, I. 121 and II. 41:

> To wage by force or guile eternal war . . .

> Whether by open war or covert guile,

17². Cf. *Paradise Lost*, II. 406–7:

> And through the palpable obscure find out
> His uncouth way,

18⁵⁵⁻⁸. The last four lines are pure Fairfax. Cf. Carew:

> Much like the storms of broylly whistling iarre,
> Whom native caves foorth from their intrayls send,
>   To darke the welkin, and a warre to band,
>   Against the great Realmes, both of sea and land.

20⁴. Cf. *Comus*, l. 40, 'And here their tender age might suffer peril'.

22. Lines 3 and 6 are Fairfax additions.

24². Cf. *Paradise Regained*, I. 377–8:

> though I have lost
> Much lustre of my native brightness,

25⁵. Cf. *Samson Agonistes*, l. 1004:

> Yet beauty, though injurious, hath strange power,

and, *Paradise Lost*, VIII, 533–4:

> here only weak
> Against the charm of beauty's powerful glance.

29⁷. 'Guidos' must surely be an error for 'Gnidos', where the famous statue of Aphrodite was.

29–32. These stanzas are almost completely rewritten. Cf. Carew's close rendering:

> Not *Argos, Cyprus, Delos* ere present,
> Paternes of shape, or bewtie could so deere,
> Gold are her lockes, which in white shadow pent,
> Eft do but glimpse, eft all disclosde appeare,
> As when new clensde we see the element,
> Sometimes the Sun shines through white cloud uncleere,
>   Sometimes from cloud out gone his raies more bright
>   He sheads abroad, dubling the day of light.
>
> The wind new crisples makes in her loose haire,
> Which nature selfe to waves recrispelled,
> Her sparing looke a coy regard doth beare,
> And loves treasures, and hers upwympelled,
> Sweete Roses colour in that visage faire,
> With yvorie is sperst and mingelled,
>   But in her mouth whence breath of love out goes,
>   Ruddy alone and single bloomes the Rose.
>
> Her bosome faire musters his naked snow,
> Whence fire of love is nourisht and revives,
> Her pappes bitter unripe in part doe show,
> And part th'envious weed from sight deprives:
> Envious, but though it close passage so
> To eyes, loves thought unstaid yet farder strives:
>   Which outward bewty taking not for pay,
>   Ev'n to his secrets hid endeeres a way.
>
> As through water or chrystall sound the ray
> Passeth, and it devides or parteth not,
> So piercing through her closed robe a way
> His daring thought to part forbodden got,
> It roameth there, there true it doth survay,
> Of so great marvailes part by part the plot:

> Then to desire it tels, and it descrives,
> And in his breast the flames more quicke revives.

42⁴. Fairfax supplies the fourth line.

44.⁴ Cf. Milton, *On the Death of a Fair Infant*, l. 40:

> Or in Elysian fields (if such there were) . . .

45⁶. Fairfax adds the proverbial phrase: cf. Tilley, S.585.

46. The translation is culpably free: Fairfax neglects Tasso's negative in the first two lines:

> e mai né stile
> di cavalier, né nobil arte apprese,

he then works up a conceit of his own in the second half of the stanza, introducing the reference to Ares, god of war, as the husband of Cytherea, and to Satan, Lord of hell.

47⁸. The final proverb is Fairfax's interpolation. See Tilley, A.32.

51⁶. Fairfax adds the flower metaphor.

54². Cf. *Paradise Lost*, II. 960:

> [When straight behold the throne
> Of Chaos, and his dark pavilion spread
> Wide on the wasteful deep; with him enthroned]
> Sat sable-vested Night,

57. Fairfax changes the accusation from the many lovers she would have had to a specific infidelity.

59⁸. 'causeless', one might be tempted to read 'ceaseless'.

63¹⁻². Cf. *Paradise Lost*, III. 154–5:

> Father, who art judge
> Of all things made, and judgest only right.

66⁸. 'his' = those who are with the king. Cf.:

> e genti ed arme gli ministri ed oro
> contra gli Egizi e chi sarà con loro.

67. Cf. *Paradise Lost*, IV. 108–9:

> So farewell hope, and with hope farewell fear,
> Farewell remorse:

72. Doyne objects to the change of image in the final line. Cf. Carew:

> Not you my Lord, not such is your bountie,
> But tis my dest'ny, which me aie denies;
> Dest'ny dismall, fell fatall destinie,
> Yeeld eke my hated life to death a prize:

Was it (aye me) a slender injurie,
To close in youthes flowre my deere parents eyes?
  That thou must also see my kingdome reft?
  And thrald to th'axe as sacrifice me left?

73. Avoiding a reference to the power of bribes, Fairfax gets an extra turn in the last line which may have connections with Sidney and Webster.
    See *Arcadia* (1590), ed. Feuillerat, Lib. I, ch. 4: 'Lastly, whether your time call you to live or die, doo both like a prince.', and *The Duchess of Malfi*, in Webster, *Works*, ed. F. L. Lucas (1927), II. 162:

For know whether I am doomb'd to live or die
I can doe both like a prince. (III. ii. 78–9).

75. Liberties are taken, especially in the couplet. Cf. Carew:

Her cheekes with those life humours sprinckelled,
Which trickling dropt down on her vestures hemme,
Seem'd entermingled roses white and red;
If so a dewy cloud do water them,
When to calme breath their closed lap they spred,
What time first peered dawning takes his stemme,
  And morne which them beholds and in them ioyes,
  Proud with their ornament her lockes accoyes.

76. Fairfax elaborates freely and has a fresh conceit. Cf. Carew:

But that cleere humour which embellisheth
Her bosome and faire ckeekes with drops so thicke,
Workes the effect of fire, and close creepeth
Into a thousand breasts, and there doth sticke:
O miracle of love! which sparckes draweth
From teares, and harts in water kindles quicke
  With flames, past nature still his powre extends,
  But in her vertue bove it selfe ascends.

78[8]. Fairfax works in the proverb. See Tilley, T.95.

85. Fairfax adds the concluding generalization.

86[3]. Fairfax adds the proverb. See Tilley, I.94. Bell notes a possible echo of Chaucer, *Troylus and Criseyde*, II. 1276.

89–91. The translation in these stanzas is very free. For the proverbs in 89[8] and 90[8] see Tilley, D.21 and P.370. *Titan* = the sun.

92. This stanza is so freely rendered that it draws Doyne's censure: the general idea is retained but conveyed with new rhetoric. Cf. Carew:

But whiles she sweetly speakes, and laughes sweetly,
And with this two-fold sweetnes luls the sense,
Well neere she makes the soule from bodie fly,
As gainst so rare delites voyde of defence,
Ah cruell love that slayth us equally,
Where wormewood thou or hony do dispence,

> And equall deadly at all seasons bee
> Mischiefes and medcines, which proceede of thee.

The lance that heals the very wound it makes comes from the story of Telephus, which Fairfax could have found in Pliny's *Natural History*, XXXIV. xlv.

93. Fairfax adds the reference to Jason and the Golden Fleece, and also provides the final metaphor.

94. The last line is Fairfax's invention.

96. Fairfax leaves out a mention of Theseus.

V

1. Fairfax changes the couplet; cf. Carew:

> For ventrers store, and worth in generall
> Breedes doubt, nor lesse their bent in speciall.

3. Again Fairfax's couplet evades Tasso's sense and is banal. Cf. Carew:

> For in the world light and chaungeable,
> 'Tis constance oft t'ensew thoughts variable.

5. Fairfax invents an effective last line. Cf. Carew:

> For herein I reserve my sov'raignty,
> In all els, franke be his authority.

7. Fairfax avoids the 'pro' and 'con' of l. 2 and supplies padding of his own. Ae sharpens the description of their deceit by the metaphor in ll. 5–6. Cf. Carew:

> And since light harmes which from this perill grow,
> Weyd with the profit, make the ballance rise:
> Your liking had, the chosen ten shall go
> With this Damsell to that brave enterprise:
> Thus he concludes, and with guile tyred so,
> Seekes close to vayle the minde, which inly fries
>   With colour'd zeale; honours desire did move
>   The rest (as seem'd) but t'was desire of love.

10. Eustace is not persuading Rinaldo to lead the champions for the sake of the Syrian Dame but because he is ambitious to succeed Dudon: Fairfax muffs this distinction in the general compliment. Cf. Carew:

> Thee whose high lynage egals all the rest,
> Whose glory me, and merit hath out-gon,
> Nor lesse himselfe, in price of martiall quest
> To hold, disdaynes the greater *Boglion*:
> Thee I for Captaine crave, if in thee nest
> No will to be this Squadrons Champion,
>   Ne thinke I thou wilt for that honour carke,
>   Which may proceed from deeds obscure and darke.

20. Fairfax is a little free with the couplet. Cf. Carew:

> But yet thy selfe wouldst it no lesse a grace,
> Where he by craving it, doth it abase.

28. Bell notes that Boreas and the rocks are not in Tasso but are to be found in the Homeric passage which is his source, *Iliad*, II. 144.

40. Fairfax adds the epithets in ll. 6 and 8.

42⁷. Fairfax loses the force of 'palme' by his conventional 'spears'. Florio, *A worlde of words* (1598) glosses as 'glorie, conquest'. Carew has 'palmes'.

43. Fairfax extends the reference to tragedy in his last line. Cf. Tasso:

> Giudici fian tra noi la sorte e l'arme:
> fera tragedia vuol che s'appresenti
> per lor diporto e le nemiche genti.

44⁶. Tasso's fine touch, 'come folgore suol, ne l'arme splende', is lost in the English; the generalization in l. 6 is banal and padding weakens the last line.

52. References to cypress and palm are exchanged for the allusion to Cynthia's hills.

54. The couplet is freely turned. Cf. Carew:

> Deere would I hold that so it might befall
> But *Godfrey* stands an equall Duke withall.

57. The deviation in the second half of the stanza is so extreme that it amounts to error. Cf. Carew:

> If wrongers slaughter then the wrong discusse,
> Who ist that bounds can to iust furie frame?
>   Who can his blowes, and what to fault is dew,
>   In heat of bickring wey, and measure trew?

60. Fairfax slips in the ornamental reference to the sun as Titan. Cf. IV. 91.

61. Fairfax adds his own conceit of arrows and quivers to describe Armida's beauty.

62. Fairfax paraphrases boldly, shortening the falcon simile to make room for the moralizing antithesis.

66. 'Truth-revealing' is supplied by Fairfax, who also touches up the last line with the reference to Vulcan, the god of fire and forges.

69. Tasso says she was in a hurry: Fairfax has her as gracious.

70³. The metaphor is changed from whip to poisoned dart.

73. Fairfax has 'helmet' for 'urna'; Carew tries 'small pitcher'. Fairfax intrudes the quip in l. 5.

79. Fairfax does not mention the idle dreams. Cf. Tasso:

> Ma come uscì la notte, e sotto l'ali
> menò il silenzio e i levi sogni erranti,
> secretamente, com'Amor gl'informa,
> molti d'Armida seguitaron l'orma.

83. By bringing a line forward into st. 82 Fairfax gives himself space to describe the drawing of the sword. 'gentle Princesse' weakens Tasso's 'la tiranna de l'alme'.

86. Neptune is added by Fairfax.

90. For 'Greci' Fairfax has 'Turks'; this is presumably a slip.

V I

85–6. Fairfax adds the reference to Hector. Cf. *Paradise Lost*, II. 392–3:

> Great things resolved, which from the lowest deep
> Will once more lift us up in spite of fate,

9. The last line is Fairfax's invention.

22. Fairfax adds 'shining' and extends the reference to allude to Rome. 'He' in l. 8 has been emended to 'Her'.

23⁶. In the margin of the British Library copy a previous owner has suggested 'Jesse's' for 'Ishaies'.

26. Fairfax cuts out the detail of Clorinda standing on an eminence and makes a couplet out of the mention of her beauty.

28. Lines 6 and 8 are supplied by Fairfax.

32. 'Tender grass' is Fairfax's addition.

33. Fairfax omits the reference to the fury, Aletto.

34⁵. Cf. *Paradise Lost*, VIII. 466–7:

> From thence a rib, with cordial spirits warm,
> And life-blood streaming fresh;

36. 'Light-foot' is Fairfax's addition: Spenser has the epithet in *Shepheardes Calender*, June, l. 26.

38. Fairfax invents the 'sandie locks'. The introduction of the Caspian shore may hark back to *Faerie Queene*, II. vii. 14 or II. xi. 26. For the second half of the stanza cf. *Paradise Lost*, II. 714–16:

> as when two black clouds
> With heaven's artillery fraught, come rattling on
> Over the Caspian,

Waller has been here too: cf. *Instructions to a Painter*, ll. 109–10:

> As when loud winds from different quarters rush
> Vast clouds encountering one another crush.

40. Fairfax substitutes the simile of Boreas, the north wind, for Tasso's reference to Tancred and Erminia.

41². Cf. *Paradise Lost*, III. 566:

> Stars distant, but nigh hand seemed other worlds,

44. Fairfax's version is vigorous and free; he introduces the fountain comparison in place of Tasso's 'macchiato e molle'.

47. Fairfax tightens the end rhetorically. Cf. Tasso:

> e cruccioso egli ancor con quanta pote
> violenza maggior la spada rote.

Cf. *Paradise Lost*, XII. 632–3:

> High in front advanced,
> The brandished sword of God before them blazed . . .

52. Fairfax takes in an echo of Psalm 104: 23.

56. The name of Erminia's father (Aciano) is omitted.

58. Some details are redisposed between sts. 58 and 59.

60. Fairfax changes Tasso's metaphor of fire to that of the mote and the mountain.

64. The list and the formal antithesis are of Fairfax's providing.

69³, ⁵. Cf. *Paradise Lost*, XI. 651:

> But call in aid, which makes a bloody fray;

and *Paradise Regained*, I. 264 and IV. 478:

> Through many a hard assay even to the death,
> . . . .
> What I foretold thee, many a hard assay . . .

70. Cf. Waller, *Instructions to a Painter*, ll. 159–60:

> He feels no wound but in his troubled thought,
> Before for honour, now, revenge he fought.

and *To the Queen, when occasioned by the sight of Her Majesty's Picture*, ll. 45–6:

> There public care with private passion fought
> A doubtful combat in his noble thought.

73. Cf. *Paradise Regained*, II. 109:

> The while her son tracing the desert wild,

74¹. Cf. *Paradise Lost*, X. 265–6:

> Go whither fate or inclination strong
> Leads thee,

80. Fairfax introduces his own simile in the second half of the stanza in place of Tasso's description of the easy intimacy between Erminia and Clorinda.

85. Lines 5 and 6 represent Fairfax's elaboration of Tasso's 'riposariansi'.

89. Fairfax slips in the detail of the rafters.

93³. Fairfax supplies the homely parenthesis.

103. It is possible that the deviation here indicates a slip on Fairfax's part. Hunt (ll. 892–3) translates ll. 5 and 6:

> In passion's mazes lost, th'enamoured Dame
> Gave pensive utt'rance to her ill-starred flame.

Tasso:

> L'innamorata donna iva co 'l cielo
> le sue fiamme sfogando ad una ad una,
> e secretari del suo amore antico
> fea i muti campi e quel silenzio amico.

Fairfax takes the reference to light literally after the description of the moonlight, whereas Tasso seems to use 'fiamme' metaphorically. On the other hand the English could be accounted for as ambiguous, and therefore free. Cf. Waller, *On St James' Park, as lately improved by His Majesty*, ll. 71–4:

> In such green palaces the first kings reigned,
> Slept in their shades, and angels entertained,
> With such old counsellors they did advise,
> And, by frequenting sacred groves grew wise.

104. Fairfax adds 'castle-like pavilions' and inserts a metaphor in l. 6.

106. Fairfax adds the parenthetic 'poore soule', but loses the distinction of Tasso's couplet:

> e la gran tigre ne l'argento impressa
> fiammeggia sì ch'ognun direbbe: 'È dessa.'

111. Fairfax adds 'watrie': cf. VII. 54.

112. Fairfax introduces his own idea in the last line and shortens the message. Cf. Tasso:

> e mandò con l'aviso al campo un messo
> che non armento od animal lanuto,
> né preda altra simìl, ma ch'è seguita
> dal suo german Clorinda impaurita;

VII

4. According to Tasso, love troubled her even in sleep; Fairfax changes to the idea of protection.

6. The parenthesis is added by Fairfax.

7[4]. For her golden hair, Fairfax substitutes 'visage'.

12[3]. 'Crime' appears to be used in the more general sense which is to be found in *Faerie Queene*, II. xii. 75, where the rhyme is equally convenient.

12[8]. The moralizing is contributed by Fairfax.

18. Fairfax follows the sense at the end of the stanza, but evades the elegant circumlocution of the Italian:

> e da l'irsute mamme il latte preme
> e 'n giro accolto poi lo stringe insieme.

There may well be an echo in l. 2 of *Faerie Queene*, I. iii. 4:

> Her angels face
> As the great eye of heaven shyned bright,
> And made a sunshine in the shadie place.

19. Fairfax adds the reference to Cupid.

22[6]. Fairfax adds the contrasting fires.

27. The English leaves out any mention of the whip. Tasso:

> Scotea mobile sferza, e da le spalle
> pendea il corno su 'l fianco a nostra usanza.

28. The final conceit is Fairfax's invention.

29. 'The Countie of Cosenza' is Boemond.

35. Fairfax muffs the last line. Tasso:

> e manderollo a i duci franchi in dono,
> s'altro da quel che soglio oggi non sono.

Cf. Hunt, ll. 291–2:

> And I, unless my wonted pow'r be fled,
> Send to the Christian Chief thy gory head.

41. Fairfax has the wound on the right side; Tasso on the left.

43[3-4]. Fairfax blurs a telling detail: Rambaldo imagines the steel going through him in anticipation of the blow; Fairfax speaks of fear in general terms'

44[5]. Fairfax misses out the parenthesis: '(al fuggitivo alto soccorso)'.

45⁴. Cf. *Samson Agonistes*, l. 732:

> With doubtful feet and wavering resolution . . .

48. Fairfax does not record that Tancred blamed his own stupidity.

50⁶. Cf. *Paradise Lost*, IV. 15–16:

> Begins his dire attempt, which nigh the birth
> Now rolling, boils in his tumultuous breast,

52. The details of the comet simile are taken very freely. Cf. Tasso:

> Qual con le chiome sanguinose orrende
> splender cometa suol per l'aria adusta,
> che i regni muta e i feri morbi adduce
> a i purpurei tiranni infausta luce;

Cf. *Paradise Lost*, II. 707–11:

>   Satan stood
> Unterrified, and like a comet burned,
>   . . .
>   and from his horrid hair
> Shakes pestilence and war.

44. Fairfax adds 'watrie'. Cf. VI. 108.

57. Fairfax adds the allusion to Olympus, the mountain of the gods.

58⁸. 'That strong prince' is Rinaldo.

63. Fairfax supplies the reference to Bellona, goddess of war.

66. Fairfax makes a mistake in calling the two Guidi 'the Gerrards twain'.

72. Fairfax mistakes 'rubello', rebel, for a proper name. Hunt notes that the man was Rudolph, Duke of Bavaria and Saxony.

77. The touch about not bending the grass is Fairfax's fancy.

78. Fairfax chooses not to mention the Vale of Terebinthus where David slew Goliath.

79. Fairfax loses Tasso's simile of the prayers ascending naturally, like fire.

94. Fairfax omits Raimondo's reference to himself as the third champion.

85¹. The quip 'still in bed' is supplied by Fairfax.

88–9. The description of the encounter is freely rendered. Fairfax leaves out the allusion to Raimondo's fear of being overpowered by Argantes' weight and adds a touch of his own in l. 4.

91. Fairfax does not choose to say that Argantes was untiring in his fury.

100. Fairfax has this stanza which distinguishes the Osanna edition from that of Bonnà. See above, p. 20.

102⁵. Fairfax changes Tasso's understatement, 'né quegli in dubbio stette', to the extravagant positive 'did laugh and skip'.

111. Fairfax changes Tasso's 100 hands and arms with their 50 shields and 50 swords to 500 men.

122. Fairfax alters the couplet; Tasso describes the two forces; Fairfax refers to Clorinda's feat. Cf.:

> la pioggia a i gridi, a i venti, a i tuon s'accorda
> d'orribile armonia che 'l mondo assorda.

VIII

9. Fairfax supplies the proper name, Corbana, for the Persian.

17⁶. Cf. *Paradise Lost*, IV. 979–82 and I. 546–7:

> and began to hem him round
> With ported spears, as thick as when a field
> Of Ceres ripe for harvest waving bends
> Her bearded grove of ears,

> with them rose
> A forest huge of spears:

18³⁻⁴. Fairfax turns Tasso's lines to give a different effect:

> molti d'essi piagati e molti spenti
> son da cieche ferite a l'aer bruno;

Cf. Hunt, l. 158:

> Unnumber'd wounds were dealt amid the gloom.

32. Fairfax adds l. 4 and then devises a simile referring to the moon's wooing of Endymion which is hardly in keeping with Tasso's concentration upon the vision of Sweno's corpse.

56. Fairfax does not translate Tasso's 'il monco busto', the mangled remains.

61. It is Fairfax who adds the reference to Lethe, the river of forgetfulness.

64. The couplet is invented. Cf. Hunt, ll. 576–7:

> Yet this by fraudful arts the Frank obtain'd
> And perfidy enjoys what valour gain'd.

82. Fairfax sharpens a phrase, 'bright swords on every side'. Cf. Tasso:

> e ch'ebbe al ferro, a l'aste ed a la face
> che 'l furor ministrò.

83. Cf. Waller, *Panegyric to my Lord Protector*, ll. 165–8:

> So when a lion shakes his dreadful mane,
> And angry grows, if he that first took pain
> To tame his youth approach the haughty beast,
> He bends to him but frights away the rest.

84. Fairfax adds 'lukewarme'.

IX

1[8]. Cf. *Paradise Lost*, II. 837, 'Might hap to move new broils'.

7. Koeppel notes that Fairfax is misleading; it is the Sultan's men who bar the way, not Godfrey's troops.

12[2]. A note in the copy of the first edition in the British Library (82.g.16) reads:

> So / Waller from his frequent use of this word *so* at the end of a verse, and in the same manner got the name of Waller So-So. Hence the *Advice to a Painter* under the name of Denham. Denham saith *Thus*, then Waller always *so*.

15. Cf. l. 8 with Ariel's repetition of Ferdinand's cry in *The Tempest*, I. ii. 214–15:

> Hell is empty,
> And all the devils are here.

17. Fairfax intrudes the tennis metaphor.

18. Fairfax adds the mention of wine and dregs.

19. Fairfax supplies the scythe simile.

21[6]. Cf. *Paradise Lost*, II. 788–9:

> Hell trembled at the hideous name, and sighed
> From all her caves, and back resounded Death.

22. Fairfax adds the reference to Boreas, the north wind. Cf. *Paradise Lost*, II. 285–6:

> as when hollow rocks retain
> The sound of blustering winds,

23[3]. Fairfax leaves out the sense of Tasso's third line, 'I could say more but it would sound like a falsehood.'

25. Fairfax loses a detail: Tasso's dragon on the helmet seemed to stretch and writhe.

29. Fairfax adds the reference to the lamb and the final phrase.

33. The bird-cage simile is Fairfax's invention; he uses it again in XIX. 45. He could have picked this up from *Faerie Queene*, III. xi. 12.

34. Fairfax adds that it was Picus who was headless. A marginal note in the British Library copy reads: 'From Vergil, Aen. X Vos etiam. etc [ll.] 390–3'.

35. Fairfax elaborates slightly, and adds the concluding moralization. Samuel Say notes in the margin of the British Library copy that he is reminded of the way Dryden turns a paradox in his translation of *Aeneid*, X. 1185, 'What time the Father, now no Father stood' [*sic*], 'Mean time his Father, now no Father, stood.'

38. Fairfax invents the last line.

41. Fairfax substitutes Engerlan for Ottone.

42. Fairfax supplies 'in his armed tent'.

44. Fairfax interpolates the wolf/fold metaphor.

45⁴. Fairfax adds a simile of sheep that is reminiscent of *Faerie Queene*, I. viii. 35.

46. Fairfax supplies the proper name, Vesulus. Cf. Chaucer, 'Doun at the roote of Vesulus the colde', *Clerkes Tale*, l. 58.

48². The echo of Psalm 80: 13 is Fairfax's doing.

49. Mars is added in the English version.

50. Fairfax alters the construction and adds 'strength with courage'. The British Library copy has a note in the margin: 'hence Waller 'Virtue with Rage, Fury with valour strove" '.
    See *Epitaph on Colonel Charles Cavendish*, l. 27.

54. The simile is supplied by Fairfax. Cf. Webster, *The Duchess of Malfi*, IV. ii. 346–7:

> and your vengeance,
> (Like two chain'd bullets), still goes arme in arme.

57. Fairfax's handling of this difficult stanza is not very satisfactory. Stanza 56 ends:

> Ha sotto i piedi il Fato e la Natura,
> ministri umili, e 'l Moto e Chi 'l misura,

continuing in st. 57:

> e 'l Loco e Quella che, qual fumo o polve,
> la gloria di qua giuso e l'oro e i regni,
> come piace là su, disperde e volve,
> né, diva, cura i nostri umani sdegni.

Fairfax sees that Tasso's 'Chi 'l misura' at the end of st. 56 means Time, but he then thinks fit to add 'Place'. This looks neat, but it misses the way in which Tasso's sense carries over to st. 57 where ''l Loco' means 'Space' and

'Quella' is evidently 'Fortune', whose ways are to be described. The first half of st. 57 refers to the subversive action of Fortune, and not to the Deity.

Hunt's version gets into line better:

> There, on Eternity's majestic throne
> The Godhead sits, unbounded and alone,
> A triple light, concentrated in one.
> Fate at his feet, and plastic Nature stand;
> Time, Place, and Motion wait his high command;
> And She, the Goddess, whose inconstant will,
> Capricious arbitress of good and ill,
> Proud states and realms by turns erects, o'erthrows,
> And Gold, the sov'reign joy, withdraws, bestows;
> Like smoke and dust that to the winds are hurl'd,
> She mocks the glories of this nether world,
>   And sporting with her victim, Man, below,
>   Confounds our triumphs, and derides our woe
>   (ll. 525–37).

62. In place of the shining countenance Fairfax has flames for the angel's eyes. He adds the moonshine. Cf. *Comus*, l. 127:

> Which these dun shades will ne'er report.

62⁸. Cf. *Comus*, l. 80:

> Swift as the sparkle of a glancing star,

and *Paradise Lost*, IV. 556–7:

> Swift as a shooting star
> In autumn thwart the night,

65. Fairfax amplifies the couplet by his mention of Hesperus, the evening star.

68. Fairfax omits the nonce reference to the name of Gallo. Cf.:

> poi fère Albin là 've primier s'apprende
> nostro alimento, e 'l viso a Gallo fende.

71. Fairfax adds Bellona, goddess of war.

92. Fairfax interpolates Briareus, the hundred-handed monster who came to the aid of the Olympians against the Titans.

93¹. Cf. *Paradise Lost*, I. 557–8:

> and chase
> Anguish and doubt and fear and sorrow and pain . . .

96⁴. Fairfax takes 'barbaro tiranno' to be Aladine: Hunt identifies him with the Syrian King. If this is a slip on Fairfax's part it is a venial one.

98². Cf. *Paradise Lost*, IV. 18–19: 'horror and doubt distract / His troubled thoughts'.

X

6⁴. Cf. *Paradise Lost*, IV. 806–7: 'thence raise / At least distempered, discontented thoughts'.

7⁶. Cf. *Samson Agonistes*, ll. 665–6:

Secret refreshings, that repair his strength
And fainting spirits uphold.

12⁶. Cf. *Paradise Lost*, X. 468–9: 'by my adventure hard / With peril great achieved'.

17⁴. The moon as Cynthia is Fairfax's contribution.

20⁸. The moralizing is Fairfax's.

23. 'an angle strate', Tasso's 'uno angusto giro', is Cyprus.

26. Fairfax adds 'some ragged Peasant' and 'webs of lead'. Cf. *Shepheardes Calender*, June, l. 89, October, l. 63, and November, l. 59 for the latter expression.

28. Fairfax substitutes 'bushie' for Tasso's 'scoscesa', precipitous.

33. Fairfax adds the Biblical comparison (*see* Matthew 19: 24).

56. 'grombling in his place' is Fairfax's touch.

64. Cf. *Paradise Regained*, II. 339–55:

In ample space under the broadest shade
A table richly spread, in regal mode,
With dishes piled, and meats of noblest sort
And savour, beasts of chase, or fowl of game,
In pastry built, or from the spit, or boiled,
Grisamber-steamed; all fish from sea or shore,
Freshet, or purling brook, of shell or fin,
And exquisitest name, for which was drained
Pontus and Lucrine bay, and Afric coast,
. . . .
And at a stately sideboard by the wine
That fragrant smell diffused, in order stood
Tall stripling youths rich-clad, of fairer hue
Than Ganymede or Hylas, distant more
Under the trees now tripped, now solemn stood
Nymphs of Diana's train, and Naiades . . .

66³. For Tasso's 'novo pensier' Fairfax has 'no pleasure'. He adds the shields of brass.

68⁸. Fairfax omits the last torment, 'o vesta irsuta fronte'.

69. Fairfax contributes the echo from Psalm 107: 10, according to the Coverdale version preserved in the *Book of Common Prayer*.

70. Fairfax supplies the proverb in the first line (cf. Tilley, M.1012). He evades Tasso's sense in l. 5. Tasso:

> e (s'io n'intesi il vero)
> di seco trarne da quell'empia ottenne
> del signor di Damasco un messaggiero,

78. Fairfax has a quite independent first half to this stanza focusing attention on Godfrey, not on Peter. Cf. Tasso:

> Qui dal soggetto vinto il saggio Piero
> stupido tace, e 'l cor ne l'alma faccia
> troppo gran cose de l'estense altero
> valor ragiona, onde tutto altro spiaccia.

XI

5. Fairfax invents the fourth line.

8. Protestant Fairfax adds 'they say' with reference to Peter.

9. The damaging reference to hermits and nuns and the parenthesis in l. 6 are Fairfax's doing. Contrast Sir G(ilbert) T(albot's) rendering:

> On Christ's deare handmayd, who had learned so well,
> To make election of the better part;
> On those chaste Virgins in theyre cloister'd Cell,
> Who from theyre heavenly Nuptials never start;

11. Cf. *Paradise Lost*, I. 314–15:

> He called so loud, that all the hollow deep
> Of hell resounded,

13. Fairfax avoids a simple bird simile and invents the third and fourth lines. A marginal note in the Bodleian copy (Antiq. d.E. 1600/2) remarks of l. 3, where the musical powers of Apollo and Pan are contrasted, 'The original has nothing corresponding to this line.'

20. Fairfax does not mention the greaves that Godfrey discarded.

27. Fairfax supplies the reference to Colossus, the bronze statue of Apollo bestriding the harbour at Rhodes, and to Cynthia, the moon.

28. It is Fairfax who introduces by name the daughter of Latona, that is, Artemis, who revenged herself and her brother upon Niobe in response to Niobe's boast that her own twelve children could match the twins of Leto, or Latona.

34. See the Index of Proper Names for a note on Alcasto.

38. The Bodleian copy (Antiq. d.E.1600/2) draws attention to Fairfax's mistake: it was not the weight thrown *by* the Christian forces but the weight

that falls *upon* them. Fairfax gives the name of the Spartan mountain, Taigetus, for Tasso's description of the shell of interlocked shields.

40[8]. Fairfax adds the moralizing.

41. Tasso says precisely that she shot seven times.

43[5]. Fairfax fails to make it clear that Roberto, the 'Flemmings guide' was hit while he was manœuvring not his horse but the battering-ram.

44. Fairfax leaves out the mention of the full fount, 'ampio lavacro'.

48. Fairfax adds the bees. He foreshortens Tasso's simile to a metaphor in l. 3. Cf. Hunt's version (ll. 440–2):

> Two clouds with shock unwonted, met on high,
> And backward with strange repercussion sent,
> Thither, whence first it came, each weapon went.

51. Fairfax adds the second line.

52. Cf. Waller, *Of the danger His Majesty (being Prince) escaped in the Road at St. Andrews*, ll. 75–6:

> So men with rage and passion set on fire,
> Trembling for haste, impeach their mad desire.

53. Fairfax does not make it clear that Godfrey changed his arms for lighter ones.

54. Fairfax makes no mention of the pain of the wound.

57. Fairfax invents the last line.

60[5-6]. Cf. *Paradise Lost*, VI. 592–3:

> That whom they hit, none on their feet might stand,
> Though standing else as rocks, but down they fell.

61. Fairfax takes the stanza very freely and does not attempt the final gibe, 'O Franchi no, ma Franche'.

72. Dictamnum, or dittany, of Crete was famous for its healing properties and its power to expel weapons. There may be an echo in *Comus*, ll. 630–2:

> The leaf was darkish, and had prickles on it,
> But in another country, as he said,
> Bore a bright golden flower . . .

74. 'Panacea', a fabulous herb healing all diseases.

75. Tasso's 'ostro', purple, is weakened to 'Pretious'. Fairfax's 'sturdie lance' loses the hyperbole of tossing the immense spear. Cf. 'e l'asta crolla smisurata'.

81. Fairfax avoids 'scelce', pebblestone, in l. 2 and has no more than a hint of Tasso's metaphor of the spinning-top in his 'wheeling round'.

82. The English substitutes stock phrasing for Tasso's more sensitive description of night's intervention, 'Sotto il caliginoso orror de l'ali'.

Cf. with l. 3 *Paradise Lost*, II. 959–60: 'the throne / Of Chaos, and his dark pavilion spread . . .'.

XII

12. Fairfax works in his own sixth line.

21. The conceit in the couplet is Fairfax's. Cf. Tasso, 'che bruna è sì, ma il bruno il bel non toglie'.

29^r. Cf. *Comus*, l. 428:

By grots and caverns shagged with horrid shades.

33^2. Cf. *Canterbury Tales*, A.3890:

Syn that my tappe of lif began to renne.

40^5. It is perhaps intentional that Fairfax should omit to translate 'Forse e la vera fede'.

43. Tasso says that the watch demanded the password.

46^8. Cf. *Paradise Lost*, IX. 136–8:

in one day to have marred
What he almighty styled, six nights and days
Continued making,

51. The margin of the British Library copy (82.g.16) marks 'Waller'. The lines come from *Instructions to a Painter*, ll. 23–4:

So hungry wolves, though greedy of their prey,
Stop when they find a lion in the way.

61. Cf. *Paradise Lost*, IX. 1067:

O Eve, in evil hour didst thou give ear . . .

64. Fairfax adds the reference to the cedar.

69. The last line is Fairfax's invention.

83. Fairfax changes Tasso's bandages, 'fasce', into a reference to hair and face.

91^4. 'Not out of knowledge was her lovely shaid': Still she was recognizable. Away from the Italian Fairfax's line is not clear. Cf. Tasso:

ma lo splendor celeste
orna e non toglie la notizia antica;

92. Fairfax supplies the precise reference to Abraham's bosom (cf. Luke 16: 23).

94. According to Tasso the tomb was of choice stone and when time allowed it was carved. Fairfax has his own elaboration; instead of the simple reference to Daedalus, the legendary craftsman, he substitutes Scopas, the Greek sculptor of the fourth century B.C.

This use of 'viride', green, is the first to be noted in *O.E.D.* The earliest cited instance of 'Spartan stone', that is, Peloponnesian marble, is from Evelyn's Diary (June 1645). Fairfax must have been reading Pliny's *Natural History*, Bk. XXXVI, in Latin. There he would have found an account of the work of Scopas (chs. v and xix). See ch. vii as translated by Philemon Holland (1601), ii. 573 a: 'But the greene marble that commeth from Lacedaemon, is esteemed most precious, and to bee more gay and pleasant than all other.'

99. Fairfax has his own last line. Cf. Tasso:

Oh se sperar ciò lice, altera sorte!

Cf. ll. 1–2 with *Paradise Lost*, X. 771–2: 'O welcome hour whenever! Why delays / His hand . . .'.

104. Fairfax adds the wolves.

XIII

4. Florio, *A world of words* (1598), glosses 'strega' as 'witch, sorceresse, also a hag or fairie, such as our fore-elders thought to change the favour of children'. Fairfax goes further and has 'ghosts and gobblins'. He avoids the reference to them as coming in the form of a dragon or goat and says more elusively, 'with dragon wings . . . some nimbly runne'.

6. Fairfax does not say that Ismen was ungirt. He supplies the parenthesis.

11[6]. Fairfax is free: Tasso's sense is that they were forbidden to take part in the war.

14. Fairfax simplifies Tasso's 'adusti Nasamoni o i Garamanti'; the Libyan peoples, to 'those of Inde'.

20[2]. Cf. *Comus*, l. 7:

Confined, and pestered in this pinfold here.

27. Fairfax leaves out the mention of Dis.

31[6]. Tasso says that he tried for three days.

37[5]. Cf. *Paradise Lost*, II. 743:

Me father, and that phantasm call'st my son.

38. Fairfax changes the setting slightly from Tasso's amphitheatre, empty but for the cypress.

For l. 3 cf. *Paradise Lost*, VII. 478:

> In all the liveries decked of summer's pride . . .

55. Fairfax inserts 'his Clytie dear', presumably alluding to Cleitus, the favourite whom Alexander accidentally killed; he then composes his own couplet with its reference to Clymene's son, that is to Phaeton, who perished in his rash attempt to drive the sun's chariot.

56. Fairfax adds the reference to Sodom (Genesis 18: 16).

60[4]. Cf. Milton's sonnet XV, 'whose bones / Lie scattered on the Alpine mountains cold'.

75. Fairfax adds the reference to Elijah, the prophet (1 Kings 18).

XIV

4. The description of the vision is taken freely. For 'un sereno candido', the Milky way, Fairfax has 'christall wide'.

16. The rhyme of the couplet is, for some ears, echoed in *Lycidas*, ll. 163–4:

> Look homeward angel now, and melt with ruth,
> And, O ye dolphins, waft the hapless youth.

See A. B. Giamatti, *Revue de littérature comparée*, xl (1966), 613–15.

20. Fairfax intrudes moral touches into ll. 4 and 8.

36[8]. Fairfax supplies the scriptural names.

39. Fairfax adds the stars.

43. Fairfax amplifies by alluding to Vulcan, the smith god. For l. 4 cf. *Comus*, l. 979: 'There I suck the liquid air . . .'.

44. See the Glossary for the terms in l. 7.

45[4]. Cf. *Paradise Lost*, II. 621:

> Rocks, caves, lakes, fens, bogs, dens and shades of death.

50[5–6]. Fairfax supplies his own details about Armida's 'tenaci nodi'.

61. Fairfax avoids Tasso's theatre metaphor and substitutes 'twylight' and a 'Faerie queene'. Cf. Tasso:

> Così dal palco di notturna scena
> o ninfa o dea, tarda sorgendo, appare.

62. Fairfax has his own idea in l. 4, and changes 'la tenerella mente' into

tender limmes': he substitutes fishes and birds for Tasso's more general statement. Cf.:

> Solo chi segue ciò che piace è saggio,
> e in sua stagion de gli anni il frutto coglie.

There may be an echo in Phineas Fletcher's *Brittain's Ida*, II. 8.

68. Fairfax adds the dragons. Cf. XVI. 69.

69. Fairfax gives the Dead Sea its other name, Asphaltes lake.

72. 'Iparted' ('iparted', 1624) presents a difficulty. Tasso has 'a pena sorti'; Fairfax adds the reference to Tiphis, the pilot of the Argo, and to Palinure, Aeneas' pilot, in place of Tasso's assurance that the guide would also be good for the return. He has an elaborate circumlocution for the eagle in l. 6, and changes Tasso's lightning to 'aire and winde'.

X V

1. Fairfax has different details for the dawn, and could be recalling *Faerie Queene*, I. ii. 7.

2. For Tasso's 'robuste' Fairfax gives 'tender'.

6. The choice of 'shallop' for Tasso's 'curvo pino' suggests a memory of *Faerie Queene*, III. vii. 27.

7. Fairfax misses the metaphor of the bit ('morso').

12. Cf. Waller, *Of the danger His Majesty (being Prince) escaped in the Road at St. Andrews*, ll. 41–2:

> With painted oars the youth begin to sweep
> Neptune's smooth face, and cleave the yielding deep.

15. Raphias is modern Refah; Rinocere is modern El Arish on the coast of Sinai. Fairfax supplies the name Casius and the half-line about Jove's temple. Dyce notes that Fairfax errs; Refah is first seen as a man passes *to* Syria *from* Egypt.
    Cf. *Paradise Lost*, II. 592–3:

> that Serbonian bog
> Betwixt Damiata and Mount Casius old,

16. Fairfax supplies the name for Alexandria but slips up when he tranlsates 'faro', the light-house, as '*Pharos* towre'.

17. 'La Mamarica rade, e rade il suolo' is omitted for the sake of a further description of Cyrene in l. 6. Ptolemais is Tolmetta, north-east of Benghasi.

18. 'The greater Sirtes' is the Gulf of Sidra; 'cape Judeca' is the headland anciently called Cefale in the Gulf of Sidra; 'flood Magras streame' (Tasso's

'Foce di Magra') is a river in the territory of Tripoli; 'little Sirtes' is the Gulf of Gabes; 'Alzerbes ile' is Gerba.

19. 'Lilebenni' is a promontory on the West coast of Sicily. The parenthesis is Fairfax's.

29. Fairfax interpolates the sense of l. 2 and avoids a later reference to 'fé di Piero'.

32. Cf. Waller, *To the King, on his Navy*, l. 1:

> Where'er thy navy spreads her canvas wings.

35–6. Cf. Waller, *The Battle of the Summer Islands, passim.*

35$^{4-5}$. Cf. *Paradise Lost*, IV. 412–15:

> needs must the power
> That made us, and for us this ample world
> Be infinitely good, and of his good
> As liberal and free as infinite,

37. Fairfax supplies the reference to Africa. For l. 3 cf. *Paradise Lost*, III. 567–8:

> or happy isles
> Like those Hesperian gardens famed of old,

41. It is Fairfax who adds 'sheds had built of clay' and 'or wanton nymphs'.

44. Fairfax omits to say that 'the one hour' was 'matutina'.

48. Cf. *Paradise Lost*, IX. 498–583. See A. B. Giamatti, *Revue de littérature comparée*, xl (1966), 613–15.

51. For Tasso's 'Ercinia', the Black Forest, Fairfax gives 'Hircania' and repeats it to translate Tasso's 'ircane selve', the Persian woods of Hircania.

52. Fairfax changes Tasso's 'little whistle and glimpse', 'Picciol fischio . . . breve vista', for 'a shake of the wand'.

53. The spikenard and balm are Fairfax's details. Cf. XVIII. 15.
  For l. 5 cf. *Paradise Lost*, V. 292–3:

> through groves of myrrh,
> And flowering odours, cassia, nard, and balm;

54. Instead of Tasso's reference to heat Fairfax has a storm: did he feel it could never be too hot?

56. Fairfax adds the golden sands and the epithet 'silken'.

60–2. The phrasing in these stanzas suggests that Fairfax remembered how Spenser had used the passage in *Faerie Queene*, II. xii. 65–8:

> As that faire Starre, the messenger of morne,
>   His deawy face out of the sea doth reare:

Or as the *Cyprian* goddesse, newly borne
Of th'Oceans fruitfull froth, did first appeare:
Such seemed they, and so their yellow heare
Christalline humour dropped downe apace.
Whom such when *Guyon* saw, he drew him neare,
And somewhat gan relent his earnest pace,
His stubborne brest gan secret pleasaunce to embrace.

The wanton Maidens him espying, stood
  Gazing a while at his unwonted guise;
  Then th'one her selfe low ducked in the flood,
  Abasht, that her a straunger did a vise:
  But th'other rather higher did arise,
  And her two lilly paps aloft displayd,
  And all, that might his melting hart entise
  To her delights, she unto him bewrayd:
The rest hid underneath, him more desirous made.

With that, the other likewise up arose,
  And her faire lockes, which formerly were bownd
  Up in one knot, she low adowne did lose:
  Which flowing long and thick, her cloth'd arownd,
  And th'yvorie in golden mantle gownd:
  So that faire spectacle from him was reft,
  Yet that, which reft it, no lesse faire was fownd:
  So hid in lockes and waves from lookers theft,
Nought but her lovely face she for his looking left.

Withall she laughed, and she blusht withall,
  That blushing to her laughter gave more grace,
  And laughter to her blushing, as did fall:
  Now when they spide the knight to slacke his pace,
  Them to behold, and in his sparkling face
  The secret signes of kindled lust appeare,
  Their wanton meriments they did encreace,
  And to him beckned, to approch more neare,
And shewd him many sights, that courage cold could reare.

note specially 'fruitfull froth'; 'ivorie soft and white'; 'mantled in gold'.

61. Fairfax does not convey the conjunction of gaiety and shame in Tasso's 'lieta e vergognosa'.

62. Fairfax substitutes a reference to her hair falling over her face; Tasso has the colour suffusing her cheeks:

> e nel riso il rossor che le copria
> insino al mento il delicato viso.

64. The 'down and lilies' elaborate Tasso's plainer mention of meadow grass.

XVI

1. Fairfax adds the references in l. 8. Porsenna's grave is explained by a passage in Pliny's *Natural History*, Bk. XXXVI, ch. xiii (in Philemon Holland's translation (1601), II. 579 D):

... for meet it is that I should write somewhat also of our Labyrinth heere in Italie, which *Porsenna*, K. of Tuscane, caused to be made for his own sepulchre; and the rather, because you may know that forrein kings were not so vain in expences, but our princes in Italie surpassed them in vanitie: but for that there goe so many tales and fables of it which are incredible, I thinke it good in the description thereof to use the verie words of my author *M. Varro*: King *Porsenna* (quoth he) was interred under the cittie Clusinum in Tuscane, in which verie place he left a sumptuous monument or tombe built all of square stone; thirtie foot it caried in breadth on everie side, and fiftie in heigth; within the base or foot whereof (which likewise was foure square) hee made a Labyrinth so intricat, that if a man were entered into it without a bottom or clue of thread in his hand, and leaving the one end thereof fastened to the entrie or dore, it was impossible that ever he should find the way out again. Upon this quadrant there stood five Pyramides or steeples, foure at the foure corners, and one in the mids, which at the foot or foundation caried 75 foot everie way in bredth, and were brought up to the heigth of 150: these grew sharpe spired toward the top, but in the verie head so contrived, that they met all in one great roundle of brasse which raught from one to the other, and covered them all in manner of a cap, and the same rising up in the mids with a crest most stately: from this cover there hung round about at little chains, a number of bells or cymbals which being shaken with the wind, made a jangling noise that mought be heard a great way off, much like unto that ring of bels which was devised in times past over the temple of *Jupiter* at Dodona: and yet are we not come to an end of this building mounted aloft in the aire, for this cover over head served but for a foundation of foure other Pyramides, and everie one of them arose a hundred foot high above the other worke: upon the tops whereof there was yet one terrace more to sustaine five Pyramides, and those shot up to such a monstrous heigth, that *Varro* was ashamed to report it: but if wee may give credit to the tales that goe currant in Tuscane it was equall to the whole* building underneath. O the outragious madnesse of a foolish prince, seeking thus in a vainglorious mind to be immortalized by a superfluous expence which could bring no good at all to any creature, but contrariwise weakned the state of his kingdome! And when all was done, the artificer that enterprised and finished the worke, went away with the greater part of the praise and glorie.

2⁴. Cf. *Paradise Lost*, V. 255, 'On golden hinges turning'.

4. Fairfax has an easier sense in l. 6 avoiding reference to the isle of Leucate = Santa Maura. There is a certain likeness to *Antony and Cleopatra*, II. ii. 195–6. Dryden may have had Fairfax in mind in *Annus Mirabilis*, ll. 603–4:

Like a rich bride does to the ocean swim,
And on her shadow rides in floating gold.

5. There is a possible echo in Phineas Fletcher's *Brittain's Ida*, II. 8.

* [Marginal note]: which was 250 foot: so that the whole was 500 foot.

8. Fairfax works in the reference to Theseus and Ariadne's thread which was to guide her out of the labyrinth.

9⁸. Cf. *Faerie Queene*, II. xii. 58.

10. Fairfax does not say that it was the enchantress who determined the breeze.

12. Cf. *Faerie Queene*, II. xii. 71.

14. Cf. *Faerie Queene*, II. xii. 74-5, and Daniel, *Delia*, Sonnet 31, and Southwell, 'Optima Deo'.

17. Fairfax weakens the effect by padding in the phrase 'ease and leasure' and leaving out the mention of the knight in the lady's lap.
   For l. 2, cf. *Paradise Lost*, V. 296-7:

> Her virgin fancies, pouring forth more sweet,
> Wild above rule or art;

19. Cf. *Faerie Queene*, II. xii. 78.

20. Fairfax has a bold but effective transposition. Tasso's parenthetic, 'estranio arnese', unaccustomed equipment, is worked in later to the ironic expression, 'noble Page, graced with that service great'.

21³. Both editions have '(she said)', whereas in Tasso it is clear that it is the man who speaks:

> Volgi,—dicea—deh volgi—il cavaliero—
> —a me quegli occhi onde beata bèi,
> chè son, se tu no 'l sai, ritratto vero . . .

24. Tasso's difficult couplet is evaded and a completely new one fabricated:

> Diè corpo a chi non l'ebbe; e quando il fece,
> tempre mischiò ch'altrui mescer non lece.

   Cf. Hunt (ll. 222-5): who quotes Fairfax's invention with a sneer:

> Her skill, all skill excelling, could supply
> To incorporal things, reality,
> And temper many a potent charm unknown,
> And spells, familiar to herself alone.

   I have failed to find any reference to 'Tuscan Guilla', even if one supposes it to be a misprint for 'Giulia'.
   Cf. Waller, *Of a Brede of divers colors, woven by Four Ladies*, ll. 5-8:

> Not Juno's bird, when, his fair train dis-spread,
> He wooes the female to his painted bed;
> No, not the bow, which so adorns the skies,
> So glorious be, or boasts so many dyes.

26. Fairfax gives a different turn to the last line, 'se non quanto è con lei, romito amante'. Cf. Hunt, l. 243:

> An hermit-lover when his love was gone.

30. It is Fairfax who adds 'Bewrapt with flowres'.

41. Fairfax does not translate the stanza, 'Dissegli Ubaldo allor . . .', given in modern texts as no. 41. It is found only among the rejected verses in Osanna's edition.

57. Xenocrates was a disciple of Plato, famed for his austere continence.

68. Fairfax adds the Fury, Tisiphone.

69. Fairfax adds the serpents, cf. XIV. 68. He omits to mention that the dreams are those of a sick man.

XVII

3^1. Cf. *Paradise Lost*, I. 376:

> Say, Muse, their names then known, who first? who last.

6. Hunt notes that Maremma is more properly a district near the sea-shore. Cf. XX. 142.

31^5. Cp. Ben Jonson, 'Prince Henry's Barriers', l. 285,

> Yet rests the other thunder-bolt of warre.

43^4. This is a blurred rendering of Tasso's 'indegno / già di reina il guer-reggiar non parmi': it does not seem to me improper for a queen to fight.

56^{7-8}. Cf. *Paradise Lost*, IV. 177:

> bushes had perplexed
> All path of man or beast that passed that way:

69. Fairfax leaves out the allusion to Hector.

70. Fairfax mistakes the place, Altino, for a person.

71. Fairfax evades the reference to the Alani and has his own generalization in l. 6.

88^{1-2}. Cf. *Paradise Lost*, X. 840, 'Beyond all past example and future', noting the accentuation of 'future'.

XVIII

2. Fairfax adds 'his grave, Forgetfulnes'.

9^3. Cf. *Paradise Lost*, I. 523, 'but with looks / Downcast and damp . . .'.

12. Cf. *Faerie Queene*, VII. vi. 23–8.

13. The second half of Fairfax's stanza is too free and to a quite different purpose. Cf. Tasso:

> ma non é chi vagheggi o questa o quelle,
> e miriam noi torbida luce e bruna
> ch'un girar d'occhi, un balenar di riso,
> scopre in breve confin di fragil viso.

Cf. Hunt, ll. 111–16:

> yet erring man and blind,
> No beauty in these glorious orbs can find;
> On things of clay we fix our vain desire,
> And those faint beams of cloudy light admire
> From woman's darkly-glancing eyes that roll,
> And to a transient smile resign the soul.

32. Fairfax pads in l. 4; he avoids referring to the brambles and invents his own last line.

37[7]. Fairfax misses the allusion to 'noce' as a walnut-tree, believed to be favoured by witches; he gives only a general sense.

41. We have emended 'elect' to 'erect', though Singer retains the 1600 reading.

44. Fairfax goes all out to supply technical terms.

45. Fairfax adds the reference to Clorinda.

50[1]. 'nolte' = ne wolt, possibly a mistake for 'ne wot'.

52[2]. Fairfax changes Tasso's fourth and fifth day to third and fourth.

67. Fairfax adds 'to the mountain height'.

70. Fairfax muffs this difficult stanza:

> Ma non togliea però da la difesa
> tanto furor le saracine genti:
> contra quelle percosse avean già tesa
> pieghevol tela e cose altre cedenti;
> l'impeto, che 'n lor cade, ivi contesa
> non trova, e vien che vi si fiacchi e lenti;
> essi, ove miran più la calca esposta,
> fan con l'arme volanti aspra risposta.

Cf. Hunt, ll. 598–605:

> Yet, undismay'd, the misbelieving host
> Stand to their arms, nor quit the dang'rous post.
> Materials soft and yielding, to receive
> The furious batt'ry, from aloft they heave;
> Innoxious there the deaden'd impulse fell,
> Wasted amid the substance flexible;
> And where expos'd the hostile crowds they spy,
> Their feather'd arrows make a sharp reply.

76. Fairfax's last line is open to misconstruction; Tasso says 'ma 'l valore e la sorte è diseguale'.

80. Fairfax omits the tortoise image in the couplet; cf. Hunt, ll. 696–7:

> Now, tortoise-like, within its shell it goes,
> Now its protruded head, emerging, shows.

85. Fairfax adds Vulcan, the smith god.

87. Fairfax makes Tasso's two witches into wizards and leaves out Charon.

96. Fairfax uses his own simile in the couplet.

100. The English is very free. Cf. Tasso:

> La vincitrice insegna in mille giri
> alteramente si rivolge intorno;
> e par che in lei più riverente spiri
> l'aura, e che splenda in lei più chiaro il giorno;
> ch'ogni dardo, ogni stral ch'in lei si tiri,
> o la declini, o faccia indi titorno:
> par che Siòn, par che l'opposto monte
> lieto l'adori, e inchini a lei la fronte.

Cf. Hunt, ll. 858–65:

> Of vict'ry proud, the conscious banner roll'd
> Exultant to the winds, its streaming fold:
> Seem'd as the passing gales with rev'rence blew;
> Seem'd as the admiring day more radiant grew
> To gild the flag divine: innoxious came
> Each feather'd shaft, each javelin miss'd its aim:
> Thy head, adoring Sion, seem'd to bow,
> And joyful Moriah bent her sacred brow.

XIX

1. (In *A Bibliographical and Critical Account of the rarest books in the English language* (London, 1865), i. 106) Collier singles out this stanza as an example of Fairfax's felicity in making his translation 'read like an original poem'.

8. Fairfax devises his own conceit in ll. 3–4 and elaborates Tasso's simple statement that the path winds.

12. Fairfax's 'bold' hardly gets the force of Tasso's 'disteso'. Thyer believed that Milton's 'dilated' (*Paradise Lost*, IV. 986) owes something to Tasso. See *Poetical Works*, ed. H. J. Todd, ii. (1842), 111.

22. Cf. Waller, *Instructions to a Painter*, ll. 95–6:

> Thus flourish they, before the approaching fight,
> As dying tapers give a blazing light.

25. Fairfax lacks precision, the wound was to the heel.

30. 'Amber' is Fairfax's addition.

35$^{1-4}$. Cf. *Paradise Lost*, IV. 183–7:

> As when a prowling wolf,
> Whom hunger drives to seek new haunt for prey
> Watching where shepherds pen their flocks at eve
> In hurdled cotes amid the field secure,
> Leaps o'er the fence with ease into the fold:

47. Fairfax's English is misleading because he follows Tasso's syntax: it is the storm, not the shepherd, that is raging. It is possible, however, that 'raging' is a misprint for 'ranging'. The parenthesis in l. 3 is Fairfax's.

58. Fairfax has his own colours for the tents, 'azzurri e persi e gialli'.

69. Dyce notes that Fairfax seems to have misread Tasso's 'scorge' = perceived, as 'sorge' = arose. The English expression 'a milken way' goes beyond Tasso's 'un bel vel secreta via'.

80. Fairfax works in the card metaphor.

91^{4}. Cf. *Paradise Lost*, IV. 108:

> So farewell hope, and with hope farewell fear.

95. Fairfax supplies the final image, cf. IX. 33.

103. Fairfax does not make it clear that on second thoughts Vafrino had doubts, 'Più il mise poscia il vestir bruno in forse . . .'.

105^{4}. Cf. *Faerie Queene*, I. ix. 40.

109. Fairfax adds the reference to torn tresses.

111^{4}. Fairfax intrudes the moralizing.

121. Fairfax names the Jordan.

126. Fairfax advances a point from st. 127: the mention of a plot against Godfrey's life.

XX

12^{5}. Cf. *Samson Agonistes*, l. 647:

> Nor am I in the list of them that hope.

22. Fairfax adds the new moon.

24. The contrasts in l. 4—praises and reproaches, pains and prizes—have been evaded.

30. R. W. Dent has suggested a connection with Webster's *Monumental Column*. See above, General Introduction, Section V.

32. Fairfax treats 'ircano', Persian, as a proper name.

37. Fairfax mistakes the pronoun in l. 3: it was Odoardo ('egli'), not Gildippe, who killed Artabano.

44. The wolf/dog simile is treated freely; Fairfax loses Tasso's vivid touch about the tail clapped to its belly.

48. Fairfax supplies the names in the last line.

50$^{1-2}$. Cf. *Paradise Lost*, VI. 245: 'Long time in even scale / The battle hung'.

54^7. The hyperbole is Fairfax's.

55. It is not clear that Fairfax sees what Tasso means about the speed of the serpent's tongue which seemed like three tongues at once. Cf.:

> Qual tre lingue vibrar sembra il serpente
> ché la prestezza d'una il persuade,

56. Fairfax's antithesis in the couplet is a little out of alignment with Tasso's sense, which is that one part used their swords to kill, the other their throats (to yell).

60. Fairfax changes Tasso's pliant twigs to ears of ripened corn.

63. Fairfax supplies l. 6 with its moralizing antithesis.

75. The addition of 'to rise again more blest' is hardly in keeping for the Souldan.

77. The parallel phrase 'from eie to eie' is used for Tasso's 'from first to last'.

89. The final quip is Fairfax's.

95^8. For Tasso's 'vago', lover, Fairfax substitutes 'spear'.

96$^{1-2}$. Cf. *Paradise Lost*, VI. 340–1:

> Gnashing for anguish and despite and shame
> To find himself not matchless,

98. Cf. Waller, *Of a War with Spain, and a Fight at Sea*, ll. 81–2:

> Then laid him by his burning lady's side,
> And, since he could not save her, with her died.

103. Fairfax adds the comparison to a tower. Cf. *Faerie Queene*, I. ii. 20.

114. Cf. Waller, *To my Lord Falkland*, ll. 37–9:

> A lion so with self-provoking smart,
> (His rebel tail scourging his noble part)
> Calls up his courage . . .

117. Fairfax misses the comparison with the greyhounds and has, more tamely, 'guides'.

124. Fairfax's couplet is his own: Hunt (ll. 1068–9) is closer to Tasso's sense.

> Its soft and yielding texture Love can tell;
> There never yet in vain his arrows fell.

129. Cf. Waller, *To the Queen, on Her Majesty's Birthday, after her happy recovery from a dangerous sickness*, ll. 35–6:

> On your pale cheek he dropped the shower,
> Revived you like a dying flower.

136. Fairfax caps the stanza with his own last line.

FAIRFAX'S
ORIGINAL POEMS

INTRODUCTION

Little has survived of Edward Fairfax's original poetry. Two of his eclogues, *Eglon and Alexis* and *Hermes and Lycaon* have come down to us complete, while a scrap from a further eclogue turns up in Gough's edition of Camden's *Britannia* (1789). There is also a poem entitled *Epitaph upon King James* and a short epitaph on his sister-in-law, Baroness Fairfax, and there seems little reason to doubt that he was the author of the complimentary verses to Queen Elizabeth and Prince Charles first printed in the 1600 and 1624 editions respectively of *Godfrey of Bulloigne*. A long fragment of a further eclogue *Ida and Opilio* has been attributed to him.

It seems that Edward Fairfax wrote twelve eclogues. Brian Fairfax in his letter to Atterbury (12 March 1704/5) quotes the following account by the poet's son, William:

These Bucolickes were written in the first yeare of the reigne of K.James, and from their finishing they lay neglected 10 yeares in my Fathers study untill Lodowic the late Noble Duke of Richmond and Lenox desired a sight of them, which made the Author to transcribe them for his Grace's use. That copy was seen and approved by many learned men, and that Reverend Divine Dr. Field now Bp. of Hereford, wrot verses upon it. and these follow-ing were writ by Wilson, Scoto-britannus.

Et Phoebum, castasque docis Fairfaxe, sorores
Salsa verecundo verba lepore loqui
Ulla nec in toto prurit lascivia libro
Pagina non minus est quam tibi vita proba.

Chaste is thy Muse as is a Vestal Nun
And thy Appollo spotless as ye Sun
No wanton thought betrayd by word or look
As blameless is thy life, as is thy Book.

But the Book itselfe and the Bishops encomium perished in the fire, when the Banquetting house at Whitehall was burnt, and with it part of the Dukes lodgings where the Book was. but with my Fathers help I recovered them out of his loose papers &c.

At the end of his letter Brian Fairfax says: 'I wish I had his letters to Dorrell, to show you; but I have his Eclogues.' Thus a manuscript of the whole set of the *Eclogues* was extant in the early eighteenth century. This may have been the manuscript which Mrs. Cooper used for the text of *Eglon and Alexis* which she printed in her anthology, *The Muses Library* in 1737. Her note on the Eclogues gives us a little more information.

The *Eclogues* . . . are in Number Twelve; all of them wrote after the Accession of King *James* to the Throne of *England*, on important Subjects, relating to the Manners, Characters, and Incidents of the Times he lived in; They are pointed with many fine Strokes of Satire; dignify'd with wholesome Lessons of Morality, and Policy, to those of the highest Rank; and some modest hints even to Majesty itself . . . As far as Poetry is concern'd in them, the very name of *Fairfax* is the highest Recommendation, and the Learning they contain, is so various, and extensive, that, according to the Evidence of his Son, (who has written large Annotations on each) No Man's Reading, beside his own, was sufficient to explain his References effectually.

(*The Muses Library*, p. 363.)

The other complete surviving eclogue, *Hermes and Lycaon*, has come down to us in a manuscript containing poems by Thomas, third Baron Fairfax, and apparently in his hand. The heading states that it was 'made by my uncle Mr. Edward Fairfax'. Both these eclogues are religious allegories. The pastoral convention provides a setting, dramatis personae, and the outlines of a narrative, but the imaginative world in which these are set is not the idealized natural world of classical or Spenserian pastoral. Indeed, these poems hardly pretend to make sense on the literal level. In *Eglon and Alexis*, the fox, instead of seeking to eat the lamb, fornicates with her, clips her fleece, and dresses her in a coat of many colours; while the nymphs adored by the shepherds, Hermes and Lycaon, belong to the world of the Book of Revelation. The main allegory is complicated by independent emblematic detail—e.g. the coat of many colours in *Eglon and Alexis*, or architectural images in *Hermes and Lycaon*.

To criticize such poems for a lack of consistency on the literal level would be like criticizing emblem book illustrations for their lack of pictorial realism. The point is that Fairfax's eclogues do achieve a certain imaginative coherence: the seducer fox does exist as a creature in his own right and not merely as a metaphor for Satan; Psyche and Flora do come to life as persons, and do not remain mere personifications. The setting, too, is imaginatively realized and provides Fairfax with an opportunity for some of his most striking and original writing.

One salient characteristic of both these eclogues is the prevalence of obscure allusions. Fairfax does not so much use exceptionally recondite sources (Pliny's *Natural History*, Plutarch's *Lives* and *Moralia*, and Hakluyt's travels, which seem to be his major sources, were far from inaccessible to his contemporaries) as pick on details in them which were unlikely to be widely known. There is, in fact, a good deal of deliberate mystification, but it always seems to serve a genuine poetic purpose.

Over and above the main metaphors of the allegory and the emblematic metaphors which are mixed up with it there are a number of conceits after the manner of Du Bartas, or the Metaphysical poets; as in the lines:

The sweatie sith-man with his rasor keene
Shore the perfumed beard from medowes greene
(Hermes and Lycaon, ll. 1–2.)

or

All night he couched on her tender Brest,
Till timely Day-spring with her Morning-Broom
Had swept the Silver Motes from Heav'ns Steel-Flore,
And at the key-hole peeped through theyr Dore.
(Eglon and Alexis, ll. 158–61.)

It is perhaps fanciful to feel that there is a certain Marvellian quality about the first of these.

Fairfax's reputation as a writer of 'smooth verse' and a forerunner of Waller was based on *Godfrey of Bulloigne*. It is interesting to see how his couplet verse (as in *Hermes and Lycaon*) compares with Waller's. Isolated couplets do indeed have something like Waller's almost Augustan ring about them: e.g.

Yee sedgie lakes, and peble-paved wells,
And thou great Pales in these feilds that dwells . . .
(Hermes and Lycaon, ll. 15–16.)

It is true that there is little running-on from line to line, and less from couplet to couplet; but one need only read on from the lines quoted to see that their regularity and balance were not routine:

How oft have you hid in the shadie spraies,
Listned Lycaon's songes, his Loves and Lays . . .
(ibid. 17–18.)

Line 18, indeed, demonstrates a favourite trick of Fairfax's which has distinctive consequences for the rhythm and melody of the line: he gives us three words which are grammatically parallel, so that the reader is forced to give pretty well equal stresses to 'songs', 'Loves and Lays'. The result is a monotony which Waller would have studiously avoided.

These two eclogues contrast strongly with the long fragment *Ida & Opilio*. Here the subject is secular (a debate between an 'ancient' and a 'modern' about the sixteenth-century voyages of discovery) and the method is literal, without any obvious allegory. The setting is beautifully, if conventionally, pastoral (suggesting a classical rather than an English landscape), but the debate has nothing whatever to do with it, so that the fragment seems to lack the kind of imaginative unity achieved in the other two eclogues. There is a certain appeal to common sense and a confidence of tone about this poem which sets it apart; and even the use of learned allusion seems less based on a desire to mystify than on an attempt to inform. Rhythmically, too, the poem has a power and an urgency we would not necessarily have expected from Edward Fairfax. On the other hand, it lacks the depth and imaginative richness of the other two eclogues. If it were to turn out that this brilliant and lively poem was indeed his work we would have to concede that he was a far more versatile poet than one might have suspected from his other work.

The two lines of Fairfax's fifth eclogue, quoted in Gough's edition of Camden's *Britannia* (1789) do not add greatly to our knowledge of Fairfax as a poet. Gough seems to have copied the lines from a manuscript note on p. 311 of Dr. John Ward's copy of John Horsley's *Britannia Romana* (1732), which states 'Mr. Fairfax's V Eclogue MS begins thus', and quotes the lines exactly as Gough gives them. Ward had evidently found them in Samuel Woodforde's manuscript collection of Roman inscriptions found in Britain, 'Inscriptionum Romanarum Britannicarum Conlectio', which Ward describes in a leaf of the manuscript notes. Woodforde was of Wadham College, Oxford. The collection of Roman inscriptions was dated 1658 and after Woodforde's death eventually passed into the Rawlinson collection in the Bodleian Library. There is nothing to show whether Woodforde saw Edward Fairfax's fifth eclogue as a whole, or was merely supplied with the quotation about 'Verbeia' by Edward's son William.

Apart from the eclogues, the only minor poem of any length that survives, *The Epitaph on King James*, is printed in *The Fairfax Correspondence* (ed. George Johnson, 1848). The manuscript seems to have been one of a collection of Fairfax papers purchased by John Newington Hughes, which had allegedly been sold by the owners of Leeds Castle to a cobbler, a romantic tale which probably conceals the systematic private selling-off of Fairfax manuscripts during the 1820s. Many of these at length found their way to the British Library, but not, unfortunately, the MS. containing the poem. It appears as item 195 in the catalogue of the Hughes sale (Sotheby, Wilkinson, & Hodge, 1877) when it was purchased by Lord Houghton; perhaps it perished in the Fuyston library fire. We do not know on what evidence the editors of the Fairfax Correspondence ascribed this poem to Edward Fairfax; but it is a poem of some beauty and wit, rising to a passionate climax. The epitaph on Baroness Fairfax is found in the British Library Additional MS. 39. 922, in what appears to be a transcript of a letter by Brian Fairfax the elder to his grandchildren.

The complimentary verses to Elizabeth I and Prince Charles are both poems of wit and originality, and the first, in particular, shows the poet's skill as a metrist.

Taken all in all, these minor poems show Fairfax as a poet of considerable talent and some ingenuity. The disappearance of the bulk of his original poetry is much to be regretted.

Eclogue IV

Eglon and Alexis

WHILST, on the rough, and Heath-strew'd Wilderness,
His tender Flocks the Rasps, and Bramble cropp,
Poor Shepherd *Eglon*, full of sad Distress!
By the small Stream, sat on a Mole-Hill-Topp;
Crown'd with a Wreath of Heban Branches broke: 5
Whom good *Alexis* found, and thus bespoke.

Alex. My *Friend*, what means this silent Lamentation?
Why on this Field of Mirth, this Realm of Smiles
Doth the fierce War of Greife make such Invasion?
Witty *Timanthes* had he seen, ere whiles,   10
    What Face of Woe thy Cheek of Sadness bears,
    He had not curtain'd *Agamemnon*'s Tears.

The blacke Ox treads not yet upon thy Toe,
Nor thy good Fortune turnes her Wheele awaye;
Thy Flocks increase, and thou increasest so;   15
Thy stragling Goates now mild and gentle ly;
    And that Foole *Love* thou whip'st away with Rods:
    Then what sets thee and *Joy* so far at ods?

Egl. Nor *Love*, nor Loss of ought that Worldings love,
Be it Dress, Wealth, Dream, Pleasure, Smoak or Glory,   20
Can my well-settled Thought to Passion move:
A greater Cause it is that makes me sorry.
    But known to thee it may seem small or none;
    Under his Fellow's Burden who needs grone?

Alex. Yet tell me, *Eglon*, for my Ram shall dy   25
On the same Altar, where thy Goat doth burn;
Else let these Kids my Olive-Trees lick dry,
And let my Sheep to shag-hayr'd *Musmons* turn!
    All Things with Friends are common; Grief and Sorrow,
    Men without Bond, or Interest freely borrow.   30

30 borrow < borrow.

Egl. Sufficeth to each Man his own Mishap;
    Yet for our Friends our Eye oft spends more Teares,
    Than for our selves; our Neighbour in his Lap,
    Sometimes our Grief, our Losses never beares;
        Fitter to weep than help when need requires!   35
        So soon the halting Steed of Friendship tires!

    Thou know'st I had a tender Lamb; a Cade,
    Nourish't with Milk and Morsels from my Table,
    That in my Bosom its soft Lodging made,
    And cherisht was, and fed as I was able,   40
        It was my Child my Darling and my Queen;
        And might for Shape a *Passover* have been!

    I kept it for an Off'ring 'gainst the Day
    That the great God of Shepherds *Pan* shall come,
    Not he whose Thousand Lambs did feed and stray   45
    On *Sicil*-Hills, one such at Night brought Home.
        Nor could the Ram, wonne by the Lords of *Greece*
        Compare his Guilded, with her pearled Fleece.

    But when the Sun with his intising Ray
    Allur'd her forth, from Quiet of my shed,   50
    Thorow the broken Wall she slipt away,
    Behind the Corner-stone, and thence she fled,
        Ambling along the Meads and Rivers shrill:
        And yet she thought, she knew she did no Ill.

    The *Fox*, whose Fort, *Malpardus*, border'd nie,   55
    Spi'd from his Keep the wandring Innocent,
    That, weary, in the cooling shade did lye,
    Lest the hot Beams her tender Limbs might shent;
        And soon he judged, by her harmless Look,
        It was a Fish would eas'ly take the Hook.   60

    He buskt him Boon, and, on his sanded Coat,
    He buckled close a slain Kid's hayry Skin,
    And wore the Vizzard of a smooth-fac't Goat:
    And Saint without, none spi'd the Devill within!
        With wanton Skips he boards the harmlesse Sheep,   65
        And with sweet Words thus into Grace did creep.

Dear Sister-Lamb! Queen of the fleecy Kind!
That opal Flowers, pick'st from these Emral'd-Closes,
Thy Bombace soft in silver Trammels bind,
And crown thy Lamber Horns with Corall-Roses!   70
   This Sabbath is the Feast-Day of thy Birth;
   Come be thou Lady of our *May*, and Mirth!

Break from the Prison of the austere Cell
Of thy strict Master, and his *Cynick* Diet!
And in sweet Shades of this fat Valley dwell,   75
In Ease and Wealth! Here we are rich and quiet!
   Unty these Bonds of Awe, and Cords of Duty!
   They be weake Chains to fetter Youth and Beauty!

With that he kiss'd her, and strayn'd her Hand,
And softly rays'd her from the tender Grass;   80
And, squiring her along the flowry Land,
Still made her court as thro' the Fields they pass:
   And that Bawd *Love*, Factor of shame and sin!
   Lent him a Net to catch this Woodcock in.

Close in the Bosom of a bended Hill,   85
Of faire, and fruitful Trees a Forest stood;
Balm, *Myrrh*, *Bdellium*, from their Bark distill,
Bay, *Smilax*, *Myrtle*, (*Cupid's* Arrow-Wood)
   Grew there, and *Cypress* with his kiss-sky Tops,
   And *Ferrea's* Tree whence pure Rose-Water drops.   90

The Golden Bee, buzzing with Tinsell-Wings
Suckt Amber-Honey from the silken Flower;
The Dove sad Love-Grones on her Sack-But sings,
The *Throssell* whistles from his Oaken-Tower;
   And, sporting, lay the Nymphs of Woods, and Hills,   95
   On Beds of *Heart's-Ease*, *Rue*, and *Daffadills*.

Hither the Traytor-Fox his Mistress leads,
Intising her with Sweetness of the Place,
Till on a hidden Net unwares she treads;
   Yet hurt her not; the subtile Fouler smil'd: 100
   Nor knew the *Dott'rell* yet, she was beguil'd.

87 Myrtle < Myrrh   distill < distill,

Not that false Snare, wherewith the Cuckold-Smith
Sham'd his Queen, and himself; nor that sly Gin
Astolfo caught the Eat-Man-Giant with,
Nor that *Arachne* takes her wild Fowle in,   105
  Nor those small Toiles the Morning-Queen doth set
  In every Mead, so fine were as that Net.

Thus caught, he bound her in a Chain three-fold,
And led her to a shady Arbour near;
The Chain was Copper, yet it seemed Gold,   110
And every Link a sundry Name did bear,
  Wrath, Sloth, Strife, Envy, Avarice, foul Lust
  And Pride: What Flesh can so strong Fetters bu'st?

An Hundred Times her Virgin-Lip he kiss't,
As oft her Mayden-Finger gently wrung;   115
Yet what he would, her Child-hood nothing wist;
The *Bee* of *Love* her soft Heart had not stung!
  In vain he sigh't, he glanc'd, he shook his Head,
  Those *Hierogliphicks* were too hard to read!

She did not, nay she would not understand   120
Upon what Errand his sweet Smiles were gone;
And in his borrowed Coate some Hole she fond,
Thro' which she spy'd, all was not Gold that shone.
  Yet still his Tools the Workman ply'd so fast,
  That her speed-Wing his Lime-Twig took at last.   125

Her Silver-Rug from her soft Hide he clip't,
And on her Body, knit a Canvass thin,
With Twenty-Party-Colours ev'nly strip't,
And guarded like the *Zabra*'s Rayne-Bow-Skin.
  Such Coats young *Tamar*, and fayre *Rachel*'s Child   130
  Put off, when He was sold, and She defil'd.

There mourn'd the *Blacke*, the *Purple* tyranniz'd,
The *Russet* hoped: *Green* the Wanton play'd;
Yellow spy'd Faults in such as Love disguis'd;
Carnation still desir'd, *White* lived a Mayd;   135
  Blew kept his Faith unstain'd; *Red* bled to Death
  And forlorn *Tawny* wore a Willow-Wreath.

103 Qneen < Queen

All these, and Twenty new-found Colours more,
Were in the Weft of that rich Garment wrought;
And who that charmed Vesture took and wore,   140
Like it, were changeable in Will and Thought.
    What Wonder then, if, on so smooth a Plate,
    He stamp't a Fiend, where once an Angel sate?

Thus clad, he set her on a Throne of Glass,
And spread a plenteous Table on the Green;   145
And every Platter of true Porcelan was,
Which had a Thousand Years in temp'ring been;
    Yet did the Cates exceed the Substance fine;
    So rare the Viands were, so rich the Wine!

Lucullus was a Niggard of his Meat,   150
And spareful of his Cups seem'd *Anthony*;
But, in each Morsel, which the Guests should eate,
The cruel Rat's-Bane of vile Lust did lye;
    Yet at that Board, the little-fearing-Sheep
    Eats, till she surfeit, quaffeth, till she sleep.   155

Then, drunk with Folly, to his loather Nest
He brought his Prey; and, in a dusky Room,
All Night he couched on her tender Brest,
Till timely Day-spring with her Morning-Broom
    Had swept the Silver Motes from Heav'n's Steel-Flore,
    And at the Key-Hole peeped through theyr Dore.   161

But such the Issue was of that Embrace,
That deadly Poyson thro' her Body spread,
Rotted her Limbs, and leprous grew her Face;
His Bosom's Touch so dire a Mischief bred,   165
    So venomous was not the poysoned Lip
    Of th' *Indian* King, or *Guinea's Cock's Combe-ship,*

Pherecides' small, winged Dragonets,
Ferrotine's Gentles, *Scilla's* Swarm of Lice,
The *Boghar*-Worm that Joynts asunder frets;   170
The Plague that scourged wanton *Cressed's* Vice,
    And that great Evill which Viper-Wine makes sound,
    Compar'd to hers, are but a Pinn's small Wound.

168 *Pherecides,* small, < *Pherecides'* small,

The gastly *Raven*, from the blasted Oake,
With deadly Call foreshew'd my Lamb's Mishap;   175
The *Wake-Bird* on my Chimney well-nigh spoke;
But I alas! foresaw no After-clap!
   Yet crew my Hens, sure Shepherd's Sign of Ill!
   But my fond Head in Bird-spell had no Skill.

For Help I sought the *Leach*, wise *Mardophage*,   180
I try'd the *English-Bath*, and *German-Spaw*;
To *Walsingham* I went on Pilgrimage,
And said strong Charmes that kept even *Death* in Awe!
   Yet none of these can her lost Health restore;
   Ah no, my Lamb's Recouery costeth more!   185

Alex. So vain a Thing is Man; what least we fear
That soonest haps; the Evill we present feel,
Brings greater Anguish than our Souls can bear;
Desp'rate we are in Woe, careless in Weale!
   Unfall'n, unfear'd! if Ill betide us, then   190
   Are we past Hope: So vain a Thing is Man!

Great is, I grant, the Danger of thy Sheep!
But yet there is a Salve for every Sore;
That Shepherd, who our Flocks and us doth keep,
To remedy this Sickness long before,   195
   Killed a *holy Lamb*, clear, spotless, pure;
   Whose Blood the Salve is all our Hurts to cure!

Call for that Surgeon good, to dress her Wound!
Bath her in holy-Water, of thy Tears!
Let her in Bands of Faith and Love be bound!   200
And, while on Earth she spends her Pilgrim-Years,
   Thou for thy Charm pray with the *Publican!*
   And so restore thy *Lamb* to Health again!

Now farewell *Eglon!* for the Sun stoops low,
And calling Guests before my Sheep-Coat's Dore: 205
New clad in *White*, I see my Porter-Crow;
Great Kings oft want these Blessings of the Poor:
   My Board is short, my Kitchen needs no Clerk,
   Come *Fannius!* come! be thou *Symposiarke!*

Textual Notes

The text is that published in *The Muses Library*, ed. Mrs Elizabeth Cooper (1737), pp. 364–76. We have followed it faithfully, correcting only what appear to be printer's errors, removing the footnotes to another place, and normalizing the long 's'. The following are the *Muses Library* readings from which our text departs; more substantial emendations are suggested in the notes.

23 But, known

30 borrow

87 distill

103 Queen

168 *Pherecides* small, winged Dragonets,

Commentary

(This commentary incorporates all the footnotes from the *Muses Library* text. These are here signed *M.L.*)

Eglon, a shepherd who is apparently old enough to be immune from the temptations of the flesh but not so old as to suffer from its other infirmities, complains to Alexis about a disaster that has befallen a favourite of his. The cunning fox has ensnared her in a net, bound her in a chain of the seven deadly sins, caught her with his sexual attractions, stripped her of her white fleece and dressed her in a garment of many colours, made her eat and drink to surfeit, and slept with her. As a result of his embraces she is stricken with a foul disease which seems incurable, but Alexis tells of a medicine administered by the Good Shepherd, consisting of the blood of a holy lamb. As he leaves, Alexis indicates that in his house a child has just been born.

It is not easy to say on how many levels the allegory is intended to move. The primary reference is clearly to the Fall of Man, but there may also be an allusion to the introduction of syphilis, and there could be still other levels.

5. *Heban*: either ebony, or possibly identical with Marlowe's 'hebon' (*Jew of Malta*, III. iv. 96) and Shakespeare's 'cursed Hebona' (*Hamlet*, Q1, I. v. 62), which *O.E.D.* tentatively explains as yew.

10. *Timanthes*: '*Timanthes* the Painter, who, designing the Sacrifice of *Iphigenia* threw a Veil over the face of *Agamemnon*; not able to express a Father's Anguish.' (*M.L.*) See Pliny, *Hist. Nat.* XXXV. x. 73–4; Holland's translation (1601), ii. 536.

13. *The blacke Ox treads not yet upon thy Toe*: 'You have not yet experienced

sorrow or old age.' See M. P. Tilley, *Proverbs in England in the Sixteenth & Seventeenth Centuries* (Ann Arbor 1950), p. 517.

20. *Smoak*: cf. Godfrey of Bulloigne, I. xxii. 5. An uncharacteristically 'rough' line: 'Dream' seems both metrically and semantically the odd word out.

28. *Musmons*: '*Musmon* a Kind of wild Sheep.' (*M.L.*) From Lat. *musimon*, Gr. μούσμων, moufflon, 'There is in Spain, but especially in the Isle Corsica, a kind of Musmones, not altogether unlike to sheep.' Holland's Pliny, 1601, i. 228.

44. *Pan*: For Pan as Christ, cf. Spenser, *Shepheards Calender*, May, 54.

45. *he whose Thousand Lambs did feed and stray On Sicil-Hills*: either Polyphemus; cf. Theocritus, *Idyll*, X. 34; or Corydon, the speaker in Vergil, *Eclogues* ii. 21.

52. *Corner-stone*: cf. Ephesians 2: 20, 'Jesus Christ himself being the chief corner-stone'.

55. *Malpardus*: possibly 'evil paradise'?

61. *buskt him boon*: *busk* = prepare, dress up (Scots and N. dialect). *boon*: confusion between 'boon' (v.), synonym of *busk* and often linked with it ('He did buske bowne him', *Scottish Field*, 1515). and 'boon' (adj. and adv.) = good, well. Cf. *Godfrey of Bulloigne*, III. 307: 'Flew on the villaine, who to flight him bound'. *sanded*: sandy.

62. *a slain Kid's hayry Skin*: cf. the story of Jacob and Esau, Genesis 27: 16–23.

87. *Balm, Myrrh, Bdellium*: All three are plants producing aromatic gum (Pliny, *Hist. Nat.* XII. xxv, XV–XVI and ix: Holland, i. 368–9 and 362–3).

88. *Bay, Smilax, Myrtle*: Bay (Pliny, XV. xxx: Holland, i. 452–4) has entirely virtuous associations, e.g. with triumph; Myrtle (Pliny, XV. xxix: Holland, i. 451) is associated with Venus, but not otherwise sinister; Smilax, however, (which is a kind of bind-weed) is unlucky (Pliny, XVI. xxxv: Holland, i. 481), being named after 'a damsel of that name' who 'was turned into this shrub or plant'. Moreover, the name Smilax is also given to the Yew (Pliny, XVI. x: Holland, i. 463), which is 'unpleasant & fearful to look upon, as a cursed tree'.

89. *Cypress*: a tree of funereal associations; see *Aeneid*, III. 63–5, 'stant Manibus arae caeruleis maestae vittis atraque cupresso.' However, cypresses are not generally noted for their altitude; 'kiss-sky Tops' seems to be poetic licence.

90. Ferrea's Tree: 'A Tree growing in one of the Canaries said to have

that Quality.' (*M.L.*) The tree in question grew on the isle of Ferro in the Canaries, and was noted for collecting large quantities of dew, which dripped off its leaves into a cistern. There are numerous accounts of it, e.g. in Hakluyt, *Principall Navigations*, 1598, in Thomas Nicols's description of the Canary Islands. *Rose-water* may be a pun on 'ros', dew.

91–6. C. G. Bell has pointed out the debt of this passage to Vergil, *Eclogues*, i. 53–8 (Unpublished thesis in Bodleian Library, Oxford).

99–100. To judge by the rhyme-scheme, a line is missing here.

102. *Cuckold-Smith*: Vulcan.

103–4. *Astolfo*: 'See *Ariosto*' (*M.L.*), *Orlando Furioso*, XV. 54. The giant is Caligorante.

110. *Copper*: perhaps Fairfax merely wanted an instance of something that glittered without being gold. A late compiler of symbolic meanings, Picinellus, in his *Mundus Symbolicus* (1681) gives a number of interpretations which might be relevant: 'Cuprum . . . symbolum iracundi, . . . maledici, infaelicis hominis, . . . venustatis, haereseos, spei mundanae lethalis' (in A. Henkel and A. Schoener, *Emblemata*, Stuttgart, 1967).

117. *The Bee of Love*: Cf. Anacreontea, 15. and Spenser: 'Upon a day as love lay sweetly slumbring', 'Amoretti', verses appended.

126. *Rug*: rough woollen material, frieze, thick woollen stuff.

129. *Zabra*: 'The *Zabra*, a Beast in *Congo*, of various colours.' (*M.L.*)

130. *Tamar*: the sister of Absalom (II Samuel 12: 18); *Rachel's child*: Joseph: Genesis 37: 23.

132–7. *There mourn'd the* Blacke . . . , etc. Cf. Alciati, *Omnia Emblemata* (Antwerp, 1574); *In Colores*, 117, p. 318.

Index mæstitiae est pullus color: vtimur omnes
   Hoc habitu, tumulis cum damus inferias.
At sinceri animi, & mentis stola candida purae:
   Hinc sindon sacris linea grata viris.
Nos sperare docet viridis. spes dicitur esse
   In viridi, quoties irrita retro cadit.
Est cupidis flavus color, est & amantibus aptus,
   Et scortis, & queis spes sua certa fuit.
At ruber armatos equites exornet amictus;
   Indicet & pueros erubuisse pudor.
Cæruleus nautas, & qui caelestia vates
   Attoniti nimia relligione petunt.
Vilia sunt giluis, natiuaque vellera byrris:
   Qualia lignipedes stragula habere solent.
Quem curae ingentes cruciant vel zelus amoris,
   Creditur hic fulua non male veste tegi.

Quisquis sorte sua contentus, ianthina gestet:
  Fortunae aequanimis taedia quique ferat.
Vt varia est natura coloribus ingignendis,
  Sic alijs aliud: sed sua cuique placent.

An English version is found in G. Whitney, *A Choice of Emblems*, Leyden, 1586, n.º 134.

146. *Porcelan*: 'The supposed natural plaster or paste then believed to harden into porcelain' (*O.E.D.*); '. . . which porcelain is a kind of plaster buried in the earth & by length of time congealed & glazed into that fine substance', Bacon, *Argts. Law, Impeachmts. Waste*, 1615 (in *Works* [1879], i. 616).

167. *Th' Indian King*: '*Muhamet* a King of Cambaia, whose Lip, being poison'd by Accident, was said to kill all the Women he kiss'd.' (*M.L.*) Found in several travel books, e.g. G. B. Ramusio, *Delle Navigationi et Viaggi* (Venice, 1563), fo. 171A. Purchas translates this in *Pilgrims* (1624), Pt. I, Bk. ix, ch. 7, para. 2: 'The Sultan of Cambaia . . . was named Macamat . . . He is so accustomed to poyson from his infancy, that he daily eateth some to keep it in use. And although he himselfe feele no hurte thereof by reason of custome; yet doth he thereby so impoyson himselfe, that he is poyson to other. . . . He entertaineth about foure thousand Concubines for whensoever he hath lyen with any of them, she with whom he hath lyen, is dead in the morning.'

Guinea's Cock's Combe-Ship: 'A Sea-Weed like a Cock's-Comb, found floating on the Coast of Guinea, so venomous as not to be touch'd without extreme Danger.' (*M.L.*) Possibly the Guinea Ship, a floating medusa (*Physalia pelagica*).

168. Pherecides: 'A Philosopher consum'd by flies like Dragons, bred in his own body.' (*M.L.*) Pherekydes the Syrian, who is said to have died of a disease in which lice overran his body (Aristotle, *Historia Animalium*, V. 557ª; Plutarch, *Life of Sulla*, xxxvi). The phrase 'small, winged Dragonets' may recall Plutarch's δρακόντια μικρά (*Symposiakon*, VIII. ix. 733B: in *Moralia*, trans. Minar [Loeb Classical Library, 1961], ix. 197), which describes worms breeding in the skin (though Pherekydes is not mentioned in that passage).

169. *Ferrotine*: 'A Queen of *Cyrene*, eaten alive by Maggots.' (*M.L.*). Pheretime, daughter of Battus, who died 'a foul death: her living body festered and bred worms', Herodotus, iv. 205. (Trans. A. D. Godley [Loeb Classical Library, 1921], ii. 407).

Scilla's Swarm of Lice: '*Scilla* died of the Lowsy-Disease.' (*M.L.*) 'He had an imposthume in his body, the which by process of time came to corrupt his flesh in such sort, that it turned all to lice', Plutarch, *Life of Sulla*, xxxvi: trans. North (1595), p. 520; North spells the dictator's name 'Sylla'.

170. *Boghar-Worm*: 'So called from a City of Bactria; which being swallowed

in drinking the Waters of the Place, finds a Way into the Legs; and must be drawn out gradually; an Inch a Day; and if broken in the Operation, the Patient dies.' (*M.L.*) There is an account of Bokhara and the worm by Anthony Jenkinson in Hakluyt, ed. cit., p. 331. (Presumably the Guinea-Worm, *Dracunculus Medinensis.*)

171. *The Plague that scourged wanton Cressed's vice*: an allusion to the leprosy which the gods inflict on Cresseide in Henryson's *Testament of Cresseide.*

172. *Viper-Wine*: various medicines were made out of vipers variously processed. Avicenna, *Liber Canonis* etc. (Venice 1562), II. ii. 608, says that viper boiled in wine relieves the ear-ache. Pliny, *Hist. Nat.* XXXIX, vi: Holland, ii. 366–7, describes various medicinal preparations made of viper, including a decoction allegedly effective against lice.

175–6. Cf. Vergil, *Eclogues*, ix. 14–15 (Bell, unpublished thesis).

177. After-Clap: 'Unexpected stroke after recipient has ceased to be on his guard' (*O.E.D.*).

180. Mardophage: ?dung-eater? According to Galen, the famous Asclepiades 'cui cognomen erat pharmaceon, et alia omnia medicamenta collegat, at multos impleret libros, et stercore ad multos saepe affectus utitur non modo medicamentis, quae foris imponuntur commiscens, sed iis quoque quae intro in os sumuntur.' (Latin trans., ed. Kühn, [Leipzig, 1826], xii. 290 f.)

181. Spaw: Name of a watering-place in the province of Liège. Cf. *Faerie Queene*, I. xi. 30, 'And th' English Bath and eke the German Spau'.

206. Porter-Crow: 'The Ring of the Door, call'd a *Crow*; and when cover'd with white Linen, denoted the Mistress of the House was in Travel.' (*M.L.*) 'An ancient kind of door-knocker' (*O.E.D.*).

209. Fannius: '*Caius Fannius*, who made a Law to restrain Luxury in Diet.' (*M.L.*) *Symposiarch*: leader of a convivial gathering (*O.E.D.* cites Holland's trans. of Plutarch's *Morals*, 1603, as the earliest example).

Eclogue (unnumbered)

Hermes and Lycaon

An Egloge
made by my vncle Mr Ed. Fairfax
in a Dialoge betwixt tow sheapards

Hermes & Lycaon

The Argument
Lycaon his false church extends
through all the world, wth pompe & pride
Hermes the church of Christ Comends
And to her spouse brings home his bride

The sweatie sith-man wth his rasor keene   1
Shore the perfumed beard from medowes greene
And on each bush & euery mossie stone
Iarred Maies littel daughter Tettrigone
When to the shadowes of a mountaine steepe   5
Lycaon droue his Goats Hermes his sheepe
The Shephards both were Louers, both were younge
Ther skill was like in piping, like in songe
The other groomes thatt hard, hid in the dales
Were dume for shame, like conqured Nightingales   10
Oft came the Nimphs, the Farie sisters oft
Forsooke ther mossie beds and liards soft
And oft the halfe-gods att ther musick sound
Came & ther browes wth Iuie garlands crownd.
Yee sedgie lakes & peble-paued wells   15
And thou great Pales in these feilds that dwells
How oft haue you hid in the shadie spraies
Listned Lycaon's songes, his Loues and Laies
And you high stretched Pines & Oakes of Ioue
Thou wanton Eccho tel-clock of this groue   20
How oft did you faire Psyches praise resound

When Hermes charmd wth songes loues bleeding wound
They sunge by Course & praised ther loues by turnes
Each Crickett loues the flame wherein she burnes
And whilst ther flocks bruze on the shrubs & briers 25
They tune ther pipes & thus they sing ther fiers

Lyc: Flora my queene my ioy my heauen of bliss
Se what my merit & deseruing is
I build the Temples & I feed thy sheepe
I bring thee gifts thy words as Lawes I keepe 30
My bed is ashes sackcloth is my weede
I drink wth Rechabs sonnes wth Job I feede
 For all my seruice & this suffring longe
 Loue me sweet Flora or thou dost me wronge

Herm: Psyche my deare my vndefild my doue 35
ô Comfort me for I am sick of loue
Thy sacred temple, is this wounded brest
Sin, error, folly my seruice is att best
Foule leper spotts on all my body growe
Wipe out these staines & wash me white as snow 40
 Clothe me wth Linien crown my head wth gold
 First make me worthie Loue, then Loue me bold

Lyc: Flora was younge & faire few goats she kept
Ten Kings espide her, loued her, wth her slept
And in her sweet imbrace such ioy they found 45
That wth three Diadems her head they crownd
And on seauen heapes ther wealth & tresure laid
Sett her ther on, fell att her feet & praide
 She forty months & tow ther seruice proues
 And takes them for her slaues, not for her loues 50

Herm: Psyches my virgen bare a blessed sonne
The dragon chastd her, she to desart runne,
The feend a streame of water att her flings
Earth drunk the flood she scapt wth eagles wings
Crownd wth twelue stars clothd wth the glorious Sun 55
She doth wth Roes & Hindes in Eden wonne
 Ther Psyches liues & reignes in safty plast
 Till time & times & halfe a time be past

22 loue < loues 30 they < thy

Lyc: out of the sea a scarlet beast appeard
Ten hornes he had & seuen heads proudly reard   60
His forked taile gainst all the world made wars
And smote the third of trees of floods of stars
Flora this monster caught & tamde his pride
And on his back as on a mule doth ride
    All nations feare the beast & serue the dame   65
    And sealed are with's number, marke, & name

Herm: before the gates of Psyches shepcote lies
Fowre wonderous beasts all full of wings & eyes
And round about them fowre & twentie Kings
Offer vp gold & mirrh & pretious things   70
All these do Psyches lambes keepe, cure & feed
And thousand thousands clad in milk-white weed
    Sings himmes of loue and faith & neuer ceace
    And on his brow each weares the seale of peace

Lyc: Flora once found me sick & hurt to death   75
Thrice did she cross me, thrice vpon me breath
Three times she dipt me in a liuing streame
And salued my wounds wth spitle salt & creame
A thousand saints she for my garde apoints
And all my head wth oyle and baulme anoynts   80
    Then makes me maister of her flocks & fould
    Her goats to keepe or kill or sell for gold

Herm: Psyches first tooke me soild wth mire & clay
Washd in the well of life my filth away
Theeues robd me slew me of a Lambe new slaine   85
On me she powerd the blood, I liued againe
Sence that wth bread of heauen wine of grace
She diets me her lapp my resting place
    Her sheepe my playfelowes heauen our fould
    Her spouse the doore his voyce the key of gould   90

Lyc: Itt was the fifteth yeare Flora a feast
Made for all those that loued & serued her beast
Her gests were kings & Lords of highest bearth
All that were wise & rich vpon the earth

73 loue, faith < love and faith

And all that Land, that Sea or ayre affords   95
Her caters tooke & ther wth fild her bords
   And drunk wth wine suckt from her cup of gold
   Were Kings & nations rich poore young & old

Herm: Psyche to super cald the weak the poore
The sick the lazer from the rich-mans doore   100
And att her bord sett them wth Lords & Kings
Her holy stewards wine & wafers brings
They eat & drinke by faith & thirst noe more
Except some guests forechargd wth Floras store
   Sitt ther & spider like from roses new   105
   Draw poyson wher the Bee sucks hunny dew

Lyc: Flora an orchard had of fruitfull treene
She parde the mosse she kept the branches cleane
She lett the fountains in, she kild the worme
She scard the birds she saued the bloomes from storme   110
Floursht the trees the bowes wth aples bent
She cald her seruents, to her orchard went
   Gethered to eat, but when she cutt the skin
   The fruit was ashes, imbers, dust w^{th}in

Herm: Last yeare my Psyche had a feild of corne   115
She skourd the ditches, stopt the gaps wth thorne
She tild the land enough she grew good seed
She stubd the briers pluckt vp the tares & weed
She fraid the crowes she kept the wild bore out
And when the Sun turned the years wheele about   120
   She reapt her crop & when her gaine she tould
   Found thirty, sixty & a hundred fould

Lyc: a flock of goats astray from Flora went
Doris her handmade after them she sent
But whilst the lass wth Thirsis sporting laid   125
Her dogs rann forth alone & soone they straid
And like the kind of wolues of wch they sprung
They slew & eat the goats & sucklings young
   Yet some escapt saued in the woods & rocks
   Doris went home but thus she lost her flocks   130

---

95 And that < And all that   110 saue < saued   116 gape < gaps

Herm: What Doris left & lost faire Daphne saught
And found and to her mothers shepfould brought
Ther Psyche bound ther wounds & stancht ther blood
Att first she gaue them milke then stronger food
And soone restord ther health, shepards beware   135
Wach feed defend your sheep charge asketh care
    All that is stolne or slaine you must make good
    And Floras Hylax yet lurkes in this wood

Lyc: King Salomon a Cedar pallace built
Thackd wth tyles of Floras tresses guilt   140
Her legs were siluer posts the house to beare
Her glorious thoughts the purple hangings were
Her brest the presence & her hart his throne
Her triple Crowne as Lord ther sitts alone
    Her holy doors she opes to each that knocks   145
    Her hands pure Myrrh drop on the bars & locks

Herm: Psyches faire locks wrapped in gold of proufe
Of gods high Temple is the guilded roufe,
Her eyes the Cristal windowes through each light
A smiling saint shoots in daies arrows bright   150
Her Corall Lips the doores that turne & twine
On Rubie hookes her mouth the quire deuine
    Her teeth the Iuorie seats built euen & thin
    Her tongue the siluer bell that rings all in

Lyc: that roial towne wher Flora hath her seat   155
Stands on seauen hills, well peopled, pleasant, great
Rich in all blessings all delights that can
Be giuen by fortune or be wishd by man
Quinzey the large, Dorado yitt scant seene
Her hand mads be she is the world sole queene   160
    Ioy in her streets Life in her Temples wide
    And dead & lost is all the world beside

Herm: Psyches cleare Citty was nott raised from dust
But came from heauen pure immortal iust
Stands on twelue pretious stones Iasper the wall   165
Streets gold gates Pearles bee, still ope to all

131 fain < faire   148 ther < the   159 Dorad < Dorado

Who tast the tree of Life wch ther do grow
About the towne two blessed riuers flow
    Of grace & Mercy, ouer ether flood
    Lies the faire bridge of faith, hope, doing good   170

Lyc: of shrill Heptaphones thou daughter cleare
Tell not these rocks of Floras doubte & feare
Write nott Phanetas in tomorrows stars
Her future troubles, dangers losses warrs
Least Psyches shepards should foreknow her doome   175
And kill her goats before her day be come
    These woods are hers these feilds & folds about
    Then keepe them Flora, till thy lease weare out

Herm: Sitting on Isis flowrie banke I spied
On a white horse a crowned Monarch ride   180
Vpon his thigh was write his wonderous name
Out of his mouth a sword two-edged came
Flora hir beasts & all her goats he slew
And in a lake of fire ther bodys threw
    This king is Psyches spouse wth him she went   185
    And rul'd the world for Floras lease was spent

Thus much did Hermes & Lycaon singe
The heifer lett the hearbs vntouched spring
Forgott to feed, the stags amazed stood
The siluer riuer staid her speedie flood   190
Charmed was the Adder deafe, tamde was the Lion
So trees hard Orpheus, Dolphins hard Arion.

Textual Notes

From Bodleian MS. Fairfax 40 (S.C. 28697).

    The manuscript, which was at one time in Ralph Thoresby's collection, contains poems by Thomas the third Baron Fairfax (grandson of the first Lord Fairfax and nephew of Edward Fairfax—and, incidentally, patron of Andrew Marvell) as well as his transcription of this Eclogue, which occupies pp. 647–57. Our text follows the MS. closely. It has not always been possible to be certain whether a given letter was intended to be a capital: in such cases, editorial discretion has been used. It was impossible to determine whether Thomas Fairfax intended any distinction between initial *I* and *J* (his own forms could often be taken for either), and as it seemed unlikely that the text he was copying would have made the distinction, we have uniformly printed *I*. The name *Psyche* is unmistakably so spelled in l. 35; equally unmistakably it appears on all subsequent occasions as *Phyche* or *Phyches*. It is just possible that Thomas Fairfax really meant this spelling, but far more likely that this was a persistent slip of the pen, occasioned by the difficulty of joining *P*, *s*, and *y* in his script. (In l. 35, where he gets the beginning of word right, he stumbles on the *ch*.) At all events, we have silently corrected all occurrences of *Phyche(s)*.

Commentary

The poem is a debate between a priest of the True Church (not, apparently, marked out by any distinctively Anglican features) and one of the False Church, unmistakably the Church of Rome. Fairfax follows an established Protestant tradition in interpreting the Book of Revelation as a prophecy concerning the clash between true and false religion and in identifying the Whore of Babylon as the Church of Rome; a classic version of this interpretation may be found in John Bale's *The Image of Both Churches*, ch. 19 (*Select Works of Bp. Bale*, Parker Society, 1849). It must be said that Fairfax is singularly gentle in his handling of the Scarlet Woman and her servants (compare his Flora with Spenser's Duessa, for example). He seems anxious to confine his criticism of the Roman Church to central points of doctrine, and church government. He comments on (*a*) salvation by works (27–34); (*b*) the worldly riches and secular power of the Roman church (46–50); (*c*) the excess of ritual in the Roman sacraments (75–80); (*d*) the power of the priest over his flock (100–22), and (*e*) the irresponsibility of some priests and the wickedness of others (124–8). Fairfax's restraint goes well with the Eclogue form—the awkwardness of Spenser's too obvious taking of sides in the *Shepheardes Calender* is avoided—but it sorts oddly with the copious use of imagery from the Book of Revelation. The mixture of bucolic charm and apocalyptic grandeur is perhaps something typically Fairfaxian.

The Argument: The names *Lycaon* (for the Roman priest) and *Hermes* (for the priest of the True Church) are appropriate in several ways.

(i) One version of the story of Lycaon, King of Arcadia, has it that he was changed into a wolf for sprinkling the blood of slain children on the altar of Jove on Mt. Lycaon: 'Fertur Lycaon . . . imperasse Arcadibus . . . quem Iupiter in lupum vertisse dicitur, quoniam ad aram Iouis Lycaei infante mactato humanum sanguinem libauerit.' (Natalis Comes, *Mythologiae* [1605], IX. 979.) He is thus the type of idolatrous worship of a true god.

(ii) In Acts, 14: 8–18 it is related that when Paul and Barnabas preached among the Lycaonians and Paul healed a cripple, the people wanted to worship the apostles—'And they called Barnabas, Jupiter; and Paul, Mercurius'.

(iii) Hermes, the messenger of the gods and conductor of the souls of the dead, seems in an obvious way to symbolize mediation between man and God: 'Atque vt intelligeretur à diuina natura res humanas non esse penitus sei unctas, Mercurium tanquam vinculum quoddam intercedere censuerunt, qui Deorum consilia ad homines, hominum ad Deos ipsos asportaret.' (Natalis Comes, ed. cit., X. 1032, De Mercurio.) A wide variety of Renaissance Platonic elaborations and variants on this theme are discussed by Edgar Wind, *Pagan Mysteries in the Renaissance* (1958), pp. 106–8.

(iv) Mount Lycaon (the home of Pan) and Lycaon himself, are mentioned in Theocritus, *Idyll*, 1. 123, 126; Hermes appears in the same poem, l. 77; thus the names are guaranteed to be genuinely pastoral.

4. *Tettrigone*: cicala. Pliny, XI. xxv: Holland, i. 325 speaks of a species of small 'grasshoppers' called Tettigoniae.

6. *goats . . . sheepe*: Matthew 25: 32–3.

12. *liart*: the balsam poplar.

20. *tel-clock*: one who tells the clock, hence, passes the time idly (*O.E.D.*).

21. *Psyche*: the True Church.

25. *bruze*: by context meaning 'browse', but in a spelling not recorded in *O.E.D.*

27. *Flora*: Roman Goddess of flowers, but also, in Renaissance mythography, a famous harlot (according to Cooper's *Thesaurus*, 1565): see E. K.'s Gloss to *Shepheardes Calender*, Mar., 16. Spenser made careful use of her ambivalent status in *Faerie Queene*, I. i. 48 and II. xii. 50. She is thus an excellent symbol for the False Church.

28–9. *merit and deserving*: the Catholic doctrine of justification by works.

29. *I build the Temples*: ?an allusion to the building of St. Peter's, financed out of the sale of indulgences.

32. *Rechab*: the sons of Rechab drank no wine: Jeremiah 35: 2–6.

Job: Job 3: 24, 'For my sighing cometh before I eat.'

35. *my undefiled my dove*: Song of Solomon 6: 9.

36. *Comfort me for I am sick of love*: ibid. 2: 5.

37. *temple . . . wound brest*: apparently a conflation of 1 Cor. 3: 16, Song of Solomon 5: 7 and Psalms 51: 17.

41. *linen . . . crownes of gold*: Revelation 4: 4 and 19: 8.

44. *Ten kings*: ibid. 17: 2 and 12.

46. *three Diadems*: the woman on the scarlet beast in Revelation 17 does not wear a triple crown, but Protestant representations of her, which generally identified her with the Roman Church, sometimes equipped her with the papal mitre; see for example *Faerie Queene*, I. viii. 25.

47. *seauen heapes*: Revelation 18: 9; identified with the seven hills of Rome.

49. *forty months and tow*: ibid. 13: 5.

51. *my virgen bare a blessed sonne*: ibid. 12: 2 and 5.

52. *the dragon*: ibid. 12: 3–4, 13.   *she to desert runne*: ibid. 12: 6.

53. *a streame of water att her flings*: ibid. 12: 15.

54. *Earth drunk the flood*: ibid. 12: 16.   *she scapt with eagles wings*: ibid. 12: 14.

55. *Crownd with twelve stars clothed with the glorious Sun*: ibid. 12: 1.

58. *Till time and times and half a time be past*: ibid., ch. 14.

59–60. *a scarlet beast . . . ten hornes . . . seuen heads*. There are three distinct occurrences of such a monster in Revelation (12: 3–17; 13: 1–10; 17, *passim*).

62–3. *taile . . . smote the third of trees of floods of stars*: Revelation 12: 4, with details added from 8: 7–12.

63–4. *Flora this monster caught . . . on his back . . . doth ride*: ibid. 17: 4.

66. *sealed are with's number, marke and name*: ibid. 13: 16–18.

68. *Fowre wonderous beasts*: ibid. 4: 6–8.

69. *fowre and twentie Kings*: ibid. 4: 4.

70. *gold and myrrh and pretious things*: ibid. 5: 8.

72. *thousand thousands*: ibid. 5: 11.

73. Defective line.

75–80. The details here correspond to those of the Roman Catholic form of infant baptism. *Cream* = chrism.

82. *Washed in the well of life*: baptism (without the elaborate Catholic ritual).

85–6. *slew me . . . I liued again*: evidently the process of 'dying' through becoming aware of sin, followed by spiritual rebirth (see, for example, Romans 7, *passim*).

90. *her spouse the doore*: John 10: 9.   *the key of gold*: Revelation 1: 18 and 3: 7 or Isaiah 22: 22.

91. *fifteth yeare*: every fiftieth year is a year of Jubilee (Leviticus 25: 8–15).

97. *cup of gold*: Revelation 17: 4.

105. *spider like*: cf. Donne, *Twicknam Garden*, l. 6: The spider love, which transubstantiates all.

114. *The fruit was ashes, imbers, dust within.* Such fruit are described by Josephus, *Wars*, IV. viii. 4, and by Sir John Mandeville, *The Voyages and Travailes of Sir John Maundervile, Knight*, n.d. ch. xxx, Sig. G.iii. Cf. *Paradise Lost*, X. 565–6.

115–22. *corn . . . tares . . . thirty, sixty and a hundredfold*: cf. Matthew 13: 3–43.

134. *milke . . . stronger food*: Hebrews 5: 12–14.

138. *Hylax*: the name of a dog in Vergil, *Eclogues*, VIII. 107.

139–46. The equation of Flora with Solomon's temple implies that that, too, was a 'false church'.

140. *cedar*: 1 Kings 6: 15.

141. *Her legs were siluer posts*: conflation of Song of Solomon 5: 15 and 3: 10.

142. *Her glorious thoughts the purple hangings were*—ibid. 3: 10 and possibly 7: 5.

146. *Her hands pure myrrh drop on the bars and locks*: ibid. 5: 5.

147–54. Psyche is identified with a distinctively Christian church building.

156. *seauen hills*: Revelation 17: 9; obviously Rome.

159. *Quinzey*: Quinsai, chief city of Mangi, in China; Marco Polo's account, reprinted in Purchas, tells us that its name means City of Heaven, 'for in the world there is not the like, in which are found so many pleasures that a man would think that he were in Paradise', Purchas, *Pilgrims*, Pt. II, Bk. ii, ch. 4, sec. 8 (Glasgow, 1906), xi, 279.

163–8. Revelation 21: 18–21, 22: 1–2.

171. *Heptaphones*. Pliny, XXXVI, c: Holland, ii. 581 tells of a colonnade at Olympia which had a sevenfold echo and was therefore called Heptaphonos. (The next step, that of calling Echo 'the daughter of Heptaphones' seems to be Fairfax's own periphrasis.)

173. *Phanetas*. An Orphic deity, Phanes (gen. Phanetos) is mentioned in Macrobius, *Sat.* I. xviii. 12, Lactantius, *Div. Inst.* I. v. 4–6, the Orphic hymns, and numerous Neoplatonic writings. That divinity, however, is a primal god and a god of light, and seems to have nothing to do with astrology.

Fairfax may have come across the name in Sir Thomas Elyot, *Bibliotheca Eliotae*, 1552, where 'Phaneta,—ae' is glossed as 'one of the names of Bacchus', and may have made a guess at the meaning of this name by deriving it from φαίνομαι, 'to come to light, appear'.

180–6. Revelation 19: 11–16, 20–1, 7–8; 21: 9.

Eclogue VIII

Ida and Opilio

THE ARGUMENT.

Ovilio skornes the dayes of ould
And boasts the wealth of præsent times,
Reckons what sailors brought home gould,
Or found new trades in unknowne Climes.

OPIL:

Bright may this riseing beame on Ida shine!
Crowne thy blith forhead with this wreath of beach
And bless the morning with some himne divine.
Hear'st not how Philomele her babe doth teach?
How sweet shee chirps? but sing the best shee can,   5
    There is noe Musicke like the voice of man.

IDA.

There dull conceit, who cut Terpanders string,
And his gross eare, who caus'd the Lords of Rome
To force the morning birds leave of to sing,
Could of my Musick give a fitter dome   10
Then thy deepe cunning; let my reed be still,
    Except Pans judge sitt yet on Tmolus hill.

But if thou deigne to tune thy seavenfould pipe,
Sitt in this shade or that unpollisht cave,
Where the wild vine with clusters never ripe   15
Orefrets the vault, and where the yong Nimphs have
There dancing schoole, but thrust the Ladies out,
    Or be their Orpheus while they friske about.

OPIL:

Nor is thy rubeck out of tune soe farre;
But this the fault of skilful singers is,   20
To be most squemish when most prai'd they arre,

Though unbesought they never cease; such blis,
Such comfort, in your selves you poets find;
  But that the common fault is of mankind.

But, Ida, let us sing or Rufus death,   25
Or Monforts treasons, or great Warwicks fraies,
Or to what dittie els thou list give breath;
Praise if thou wilt the sheephards of our dayes,
That find each yeare new lands, new seas, new starrs,
  And thence bring pearls in ropes and gold in barrs.   30

How is this age with wealth and wisdome blest!
How poore and simple were the elder times!
That wanted all the gould found in the west
And thought the world not wonned in three climes,
And he that of Antipodes durst tell   35
  Was tearm'd an Heretick and damn'd to hell.

They had no house with goulden [tiles which] shone,
They lackt the ransome of the Peruan king,
Pedrarias pearle and Moralis stone
And pretious trees that did in Puna spring,   40
With other blessing which those countreys yeild,
  Divine Tobacco and rich Cucheneild.

IDA.

Stay, sheephard! stay, for thou condemnest those
Thou kennest not; perdie the times of ould
Were not soe rude or poore as you suppose;   45
They wanted neither Jewels, stones nor gould,
Let Cleopatras pearle, Pithius his vine,
  Nonius his Opall, match those Jemmes of thine.

The Persian Darichs who can number them,
Talents of Greece and Sesterties of Rome?   50
Who weighes the Shekels of Hierusalem,
That did from Ophir and from Sheba come?
Doubtless our saylors noe such riches find
  In Lumaches, and Cacoas of Inde.

47 Pithins < Pithius   48 Vomins < Nonius   54 Lumaches, <
Lumaches,

Opil:

Yea but there wealth to them was nothing worth,   55
Their ignorance knew not to use their good,
They only tooke what until'd earth brought forth
When caves were howses, leaves clothes, Akornes food;
The earths rich parts, that silke, spice, unguents send,
    They kn[e]w not, Finister was ther worlds end.   60

Ida.

Perchance thou hast some curious feaster seene,
That serves his wildfoule with ther feathers on,
And wraps up Antick-like his napkins cleene,
Or know'st that Lord of France with pearle and ston
That sawceth all his meate, or hast hard tell   65
    In how rich towres Dorados Ingas dwell.

If soe, yet did those dayes our times surpass
In costly buildings, utensils and [cheare];
Let Cyrus house that earth[s] seaventh wonder was,
Let Æsops platter, Celers barball deare,   70
Let Plotius fatall perfumes witnesse bee,
    They were as rich, as wise, as mad as wee.

Nor did there knowledge with Cape Vincent end:
Plato can tell thee of Atlantis land;
The place where Salomon for gould did send   75
Is by the Parian gulfe; Eudoxus fand
The point Speranza, and those men of Inde
    Metellus saw, the Norwest streit did find.

And if that navy, which the stormes sterne blast
In the third Henries dayes to England brought,   80
King Fucusur upon this Island cast,
When from his owne expel'd new lands he sought
In ships five masted, built of Chinas mould,
    Then was the Northeast passage sail'd of ould.

Opil:

The land of Nusquam where king Nemo dwels,   85
Utopia and Lucians realme of lights,

69 Ciprus < Cyrus   71 Plotins < Plotius

Fronter Atlantis, whereof Plato tels,
And he that to the west his voiage dights
To seeke for Ophir, may teach Salomon
   To saile from Joppa, not from Ezion.   90

Noe, noe, that earths back side, that nether land,
Where like deepe fretworke in some heighroof'd hall,
The mountains hang and towres reversed stand,
If they wist whether, ready still to fall,
To our forefathers ever was unkend,   95
   They thought the earth had bounder side and end.

But wise Columbus wist the world was round,
That night was but earths shade, that the sun beame
His midnight light bestowed on some ground
Not all on waves and fishes in the streame,   100
And of the globe hee knew the sea possest
   But the seaventh part, firme land was all the rest.

Thereby [hee] gathered many people dwelt
Twixt Spaine and China, and what god they feared,
What wealth they had, what heat or could they fealt   105
He longed to discrie, and that way steard,
Where a new world he found, yet on the same
   Americk entered, and it beares his name.

I will not praise the Ruffian that first found
The calme Southsea, nor yet the man who past   110
The Ocean[s] stormy mouth, nor him to ground
That Mutezumas spatious pallace cast,
Nor the bould swinheard to his frend untrew
   Who kil'd the ransom'd king of rich Peru.

But listen, while I praise in rurall songe   115
Such hardie groomes as this faire Isle sent forth
To grope their way in darke nights halfe-years long,
To feele the July winter of the North,
To sweat at Christmas with the lines whot aire
   Or droope in six months showres by springs of Zaire.   120

The cheife of these and all the rest biside
Is he that on this ball of sea and land

112 Mutezmnas < Mutezumas

Did three long years in joyfull tryumph ride
And the vast round girt in a golden band,
Grand pilot of the world, who learn'd this feat   125
   Of the wise stearman of Noyes carrak great.

Great Amurath did to his picture bend
And at his name Rome did an earthquake feele,
Spaines Jennet proud he did to stable send,
Which stampt to powder with his brazen heele   130
The worlds halfe conquer'd globe, but now surpriz'd,
   The stall houlds him whom scant the world suffiz'd.

Noe thunders rage, no Tuffons furious rore,
Noe lions strange which rise, no spouts that fall
Dismai'd his courage, but from Albion's shore,   135
From Tarenat, from Helens garden smal
To London safe he brought his Argo backe;
   And yet this Jason doth his Orpheus lack.

His fellow rivall of his honour sought
For mines of gould on Metas unknowne side,   140
England admir'd the savages he brought,
But when his oare was in the furnace tride
It proved Marcasite, the shining rocks
   Beguile his eyes, soe fortune vertue mocks.

Oft he neigh perish't in the frozen piles   145
Of swimeing Ice, while longe he sought in vaine
A passage that way to Moluccas Iles.
Nor he that three times saild that cowrse againe,
Had better happ, but with bare hope came home;
   The time for that discovery is not come.   150

And hee the shores and creekes of new found Land
Who lett to farme and fished all the banke,
Lost his delight upon an unknowne sand,
And lost himselfe when his light frigot sanke,
And yet some say that from the Ocean maine   155
   He will returne when Arthur comes againe.

Of those that with the Russ our trade began
The first were turned by Arzinas frost

---

134 sponts < spouts   138 Orphens < Orpheus   158 Arzimas < Arzinas

To images of Ice, and some that ran
To Vaigats and Petzora there were lost;   160
Soe merciless, alas, is wave and winde,
  U[n]happy [P]akin, thou art hard to find!

    .   .   .   .   .

Textual Note

This eclogue is found in the British Library MS. Addit. 11743. Attention
was first drawn to it by A. H. Bullen in his notice on Fairfax in *The Dictionary
of National Biography*. W. W. Greg published an edition of it in *Modern
Language Quarterly*, IV (1901), 85–91, and supplemented his copious notes
with further comments, provided by R. B. McKerrow, which he printed in
M.L.Q. VI (1903), 73–4. Greg's edition was reprinted by J. C. Maxwell in
W. W. Greg, *Collected Papers* (1966), pp. 29–43, with slight verbal differences.
We print Greg's text with part of his introduction, incorporating amend-
ments proposed in his own and McKerrow's notes, and silently capitalizing
some place-names. The explanatory notes are adapted from Greg and
McKerrow, and supplemented by comments drawn from the thesis of Mr.
G. C. Bell. It must be acknowledged that many of the references remain
unexplained.

  Greg gives the following account of the manuscript and his editorial
method:

The manuscript of the eclogue is unfortunately imperfect at the end, two leaves
only being preserved, which form folios 5 and 6 of the collection in which they occur.
They are written in a very neat hand of the early seventeenth century, chiefly of an
Italian character, but with occasional English forms. The whole has been revised
and punctuated by the same hand, though in blacker ink. These corrections have
been silently introduced into the present text. The original spelling has been
retained, together with the use of capitals; the punctuation, on the other hand,
has been modernized, the original being in many cases more than usually clumsy,
nor has it been thought necessary to follow the manuscript in the use of long and
short *s*, *u* and *v*, or *i* and *j*.

  The manuscript is evidently a careful transcript from the original, but not the
work of a very educated man. Thus although *u* and *n* etc. are usually clearly dif-
ferentiated, they appear hopelessly confused in the names, having probably been
indistinguishable in the original manuscript. Thus in ll. 47 and 48, 'Pithius' and
'Nonius' appear as 'Pithins' and 'Vomins', in l. 112 we have 'Mutezmnas' for
'Mutezumas,', and in l. 158 'Arzimas' for 'Arzinas', and in l. 138 'Orphens' for
'Orpheus'! The only case of confusion, except in these names, is in l. 134 where the
manuscripts reads 'sponts' for 'spouts'; the transcriber probably had no notion
what was meant, and the apparently meaningless 'lions' in the same line may
equally be his blunder.

  The few other corrections that appeared necessary are enclosed in square brackets.
I may add that there is a bad stain at the head of the leaves which has rendered two
words in the top line on f. 5ᵛ. almost illegible. (See note on l. 37.)

Authorship

The fragment is found in a volume containing poetry by members of the Fairfax family, but it is not known whether it was included because some evidence exists that it was by Edward Fairfax or on the basis of mere surmise. It is clearly of the late sixteenth or early seventeenth century, and, like *Eglon and Alexis* and *Hermes and Lycaon*, learned and allusive. The sources of some of the learning, moreover, appear to be identical with sources used by Edward Fairfax, notably Pliny's *Natural History* and (according to G. C. Bell) the second edition of Hakluyt's travels. But Pliny's *Natural History* was an easily accessible work, as was Hakluyt, and in any case the allusions to travels could have come from other sources (notably, Peter Martyr's *Decades* and Purchas's *Pilgrims*).

Thus there is no hard evidence in favour of the ascription. Against it, one may point to the tone, style, and versification of the poem. There is a sharpness and brilliance about the writing for which the other two eclogues would not have prepared us; the verse moves briskly; and the handling of the stanza form and of run-on lines seems rather in the Spenserian tradition than in line with Fairfax's practice. As for the learned allusions, these seem, on the whole, to be used rather more directly, and for their face-value, than is the case in the other two eclogues, though it could be that some of the allusions in *Ida and Opilio* conceal further Christian–Platonic meanings (notably the allusions to Apollo, to the Cave of the Nymphs, and Orpheus, ll. 12–18).

Critical Commentary

The poem takes the form of a debate between a 'modern' Opilio and an 'ancient' Ida. Their difference however is not over the relative merits of the ancient and modern worlds, but over the extent of geographical knowledge then and now. The true subject, in fact, is exploration, and particularly the contribution of English travellers. Bell has pointed out that the 'modern' draws on sources which could be found in Hakluyt, and the 'ancient' on Pliny. Each reports marvels, and each is excited by the thought that these may really be true. We do not, unfortunately, have enough of the poem to know whether Opilio's 'humanist' remarks ('There is noe Music like the voice of man') and his complacency about the present ('How is this age with wealth and wisdome blest!') are to be taken at face-value, or whether some irony is intended.

On the evidence of what remains of the poem, one may suppose, however, that the poet is only mildly critical of Opilio, if at all, and he shares his excitement at the discovery of new worlds.

4–5. Pliny says that the nightingale teaches her young to sing (*Hist. Nat.* X. xxix).

7. *There dull conceit, who cut Terpander's string.* This line seems to be due to imperfect recollection of a passage in Plutarch's *Moralia* (*Antiqua Instituta Laconica*), which, in Holland's translation of 1603, appears as follows:

But if any man passed one point beyond this ancient musike, they would not endure him, insomuch as the *Ephori* set a fine upon the head of Terpander . . . [and] hung up his harp upon a stake or post, onely because he had set to it one string more than ordinarie . . . and when *Timotheus* at the feast *Carneia* plaied upon the harpe for to winne the prize, one of the *Ephori* taking a skeine or knife in his hand, asked him, on whether side, either above or beneath, he would rather have him to cut a two the strings which were more than seven. (p. 477, ll. 8–17.)

8. *And his gross eare, who caus'd the Lords of Rome to force the morning birds leave of to sing.* The reference is to a story told by Pliny, *Hist. Nat.* XXXV. xxxviii. Lepidus, during the Triumvirate, being entertained by the magistrates of a certain place, was lodged in a house surrounded by trees. Next day he complained of having been kept awake by the singing of the birds. Accordingly they had a dragon painted on long strips of parchment and surrounded the grove with it, which so terrified the birds that they at once became silent.

12. The reference is to the story told in Ovid's *Metamorphoses*, XI. Pan challenged Apollo to a musical contest, pipe against lyre. The judge, Tmolus, the god of the mountain of that name, decided in favour of Apollo, and his judgement was approved by all the others, except Midas, who was consequently graced with ass's ears by the slighted god. 'Pan's judge' is the judge who gave his voice in favour of Pan. The meaning of the passage therefore is: 'Do not bid me sing unless it be before such an uncritical judge as Midas.'

21, etc. So Horace: 'Omnibus hoc uitium est cantoribus, inter amicos / ut nunquam inducant animum cantare rogati, / iniussi nunquam desistant' (*Satires*, I. iii. 1).

26. *Warwick*: Richard Neville, Earl of Warwick and Salisbury (1428–71), the famous 'king-maker' of the Wars of the Roses.

34. *wonned*: i.e. inhabited. However, though in O.E. *wunian* is sometimes found with an accusative, the word never seems to have possessed a passive.

35, etc. The reference is to Virgilius, Bishop of Salzburg, said to have been burnt in the eighth century for heretically maintaining the existence of the Antipodes.

37. [*tiles which*]. The line in the manuscript is partly covered by an ink stain. A. W. Pollard read 'bales' in which case the reference would be to Atahuallpa's ransom. Greg's note continues 'All can, however, be deciphered with ease, except these two words. The second, moreover, may be taken as certain in spite of the rather unusual shape of the "*w*", and about the last three letters of the first there can also be no doubt. The second letter may be

either an *a* or an *i*, while the first is certainly a tall letter.' Greg was 'convinced that the letter is a *t*, and the word, consequently, "tiles" '. The references might then be either to 'the golden city of Manoa, called on that account "El Dorado" (cf. l. 66), or . . . the golden roofs of the temples of Japan described by Marco Polo.' McKerrow adds a reference to 'Saris's account' of Edo (Tokyo) and of the houses with their 'ridge-tiles and corner tiles richly gilded'. *The Voyage of Captain John Saris to Japan*, 1613 . . . *Hakluyt Soc.* (1900), p. 133.

38. *Peruan king*: (the *u* has been altered from *n*) Atahuallpa. The amount of his ransom actually collected amounted to 1,326,539 *pesos de oro*, besides silver, estimated at 51,610 marks (*see* W. H. Prescott's *Conquest of Peru*, Bk. III, ch. vii, ed. W. H. Munro [London, 1904], II. 164–5). The story is referred to in Montaigne's *Essays*, 3. 6.

39. *Pedrarias pearle*. Pedrarias Davila (Pedr' Arias d'Avila), after murdering Balboa (l. 108), succeeded him as governor of Darien. The pearl is described in Peter Martyr's *Decades*, trans. Richard Eden, 1555. It was bought 'euen in *Dariena* for a thousande and two hundreth Castelans of golde . . . and came at the length to the handes of *Petrus Arias* the gouernoure', who gave it to his wife. Decade III, Bk. x, fo. 141.

Moralis stone. Andreas Moralis, or Morales, a pilot of good repute at the time of the early Spanish discoveries in America obtained a famous diamond from a native on the north coast of South America. Moralis bought it from a native 'for fyue of our coûterfect stones made of glass of dyuers colours, wherwith the ignorant younge man was greatly delyted'. (See Peter Martyr, Dec. III, Bk. iv. fo. 112.)

40. *Puna*. The island of Puná is situated in the Gulf of Guayaquil, separating Ecuador from Peru. Possibly the author had in mind the passage in Montaigne:

The wonderful, or as I may call it, amazement-breeding magnificence of the never-like seene cities of Cusco and Mexico, and amongst infinite such-like things the admirable Garden of that King, where all the Trees, the fruits, the Hearbes and Plants, according to the order and greatness they have in a Garden, were most artificially framed in gold.

Florio's *Montaigne*, III. vi. The whole essay is very much on the same subject as the present eclogue. In this passage, however, a more probable source is perhaps the account of the trees of gold in Sir Walter Raleigh's *Discovery of Guiana*. See *Works* (1829 edn.), VIII. 399.

42. *Divine Tobacco*. The phrase echoes Spenser, *The Faerie Queene*, III. v. 32.

47. *Cleopatras pearle*. A reference to the well-known story of Cleopatra dissolving a pearl in a cup of wine.

Pithius: (written Pithins) properly 'Pythius', a Lydian, who gave Darius a golden plane and a golden vine (*see* Herodotus, vii. 27).

48. *Nonius*. The manuscript reads 'Nomius', or 'Nomins', or 'Nonims' (the six strokes are indistinguishable), no doubt through an error of the transcriber. Nonius was a Roman senator proscribed by M. Antonius on account of his possessing an opal of great value. Fairfax perhaps took Cleopatra's pearl, Pithius, and Nonius from Pliny, *Hist. Nat.* IV. ix. 58, xxxiii, 47, and xxxvii, 6.

54. *Lumaches and Cacoas of Inde*: two forms of currency. The first were shells used as money in the Congo. See *A Report of the Kingdome of Congo . . . Drawen out of the writings and discourses of Odoardo Lopez a Portingall, by Philippo Pigafetta. Translated out of Italian by Abraham Hartwell* . . . (1597), I. iv. 22. Reprinted in Purchas's *Pilgrims*. See also Hakluyt, 2nd edn., iii. 464.

Cacoas were used in the empire of Montezuma. 'I haue heeretefore said that their currant money is of the fruits of certaine trees, like our almonds, which they call *Cachoas*'—*The Historie of the West Indies*, 1626(?) (an enlarged edition of Eden's translation of Peter Martyr's *Decades*, 1555), Decade V, ch. iv, fo. 195.

60. *kn[e]w*. The manuscript reads 'know'.

Finister: i.e. Cape Finisterre (*finis terrae*), the north-west point of Spain.

66. *Dorado*: for 'El Dorado'.

Ingas: Incas, princes of Peru. Raleigh uses the form 'Ingas'.

68. [*cheare*]. The manuscript reads 'theare'. The scribe evidently misread the original.

69. *Cyrus house*. The house of Cyrus was reckoned among the wonders of the world.

Aesops platter: the expensive 'platter' was a dish of singing and talking birds which cost the actor Aesopus 100,000 sestertii (Pliny, *Nat. Hist.*, X. lxxii).

70. *Celers barball deare*. This must be the fish 'mullus', bought by Asinius Celer at Rome during the reign of Caligula for 8,000 sesterces. See Pliny, *Hist. Nat.* IX. xxxi. The names 'mullet' and 'barbell' are used by Cotgrave as almost synonymous.

71. *Plotius*. L. Plautius Plancus, being proscribed by the Triumvirs, was betrayed in his place of concealment at Salernum by the smell of unguents. See Pliny, *Hist. Nat.*, XIII. v. Hence his perfumes would be rightly termed 'fatall'. The form of the name is probably due to Pliny's words, 'L. Plotium, L. Planci fratrem, proscriptum . . .'.

76. *Parian gulfe*. Paria was the early name of that part of S. America now

occupied by Venezuela. The poet is alluding to the tradition that grew up after the wealth of S. America became known, that here was Solomon's Ophir. Ida maintains that far from a Spanish headland being the *Finis terrae* of the ancients, they had crossed the Atlantic westward to America and southwards to the Cape of Good Hope.

Eudoxus: Eudoxus of Cyzicus, who, according to Strabo, attempted to circumnavigate Africa. He lived *c.* 130 B.C. (Strabo, ii. 98–100).

77. *The point Speranza*: the Cape of Good Hope, named 'Cabo de bona Esperanza' by King John II of Portugal.

78. 'Plinie affimeth out of Cornelius Nepos (who wrote 57 yeeres before Christ) that there were certain Indians driven by tempest upon the coast of Germanie, which were presented by the King of Suevia unto Quintus Metellus Celer, the Proconsull of France.'—Sir H. Gilbert's 'Discourse to prove a passage by the North-west to Cathaia', ch. iv, para. 2, printed in Hakluyt (1599–1600), iii. 16. Pomponius Mela (iii. 5), quoting from the same lost work of Cornelius Nepos, makes the present come from the King of the Bæti. See Pliny, *Hist. Nat.*, II. lxvii. The poet probably alluding to an incident related by Holinshed (from Matthew Paris) as having occurred in the year 1254.

About this season [8th Feb. according to Matthew Paris] were certeine ships driuen by force of wind and weather into certeine hauens on the north coasts of England towards Barwike, which ships were of a verie strange forme and fashion, but mightie and strong. The men that were aboord the same ships were of some farre countrie, for their language was vnknowne, and not vnderstandable to any man that could be brought to talke with them. The fraught and balast of the ships was armour and weapon, as habergeons, helmets, speares, bowes, arrowes, crosbowes, and darts, with great store of vittels. There laie also without the hauens on the coast diuerse other ships of like forme, mold, and fashion. Those that were driuen into the hauens were staied for a time by the bailiffes of the ports. But finallie, when it could not be knowne what they were, nor from whence they came, they were licenced to depart without losse or harme in bodie or goods.'

McKerrow conjecturally identified King Fucusur with the person called by Marco Polo Facfur, king of Manzi (South China), who was driven from his kingdom and fled to the islands of the Ocean Sea in 1268 (Marco Polo, ed. Yule, ii. 108), though the dates do not correspond.

86. *Lucians realme of lights*: possibly the Islands of the Blest described in Book II of the *Vera Historia*, where there was no night, but a certain kind of light always filling the land, and resembling the twilight just before dawn.

87. *Fronter*. The verb 'to frontier' is not uncommon in writers of the time of Hakluyt, in the sense of to border upon. The actual form 'fronter' was used in 1586 by Ferne—'that part of the country a frontering the sea' (*Blaz. Gent.* ii. 32, quoted in *N.E.D.*). Opilus' argument is 'No, your instances

prove nothing; Plato's Atlantis is a myth, a worthy neighbour of No-man's-land, Utopia, and Lucian's fanciful realms; moreover, if you are going to place Ophir on the east coast of America, you will have to suppose that Solomon's ships sailed from some Mediterranean port such as Joppa (i.e. Jaffa), and not from the traditional Red Sea port.'

90. *Ezion*: i.e. Ezion-geber, 'on the shore of the Red Sea, in the land of Edom', 1 Kings, 9: 26.

94. *whether*: i.e. whither.

96. *bounder*: a boundary. 'Probably a corruption of 'boundure' [= border], taken as *bounder*, 'that which bounds' (*N.E.D.*). See *Godfrey of Bulloigne*, III. 57³ and XV. 25⁷.

102. *seaventh part*. The reference here is to 2 Esdras, 6: 50, etc. (English version, not in Vulgate or Douay), where the portion of the earth covered by water is given as one-seventh. Columbus, however, though relying largely on ecclesiastical arguments, based his views on the so-called Ptolemaic system, which, while exaggerating the proportion of land to sea, did not go so far as Esdras. Geography books inform us that the sea covers some three-quarters of the surface of the globe.

108. *Americk*: Amerigo Vespucci (Americus Vespucius), the famous Florentine explorer, who first realized that the land to which Columbus had shown the way, was not a part of Asia, but a New World. The name America was given to it in his honour by Martin Waldseemüller of St. Dié in 1507.

109. The first to discover the Pacific was Vasco Nuñez de Balboa, who saw it from the summit of the Sierra de Quarequa in the Isthmus of Panama, on 25 Sept. 1513.

110. Magellan, who entered the Pacific through the straits that still bear his name, on 27 Nov. 1520.

111. Hernando Cortés.

112. *Mutezuma*: i.e. Montezuma II, the last Aztec emperor of Mexico.

113. Francisco Pizarro, an illegitimate son of Gonzalo Pizarro and Francisca Gonzales, is said to have been deserted by his parents, and to have spent his youth as a swineherd. Atahuallpa had shown him and his Spaniards the greatest kindness and courtesy, in return for which he was treacherously seized, and after being made to pay an enormous ransom (cf. l. 38) was sentenced and executed on a fictitious charge of treason.

119. *line*: the equator.

120. *showres*. The word has been inserted afterwards in the same ink as the

punctuation and the other corrections, and being in the same hand as the text, makes it possible to ascribe the corrections to the original scribe.

Zaire: the old name for the Congo, now restored.

121. Sir Francis Drake, whose voyage of circumnavigation lasted from 13 December 1577 till 26 September 1580.

126. *Noyes carrak*: i.e. Noah's ark. Magellan, Drake's great forerunner, was similarly compared to Noah.

127. *Amurath*: the Sultan, more usually known as Morad III, whose reign, rendered remarkable by his weakness and cruelty, lasted from; 1574 to 1595.

129. *Spaines Jennet*: i.e. Philip II.
Jennet: or 'genet', a breed of small Spanish horses.

133. *Tuffon*: for typhon, whirlwind; Greek τυφῶν or τυφώς. Etymologically distinct from 'typhoon', a modern loanword from the Chinese *ta fung*, 'great wind'. Perhaps an allusion to the terrific storm, lasting fifty-two days, that Drake encountered after passing through the Straits of Magellan, and in which the *Marigold* was sunk, and the *Elizabeth*, being separated from the *Golden Hind* (the name assumed by the flagship, originally named the *Pelican*, on entering the straits), returned home, leaving Drake to continue the voyage alone.

135. *Albion's shore*. 'Nova Albion' was the name given by Drake to the country round San Francisco Bay, a name which continued in use for more than two centuries.

136. *Tarenat*. Ternate no doubt is meant, where Drake arrived in November 1579. It is one of the Moluccas.
Helens garden. This can only refer to the Island of St. Helena—but Drake did not call there.

138. *Orpheus*: one of the Argonauts, who accompanied Jason and recorded his deeds.

139. *fellow rivall*: Sir Martin Frobisher (1535?–94), who in 1576 made a voyage in search of the North-west Passage. He returned with some 'savages' (Esquemos) and some ore, which, contrary to the opinion of the London goldsmiths, was declared auriferous by the Italian alchemist Agello. The voyages of 1577 and 1578 were for the express purpose of collecting this ore, which, however, proved rubbish. Subsequently Frobisher commanded the *Triumph* at the time of the Armada.

140. *Meta*: i.e. Meta Incognita, the name given by Queen Elizabeth to what was at the time supposed to be the shores of a northern strait leading to the Pacific, similar to Magellan's to the south, but which later proved to be only a bay in Baffin Land.

143. *Marcasite*. The term was formerly applied to the black pyrite, which was what Frobisher collected. It is now used for the 'white iron pyrites', or iron disulphide.

147. *Moluccas Iles*. The Moluccas, or Spice Islands, a small group in the Malay Archipelago, were the only home of two of the most valued spices, the clove and the nutmeg.

148. John Davys or Davis (1550?–1605). His three voyages to the north-west were in 1585, 1586, and 1587.

153. *delight*. Sir Humphrey Gilbert's largest vessel, the *Delight*, was wrecked on 29 Aug. 1583, between Cape Breton Island and Newfoundland. Sir Humphrey himself perished a week later in the *Squirrel*, a vessel of only ten tons burden.

154. *frigot*: i.e. frigate; the form is uncommon, but is occasionally found in the sixteenth and seventeenth centuries.

157. The earliest expedition was that of 1553, consisting of three ships under Sir Hugh Willoughby commissioned to search for the N.E. Passage to Cathay and India by a 'Mystery and Company of Merchant Adventurers for the discovery of regions . . . unknown', founded in 1552. In this expedition the crews of two ships were frozen to death at Arzina (or Warsina), an inlet 'near to Kegor, where Norwegian Lapland marches with Russian' (*D.N.B.*). The third ship succeeded in reaching the White Sea, and the commander, Richard Chancelor, was allowed to proceed to Moscow, where he obtained letters-patent from the emperor. Armed with these he returned to England in 1554, and the following year the 'Company of Merchant Adventurers' became the 'Muscovy Company'. A letter from George Killingworth, their first agent, 'touching their entertainment in their second voyage', dated 27 November 1555, is printed by Hakluyt, together with the Company charters from Mary and John Vasilivich, the emperor of Russia, dated the same year.

158. *Arzinas*. The manuscript reads 'Arzimas', no doubt through an error of the transcriber.

160. *vaigats*: or Waigatz, an island in the Arctic Ocean, off the north coast of Russia, between it and Novaya Zemlya. The reference is to the voyage of Arthur Pet and Charles Jackman in 1580, in which Jackman lost his life.

Petzora: or Petchora, a river of North Russia, flowing into the Arctic Ocean.

162. *U[n]happy*. The word is miswritten 'Uphappy' in the manuscript.

[*P*]*akin*. The manuscript reads 'Takin', presumably by mistake for 'Pakin', i.e. Peking. Bacon in his *New Atlantis* uses the form 'Paguin'.

Fragment of Eclogue V

Upon Verbeia's willow-wattled brim
As Mopsus drest the wands and wickers trim.

MS. note, p. 311 of John Horsley, *Britannia Romana*, 1732, referring to
'Woodford in Ward's MS'. See Bodley MS. Rawl. C. 907. First printed in
Gough's edn. of Camden's *Britannia* (trans. and enlarged 1789), iv. 50.

An Epitaph upon King James

All that have eyes now wake and weep;
He whose waking was our sleep
Is fallen asleep himself, and never
Shall wake more till he wake ever.
Death's iron hand has closed those eyes   5
That were at once three kingdoms' spies,
Both to foresee and to prevent
Dangers as soon as they were meant;
He whose working brain alone
Wrought all men's quiet but his own;   10
Now he's at rest, O! let him have
The peace he lent us to his grave.
If no Naboath all his reign
Were for his fruitful vineyard slain,—
If no Uriah lost his life   15
Because he had so fair a wife,—
Then let no Shimei's curse or wound
Dishonour or profane this ground
Let no black-mouthed, rank-breathed cur
Peaceful James his ashes stir.   20
Princes are Gods, O! do not then
Rake in their graves to prove them men.
For two-and-twenty years' long care,
For providing such an heir,
That, to the peace we had before,   25
May add thrice two-and-twenty more—

For his days' travels, midnight watches,
For his crazed sleep, stolen by snatches,
For two fierce kingdoms joined in one,
For all he did, or meant to have done,   30
Do this for him—write o'er his dust—
James the peaceful and the just.

Commentary

13, see 1 Kings 21.
15, 2 Samuel 11.
17, 2 Samuel 16: 5.

From *The Fairfax Correspondence*, ed. George Johnson (1848), i. 2–3.

Epitaph on Lady Fairfax[1]

On my grandmother at Otley,
by my uncle, Edward Fairfax.

Here Lea's Fruitfullness, and Rachel's beauty
Here lyes Rebecca's Faith, there Sarah's duty.

From British Library Addit. MS. 39,992, fo. 383–4.

[1] Sister-in-law of Edward, wife of Sir Thomas Fairfax.

GLOSSARY

In this glossary we have tried to go some way beyond helping the reader with 'hard words'. We have attempted to note all word-forms substantially unlike their present-day descendants or cognates; all word-forms that have no present-day descendants; and usages that seem sufficiently unlike those of modern English. No doubt we have fallen a long way short of completeness, but we hope that the glossary can form at least the foundation for a study of Fairfax's English. We distinguish between forms and usages that seem to have been introduced by Fairfax; those which were introduced or revived by other poets (especially Spenser); older forms for which the *O.E.D.* gives no instances between 1550 and Fairfax (and few or none later), where it seems a reasonable inference that these were archaisms revived by Fairfax; forms and usages which Fairfax seems to be the last recorded author to have employed; and dialect forms and usages. Inevitably, we have been guided in this by the *O.E.D.*, and where even that great work is fallible we are bound to be tentative in our assessment of the state of currency of any given word. At any rate the assessments given in this glossary will do as starting-points for argument, and our account in the Introduction (pp. 53–64) of Fairfax's *lexis*, based as it is on the glossary, is likewise to be regarded as a tentative interpretation of Fairfax's normalities and abnormalities of language.

Abiect (n.) XII. 27⁴ one cast off.
abord (adv.) V. 8⁸ alongside; cf. *O.E.D.* aboard, (adv. 2), F.'s usage, however, seems influenced by the verb 'abord = to accost'.
abraid XIII. 50⁷ started up, XVI. 31 awaked; cf. Spenser, *Faerie Queene*, IV. vi. 36.
admired VI. 29⁵ wondered at.
adowne (prep.) XIII. 60² downward (poetic by 1600).
advised XIII. 33² cautious; the nearest equivalent is *O.E.D.* 'well-advised'.
affray (v.) XIII. Arg.² terrify.
affront (v.) XV. 49⁴ confront; Spenserian usage, *F.Q.* IV. iii. 22.
agone IV. 19⁷ ago (dialect/archaic).
all and some XIII. 11⁵ every single one.
allow'd IX. 13² urged on; glossed in the margin of the B.L. copy as

'loo'd them on'. See *O.E.D.*, 'halloo'. Cf. *Lear*, III. iv. 79, 'alow, loo, loo'.
amated (v.) XI. 12²; XIII. 22² disheartened.
ambassage VI. 17⁶ message conveyed by an ambassador.
ambling IV. 27⁷ walking.
angle X. 23³ an outlying spur or corner, a nook.
anmaile XX. 42¹ enamel; F's unrecorded use may be an error for 'aumaile', q.v.
annoys XIII. Arg.⁸ distresses.
Apogaeon II. 67¹ highest point. See *O.E.D.* under 'Apogee'. F. first instance quoted for this form.
appaid IX. 5⁵ pleased.
approv'd II. 93² tested.
approve XII. 24⁷ corroborate.
armipotent (L. *arma*, arms; *potens*,

armipotent (*cont.*):
power) III. 70¹ mighty in arms. Not in Spenser.

arreare (adv.) II. 40⁴ in the rear; IX. 95³ to the rear (archaic).

arreed XX. 104⁵ guess, foresee.

artillery XVII. 49⁶ discharging any missiles by engines.

aspect XIV. 43⁸ relative positions of the heavenly bodies as they appear to an observer on the earth's surface at a given time.

attempted I. 62⁴ tried, proven (participial adj. separately given in *O.E.D.*, citing Spenser and Milton).

aumaile XX. 42¹ enamel. 27. See *Faerie Queene*, II. ii. 27.

awards XIX. 14⁴ wards off.

balk XVIII. 80⁸ beam.

bands XIII. 51⁵ bonds.

banke X. 27⁷ slope.

bases VII. 41⁸ skirts of mailed armour, reaching down to the knee.

battailons I. 37¹ warlike (Spenserian).

battle (adj.) I. 43⁴ rich (of grass, soil).

beauvoir II. 48⁷ lower portion of the face-guard of a helmet when worn with a visor; but occasionally serving the purposes of both. (The unusual spelling to imply a false etymology is worth noting.)

bebled XIII. 41⁴; XIX. 102⁷ covered with blood (archaic, not in Spenser).

beforne I. 61² before.

beild; bield II. 84³; XVI. 49³ refuge, shelter (Northern).

bent¹ VI. 80⁶ reedy, rush-like grass.

bent² XVII. 35⁴ bending, curvature.

bent³ IV. 87³ either, the bending of the bow, or, force of the bent bow, or, aim, purpose.

bent⁴ XX. 9¹ hillside, slope.

besprent XVII. 35⁶ sprinkled.

bewray II. 10³ reveal, betray, expose.

blent XII. 86³ blinded.

blest IX. 67⁵ brandished. Cf. *O.E.D.*, 'bless', v.³ *obs.* (Spenserian) *F.Q.* I. v. 6 *et al.*

blist XIII. 29³ struck.

bod XI. 69¹ bade.

bombace *Eglon and Alexis*, 69 cotton.

boon (adj. and adv.) *Eglon and Alexis*, 61 good, well: see note.

bosom XIX. 8³ valley, a sense mistakenly cited by *O.E.D.* under 'bosom' 4.c. as 'concave bend in a coast-line ... a bay'.

bounders III. 57³; XV. 25⁷ boundaries.

brake XVIII. 43² ballista, catapult.

brand XIV. 27¹ sword.

brast II. 27⁷ broke (Northern form for 'burst').

bray IX. 96⁵ brae, hillside (Northern).

breathing I. 47⁴ gentle blowing.

brent II. 53⁸ burnt.

browne I. 64⁴ etc. dark.

brust XVIII. 44³ burst.

buskt VII. 37² etc. and *Eglon and Alexis*, 61, (see note), equip, dress (Northern).

buxome XV. 12² obedient.

Cade *Eglon and Alexis*, 37 a lamb left by its mother and brought up by hand; still current in Shropshire.

Can XIV. 67⁵ began (cf. **gan**).

cantel VI. 48⁴ slice.

careless XVIII. 33⁸ unconcerned.

carknet XV. 5⁶ collar of jewels.

case XIV. 77⁶ condition.

caudate (L. cauda, tail) XIV. 44⁷ tailed (F.'s is the first use quoted).

cell (variant spelling of **sell**, q.v.) III. 15² saddle; IV. 7¹ seat (archaic).

certifie V. 68² inform.

chaffer XVI. 43⁶ haggle, bandy words.

cheere XVII. 41⁴ entertainment.

chest III. Arg.⁶ coffin.

chevisance IV. 81³ undertaking, adventure (Spenserian in this sense, *F.Q.* III. xi. 24).

chickens VIII. 49³ chicks.

clap (n.) XI. 45⁴ a hit.

clear IV. 28³ beautiful (archaic).

clift¹ I. 14⁶ cleft.

clift² IV. 8², VI. 26⁵ cliff.

closely IV. 22³ etc. privately, secretly, inwardly.

closes *Eglon and Alexis*, 68 closed fields.

coast XI. 59⁶ side, direction.

cobles XX. 29⁴ round stones.

cogge XIV. 58⁷ cock-boat (Yorkshire dialect, or archaic).

comate (L. coma, hair) XIV. 44⁷ hairy. Fairfax only is cited in *O.E.D.*

compile III. 22⁶, V. 8⁴, heap up. 'Compose' is the nearest equivalent in *O.E.D.*

congee II. 94¹ etc. leave.

consent XVIII. 19⁴ harmony.

content XVII. 67⁶ acceptance.

cornet XIII. 68⁸ troop of horse.

correspond (vb. trans.) I. 29⁷ answer to, agree with.

correspondent I. 27³ consonant.

countie VII. 29⁵ count.

court of guard II. 60³ small body of soldiers on guard-duty.

crasht VII. 42⁷ gnashed.

cream *Hermes and Lycaon*, 78 chrism, the consecrated oil used in anointing (*O.E.D.*).

creeks XIX. 8³ narrow plains, or recesses in between mountains.

crinite (L. crinis, hair) XIV. 44⁷ hairy. Fairfax's use is the first cited in *O.E.D.*

crudded (1624 curded) XV. 8³ curdled.

cucheneild *Ida and Opilio*, 42 cochineal.

cumbers II. 73⁸ hindrances.

cure IX. 58⁶ care.

curious XII. 64⁶ elaborately wrought.

currer = courier VII. 29¹.

curtlax IX. 82⁶ cutlass.

damnifie VII. 18³, X. 37⁶ injure.

darrick *Ida and Opilio*, 49 a Persian coin made of both gold and silver, said to derive its name from Darius I.

deare (adj.) XIII. 20⁴ brave, bold (archaic).

defenst I. 61⁸ provided with defences.

defoil VIII. 60⁴ defile (variant of 'defoul': archaic, not in Spenser).

defy (n.) XIX. 65⁵ challenge.

denay I. 23⁷ deny.

depastred (L. depascere, to eat down) XIII. 79⁴ grazed, consumed. (F. is quoted for the first figurative use.)

descry II. 85⁵ reveal.

designment I. 24³ etc. design.

dictamnun XI. 72⁶ 'a plant, origanum dictamnus, formerly famous for its alleged medical virtues'.

dight II. 32⁸ provided, equipped, decked.

dilate XII. 60⁴ spread abroad.

dint XI. 31⁷ etc. blow, stroke of thunder.

discover II. 22⁷ etc. reveal.

discoverment XV. 39⁶ discovery. (F. only citation in *O.E.D.*)

dispos'd XII. 25¹ prepared.

dome V. 55⁸ and *Ida and Opilio* 10 judgement.

done I. 70⁷ to do.

dormant XVIII. 80⁵ fixed, horizontal beam.

dott'rell *Eglon and Alexis*, 101 a foolish person.

drearie IV. 3¹ dire ? dismal ?

drest XII. 1⁴ erected.

dripile ?dripple XX. 124⁸; cf. *O.E.D.* 'drib' = to shoot wide of the mark.

drived VII. 3¹, XV. 10¹ rode, moved swiftly.

Duke I. Arg.⁴ leader, general (archaic; latest ex. in *O.E.D.*, 1591).

eame IV. 49⁶ uncle.

ear II. 14⁴ plough.

earn'd I. 48³, II. 97⁵, XII. 43⁷ variant of 'yearned'.

earst XIII. 38⁷ formerly, once upon a time.

eath (adj. and adv.) II. 46⁵ etc. easy (archaic).

eft II. 41² etc. again, back, moreover, afterwards (noted archaism).

eft soones VI. 64² etc. again, afterwards, soon.

eild III. 35⁴, etc. age (Northern or Scots form of 'eld').

embay XII. 62⁵ bathe (Spenserian).

empries II. 77² enterprise.

enchaste XII. 57⁵ engraved.

endears XX. 136² recommends, enhances the value of.

enorme VIII. 71⁴ outrageous.

ensample XVIII. 89⁸ practical warning, (cf. *O.E.D.* (3)).

entreatance I. 19⁴ etc. entreaty.

environ (adv. and prep.) II. 80⁵ round about (archaic).

errours V. 1² winding ways and deluded courses. Advantage is taken of both senses.

espials V. 68² spies.

fact II. 19⁸ deed.

fand IV. 55⁷, XVI. 37⁵, and *Ida and Opilio*, 76 found (?Scots form).

fannes XVIII. 49⁵ wings (earlier than *O.E.D.* example, 1640).

fantasme XIII. 37⁵ ghost.

fare XVI. 19⁸ doings.

fared VI. 27³, etc. went.

faulters II. 11⁴ offenders.

feat XIII. 8⁸ activity, action.

fell (adj.) I. 83³ etc. fierce, cruel, angry.

feltred IV. 7⁵ matted.

fence XIX. 15² the art of fencing.

fine XII. 17³ of fine temper, highly purified, superior quality.

flanker III. 49² a fortification projecting so as to flank another part, or to command the flank of an assailing enemy.

flash XI. 28² sheaf.

fleet X. 62⁴ float.

flit (adj.)¹ IV. 9³ and 18⁸ light, airy, unsubstantial (Spenserian).

flit (adj.)² XIV. 72⁶, XVII. 85⁷ swift.

flit (v.)¹ IV. 9³ fly.

flit (v.)² V. 58³ fled.

foin XII. 55⁸ thrust in fencing.

fond XII. 19⁸ foolish.

footman XI. 20⁶ foot-soldier.

for I. 18⁷ etc. since.

foreknowledge XIV. 6³ memory (sense not cited in *O.E.D.*).

foreshowes (v.) IV. 49⁶ etc. predicts, warns.

foreshowes (n.) XIII. 54⁶, prognostic signs.

foreslowe I. 28⁷ and 67⁶ delay.

forlore¹ VII. 1³ lost.

forlore² III. 76⁸ forsook.

fornenst IX. 4¹ etc. right opposite (Scots and Northern).

forraid III. 14⁴ foraged.

forst not IX. 76⁶ etc. did not care about.

forth XII. 58⁴ out.

for thy XIV. 28⁷ therefore (poetic).

frame IV. 25⁸ succeed.

frie I. 32² burn with strong passion.

frigot XIV. 57⁶, XV. 7⁷, and *Ida and Opilio*, 154 light, swift vessel.

froarie II. 40² covered with foam or froth (*O.E.D.* cites only Fairfax in this sense).

front XIX. 59⁸ brow.

froward XIV. 43⁸ unpropitious.

frusht VIII. 48³ crushed, smashed.

gace II. 27² Northern dialect variant for 'gaze'.

gamut IV. 93⁸ the first note of the Medieval scale.

gan II. 1² began to.

gard (n.) XII. 68² custody.

gastly (adv.) VII. 25⁴ terribly.

gaze (n.) (at gaze) I. 47⁵ attitude of gazing.

gent II. 17³ graceful, elegant, pretty (poetic).

giglet VI. 72³ wanton woman.

girdling stead XX. 33⁵ waist (*O.E.D.* gives only 'girdlestead').

gite XIII. 54² gown.

gits XIX. 85⁶ goes. Cf. modern idiom 'get out'.

glass (v.) XIV. 77⁵ see reflected.

glave I. 50³ longsword or scimitar.

glistring XIV. 6² glittering.

glorious VI. 18² boastful.

glosing IV. 47⁵ talking smoothly and deceitfully.

gnarring IV. 8⁵ growling, snarling.

good ('how much good she knew') XVI. 13⁶ how accomplished she was.

greaves III. 6⁷ thicket (archaic/Northern).

gree III. 8⁶, X. 10⁷ favour.

greet XII. 94⁵ see **spartan.**

grift XVII. 79⁸ scion.

gromble XIII. 21⁵ growl, rumble.

gromes XI. 20⁷ grooms.

guerdon XII. 11³ reward.

guide (n.) I. 51¹ leader.

guides (v.) I. Arg.⁷ rules.

guie I. 49⁵ guide (archaic).

guilden XII. 48¹ gold, gilded.

guise XII. 25⁸ custom.

haberjon I. 72³ sleeveless coat of mail.

hags VIII. 41¹ hedges (Northern).

halfe IX. 74² etc. side.

hap XIII. 13¹ etc. chance.

haply XII. 71⁵ etc. by chance.

hardiment VI. 34⁸ etc. boldness (archaic).

hawberk I. 72³ coat of mail.

headland II. 62⁷ a strip of ploughed

field left for convenience of turning the furrow . . . in old times used as a boundary.

heed XIX. 10⁷ ?head. See *O.E.D.* 'head' (as in 'head of water' or 'head' = tidal wave; but also cf. *Hamlet*, IV. v. 101 'Young Laertes in a riotous head').

hend/hent XII. 18³, XIX. 42¹ grasp, hold.

hold (n.) I. 60³ etc. fortress.

holdfast (adj.) XIX. 17⁷ firmly holding.

holts VIII. 41¹ woods.

hordas XVII. 21⁵ hordes, i.e. 'tribes of . . . Asiatic nomads' *O.E.D.*

horrid (L. horridus, bristling) I. 39³ bristling (Spenserian, *F.Q.* I. vii. 31).

hov'red III. 16³ lingered.

ibore X. 39³ born (archaic).

icleped III. 71² called (archaic).

idea I. 48⁶ mental image.

illustrate XIX. 22⁸ render illustrious.

imbarde I. 13³ variant of 'embard', enclosed, imprisoned.

impe I. 59⁴ scion of a noble house.

impeach XI. 52⁴ hinder.

impreses XX. 28⁷ emblems or devices.

incontinent V. 51⁴ immediately.

infant XVI. 34¹ youth of noble, or gentle birth (Spenser).

Ingas *Ida and Opilio*, 66 Incas, Princes of Peru, Raleigh uses 'Ingas'.

Ingine I. 83³ genius, natural ability, intellect. (?Scots form.)

iparted XIV. 72¹ ?just emerged. See note.

ipend; ipent VI. 5³ etc. confined. Past part. of 'pen', to shut up; cf. *Shepheardes Calender*, Jan., 4, 'ypent'. (F. is first reference in *O.E.D.*).

ipight (normal form in sixteenth century) I. 48⁵ fixed; cf. *Faerie Queene*, I. ix. 33. 'ypight'.

isprong I. 37⁸, XVI. 56² sprung (archaic).

itost VIII. 45² tossed (archaic); cf. *Shepheardes Cal.* June, 12, 'ytost'.

iwrit IV. 13⁷ written (archaic).

jarres XVII. 62⁷ conflicts.

jollie I. 39¹ gallant.

keepe (n.) as in 'take keep' (1) XIV. 60³ took keep, observed; (2) XV. 12⁵ take care.

kend IV. 87³ etc. knew.

kept XI. 86⁴ etc. guarded, protected.

kest (v.) II. 96⁷ etc. cast.

kinde XIV. 42⁷ etc. nature.

lace II. 20⁶ snare.

lad (v. pret.) I. 38⁵ etc. led.

laft (v. pret.) I. 69⁴ left.

l'amber *Eglon and Alexis*, 70 amber, cf. French 'l'ambre'.

lamp XX. 20² flash of lightning.

lap II. 89⁶ fold of a garment.

large I. 84⁷ free.

latest XX. 14³ final.

lay XI. 19³, XV. 33⁶ lea, fallow land.

leaguer X. 27⁸ besieging army.

leare¹ XII. 40³ to teach.

leare² X. 25⁶ to learn.

leden XVI. 13⁴ language (perhaps reminiscent of Chaucer's 'Squires Tale', l. 407).

legier I. 70¹ representative.

let (n.) IV. 2² etc. hindrance.

let (v.) XIII. 37⁸ etc. hinder(ed).

letharge XVI. 33¹ lethargy.

liard *Hermes and Lycaon*, 12 balsam poplar.

light (v.) XI. 49¹ fell.

line *Ida and Opilio*, 119 the Equator.

lite IX. 81⁴ etc. small (archaic/Northern).

loop XI. 32⁷ loophole.

lough I. 44⁷ lake, arm of the sea.

love-toies XVI. 23² amorous gestures or expression.

lust (v.) VI. 28⁶ and IX. 57³ to will.

maine XI. 81¹ force (archaic).

make IV. 46⁵ mistress, love.

mankinde (n.) XI. 9⁶ male creature.

mankinde (adj.) XX. 95⁶ mannish.

marish VII. 90² marsh.

mark II. 97⁵ aim.

Mart II. 89⁵ Mars.

mart VI. 36⁴ battle (archaic, not in Spenser in this sense).

mature XIX. 98⁵ prompt (*O.E.D.* first citation from Fairfax).

maze II. 10⁶ bewilderment.

message XVI. 39⁷ errand.

met XV. 39⁶ measured.

mew VIII. 41⁴ hiding-place.

mickle XI. 35² much (archaic/ Northern).

mid-earth I. 79³ Mediterranean.

mildew II. 61⁸ honey-dew.

mirksome XIII. 75⁶ obscure (Spenserian).

mister wight IV. 28⁸ sort of person (archaic); cf. *F.Q.* I. ix. 23.

miswent II. 10⁶ strayed.

molde I. 25² etc. soil.

monster XII. 76⁷ showpiece, exhibit.

moorie III. 9⁴ marshy.

more (adj.) XI. 70⁶ greater.

mounture VII. 96¹, XVII. 28⁶ mount, horse.

murderment II. 17¹ act of murder- ing.

musmons (L. musmo, moufflon) *Eglon and Alexis*, 28 wild sheep, see note.

mutines I. 1⁷ (in first version) mutinies.

nar II. 88¹ nearer.

nardus XVIII. 15⁶ spikenard.

narrow III. 65⁵ close.

nathelesse XIII. 32⁵ notwithstanding.

needments VI. 91¹ necessary things, provisions (Spenser).

neeld XX. 95⁸ needle.

neglect (v.) XII. 7³ desert.

nere XII. 81⁵ etc. were not.

new ('of new') II. 24¹ again.

nice IV. 23³ refined.

nicely XVI. 30⁷ daintily.

nill XIII. 14³ will not.

nould V. 47⁷ would not.

object (v.) XI. 22³ put forward.

ofspring VII. 18³ ancestry.

or VII. 32⁸ etc. before.

oreset XIX. 1⁸ overcome.

overgone I. 45⁵ overcome.

over-ren XV. 21⁵ run beyond.

owe III. 73³ etc. own.

out braid X. 1⁵ dart out, eject. (*O.E.D.* only cites F.)

Panacea XI. 74² a fabulous herb to which was ascribed the power of healing all diseases.

parled of X. 13¹ talked to.

part IV. 15⁷ side.

passover *Eglon and Alexis*, 42 paschal lamb.

pastora VII. 17⁵ shepherdess. (Earliest use recorded by *O.E.D.*)

peece¹ IV. 50² fortified place, strong- hold.

peece² XII. Arg.⁴ siege-engine.

penticle XVIII. 74⁷ pentice, penthouse (F.'s nonce use).

pentise XI. 33³ etc. penthouse.

pheare IV. 47² mate.

pies VIII. 67⁴ magpies.

pight (v. pret. and ptc.) XIV. 57⁵ pitched, planted, arranged (cf. ipight).

pine XVI. 57⁴ torment (archaic/ Northern).

pinfoldes XIII. 20² places of confine- ment.

plained I. 89³ levelled.

pletted XIV. 68³ plaited.

poinant XI. 78⁴ piercing.

ports III. 12² etc. gates.

post (n.) VII. 27⁴ messenger.

post (in post) XV. Arg.⁵ at speed.

posted XIX. 36¹ squared for sawing.

prate (v.) XVIII. 5⁵ ?chatter, ?boast.

prease X. 35² throng.

prest I. 82³ ready.

prevents III. 1⁷ anticipates.

prick IX. 22¹ ride (archaic).

prickt II. 59⁸ impaled.

prise (n.) IV. 22¹ esteem.

proaching, proched VI. 39⁴, XIII. 47³ approach (poetic).

procured I. 67³ endeavoured.

prove (v.) II. 34¹ etc. experience.

prove (n.) V. 55⁴ proof.

provide (v.) I. Arg.⁸ etc., undertake, arrange.

puissant I. 55¹ mighty.

punchions XVIII. 44² short, upright pieces of timber, serving to stiffen a frame or support a load.

quaild XV. 25¹ brought into sub- jection.

quarry III. 49³ and 51⁸ cf. 'quarrell', a square-headed arrow. (F. is first usage cited in *O.E.D.*; but see *F.Q.* II. ix. 24.)

quite (v.) II. 52⁸ release.

quites (v.) II. 36⁴ rewards, pays.

raced V. 63⁴ razed, levelled with the ground.

racke XIII. 56⁴ driving mist of clouds.

railed III. 30⁴, IV. 74⁵ gushed, flowed (poetic).

rampire VI. 1⁸ etc. rampart.

ranke III. 18² rapid, headlong.

rasps *Eglon and Alexis*, 22 raspberries.

ray (n.) XVII. Arg.¹ array.

recomfort XIV. 15² etc. inspire with courage.

record II. 97⁴ sing, especially of birds.

recure VIII. 22⁶ hope of recovery.

refrain XII. 88⁷ restrain.

regreet¹ I. 34⁵ greet again (rare).

regreet² XVI. 25³ lament, sorrow.

relent XII. 70² soften.

remew XIII. 70³ remove (archaic).

rende-vous I. 19² meeting-place. (F. first usage quoted in *O.E.D.* for this sense.)

repass XVII. 72³ return.

repree XVI. 45⁴ reproof.

repugnes XV. 39⁴ be opposed to.

respect (in respect) V. 17³ in comparison.

respond X. 40⁸ correspond to.

resteth XIV. 78¹ remains.

retire XIV. 26⁶ return to one's usual place.

rew (v.) XIII. 70⁵ have mercy on.

rew (n.) XVII. 75⁵ row.

rives (v.) XII. 64⁵ tears. (pret. **rave** XII. 66⁵.)

roarie (L. ros, roris, dew) I. 14⁸, IV. 75⁴ dewy. (Earliest instance cited in *O.E.D.*)

rockets XI. 4⁷ rochets, vestments worn by bishops and abbots.

romble IV. 3², XIII. 26⁴ rumble, as of running water, producing low, continuous sound; moving with continuous murmuring.

rore XVIII. 18³ a rushing sound (cf. *F.Q.* I. ix. 4).

rout (n.)¹ VIII. 63⁶ root (spelling variant).

rout (n.)² XIII. 53⁴ either, sway, influence, *O.E.D.* 'rout' sb.¹ 8.c., or, root, metaphorically used.

rubeck (cf. 'rebeck') *Ida and Opilio*, 19 a kind of fiddle.

rug *Eglon and Alexis*, 126 a rough woollen material, a sort of coarse frieze (*O.E.D.*).

scaith / scath XVII. 63³ etc. harm.

scalado XI. 34⁶ scaling ladder.

scaldred XVIII. 85³ scalded (Northern).

scant of XII. 80⁷ short of.

scantly XI. 42³ etc. hardly, scarcely, with difficulty.

scored XVII. 58⁵ engraved.

scuses XII. 9¹ excuses.

sdainfull VII. 42⁵ disdainful (Spenserian: *F.Q.* III. vii. 10).

secure IX. 11⁶ free from apprehension.

seely XII. 33⁷ simple, humble.

seld XII. 24⁸ etc. seldom.

sell seat (see **cell**).

serviceage VIII. 83⁶ bondage, service.

shallop XV. 6⁷ boat for use in shallow water; cf. *F.Q.* III. vii. 27.

shaw VIII. 52² thicket, copse.

sheene I. 11³ etc. bright.

shend I. 6⁷, VI. 4⁵ injure, disgrace.

shootresse XVII. 49⁵ female shooter.

showter III. 76¹ of the yew tree, good for shooting.

side IX. 8⁶ long (archaic/dialect ? Noted in margin of B.L. copy of 1600 as Norfolk and Suffolk.)

signorise IV. 46⁶, XIII. 53² govern, control.

sindall VIII. 55¹ fine linen or silk, or lawn used for dressing wounds, or for a shroud.

sleevelesse VI. 89⁶ futile, trifling.

smart XIV. 65⁸ painful.

smooke I. 22⁵ vapour (Northern **and** Scots).

soil VI. 109² pool used as a refuge for the hunted deer.

some-deal II. 26⁷, III. 61⁶ somewhat.

sout XV. 46⁴ sweet.

sowne I. 73⁷ sound.

sparefull IV. 30³ niggardly.

sparsed V. 88³ etc. dispersed.

spartan greet XII. 94⁵ Peloponnesian marble (see note).

speed XVIII. 52⁸ success.

sphynges XIII. 18⁸ plural of Sphinx.

spiall I. 67¹ spy, scout.

splendant XIII. 9¹ shining.

spright V. 52¹ spirit.

spring (n.)¹ I. 30⁵ origin.

spring (n.)² XIII. 5² and 23² grove.

square XII. 64⁶ a square piece of material covering the bosom; the breast-piece of a dress.

stay I. 76⁵ etc. stop, stand, wait.

steepie VIII. 51⁴ steep.

sterne XV. 50⁵ tail.

sterve II. 17² die.

store XV. 8⁵ volume.

stound XIX. 28¹ a short time.

stowre I. 55⁷ combat (archaic).

strange X. 5⁶ various.

streat XV. 30² strait.

strive I. 30¹ strife.

strouting IX. 8⁴ sticking out.

studdes XVIII. 44² posts, props.

sublime XVIII. 54³ very high.

sullen I. 7¹ gloomy.

suretie I. 28⁶ freedom from care.

suspect (n.) XII. 24⁷ suspicion.

swage II. 88⁶ assuage.

sway XIV. 30⁶ momentum.

tackling XII. 63⁷ stand to one's tackling = hold one's ground. *O.E.D.* 'tackling' 3.

talent VII. 96⁸ talon.

tap (sb.) XII. 33² liquid drawn through a tap (cf. Chaucer, Reeve's 'Prologue', l. 36).

tapisht VII. 2³ lurk, lie hid (hunting term).

targe XVI. 30¹ shield.

tariance XV. 38² delay.

teene X. 25⁵ vexation.

tel-clock *Hermes and Lycaon*, 20 one who tells the clock, hence to pass the time idly (*O.E.D.*).

temper XII. 17³ composition.

termes XVII. 84⁶ to stand on termes = to stand on ceremony.

thorow VIII. 64³ through.

thorpe XII. 32³ hamlet (archaic).

thought (v. impersonal) XIII. 40³ seemed.

thundred (ptc.) XX. 103⁸ struck by thunder (earliest quoted instance).

tising XV. 58⁸ enticing.

tofore I. 37⁶ etc. before, ahead of. (*O.E.D.*'s latest instance.)

tort I. 30⁶ injury, wrong.

tought XI. 37⁷ tough (dialect).

tout / toot X. 56⁶, XIV. 66⁸ peer, gaze.

tract VII. 23⁵ path.

trade (p.p.) VII. 45⁵ tread.

traine I. 74² snare, trap.

travaile¹ I. 66¹ etc. journey.

travaile² VII. 24⁶ effort.

traverst XIX. 11⁵ moved from side to side (fencing term).

tree XVIII. 98³ any kind of wooden structure, bridge.

treene XVIII. 23⁷ trees, *F.Q.* I. ii. 39 etc. (Archaic/dialect ?)

tries (v.) I. 57⁶ experiences.

trigon II. 51⁵ triangle (F. first instance cited in *O.E.D.*).

triple (n.) XVIII. 24⁵ treble voice. (Cf. *O.E.D.* 5. F. only instance cited.)

truchman XX. 24³ interpreter (also in Richard Carew).

trumpe XIX. 80³ trump card, trick.

tuch II. 93² touchstone.

twined (v.) XVIII. 12⁶ turned.

twist (n.) XIII. 27⁴ etc. twig, branch.

unadvised I. 45⁶ unexpected, unsought.

unbesought XIV. 21⁴ not sought after (*O.E.D.*'s first citation is Milton, 1667).

unbodied XII. 71¹ released from the body.

uncompaned I. 48⁴ unaccompanied.

uncouth II. 38³ unknown.

underbound XIX. 18⁶ kept down.

uneath (adv.)¹ IV. 59⁸ almost, virtually. (*O.E.D.* cites this as an erroneous use, also found in Spenser: *F.Q.* I. x. 31 etc.)

uneath (adv.)² V. 86⁶ scarcely.

unfeared I. 52² fearless.

unkend XV. 31⁴ unknown.

unmarkt IV. 70² unnoticed.

unremoved IX. 31⁶ fixed in one place, firmly stationed.

unsprong I. 49⁴ not having sprouted.

unwroken VIII. 66² unavenged.

uphent XII. 72⁷ lifted.

upright V. 55⁸ just.

uprold XIII. 57² rolled up, concentrated.

ure III. 32¹ species of wild ox, now extinct.

use XIII. 8⁸ habitual practice.

Vale / vaile (v.) II. 48⁷, XX. 42³ lower.

vamure (A. Fr. vannt mure, before the

walls) XI. 64⁷ earthworks thrown up in front of main fortifications.

vantbrace XX. 139⁴ armour to protect the forearm.

ventall VI. 26⁷ etc. mouth-piece of a helmet.

vilde XII. 27⁴ etc. vile.

virago III. 145⁵ female warrior.

wained I. 59⁴ weaned.

wannish IV. 1⁴ somewhat pale.

wanted VIII. 53¹ was missing.

ward (n.) XIX. 11⁶ defensive position.

web (of lead) X. 26⁶ sheet.

web (of a sword) II. 93¹ etc. blade. (Earliest use of this sense recorded in *O.E.D.*)

weede IV. 94² garment.

weet (v.) V. 86⁷ know.

welneare III. 36⁴ well-nigh.

wend (v.) VI. 109⁵ go.

whether *Ida and Opilio*, 94 whither.

whilome XIII. 7¹ once upon a time.

wight I. 33⁵ etc. creature, person, man.

windelais XIV. 34⁴ circuits.

winkte XVIII. 97¹ closed his eyes.

wonne IX. 28⁸ dwell.

wontes XI. 20⁴ etc. is accustomed.

wood II. 22⁵ mad.

writhen X. 9³ contorted.

yawle IV. 5³ cry, howl.

yond I. 55⁵ fierce (Spenserian: *F.Q.* II. viii. 40).

yood XIV. 33⁸ etc. went (archaic). Cf. 'yod', *F.Q.* I. x. 53 etc.

INDEX OF PROPER NAMES

Names are given in Tasso's form, followed by Fairfax's equivalent when the English form differs in any way likely to mislead or throw out alphabetical reference. Numbers in brackets refer to places where the proper name is not used in the translation. Names in brackets refer to persons mentioned, but not belonging to dramatis personae of the poem , e.g. historical and genealogical or legendary and literary references.